Object-Oriented Databases with Applications to CASE, Networks, and VLSI CAD

Object-Oriented Databases with Applications to CASE, Networks, and VLSI CAD

Editors:

Rajiv Gupta
GE Corporate Research and Development

Ellis Horowitz
University of Southern California

Prentice Hall Series in Data and Knowledge Base Systems
Dennis McLeod, Series Editor

Prentice Hall, Englewood Cliffs, NJ 07632

Library of Congress Cataloging-in-Publication Data

Object-oriented databases with applications to CASE, networks, and
  VLSI CAD / edited by Rajiv Gupta and Ellis Horowitz.
     p.   cm.
   Includes bibliographical references and index.
   ISBN 0-13-629833-8
   1. Object-oriented data bases. 2. Computer-aided software
engineering. 3. Computer networks. 4. Integrated circuits--Very
large scale integration--Design and construction--Data processing.
5. Computer-aided design. I. Gupta, Rajiv. II. Horowitz, Ellis.
QA76.9.D3026 1991
005.75--dc20   90-39302
                                                           CIP

Editorial/production supervision and
interior design: Jennifer Wenzel
Manufacturing buyers: Linda Behrens and Patrice Fraccio

©1991 by Prentice-Hall, Inc.
A Division of Simon & Schuster
Englewood Cliffs, New Jersey 07632

Printed in the United States of America

10 9 8 7 6 5 4 3 2 1

ISBN   0-13-629833-8

Prentice-Hall International (UK) Limited, *London*
Prentice-Hall of Australia Pty. Limited, *Sidney*
Prentice-Hall Canada Inc., *Toronto*
Prentice-Hall Hispanoamericana, S. A., *Mexico*
Prentice-Hall of India Private Limited, *New Delhi*
Prentice-Hall of Japan, Inc., *Tokyo*
Simon & Schuster Asia Pte. Ltd., *Singapore*
Editora Prentice-Hall do Brasil, Ltda., *Rio de Janeiro*

Contents

Preface

Object-oriented has become one of the most important buzzwords in the computer science arena. This is no accident. To a practitioner in software engineering the term promises a substantial body of proven concepts such as data abstraction, encapsulation, inheritance, polymorphism, extensibility, generic programming, information hiding, code reusability, modularity, exception handling, and so on. The list goes on, if only because there is no clear consensus on "what" is object-oriented programming.

One stream of research in the object-oriented field is object-oriented *databases*, (abbreviated here as OODBs). OODBs, which are a radical departure from conventional data structuring paradigms, are the primary focus of this book. Since language, database, and software engineering issues are intricately intertwined, a few chapters in the book are devoted to object-oriented languages. However, the overall view is distinctly database oriented.

Relational database technology has dominated the database field for the past decade, and more. There are now many commercially available relational systems. Researchers have long recognized the limitations of relational systems in managing data for applications such as CAD CAM, office information systems, and CASE. The incorporation of the object paradigm in database management systems is a direct consequence of this realization.

Many journal articles have been published that deal with numerous aspects of this new class of data management software. However, "real" object-oriented databases are just now appearing and several others are about to make their debut. In the absence of any torch bearers when it comes to actual software, and any book that presents the big picture, buzzwords abound and the Tower of Babel syndrome is clearly discernible. It is our ambition in this book to take some of the "buzz" out of these buzzwords that are so prevalent in this fast-breaking field and expose the concepts behind them.

The purpose of this book is fourfold.

1. It provides the reader with a perspective on various object-oriented concepts. These concepts, which have been under development in a diverse set of fields such as artificial intelligence, database theory, programming languages and compiler theory, form the backbone of the object paradigm. Illustration of their power, implementation, and use is a primary objective of this book. This book presents several issues of practical importance which are still in research/development stages. Issues such as benchmarking, schema evolution through learning, and incorporating and promoting the object paradigm in a corporation, are covered.

2. The book provides the reader an overview of existing OODBs, including examples of their use and comparison of their strengths and weaknesses. Besides a survey, three OODBs are selected for closer scrutiny. We believe that these three databases adequately represent the three evolutionary tracks taken by OODB research. As the reader will find out, the core concepts embodied in most OODBs are very similar. Instead of restating the same concepts over and over, the book presents three different facets of these databases.

3. The book provides a series of real-world examples and shows how they are mapped onto an object-oriented framework. The idea is to show the concepts in action. A diverse set of application areas is chosen so as to exemplify the universal applicability of the object paradigm.

4. C++, even though it is not an OODB, has been a prime mover in this field. Several yet-to-be-released OODBs have either adopted C++ as their primary data manipulation language, or are implementing object persistence directly into the language. The book presents a brief overview of the language, its power and limitations. It then presents two quite different approaches to *making a database out of* C++.

A number of object-oriented systems are covered in this book. These include Vbase (TDL and COP), GemStone and OPAL, Statice, ONTOS, IRIS, ORION, ODE, SIM, and C++. We do not expect the reader to be familiar with any of these systems. The overall coverage, though intentionally detailed at places, is quite self-contained. The book, however, does assume a degree of maturity about the "software-in-the-large" and knowledge of any one high-level language.

Advice to the Reader

The reader of this book will doubtlessly be someone who is a computer professional. Let us first assume that the reader has had no exposure to object-oriented concepts, but has an interest and knowledge of databases. He is advised to "begin at the beginning". Part I introduces the main concepts of object-oriented programming and object-oriented databases. For a reader just starting out in this field, the lay of the land is important. For such a reader, of special merit would be the articles by Gupta and Horowitz, McLeod, and Berre as they assume a beginning reader. In Part II the "Overview" article by Horowitz and Wan also would be appropriate for this person. Afterwards the reader might either move into the more in-depth material on Statice, Vbase and GemStone, or move to the applications of Part III.

Alternately, let us assume that our reader is interested in using an OODB for an application. Readers who have a specific interest, such as VLSI CAD, CASE or network management might begin with the surveys in Part I and II and then go to the article in Part III that deals specifically with their application. Here he can read about several serious attempts to use OODBs, the successes and the failures. He might then go to Part IV and examine the latest attempts to add persistence to C++.

Acknowledgments

This book would not have been possible without the wisdom and cooperation of the contributing authors. Special thanks go to the staff at Ontologic, Inc. for providing us with software and documentation which is eminently useful. Thanks also go to our editors at Prentice Hall. Special thanks to Dan Olson for providing help with PHtex macros. The University of Southern California has been a stimulating environment for writing this book.

Rajiv Gupta and Ellis Horowitz

To my wife, Lupe,
and to Samantha—the greatest thing that happened to
us since this book was begun—with a request.

    "Child! do not throw this book about;
Refrain from the unholy pleasure
Of cutting all the pictures out!
Preserve it as your chiefest treasure"
[Hilaire Belloc, Bad Child's Book of Beasts]

Rajiv Gupta

To Ira Horowitz,
    the object of my parental affection.

Ellis Horowitz

About the Editors

RAJIV GUPTA is a computer scientist at the General Electric Corporate Research and Development Center, Schenectady. Prior to his position at GE, he was a Research Assistant Professor of Electrical Engineering—Systems at the University of Southern California, Los Angeles from 1988 to 1990. Dr. Gupta served as a Post Doctoral Research Fellow in the VLSI Test Group at USC from July 1987 to June 1988, and as a Junior Software Engineer at Tata Burroughs Ltd, Bombay from March 1982 to July 1982.

Dr. Gupta received his B.E. (Hons.) degree in Electrical and Electronics Engineering and his M.Sc. (Hons.) degree in Physics from Birla Institute of Technology and Science, Pilani, India, both in 1982. He received his M.S. and Ph.D. degrees in Computer Science from the State University of New York at Stony Brook, where he was a Research Assistant from August 1982 to July 1987.

Dr. Gupta's primary research interests include object-oriented frameworks for VLSI CAD, VLSI design and testing, system-level fault diagnosis and reconfiguration, and fault-tolerant computing. He is currently investigating databases for organizing and integrating CAD information. As an experimental testbed for integrating VLSI CAD tools, he has designed and implemented a prototype framework called Cbase. Dr. Gupta has published numerous research articles on subjects ranging from system reconfiguration, fault diagnosis, VLSI testing, and logic programming to object-oriented databases for VLSI CAD.

Dr. Gupta is a member of IEEE Computer Society and a recipient of the National Science Talent Search Scholarship awarded by the Government of India.

ELLIS HOROWITZ received his B.S. degree from Brooklyn College and his Ph.D. in computer science from the University of Wisconsin. He was on the faculty there and at Cornell University before assuming his present post as Professor of Computer Science and Electrical Engineering at the University of Southern California. He has also been a visiting Professor at M.I.T. and the Israel Institute of Technology (Technion). Dr. Horowitz has held numerous administrative jobs including Associate Chairman of Computer Science at the University of Wisconsin and at U.S.C. He was also acting chairman of the Computer Science Department at U.S.C. He is the author of six books and over sixty research articles on computer science subjects ranging from data structures, algorithms, and software design to computer science education. Dr. Horowitz has been a principal investigator on research contracts from NSF, AFOSR, ONR, and DARPA. He is a past associate editor for the journals *Communications of the ACM* and *Transactions on Mathematical Software*. He currently serves on the technical advisory boards of several software companies and is an IBM scholar.

1 A Guide to the OODB Landscape

Rajiv Gupta and Ellis Horowitz

1.1 INTRODUCTION

In the wake of the Falkland Islands war it was reported that the British destroyer HMS Sheffield was sunk on high seas because the database in its warning system was incorrectly programmed. Gemini V landed miles away from its designated landing point because of a flaw in its guidance program. Stories about false alarms from North American Aerospace Defense Command because of situations unanticipated by the C^3 software are disquietingly common in software engineering folklore. What is described as the "software crisis" is quite real. The above mishaps, which can all be traced to buggy software, would convince even the most optimistic practitioner of the craft that present day large-scale programs can at best be regarded as fragile contraptions [Lin85].

Development of high-quality, large-scale software is widely acknowledged as a tough undertaking. Design methodologies that promise to improve the quality of software—notwithstanding the debate over how to measure software quality in terms of correctness, robustness, extensibility, ease of integration, reuse and maintenance—are of great interest to the design community.

Of the current software design methodologies, top-down decomposition of the function to be implemented, with stepwise refinement, is by far the most widely practiced. This design methodology starts with a very high-level description of the problem or task, and gradually refines it into a set of subtasks until the problem is reduced to a sequence of manageable pieces. This leads to a tree-like decomposition of the original problem.

Experience over the past three decades has shown that this paradigm for software construction leads to quick development of *a* program for the task at hand as it concentrates on *what* needs to be done. However, the resulting programs are less maintainable as the methodology concentrates on a very chameleonic aspect of the program, viz., its function. Over the lifetime of the program, the original function invariably changes and becomes one of the many functions provided by the program. Also, the tree-like decomposition, based on a premise that will change over time, divides the program along procedural lines with data structures and future reusability being second-order concerns. A number of empirical studies have shown (see, for example [Boehm81]) that in such an environment the effort required in constructing large-scale software increases rapidly with the size of the program.

1.1.1 Object Paradigm in a Nutshell

The object-oriented paradigm for program construction builds on the simple premise that software organized along modular, self-contained "objects" is more maintainable, extensible and reusable than the conventional "action-oriented" approach where software is divided around procedural lines. This is a radical shift from the traditional top-down approach. Instead of concentrating on what functions need to be performed, the focus is shifted to the entities on which functions have to be performed. The object-oriented design methodology leads to an architecture that is based on objects every system or subsystem manipulates.

There are several key advantages of shifting the emphasis from actions to objects. First, the basic objects in any application, in general, change much less frequently than the functions the application is required to perform. This is especially true of database programs. Even when the basic data entities do change, the change either introduces new types of objects or is localized to a few object types. Ease of software integration is another argument in favor of the object-oriented approach. It is difficult to combine actions if the data structures used by them are incompatible. In this respect, pre-agreed object modules hold a distinct advantage over pre-agreed function modules. The same argument holds for reusability of software. The users of the system-provided objects do not have to reinvent the wheel every time a new facility is needed.

Object-oriented program construction begins with the identification of objects that the applications will manipulate. Thus the key question the designers need to ask is, "What are the basic entities that the program will need?" rather than "What function will the program perform?" Once the set of objects and their characteristics are identified, *classes* of objects sharing similar characteristics are defined. These classes are typically organized in an *inheritance* hierarchy or lattice to describe interrelationships among them.

A class should be viewed as a self-contained modular unit that specifies what can be stored with objects of this class, and provides *operations* or *methods* that can be performed on these objects. Thus the notion of class is quite close to that of an *abstract data type*. In fact the object-oriented design of software systems can be thought of as a collection of well-integrated abstract data types providing a core of functionality around which complex systems can be built.

The basic tenets of the object paradigm are summarized below.

1. Make the system modules correspond to the data structures to be used. These modules should be self-contained as far as possible.

A Guide to the OODB Landscape   Chap. 1

2. Implement each module as an abstract data type. Every module should correspond to a class of data objects. The interface to the object implemented by a module should be explicit and concise. In addition, the user of the module should be given access to minimal information about the object, preferably through some layers of abstraction (information hiding).

3. Organize the modules in a hierarchy/lattice reflecting the commonality among the object classes they correspond to.

4. Provide a set of generic operations which can act on objects of various classes.

One look at the above steps for object-oriented software construction would confirm that they can be applied just as effectively to a database management system. The only difference is that in the latter case the objects in question are *persistent* and outlast the invocation of any individual program. This, however, lends further credibility to the basic premise of the object paradigm that the data structures change less frequently than the programs that manipulate the data.

On the surface the object paradigm for software construction in general, and database management in particular, appears to be a marriage of software engineering principles that have been known for a long time. Most of the concepts mentioned above have been discussed at great length in the research literature in the past quarter century. All these concepts, in one form or another, were present in early efforts such as Simula 67 (1966), Smalltalk (first version in 1972), CLU (mid-1970s), Mesa (1979), Modula-2 (1982), Ada (1983), and several others.

Is object orientation an old wine in a new bottle? Even though some in the community view it that way, we differ with this characterization. Even if the parts of the solution existed—and that should be no surprise as we are addressing the same problems in large software design as those that existed 25 years ago—it is this coming together of these disparate concepts that have given some a glimmer of hope. What makes the object paradigm powerful and exciting is the symbiotic fusion of many basic solution strategies that promises a concerted attack on the large software development problem. From this point of view, many vintage wines, aged to perfection and harmoniously blended, in a new bottle is perhaps a better description of the object paradigm.

1.1.2 Object-Oriented Databases

The last decade has witnessed the emergence of practical, general-purpose, relational database management systems (DBMSs) and associated fourth-generation database languages as state-of-the-art technology. Commercial DBMSs based on relational and pseudo-relational concepts are now widely utilized in a variety of application environments, on computers ranging from large-scale mainframes to small personal computers.

Recent research and development efforts have resulted in yet another generation of database technology: the so-called semantic and object-oriented database (OODB) systems. These advanced systems, now beginning to appear as commercial products, provide further database management capabilities and address some of the limitations of relational and other record-oriented DBMSs (e.g., those based on hierarchical and network data models).

This book is about this new generation of database technology that incorporates the object paradigm in a database management system. Several issues are important in the study of OODBs. What object-oriented concepts can be applied to databases? How are these concepts incorporated in an OODB? How are OODBs constructed and used? Can database management capabilities be merged into an object-oriented programming language? The chapters that follow will provide answers to these and many other questions.

1.2 TOPICS IN THE STUDY OF OODBs

Our brief introduction to the object-oriented concepts pointed out that applying these concepts in a database setting is what this book is all about. In this section we discuss the key object-oriented concepts as they appear in the database context. Various issues pertinent in the study of OODBs are outlined and an attempt is made to show how the various chapters of the book address these issues. This section is as much an introduction to the book as it is to the field. We hope that by highlighting the salient points of the various chapters the reader will be pointed in the proper direction.

1.2.1 The Basics

Part I of this book is a collection of chapters which talk about the basic OODB concepts in general. Starting with an evolutionary history of OODB concepts, the steps involved in logical design of an object-oriented schema are covered. This part then presents the issues pertinent in schema evolution and benchmarking. Finally, guidelines for harnessing this new technology in an environment dominated by conventional data structuring paradigms are discussed.

The evolution of OODB concepts. The concepts that OODBs bring together have been under development in diverse fields such as programming languages, compiler theory, database theory and artificial intelligence. How these concepts evolved from early semantic networks and relational models into object-oriented programming languages, and then into OODBs, makes a fascinating story.

The book begins with an overview of the field from an evolutionary perspective. In the chapter "A Perspective on Object-Oriented and Semantic Database Models and Systems," Dennis McLeod, a pioneer in the field of semantic data models, traces the evolutionary history of OODBs. The chapter is of a general nature. It requires no prior knowledge of OODBs and is suitable for a wide audience.

Object-oriented schema design. A key step in the design of OODBs is the derivation of classes that describe the data objects required by the applications and the specification of interrelationships among them. This activity is referred to as the logical design of an object-oriented database schema. Most applications require a wide variety of changes before converging to an acceptable schema. In general, the users of OODBs arrive at the desired schema for objects through trial and error.

Schema design has not been thoroughly addressed in the database literature to date even though a considerable body of research exists in the areas of AI knowledge representation, dependency theory, AI theorem proving, and graph algorithms to solve some of the most fundamental problems in schema design. A unified framework for logical design of an OODB schema that synthesizes existing research results from these areas is essential for deriving schemata that are efficient, consistent and non-redundant.

The third chapter by Hyoung-Joo Kim, "Algorithmic and Computational Aspects of Object-Oriented Schema Design," looks at the issues and problems involved in logical schema design in an OODB. The basic steps involved in schema design are discussed. Three fundamental problems in the process are identified and their computational complexity studied. The latter portion of this chapter is quite detailed and readers may wish to skip it in the first reading without any loss in continuity.

Schema evolution. Large applications such as weather simulation software, embedded computer systems for real time flight guidance, office information systems, and payroll and accounting packages are never written in their final form the first time around. An important issue in this respect is the ability to make a wide variety of changes to the database schema dynamically. This process is called *schema evolution*. For practical applications of object-oriented databases, which evolve over time, some form of schema evolution is indispensable. Unfortunately, changes to the schema, which are common in many application environments, are in general inadequately supported by existing database systems.

This fundamental problem concerning changes to the conceptual structure (metadata/knowledge) of a database is addressed in Chapter 4, "Conceptual Database Evolution through Learning." In this chapter, Li and McLeod explore methods for automatic object flavor evolution using machine learning techniques.

Performance and benchmarking. For any new technology that claims to solve some of the most nagging problems of an existing one, good performance is a crucial condition for survival. If modeling power and methodological elegance are the jewels in the OODB crown, performance, at least so far, has been its Achilles' heel. Improving performance is the central issue facing OODBs today. Another important need is a method for unbiased evaluation in an environment for which OODBs are targeted. Since most object-oriented databases are aimed to meet the needs of engineering applications such as CAD and CASE, an application-oriented approach is more suitable. The chapter entitled "The HyperModel Benchmark" describes such an approach to database evaluation. In this chapter, a generic benchmark that can be used to measure the performance of any OODB is described at a conceptual level.

Transition to the object paradigm. In the past few decades very large systems have been built using the relational and other conventional database management systems. These systems represent an astronomical investment in terms of effort, time, and money. From this point of view a transition to object-oriented development and promoting this new paradigm in the relational world is an important issue. In fact, for a very large system, it is not clear what exactly is meant by the word "transition." Should the new applications embrace the new paradigm and the old ones be left untouched? Is it possible for the two to co-exist in the first place? How does one go about convincing the upper-level management that a change to object-oriented technology is warranted?

These are some of the questions that will confront software managers more and more as this new technology comes into the mainstream.

The last chapter in this part is concerned with the transition to the object technology in a hitherto relational world. Step by step guidelines in terms of process, methodology, tools and management are provided for harnessing this new technology.

1.2.2 Some Real OODBs

Many OODB systems have already appeared on the scene. These include, to name a few, Vbase, GemStone, SIM, Iris, ODE, Statice, ONTOS, and ORION. These systems, though radically different in their syntax, provide features that are quite close to each other semantically. A study of features provided by some, if not all, of these OODBs is essential to understanding the object paradigm *in situ*. The purpose of Part II is to collect together in-depth material on existing OODBs. The first chapter in this part, entitled "Some Real Object-Oriented Databases," surveys many of the existing OODB systems. For each system an overview is presented and a small example is included to show how types are defined and how objects are manipulated. The latter chapters cover in detail different aspects of the Statice, Gemstone, and Vbase systems.

One can loosely view the evolution of real OODBs as having taken three distinct evolutionary tracks. A typical development pattern is to start with an existing programming language and enhance it with object persistence to get an OODB. To date, systems based on C, Smalltalk and Lisp have been announced. The C track has led to systems such as Vbase and ONTOS; the Smalltalk track has resulted in systems such as Gem-Stone; and the Lisp track has led to Lisp-based systems such as Statice. The basic semantics, the language interface, and the techniques used to implement concurrency control, recovery, and access to objects provided by these OODBs using three very different "host" languages makes a fascinating study. The book provides an in-depth discussion of a representative OODB taken from each track.

From Lisp to OODB. Statice is an OODB system designed to support the Genera integrated programming environment by providing objects that are persistent and shared between workstations. Statice has a clear and natural interface to the host language, Symbolics Common Lisp. In the chapter entitled "An Object-Oriented Database System to Support an Integrated Programming Environment," the basic semantics and the language interface of Statice are described and then illustrated with examples. Following that there is a discussion of the techniques used to implement concurrency control, recovery, and efficient access to data. Statice has been used on several real projects and the authors describe some of them.

From C to OODB. In Chapter 9, Tim Andrews provides the reader with a working knowledge of Vbase [Ontologic88a]. Vbase has two separate languages, TDL for type definition and COP for object manipulation. TDL adds object types to an initial database that consists of predefined types such as `Integer`, `Real` and `String`. After the TDL is compiled, the database contains all the meta-information it needs to work with objects. COP, which is an extension of the C programming language, is used for creation, deletion and manipulation of objects. These extensions allow COP to handle persistent objects, exceptions and iteration over object aggregates.

There are many reasons for discussing Vbase in detail, despite the fact that many of its features are either modified, upgraded, or unsupported in its newer incarnation ONTOS (Chapter 21). First, Vbase was one of the first systems that introduced features such as inheritance, polymorphism, data abstraction, exception handling, triggers and elision in a database environment. The merger of a programming language and a database in Vbase was unprecedented at the time of its release. Thus a study of its features makes it especially interesting to OODB researchers. Secondly, from a pedagogical standpoint, its type definition language is quite readable and leads to natural object type descriptions. In addition, Vbase's programming interface is through an extension to the C programming language. C has become the *lingua franca* for a wide segment of the computer engineering community. Thus Vbase programs should be easily followed by most readers.

From Smalltalk to OODB. OODBs have been hailed as great "integrators." For this to be true, they must provide simple interfaces to both procedural and object-oriented languages. One of the pioneering OODBs in this respect is GemStone. It incorporates a successful interface between an object server and two procedural languages (C and Pascal). The interaction of cache, transaction, and message management strategies, which makes the implementation quite nontrivial, is elegantly solved. In the chapter entitled "Integrating an Object-Server with Other Worlds," Purdy et al. discuss the integration aspects of GemStone, an OODB that has its roots in Smalltalk.

Storage management in OODBs. Despite the fact that one of the major historical precursors to object technology comes from data abstraction languages, most object-based systems do a poor job of data abstraction [Wegner87]. One can improve data abstraction by providing a mechanism for separating an object's abstract specification from its implementation details. This mechanism should consist of a specification that includes a notion of object state (rather than just operational behavior) and a model for representation. The database should provide a mapping of specification onto representation that allows for object-oriented inheritance.

In the chapter entitled "Abstract State and Representation in Vbase," Damon and Landis discuss the semantic foundation of one such mechanism in the context of Vbase. The main thesis of this chapter is that the abstract notion of state and its implementation are two distinct entities and should be treated differently. They show that strict encapsulation of implementation details behind an abstract interface specification enhances both safety and maintainability.

Query processing in OODBs. Most databases provide some kind of querying facility besides data definition and data manipulation languages. SQL, along with its look-alikes and variants, is by far the most widely used query language. Even though SQL has in the past been used only with relational or pseudo-relational databases, it can be adapted for querying an OODB. The chapter by Craig Harris and Joshua Duhl discusses the motivation, extensions and several pragmatic considerations in the implementation of Object SQL.

1.2.3 Applications of OODBs

Since OODBs are a new technology it is fair to ask if it has been tested on some serious examples. In Part III, "Applications", there are a series of chapters that deal with real uses of OODBs. The areas include the fields of VLSI CAD, CASE, Networks, and geographical information processing. As such they constitute a significant number of applications of this new technology. Both the pros and cons of using OODBs to solve the problem are discussed in order to provide a balanced perspective.

The main intent of this part is to show the object-oriented concepts in action by describing how a set of real world problems were solved using the OODB approach. The authors describe the problem and then discuss how they implemented their system. These examples take the concepts of the object paradigm one step further and actually show how they are used, something which research publications in this field are often unable to do.

We review the applications covered by this part next.

Integrated design environments.   Much has been said about using an object database to build integrated design environments. A wide variety of tools are needed to support the various phases of product development and deployment. This has led to a desire for an environment capable of integrating these tools. However, the lack of generality present in the tools, combined with the lack of a suitable substrate product, has inhibited the evolution of such an environment. Object database technology, which combines the modeling abstractions of objects and the storage mechanisms of databases, is shown to offer potential as a platform for building integrated environments. Two critical elements are deemed necessary: open architecture and very good separation of the model from the implementation.

VLSI CAD.   Designing a VLSI chip is a complex activity characterized by very large data volumes, several views/perspectives to the design data, and a multitude of tools to process this data. Using an object-oriented database to integrate the design data and to provide a common framework for CAD tool integration has been suggested by several researchers. The chapter by Gupta et al. describes one such framework called Cbase.

Cbase is a multilayered system that provides a common repository of both VLSI objects and their associated operations, a tool interface for writing new applications, and a user interface for invoking applications or viewing objects in the database. It provides a platform for creating, displaying, manipulating and maintaining large digital designs. The system interfaces to a set of existing tools for circuit analysis which are written in a diverse set of languages including C, Pascal and Lisp. The advantages of using OODBs to build an integrated VLSI CAD framework are illustrated with the help of actual code segments taken from the system.

CASE.   Object database support for CASE is another important application area. An OODB provides only a kernel set of capabilities. Data management requirements related to software project management need to be defined and then represented using object concepts. The DesignNet model in this book shows how the concepts of the work breakdown structure, project history, event monitoring, and re-initiation of tasks are realized in a specific object-oriented system. Limitations of existing object-oriented database systems are identified, with respect to implementing these concepts. Based upon an actual prototype, recommendations are made for enhancing future object-oriented systems.

Network management. Most networks today lack management tools that support automated identification of faults and bottlenecks and support effective recovery procedures. The NetMATE project addresses the issues related to distributed network management of large, heterogeneous networks. NetMATE employs a modular, object-oriented approach to develop extensible management tools and a model for network information. The first prototype of the system confirms the elegance of the design.

Geographical information management. GIS is an object-oriented geographical information system. An object-oriented model and prototype for an image exploitation environment have been developed. The model captures those elements of a geographic information system that are relevant to the image analysis and exploitation process. The prototype was developed using the Vbase object-oriented database environment and a standard window interface library, X-windows.

1.2.4 The Challenge: From C++ to OODB

What is in the near future of OODBs? The growing popularity of C++ as an object-oriented programming language has made it the ideal candidate as the base for an OODB. Many of the serious attempts to build an object-oriented database today are being done using C++ as the base language. Part IV is a special section on C++ and attempts to incorporate persistence in it.

The C++ programming language. C++ is the current most popular object-oriented programming language. C++ was developed by B. Stroustrup at AT&T Bell Labs. As an upwardly compatible superset of C, its incorporation of object concepts has proven to be a large stimulus to the programming community to embrace these concepts. Part IV begins with a brief introduction to C++. Features of C++, and how it enhances C, are introduced. The exposition—which is geared towards describing the core functionality rather than the details of C++ syntax—assumes a knowledge of C. Pointers to more detailed sources are provided when appropriate.

Limitations of C++ as a database language. Following that, the article by C. Damon compares and contrasts two object-oriented programming languages, COP (of Vbase) and C++. The comparison is interesting as it contrasts a language that has been specifically designed for an OODB with an object-oriented programming language with no database support. COP is an example of the former, and C++ an example of the latter. The comparison between the two highlights shows these two different starting points led to many different features.

C++ with persistence: the ODE approach. R. Agrawal and N. Gehani introduce extensions to C++ to support persistence in the chapter entitled "ODE: The Language and the Data Model." This chapter describes a database system and environment based on the object paradigm. ODE offers one integrated data model for both database and general purpose manipulation. The database is defined, queried and manipulated in the database programming language O++ which is based on C++. O++ borrows and extends the object definition facility of C++. One of the special aspects of ODE not previously discussed is the versioning of objects. Other interesting features include the definition of and iteration over sets. As with Vbase, ODE provides facilities that associate constraints and triggers with objects.

C++ with persistence: the ONTOS approach. In the final chapter in this part, T. Andrews, C. Harris, and K. Sinkel talk about ONTOS, the successor product to the Vbase object database. ONTOS is a distributed object manager with very high performance. It incorporates a version and alternative mechanism, nested and shared transactions, an out-of-line exception handling mechanism and object extensions to SQL. The objects stored in ONTOS can be accessed and manipulated using C++ through a member function-style interface. The chapter describes the main features of ONTOS and how it extends C++.

1.2.5 Some Miscellaneous Topics

Finally we observe that though the book is quite comprehensive in covering most of the real systems and concepts, some specialized niches have been dealt with only in the context of existing databases. Object versioning is discussed only in connection with ODE and ONTOS; concurrency control and recovery are detailed only for the Statice system; and object distribution is talked about only in the context of ONTOS. References at the end of the book provide pointers to more detailed literature on these topics.

1.3 SOME FINAL THOUGHTS

OODBs are an up-and-coming technology. There are many reasons to believe that they hold great promise. As the next score of chapters will show, they hold an edge in several important areas such as, to name a few, data modeling, extensibility, generic programming, and information hiding where their capabilities are more suitable than conventional database construction methodologies. Certainly there are many others.

However, rather than paint a euphoric picture throughout the book, we prefer to add a note of caution. Much work remains to be done and several key problems have to be solved before this technology can become a dominant database construction paradigm. There are issues pertaining to the interfaces to existing programming languages and applications. There is little that the object paradigm tells us about how one should go about structuring the data types in a complex system. This step is still more an art than science. Performance is another major issue. Though the performance of object-oriented languages, both in terms of speed and size of the compiled code, has become quite competitive, OODBs still need further enhancements. Some of the early prototypes, which turned out to be too slow and too large, have proved the simple truth that all nice features have a cost. The bigger challenge, therefore, is not in inventing more and more features; rather it is in discovering the right mix of features.

Database technologies do not establish themselves in an overnight coup. They take years, sometimes decades, to mature. Object-oriented databases will be no exception.

2 A Perspective on Object-Oriented and Semantic Database Models and Systems

Dennis McLeod

2.1 INTRODUCTION

Computerized databases are essential and inseparable components of a vast majority of today's information systems. Database systems are utilized at all levels of management, research, and production to provide uniform access to and control of consistent information. Applications in which the use of database systems are critical include large "commercial" applications such as banking, reservations, personnel, and inventory systems. However, other database-intensive applications are becoming more-and-more important, including those to support computer-aided design, software engineering, computer integrated manufacturing, personal information management, and computer-supported cooperative work.

The past decade has witnessed the emergence of general-purpose relational database management systems (DBMSs) and accompanying fourth generation database manipulation languages as viable and practical tools. This generation of database technology represents significant breakthroughs in the generality, efficiency, evolvability, user friendliness, and mathematical foundations of such systems over their historical predecessors. Relational, pseudo-relational, and other record-oriented database management systems are now widely utilized in a wide variety of application environments, and on computers ranging from large-scale mainframes to personal machines.

We are now seeing another generation of database systems, the so-called "semantic" and "object-oriented" database systems [Andrews87, Bancilhon88, Banerjee87b, Fishman87, Jagannathan88], which provide additional capabilities above and beyond those of relational technology, and which address many of the limitations thereof. The tools and systems of this new generation of database systems supply additional modeling and abstraction power, explicitly support semantic integrity constraint specification and enforcement, more substantively facilitate graceful database evolution, support a wider diversity of modalities of database objects, and provide for higher level user and program interfaces.

In this chapter, we explore this new generation of database systems. Emphasis is placed on the important concepts, principles, and techniques of object-oriented and semantic databases systems. The relationships of this technology with more traditional database management approaches are examined. A historical perspective on the evolution of database technology as related to object-oriented and semantic database systems is provided.

2.2 DATABASE SYSTEMS AND DATABASE MODELS

The concepts underlying "object-oriented" and "semantic" databases are best examined in the context of general-purpose database management systems (DBMSs). A general-purpose DBMS can be viewed as a generalized collection of integrated mechanisms and tools to support the definition, manipulation, and control of databases for a variety of application environments. In particular, a general-purpose DBMS is intended to provide the following functional capabilities:

1. Support the independent existence of a database, apart from the application programs and systems that manipulate it;
2. Provide a conceptual/logical level of data abstraction;
3. Support the query and modification of databases;
4. Accommodate the evolvability of both the conceptual structure and internal (physical) organization of a database, in response to changing information, usage, and performance requirements;
5. Control a database, which involves the four aspects of semantic integrity (making sure the database is an accurate model of its application environment), security (authorization), concurrency (handling multiple simultaneous users), and recovery (restoring the database in the event of a failure of some type).

While the emphasis here is on discussing the capabilities of general-purpose database management systems (DBMSs), it should be noted that the concepts examined here also apply to database systems tailored to specific application environments.

At the core of any database system is a database model (data model), which is a mechanism for specifying the structure of a database and operations that can be performed on the data in that database. As such, a database model should: allow databases to be viewed in a manner that is based upon the meaning of data as seen by its users; accommodate various levels of abstraction and detail; support both anticipated and unanticipated database uses; accommodate multiple viewpoints; and be free of implementation and physical optimization detail (physical data independence).

Abstractly speaking, a database model is a collection of generic structures, (semantic integrity) constraints, and primitive operations. The structures of a database model must support the specification of objects, object classifications, and inter-object relationships. The semantic integrity constraints of the database model specify restrictions on states of a database or transitions between such states, in order that the database accurately reflect its application environment. Some constraints are embedded within the structural component of a database model, while others may be expressed separately and enforced externally to the DBMS. We can refer to the specification of a particular database constructed using these general-purpose structures and constraints as a (conceptual) schema.

The operational component of a database model consists of a general-purpose collection of primitives that support the query and modification of a database; viz., given a database with an associated conceptual schema, the operations facilitate the manipulation of that database in terms of the schema. Such primitives may be embodied in a stand-alone end-user interface or a specialized language, or embedded within a general-purpose programming language. Database-specific operations (transactions) can be constructed utilizing the primitives of the database model as building blocks.

2.3 RECORD-ORIENTED DATABASE MODELS

Record-oriented database models, which dominate the database systems in practical use today, include the relational model as well as partially relational models (pseudo-relational models), and hierarchical and network models. While there is considerable variation among the versions of these models embodied in particular DBMSs, the key point they have in common is the use of the record construct as the foundation of the model.

The variety of DBMSs which embody hierarchical and network type database models offer inter-record link types in addition to the record as a basic modeling construct; these link types explicitly express inter-record relationships. Traditionally, such systems suffer from a lack of physical data independence, but this need not be the case in principle. By contrast, DBMSs based upon the relational model capture inter-record relationships in a uniform manner: by means of common data values. In fact, the simplicity and uniformity of the relational database model is a fundamental goal of that model. Other important aspects of the relational approach are also quite significant, although these are not necessarily tied to the model itself; these include the importance of physical data independence, high-level general-purpose operational primitives, set-at-a-time (as opposed to record-at-a-time) orientation, and a firm mathematical foundation [Codd70, Codd79, Date82].

To serve the purpose here of a state-of-the-art record-oriented model, the basic structures and constraints of the relational model can be considered. A relational database consists of a number of n-ary relations and a collection of underlying domains. A relation can be crudely viewed as a table containing a fixed number of columns (attributes) and a variable number of rows (tuples).[1] Figure 2.1 presents four example relations, indicating a name for each relation (table) and column.

This simple example database includes information on restaurants, persons, the food specialties of restaurants, and recommendations of restaurants by persons.

---

[1] Strictly speaking, a table depiction of a relation is an approximation; e.g., rows and columns are unordered, and no duplicate rows are allowed.

Figure 2.1 An example relational database.

Also indicated in Figure 2.1 are examples of three fundamental relational model constraints, which we will term domain, entity, and referential integrity. Domain integrity involves specifying the set of possible values a column entry may take; the values that may appear in a given column are those that are members of the underlying domain of that column. Underlying domains are sets of atomic data values, which may be built-in (e.g., Numbers, Strings) or user-defined (e.g., Phone#s). Entity integrity involves specifying a column or collection of columns whose values taken together uniquely determine rows in the relation; such a column or column collection is termed a primary key (logical unique identifier) and is underlined in the figure. For example, the primary key of RECOMMENDATIONS is the combination of Restaurant and Person, which means that given the name of a restaurant and the name of a person, there is at most a single value of Rating for that pair. (Note that the relations in Figure 2.1 are in third normal form [Date82, Ullman82].) Referential integrity constraints, indicated by dashed lines in the figure, specify that the values in some column must occur as values in some other column. For example, the arrow from Restaurant in RECOMMENDATIONS to Name in RESTAURANTS means informally that for a recommendation to exist for a restaurant, that restaurant must exist in the RESTAURANTS relation; more precisely, the name of the restaurant as indicated in RECOMMENDATIONS must also exist as the name of the restaurant in RESTAURANTS.

To illustrate the operational component of a typical relational DBMS, Figure 2.2 contains an example database query expressed in an SQL-like notation.

```
select Name, Telephone, Specialty
from RESTAURANTS, SPECIALTIES
where Name = Restaurant
     and Name is in
          select Restaurant
          from RECOMMENDATIONS
          where Person = "Laurie Anderson"
```

Figure 2.2 An example relational database query.

This query informally retrieves the name, telephone, and specialties of each restaurant that has been recommended by the person named "Laurie Anderson". The query produces a ternary relation, with columns containing a restaurant name, the telephone of the restaurant, and a specialty of that restaurant. Note that the RESTAURANTS and SPECIALTIES relations are being in effect joined on matching restaurant name, and that a subset of this join is selected corresponding to those restaurants for which a recommendation by Laurie Anderson exists. Also note that if a restaurant has no specialties, its name and telephone will not appear in the query result.

2.4 SEMANTIC AND OBJECT-ORIENTED DATABASE MODELS

Given the preceding brief view of record-oriented database models, it is now possible to consider semantic and object-oriented database models. When applied to database models, the terms "object-oriented" and "semantic" are used to refer to many characteristics and mechanisms [Abiteboul87, Afsarmanesh86b, Andrews87, Banerjee87b, Fishman87, Gibbs83, Hammer81, Hull87, Jagannathan88, Zdonik84]. We shall attempt here to use them somewhat precisely. In particular, we place object-oriented database systems in contradistinction to record-oriented database systems, and consider object-oriented features such as object identity, object classification, inheritance, etc.

Specifically, we use the term object-oriented to refer to the following characteristics, as exhibited by a database model and a database system that embodies that model:

1. **Individual object identity:** Abstract objects can be directly represented and manipulated in a database, independent of symbolic surrogates for them [Codd79a, Hammer81, Kent79, Smith87]. Objects at various levels of abstraction and of various modalities (different media) can be accommodated.

2. **Explicit semantic primitives:** Primitives are provided to support object classification, structuring, semantic integrity constraints, and derived data. These primitive abstraction mechanisms support such features as aggregation, classification, instantiation, and inheritance. The roots of these semantic primitives are in the "semantic" data models" [Codd79, Hammer81, King85a, Mylopoulos80a, Shipman81, Smith77] and in artificial intelligence knowledge representation techniques [Brachman85a, Brodie86, Woods75].

3. **Active objects:** Database objects can be active as well as passive, in the sense that they can exhibit behavior. Various specific approaches to the modeling of

object behavior can be adopted, such as an inter-object message passing paradigm (e.g., as described in [Purdy87, Stefik86]), or abstract datatype encapsulation (e.g., [Andrews87]). The important point is that behavioral abstraction and encapsulation are supported, and procedures to manipulate data are represented in the database.

4. **Object uniformity:** All information (or nearly all) in a database is described using the same object model [Afsarmanesh85a, Banerjee87b]. Thus, descriptive information about objects, referred to here as meta-data, is conceptually represented in the same way as specific "fact" objects.

Since practical semantic and object-oriented DBMSs are now only beginning to appear, it is logical that only some of the above aspects of object-orientation are handled by them. The first two, object identity and explicit semantic primitives, can be ascribed to a "semantic DBMS" which has a structural object-orientation; the last aspect, object uniformity is also addressed to some extent by these new systems. Behaviorally object-oriented systems also address the issue of active objects, viz., accommodating application-specific methods or procedures on objects in the database itself [Bancilhon88, Purdy87]; further, some significant differences exist between the way semantic primitives are handled in structurally and behaviorally object-oriented systems (e.g., inheritance).

2.5 FUNDAMENTALS OF A SEMANTIC DATA MODEL

The fundamental components of a semantic, structurally object-oriented database model can be generally characterized as follows:

1. Objects are abstract or atomic entities which correspond to things in the application environment being represented in the database, and may be at various levels of abstraction and of various modalities (media).

2. Inter-object relationships describe associations between objects. Such relationships are modeled as attributes of objects (logical mappings from one object to another) and their inverses, as well as by association objects (objects that view relationships as entities in their own right).

3. Object classifications group together objects which have some commonalities. The term object type is often used to refer to such a classification, and the term class to the set of objects classified according to the type.[2] Relationships between object classifications specify inter-classification associations, e.g., the subtype/supertype inter-type relationship supports specialization/generalization. Object types or classes can themselves be considered objects at a higher level of abstraction, e.g., with attributes of their own.

To examine in more detail the fundamentals of a semantic, structurally object-oriented database model, we again consider the example application environment involving restaurants, persons, restaurant recommendations, etc.

---

[2]The term type and class are sometimes informally used somewhat synonymously.

Figure 2.3 illustrates the concepts of types and attributes. Types are classifications of objects, and attributes are mappings from one object type to another. In this figure, types are indicated as ovals. Example types include abstract entity classifications, such as Restaurants, Persons, Recommendations, and Specialties, as well as atomic/printable value types such as Phone#s, R-names (restaurant names), P-names (person names), and Ratings.

In Figure 2.3, attributes are indicated by labelled directed arrows from the described type to the describing type (value type). Attributes are labelled with a name, and are indicated as single-valued (1) or multi-valued (m); attribute inverses are specified by a line connecting two small open circles. An attribute A from a type T1 to a type T2 means that an object classified as being of type T1 may be related to object(s) of type T2 via A; the inverse of A, which is always logically present, may be explicitly indicated and named. For example, type Restaurants has an attribute called has-specialties which is multi-valued; for a given restaurant object, its specialties are indicated by the value of this attribute, which relates the restaurant to zero or more objects of type Specialties. The inverse of this attribute is called is-specialty-of of Specialties, which is also multi-valued. Another example is the attribute phone# of Restaurants, which is single-valued; its inverse is not explicitly present here, but can be referenced as "the inverse of phone# of Restaurants", which is of course an attribute of type Phone#s.

One-to-one, one-to-many, many-to-one, and many-to-many binary relationships between object types can be expressed by attribute and attribute inverse pairs. The many-to-many relationship between types Restaurants and Specialties is represented by the multi-valued attribute has-specialties of Restaurants and its multi-valued inverse, is-specialty-of of Specialties. An example of a one-or-many relationship is indicated between the Restaurants and Recommendations types by the single-valued attribute restaurant of Recommendations and its multi-valued inverse attribute recommendations of Restaurants; this means informally that an object of type Recommendations

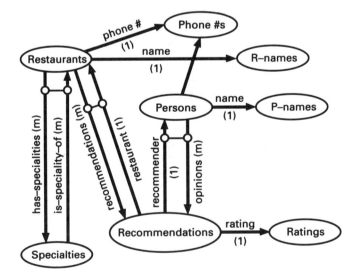

Figure 2.3 Types and attributes.

represents the evaluation of a single restaurant, and that a given restaurant may have many evaluations. An example of a one-to-one relationship, although not indicated as such in Figure 2.3, might be between Restaurants and R-names; here, the attribute called name of Restaurant is single-valued, and its inverse (from R-names to Restaurants, e.g., called is-name-of) would also be single-valued.

Figure 2.4 illustrates the Recommendations type in more detail.

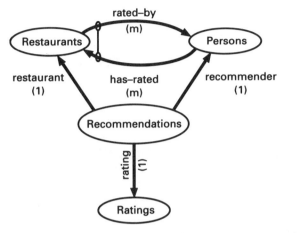

Figure 2.4 Association objects.

We see here that Recommendations has three attributes (restaurant, recommender, and rating), each of which is single-valued. Objects of type Recommendations represent abstract entities that correspond to recommendations of restaurants by persons with a given rating; they in effect model a ternary relationship. It is also possible to consider a derived attribute called rated-by of Restaurant and its inverse (has-rated of Persons), both of which can be derived from information carried by the values of the attributes of Recommendations. This is an example of derived data in general, and derived attributes in particular; note that attribute and attribute inverse pairs are in a sense also derived, or more precisely, logically redundant information [Hammer81, Hudson88]. A database system supporting a semantic database model must of course support this redundancy, and maintain consistency in its presence.

The concept of specialization (and its inverse, generalization) is an important kind of inter-type relationship, which may be supported by the subtype/supertype construct. Figure 2.5 illustrates this relationship between a type and its subtype(s), using a thick arrow from a type to a subtype.

In the example, the type Restaurants has two subtypes, viz., Indian Places and Sushi Bars. Sushi Bars in turn has a subtype itself, namely Good Sushi Bars. Attributes are inherited by a subtype from its supertype, and the subtype may have additional attributes as well. Thus, Indian Places has the attribute Indian-variety, and also the attributes called name, has-specialties, recommendations, and phone, which are inherited from Restaurants.[3]

The objects classified by a type may be termed the instances of that type. The set of instances of a subtype must be a subset of the set of instances of its supertype. In

---

[3]For simplicity in the figure, the value types of some attributes are omitted.

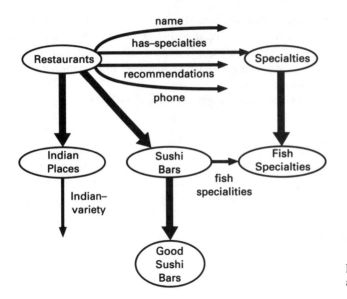

Figure 2.5 Subtypes, supertypes, and attribute inheritance.

Figure 2.6, we see that there are some instances of type Restaurants, indicated as R1, R2, R3, R4, and R5.

Sushi Bars has instances R2, R3, and R5, while Good Sushi Bars has the single instance R5. Note that the same restaurant object R5 is an instance of three types; it can be viewed as a restaurant, a Sushi bar, and a good Sushi bar. The subset constraint involving instances of a subtype must of course be enforced by the database system.

It is also possible for a type to have multiple supertypes. In this case, the specialization structure among types is not necessarily a tree, but rather a directed acyclic graph. For example, suppose that Friends and Colleagues are defined as subtypes of Persons; the type Friends at Work might then be defined as a subtype of both Friends and

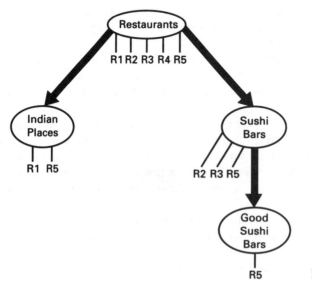

Figure 2.6 Subtypes and instances.

Colleagues. In this example, the instance subset constraint implies that the instances of Friends at Work must be a subset of the instances of Friends as well as a subset of the instances of Colleagues. When multiple supertypes are permitted, some rules must be present in the database model to accommodate the problem of multiple inheritance (viz., the inheritance of attributes from more than one supertype).

It is clear that a number of semantic integrity constraints are embedded as an integral part of a semantic database model. Attribute values can be any objects, not just atomic, symbolic data values as in record-oriented database models; thus, the analog of referential integrity constraints for the relational database model is the notion of object-valued attributes in a semantic database model. The subtype construct also supports constraints, such as the instance subset constraint. Additional constraints on the relationship among subtypes may also be supported, e.g., that two or more subtypes are disjoint (mutually exclusive) and/or collectively exhaustive. Figure 2.7 provides an example of a subtype disjointness constraint between the subtypes of Restaurants called Winners and Losers.

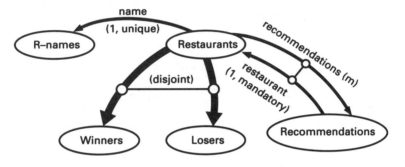

Figure 2.7 Example constraints.

Constraints on attributes are also present in a semantic database model, such as single-valued and multi-valued. An additional useful attribute constraint is to require that an attribute value is mandatory (not null). It is also useful to specify that an attribute is a logical unique identifier for the objects in the class it describes, or that a collection of such attributes is a logical unique identifier when their values are considered as a unit. Figure 2.7 provides several such examples, e.g., stating that the attribute called name of Restaurants is single-valued and unique, and the attribute restaurant of Recommendations is single-valued and mandatory.

Figure 2.8 contains an example specification of an operation on the example semantic database model schema; this is the same query as used above for the relational model, viz., to find the name, phone# and specialties of each restaurant recommended by Laurie Anderson.

Note here that the composition of attributes is being used in place of explicit value-based joins in the relational database model example. In particular, we obtain the name of the recommender of recommendations of Restaurants, and compare that name to the constant "Laurie Anderson". Further, the result of the query contains two single-valued attributes (name and phone#) and one multi-valued attribute (has-specialties). Subtyping and inheritance also play a prominent role in the specification of operations; for example,

```
retrieve
    name, phone#, has-specialties
        of Restaurants
where
    name of recommender
        of recommendations
        of Restaurants
    = "Laurie Anderson"
```

Figure 2.8 Example operation specification.

to change the above query to refer to Sushi Bars would require a very small modification due to attribute inheritance. In general, we note that the manipulation primitives of a semantic database model correspond to the structures of that model.

To conclude our discussion of the fundamentals of a semantic database model, Figure 2.9 provides a graphical description of a portion of a conceptual schema constructed with the SDM database model [Hammer81].

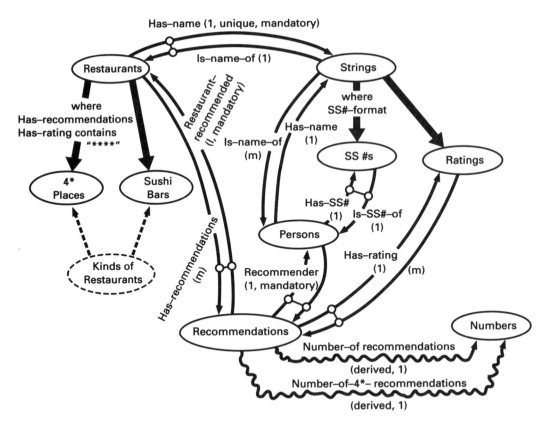

Figure 2.9 An SDM schema example.

In this figure, we see several additional concepts not discussed above. For example, the subtype of Restaurants called 4* Places is a predicate-defined subtype; a predicate, shown on the subtype arrow, specifies the instances of 4* Places by computation rather than via enumeration by users. Figure 2.9 also shows a type named Kinds of Restaurants, which is a higher-order type, in the sense that its instances are other types. Subtypes of symbolic data values (Strings) are also shown here. Two derived attributes that apply to a type as a whole, as opposed to the instances of that type, are also shown for the type Recommendations. Further discussion of these and other additional semantic database model features can be found in [Afsarmanesh84, Hammer81, Hull87, King85a].

2.6 A VIEW OF TWENTY YEARS OF DATABASE SYSTEM TECHNOLOGY

To provide a historical perspective on state-of-the-art semantic and object-oriented database models and systems, Figure 2.10 shows a twenty-year timeline with descriptive terms highlighting some of the most significant developments and the major conceptual trends underlying them.[4]

In Figure 2.10, we note on the top left of the upper portion of the figure the introduction and subsequent development of the relational database model. Work on normalization focused on the design of "good" relational conceptual schemas, while work on constraints for the relational model addressed the problem of adding additional semantics to the simple relational structures. Following to the right, we see RM/T, the structural model, SAM/SAM*, and GEM, which are extensions of the relational model to capture more meaning.

Functional models explored the use of mappings from one data set to another, and are related to the binary relational models. The data semantics model was an early binary semantic model. The entity-relationship model was originally introduced as a design tool for record-oriented databases (as were many of the semantic database models), and the SHM (semantic hierarchy model) focused on the importance of aggregation and generalization primitives. SDM was a complex semantic database model, containing a rich collection of modeling primitives, and supporting a variety of semantic integrity constraints and derived data specifications.

On the bottom left of the upper portion of Figure 2.10, we see work on semantic networks which represented a significant step in the structuring of knowledge for artificial intelligence applications; subsequent work on the ADD and Taxis systems explored more directly the applicability of fundamental semantic model primitives (such as "is-a" or generalization) to database systems. Work on abstract datatypes and Smalltalk in the programming language arena developed the importance of behavioral abstraction. SHM+ and the event model incorporated behavior modeling notions into the semantic database model framework. The 3DIS incorporated ideas of merging schema and data into a uniform framework (as did work on Smalltalk and early work on Orion). IFO was introduced as a model formalizing many of the important semantic database model primitives.

---

[4]Note that the developments and trends noted here clearly do not cover all important work in the field; further details, discussion, and citations can be found in [Afsarmanesh86b, Brodie84b, Hull87, King85b].

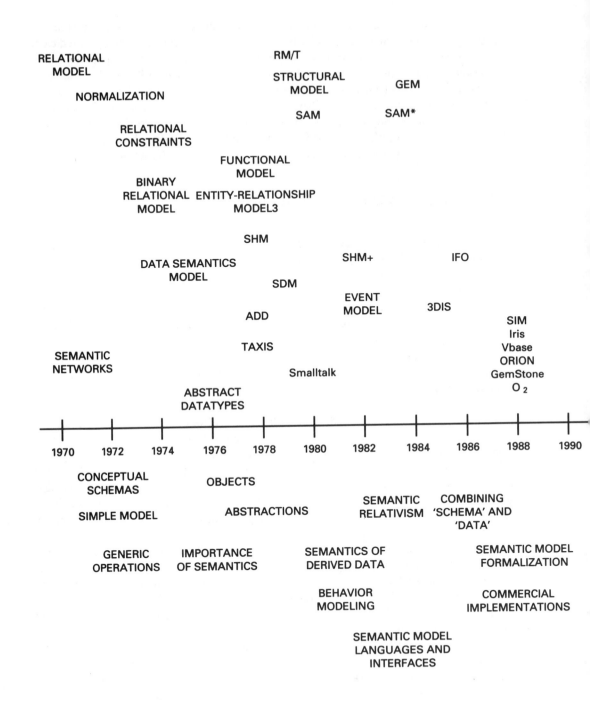

Figure 2.10 Twenty-year research and development trends.

Significantly, we note that commercial implementations of semantic and object-oriented database models are now beginning to appear. In the bottom right of the top portion of Figure 2.10, we see several systems listed. In particular, SIM [Jagannathan88] is an implementation of a full-scale database management system based upon a semantic database model. Gemstone [Purdy87] is an implementation of a Smalltalk-like object-oriented database model, with supporting database server facilities. Vbase [Andrews87] is a database management tool and development environment based upon a semantic, object-oriented database model, which includes some fundamental aspects of abstract datatypes [Liskov77]. Several other comprehensive database systems which may soon become commercial products are also under development (e.g., Iris [Fishman87], O2 [Bancilhon88], and Orion [Banerjee87b, Kim87]).

In the bottom portion of Figure 2.10, we see a summary of some of the major conceptual highlights during the twenty-year period leading to commercial semantic and object-oriented database systems. Here, we see early recognition of the importance of conceptual schemas (viz., separating a meaning-based specification of a database from physical implementation detail), the utility of a simple uniform model of data, and the notion of a (complete) generic set of manipulation operations. The importance of semantics, and the specific notions of objects and abstractions were then noted. The modeling of behavior and the semantics of derived data were then integrated into database models, and the importance of accommodating multiple points of view on data semantics (semantic relativism) was observed. Languages and interfaces for databases structured with semantic and object-oriented database models were devised. The utility of a uniform model of "schema" (meta-data) and "data" was noted. Semantic database model notions were then formalized. Finally, we see the existence of practical, commercial systems based upon semantic and object-oriented database models. Clearly, experience will be gained in the near future with the practical use of these systems.

3 Algorithmic and Computational Aspects of OODB Schema Design

Hyoung-Joo Kim

3.1 INTRODUCTION

The successful use of database management systems in data-processing applications has created a substantial amount of interest in applying database techniques to such areas as knowledge bases and artificial intelligence [Stefik86, Ballou88], software engineering [Snyder86], computer-aided design (CAD) [Afsarmanesh86a, Kemper87], and office information systems [Lochovsky85, Ahlsen84, Meyrowitz86, Woelk86]. In order to provide the additional semantics necessary to model these new applications, many researchers, including those referenced above, have adapted the object-oriented programming paradigm [Goldberg83, Bobrow86, Bobrow83, Curry84, Symbolics84] to provide a data model.

In order to use the object-oriented approach in a database system, it was necessary to add persistence and sharability to the object-oriented programming paradigm. Several database systems based on this approach are currently available, including Vbase [Ontologic88], GemStone [Maier86a], IRIS [Fishman87], ONTOS (Chapter 21), and ORION [Banerjee87b]. In order to meet requirements of new database applications, each of these recent database systems has its own *advanced functions* (such as version control, schema evolution, etc.) that were not available in conventional database systems such as System/R [IBM81] and INGRES [Stonebraker76].

One of the advantages of object-oriented programming over conventional control-oriented programming is supporting the notion of a *class hierarchy* and *inheritance* of properties (instance variables and methods) along the class hierarchy. A class hierarchy captures the IS-A relationship between a class and its subclass (equivalently, a class and its superclass). A class inherits all properties defined for its superclasses, and can have additional properties local to itself. The notion of property inheritance and class hierarchy enhances application programmer's productivity by facilitating top-down design of the database as well as applications.

Recently there has been a flurry of research activity regarding various issues of object-oriented databases. However, the logical design of object-oriented database schema has not been addressed adequately in the database literature. Class hierarchy design is the main theme of schema design for object-oriented databases. In section 3.3, we present a unified framework for object-oriented database schema design that utilizes research results in the areas of AI knowledge representation, database dependency theory, AI theorem proving, and graph algorithms. Three fundamental problems that need to be solved efficiently in order to keep the database schema correct and consistent are introduced and their computational complexity studied (section 3.3.4).

The practical applications of object-oriented databases, such as CAD/CAM, AI, and multimedia office systems, require the ability to make a wide variety of changes to the database schema dynamically; this process is called *schema evolution*. The types of schema changes required include creation and deletion of a class, alteration of the IS-A relationship between classes, addition and deletion of an instance variable and a method, and others. The users tend to arrive at the desired schema for objects through trial and error. Therefore, schema evolution can be thought of as an interim process for the logical design of object-oriented database schema: schema change operations are used for designing a desired schema.

Subclassing is the most frequently used schema change operation. A new class needs to be created from a class when a new concept, which cannot be accommodated in the existing classes, has to be introduced. Most subclassings involve the imposition of restrictions on instance variables of a parent class. The constraints that accompany these subclassings, also known as *subclassing conditions*, are predicate expressions on instance variables.

In sections 3.5, 3.6 and 3.7, we shall present several issues related to subclassing. First, we present a taxonomy of subclassing and the semantics of each case. Second, we address the issue of subclassing condition management because most subclassings are accompanied by subclassing conditions. As a database and schema grow in size and complexity, it is very difficult to maintain consistent class hierarchies without taking advantage of subclassing conditions. We also consider the inverse operation of subclassing, *desubclassing* (dropping an existing class). Finally, all subclassing conditions are useful in many applications of object-oriented databases; we identify such applications and introduce techniques for applying subclassing conditions to them.

3.2 OBJECT-ORIENTED DATA MODELS

This section reviews the core concepts of object-oriented data models. We also indicate some assumptions or conventions in the data model which will be used in this chapter.

3.2.1 Core Concepts

Object-oriented data models support the usual features of object-oriented languages, including the notions of classes, subclasses, class hierarchies, and objects. Each entity in a database is an *object*. Objects include *instance variables* that describe the state of the object. Instance variables may themselves be objects with their own internal state, or they may be *primitive objects* such as integers and strings which have no instance variables. Objects also include *methods* which contain code used to manipulate the object or return part of its state. These methods are invoked from outside the object by means of *messages*. Thus, the public interface of an object is a collection of messages to which the object responds by altering its state or returning an object.

Although each object has its own set of instance variables and methods, several objects may have the same *types* of instance variables and the same methods. Such objects are grouped into a *class* and are said to be *instances* of the class. Usually each instance of a class has its own instance variables. If, however, all instances must have the same value for some instance variable, that variable is called a *shared-value variable*. A default value can be defined for a variable. This value is assigned to all instances for which a value is not specified. Such variables are called *default-valued variables*. The *domain* of an instance variable is a class and can be bound to a specific class and all subclasses of the class.

Similar classes are grouped together into *superclasses*. The result is a directed acyclic graph (DAG) containing an edge (C_1, C_2) if class C_1 is a superclass of C_2. A class inherits properties (instance variables and methods) from its immediate superclasses, and thus, inductively, from every class C for which a path exits to it from C. The class-superclass relationship (C_1, C_2) is an "IS-A" relationship in the sense that every instance of a class is also an instance of the superclass. Using the terminology of the entity-relationship model, we say that C_1 is a *generalization* of C_2 and C_2 is a *specialization* of C_1.

As the classes are arranged in a DAG to represent the IS-A relationship among them, it is possible for a class to inherit properties from several superclasses. This is called *multiple inheritance* in [Stefik86]. Multiple inheritance leads to possible naming conflicts between properties inherited from various superclasses. Another source of conflict arises from the possibility that a locally-defined class variable or method may have the same name as the one that is inherited. These conflicts are resolved by giving the local definition precedence. Other conflicts are resolved based upon a user-supplied total ordering of the superclasses. This ordering can be changed at any time by the user. Furthermore, the user may override the default conflict resolution scheme either by renaming or by explicitly choosing from which superclass the property or the method should be inherited.

3.2.2 Instances with One and Only One Type

The inheritance mechanism causes inclusion relationships among sets of instances. For example, if a class S is a subclass of a class C, then any instance of S is also an instance of C. These inclusion relationships should be maintained to make IS-A relationships among the classes of a class hierarchy meaningful.

There are two ways of positioning (physically storing) instances in class hierarchies. One can allow an instance to belong to more than one class, or mandate that an instance belong to *one and only one* class. While some object-oriented systems, such as GALILEO [Albano85], ADAPLEX [Smith80], and TAXIS [Mylopoulos80], follow the former approach, others, such as ORION [Banerjee87b], GemStone [Maier86a], and CommonLoops [Bobrow86] follow the latter approach. The class hierarchies in Figure 3.1.a and 3.1.b illustrate the former and latter approach respectively. In the figures, an arrow from x to y denotes that "y is–a x" or y is a subtype of x.

There are reasons to believe that requiring instances to belong to one and only one class is better in applications that involve many instances (i.e., data-intensive applications). The basic reason is data redundancy. By allowing instances to belong to more than one class, both storage and update costs are increased. As shown in Figure 3.1.a., if the user deletes an instance (e.g., H.J. Kim) from the UNIVERSITY-PERSON, the system must also delete corresponding instances from all subclasses of UNIVERSITY-PERSON, i.e., GRAD-STUDENT, STAFF, and TA, in order to keep the database in a consistent and meaningful state. The same argument applies to insert and update operations. One disadvantage of requiring instances to belong to one and only one class is that the data querying is more complicated (addressed in the next section); two types of retrieval and update operations are needed [Banerjee87b].

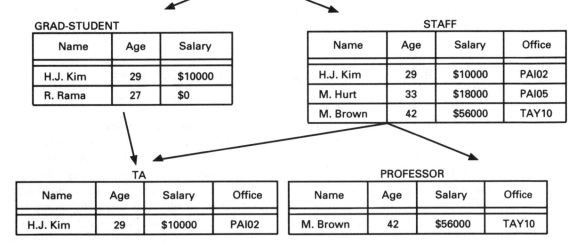

Figure 3.1.a Instances belonging to more than one class.

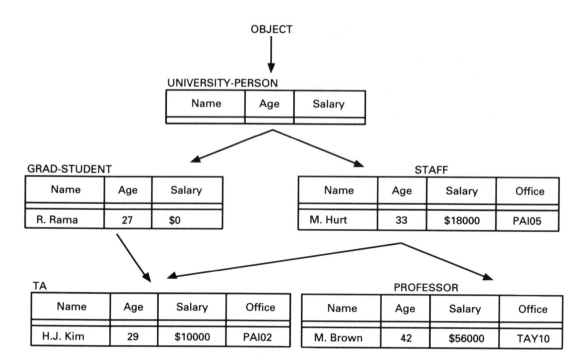

Figure 3.1.b Instances belonging to one and only one class.

The difference between the two approaches can also be seen in Figure 3.2. In Figure 3.2.a, the object 09 can belong to NUCLEARVEHICLE and WATERVEHICLE (and, of course, to VEHICLE), whereas in Figure 3.2.b, a new class, called NUCLEAR-WATERVEHICLE, must be created for capturing the object 09 in a single class.

In this chapter, we follow the approach in Figure 3.1.b and Figure 3.2.b and assume that instances cannot belong to more than one class.

3.3 A UNIFIED FRAMEWORK FOR OBJECT-ORIENTED DATABASE DESIGN

In object-oriented databases, the notion of generalization (class hierarchy) is borrowed from the knowledge representation area of AI. However, class hierarchies in knowledge representation schemes may not necessarily be accurate due to the heuristic nature of AI, whereas class hierarchies in object-oriented databases must be accurate. Object-oriented database schemas should be *consistent* and *non-redundant* (to be addressed shortly). Object-oriented database schemas tend to be modified frequently during the lifetime of a database and users tend to arrive at a preliminary design through trial and error using the schema change operations [Banerjee87]. After the user modifies the class hierarchy, the resulting class hierarchy must also be in a consistent and non-redundant state. The steps involved in object-oriented database design are considered next.

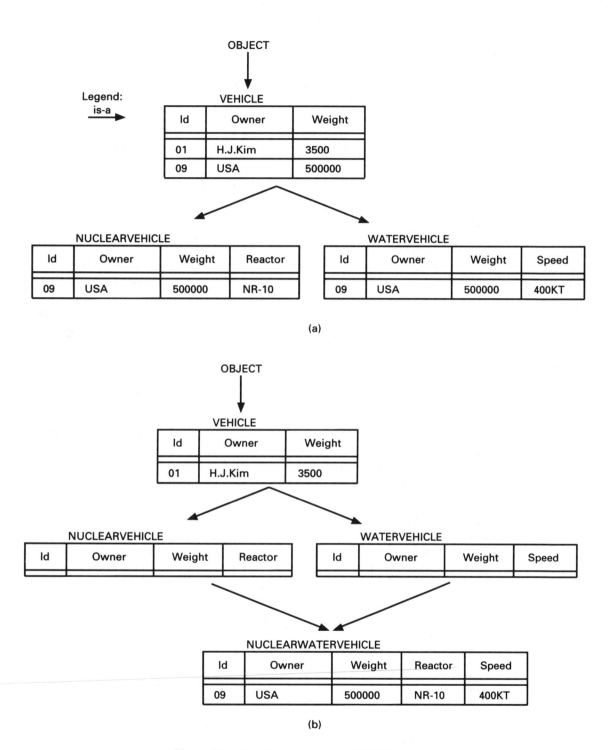

Figure 3.2 Modeling instances in VEHICLE database.

3.3.1 Object-Oriented Database Design Steps

Object-oriented database schema design can be viewed as an iterative process with 6 basic steps. Steps 4, 5 and 6 are repeated iteratively during the lifetime of a database.

> **(Step 1) Initial Design**: The user specifies a collection of classes and a set of constraints among them. Each class definition consists of a set of superclasses, a set of instance variables, and a set of methods. Constraints that will be considered in this chapter are: IS-A, Disjointness, and Covering constraints (to be defined shortly).
>
> **(Step 2) Class Compilation**: Each class definition is compiled so that it inherits instance variables and methods from its superclasses. During compilation, conflicts among inherited instance variables (and methods) and locally defined ones are resolved by a given set of conflict resolution rules. The compiled version of a class consists of only a set of instance variables and a set of methods, without a superclass declaration.
>
> **(Step 3) Schema Verification**: The initial design is checked for consistency and non-redundancy. For each declared constraint, an appropriate verification should be performed. Typical verification tasks in this step are: "Is the set of constraints consistent?", "When a user declares $A \stackrel{isa}{\Longrightarrow} B$, can A really become a subclass of B?", "Are there any equivalent classes or redundant IS-A relationships in the set of constraints?," etc.
>
> **(Step 4) Schema Querying**: During the lifetime of a database, the user can query against a schema and the constraints on that schema. This step is necessitated by the need to understand non-obvious aspects of the current class hierarchy and to prepare for the next schema change operation. Typical queries raised by the user in step 4 are: "Is A a subclass of B?", "What are subclasses of A?", "Is A disjoint with B?", etc.
>
> **(Step 5) Schema Modification**: Typical schema change operations are: "create a new class", "create a new IS-A relationship among classes", "drop an existing class", etc. All the schema change operations in the taxonomy, to be described shortly, can be applied to the schema. Constraints on the schema also can be changed.
>
> **(Step 6) Schema Verification**: The schema resulting from schema change operations and constraint modifications must be rechecked for consistency and non-redundancy. Typical verification tasks in step 6 are the same as those in step 3.

3.3.2 Schema Change Operations in Object-Oriented Databases

A schema change taxonomy for object-oriented databases is given below. All the operations in the following taxonomy have been implemented in ORION system [Banerjee87b]. Readers interested in further details concerning the semantics of schema change operations are referred to [Banerjee86, Banerjee87a].

(1) Changes to the contents of a node (a class)

    (1.1) Changes to an instance variable

        (1.1.1) Add a new instance variable to a class

        (1.1.2) Drop an existing instance variable from a class

        (1.1.3) Change the name of an instance variable of a class

        (1.1.4) Change the domain of an instance variable of a class

        (1.1.5) Change the inheritance of an instance variable (inherit another instance variable with the same name)

        (1.1.6) Change the default value of an instance variable

        (1.1.7) Manipulate the shared value of an instance variable

            (1.1.7.1) Add a shared value
            (1.1.7.2) Change a shared value
            (1.1.7.3) Drop a shared value

    (1.2) Changes to a method

        (1.2.1) Add a new method to a class

        (1.2.2) Drop an existing method from a class

        (1.2.3) Change the name of a method of a class

        (1.2.4) Change the code of a method in a class

        (1.2.5) Change the inheritance of a method (inherit another method with the same name)

(2) Changes to an edge

    (2.1) Make a class S a superclass of a class C

    (2.2) Remove a class S from the superclass list of a class C

    (2.3) Change the order of superclasses of a class C

(3) Changes to a node

    (3.1) Add a new class

    (3.2) Drop an existing class

    (3.3) Change the name of a class

3.3.3 Constraints in Object-Oriented Databases

In the schema object-oriented databases, the following four types of constraints arise. The user declares constraints initially and modifies them later. The system verifies whether the constraints are correctly declared and modified. The user can ask the system if a particular constraint can be derived from a given set of constraints.

1. **Single Inheritance Constraint (SIC):** Given two classes A and B, $A \xrightarrow{\text{isa}} B$ means that A is a subclass of B and every instance in A is an instance of B. Let ISET denote a set of instances. Consequently, $\text{ISET}(A) \subseteq \text{ISET}(B)$.

2. **Multiple Inheritance Constraint (MIC):** Given three classes $A, B,$ and C, $A \xrightarrow{\text{isa}} B \cap C$ means that A is a subclass of B and also a subclass of C and every object common in B and C is an object of A. $A \xrightarrow{\text{isa}} B \cap C$ implies $(A \xrightarrow{\text{isa}} B) \wedge (A \xrightarrow{\text{isa}} C)$. Consequently $\text{ISET}(A) \subseteq \text{ISET}(B) \cap \text{ISET}(C)$.

3. **Disjointness Constraint (DC):** Given two classes A and B, $A \xleftrightarrow{\text{disjoint}} B$ means that there is no common object in A and B. Therefore, $\text{ISET}(A) \cap \text{ISET}(B) = \emptyset$.

4. **Covering Constraint (CC):** Given three classes, $A, B,$ and C and two SICs, $B \xrightarrow{\text{isa}} A$ and $C \xrightarrow{\text{isa}} A$, $A \xrightarrow{\text{cover}} B \cup C$ means that every instance of A must be either an instance of B or an instance of C. Therefore, $\text{ISET}(A) \subseteq \text{ISET}(B) \cup \text{ISET}(C)$. From the given SICs, $\text{ISET}(A) \supseteq \text{ISET}(B)$ and $\text{ISET}(A) \supseteq \text{ISET}(C)$. Therefore, $\text{ISET}(A) \supseteq \text{ISET}(B) \cup \text{ISET}(C)$. Hence, $\text{ISET}(A) = \text{ISET}(B) \cup \text{ISET}(C)$.

Disjointness constraints and covering constraints are first suggested by Israel and Brachman in [Isreal84] and their formal properties are investigated by Lenzerini [Lenzerini87] and Atzeni and Parker [Atzeni86].

Example 3.3.1

The VEHICLE class hierarchy in Figure 3.3 illustrates the above four notions. A dotted arrow means a disjointness constraint and a normal arrow means an IS-A constraint. An arc implies a covering constraint. AUTO, WATERVEHICLE, and NUCLEARVEHICLE are subclasses of VEHICLE (SICs). SUBMARINE is a subclass of NUCLEARVEHICLE and WATERVEHICLE (MIC). AUTO is disjoint with WATERVEHICLE and NUCLEARVEHICLE (DCs), i.e., any instance of AUTO must not be an instance of WATERVEHICLE or an instance of NUCLEARVEHICLE. AUTO covers 2DOOR, 4DOOR, and WAGON (CC), i.e., every instance of AUTO must be an instance of 2DOOR, 4DOOR, or WAGON.

3.3.4 Three Fundamental Problems

The following three fundamental problems reside in the core of object-oriented database design.

Computation among type descriptions. If the user declares a constraint among classes, the system should make sure that the constraint is really true. We consider three types of computation among type descriptions. The terms "type description" and "class definition" will be used synonymously. We shall use $T(C)$ for denoting type

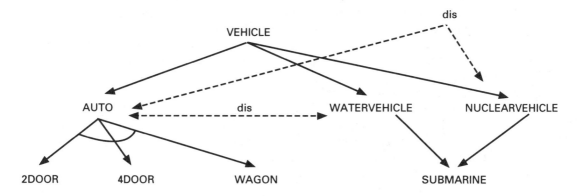

Figure 3.3   A sample class hierarchy with various constraints.

description of a class C, and $\lambda(C)$ for denoting a logical formula describing type description of a class C using a certain type representation formal language. Three type computation problems are defined below.

Given two class definitions T(A) and T(B), if the user declares $A \overset{\text{isa}}{\Longrightarrow} B$, then T($A$) should be subsumed by T(B): that is, suppose $\lambda(A)$ and $\lambda(B)$ are both formulas of a type representation language, a new formula $\lambda(A) \to \lambda(B)$ should hold where $\to$ means 'implication'. This is referred to as the "*type subsumption problem.*"

Given two class definitions T(A) and T(B), if the user declares $A \overset{\text{disjoint}}{\Longleftrightarrow} B$, then T($A$) and T($B$) must be disjoint: that is, suppose $\lambda(A)$ and $\lambda(B)$ are both formulas of a type representation language, a new formula $\lambda(A) \to \neg \lambda(B)$ (or $\lambda(B) \to \neg \lambda(A)$) should hold. We call this, the "*type disjointness problem.*"

Given three class definitions T(A), T(B) and T(C), if the user declares $A \overset{\text{cover}}{\Longrightarrow} B \cup C$, then T($A$) must be equivalent to T(B) $\cup$ T(C): that is, suppose $\lambda(A)$, $\lambda(B)$, and $\lambda(C)$ are all formulas of a type representation language, a new formula $(\lambda(A) \to \lambda(B) \vee \lambda(C)) \wedge (\lambda(B) \vee \lambda(C) \to \lambda(A))$ should hold. We call this, the "*type covering problem*".

The common core in the three type computation problems (type subsumption, type disjointness, and type covering) is essentially to *prove a well formed formula* in a type description language. Further, the type disjointness problem and the type covering problem can be viewed as special cases of the type subsumption problem. Therefore it suffices to consider only the type subsumption problem for which an in-depth review is presented in section 3.4.1.

Constraint membership problem.   Given a set of constraints provided by the user, new constraints can be derived using the associated inference rules (to be defined shortly). The user can pose queries concerning the class hierarchy and the constraints on the class hierarchy. These queries are typically to check if a particular constraint is a member of the closure of a given set of constraints, i.e., to check if the particular constraint can be derived from the given set of constraints. For example, suppose the user asks the system whether SUBMARINE is a subclass of VEHICLE in the VEHICLE class hierarchy of Figure 3.3. In order to process this query, the system needs to check whether SUBMARINE $\to$ VEHICLE is a member of the closure of the IS-A relationships in the VEHICLE class hierarchy of Figure 3.3.

Undesirable property detection problem. There are three types of undesirable properties in class hierarchy design which should be detected and reported.

Consider the situation where there are three classes A, B, and C and the user has declared A to be a subclass of both B and C, and B and C to be disjoint. Then clearly, the class A is invariably empty as B and C are disjoint. We refer to such a schema or a class hierarchy, in which a class cannot have an instance as being *inconsistent*.

Consider another situation in which the user, for three given classes A, B, and C, declares A to be a subclass of B, B to be a subclass of C, and C to be a subclass of A. This situation is undesirable because in this situation A, B, and C are actually the same class. Since a class hierarchy must be a DAG (directed acyclic graph), cyclic structures should be avoided. We call such classes *redundant classes*.

Finally, consider the case when user declares A as a subclass of B, B as a subclass of C, and A as a subclass of C. Since IS-A relationship is transitive, the last declaration "A is a subclass of C" is redundant in the sense that it can be derived from other IS-A relationships. We call this a *redundant IS-A*.

In summary, inconsistent schema, redundant classes, and redundant IS-As should be detected and avoided while designing an object-oriented database schema.

We note that the Constraint Membership Problem is associated with step 4 whereas the Type Subsumption Problem and the Undesirable Property Detection Problem are associated with step 3 and step 6. We examine below each of these problems in greater depth. We believe that the above problems should be solved automatically by the system, and not by the database designer. Fortunately, these problems have been addressed in the past, even though their solutions have been scattered in several areas such as AI knowledge representation, database dependency theory, AI theorem proving and graph algorithms.

3.4 COMPUTATIONAL ASPECTS OF THE THREE FUNDAMENTAL PROBLEMS

In this section we study the algorithms and the algorithmic complexity of the three fundamental problems encountered in the design of object-oriented schema. For the type subsumption problem several results from the literature are given. The other two problems, viz., constraint membership and undesirable property detection, are characterized using the formalisms borrowed from three formal systems: inference rules, first order logic and graph theory.

This section covers the three problems in depth and requires a degree of mathematical and algorithmic maturity. The reader may skip this section in the first reading without any loss of continuity (Eds.).

3.4.1 Type Subsumption Problem

As mentioned earlier, the type subsumption problem requires proving an implication formula ($\alpha \rightarrow \beta$, where α and β are formulas of a type description language) written in a type description language. An important issue here is that there is a fundamental tradeoff between the expressive power of the type representation language and the computational complexity of the type subsumption decision of the implication formula.

If a type representation language has the full power of first order logic, the decision problem of type subsumption is *intractable* because deciding the truth value of an arbitrary first order logic formula is intractable. In the knowledge representation area, several attempts have been made to find a type representation language which has both a reasonable expressive power and a reasonable computational overhead. Fortunately, researchers in artificial intelligence have found a good solution for the type subsumption problem.

Below we introduce a recent result by Levesque and Brachman [Levesque86]. Levesque and Brachman designed two type description languages which are almost the same at first glance. However, the computational complexity of type subsumption in one language is $O(n^2)$ whereas the other language has intractable (exponential) time complexity. Here are the BNF forms of the two type representation languages from [Levesque86].

```
(TR-1)
    <type> ::=     <atom>
                 | (AND <type1>...<type2>)
                 | (ALL <attribute> <type>)
                 | (SOME <attribute>)
    <attribute> ::= <atom>
                 | (RESTRICT <attribute> <type>)
(TR-2)
    <type> ::=     <atom>
                 | (AND <type1>...<type2>)
                 | (ALL <attribute> <type>)
                 | (SOME <attribute>)
    <attribute> ::= <atom>
```

Note that atoms are primitive types. The semantics of AND is that x is an (AND t_1 t_2 ... t_n) iff x is a t_1 and a t_2 and ... and a t_n. ALL and SOME restrict values of an attribute, e.g., x is an (ALL a t) iff each a of x is a t, that is, the domain of attribute a of the type x is a type t; and x is a (SOME a) iff x has at least one a. RESTRICT constrains attributes by the types of their values, e.g., y is a (RESTRICT a t) of x iff y is an a of x and y is a t.

The use of the two type description languages above will become clear by the following two examples from [Brachman84].

Example 3.4.2 [Brachman84]

Suppose we have five given types: PERSON, MALE, FEMALE, LAWYER, and DOCTOR. Let Child be an attribute of the type PERSON. Then, the TR-1 representation of "a person with at least one child, and each of whose sons is a lawyer and each of whose daughters is a doctor" is:

```
(AND PERSON
            (SOME Child)
            (ALL (RESTR Child MALE) LAWYER)
            (ALL (RESTR Child FEMALE) DOCTOR))
```

Example 3.4.3 [Brachman84]

Assume that we have two more basic types RICH and SURGERY and Specialty is an attribute of the type DOCTOR. Let $D1$ correspond to "a person whose children are all doctors". Let $D2$ correspond to "a person whose children are all rich, and a male each of whose rich children is a doctor with surgery as a specialty". $D1$ subsumes $D2$, i.e., $D1$ is more general than $D2$. In other words, $D2$ is a subclass of $D1$. TR-1 representations of $D1$ and $D2$ are:

```
D1 = (AND   PERSON
             (ALL Child DOCTOR))
D2 = (AND
             (AND PERSON
                  (ALL Child RICH))
             (AND MALE
                  (ALL (RESTR Child RICH)
                       (AND DOCTOR
                            (SOME (RESTR Specialty
                                   SURGERY))))))
```

Theorem 3.4.1.   Type subsumption in TR-1 is NP-complete [Levesque86].

Proof. Levesque and Brachman defined a mapping from propositional formulas in conjunctive normal form to languages in TR-1.

Theorem 3.4.2.   Type subsumption in TR-2 is $O(n^2)$ where n is the number of elements in the longest type [Levesque86].

Proof. The following algorithm by Levesque and Brachman [Levesque86] establishes the bound.

Subsumption Algorithm for TR-2: SUBSUME?(exp_1, exp_2)

1. Flatten both exp_1 and exp_2 by removing all nested AND operators. For example, after flattening (AND x (AND y z) w) will become (AND x y z w).
2. Collect all arguments to an ALL for a given role. After this operation, terms such as (AND (ALL r (AND a b c)) (ALL r (AND e f))) will become (AND (ALL r (AND a b c e f))).
3. Assuming exp_1 is now (AND a_1 ... a_n) and exp_2 is (AND b_1 ... b_m), return true iff for each a_i,
   a. if a_i is an atom, then one of the b_j is subsumed by a_i.
   b. if a_i is a SOME, then one of the b_j is subsumed by a_i.
   c. if a_i is (ALL r x), then one of b_j is (ALL r y), where SUBSUME?(x, y).

Clearly, step 1 takes linear time. Step 2 requires traversals of exp_1 and exp_2. Steps 3.a and 3.b compare atomic types which are represented in a table or a type graph (class hierarchy for atomic types). This step can be solved in two ways: (1) using inference rules and (2) using DAG traversal.

1. Inference Rules: (1.) Given a type A, $A \overset{\text{isa}}{\Longrightarrow} A$, and (2.) Given three types A,B, and C, if $A \overset{\text{isa}}{\Longrightarrow} B$ and $B \overset{\text{isa}}{\Longrightarrow} C$, then $A \overset{\text{isa}}{\Longrightarrow} C$ (i.e., transitivity). The subsumption problem between two atoms is, therefore, the membership checking problem.

2. Graph Traversal: If atoms are nodes of a DAG, the subsumption problem between two atoms is the reachability problem.

Both solutions take linear time. Step 3.c requires a traversal of exp_1 for each element of exp_1. Steps 2 and 3.c can be done in $O(n^2)$ time where n is the number of elements in the longest expression.

Normally, a class definition is composed of a set of superclasses, a set of instance variables, and a set of methods (operations). TR-1 and TR-2 can represent only superclasses and instance variables. Therefore, a mechanism for deciding subsumption between methods is needed. Deciding subsumption between methods can be understood as follows. We follow Cardelli [Cardelli83].

Definition 3.4.1. A method M has a set of input parameters $I_1, I_2, ..., I_n$ and a set of output parameters $O_1, O_2,..., O_n$, i.e., M: domain(I_1) $\times$ domain(I_2) ... $\times$ domain(I_n) $\Rightarrow$ domain(O_1) $\times$ domain(O_2) ... $\times$ domain(O_n). Let M': domain(I_1') $\times$ domain(I_2') ... $\times$ domain(I_n') $\Rightarrow$ domain(O_1') $\times$ domain(O_2') ... $\times$ domain(O_n'). Then M subsumes M' iff for all i, domain(I_i') subsumes domain(I_i) and domain(O_i) subsumes domain(O_i') respectively.

Figure 3.4 shows the subsumption between methods. Obviously the computational overhead for method subsumption depends on the representation language for input and output parameters. Hence we can make use of TR-1 or TR-2 for representing methods.

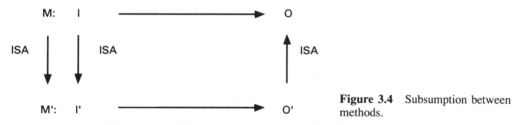

Figure 3.4 Subsumption between methods.

Example 3.4.4 [Cardelli83]

Let M: VEHICLE $\rightarrow$ VEHICLE and M': CAR $\rightarrow$ OBJECT. Since VEHICLE subsumes CAR (i.e., CAR is a VEHICLE) and OBJECT subsumes VEHICLE (i.e., VEHICLE is a OBJECT), M subsumes M' (i.e., M' is a M).

3.4.2 Constraint Membership Problem

We can characterize the constraint membership problem in three different formal systems: inference rule system, first order logic system, and graph theory system.

Inference rule system. The four types of constraints have their own inference rules. The most important issues in an inference rule system are whether every valid constraint can be generated by the inference rules (completeness), and whether the inference rules generate only valid constraints (soundness). Fortunately, the soundness and completeness of the inference rules for the four constraints (SIC, MIC, CC and DC) were proved in the literature [Arisawa86, Atzeni86, Lenzerini87]. Another important issue is how fast a new constraint can be derived from a given set of constraints. The computational complexities of the membership checking algorithms were also investigated in [Arisawa86]. Here we summarize these results and clarify the connections among the four types of constraints.

Definition 3.4.2. We call a set of constraints given by the user $CSET$. The definitions of inference rules for each constraint, as originally introduced in [Arisawa86, Atzeni86, Lenzerini87], are as follows.

1. Inference Rules for single inheritance constraint:

   SIC-R1: Given a class A, $A \overset{\text{isa}}{\Longrightarrow} A$.

   SIC-R2: Given three classes A,B, and C, if $A \overset{\text{isa}}{\Longrightarrow} B$ and $B \overset{\text{isa}}{\Longrightarrow} C$, then $A \overset{\text{isa}}{\Longrightarrow} C$ (transitivity).

   SIC-R3: Given classes A, B_1, B_2, ..., B_n, if $A \overset{\text{isa}}{\Longrightarrow} B_1 \cap B_2 \cap ... \cap B_n$, then $A \overset{\text{isa}}{\Longrightarrow} B_i$ for every $i = 1, ..., n$.

2. Inference Rules for multiple inheritance constraint:

   MIC-R1: Given classes A, B_1, B_2, ..., B_n, if $A \overset{\text{isa}}{\Longrightarrow} B_i$ for every $i = 1, ..., n$, then $A \overset{\text{isa}}{\Longrightarrow} B_1 \cap B_2 \cap ... \cap B_n$.

3. Inference Rules for covering constraint:

   CC-R1: Let G be a set of classes. If $A \in G$, $A \overset{\text{cover}}{\Longrightarrow} G$.

   CC-R2: Let $G1$ and $G2$ be sets of classes, if $A \overset{\text{cover}}{\Longrightarrow} G1$ and $B \overset{\text{cover}}{\Longrightarrow} G2$ and $B \in G1$, then $A \overset{\text{cover}}{\Longrightarrow} (G1 - B) \cup G2$.

4. Inference Rules for disjointness constraint:

   DC-R1: Given two classes, A and B, if $A \overset{\text{disjoint}}{\Longleftrightarrow} A$, then $A \overset{\text{disjoint}}{\Longleftrightarrow} B$.

   DC-R2: Given three classes, A,B, and C, if $A \overset{\text{disjoint}}{\Longleftrightarrow} B$ and $C \overset{\text{isa}}{\Longrightarrow} A$, then $C \overset{\text{disjoint}}{\Longleftrightarrow} B$.

   DC-R3: Given two classes, A and B, if $A \overset{\text{disjoint}}{\Longleftrightarrow} A$, then $A \overset{\text{isa}}{\Longrightarrow} B$.

DC-R1 and DC-R3 may seem unreasonable initially. However, these rules are never used in a consistent schema because their if-clause is always false [Atzeni86].

Theorem 3.4.3. The following are true:

1. SIC-R1 and SIC-R2 are sound and complete with respect to SICs [Arisawa86].
2. SIC-R1, SIC-R2, SIC-R3, and MIC-R1 are sound and complete with respect to SICs and MICs [Arisawa86].
3. DC-R1, DC-R2, and DC-R3 are sound and complete with respect to DCs [Atzeni86].
4. SIC-R1, SIC-R2, DC-R1, DC-R2, and DC-R3 are sound and complete with respect to SICs and DCs [Atzeni86].
5. CC-R1 and CC-R2 are sound and complete with respect to CCs [Lenzerini87].

Lemma 3.4.1 SIC-R1, SIC-R2, CC-R1, CC-R2, DC-R1, DC-R2, and DC-R3 are sound and complete with respect to SICs, CCs and DCs.

Proof. CCs and SICs are independent in that CC rules do not depend on any SICs and also SIC rules do not depend on CCs. The same argument is applied to CCs and DCs.. By Theorem 3.4.3(5), the soundness and completeness of CC rules are guaranteed. DC rules depend on SICs. By Theorem 3.4.3(4), the soundness and completeness of SIC rules and DCs with respect to SICs and DCs are guaranteed.

Theorem 3.4.4. SIC-R1, SIC-R2, SIC-R3, MIC-R1, CC-R1, CC-R2, DC-R1, DC-R2, and DC-R3 are sound and complete with respect to SICs, MICs, CCs and DCs.

Proof. Every MIC can be transformed into a set of SICs by the rule SIC-R3. By Lemma 3.4.1, this theorem holds.

As we mentioned earlier, an important issue of the constraint membership problem is to determine how fast a member (new constraint) can be derived from the given set of constraints. The following results shed some light on this problem.

Theorem 3.4.5. Testing the membership of SICs is $O(k)$ where k is the number of SICs in the given set $CSET$ [Arisawa86].

Theorem 3.4.6. Testing the membership of SICs and MICs is $O(k)$ where k is the number of SICs and MICs in the given set $CSET$ [Arisawa86].

Theorem 3.4.7. Testing the membership of CCs is $O(k)$ where k is the number of CCs in the given set $CSET$ [Lenzerini87].

Theorem 3.4.8. Testing the membership of DCs is $O(nk)$ where k is the number of SICs and MICs and n is the number of DCs in the given set $CSET$.

Proof. The following algorithm is for testing the membership of a DC $A \overset{\text{disjoint}}{\Longleftrightarrow} B$ in $CSET$. We assume that the given constraints are logically consistent. Owing to Theorem 3.4.3 and Theorem 3.4.6, the algorithm becomes simple. The algorithm is correct in accordance with Theorem 3.4.3 (Completeness and Soundness of SIC and DC inference rules) because the inference rules of SIC and DC are implemented in the algorithm. More precisely, the algorithm implements only SIC-R2 (line 5), SIC-R3 (line 1) and DC-R2 (line 3 and 5) because SIC-R1, DC-R1 and DC-R3 are trivial inference rules.

```
DISJOINT?(A,B)
/* A,B: Classes */
begin
1 transform all MICs in CSET into SICs and assign them
       to EXTRA;
2 CSET ← CSET ∪ EXTRA;
3 foreach DC X ⟺ Y in CSET: do
4     begin
```

```
5       if (( A ⇒ᶦˢᵃ X can be derived from CSET) ∧
              ( B ⇒ᶦˢᵃ Y can be derived from CSET)) ∨
            (( B ⇒ᶦˢᵃ X can be derived from CSET) ∧
              ( A ⇒ᶦˢᵃ Y can be derived from CSET))
6       then return ("YES");
7       end
8 return ("NO");
 end
```

Since the steps in line 1 and 5 take $O(k)$ where k is the number of SICs and MICs and the foreach loop halts in $O(n)$ where n is the number of DCs in the given set $CSET$, in total, this algorithm takes time of $O(nk)$.

First order logic system. The above four types of constraints can be expressed with formulas of the first order theory [Lenzerini87]. The formulas are universally quantified and include only unary predicates and no function symbols.

$A \overset{\text{isa}}{\Longrightarrow} B$	is transformed into	$\forall\, x\ (A(x) \to B(x))$
$A \overset{\text{isa}}{\Longrightarrow} B \cap C$	is transformed into	$\forall\, x\ (A(x) \to B(x) \land C(x))$
$A \overset{\text{disjoint}}{\Longleftrightarrow} B$	is transformed into	$\forall\, x\ (A(x) \to \neg\, B(x))$
$A \overset{\text{cover}}{\Longrightarrow} B \cup C$	is transformed into	$\forall\, x\ (A(x) \to B(x) \lor C(x))$

We denote a set of first order theory formulas which are provided by the user as $ASET$ (the axiom set). Constraint membership problems can now be reconstructed as follows.

1. Testing the membership of a SIC $A \overset{\text{isa}}{\Longrightarrow} B$ is equivalent to proving $ASET \vdash \forall\, x$ $(A(x) \to B(x))$.

2. Testing the membership of a DC $A \overset{\text{disjoint}}{\Longleftrightarrow} B$ is equivalent to proving $ASET \vdash \forall$ $x\ (A(x) \to \neg\, B(x))$.

3. Testing the membership of a CC $A \overset{\text{cover}}{\Longrightarrow} B \cup C$ is equivalent to proving $ASET \vdash$ $\forall\, x\ (A(x) \to B(x) \lor C(x))$.

Graph theory system. Constraint membership problems can also be reconstructed using graph theory. Let G denote a class hierarchy with SICs, DCs and CCs.

Testing the membership of a SIC $A \overset{\text{isa}}{\Longrightarrow} B$ is equivalent to finding a direct path (reachability problem) between the node A and the node B in G.

Testing the membership of a DC $A \overset{\text{disjoint}}{\Longleftrightarrow} B$ is equivalent to checking whether G includes the graphs in Figure 3.5 as subgraphs (subgraph matching problem) [Atzeni86].

Testing the membership of a CC involves computing a closure on the graph of given CCs. Consider the graphs in Figure 3.6. Figure 3.6.a has three CCs $A \overset{\text{cover}}{\Longrightarrow} B \cup C \cup D$, $C \overset{\text{cover}}{\Longrightarrow} E \cup F \cup G$, and $E \overset{\text{cover}}{\Longrightarrow} H \cup I$; Figure 3.6.b has two CCs $A \overset{\text{cover}}{\Longrightarrow} B \cup E \cup F \cup G \cup D$, and $E \overset{\text{cover}}{\Longrightarrow} H \cup I$; Figure 3.6.c has two CCs $A \overset{\text{cover}}{\Longrightarrow} B \cup C \cup D$, and $C \overset{\text{cover}}{\Longrightarrow} H \cup I \cup F \cup G$; and finally Figure 3.6.d has one CC, $A \overset{\text{cover}}{\Longrightarrow} B \cup H \cup I \cup F$

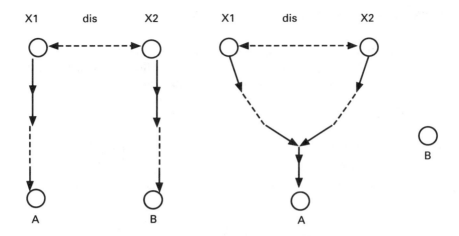

Figure 3.5 Disjointness constraint derivations.

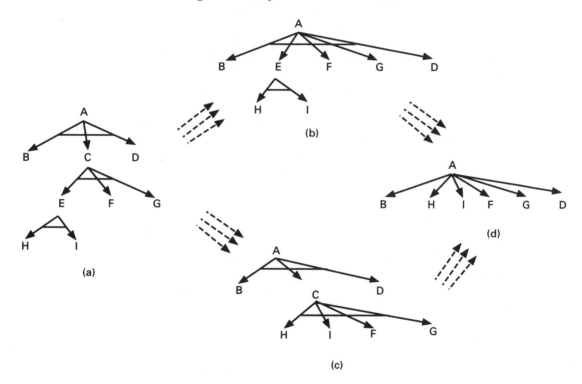

Figure 3.6 Graph associating CCs.

∪ *G* ∪*D*. One-level trees of Figure 3.6.a-3.6.b are the closure of CCs in Figure 3.6.a. Therefore, testing the membership of a CC can be viewed as a graph matching problem.

Thus testing various types of memberships can also be posed as some well studied problems in graph theory. In order to solve the above problems, existing graph algorithms may be used directly or may have to be slightly modified for the above problems.

3.4.3 Undesirable Property Detection Problem

As we can solve the constraint membership problem in three ways (inference rules, first order logic, and graph algorithms), we also can solve the undersirable property detection problem in three different formal systems. As mentioned earlier, we consider three cases of undesirable properties: inconsistent schema, schema with equivalent classes (cyclic structures), and schema with redundant IS-A relationships.

Inference rule system. The inconsistency checking problem is equivalent to checking whether for a certain class x, $x \overset{\text{disjoint}}{\Longleftrightarrow} x$ can be derived from $CSET$ [Atzeni86].
The redundant class problem is equivalent to running the following algorithm:

```
begin
foreach class x in CSET:
  if {x}^+ includes x
  then x is a redundant class
end
```

where $\{x\}^+$ denotes the transitive closure of SICs whose left-hand sides are x (excluding the starting x).

The redundant IS-A problem is equivalent to running the following algorithm:

```
begin
foreach SIC {i} in  CSET:
  if i can be derived from CSET - {i}
  then i is a redundant IS-A relationship
end
```

First order logic system. The inconsistency checking problem is equivalent to checking whether formulas in $ASET$ are satisfiable. Lenzerini [Lenzerini87] showed that a set of universally quantified formulas of first order theories with unary predicates and no function symbols can be mapped (1-to-1) into propositional formulas in conjunctive normal forms. As it turns out, the first order logic formulas of SICs, MICs and DCs have exactly two unary predicates. Formulas of CCs can have more than two unary predicates. This minor difference causes enormous difference in computational complexity of constraint membership problem.

Theorem 3.4.9. The satisfiability problem with respect to SICs, MICs and DCs has polynomial time complexity.

Proof. SICs and DCs are transformed into first order logic formulas having exactly two unary predicates. Every MIC can be transformed into a set of SICs and the SICs in this set, in turn, are transformed into formulas having two unary predicates. Now every transformed formula has only two unary predicates and the satisfiability problem of such formulas, popularly known as the 2-SAT problem, can be solved in polynomial time (unlike the corresponding 3-SAT problem) [Aho76].

Theorem 3.4.10. Satisfiability problem with all four constraints, i.e., with respect to SICs, MICs, DCs and CCs, is NP-complete.

Proof. CCs are transformed into formulas having more than two unary predicates and all unary predicates are connected with $\vee$. For example, $A \overset{\text{cover}}{\Longrightarrow} B \cup C$ is transformed into $\forall x ((\neg A(x)) \vee B(x) \vee C(x))$. Obviously, such formulas cannot be transformed into formulas having only two unary predicates. As we mentioned earlier, a set of universally quantified formula with unary predicates and no function symbols can be mapped (1-to-1) into propositional formulas in conjunctive normal forms. Now some of the transformed propositional formulas have more than two unary predicates and the satisfiability problem of such formulas is called the 3-SAT problem. Since 3-SAT is NP-complete [Aho76], the theorem holds.

The redundant class problem is equivalent to running the following algorithm:

```
begin
foreach i of the form (∀ x A(x) ⇒ B(x)) in ASET:
  if ASET ⊢ (∀ x ( A(x) ⇒ B(x) ∧ ( B(x) ⇒ A(x))))
  then A and B are equivalent classes
end
```

The redundant IS-A problem is equivalent to running the following algorithm:

```
begin
foreach i of the form (∀ x A(x) ⇒ B(x)) in ASET:
  if ( ASET - i)⊢ i
  then i is a redundant IS-A relationship
end
```

Graph theory system. The inconsistency checking problem is equivalent to checking whether one of the graphs in Figure 3.7.a is a subgraph of G.

The redundant class problem is equivalent to finding a cycle in G. The cycle checking algorithm runs in $O(k)$ where k is the number of edges in G. The cycle checking algorithm is based on depth-first search. However, finding out all cycles and printing out all classes involving cycles is computationally hard (exponential time).

The redundant IS-A problem is equivalent to checking whether one of the graphs in Figure 3.7.b is a subgraph of G. The following is the graph algorithm for the redundant IS-A problem.

```
begin
foreach edge (x, y) in G:
    delete the edge (x, y) from G;
    add a new edge ( y, x) to G;
    run cycle detection algorithm starting from y;
    if a cycle is found then the IS-A from x to y
        is redundant;
end
```

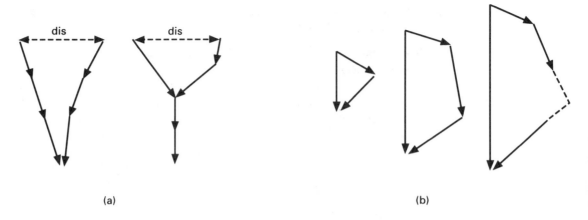

(a)   (b)

Figure 3.7   Graph associating undesirable properties.

This algorithm has $O(k^2)$ run-time where k is the number of edges in G. However, finding out all classes involving redundant edges is computationally hard, as is finding all cycles.

Implementation.   The formal systems used above implicitly suggest an implementation style. For inference rules system based solutions, a PROLOG interpreter seems the best vehicle for implementation. For first order logic system based solutions, general theorem provers for first order logic (say, resolution theorem prover) can be used. However, we suspect that database environment cannot allow the use of theorem provers because of performance reasons. For graph theory based solutions, any general programming language can be used.

3.5 SUBCLASSING

In order to achieve a consistent and optimal class hierarchy which implements the desired semantics, one has to apply various schema change operations outlined in the previous section. Among the operations in the taxonomy, "(3.1) Add a new class" or subclassing is the most frequently used operation in object-oriented applications. In the rest of this chapter we examine subclassing in greater detail.

A new class needs to be created when a new concept has to be introduced in the system. The new class may be a specialization of an existing class or classes. These latter classes, then, have to be specified as the superclasses of the new class. All instance variables and methods of the superclasses are inherited by the new subclass. Typically, either some changes to the inherited instance variables or methods are needed, or new instance variables or new methods have to be added to the new subclass.

We identify three cases in which subclassing is needed.

Case 1: The user (database designer) needs to create a new subclass from a class C in order to partition existing instances of the class C for conceptual convenience. In this case, C is the unique superclass of the new subclass. For example, a user may want to classify expensive and cheap automobiles from AUTOMOBILE class. Two refined class definitions of AUTOMOBILE class are needed for expensive and cheap automobiles respectively; if the price of an automobile is more than $10,000, then the automobile is an expensive automobile, otherwise it is a cheap automobile. Instances of AUTOMOBILE class must be moved down to the two new subclasses because an instance cannot belong to more than one class.

In general, partitioning of the instances of a class can be achieved by applying some predicates (we shall call them *subclassing conditions*) to existing instances of the class. If partitioning is determined by predicates on an instance variable, we call such variable *partition-control instance variable*. In the above example, the price instance variable is a partition-control instance variable.

Case 2: When a designer wants to insert an instance to a database, if more than one class can accommodate the instance and the classes do not have IS-A relationship, a new class must be created due to the restriction that an instance cannot belong to more than one class. For example, if the user wants to insert an instance I to a database, and I can belong to two existing classes C_1 and C_2 between which there is no IS-A relationship, then a new subclass having C_1 and C_2 as superclasses needs to be created for storing I. In this case, a test must be performed by either the user or the system to determine whether I belongs to more than one class.

Case 3: When a designer wants to insert an instance to a database, if no existing class can accommodate the instance, a new class must be created for storing the new instance. Again, either the user or the system can check whether or not the instance belongs to any existing class.

We shall present subclassing algorithms for the above three situations in section 3.5.2. As mentioned earlier in this section, a new class definition accompanies *restrictions*, such as declaration of new instance variables and modifications on inherited instance variables. The new class definition also accompanies declaration of new methods and modifications of inherited methods. However, in this chapter, we concentrate on instance variable-oriented restrictions. We discuss below the types of restrictions and the semantics of each type.

3.5.1 Taxonomy of Restriction

The following types of restrictions can be identified.

     (1) Predicate-based
          (1.1) Interval Reduction
          (1.2) Value Isolation
          (1.3) Value Negation
          (1.4) Instance Variable Comparison
     (2) Domain Reduction
     (3) Instance Variable Overriding
     (4) Instance Variable Addition

Subclassing combines one or more of the above cases. The sub-cases of (1) involve application of predicates to domains of instance variables of a parent class. Interval reduction (1.1) type of restriction reduces the interval domain of a partition-control instance variable of a superclass, whereas value isolation (1.2) and value negation (1.3) involve specifying and excluding a particular value in the domain of a partition-control instance variable, respectively. Instance variable comparison (1.4) entails comparing values of two different variables to select out instances.

For examples of (1), consider Figure 3.8. A new class BIG-ENGINE-AUTO may be created from the class AUTOMOBILE by specifying a predicate (Size $\geq$ 300). A new class TWO-DOOR-AUTO may be created from the AUTOMOBILE class by specifying a predicate (NoDoors = 2) whereas NON-TWO-DOOR-AUTO by a predicate (NoDoors $\neq$ 2). These examples represent (1.1), (1.2) and (1.3) types of restrictions, respectively. As an example of (1.4), consider PEOPLE class with three instance variables ($name, income, outgo$). A new class DEBTER can be defined as people who spent more money than what they earned (i.e., $income < outgo$).

Domain reduction (2) is to change the domain D of an inherited instance variable to a subclass of D. Again in Figure 3.8, WATERVEHICLE class inherits three instance variables of VEHICLE class, but changes the domain of Manufacturer instance variable from COMPANY to SHIPBUILDER which is a subclass of COMPANY class.

Instance variable overriding (3) is used to override the domain of an inherited variable with a different domain, (i.e., change the meaning of the instance variable). For example, suppose BUS class is created from AUTOMOBILE class. The meaning of Size in AUTOMOBILE is engine size. The designer can change the meaning of Size to "number of people which can be accommodated in a bus" as shown in Figure 3.8. Instance variable addition (4) is to add new instance variables while subclassing. As shown in Figure 3.8, AUTOMOBILE class has three new instance variables as well as three inherited instance variables from the VEHICLE class.

3.5.2 Subclassings and Subclassing Conditions

In practice, a large number of subclassings involve the predicate-based restrictions in (1). In this section we shall elaborate on predicate-based restrictions.

Conceptual subclassing condition vs. actual subclassing condition.
Suppose AUTOMOBILE class has two subclasses, BIG-ENGINE-AUTO and SMALL-ENGINE-AUTO, as shown in Figure 3.9.a. AUTOMOBILE class has four instance variables: `Id` (Positive Integer), `Manufacturer` (String), `Engine-size` (Positive Integer), and `Price` (Real).

Assume that the subclassing condition of AUTOMOBILE class is (150 $\leq$ `Engine-Size` $\leq$ 450) $\wedge$ (5000.00 $\leq$ `Price` $\leq$ 40000.00) and let this predicate be denoted by P. Suppose BIG-ENGINE-AUTO class and SMALL-ENGINE-AUTO are for automobiles whose engine size is bigger than 300 cubic inches and smaller than or equal to 300 cubic inches, respectively. Then the subclassing conditions of BIG-ENGINE and SMALL-ENGINE are P $\wedge$ (`Engine-Size` > 300), and P $\wedge$ (`Engine-Size` $\leq$ 300), respectively. Note that P is inherited by BIG-ENGINE and SMALL-ENGINE. As all properties of a class such as instance variables or methods are inherited into subclasses, subclassing conditions should also be inherited. Subclassing conditions are inherited in a conjunctive form.

Clearly both P $\wedge$ (`Engine-Size` > 300) and P $\wedge$ (`Engine-Size` $\leq$ 300) imply P. IS-A relationships between AUTOMOBILE and BIG-ENGINE and be-

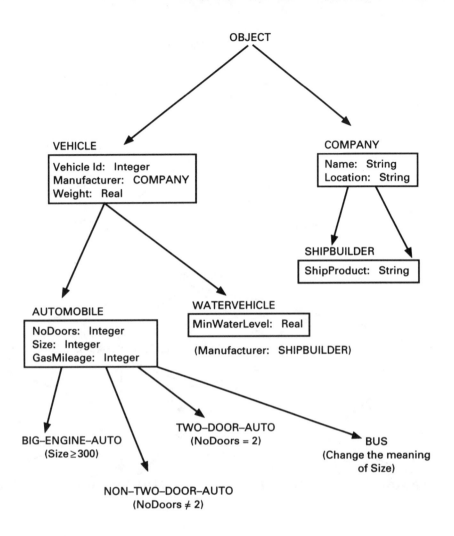

Figure 3.8 VEHICLE and COMPANY class hierarchies.

tween AUTOMOBILE and SMALL-ENGINE-AUTO make sense, i.e., every automobile with engine size bigger than 300 and smaller than or equal to 300 is an automobile. We call P, P ∧ (Engine-Size > 300), and P ∧ (Engine-Size ≤ 300) the *conceptual subclassing condition predicates* (denoted CSCP) of AUTOMOBILE, BIG-ENGINE-AUTO, and SMALL-ENGINE-AUTO, respectively.

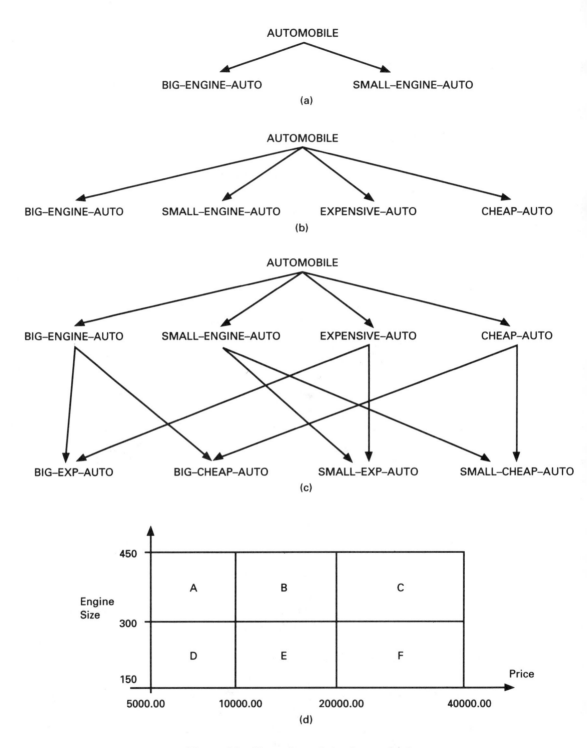

Figure 3.9 Illustrating subclassing mechanism.

As mentioned earlier, an instance must belong to (in order to be physically stored) one and only one class. Again in Figure 3.9.a, none of the automobile instances are physically stored in the AUTOMOBILE class. That is because an automobile, which is an instance of both AUTOMOBILE and BIG-ENGINE-AUTO, is stored in BIG-ENGINE-AUTO while an automobile, which is an instance of both AUTOMOBILE and SMALL-ENGINE-AUTO, is stored in SMALL-ENGINE-AUTO. This gives rise to another concept called *actual subclassing condition predicates* (denoted ASCP) which define membership in a class but in no subclasses.

The actual subclassing condition predicates of AUTOMOBILE, SMALL-ENGINE-AUTO and BIG-ENGINE-AUTO are $P \wedge \neg$ (Engine-Size > 300) $\wedge \neg$ (Engine-Size $\leq$ 300), $P \wedge$ (Engine-Size $\leq$ 300), and $P \wedge$ (Engine-Size > 300), respectively. The actual subclassing condition of AUTOMOBILE is unsatisfiable (i.e, always false) and no instance can belong to AUTOMOBILE. Only instances, which satisfy ASCP of a class C, can belong to the class C. It should be noted that ASCPs of AUTOMOBILE, SMALL-ENGINE-AUTO, and BIG-ENGINE-AUTO are mutually disjoint.

In summary, conceptual subclassing conditions define membership in a class and its subclassess; actual subclassing conditions define membership in a class but not in subclasses. The relationships among various predicates in Figure 3.9.a are given below.

CSCP(BIG-ENGINE-AUTO) implies CSCP(AUTOMOBILE)
CSCP(SMALL-ENGINE-AUTO) implies CSCP(AUTOMOBILE)
ASCP(BIG-ENGINE-AUTO) $\wedge$ ASCP(AUTOMOBILE) is unsatisfiable
ASCP(SMALL-ENGINE-AUTO) $\wedge$ ASCP(AUTOMOBILE) is unsatisfiable
ASCP(BIG-ENGINE-AUTO) $\wedge$ ASCP(SMALL-ENGINE-AUTO) is unsatisfiable

CSCPs and ASCPs are important in that they are used to keep class hierarchy consistent and nonredundant. We now present three different subclassing algorithms and show how CSCPs and ASCPs should be managed.

Case 1: Subclassing for partitioning instances. Now we consider the case of subclassing which stems from a need to partition existing instances. As mentioned earlier, in this case the designer specifies a superclass of a new subclass and some restrictions on the superclass; the superclass is the unique superclass of the new subclass.

Consider the class hierarchy in Figure 3.9.a. Instances of AUTOMOBILE class are presently partitioned into two classes by the partition-control instance variable Engine-Size, i.e., the instances in the regions A,B, and C of Figure 3.9.d are positioned in BIG-ENGINE-AUTO whereas the instance of D,E, and F are positioned in SMALL-ENGINE-AUTO. Suppose the designer is trying to create EXPENSIVE-AUTO class and CHEAP-AUTO class for distinguishing automobiles having a price between $5000.00 and $10,000.00 and between $20,000.00 and $40,000.00, respectively. Then the resulting class hierarchy would be the one in Figure 3.9.b. Now the designer has to partition instances of the AUTOMOBILE class using the partition-control instance variable, Price. An automobile whose engine size is 350 cubic inches and price is $34,000.00 should appear in two classes, EXPENSIVE-AUTO and BIG-

ENGINE-AUTO. Therefore, the class hierarchy in Figure 3.9.b is not allowed. In this case, either a new subclass is created for accommodating instances belonging to both EXPENSIVE-AUTO and BIG-ENGINE-AUTO, or the request must be rejected. The class hierarchy in Figure 3.9.c is allowed in that every instance belongs to one and only class.

Whenever a new class S is created as a subclass of C, CSCP(S) should imply CSCP(C) for a meaningful IS-A relationship. At the same time, ASCP(S) should be disjoint with ASCPs of existing classes of the database; otherwise either the creation request of S is rejected or an additional class needs to be created for preserving the property "an instance belongs to one and only one class". We present below the algorithm for Case 1 followed by a brief explanation of various steps.

```
SUBCLASSING-CASE-1 (C,S,P)
/* C : parent class of S */
/* S : new subclass */
/* P : conceptual subclassing condition predicate of S */
   begin
1  if IMPLY(P,CSCP(C)) then
     begin
2       create C such that CSCP(C) is P and ASCP(C) is P;
3       foreach I ∈ existing instances of C:
4          if ASCP(S) is satisfied with I then
5              move the instance I from C to S;
6       update ASCPs of C's superclasses;
7       foreach S' ∈ U - {C and superclasses of C}:
          /*U is the set of all classes in the database */
8          if (there is an instance satisfying both
                 ASCP(S) and ASCP(S')) then
             begin
9              create another new class S* having S and S'
               as immediate superclasses and CSCP(S*) and
               ASCP(S*) are both (ASCP(S)∧ASCP(S'));
11             foreach I ∈ instances of S':
12                if ASCP(S*) is satisfied by I then
13                    move the instance I from S' to S*;
14             update ASCPs of superclasses of S* properly;

           end;

        end;

     end;
```

- In line 1, we used IMPLY(p,q) as a built-in procedure to test if the predicate p implies the predicate q, i.e., to see if $\neg p \vee q$ is true. If a class S is a subclass of a class C, IMPLY(CSCP(C),CSCP(S)) should be true. We shall elaborate on IMPLY in section 3.6.

- Line 6 is to test whether there is an instance belonging to more than one class.

- Lines 3-5 and 11-13 shows repositioning instances from a class to a new subclass. The system may automatically perform "MOVE" operation according to subclassing conditions. Unless subclassing condition predicates are provided, the system cannot partition instances automatically. In that case we assume that the user is responsible for partitioning instances.

- After creating subclasses, ASCPs of existing classes should be updated. The details of Lines 6 and 14 (updating ASCPs) will be discussed in section 3.6.

Case 2: Subclassing for a new instance having more than one corresponding class.   Case 2 is concerned with the creation of a new subclass for a new instance which can be accommodated by more than one existing class. When a new class is created and added to a database, the appropriate taxonomic location (superclasses of the new class) should be identified by the system unless the user specifies the superclasses for the new class. We present two algorithms, denoted by Case 2A and 2B, for these two situations. Case 2A is used when the designer specifies superclasses of the class which will accommodate the new instance; Case 2B is for the case when the designer consults the system to find out the superclasses of the new class.

First, consider the case when the user provides a list of superclasses. If CSCPs of any two of superclasses are unsatisfiable, the user's request should be rejected as no instance can belong to the new class. Also if there is any IS-A relationship between any two of the classes that are provided by the user as superclasses of the new class, the request should be rejected because the resulting class hierarchy has redundancy in it. For example, suppose the user declares both BIG-ENGINE-AUTO and AUTOMOBILE in Figure 3.9.a as immediate superclasses of a new class C. The IS-A relationship between C and AUTOMOBILE is redundant in that AUTOMOBILE is already a superclass of C because AUTOMOBILE is a superclass of BIG-ENGINE-AUTO and, in turn, BIG-ENGINE-AUTO is a superclass of C. The complete algorithm for this case is given below.

```
SUBCLASSING-CASE-2A (I,C,P)
/* I : a given instance */
/* C : a given class */
/* P : user-specified superclasses of C*/
begin
1        foreach C_i,C_j ∈ P:
2            if IMPLY(TRUE,¬(CSCP (C_i) ∧CSCP (C_j))) then
             begin
3                reject the request;
4                return;
             end
5        foreach C_i, C_j ∈ P:
```

```
6          if (C_i is a superclass of C_j ) ∨ (C_j is a
               superclass of C_i ) then
           begin
7            reject the request;
8            return;
           end
9        create the new class C;
10       insert I as an instance of C;
11       update ASCPs of superclasses of C properly;

  end;
```

- Lines 2-4 test the satisfiability of CSCPs of any two superclasses which are provided by the user. If any two CSCPs are unsatisfiable, the subclassing request must be rejected.
- Lines 5-8 detect redundant IS-A relationships.
- Refer to section 3.6 for the details of line 11.

Consider now the second case where the user does not specify superclasses of the class for the new instance I. The system should find classes which can accommodate I and collect them in the superclass-set set variable. If there is only one class, the instance I should be inserted into the class. Otherwise a new class C having classes in the superclass-set as immediate superclasses should be created and the instance I inserted into C.

```
SUBCLASSING-CASE-2B (I)
/*  I : a given instance */
  begin
1    superclass-set ← ∅;
2    foreach leaf to root path in the class hierarchy:
3        foreach class C in the path:
4            if (C can accommodate I) then
5            begin
6              superclass-set ← superclass-set ∪ {C};
7              break the foreach loop in line 3;
             end;
8    if (there is only one class in the superclass-set)
9    then insert I as an instance of the class;
10   else begin
             /* more than one class can accommodate I */
11           create a new class C' having the classes as
             superclasses;
12           insert I as an instance of C';
13           update ASCPs of superclasses ofC' properly;
         end;
    end;
```

- In lines 1-7, the system returns a set of classes which can accommodate I. Redundant IS-A relationships cannot be made because once C is found to be a class which can accommodate I, then the superclasses of C are skipped.
- Refer to section 3.6 for details concerning line 13.

Case 3: Subclassing for a new (exceptional) instance having no corresponding class. In this case the procedure for consulting with the system to find out the corresponding classes for the new instance is difficult to automate because the new instance may have instance variables which do not occur in any existing class. In this situation it is the user's responsibility to provide corresponding superclasses. Thus the algorithm is the same as SUBCLASSING-CASE-2A described earlier.

3.6 SUBCLASSING CONDITION MANAGEMENT

Earlier sections have implicitly used two built-in procedures about predicates. In this section, we discuss the two built-in procedures—'update ASCPs' and 'IMPLY'—in greater detail.

3.6.1 Update Actual Subclassing Condition Predicates

After a new subclass S of a class C is created, the actual subclassing conditions of C's superclasses should be updated recursively. In the previous section, the three subclassing algorithms contain a statement, 'update ASCPs of superclasses of a class C'. The following procedure can be used to do this job.

```
UPDATE-PROPAGATION(S,P)
/* S : a new subclass */
/* P : ASCP of S */
  begin;
      foreach S' ∈ immediate superclasses of S:
          begin;
              ASCP(S') ← (ASCP(S) ∧ ¬ASCP(S'))
              UPDATE-PROPAGATION(S', ASCP(S'));
          end;
  end;
```

3.6.2 IMPLY Processing

IMPLY is a built-in procedure to test if a predicate p implies a predicate q. The implication problem can be rephrased as the unsatisfiability problem, because checking if $p \Rightarrow q$ is equivalent to checking the unsatisfiability of $\neg (p \Rightarrow q)$. In particular, we are interested in testing if a conjunction of two predicates $P1$ and $P2$ is satisfiable, that is IMPLY(true, $P1 \land P2$). Similarly, to see if a conjunction of two predicates $P1$ and $P2$ is unsatisfiable is to prove IMPLY(true, $\neg (P1 \land P2)$).

As mentioned earlier in the type subsumption problem section, testing satisfiability or proving arbitrary predicates in first-order predicate calculus is an intractable problem.

As such, adopting the first-order predicate calculus for managing subclassing conditions is not desirable. Therefore, the issue is to characterize a subset of first order predicate logic expressions which is powerful enough for expressing subclassing conditions and in which the satisfiability problem can be processed efficiently.

Subclassing conditions can be represented with the "simple predicates" of Eswaran et al. [Eswaran76]. The BNF of simple predicates (S-P) is as follows:

$$\langle \texttt{S-P} \rangle ::= \langle \texttt{S-P} \rangle \wedge \langle \texttt{S-P} \rangle \mid \langle \texttt{S-P} \rangle \vee \langle \texttt{S-P} \rangle \mid \neg \langle \texttt{S-P} \rangle \mid \langle \texttt{predicate} \rangle$$
$$\langle \texttt{predicate} \rangle ::= \langle \texttt{variable} \rangle \langle \texttt{comparison-op} \rangle \langle \texttt{right-hand side} \rangle$$
$$\langle \texttt{comparison-op} \rangle ::= \; = \mid \neq \mid < \mid \leq \mid > \mid \geq$$
$$\langle \texttt{right-hand side} \rangle ::= \langle \texttt{constant} \rangle \mid \langle \texttt{variable} \rangle \mid$$
$$\langle \texttt{variable} \rangle + \langle \texttt{constant} \rangle$$

Rosencrantz and Hunt [Rosenkrantz80] showed that the satisfiability problem of the set of simple predicates is NP-hard. However, they showed that conjunctive unequals-free predicates (simple predicates that do not contain $\neq$ and $\vee$) can be processed efficiently (polynomial time). It is interesting to note that a large class of subclassing conditions can be represented with conjunctive unequals-free predicates.

The following is the algorithm, called Satisfiability-Unequalsfree-Conjunctive-Predicates or SUCP, for testing in polynomial time the satisfiability of a conjunctive containing no $\neq$ operations [Rosenkrantz80].

SUCP (P)
```
/* P is a conjunctive unequalsfree predicate */
begin
```

1. Transform P into an equivalent predicate P' containing only the $\leq$ operator in the following manner. $V1$ and $V2$ stands for variables while $C1$ stands for a constant.
   - $V1 = V2$ is transformed into $(V1 \leq V2 + 0) \wedge (V2 \leq V1 + 0)$
   - $V1 < V2$ is transformed into $V1 \leq V2 + (-1)$
   - $V1 \leq V2$ is transformed into $V1 \leq V2 + 0$
   - $V1 > V2$ is transformed into $V2 \leq V1 + (-1)$
   - $V1 \geq V2$ is transformed into $V2 \leq V1 + 0$
   - $V1 = C1$ is transformed into $(V1 \leq 0 + C1) \wedge (0 \leq V1 + (-C1))$
   - $V1 < C1$ is transformed into $V1 \leq 0 + (C1 - 1)$
   - $V1 \leq C1$ is transformed into $V1 \leq 0 + C1$
   - $V1 > C1$ is transformed into $0 \leq V1 + (-C1 - 1)$
   - $V1 \geq C1$ is transformed into $0 \leq V1 + (-C1)$
   - $V1 = V1 + C1$ is transformed into $(V1 \leq V2 + C1) \wedge (V2 \leq V1 + (-C1))$
   - $V1 < V2 + C1$ is transformed into $V1 \leq V2 + (C1 - 1)$
   - $V1 \leq V2 + C1$ is transformed into $V1 \leq V2 + C1$
   - $V1 > V2 + C1$ is transformed into $V2 \leq V1 + (-C1 - 1)$
   - $V1 \geq V2 + C1$ is transformed into $V2 \leq V1 + (-C1)$

2. Transform P' into a weighted directed graph. The graph has a node for each variable, plus a node for a constant zero. Transformation is as follows:
   - Each var-1 $\leq$ var-2 + const-1 corresponds to an edge whose weight is const-1 from a node var-1 to a node var-2.

- Each var-1 $\leq$ 0 + const-1 corresponds to an edge whose weight is const-1 from a zero node to a node var-1.
- Each 0 $\leq$ var-1 + const-1 corresponds to an edge whose weight is $-$const-1 from a zero node to a node var-1.

3. If there is more than one edge from one node to another, retain the minimum weight edge, and discard the others.

4. Apply Floyd's all shortest path algorithm to the constructed graph to see if the graph has a negative weight circuit.

end

Rosencrantz and Hunt [Rosenkrantz80] showed that P is satisfiable if and only if its transformed weighted directed graph has no negative weight cycles. In the above algorithm, the steps 1, 2, and 3 are processed in a linear time. The step 4 (Floyd's all shortest paths algorithm) takes $O(k^3)$ for a k node graph. As such the above algorithm runs in $O(k^3)$ where k is a number of variables in the predicate P.

There are two restrictions in the above algorithm. First, each variable should be integer valued; and second, predicates cannot have $\neq$ operators. Fortunately, many of subclassing conditions involve integer valued domains such as engine size, price and number of doors.

For $\neq$ operators, Böttcher et al. [Bottcher86] have suggested a simple mechanism to include $\neq$ comparisons into the SUCP algorithm. Their algorithm first sorts the comparisons of each conjunction such that $\neq$ comparisons are located last, processes conjunctions without $\neq$, and then does additional tests for conjunctions with $\neq$. Here is the algorithm.

Satisfiability-Conjunction-Predicate(P)
```
/* P :conjunctive predicates including ≠ */
begin
```
1. Sort P into $P1 \wedge P2$ where $P1$ is conjunctive predicates without $\neq$ and $P2$ is conjunctive predicates with $\neq$

2. Perform SUCP($P1$)

3. *if* (the graph for *P1* contains no negative cycles) *then*
```
      begin
      foreach var-1 ≠ var-2 ∈ P2:
          if (the graph contains zero weight cycle
          between nodes var-1 and var-2) then
            return(''P is unsatisfiable'');
      foreach var-1 ≠ const-1 ∈ P2:
          if the graph contains zero weight cycle
              between var-1 node and zero node then
          return(''P is unsatisfiable'');
      end
   return(''P is satisfiable'');
```

end

This algorithm runs in $O(k^3)$. However, it is only partially correct in that if P is satisfiable, the algorithm always says P is satisfiable, but if P is unsatisfiable the algorithm may say P is satisfiable. This is acceptable because of the following reasons.

1. Whenever the algorithm says "P is satisfiable", search the database to see if there is really an instance satisfying P. If there is no instance satisfying P, then conclude P is unsatisfiable. In this way, the algorithm can be corrected.
2. In practice, subclassing conditions involving $\neq$ are not very prevalent.

3.6.3 Properties of Subclassing Conditions

Now we summarize the properties of subclassing conditions formally.

Criteria for consistent schema design. The following properties should hold in consistent object-oriented database schemas.

1. $\text{ASCP}(C) = \text{CSCP}(C)$ if C is a leaf class
2. $\text{CSCP}(C) = (\bigvee_{S \in immediate\ subclasses\ of\ C} \text{CSCP}(S)) \vee \text{ASCP}(C)$
3. $\text{CSCP}(C) = \text{ASCP}(C) \vee (\bigvee_{S \in superclasses\ of\ C} \text{ASCP}(C))$
4. $\nexists$ instance satisfying $(\text{ASCP}(C_i) \wedge \text{ASCP}(C_j))$ for $C_i \neq C_j$
5. $\text{IMPLY}(\text{ASCP}(C), \text{CSCP}(C))$ is true for any C

Useful rules for IMPLY processing. The following rules are useful for optimizing algorithms which are introduced so far.

1. $\text{IMPLY}(Pi, Pi)$ is true for any Pi
2. $(\text{IMPLY}(Pi, Pj) \wedge \text{IMPLY}(Pj, Pk)) \Rightarrow \text{IMPLY}(Pi, Pk)$
3. $Pi \wedge Pi$ is satisfiable for any Pi
4. $(Pi \wedge Pj$ is satisfiable) if and only if $(Pj \wedge Pi$ is satisfiable)
5. $(Pi \wedge Pj$ is satisfiable) $\wedge \text{IMPLY}(Pj, Pk) \Rightarrow (Pi \wedge Pk$ is satisfiable)

3.7 DISCUSSION

3.7.1 Desubclassing

In this section, we discuss the inverse operation of subclassing, *desubclassing* (i.e., dropping an existing class). As shown in section 3.5, the designer cannot create an arbitrary class because of the assumption "an instance belongs to one and only one class". By similar reasoning, arbitrary desubclassing is not allowed. For example, in Figure 3.9.c BIG-EXP-AUTO is not allowed to be dropped as long as instances of BIG-ENGINE-AUTO exist because BIG-EXP-AUTO was created to accommodate common instances belonging to both BIG-ENGINE-AUTO and EXPENSIVE-AUTO. In general, a class with more than one superclass cannot be dropped as long as instances remain in the class.

When a class C is dropped, instances of C are moved up to its superclass and ASCP of superclasses of C should be updated properly. Here is an algorithm for desubclassing.

```
DESUBCLASSING(C,P)
/* C: A Class to be dropped*/
/* P: ASCP of C */
begin
if ( C has more than one superclass)
    then if (instances remain in C)
            then reject the request
            else begin
                drop C;
                UPDATE-ASCP-AFTER-DESUBCLASSING( C,P);
                end
    else begin
        drop  C;
        move instances of C to its superclass;
        UPDATE-ASCP-AFTER-DESUBCLASSING( C,P);
        end
end


UPDATE-ASCP-AFTER-DESUBCLASSING(C,P)
/* C: A Class */
/* P: ASCP of C */
begin
    foreach S' ∈ immediate superclasses of S;
        begin
        ASCP( S')← ASCP(S)∨ ASCP( S');
        UPDATE-ASCP-AFTER-DESUBCLASSING(S',ASCP(S'));
        end
end
```

3.7.2 Applications of Subclassing Conditions

A major motivation behind keeping track of subclassing conditions was to maintain consistent class hierarchies and partition instances properly. Fortunately, there are many other important applications which can benefit substantially from utilizing subclassing conditions. In this section we introduce a couple of feasible applications of subclassing conditions.

Query optimization. A query processor needs to visit a target class and its subclasses for processing queries in object-oriented databases. For efficiency reasons it is not desirable to let the query be processed with instances of the target class and all of its subclasses. An interesting problem in query optimization is to find the minimal set of classes sufficient to process a query. Another problem is to simplify a query predicate when it contradicts or is implied by subclassing conditions.

Suppose a query (based on a predicate P) were posed against a class C and C's subclasses. The following algorithm finds a minimal set of classes for the query.

```
QUERY-PROCESS(C,P)
/* C: Target Class */
/* P: Query Qualification */
begin
    if (C is not marked)∧(CSCP(C)∧P)) then
        begin
        mark C;
        if(ASCP(C)∧P) then
            begin
            P←(ASCP(C)∧P);
            select instances of C satisfying the query
                    qualification P;
            end
        foreach S ∈ {immediate subclasses of C}:
                QUERY-PROCESS(S,P);
        end
    else foreach S* ∈ {subclasses of C}:
            if (S* is not marked) then mark S*;
end
```

Access control. Subclassing conditions can also be used to control the access of a user to the database (also known as "Authorization"). Suppose the user U has the access right $AR(U,C)$ against a class C and the user U poses a query with predicates $Q(C)$ to the class. The query is allowed to be processed only if $(Q(C) \wedge AR(U,C) \wedge ASCP(C))$ is satisfiable. Otherwise the query is rejected. If $(Q(C) \wedge AR(U,C) \wedge ASCP(C))$ is satisfiable, an associated problem, that concerns efficiency of processing, is to determine if there exists a simpler predicate which is equivalent to $(Q(C) \wedge AR(U,C) \wedge ASCP(C))$.

3.8 SUMMARY

This chapter established a unified framework for the logical design of object-oriented database schema by synthesizing research results of the areas such as AI knowledge representation, database dependency theory, AI theorem proving, and graph algorithms. We identified three problems, viz., type subsumption problem, constraint membership problem, and undesirable property detection problem, which are essential to the design of object-oriented schemas. A recent result by Levesque and Brachman [Levesque86] was used for the type subsumption problem. Further, we characterized the constraint membership problem and the undesirable property detection problem in the three different formal frameworks: inference rule system, first order logic system, and graph theory system.

Subclassing in object-oriented databases, a frequently used schema change operation, was considered in detail. We defined the semantics of various types of subclassing.

Most subclassings are accompanied by associated constraints called *subclassing conditions*. We investigated how to use and maintain subclassing conditions.

A major application of subclassing conditions is the maintenance of a class hierarchy in a semantically correct manner. Managing huge class hierarchies having hundreds of thousands of classes in a consistent way is almost impossible without the aid of subclassing conditions. A related problem, called *knowledge-base classification problem*, is an important research issue in AI [Finin84].

As shown in this chapter, many stages of object-oriented database design and subclassing related tasks need the capability of proving the truth value or the satisfiability of a formula in the first order logic. A proving facility (say, *predicate manager*) which can support the three fundamental problems of type subsumption, constraint membership, and undesirable property detection, and subclassing management is required. To the best of our knowledge, none of the existing object-oriented systems has such a predicate manager. The design and implementation of a predicate manager for object-oriented database systems, however, is beyond the scope of this chapter.

ACKNOWLEDGMENTS

The author gratefully thanks his advisor, Hank Korth, for his insightful comments on earlier drafts of this chapter. The author is grateful to Rajiv Gupta who helped to make this paper more readable. This research was partially supported by NSF Grant DCR-8507724 (Principal Investigators: Avi Silberschatz and Henry F. Korth, University of Texas at Austin). This work was performed while the author was at the University of Texas at Austin.

Figures 3.5 and 3.7 of this chapter have been reproduced, with permission, from the paper "Formal Properties of Net-Based Knowledge Representation Schemes," by P. Atzeni and S. Parker, Data-Engineering Conference Proceedings, 1986. The BNF forms on page 37 have been reproduced with permission, from the paper "The Tractability of Subsumption in Frame-based Description Languages," by H. Levesque and R. Brachman, AAAI Conference Proceedings, 1984.

4 Conceptual Database Evolution through Learning

Qing Li and Dennis McLeod

4.1 INTRODUCTION

A current very significant research activity in databases involves extending database capabilities to meet the needs of emerging data-intensive applications such as office information systems [Gibbs83, King85a], personal databases [Cattell83, Lyngbaek84b], design engineering databases [Afsarmanesh85a, Batory85], and artificial intelligence systems [Brodie86, Stefik86]. One of the important advanced functions that these applications require is *conceptual database evolution (CDE)*: the ability to dynamically change meta-data (conceptual database structure). The user may want to change the conceptual database structure when the application environment that the database models evolves, or when his/her view of that environment changes. Evolution may also be required when new usage patterns are encountered (e.g., an attribute/a relationship is later on used as an entity/object), or when more information/knowledge is obtained from the user (e.g., a person name is later known to have last name and first name components, not just a non-decomposable string).

Several research efforts have addressed the problem of providing facilities for the user to dynamically change the conceptual structure of a database (e.g.,[Banerjee87b, Li88a, Penney87]). The bulk of this research has been in the context of "object-oriented" database systems. In [Penney87], particular attention has been paid to kinds of changes to an object class (type), and to modification of the class/subclass hierarchy. [Banerjee87b] also addresses a variety of object class changes. In [Li88a], another particular kind of meta-data changes, termed OFE (object flavor evolution), has been studied. This kind of evolution involves changes to the fundamental semantics of objects. For example, a real-world concept modeled in a database as a symbolic object (e.g., the name of person), may later on evolve to or be alternatively viewed as an abstract object (e.g., a person entity). Most proposed approaches to accommodating dynamic evolution are, however, passive, as opposed to active. Consequently CDE is still a difficult and tedious task for the user: the user has to know "how to evolve", "what to evolve", and "when to evolve".

We are interested here in providing a database system with capabilities to actively support and conduct CDE for the end-user. In [Li88b], we proposed an *active* approach to support OFE for the end-user in a simple, extensible object-oriented database system called PKM[1] currently being implemented on top of Vbase [Ontologic88a]. Our approach is realized by incorporating machine learning techniques [Michalski83a, Michalski86b] into the PKM architecture, which is composed of a low-level object-oriented model (kernel model), and a high-level semantic model. The OFE problems have been studied mainly at the kernel level model. For the high-level model, there are also kinds of CDE that need to be studied. The kinds of CDE to be studied may be accordingly termed as "high-level"; an example is the evolution of a binary relationship to a ternary relationship. In this chapter, we explore the use of learning techniques to actively support such kinds of CDE in the context of the high-level PKM model.

The remainder of the chapter is organized as follows. In section 4.2, we summarize the overall PKM system architecture to support CDE through learning. In section 4.3, we study certain cases of high-level CDE, in which learning plays a key role. In section 4.4, we discuss related applications of CDE, including schema integration in the distributed autonomous database environment. Conclusions and research directions are offered in section 4.5.

4.2 OVERALL SYSTEM ARCHITECTURE

By applying learning techniques to the problem of conceptual database evolution (CDE), we address two goals. The first is to partially automate certain kinds of CDE. The second is to have the system learn more knowledge about the objects from various CDE cases. This leads us to an overall system architecture illustrated in Figure 4.1.

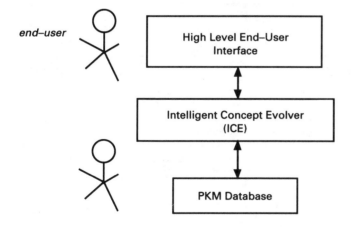

Figure 4.1 The overall PKM system architecture.

[1]PKM stands for "personal knowledge manager".

Here, end-users interact with a high-level interface, which utilizes an *intelligent concept evolver (ICE)* to support individual CDE cases, based upon three fundamental learning techniques and a set of learning heuristics. ICE also serves as an *interpreter* that translates high-level user transactions into the low-level kernel database operations.

Figure 4.2 illustrates the architecture of the intelligent concept evolver (ICE). Within ICE, three general machine learning techniques are utilized: *learning from instruction (LFI)*, *learning from exception (LFE)*, and *learning from observation (LFO)* [Carbonell83b, Hass83, Michalski86b, Michalski83b]. These three learning techniques are used to support CDE as follows:

1. LFI is a kind of *passive* learning: learning processes are explicitly initiated by the user. LFI processes acquire knowledge from the user, transform the knowledge from the high-level language to the internally-usable representation, and integrate the new information with prior knowledge for effective use. Hence, LFI processes are dialogue-based, and typically involve some inference.

2. LFE is also a kind of *passive* learning: learning processes are triggered by violations of constraints or definitions of objects in the database. LFE processes obtain knowledge from the transactions that caused the violations, from the definitions of objects, and/or from the user. Therefore, LFE processes are interactive or automatic, and they usually involve more inference than LFI processes.

3. LFO is a type of *active* learning: learning processes actively check whether there is any evolution that should be conducted, given some metrics of "improvement".

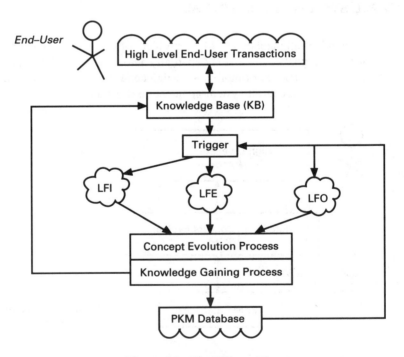

Figure 4.2 The ICE module.

This is a very general form of inductive learning that includes the discovery of an evolution target. Hence, LFO processes are automatic. This form of learning involves more inference than LFI and LFE.

In Figure 4.2, the *concept evolution process* supports changes to the definitions of objects (e.g., creating attributes of objects, modifying class/type definition predicates, etc.). The *knowledge gaining process* infers new knowledge about the objects in the database, based on the three learning techniques and a set of simple learning heuristics (described below). The knowledge inferred is then stored in the ICE knowledge base (KB)[2]. The *trigger* block of ICE is basically a collection of rules that specifies which learning processes are to be triggered for a given user transaction or CDE case.

4.3 HIGH-LEVEL EVOLUTION CASES

In this section, we study several important CDE cases in the context of the high-level PKM database model, and show how learning can ease evolution tasks for the user; we also examine what the system can learn from various evolution cases. The high-level PKM model is a simple semantic/object-oriented data model [Banerjee87a, Fishman87, Lyngbaek84b, Smith87] in which the modeling constructs type (**T**), sub/supertype (**S**), attribute (**A**), and instance (**I**) are supported. Figure 4.3 shows a portion of an example **Student Affairs Office** database of a university, defined using this data model.

In Figure 4.3, there are four type **T** objects: **Persons**, **Students**, **Courses**, and **Strings**. Type **Persons** has an attribute (**A**) **has-name** whose value range is the type

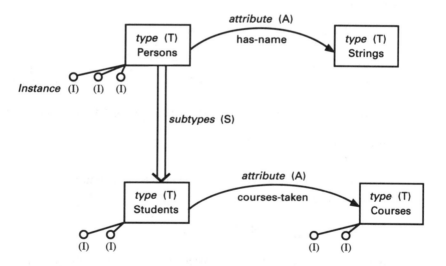

Figure 4.3 An example PKM database.

[2]Conceptually, the KB is distinct from the kernel database, but physically, the knowledge in the KB can be stored in the database as well, using the "abstract triplet" technique described in [Li88b]. Details of our approach to managing the contents of the KB are beyond the scope of this chapter.

Strings. Type **Students** is a subtype (**S**) of **Persons**. In addition to the attribute **has-name** inherited from its supertype **Persons**, **Students** has the attribute **courses-taken** whose value range is the type **Courses**. Each type object has certain instances (**I**), and the instances of a supertype include all the instances of its subtypes.

The nine kinds of CDE described below are based upon the four basic modeling constructs described above. As shown in Figure 4.4, we are interested here in examining possible evolution cases involving relationships among modeling constructs. Specifically, an arrow in Figure 4.4 indicates an evolution path of possible interest. For example, the evolution path from **T** to **S** might involve the decomposition of a type into two or more subtypes. Note that the CDE cases we consider are not exhaustive: there are other possible CDE cases in the context of such a data model. Our intention here is to present simple, fundamental CDE cases, to provide a general picture of how CDE can be actively supported through learning in a typical object-oriented database system. Further research is being conducted to identify other CDE cases which can be supported based upon our approach, and to examine in detail the relationships among such heuristics.

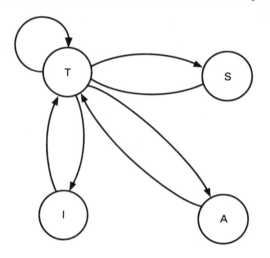

Figure 4.4 Kinds of CDE studied.

In the description of evolution cases below, we specify the following:

1. the informal *semantics* of each evolution case,
2. a *sample situation* for the evolution case,
3. the *learning techniques applied* in the course of evolution,
4. the *learning heuristics used.*[3]

(1) **Type** $\Rightarrow$_{specialize} **Subtypes**:

1. **Semantics:** Specialize a type object O_i into several subtypes. This kind of evolution is needed when the user wants to consider certain groups of instances of O_i as a whole (e.g., to define attributes exclusive to those instances, when certain transactions or constraints apply only to certain instances of O_i, etc.).

---

[3]Note that in the interest of brevity, the heuristics are described relative to the sample situation.

2. **Sample Situation:** Suppose there exists a type object **Students** in the database that has three attributes: **has-id#, courses-taken**, and **marriage-status**. Suppose further that the user decides to add a new attribute **has-spouse** to **Students**. Observing that all instances of **Students** whose **marriage-status** = "single" have null values on the newly added attribute **has-spouse**, ICE's LFO (learning from observation) process suggests specializing the type **Students** into two subtypes: one with **marriage-status** = "single" and one with **marriage-status** = "married"; the attribute **has-spouse** is associated with the second subtype (i.e., married students) only.

3. **Learning Techniques Applied:** LFO

4. **Learning Heuristics Used:** For a type object O_i, if some of its instances have null value for a given attribute A, then suggest specializing that type into subtypes O_j and O_k, with one of them (O_j) containing the instances of O_i that have null value for A; migrate A from O_i to subtype O_k.

(2) **Types $\Rightarrow$ merge Supertype:**

1. **Semantics:** Merge two type objects O_i and O_j that have the same attributes into a supertype. This kind of evolution is useful when we want to reduce the depth of sub/supertype hierarchy by removing unnecessary subtypes.

2. **Sample Situation:** Suppose that the type object **Persons** in the database has two direct subtypes: **Male** and **Female**. Discovering that the two direct subtypes of **Persons** have the same attributes, LFO suggests merging them into their supertype **Persons** by introducing a new attribute to the type **Persons**. With the user's approval, LFI (learning from instruction) is used to acquire the definition of the attribute from the user, which yields the new attribute **has-sex**; note that user approval is required, since **Male** and **Female** may exist for other reasons, e.g., **Male** may be the value range type of an attribute of some other type.

3. **Learning Techniques Applied:** LFO, LFI

4. **Learning Heuristics Used:** For any two type objects O_i and O_j that have the same attributes, suggest merging them into their direct supertype O_k by associating a new attribute with O_k; if O_i and O_j do not have the same direct supertype O_k, then suggest that one be created.

(3) **Types $\Rightarrow$ generalize Supertype:**

1. **Semantics:** Generalize two type objects O_i and O_j that have certain common attributes into a newly introduced supertype. This is useful when we want to abstract a new type from two closely related types.

2. **Sample Situation:** Suppose there are type objects **Faculty** and **Staff** in the database. Discovering that these two types have certain common attributes (e.g., **employee#, salary**, etc.), LFO suggests generalizing them to a new supertype. With the user's approval, LFI is used to acquire the name (e.g., **Employee**) and the attributes of this new type.[4] Note that this may be regarded as a more gen-

---

[4]The attributes of the new type object are by default the common attributes of the two types being generalized.

eral case of the previous one: for generalizing two types, only certain common attributes are required, whereas for merging two types, all the attributes must be the same. A fundamental difference, however, is that the two types participating in the generalization will not disappear from the database, but rather will become two direct subtypes of the newly introduced type.

3. **Learning Techniques Applied:** LFO, LFI
4. **Learning Heuristics Used:** For any two type objects O_i and O_j that have no sub/supertype relationship, if they have certain common attributes, then suggest generalizing them into a new supertype O_k whose attributes are those common attributes of O_i and O_j (by default).

(4) Attribute $\Rightarrow_{\text{objectify}}$ Type:

1. **Semantics:** Evolve an attribute A to a type object. This often implies that a binary relationship is evolved to a ternary (or higher order) relationship. It is useful if the user wants to view an attribute as a type object, and is necessary when the user wants to associate an attribute with an attribute (or equivalently, with a binary relationship).
2. **Sample Situation:** Suppose at first the type **Students** has an attribute **courses-taken** whose value range is the type object **Courses**. Now the user wants to associate an attribute **has-grade** with the attribute **courses-taken** to record the grades students received in the courses they took. This transaction, however, violates the definition of an attribute [5]; LFE (learning from exception) is used to handle this problem. Specifically, LFE is used to evolve the attribute **courses-taken** to a type object (possibly with a name change, e.g., to **Enrollments**); instances of **Enrollments** are created for each attribute mapping occurrence from **Students** to **Courses**. The attributes of the new type object **Enrollments** include **has-student** and **has-course**.
3. **Learning Techniques Applied:** LFE
4. **Learning Heuristics Used:** If an attribute A (of a type object O_i, with the value range O_j) is to be considered as a type, objectify A by creating a new type O_k with attributes **has-O_i** and **has-O_j**. Create instances of O_k for each attribute mapping occurrence defined by A; A is then deleted (alternatively, A; could be retained redundantly, with an appropriate integrity constraint specified).

(5) Type $\Rightarrow_{\text{deobjectify}}$ Attribute:

1. **Semantics:** Evolve a type object O_i to an attribute. This kind of evolution is useful when the user wants to highlight the relationship between two indirectly related types, or to eliminate unnecessary types.
2. **Sample Situation:** Suppose that there is a type object **Application-Letters** that only has two attributes: **has-sender** (whose value range is the type object **Applicants**) and **has-receiver** (whose value range is **Departments**). LFI is employed,

---

[5]In the model we use, an attribute cannot itself have attributes.

which evolves the type object **Application-Letters** to an attribute of **Applicants** (possibly with name **applied-to**). The inverse of **applied-to**, viz., **has-applicants** of **Departments** can optionally be redundantly introduced (with an appropriate integrity constraint specified).

3. **Learning Techniques Applied:** LFI
4. **Learning Heuristics Used:** For a type object O_k that only has two attributes whose value ranges are two type objects O_i and O_j, O_k can be evolved to be an attribute from O_i to O_j (and/or from O_j to O_i).

(6) Instance $\Rightarrow_{\text{promote}}$ Type

1. **Semantics:** Promote an instance object O_i to a type object, so that instances of O_i can exist.
2. **Sample Situation:** Suppose that there is a type object **CS-Courses** which contains all the courses offered by the computer science (CS) department (e.g., **CS101**, **CS201**, etc.). The course **CS557** was initially offered with one section. Noticing that the course has too many students for one section, the CS department decides to partition this course into two sections: **CS557a** and **CS557b**. The user wishes to create two objects, and wants them to be instances of the object **CS557**. LFE is used to help the user to accomplish this goal, which results in the instance object **CS557** being evolved to a type object, with the objects **CS557a** and **CS557b** as its instances; the default attribute values of **CS557a** and **CS557b** will be the attribute values of **CS577**.
3. **Learning Techniques Applied:** LFE
4. **Learning Heuristics Used:** If some instance objects $O_1,...,O_k$ are to be made instances of a non-type object O_n, evolve O_n to a type object and add $O_1,...,O_k$ to it, with their default attribute values being the attribute values of O_n.

(7) Type $\Rightarrow_{\text{reduce}}$ Instance

1. **Semantics:** Reduce a type object O_i that has only one instance or has zero instances to an instance object. This kind of evolution is useful when the user wants to eliminate unnecessary types.
2. **Sample Situation:** Suppose that there is a type object **Senior-Faculty** containing all the faculty members who have tenure. Observing that it has only one instance **George White**, ICE suggests evolving **Senior-Faculty** to an instance object, with **George White** being its synonym.
3. **Learning Techniques Applied:** LFO
4. **Learning Heuristics Used:** For a type object O_i that has only one instance or zero instances, suggest evolving O_i to an instance object.

(8) Types $\Rightarrow_{\text{combine}}$ Type:

1. **Semantics:** Combine types that have the same instances into one type. This is useful in identifying equivalent type objects, and reducing redundant types. (It is

also very useful in "schema integration" of multiple databases; see the discussion in section 4.2.)

2. **Sample Situation:** It is not unusual for the user to employ different names to denote the same or similar things at different times. Suppose there was a type object **Departments** with three attributes: **has-name**, **has-office**, and **owns**, with value ranges **Names**, **Offices**, and **Machines** (respectively). Later, an additional attribute **contains** of **Departments** is created, whose value range is the type object **Equipment**. Observing that the instances of the type **Equipment** are exactly the same as the type object **Machines**, LFO suggests combining the types **Equipment** and **Machines** into a single type.

3. **Learning Techniques Applied:** LFO

4. **Learning Heuristics Used:** For any two type objects O_i and O_j, if they have the same instances, then suggest combining these two types into one type O_i, with possible new attributes from O_j.

(9) Type $\Rightarrow_{expand}$ Subtypes:

1. **Semantics:** Expand a type object O_k into subtypes to accommodate heterogeneity among the instances of O_k. This kind of evolution is useful when the user wants to expand the definition of a type.

2. **Sample Situation:** Suppose the type object **Applicants** has three attributes: **has-name**, **has-GPA**, and **has-address**, having value ranges **Names**, **GPA**, and **Addresses** (respectively). Assume that the user wants to make the object **Robert Chen** an instance of **Applicants** with "Chen, Robert" as his name, "85.00" as his GPA, and "1210 Adams St." as his address. This transaction however, cannot be accomplished because the GPA "85.00" is not compatible with the definition of the type **GPA** (which is 4-scaled, rather than 100-scaled). LFE handles this problem, by obtaining from the user the information that GPA can be either 4-scaled or 100-scaled. The two new type objects **4-Scaled** and **100-Scaled** are introduced, as subtypes of the type object **GPA**.

3. **Learning Techniques Applied:** LFE

4. **Learning Heuristics Used:** If new instances that violate its definition are to be added to a type O_i, then expand the definition of O_i by introducing subtypes of O_i.

The above description provides us with a general picture of how learning techniques can be used to actively support conceptual database evolution (CDE) for the user. It is significant to note that CDE occurrences have varied causes: some are caused by user intentions, in which LFI is typically involved (e.g., case 5); some are triggered by user transactions unintentionally, in which the LFE technique is typically used (e.g., cases 4 and 6); some are suggested by ICE's learning processes (LFO), which indicate possible "candidates" for the user to consider[6]. Therefore, although some evolution cases (e.g., cases 4 and 5) are in some sense duals of each other, long or infinite looping of the application of heuristics is unlikely.

---

[6]Certain evolution candidates suggested by ICE may not be accepted by the user, because they might produce undesired side-effects.

4.4 APPLICATIONS OF OUR APPROACH

Our approach to supporting CDE through learning can be utilized in several contexts. Below, we examine possible applications of our approach to a single database, and to sharing among multiple databases.

4.4.1 The Single Database Context

An obvious direct application of our approach in a single database context is to support changes in data semantics, new requirements, and additional information. Further, learning based CDE supports "cooperative behavior" on the part of the system and user. For example, we would like to have the database system be tolerant of occasional deviations from the constraints imposed by the conceptual database structure; this is the problem of accommodating exceptional information [Borgida85]. Another example of cooperative behavior involves handling query failure problems [Motro86a]; in particular, queries/transactions involving new concepts are no longer necessarily "illegal"; rather, they might be evaluated successfully with appropriate learning and evolution processes [Li88a, Li88b].

Figure 4.5 shows the overall structure of an experimental single-PKM system prototype currently being implemented. This prototype is based upon the Vbase system, running on a SUN 3 workstation. For the end-user interface, we are using the SunView system [Sun86] to provide the user with a convenient and powerful interaction tool.

Note that the ICE module interacts with the PKM database at both the kernel and the high level, in order to deal with both the OFE problems described in [Li88a], and high-level CDE problems examined in this chapter.

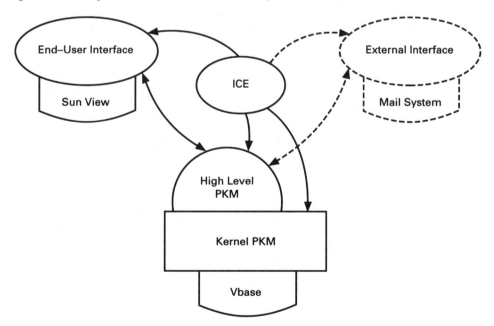

Figure 4.5 Overview of the PKM prototype.

The implementation of the kernel model and the high-level model has been greatly facilitated by the Vbase system. In particular, Vbase has been utilized to provide an implementation base for our prototype, which avoids much low-level database development that is not a main part of this research.

The overall structure of the PKM implementation based on Vbase can be described in three levels, as shown in Figure 4.6. The top level is the interface through which the high-level end-user interface can call the PKM operations for managing objects and their evolution. At level 2, the methods for the types are provided, and the PKM operations are implemented in the Vbase "C" operations (**COP**) language. All type definitions are given at the bottom level in the Vbase type definition language (**TDL**).

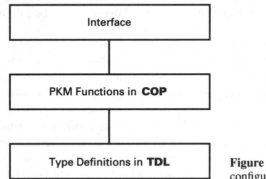

Figure 4.6 PKM system configuration.

An important issue in the design of ICE concerns the order of application of the heuristics (rules) provided for different CDE cases. In particular, objects may satisfy more than one "evolution condition" at the same time, which means they can evolve in different directions. For example, suppose type objects O_i and O_j have the same attributes; then both rule (2) and rule (3) (see above) can be applied, which may yield different results. This happens since rule (3) concerns a more general situation than rule (2). In our prototype, we take the point of view that more specific rules should have higher priority. In this example, rule (2) will be fired. There are, of course, other relationships among rules: An investigation is currently being conducted to more precisely analyze potential significant relationships and interactions among the rules.

Another significant problem is to deal with old versions of evolved objects. Old (or historical) objects are often useful and important. A mechanism is provided by ICE to retain old information objects (as well as their relationships with evolved objects); this historical information is kept in the ICE knowledge base (KB). Historical information is not only useful in answering user queries involving history, but also can aid in inferring more accurately new definitions of evolved objects [Li88b]. Another reason to keep historical information is to allow the system to be compatible with transactions that could be performed prior to evolution [Skarra86, Kim88a].

4.4.2 The Multiple Database Context

A current very important trend in information management is towards an environment consisting of a network of autonomous databases [McLeod85]. As shown in the broken line portion of Figure 4.5, an inter-PKM sharing mechanism, based initially upon current mail system facilities, is being developed. Typically in such a logically decentralized database network environment, information sharing patterns are highly dynamic, and only partial database integration and coordination are appropriate [Heimbigner85, Lyngbaek84a]. Such an environment turns out to be, in fact, a very appropriate application domain for our approach. In particular, the problems of meta-data (schema) integration can be very much eased and simplified with system support for structural evolution through learning.

The basic problems to be addressed during (partial) integration stem from the structural and semantic diversities of the databases to be (partially) merged [Batini86]. Below, we examine several kinds of diversity, discuss how they are related to the problems of conceptual database evolution (CDE) in a single database context, and show how our approach might aid in addressing such diversity.

1. **Equivalence Among Objects:** In a typical database model, significant degrees of modeling freedom are provided, vis-à-vis the conceptual representation of the same real world objects. For example, to represent the information that persons can be either male or female, one database (DB1) may use a generalization hierarchy in which a type objèct **Persons** serves as the supertype, and type objects **Male** and **Female** as two direct subtypes of **Persons**. Another database (DB2) may, however, model this information by associating the attribute **has-sex** with the type object **Persons**. These two **Persons** are not exactly the same since they use different modeling constructs, but they are similar in terms of information capacity. This kind of diversity can be handled by cases 1 and 2 above (specialize and merge).

2. **Different Perspectives:** It is only natural that users of different databases may adopt their own viewpoints in modeling real world objects and their interrelationships. For example, suppose that a user of database DB1 wants to utilize from DB2 information about the relationship between faculty members and equipment. Assume that in DB1, this information is modeled via a type object **Persons** with attribute **has-equipment**. In DB2, the information is represented via a type object **Equipment-Assignments** with attribute **has-faculty** and **has-device**. The principal difference between these two groups of constructs is that DB2 views the attribute **has-equipment** of **Persons** in DB1 as a type object (**Equipment-Assignment** in DB2). Note that such schema diversity is addressed by cases 4 and 5 above (objectify and deobjectify).

3. **Naming Conflicts:** It is common that different databases label the same or similar data using different terminology and names. In case 8 above, we have tackled the *synonym* problem which also occurs in the multiple database context. Here, we consider another kind of naming problem, the *homonym* problem, which often occurs in the multiple database context. A homonym problem occurs when the same name is used for two different concepts, which gives rise to inconsistency unless detected. For instance, suppose there is a type object **Fee-Bills** in DB1 that refers to all student registration fee bills, whereas in DB2 there is a type object **Fee-Bills** that refers to all kinds of fee bills (including staff and faculty parking fee bills, student registration fee bills, medical insurance fee bills, etc.). It is obvious that merging two such types in the integrated schema would result in producing a

single type object for two conceptually distinct kinds of objects. To deal with such problems, learning techniques can be applied to analyze the relationships between these two type objects.

4. **Mapping Compatibility:** Different databases may have different constraints on the same or similar relationships among objects. An important constraint is the *mapping constraint*, which enforces certain restrictions on the nature of a mapping. For example, DB1 may have a mapping constraint that the attribute **has-spouse** of type object **Married-Students** is one-to-one, whereas DB2 allows marriage to be one-to-many (a person can have several spouses at the same time). Clearly for DB2, the constraint on **has-spouse** of DB1 is compatible for integration, but not in the other direction. Learning techniques can be applied to identify such mapping compatibilities for the user.

4.5 CONCLUSIONS AND RESEARCH DIRECTIONS

In this chapter we have presented an active approach to supporting certain specific kinds of high-level conceptual database evolution (CDE) in an experimental object-oriented database system called PKM. First, the overall PKM system architecture that supports CDE through learning was described, with emphasis on the learning module called ICE. Then, we studied high-level CDE cases and showed how they are supported by applying learning techniques. Finally, we examined possible applications of our approach in the single and multiple PKM database contexts.

An important current direction of our research involves supporting cooperative behavior of the system and the user. In particular, a high-level end-user interface mechanism for ICE is being designed and implemented, and learning techniques employed to handle query failures and exceptional information. We also intend to apply our approach to the problem of "partial database integration" in the distributed, autonomous database environment, as described above.

5 The HyperModel Benchmark for Evaluating Object-Oriented Databases

Arne J. Berre and T. Lougenia Anderson

5.1 INTRODUCTION

Advanced database management systems (DBMSs) such as GemStone, Vbase, ONTOS, and others were developed primarily to meet the requirements of engineering applications. An important question to answer then is how well do these advanced DBMSs meet the needs of the applications for which they were developed. The best evaluation and benchmarks for a specific application can only be given by implementing the application itself for different DBMSs. This will almost always turn out to be too expensive. A second alternative is to find one generic application that represents common requirements for a larger set of applications. This is the approach we are taking in our evaluation strategy for DBMSs.

This chapter presents an application-oriented approach to evaluation and benchmarking of database management systems aimed at engineering applications. Our generic application is based on an extended hypertext model, which we call the HyperModel. HyperModel is described at a conceptual level and how it can be realized using an example object-oriented database system is shown.

Hypertext is a generic graph structure consisting of nodes and links. The nodes may contain text or other kinds of data such as bitmaps. The links are used to describe references between the nodes. Hypertext has been proposed as a good model for use in Computer Aided Software Engineering (CASE) because it is possible to store software and documentation as hypertext graphs. We chose hypertext as the basis for our evaluation strategy because the requirements it places on the DBMS are quite similar to the requirements for other kinds of engineering applications. For example, a recent development reported in [Gallo86] has shown that a data model to be used in software engineering environments is very similar to the node-link concept in hypertext models.

We have extended the basic hypertext model with two aggregation relationships, a one-to-many and a many-to-many relationship, typical of those found in part-of hierarchies. Thus it is a model that incorporates the three most commonly found relationship-types: one-to-many, many-to-many, and many-to-many with attributes. Together with operations to be performed on text-nodes and bitmap-nodes in the structure, it is a model that is mapable to a variety of engineering applications.

Historically, evaluation of DBMS systems has been concerned with performance issues [Bitton83]. However, performance is not the only factor to consider, though it is certainly a very important one. Functionality is as important to an application builder, and economic/market-factor analysis must also be considered. In our evaluation we are studying each of these factors. However, only the design of a part of the evaluation study is covered in this chapter.

We begin with an outline of the important functionality requirements for design applications in section 5.2. Section 5.3 briefly describes the related work presented in [Rubenstein87], and in section 5.4 we introduce the HyperModel benchmark design as an extension to this work. We show how a TDL-schema is derived from the general schema in section 5.5, and discuss how the HyperModel has been realized in Vbase in sections 5.6 and 5.7. Finally we conclude with some comments about Vbase in relation to the requirements from the HyperModel and a section on future work. Readers may wish to skip the Vbase related sections in the first pass and come back to them after the Vbase system has been introduced (chapters 7 and 9).

5.2 FUNCTIONALITY REQUIREMENTS FOR DESIGN APPLICATIONS

Engineering applications exhibit many of the requirements of traditional DBMS applications as well as a number of new requirements. We have, in fact, identified some thirty requirements in Tektronix in-house survey of engineering applications. This section summarizes some of the more critical DBMS requirements found by this survey. We divide the requirements into two types: data model requirements and database system requirements.

5.2.1 Data Model Requirements

One of the most obvious requirements in this area is the ability to model complex object structures. Recursive structures, nesting of objects, multi-valued relationships between objects, and object sharing all abound in engineering applications. In addition, these relationships between objects are often ordered (e.g., the sequence of sections in a document), and require attributes themselves (e.g., the date a relationship was last updated).

Engineering applications require more complex data types than are found in conventional applications. For this reason the data model must be extensible to capture new data types, such as text, engineering drawings, or cartographic maps. Also, the operations on these new data types are complex (project, select, and join with limited arithmetic are not adequate to describe these operations succinctly) and will require a full programming language to capture their semantics. Ideally, the programming language used to describe the engineering applications and the language used to describe these complex operations on the stored data structures should be the same [Maier84]. Finally, engineering applications require data model support for versioning and variation. For example, it should be possible to associate a time with all changes to an object, to model parallel versions of an object, and to support configuration structures.

5.2.2 Database System Requirements

The most important requirement in the system area is performance. Users will not accept performance that is significantly lower than the performance obtained when running the application in single-user mode on their own workstation. Since many engineering applications are interactive, this implies the need to access in the range of 100 to 10,000 objects per second, where each object is on average 100 bytes in size.

In addition, there is a requirement for conventional concurrency control (i.e., short transactions with some form of locking) as well as support for cooperation (i.e., long transactions and collaborative work on shared structures) among users. Of course, the engineering user does not want to lose work, so there is also the traditional requirement for logging, backup, and recovery.

Finally, all of this must run in a distributed environment, since typical engineering applications run on workstations which are in turn networked with other workstations. The important question here is the location of the DBMS: should it be on a central server or distributed among the workstations? Most multi-user concurrency control mechanisms require centralized control. However, performance requirements for interactive applications in the workstation environment will probably mandate more sophisticated solutions than the centralized server.

5.3 PREVIOUS WORK

The most well-known database-benchmark aimed at engineering applications "Benchmarking simple database-operations" is found in [Rubenstein87]. The application-model chosen here is document-authorship represented by documents and persons with a many-to-many relationship between them.

On this structure seven different operations are measured. They are:

1. Name Lookup
2. Range Lookup
3. Group Lookup
4. Reference Lookup
5. Record Insert
6. Sequential Scan
7. Database Open and Close

These operations give useful information about the performance of the database system, but the data model is too simple to measure transitive closures and other traversal operations that are common in engineering applications. We use this benchmark as a starting point for our work, and extend the model with more relationships, more complex object-types and additional operations appropriate for this more complex structure.

5.4 THE HYPERMODEL APPLICATION

The HyperModel presented in [Berre88] is a high-level description that can be mapped into an implementation on different database systems (see Figure 5.1). The Object Modeling Technique (OMT) described in [Blaha88] and [Loomis87] is used to give this high-level description.

The model shows that a Node has a set of attributes and that nodes are related by three different relationships, a one-to-many (1:N), a many-to-many (M:N) and a many-to-many with attributes (M:NATT). The relationship father/children is a one-to-many ordered relationship. The black circle shows a "many" end, the white a "one" end, and the arrow points towards aggregate-components. The circle on the relationship line means that the relationship is ordered. The partOf/parts relationship also describes an aggregation, but is many-to-many and allows for a Node to be partOf multiple Nodes.

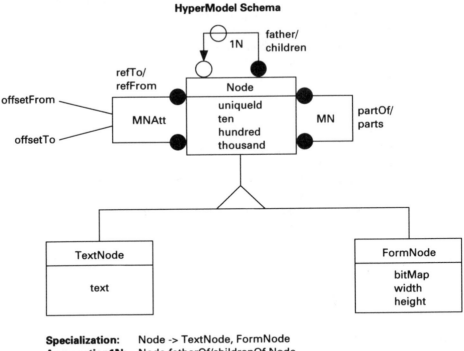

Specialization: Node -> TextNode, FormNode
Aggregation1N: Node fatherOf/childrenOf Node
AggregationMN: partOf/parts
AssociationMN: Node Ref-to/from Node

Figure 5.1 The HyperModel schema.

The refTo/refFrom relationship is many-to-many with two attributes. Aggregation in the OMT-model is an assembly-component or a-part-of relationship, which might be multilevel and recursive. Aggregation is used to combine low-level objects into composite objects.

There are two subtypes of `Node`, `TextNode` and `FormNode`, which contain text or bitmap contents with appropriate operations. The fact that some nodes contain text or a form (bitMap) is described by a generalization/specialization relationship between the `Node-class` and the `TestNode-` and `FormNode-classes`. The triangle on the lines between the classes symbolizes generalization.

5.4.1 Test-database generation

Different test-databases can be generated based on this schema. For example, for the benchmark we created three different sized databases with this structure. One of the aggregation-relationships describes a hierarchical 1:N tree-structure, while the other describes a hierarchical M:N structure with shared sub-parts. The 1:N relationship is used to create the primary structure of the test-database.

The test-database has a fan-out of five new nodes for each level in the aggregation hierarchy, and there are seven levels (0-6) in the structure of the largest test-database. This gives the following number of nodes on each level: 0(1), 1(5), 2(25), 3(125), 4(625), 5(3125), 6(15525), and a total of 19,531 nodes. The lowest level consist of text-nodes and form-nodes. There is one form-node per 125 text-nodes, giving 125 form-nodes and 15,500 text-nodes.

In order to make it easier to generate the structure and specify random objects, each node has a uniqueId-attribute, running sequentially from 0 for the first node. Such an attribute is not necessary in a system having system-supported object-identifiers, but makes it easier to specify operations. Based on a fixed fan-out for each node, and having the root-node start with 0, it is easy to figure out the level in the one-to-many hierarchical structure to which a node belongs, since the id-numbers will increase with the power of the fan-out for each level.

Two aggregation-hierarchies are imposed on the created nodes. The 1:N hierarchy is as just described, while the M:N hierarchy is created by relating each node to five random nodes from the next level in the 1:N aggregation-hierarchy. This is done for all nodes except the leaf nodes. This gives a number of 1:N and M:N relationships equal to one less than the number of nodes. This also makes it possible to measure the effect of an eventual clustering along one of the aggregation-hierarchies. If the system supports clustering, clustering is done along the 1:N relationship-hierarchy.

The ten-, hundred-, thousand-, and million-attributes of each node are randomly assigned to integers in the corresponding interval.

The refTo/refFrom relationships are created by visiting each node once and creating a reference to another random node. The values of the offset-attributes are random integers between 0 and 9. This will give a number of M:N-attribute relationships equal to the number of nodes.

Each text-node contains a text-string of a random number (10–100) of words, the words separated by a space and consisting of a random number (1-10) of random small characters. The first, middle and last word are "version-1", to allow for string search and substitution operations on the nodes. Each form-node is initially all white (all 0's), with a bitmap size varying randomly between 100x100 and 400x400.

Finally, we created test-databases of three different sizes, with five, six, or seven levels, respectively.

5.5 MAPPING BETWEEN THE OMT-MODEL AND VBASE TDL

The OMT-model can be mapped into TDL as follows:

```
define Type Node
     import Link;
     supertypes = {Entity};
     properties ={
          uniqueId: Optional Integer;
          ten: Optional Integer;
          hundred: Optional Integer;
               define set triggers (HundredSetTrigger);
          thousand: Optional Integer;
          million: Integer
               define set triggers (MillionSetTrigger);
          father: Optional Node;
          children: Optional LIST[Node];
          fromLinks: Optional SET[Link];
          toLinks: Optional SET[Link];
          parts: Optional SET[Node];
          partOf: Optional SET[Node];
};
operations = {
 /* Node-operations - for closure .. */
};
 end Node;
```

The ordered one-to-many father/children relationship can be specified as a List down the hierarchy, and as a pointer upwards. It would have been possible to represent this relationship in Vbase as an inverted link, as shown below, if there had not been an additional requirement to maintain an order on the linked objects.

```
father: Optional Node inverse $Node$children;
children: Optional distributed Set{Node} inverse
          $Node$father;
```

This would have insured an automatic update of the inverse when one side is changed. However, since this relationship is represented as an ordered list one must specify where in the list a reference is to be placed. Such automatic update for ordered sets with inverses may eventually be realized by a special set-method.

The many-to-many parts/partOf relationship can be specified by using a Set in both directions as shown above. The many-to-many relationship with attributes requires the definition of a Link-type to hold the attributes.

```
define Type Link
  import Node;
  supertypes = {Entity};
  properties = {
     toNode: Node;
     fromNode: Node;
     offsetTo: Integer;
     offsetFrom: Integer;
     };
  operations = {
};
  end Link;
```

Each relationship with attributes is handled by a separate object. In the Node type we have chosen to represent outgoing and incoming (fromLinks and toLinks) relationships in two different set-valued attributes. They could also have been handled by the same set, with the link-object asking for the toNode and fromNode each time.

5.6 CREATION OF THE TEST-DATABASE

Figure 5.2 shows the data structures used to implement the Hypermodel in Vbase.

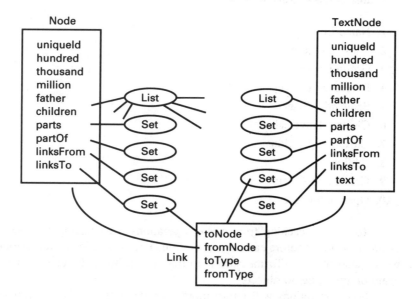

Figure 5.2 The HyperModel in Vbase.

Creation of the test-database is also used as a test case for measuring creation times. Five operations with their associated commit are measured:

```
Create the Aggregate-nodes:
Create the Leaf-nodes (text and form-nodes)
Create the 1:N relationship between nodes
Create the M:N relationship between nodes
Create the M:NATT relationship between nodes
```

As the data structure shows, for each node in the test-database six or more Vbase-objects are created. One (Node), two (TextNode) or three (FormNode) objects will be created to hold the contents, and five objects will be created to hold the relationship-pointers.

It is possible in Vbase to cluster sub-objects at entity-creation time by using the where: and hownear: parameters to the create routine as shown below.

```
node = Node$[uniqueId; name, where: parent, hownear:
              $Segment];
```

This is done for clustering along the one-to-many father/children aggregation-hierarchy.

5.7 BENCHMARK-OPERATIONS

The following ten categories of operations contain the operations to be executed on the structures in the test-database:

1. Name Lookup
2. Range Lookup
3. Group Lookup
4. Reference Lookup
5. Sequential Scan
6. Closure Traversal
7. Closure Operations
8. Editing
9. Create-and-Delete
10. Open-and-Close

To prevent caching from earlier operations from having an effect on timing, the database is closed before each new operation. Each operation is run 50 times on randomly picked start-objects. To measure the effect of caching, the operation is then run once again on the same 50 objects.

Some operations will return more than one object. The benchmark requires that the return-result be in a form that is storable in the database. For Vbase this means that a

Set or Array-object has to be created, and the resulting objects put into the collection. In many cases, however, an application does not need all result-objects at once, and could take advantage of the Iterator-construct provided by Vbase. This will save the extra time it takes to create a collection-object, and the time to put objects into the collection.

The generic set up for measuring a benchmark-operation is:

```
get 50 random object-identifiers
  for each object do the operation (not cached)
use the same 50 object-identifiers
  for each object do the operation again (cached)
```

We report the total time for each operation, the number of nodes involved, and the average time per node. This is done first for non-cached objects, then for cached objects.

The following describes each operation-group, and how it has been realized in the Vbase system.

5.7.1 Name Lookup

This operation finds the hundred-attribute of a node based on a reference to it. The reference can either be given by the value of a unique attribute (key), or by a system-generated identifier. Both kinds of lookup are measured if applicable.

These operations require retrieval of objects based on a unique attribute-value of a node, or by using Vbase's own object-pointer. To return nodes based on a unique attribute-value, an UnorderedDictionary is used. Each time a node is created it is put into the dictionary with the corresponding attribute as a key.

```
define UnorderedDictionary InitNodeDict
  memberspec= Node;
  indexspec = Integer;
end;
define Variable NodeDict:
  UnorderedDictionary[Node, Integer] := InitNodeDict;
```

Each node is put into this dictionary when it is created, e.g., by the use of a trigger-method for the creation-routine. The unique-Id of the node is used as the indexspec, and a lookup can be done by getting the dictionary element for this id:

```
node = UnorderedDictionary$GetElement($NodeDict, id);
```

The dictionary is stored in a database-variable, and used each time a node is to be looked up based on the value. Since in this case the unique attribute is an integer running sequentially from 0, an array with that integer as index could also have been used.

5.7.2 Range Lookup

This operation finds the nodes satisfying a range-predicate based on the values of the hundred- or million-attribute. The range lookup has a selectivity of 10% for the hundred-attribute and 1% for the million-attribute, and allows for the use of an indexing-mechanism on the hundred- and million-attributes.

There is no built-in or predefined indexing-mechanism in Vbase, but the concept of trigger-methods makes it possible for the application programmer to define his own, and have the structure updated each time a value is changed.

A simple solution in this case is to use an array with lists of objects, where there is a mapping between attribute-values and indexes in the array, a better solution would be to implement a B-tree mechanism. For the hundred-attribute the easiest solution is to use an array of hundred elements, while for the million-attribute a mapping to an array of a thousand elements could be used. Both arrays can be declared as database-variables and stored in the database. The following shows the indexing-structure for the million-attribute, and the structure for the hundred-attribute can be realized the same way.

```
million: Integer
   define set triggers (MillionSetTrigger);
define List EmptyList
     MemberSpec = Node;
end EmptyList;
define Array MillionArrays
     memberspec = List;
     lowerbound = 0;
     upperbound = 999;
     fill = $EmptyList;
end MillionArrays;
```

One must also define a trigger-method for creation and deletion similar to the set-trigger method.

```
void method MillionSetTrigger(node, anInt, theProp)
obj $Node node;
obj $Integer anInt;
obj $PropertyType theProp;
{
/* Call the original set-operation: */
    $$(node, anInt, theProp);
/* Update the indexing-structure with the new value and
        node */
}
```

An iterator is specified and implemented to return objects from this structure, based on a low and a high entry.

```
define iterator MillionRange(low: Integer,
    high: Integer)
    yields(Node)
```

```
     method(MillionIter)
  end MillionRange;
iterator obj Node MillionIter(low,high)
obj Integer low;
obj Integer high;
{
 Find the first and last item in the indexing-structure
  corresponding to low and high
 iterate through the possible elements
  yield each element satisfying the interval-conditions
}
```

This iterator is used each time one wants objects having the attribute-value in an interval low/high. Since trigger-methods can be specified, the programmer can trap all updates, initializations and deletions. This approach requires some programming the first time, but will be easier as a library of indexing-mechanisms is built up. The following shows the use of the iterator:

```
nrf = 0;
iterate (node = Node$MillionRange(lowbound, highbound))
{
        fndnr = node.million;
        nrf++;
}
```

If one wants to return the set of objects found instead of iterating through each one of them, a collection should be created and the found objects stored into it.

5.7.3 Group Lookup

In group lookup we follow the defined one-to-many, many-to-many, and many-to-many with attribute-relationships from random nodes and measure the average time per node to retrieve a reference to the related nodes. The return-object contains references to the nodes found, and it is storable in the database. If there is an iterator construct that gives access to nodes one at a time, the corresponding timing should also be given.

Vbase again has different possibilities for return-objects. One can either directly return the actual collection-object holding the pointers to related objects, or return a copy of it, or iterate through the collection.

```
iterate (found = node.children)
{  nr = found.hundred;
}
```

In the many-to-many relationship with attributes, one needs to find the link-objects and find the corresponding nodes from them:

```
iterate (link = node.fromLinks)
{ holdNode = link.toNode;
}
```

5.7.4 Reference Lookup

This is the inverse of group-lookup, given by following the 1:N, M:N and M:NATT
relationships in the direction opposite to that of groupLookup.

5.7.5 Sequential Scan

This operation finds the average time per object to look up the ten-attribute when all
objects of the test-structure are visited. The database should be allowed to have other
instances of class Node, (e.g., a second copy of the test-database) so the direct extension
allInstances-of-Node cannot be used to do the sequential scan. Thus one cannot
use the Class property belonging to each type to iterate through its elements. This
would give all instances of type Node, not only those belonging to the test-structure.

   If the database supports contexts or object-spaces this can be used, but the requirement is that the application-programs be able to simultaneously access other node-objects
not in the test-database. Two other possibilities are to iterate through the value-elements
of the UnorderedDictionary used for name-lookup, or to traverse the one-to-many
father/children hierarchy.

5.7.6 Closure Traversals

These operations will start with a random node, and find the nodes transitively reachable
by a certain relationship from the given node. For all the operations, we measure the
average time per node returned by the operation. These operations are defined to start in
a random node on level 3 (id 31-155) in the test-database, and then to follow either the
one-to-many relationship or one of the many-to-many relationships to a certain depth.

   The 1:N-closure is required to preserve the order of the sub-node relationships,
and deliver a list of references according to a pre-order traversal of the structure. The
list should be storable in the database. This could, for instance, be used to generate a
simple table of contents for the structure. Both the 1:N and the M:N relationships are
traversed all the way down to the leaves. The M:NATT relationship will never reach a
node without outgoing relationships (i.e., no terminating condition exists) and is specified
to traverse to a depth of 25.

   These closure-operations will typically be implemented as recursive methods with
the following generic structure:

```
for object x
  do the operation for me
  add my-result to the result
 do the operation for my related objects if any,
   when the depth is > 0
  add the result from each related object to the result
 return the result
```

Since object-creation tends to take much time, we pass a result-array and an array-index as parameters to each method call instead of creating intermediate temporary result-objects.

5.7.7 Closure Operations

These operations will start with a random node, and also perform operations on the nodes transitively reachable by a certain relationship from this node. For all the operations, we measure the average time per node involved in the operation. These operations do more than just return the nodes found in the closure, e.g., by summing up or setting values.

- **closure1NAttSum:** Get the sum of the hundred-attribute of all nodes reachable from a random node on level 3 (31-155) by following the 1:N-relationship recursively.

- **closure1NAttSet:** Set the hundred-attribute to the absolute-value of 99 minus the current value (by doing this twice the attribute is restored to its original value) for all nodes reachable from a random node on level 3 (31-155) by following the 1:N-relationship recursively.

- **closure1NPred:** Get a reference to all nodes reachable from a random node on level 3 (31-155) by following the 1:N-relationship recursively, and excluding nodes as well as terminating recursion at the nodes that have the million-attribute in the range x..x+9999. (1%).

- **closureMNATTOIDLINKSUM:** Get the total distance, measured by the toLink-attribute, to all nodes reachable from a random node on level 3 (31-155) by following the M:NATT-relationship recursively to a depth of 25. Return a list of object-reference/distance-pairs.

These operations follow the same recursive method-call structure as above, and do the appropriate operation for each object.

5.7.8 TextNode-Editing

The editing-operations are intended to demonstrate the power of the database-programming language and to test if any statements have to be executed in another programming language. The operation for `TextNodes` is to get a random textNode and substitute the occurrence of substring "Version1" with "Version-2" in the first run, then substitute back again in the second run. This requires that the text-structure be extended or replaced by a new structure. For systems that support handling of versions and variants, the editing-operations can also be used to demonstrate these features.

The `TextNode` is defined as follows:

```
define Type TextNode
    supertypes = {Node};
    properties ={
        text: Optional Dynarray[Character];
};
    operations = {
```

```
        substitute(tn: TextNode, old: String, new: String)
        method (TextNodeSubstitute)
    };
    end TextNode ;
```

In the case of basic data-types such as integers and characters, the application programmer can choose to convert between C data structures and Vbase data structures and do much of the operation-implementation in C, or to do as much as possible in Vbase-TDL/COP. A dynamic array of characters can be handled in a fashion similar to a character-array in C, and it is natural to realize the operations using Vbase data structures for the TextNode-operations. However, a conversion to C is required for the FormNode-operations.

Initially a TextNode is created with random text according to the set-up specified earlier. The substitution-method will check for any occurrences of the old substring, eventually adjust the high bound, and replace the old substring with the new.

5.7.9 Bit-Editing

The FormNode is a node-type that contains a bitmap realized by the Form-type. The edit-operation is inversion of a sub-rectangle of the bitmap. The FormNode is defined as follows:

```
define Type FormNode
    supertypes = {Node};
    properties ={
        form: optional Form;
        };
    operations = {
        bitinvert(fn: FormNode, r: Rectangle)
        method (FormNodeInvert)
            };
    end FormNode;
```

The type Form is a general type for handling bitmaps. It could also be directly defined in the FormNode-class, but it is assumed to be a type of general interest and multiple implementations will eventually exist.

```
define Type Form
    supertypes = {Entity};
    properties ={
                bitMap: optional Array[Integer];
                height: optional Integer;
                width: optional Integer;
                };
    operations = {
                invert(f: Form,x1:Integer, y1: Integer,
```

```
                    x2:Integer, y2:Integer)
                    method (FormInvert);
                getPoint(f: Form, x: Integer, y: Integer)
                  returns(Integer)
                    method (FormGetPoint);
                setPoint(f: Form, x:Integer, y:Integer,
                    val: Integer) method (FormSetPoint);
    };
        define Procedure Create(T: Type,
                keywords
                    optional bitMap: Array[Integer],
                    optional height: Integer,
                    optional width: Integer)
                returns(Form)
                raises (BadCreate)
                triggers(FormCreateTrig)
                supertypes = {$Entity$Create};
        end Create;
    end Form;
```

The trigger-method, `FormCreateTrig`, takes care of creation of representation objects. In this case the bitmap is represented in an array of integers. Based on the height and width, the size of the array is calculated and an appropriate-sized array created.

The methods `getPoint` and `setPoint` find the correct word in the array and find the correct bit using bit-operations on the integers. Since the Vbase integer type does not support bit-operations, each Vbase-integer is converted to a C-integer, then the bit-operations are done in C, and the result is converted back. The Vbase `BitString` type does not support some of the needed operations like And and Or. A possibility for enhancing performance would be to create a special storage-manager for bitmaps, and to implement specialized raster operations. The separation between specification and implementation in Vbase with the additional possibility of different storage managers make this a viable option.

The invert-method finds the first word and the last word in each raster-line and inverts the corresponding bits. Since this requires a lot of conversions between Vbase and C, much higher performance would be expected from a specialized storage manager.

5.8 VBASE EVALUATION

The following are some comments on how Vbase meets twelve requirements for data model and database system support, as extracted from the requirements described in section 5.2.

1. **Modeling of complex object-structures—** The power of the Vbase datamodel makes it easy to specify the types required by the HyperModel. There is no special support for complex objects/aggregation-relationship, but clustering may be specified at creation-time.

2. **Description of different data-types—** Since user-defined types can be created and collections such as set and array are basic types, all the specified types are defined.

3. **Integration with application programming languages—** There is a natural integration with C through COP, but no support for C++, Smalltalk-80 or other languages. The programmer needs to know three languages: C, COP and TDL.

4. **Dynamic modifications to the database schema—** New types may be added to the database, and migration of objects after a schema-change is possible in some cases.

5. **Support for Versions and Variants—** Versions and Variants are not directly supported in Version 1.1 of Vbase.

6. **An architecture of workstations and servers—** For the HyperModel application, the architecture should support multiple users in a network of workstations and servers. Version 1.1 of Vbase runs only on a single processor, and requires simultaneous users to make use of shared memory on this processor.

7. **Concurrency Control—** Version 1.1 supports a transaction-mechanism for multiple users on a single processor with shared memory, which is based on an optimistic concurrency control mechanism.

8. **Cooperation between users—** Synchronization primitives lock, sequencer, and event-count may be used by the application-programmer and are similar to the use of semaphores. These might be building-blocks in a long-transaction-mechanism, but an automatic abort in the case where one user reads something another has written may cause problems.

9. **Logging, backup and recovery—** The environment-utilities contain backup and restore facilities.

10. **Access-control—** There are no access-control facilities.

11. **Ad-Hoc Query Language—** There is a query-language, Object SQL, which is end-user oriented but does not support a programming-interface.

12. **Comments on benchmark-operations—** Since there is no indexing-mechanism to support range-queries, such a mechanism has to be developed by the application-programmer. When indexing-structures and trigger-methods have to be defined and implemented for each property/attribute to be indexed, the program becomes larger and more difficult to comprehend.

The clustering-mechanism can be used for nodes in the same aggregation-hierarchy, and possibly give better performance for some of the transitive closure queries.

The major restriction with Vbase for the HyperModel benchmark is that it is executing on a single processor. The ideal environment for this benchmark would have two or more active workstations editing data in a shared database.

5.9 CONCLUSIONS AND FUTURE WORK

The HyperModel seems to be an adequate model for discussing several of the essential requirements for database-support for engineering applications. The HyperModel has been implemented for Vbase and Servio Logic's Gemstone, and there are plans to do it for a relational system following the methodology in [Blaha88], and for some of the recent European Object-Management-Systems, like DAMOKLES [Dittrich86] and PCTE-OMS [Gallo86].

We are also implementing "The simple db-operations benchmark" [Rubenstein87], and the "Wisconsin benchmark" [Bitton83] on some of these systems to compare them with each other and with the results from the HyperModel benchmark.

ACKNOWLEDGEMENTS

This work was done during the "Database Year" 1987–88 at Oregon Graduate Center in cooperation with Tektronix's task force on engineering databases. Special thanks is due to Professor David Maier for arranging the "Database Year" and providing numerous valuable discussions for the benchmark design.

Thanks also to Rick Cattell and the other participants at the "Workshop on Object-Oriented Database Benchmarking" in March 1988, arranged by the Oregon Database Forum. Also, Ontologic provided useful suggestions for the Vbase realization.

Arne-J Berre was sponsored by a fellowship from the Royal Norwegian Council for Scientific and Industrial Research during the "Database Year". Both the authors were affiliated with Tektronix, Inc., USA at the time of writing this paper.

6 Transition to Object-Oriented Development: Promoting a New Paradigm

George Konstantinow

6.1 INTRODUCTION

Recently, there has been a tremendous surge in the popularity of object-oriented software systems. Object-oriented design is finding a place among more traditional structured analysis and design methods. Object-oriented programming languages are gaining respect in wide-ranging application settings. Object management systems are being introduced which promise to repair or eliminate the shortcomings of standard database management systems in virtually any type of application.

In the midst of all this activity, system developers are faced with the dual challenge of understanding the implications of an "object-oriented technology" and determining whether object-oriented methodologies are really relevant to their particular application requirements. This challenge applies to real-time system construction as well as to business-oriented application development, regardless of system type. Developers ask: "What will object-orientation do for me?" and "How can I incorporate object-oriented notions into my current development environment?"

The theme of this chapter is, that, in determining how the object-oriented paradigm may be applied, an organization should plan for a transition to object-oriented development, not a radical replacement of existing development techniques. Indeed, object-orientation can be beneficial in building any type of application; but a more important issue is the way object-oriented approaches are promoted within an organization and incorporated to support (or perhaps even establish) a software development environment.

Now, an object-oriented approach to system development is not an end in itself. Any methodology can be applied only relative to a development process. A process is formulated in terms of a software development life cycle model and corresponding life cycle management requirements. Problems in system development arise when the development process is ignored or never established, when a methodology is adopted without concern for the underlying process which it is supposed to support, or, worse yet, when tools are implemented without regard for a methodology which they are supposed to automate.

Such problems in development may be compounded by the complexity of the development process itself. The following factors (among others) characterize this complexity:

1. **Multiple application types**— Often, large systems evolve as hybrid systems, with their development based on interwoven scientific, engineering, and business DP computing models.

2. **Multiple system representations**— System development environments must accommodate and coordinate functional, behavioral, and data-oriented representations of the system.

3. **Interconnected technical activities**— Development environments must provide for extensive communication and smooth flow of information among design, programming, and database activities.

4. **Interconnected management activities**— Development environments should offer services for managing the process of, products of, and resources for development.

Proponents of object-oriented methodologies claim that an object-oriented paradigm can be a huge help in addressing the complexities of system development successfully. Such a paradigm can support standard models for processes, data, and agents to be represented in the system. Moreover, by the very nature of their construction, these representations may often be reused in applications and even shared among different application types.

This chapter discusses object-oriented paradigms as applied to system development. It addresses requirements for adopting an object-oriented development approach and gives guidelines for promoting an object-oriented development environment.

6.2 REQUIREMENTS FOR OBJECT-ORIENTED DEVELOPMENT

Large scientific applications (such as weather simulation programs), large engineering applications (such as embedded computer systems for real-time flight guidance), and large commercial applications (such as payroll systems) all share common attributes in system development. Each is designed and constructed according to a development process, or series of activities required to produce and validate the system. In each case the process is carried out according to a development methodology, or series of techniques which support the process steps. Structured analysis and design, rapid prototyping, and use of an underlying database management system (DBMS) are examples of development methodologies. Finally, each development effort may call on a set of tools associated with the methodology to automate system design, construction, and validation optimally.

Consider, for example, the following description of one particular approach to system development:

To build a large commercial application (such as a payroll system), it is usually most efficient to adopt a structured design and programming methodology for system design and construction. COBOL is useful for programming such applications, since its structured programming constructs reflect that methodology. Finally, a relational database management system which is part of the system architecture and is accessible by COBOL through a callable interface may also be useful for supporting the creation and management of data entities within the system.

How does this sound when it is translated and generalized to relate to an object-oriented paradigm?

To build a large scientific, engineering, or commercial application, it is feasible and highly beneficial to adopt an object-oriented methodology for system design and construction. An object-oriented programming language is required for programming such applications, since its constructs reflect that methodology. Finally, an object-oriented database management system which is part of the system architecture and is accessible by the language through a programming interface is essential for supporting the creation and management of system objects.

The premise in the rephrasing is first that an object-oriented approach is applicable to large-scale system development ("feasible") and second that it actually can help in building reliable and maintainable applications ("highly beneficial").

6.2.1 Is this premise accurate?

This question is addressed below. How object-oriented methods apply to system development is discussed in terms of design, programming, and database management.

Design.   Three actions precede the design of a software system:

1. analyze user requirements;
2. specify the system architecture;
3. plan for managing software elements.

In practice, these actions are interrelated and iterative. In some cases, they are even continued throughout the life of the software. Rapid prototyping is one example of a methodology which accommodates these actions. Object-oriented design is another methodology that can help "orient" these system description activities towards "good" design—that is, towards the design of program components which are correct, satisfy system specifications, and can be maintained effectively throughout development.

A useful model for object-oriented design was offered by Ledgard [Ledgard81] and made popular by Booch [Booch86b] as an Ada program development method (Figure 6.1).

Users and developers interact by discussing a problem to be solved (or mission to be accomplished, or capability to be established). This discussion (analysis of user requirements) involves objects and actions in a "real-world" problem space: users describe

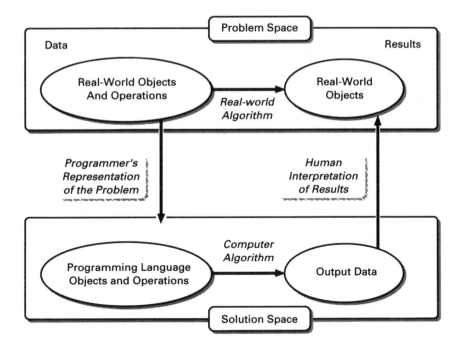

Figure 6.1 A model for object-oriented design.

data which they deal with and procedures which access or transform the data. Developers then represent the problem (or mission, or capability) in a computer-based solution space: they specify structures and operations which represent the real-world objects and actions, and propose algorithms in the solution space which match the transactions and transformations in the problem space.

When a traditional development approach is applied to this model, two biases persist. First, there is often an overwhelming urge to offer a functional decomposition of "the system" as a means for understanding user requirements. The user says "I want the system to do this and this," and the developer responds "We need a subsystem to do this and this." Often, the user really means "I want to do this and this—with these things" (irrespective of any computer application). The developer may elicit this simply by asking "What things do you deal with and what do you do with them?"

A second bias is that system requirements may be constrained too early by the features of a particular programming language. Often the tendency is to describe real-world objects immediately in terms of data structures and to isolate the operations which apply to those objects in terms of functions or procedures allowed by the language. One could argue that this is exactly the opposite of the method described above: the user is asked to represent the developer's structures in terms of real-world objects!

In object-oriented design, the emphasis is shifted to the data or "objects" which comprise the system, the operations which apply to the objects, and the interfaces among the objects identified. Users and developers use these object descriptions as a common language to communicate and understand system requirements together. Specifications, which can be stated in the same language used to determine requirements, then allow users to verify that their requirements have been understood and developers to validate later their design of system objects as being consistent with system requirements. Implementation of the objects in the solution space is relegated (as it should be) to later steps in the development process.

In object-oriented design, the developer focuses on the specification of a software architecture rather than immediately (and perhaps prematurely) producing a high-level system design as a hierarchical decomposition of the system into "modules" which perform certain functions. This architecture is important not just for organizing the technical specifications of the system (as a foundation for design and implementation) but also for planning how the resulting software elements are to be managed. The architecture indicates how objects interrelate within the system, how changes in one part of the system may affect other parts, how objects share and inherit common attributes, and how software components may be reused among applications. Even early in design, the importance of specifying an object management system as a significant part of the software architecture becomes apparent.

Programming. The requirements for an object-oriented programming language intended for use in system development are relatively straightforward. The language must support a methodology for identifying objects and their interrelationships (preferably in a manner useful for high-level system description and design in addition to program construction) and for managing the objects in a development environment. Note the distinction which Bjarne Stroustrup, designer and primary proponent of C++, makes regarding the degree of support which must be offered:

> "A language supports a programming style if it provides facilities that make it convenient (reasonably easy, safe, and efficient) to use that style. A language does not support a technique if it takes exceptional effort or skill to write such programs; in that case, the language merely enables programmers to use the technique. For example, you can write structured programs in FORTRAN and type-secure programs in C, and you can use data abstraction in Modula-2, but it is unnecessarily hard to do so because those languages do not support those techniques [Stroustrup88a]."

For effective implementation of a system designed according to an object-oriented paradigm, an object-oriented language must support at least the definition and use of classes, inheritance mechanisms for defining object attributes and operations, features for type definition, and constructs for procedural computation. A good object-oriented language should also support features which embody modern software engineering principles for the design of reliable systems, such as data abstraction, modularity, information hiding, and reusability. This is especially important for large-scale system development and maintenance. Note once again the implied reliance on a strong underlying object management system, tied in with the language itself if possible.

Any object-oriented language necessarily reflects an underlying programming methodology. Most languages (for example, C++ and Eiffel) are defined according to the abstract data type (ADT) model, providing built-in mechanisms to define and control user-defined structures. Similar to the ADT model is the object-message model, made popular by Smalltalk, which is intuitively easy to understand and lends itself well to producing prototypes of systems. Objects in this paradigm are defined as modules which encapsulate data and procedures and which communicate with one another via passed messages. This is analogous to the ADT model with packaged operations on the data types, with possible differences in compile-time or run-time type checking. A variant on the object-message model is the software-IC model [Cox86], which emphasizes information hiding, well-defined public interfaces for message passing, and reusability of software components. This approach is modeled after the way integrated circuits (IC's) are constructed from electronic hardware components.

Although itself not a "true" object-oriented language, Ada was designed with features which are important to object-oriented programming. In particular, the definition of packages in Ada promotes modularity and encapsulation in design, user-defined data types and associated operations correspond to ADTs, the availability of generics offers some support for class definition and inheritance, and program unit construction (with separately compilable specification and body, and visible and private parts) reflects the notions of information hiding and flexible interface specification. Ada is also useful for combining object-oriented design with Dijkstra's concept of "layered virtual machines," a generalization of ADT. According to this model, programs are decomposed into modules, each of which is executed by its own virtual machine (which has just the necessary instructions and variables for that portion of the problem to be solved) [Bardin87].

Database. In object-oriented system development, perhaps even more important than the choice of an object-oriented programming language is the installation of an object-oriented DBMS, or object management system (OMS). An OMS serves a dual purpose in development, first for managing the objects within the application and second for managing the products of development themselves. In traditional system development, the programs comprising the system and the data which these programs manipulate are considered separate entities. "Managing" the data is a function of the programs, whereas managing the programs is a function of some external organization. In object-oriented development, data and procedures are closely connected; so that, in effect, the same database that is used in production to support communication among objects in the application can also be used to establish and control dependencies among the objects as they are being developed.

The major benefit of using an OMS to support system development is that an OMS allows the developer to create an application-specific model of real-world constructs for the application. It can be extremely useful for large systems with stringent maintenance requirements to have the actions which take place among objects represented as part of the information model for the system. For example, Vbase, an OMS from Ontologic Corporation, combines an object-oriented programming language with a database system geared toward the representation of "persistent objects" through the language - objects which can then be shared among multiple applications. The OMS provides for representation and management of objects, properties (or attributes) of objects, relationships among objects, and operations. It also provides support for standard user interfaces (interactive database definition and data manipulation, callable interfaces to standard programming languages, and an interface via SQL for relational queries) [Ontologic88a].

Another benefit of a system such as Vbase for information modeling is that, in general, an OMS allows the developer to represent different data models (hierarchical, network, and relational) according to the possibly different data requirements of the application. A good example is the applicability of an OMS for managing data generated in computer-aided design (CAD) of mechanical systems [Cammarata86]. The hierarchical structure of mechanical objects (assemblies and parts) may be represented well by a hierarchical data model and the objects stored in a hierarchical parts database. Other data requirements, however, related to bill-of-material processing, require access to and extensive query on attributes of parts, which may be handled better by a relational model. A traditional solution to the problem of representing this duality (short of implementing two databases and suffering from unavoidable redundancy and synchronization problems) is to represent either data model in terms of the other. Such a "solution" could easily lead to an ineffectual and potentially unmaintainable implementation. A better approach is to exploit the duality inherent in an OMS (as described above) which associates attributes and relations with an object. The user may then create different views of objects in the system (or their attributes) dynamically rather than access objects only through a relatively inflexible database structure.

The importance of an OMS for system development may be summarized by noting that an OMS can provide for an "integrated" object-oriented model:

1. a DBMS (including information model) for managing objects in the application
2. an Application Manager (including tools) for managing software objects in development and production
3. a User Interface to the OMS and the applications

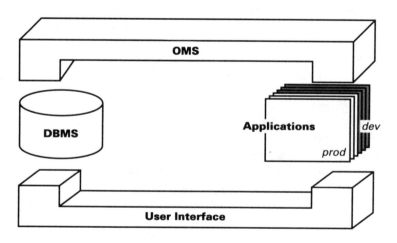

Figure 6.2

6.3 PROMOTING AN OBJECT-ORIENTED DEVELOPMENT ENVIRONMENT

The goal of investigating object-oriented approaches is planning for a transition to object-oriented development within an organization. The objective is the establishment of a software development environment which embodies object-oriented principles. A strategy for promoting object-oriented approaches is to start by focusing on the usefulness of such approaches in system design, next introduce object-oriented data modeling techniques and OMSs, and finally select an object-oriented programming language for system construction. This pathway is probably least disruptive to any development practices and procedures which may already be in place within an organization, since it provides a smooth transition to an evolving development environment.

Below are some guidelines for promoting an object-oriented paradigm in system development. These are categorized in terms of process, methodology, tools, and management.

6.3.1 Process

1. Outline an object-oriented development life cycle which suits the overall development environment of the organization. Match this with any practices or procedures already established, whenever possible.

2. Investigate how an object-oriented paradigm may apply to different application types (scientific, engineering, business DP) encountered in the organization. Note that, even within a particular application area, the applicability may change. For example, a compute-intensive scientific application based on a few deterministic formulas may not lend itself to object-oriented design; however, a large-scale simulation with autonomous but intricately connected communicating agents certainly could benefit greatly from an object-oriented approach.

3. Demonstrate how an object-oriented paradigm applies well to the different functional, behavioral, and data-oriented representations of system.

6.3.2 Methodology

1. Demonstrate the technical utility of an OMS. Show how the constructs of an OMS both support object-oriented design and provide analogs or connections to other standard database models and information management systems within the organization.

2. Set forth requirements for object-oriented programming support to extend the functions of an OMS in system development. Define the minimum requirements (based on the organization's information structure) for a data definition language (DDL), a data manipulation language (DML) within the OMS, an object-oriented procedural language, and interfaces to standard 3GLs and 4GLs (including DDLs and DMLs) used in the organization. Ask what features such languages should have and how they relate to other programming methodologies adopted.

3. Analyze requirements for a flexible user interface to the OMS and development systems. New methodologies for object management, prototyping, and the like

may require different presentations to developers and different database access mechanisms than are normally encountered in the organization.

6.3.3 Tools

1. Establish guidelines for evaluating toolsets which integrate object-oriented programming languages with OMSs. Recommend selection of an OMS with languages already integrated (as specified above).
2. Evaluate tools which offer programming extensions to 3GLs and 4GLs already accepted within the organization. The purpose is to ease the transition from standard development techniques to an object-oriented approach; in some cases, it may even be appropriate to introduce object-oriented constructs through standard programming languages [Meyer88].
3. Plan for computing system, networking, and workstation support before introducing an integrated OMS. Delineate any expected differences between installing an OMS and a standard DBMS (along with its accompanying support environment) for use in a development environment. Show how OMS administration corresponds to or varies from database administration for DBMSs already in use within the organization.

6.3.4 Management

1. Demonstrate the capability and usefulness of an integrated OMS for coordinating technical activities (design, programming, and database) in system development.
2. Promote a system development plan which incorporates an integrated OMS for managing reusable objects and applications. Note that designing for reusability calls for special considerations concerning the development life cycle, identification and management of reusable components, and strong underlying database support which can be tied in naturally with the OMS. The emphasis here is that design for reusability is not just a technical issue but has special significance for software management as well.
3. Formulate a strategic plan for managing information for all enterprises of the organization on the basis of object-oriented systems.

6.4 CONCLUSIONS

Object-oriented methodologies will continue to play a prominent role in addressing the complexities of system development. They may be applied to many types of applications and system representations, and can offer the advantage of connecting technical and management activities during development. These methodologies offer tremendous potential for realizing a major software engineering goal: building reliable applications from reusable components in a way that, in the long run, will prove to be less expensive and more efficient than traditional methods.

7 An Overview of Existing Object-Oriented Database Systems

Ellis Horowitz and Qiang Wan

7.1 INTRODUCTION

Relational database technology has dominated the database field for the past decade, and more [Abrial74, Codd70, Codd79, Date82]. The conventional record-oriented database system often reduces application development time and offers good storage management capability. Besides improved reliability and security, the record-oriented DBMS provides other advanced features such as a uniform model of data, non-procedural data manipulation, physical data independence, a certain level of data abstraction, separation of conceptual data representation and implementation, and support of data sharing among applications. However, these DBMSs are subject to the many serious limitations that make the emergence of a new generation of database technology inevitable [Breuer88, Maier86a].

We briefly summarize the limitations of relational systems (see [Kent79] for a detailed discussion).

1. Record based systems are severely restricted in their modeling power. Some objects cannot be adequately represented (e.g., fields which can have values from two domains), while others are over represented (e.g., fields invented by the programmer to circumvent the single domain restriction, where any alpha-numeric value can be stored).

2. Record based systems assume horizontal homogeneity, meaning that each record of a certain record type is assumed to be composed of the exact same fields.

3. Relational systems assume vertical homogeneity, i.e., each field should be from the same domain in all the records.

4. Only a fixed set of operations are allowed on atomic data values, such as arithmetic and comparison operations, and tuple-oriented operations. It is not possible to add new operations and make those operations appear syntactically similar to the built-in operations.

5. Meta-information is generally not accessible. This results in program text that includes hard coded data based on prior knowledge of the schema, making alterations in both the schema and the program difficult to manage.

6. Dynamic objects such as sets have to be implemented using several records and join operations, causing inefficiency.

7. Transaction time for design objects (e.g., data from VLSI CAD or software development) is often long, spanning several hours or days, and not uncommonly, weeks or months. This is in marked contrast to business data processing transactions, which are assumed to be short-lived. Concurrency control primitives and protocols (such as two-phase locking) supported by relational databases are not particularly suitable for long-lived transactions.

Researchers have realized the limitations in relational database systems and have put forward the notion of an object-oriented database system as a powerful alternative [Andrews87, Breuer88, Afsarmanesh85a, Batory84]. These advanced systems, now beginning to appear as commercial products [Ontologic88a, Penney87, Maier86a], provide further database management capabilities and address many of the limitations mentioned above. Incorporation of object-oriented technology into database systems improves the modeling power and integrity of systems. Some key advantages of the object-oriented approach are listed below.

1. Integration - all application/tools have a common view of the data.

2. Natural Representation - supports a representation which is close to the entity being modeled.

3. Code Reusability - promotes code sharing.

4. Generic Programming - old utilities work even when new components and devices are added to the database, i.e., code is generic and not dependent on any particular representation.

5. Elision - data hiding is an important software engineering concept which is supported by such databases.

6. Self-Documenting (to some extent) - object schema definition and the corresponding methods automatically constitute an up-to-date documentation for the system.

7. Meta Information - not only data, but the schema used to store data in the database is available to programs. This is an improvement over file and relational systems where the information about file and record formats is not usually explicitly available.

8. Explicit expression of more meanings of data, higher levels of abstraction, a notion of abstract objects apart from symbolic surrogates (or object identity), constraint encapsulation, and support of polymorphic routines.

9. New data types are indistinguishable from system supplied types for the purposes of application programming.

10. The notion of object-oriented operation also protects integrity of the database by system enforced constraint checking and elimination of update anomalies.

Despite all of these advantages, many issues remain to be solved before object-oriented databases become fully useful. For example, adequate support for a multi-user environment is needed with mechanisms for managing long transaction time and concurrent access. In the case of system failure and violation, a database system must be able to restore the database to a consistent state while minimizing the amount of computation lost. Performance is another challenging issue for OODBs. One direct impact is the physical storage management design. Physical storage transparency is desirable to reduce programming effort, however, storage clustering should be specifiable by the programmers to improve the performance of database access. The other impact of the performance issue is the recognition of the importance of an interface to procedural languages like C and Pascal for efficient implementation of operations. Finally, there is no agreed upon standard for a user interface to an object-oriented database system.

The following sections of this chapter are devoted to a closer examination of five of the representative OODB systems: Vbase, GemStone, SIM, Iris and ORION. For more information on Vbase, the reader should consult Chapters 9 and 10. Gemstone is covered in greater detail in Chapter 12.

7.2 Vbase

Vbase is a commercial OODB from Ontologic, Inc.[Ontologic88a]. The platforms it runs on are UNIX and VMS. Vbase offers a language for schema definition and abstract object interface specification, and another language for object manipulation. The first language is called TDL, the Vbase Data Type Definition Language. It is an object-oriented declarative language with strong type checking, and explicit expression for describing attribute constraints. Vbase objects are manipulated through a compiled procedural language, COP, which is an object-oriented extension of the C language for method implementation and application programming. Unlike the classic object-oriented programming languages like Smalltalk-80, Vbase does not use the *message* paradigm to describe object behaviors. In Vbase, object behaviors are classified into *static* and *dynamic*. Static behaviors are modeled by the attributes (or properties, as used in Vbase) where the standard dot notation is used for the *set value* and *get value* operations. Dynamic behaviors are represented by operations and procedures where C-like function format is used for invocation and parameter passing.

7.2.1 TDL

TDL is a block structured declarative language. It is roughly analogous to data definition languages of traditional databases. It is used to specify a schema or data model for a Vbase application. From the perspective of an object-oriented system, TDL is the class definition language which extends the hierarchy of system defined classes (or types, as used in Vbase) in the Vbase kernel database, and specifies the relationships and semantics of the data objects. TDL is used to specify an abstract interface to the attributes of new data types which may be instantiated and the operations which may be performed on these instances. Here is a sample TDL definition:

```
define Type Employee
        supertypes = {Entity};
        properties = {
                name: String;
                employee_number: Integer;
                salary: Integer;
                office: Room;
        };
        operations = {
                display(e:Employee)
                method(EmployeeDisplay)
                raises(EmployeeNotFound);
        };
end Employee;
```

There are several advantages of having TDL separated from the implementation language:

1. There is a natural separation of data type definition from method implementation in database systems, where data type (or schema) definition is mainly performed at the *design phase* and requires infrequent changes once it is done.

2. The concept of strong typing in data type definition is different from that in the manipulation language. The manipulation language represents a procedural process where the object types encountered in each step are determined by the context; the data type definition language, on the other hand, should allow some unknown data types to be referenced in a definition block in order to overcome the barrier created by sequential compiling. The object type Room in the above sample definition block is a good example of the latter.

3. Since TDL is used to describe an abstract interface and general features of objects, it is desirable for the language to be more narrative than the implementation language so that it is suitable to be used as a *specification language* by application programmers.

4. The narrative feature of TDL makes the major parts of Vbase applications *self-documenting*, which is very desirable in a software engineering environment.

Vbase's TDL can also be used to create instances of user defined or system supplied types. That is, TDL can be used both for specifying schema, or meta-data for the database, and for populating the database with concrete data objects. In conventional database systems, it would be impossible to support these two kinds of operations under the same syntax. In an object-oriented environment, however, it is natural to have these two operations syntactically indistinguishable, since like the data objects, data schema themselves are nothing but *objects*.

7.2.2 COP

COP is the implementation language of Vbase. It is a super-set of the C language with extensions to access database objects. Choosing C as the platform of COP allows Vbase programmers to incorporate many existing UNIX-based application packages into their applications smoothly without sacrificing efficiency. Also, the programmers have the choice of using a familiar programming environment for application development.

COP extends C by the following special features:

1. **Object Identification, Operation Invocation, and Property Access**— COP provides naming conventions that serve both to distinguish database names from standard C identifiers and to reflect the database object hierarchy. COP recognizes an identifier as a database name if it is preceded by a dollar-sign. Database names may be concatenated to reflect the nested structure of the object or of the operation in the type hierarchy. This naming convention provides a *seamless* connection between database objects and application programs by allowing the application programmer to *directly* address the database objects. The other kind of object referencing is done by using variable object names. COP introduces a new storage class called **obj**, which is used to declare a temporary variable for holding references to database objects of a certain type (or its subtypes). Property access is done by using the dot notation that is similar to a record field access in Pascal.

2. **Database Name Visibility**— As the result of a disk-based database system, certain database names must be made visible explicitly to the application program to overcome the barrier created by clustering. This is achieved by using one of the two declarations **import** and **enter module**.

3. **Iterators**— Iterator is a coroutine which performs the operation that iterates over an aggregate of objects yielding each object in turn. The following program section calls the **display** operation for all employee objects assigned to some office object:

```
{
        obj $Employee anEmployee;
        obj $Room aRoom;
        ...
        iterate( anEmployee = aRoom.occupants){
                $Employee$Display(anEmployee);
        }
        ...
}
```

4. **Exception Handling**— Potential problems that occur in the usage of operations are defined as exceptions, and Vbase provides the mechanism for handling these exceptions. The kinds of exceptions that the programmers anticipate can be described in TDL by extending the hierarchy of the system type **Exception**. In COP, the programmer can write an exception handler with the **except** statement. During the execution of a method, if an error is detected, the method indicates this via the COP **raise** statement. The flow of the program is then interrupted, and the

system starts searching for an exception handler immediately after the statement that caused an exception to be raised.

5. **Method Combination—** Vbase provides the mechanism for method combination to produce desired behavior. A series of methods can be nested to combine a base method with a set of triggers, and the way these methods are nested are described in TDL definitions. This mechanism also allows programmers to customize system supplied operations, in which case the base method is the one that implements the system supplied operation.

6. **Keyword Arguments—** Besides positional formal arguments, functions in COP may also have keyword arguments for object referencing. In the function invocation, the keyword formal arguments are addressed by their names instead of their positions.

7. **Optional Argument—** An optional property can be explicitly specified in TDL by using the keyword **optional**. In COP, the statement **hasvalue** can be used to check if the optional property holds any value.

8. **Object Type Conversions—** COP supports conversions of object types by providing the function **assert** which converts an object reference to one of its subtypes as specified by the programmer.

9. **Concurrent Access to Database Objects—** The notion of transaction is supported in Vbase to deal with concurrent access to the database.

10. **Parameterization—** Another significant capability of Vbase is the so-called type parameterization. This means that the types of objects contained in aggregate objects (like array, set, dictionary, etc.) can be specified by means of parameters. This capability is important for maintaining a strong typing system without sacrificing modeling power. For example, a set of employees can be declared as follows:

```
obj $Set[obj $Employee] employeeList;
```

7.2.3 Object SQL/Vbase

Many people consider SQL to be an important metric in judging the data manipulation capability of a database management system. Object SQL is the Vbase implementation of the SQL query language. The main query operation supported by Object SQL is via the three major clauses *SELECT*, *FROM* and *WHERE*. Syntactically, object and relational implementations of the *SELECT* clause are equivalent. However, the object implementation may reveal more information as a result of the rich interconnection among the objects in the underlying object-oriented database. Vbase's Object SQL is a separate tool provided for application development. Application programmer is not able to link any Object SQL function with application program. Also, any application dependent refinement, like the triggers, is not visible in the Object SQL. Here is a sample query in Object SQL:

```
SELECT Name
FROM $Employee
WHERE salary > 20000
```

This will display names of all employees whose income is over $20,000. Vbase will display the result in a tabular format.

Object SQL can be used to directly invoke operations. For example,

```
SELECT Name
FROM $Employee
WHERE $String$SubString(phoneNumber, 0, 3) = '818'
```

will display names of all employees whose phone number is in the 818 area-code. A more detailed examination of Object SQL can be found in Chapter 12.

7.3 GemStone

GemStone is a commercial OODB system from ServioLogic [Purdy87, Maier86a]. The platform runs on a network involving a VMS system as file server (or GemStone object server), and one or more IBM PC and Smalltalk-80 workstations. Unlike Vbase, GemStone offers one uniform language to its programmers: OPAL. OPAL is a modified version of Smalltalk-80. It is a computationally complete language with assignment, conditional, and iteration constructs. The uniform language approach of GemStone helps to avoid the problem of *impedance mismatch* where information must pass between two languages that are semantically and structurally different. GemStone also provides an interface to procedural languages like C and Pascal (see Chapter 12).

7.3.1 OPAL

In OPAL, data definition and data manipulation facilities are combined in one language whose style borrows heavily from Smalltalk-80. We will see how the familiar notions of *classes*, which consists of data structure definition, and a collection of operations, called *methods* are described. Each method is defined for a particular class, and it applies to *instances* of that class and subclasses. Object manipulation in OPAL uses the *message* paradigm, where operations are invoked on objects via messages.

A procedure in OPAL is called a *method*. The form of a method definition is:

```
method <class name>
    <message format>
    <body of method>
%
```

The *class name* is the class to which the method applies. The *message format* is the name of the methods and/or the names of its parameters, and the *body of method* is the OPAL code that is executed whenever the method is called. There are system predefined methods, such as **new** and **remove**, that are understood by all classes. Formal arguments in *message format* may be named or positioned.

The following OPAL segment declares a class *EmpType*:

```
Object
    subclass: 'EmpType'
    instVarNames: #['name', 'empNumber', 'salary']
    constraints: #[
        #[ #name, String],
        #[ #empNumber, Integer]
        #[ #salary, Integer]
    ].
```

Unlike Vbase, OPAL does not make the distinction between *static* and *dynamic* behaviors. All behaviors are modeled by using the *message-method* paradigm. So in OPAL, even the most primitive operations (except the **new** and **remove** operations for classes) must be described for each class defined. For example, the basic *set value* and *get value* operations for the **salary** attribute in the class **EmpType** have to be explicitly specified as:

```
method: EmpType
    getSalary
            ^salary
%
method: EmpType
    setSalary: n
            salary := n
%
```

GemStone provides a C and Pascal callable object module (called Procedural Interface Module,or PIM) which the designer links with applications running on an IBM PC. PIM is essentially a collection of functions which implement remote procedural calls to the GemStone object server. The PIM hides the network communications protocols and provides access to the GemStone object database from a procedural environment.

7.3.2 Database Features

Smalltalk is a single-user, memory-based, and single-processor system. There are certain enhancements in the implementation of OPAL to meet the requirement of a database system. GemStone combines the database management features common to most commercial database systems. Its main database features include:

1. **Sharing of Objects**— GemStone provides each user with a distinct list of dictionaries called a **symbolList**. The dictionary allows the sharing of the objects contained in that dictionary.

2. **Centralized Server**— Unlike Vbase, GemStone has a centralized server for a database of objects.

3. **Security**— GemStone secures the object database from unauthorized access by authenticating each user through a user name and password. Along with authentication, groups of objects may be explicitly marked as either read only, read/write,or no privileges for selected users.

4. **Resilience to Common Failure Modes**— Besides normal failure modes protections, GemStone also offers the ability to selectively replicate the stored objects on-line, ensuring the database survives single-point disk failures.

5. **Multiple Concurrent Users**— GemStone employs some concurrency control mechanisms to manage the transactions in a shared database.

6. **Primary and Secondary Storage Management**— GemStone hides from application designers the paging of objects between secondary and primary storage, and supports objects that are larger than what can fit in the server's primary memory.

7. **Method Execution**— GemStone gives the application designer a choice: copy an object's state to the workstation for manipulation, or execute messages remotely on the GemStone server.

8. **Fast Associative Access**— GemStone allows dynamic addition and removal of associative access structures to accelerate membership tests.

7.3.3 OPAL/GemStone Queries

OPAL's version of database query is essentially a method implementation of the SELECT, FROM and WHERE clauses. OPAL provides some system predefined operations on set objects. The purpose is to provide some database query capability under the assumption that most relations are modeled in OPAL as set objects which play the roles of *records* in relational databases.

OPAL provides several ways of exploring all the members of an object that are a set. One is by a method whose parameter name is **select:**. The parameter of a selection is a block of code with a single local variable that takes on, in turn, each of the members of the set as its value.

The form of the message is:

```
select: [ :X | <code involving X and returning true or
                      false> ]
```

where :X, followed by a bar, declares X to be a local variable. The functionality of the **select** message is much like that in relational database management systems, with the *code body* representing the *WHERE* clause, and the receiver of the message being the *FROM* clause. For example, suppose all *employee* objects are stored in a set called **Employees**. Then, the query "find all the employees whose salary is over 20000" can be written as:

```
highPayEmps := Employees select: [:e | (e getSalary) >
                      20000 ]
```

Notice that *select:* is not equivalent to the Vbase *iterate*, since *select:* will go over all the members of the set and return the selected members as a subset. Another method for performing a query on a set object is *detect:*, which is executed with its local variable equal to each member of the set, in some order, until a member x that makes the message block true is found. Then, x is produced as a value. Note that unlike the *select:* method, which produces a subset as value, *detect:* produces an element of the set. For example:

```
anEmp := Employees detect: [:e | (e getName) = 'John
           Adams' ]
```

will obtain the information for an employee John Adams and assign the values to the
variable **anEmp**.

7.4 SIM

SIM is a commercially available object database system from Unisys. It is based on
a semantic data model similar to Hammer and McLeod's SDM [Maier86a]. The goal
of the system is to allow the semantics of data to be defined in the schema and make
the database system responsible for enforcing its integrity. SIM provides a rich set of
constructs for schema definition, including those for specifying generalization hierarchies
modeled by directed acyclic graphs, inter-object relationships and integrity constraints.

7.4.1 Schema Definition in SIM

The primary unit of data encapsulation in SIM is a *class*, which represents a meaningful
collection of entities. The notion of subclass is also supported, which *inherits* all the
attributes of all its ancestor classes in its generalization hierarchy. In SIM, every base
class has a special system-maintained attribute called its *surrogate*. It is used in the
implementation of generalization hierarchies and entity relationships. SIM makes the
distinction between *data-valued attributes*, or *DVA*, and *entity-valued attributes*, or *EVA*.
A DVA describes a property of each entity in a class by associating the entity with a
value or a set of values from a domain of values. An EVA, on the other hand, describes
a property of each entity of a class by relating it to an entity or entities of another or
perhaps the same class. An EVA represents a binary relationship between the class that
owns it (domain) and the class it points to (range). This distinction is unique in SIM.
In most (or almost all) other systems, all attributes are conceptually modeled as Entity
Valued Attributes, but those system-supplied classes like Integer, Real, and String are
implemented as Data Valued Attributes, and it is the programmer's responsibility to clear
the confusion.

One important feature of SIM is its strong support for the *inverse* relationship. SIM
automatically maintains the inverse of every declared EVA and ensures that an EVA and
its inverse will stay synchronized at all times. The inverse can also be explicitly specified
by the user.

Here is a sample SIM data schema:

```
Class Person(
    name:  string[30];
    soc-sec-no:  integer, unique, required;
    birthdate: date;
    spouse:  person inverse is spouse;
    profession: subrole (student, instructor) mv );
```

The following keywords, called attribute options in SIM, are used to describe data value constraints that are imposed on an attribute:

- **required**—this option implies that the value of the attribute cannot be null.
- **unique**—this option implies that no two entities of the class can have a value in common for this attribute. Null values are omitted from uniqueness considerations.
- **mv**—this option indicates that an attribute is multi-valued. By default, attributes are single-valued.
- **distinct**—this option on a multi-valued attribute implies that the attribute contains a set of values instead of a multiset.
- **max**—this option limits the number of values an MV attribute can take, which by default is unbounded.
- **inverse**—this option specifies an inverse relationship between the attributes and another attribute, possibly in the same class. Depending on the type of value of the specified attribute, the **inverse** may be used to model 1:1, 1:many, or many:many relationships among objects.

Another important feature of the SIM data model that we can see from the above sample schema is the use of *subrole*. SIM requires that every class that has subclasses have a special attribute of the subrole type declared with it. A subrole is a special case of enumerated types and its value set must contain the names of all the immediate subclasses of the class in which it is used. Subrole attributes are system-maintained and can only be read.

7.4.2 Data Manipulation in SIM

Unlike the data manipulation languages we have seen so far in other object-oriented DBMSs, SIM DML is a high-level, non-procedural language. It is basically a database query language whose style is similar to DAPLEX. SIM DML consists of a RETRIEVE clause, some aggregate functions like AVG, COUNT, etc., and some update statements like INSERT, MODIFY, and DELETE.

To support a query, the notion of *perspective class* is used in SIM. The assumption is, when formulating a query, a user is primarily interested in one class, called the perspective. Other classes in the database are viewed based on their relationship to the perspective class, and the link is established by applying *qualifications* on the attributes. For example, the request "print the name of each student and the name of his/her advisor, if any" is expressed in SIM DML as

```
FROM Student
RETRIEVE Name, Name of Advisor
```

Here, the perspective of the query is STUDENT. NAME OF ADVISOR refers to an extended attribute, and is connected to the perspective by using the qualification **of**. It is interesting that SIM also supports a shortcut of the qualification, if there is no ambiguity. For example, the query " find out the advisor's name and salary" can be formulated as

```
FROM Student
RETRIEVE Name of Advisor of Student, Salary of Advisor
            of Student
```

or, it can be simplified as

```
FROM Student
RETRIEVE Name of Advisor, Salary.
```

7.4.3 SIM User Interface

SIM offers its user database query capability in its data manipulation language. The SIM DML basically contains a RETRIEVE clause, some aggregate functions, and a set of update functions.

The syntax of the retrieve queries is of the form:

```
[ FROM <perspective class list> ]
RETRIEVE [ TABLE [DISTINCT] | STRUCTURE ]
     < target list >
[ ORDERED BY  < order list > ]
[ WHERE  < selection expression >  ].
```

Perspective class list is the list of perspective classes for a query with optional associated reference variables. *Target list* and *order list* are lists of expressions made up of constants, immediate, inherited and extended attributes of the perspectives (aggregate and other functions apply on these attributes).

The concept of *range variables* is used in SIM DML to bind attribute and class names.

7.5 IRIS

Iris is a research prototype of an object-oriented database system built at the Hewlett-Packard Laboratories. It is designed to be accessible from many programming languages, and by stand-alone interactive interfaces. Construction of interfaces is made possible by a set of C language subroutines that defines the object manager interface. Iris currently supports two interactive interfaces. One is OSQL, or Object SQL, which is an extended version of the SQL, and the other is called Inspector, which is an extension of a LISP structure browser and a precursor to a graphical interface.

Iris object manager implements the Iris data model by providing support for schema definition, data manipulation, and query processing. The data model, which is based on the three constructs *objects, types,* and *operations,* supports inheritance and general properties, constraints, complex or non-normalized data, user-defined operations, version control, inference, and extensible data types.

7.5.1 Iris Data Model and Operations

The Iris type structure is a directed acyclic graph. A given type may have multiple subtypes and multiple supertypes. Besides the common definition for *objects, classes,* and *operations*, the Iris data model distinguishes between *literal objects* and *non-literal objects*. Examples of literal objects are strings and numbers, examples of non-literal objects are persons and departments. The Object Manager provides operations for explicitly creating and deleting non-literal objects, and for assigning values to their properties. Referential integrity is supported by allowing objects to be deleted only if they are not being referred to. Therefore, Iris offers a strong support for the inverse relationship among objects, thus maintaining the referential integrity of the system.

Here is a sample Iris type definition for a class `Person`, and one of its subclasses `Student`:

```
CREATE TYPE Person
    (name Charstring REQUIRED,
     address Charstring,
     phone Charstring);
CREATE TYPE Student SUBTYPE OF Person
    (student_id  Charstring REQUIRED,
     takes Course MANY);
```

The concept of property in Iris is modeled and implemented by a *function* that returns a value when applied to that object. Functions in Iris are implemented by *operations*. An Iris operation is a computation that may or may not return a result. Operations are defined on types and are applicable to the instances of the types. The specification of an Iris operation consists of two parts, a *declaration* and an *implementation*. A declaration specifies the name of the operation and the number and types of its parameters and results. An implementation specifies how the operation is implemented. Here is a sample Iris function definition:

```
NEW FUNCTION  marriage(p/Person)=(spouse/Person,
                                   date/Charstring)
```

This function declares a function called marriage. A function can also return a compound result, as in the above example where the result of the function contains both the spouse and the date of the marriage. This function can be called in Iris as follows:

```
(s,d) = marriage(bob)
```

Iris mixes the notions of database query functions with object-oriented operations, and supports the notions of:

1. **Stored functions**—A stored function in Iris is implemented as a table. It maps input values to their corresponding result values, and may be accessed using standard relational database techniques.

2. **Derived functions**—The definition of a function may be specified in terms of other functions, for example,

```
DEFINE manager(e/employee) = FIND m/employee
   WHERE m = department-manager(department(e))
```

This definition specifies how the manager of an employee may be derived. In Iris, function definitions may contain arbitrary queries. These definitions are compiled by the Object manager into an internal relational algebra representation that is interpreted when the function is called.

3. **Foreign functions**—In Iris, new data types and operations are defined by using the existing data types and operations. For operations that are too difficult to be modeled by existing ones, Iris treats them as *foreign functions* and extra work has to be done to link them into the database.
4. **Compound functions**—Iris developers are considering allowing users to define operations containing sequences of operations.
5. **Update functions**—This is a set of operations that changes the future behavior of the database functions.

7.5.2 Iris Storage Manager

The Iris prototype is built on top of a conventional relational storage manager. The system supports transactions with *savepoints* and *restores to savepoints*, concurrency control, logging and recovery. The Storage Manager is actually a collection of Index manager, Lock Manager, Buffer Manager, Log Manager, and Record Manager.

7.5.3 Object SQL/Iris

Object SQL in Iris is an interactive interface. There are two main extensions Iris has made beyond SQL to adapt it to the object and function model:

1. Direct references to objects are used rather than their keys. Interface variables may be bound to objects on creation or retrieval and may then be used to refer to the objects in subsequent statements.
2. User-defined functions and Iris system functions may appear in WHERE and SELECT clauses to give concise and powerful retrieval.

There are also some changes in keywords. Here is a sample Iris OSQL for the query "find all the students who are taking Robinson's course":

```
SELECT name
FOR EACH student s
WHERE Robinson = isInstructorOf(s)
```

7.6 ORION

ORION is a prototype object-oriented database system built at MCC [Kim88b]. It is intended for applications from the fields: AI, multimedia documents, and computer-aided design domains. Functions supported in ORION include versions and change notification, composite objects, dynamic schema evolution, transaction management, associative queries, and multimedia data management.

ORION has been implemented in Common LISP on a Symbolics 3600 Lisp machine, and has also been ported to the SUN workstation under the UNIX operating system. ORION extends Common LISP with object-oriented programming and database capabilities.

The schema of an ORION database is a class hierarchy, actually a directed acyclic graph. ORION contains most of the data schema definition capabilities we have seen in the other OODBs, and in addition, supports the following features:

1. **Composite Objects**—ORION uses the notion of Composite Objects to capture the modeling of IS-PART-OF relationship between objects. This can be viewed as a specialized realization of the inverse constraint.

2. **Versions**—The ORION objects can be either versioned or non-versioned. ORION distinguishes transient versions from working versions.

3. **Dynamic Evolution**—ORION offers such commands like **add-superclass, remove-superclass**, and **change-attribute** to dynamically modify data schema.

ORION also extends Lisp by limited support of database query capabilities, and the notion of transaction to support concurrent access to the database.

In ORION a set of predefined messages is provided for forming queries and performing update operations. These messages include select (or select-any), change and delete.

The message select returns a set (possibly empty) which contains all instances of a class that satisfy a given query expression:

```
(select    Class   Queryexpression)
(select-any    Class   Queryexpression)
```

The query expression is a Boolean expression of predicates. For example,

```
(select   'Student '(> GPA 3.6)
```

returns all student objects with a GPA over 3.6.

To delete all instances of a class that satisfy a given query expression, a delete message is used.

```
(delete   Class   Queryexpression)
```

Similarly, a change message is used to replace the value of an attribute of all instances of a class that satisfy a given Boolean expression:

```
(change  Class [QueryExpression]
                AttributeName NewValue)
```

7.7 CONCLUSIONS

This chapter has attempted to give you a brief technical overview of several popular object-oriented databases. One conclusion to draw is that as yet there is no standard in the field. A second conclusion is that the core programming language greatly influences the underlying database model. Though early efforts have chosen Smalltalk and Lisp, there has been a great deal of support for C-based extensions, mostly because of the popularity of C and UNIX. Newer implementations of object-oriented databases using C or C++ are presented in the last section of this book.

8 An Object-Oriented Database System to Support an Integrated Programming Environment

Daniel Weinreb, Neal Feinberg, Dan Gerson,
and Charles Lamb

8.1 INTRODUCTION

Statice is an object-oriented database system. It runs on the Genera operating system on Symbolics workstations, and it is written in Symbolics Common Lisp, which includes the Flavors object-oriented programming language extension. Statice was created to be a basis for new tools in the Genera programming environment.

This chapter starts by explaining why an object-oriented database system is an important basis for a programming environment such as Genera. It then describes the data model of Statice: how Statice looks to a programmer. Next, it outlines how Statice is implemented. Finally, it discusses conclusions, and the current status of the product.

8.2 GENERA AND DATA-LEVEL INTEGRATION

The purpose of the Symbolics Genera integrated programming environment [Walker87] is to let programmers build complex and innovative software systems much more productively than they can with conventional environments. Part of Genera is an extensive suite of *tools*: interactive programs used by programmers, including advanced editors, debuggers, browsers, inspectors, configuration managers, and project management and communication utilities.

Genera is based on *data-level integration*. All information is represented as objects in a virtual address space shared by all Genera tools. The different tools communicate with each other by sharing and manipulating these objects. Many processes can work simultaneously on many activities in many windows, and all access the same object base and share the same data structures. This makes Genera tools more tightly integrated than tools of conventional environments.

Data-level integration has several weaknesses when it is based on shared virtual memory.

1. Objects are volatile, and cease to exist when the user session ends or the workstation is shut down or crashes. Any information that needs to be persistent must be converted to text or binary strings and stored in files.

2. Although objects are shared among different tools in one user's environment, they cannot be shared between the environments of many users using different workstations. Communication between users must be done by transmitting raw bytes through the file system, networks, or pipes.

3. Virtual memory is never big enough to hold everything you might ever want to use. Mechanisms must be added to move objects into and out of virtual memory, imposing burdens of complexity on the implementors and slowness on the user.

Using files to deal with these problems has several drawbacks. Explicit copying of information makes tools hard to use and introduces many opportunities for error. Information must be translated from a virtual memory format to a raw byte format, and back. This can be difficult with structured information that contains pointers, particularly when circular structure is allowed. Files are generally read and written as a unit, which makes access and update slower for larger files. Concurrency control is crude and overly restrictive. Objects not stored in files must be re-created by each user, for each session, by running the compiler or analysis tools, which is also slow.

8.3 GOALS AND PHILOSOPHY

To solve these problems, and retain the benefits of data-level integration, the integration must go beyond the limits of the virtual address space. Objects must be *shared* among users on different workstations, and must be *persistent* from one session to the next and in the face of system failure.

Statice is an object-oriented database system that provides shared, persistent objects to Genera. By using Statice as the basis of data-level integration, future tools will be able to solve the problems described above. Statice also works as part of the Genera substrate, so both Genera tools and user programs, can use Statice.

Statice has the following additional goals:

1. Concurrency control: many processes, on one or many workstations, are able to access shared objects without interfering with each other.

2. Recovery: the effects of a group of operations on shared objects are made persistent when the operations complete, or must have no effect at all if they do not complete.

3. Associative access: associative searches over many objects, including range searches as well as equality searches, are efficient for large databases.

4. Direct access: operations on single objects, such as direct access to an object's contents from a reference to the object, are very efficient.

5. Query language: there is a way to express queries that can be optimized for efficient execution, as in a relational database system.

6. Data independence: the data model of information is abstract, making only the semantic information content visible and hiding the underlying organization. This is a fundamental principle of relational database systems.

7. Object semantics: Statice objects have identity, inheritance, and methods, and otherwise provide a true object-oriented programming capability.

8. Natural programming: using Statice from an application is natural and easy, fitting into the Common Lisp language and the Genera environment in a straightforward way.

The concurrency control and recovery goals were combined into the single goal of providing general transactions [Bernstein87]. The associative access goal refers to using various 'access methods', or storage formats, developed for conventional DBMSs, to allow fast content-addressed lookup in large databases. In general, Statice aims at retaining the traditional benefits of conventional database systems while adding the new benefits of object-oriented database systems.

At first we thought that the natural programming goal meant that the data model of Statice should be exactly the same as that of Lisp. However, we found that this was in strong conflict with the data independence goal. Lisp does not separate real information from underlying organization. For example, lists and vectors really represent the same underlying semantics, namely a sequence. The only difference between them lies in the implementation, and mainly reflects performance (speed of insertion versus speed of accessing the nth element). The purpose of data independence is to hide such differences, but Lisp makes them quite visible.

Also, for many types of objects in Lisp, it's not clear what it would mean to store them as shared, persistent objects. Some objects, such as processes and indirect arrays, depend on the virtual memory for their meaning. Others objects, like most symbols and many of the pre-created structures in Lisp, must exist separately for every Lisp environment, and so cannot be shared in a straightforward manner. Some other related problems are discussed in [Vegdahl86].

To provide data independence, and avoid these pitfalls, we adopted a more abstract, object-oriented data model, described in the next section. This data model is based primarily on DAPLEX [Shipman81,CCADaplex84]. We were also substantially influenced by [Cattell83] and [Kent79]. A similar model is used by [Kempf86].

8.4 DATA MODEL

Statice information is stored in *databases*. Each database has a *schema*, which is a description of the kinds of information stored in the database. For example:

```
(define-schema university (person student course
        instructor department))
```

This form defines a schema called university. A university database contains objects of five *entity types*: person, student, course, instructor, and department.

```
(define-entity-type person ()
  ((name string :unique t :no-nulls t :read-only t
         :inverse person-named :inverse-index t)))
```

This form defines an entity type called person. The person entity type has one *attribute*, named name, whose type is string. In other words, every person has a name, and the name is represented as a character string. Attributes model both the properties of entities, and the relationships among entities.

The :unique option means that no two person entities in the database can have the same value for the name attribute. In other words, the relation between person entities and names is one-to-one.

The :no-nulls option means that the value of the name attribute of a person entity cannot be the *null value*. The null value is a distinguished value that an attribute can have, regardless of type, meaning 'unknown' or 'not applicable'. Forbidding the null value is like saying that the attribute is 'required'.

The :read-only option means that the attribute's value can be examined but not changed after the entity is created. The :inverse option defines an inverse accessor function, and the :inverse-index option creates an index; this is discussed further below.

```
(define-entity-type student (person)
  ((dept department :inverse students-in-dept)
   (courses (set-of course) :index t
            :inverse course-students)))
```

The student entity type inherits from the person entity type. In other words, every student is also a person. Student entities inherit the attributes of person, so every student has a name.

The type of the dept attribute is department, which is one of the other entity types of the schema. This means that the value of the dept attribute of a student entity is a department entity.

Since the :unique option is not specified, many students can be in the same department. The dept attribute is many-to-one.

The attributes we've discussed so far are all *single-valued*. The courses attribute is *set-valued*, because a student can be taking many courses. :unique is not specified, because many students can be taking the same course; this is a many-to-many relation.

```
(define-entity-type course ()
  ((title string
          :inverse courses-entitled)
   (dept department)
   (credits integer)
```

```
         (instructor instructor
                     :inverse courses-taught-by
                     :inverse-index t))
          (:multiple-index (title dept) :unique t))
       (define-entity-type instructor (person)
          ((dept department :no-nulls t)
           (visiting boolean)
           (salary single-float)))
       (define-entity-type department ()
          ((name string :unique t
                 :inverse department-named :inverse-index t)
           (head instructor))))
```

These forms define the rest of the entity types. `:multiple-index` is an option that applies to the whole entity type, specifying an index on two attributes (indexes are discussed below).

In addition to defining Statice entity types and their attributes, `define-entity-type` also defines a *class* of the Common Lisp Object System (CLOS) [DeMichiel87,Moon88]. CLOS is an object-oriented extension to the Common Lisp language. Statice inheritance and CLOS inheritance work the same way (including multiple inheritance). The entity classes don't have any slots; Statice attribute values are stored in the database, not in Lisp's virtual address space.

An instance of such a class is called an *entity handle*. An entity handle is a Lisp object that refers to a Statice entity. Entity handles reside in Lisp's virtual memory, whereas entities reside in databases. A particular Lisp world has only one entity handle (or none) for any entity, so the Lisp concept of identity maps directly to the Statice concept of identity. For example, the Lisp `eql` function can be used to compare the identity of Statice entities. Entity handles continue to exist outside transactions, and can be kept in Lisp data structures.

8.4.1 Types

The Statice type system maps directly into the Common Lisp type system, so the familiar Common Lisp operators such as `typep`, `typecase`, and `check-type` can be used in the natural way for entity handles. Programs using Statice can define methods on entity classes, just like any other class. The type specifiers used to name types of Statice attributes are Common Lisp *type specs* [Steele84]. Thus, Statice fits smoothly into the object-oriented programming system already provided by the Lisp language.

Statice types have the same semantics as Common Lisp types, as well as the same names. For example, strings can be of any length, and can include style (family, face, and size) information and use many character sets. Integers can be of arbitrary precision. (Storage formats are arranged so that common cases, such as small integers and strings without style information, are stored efficiently.) Statice supports all Common Lisp numeric types, including rational and complex, as well as integer subranges, enumerated types (the Common Lisp `member` type), and others. Another type holds an arbitrary-length vector of 32-bit words, for storing arbitrary binary data. A general union type can represent a wide range of Lisp objects, by utilizing the same binary dumper that the Lisp compiler uses to store constants. Pictures in the form of diagrams from Genera's graphics system [Genera88] and bitmap images can also be stored as values.

Statice application programs can extend the type system, defining their own types, in two ways. To define a *logical* type, a program defines encoder and decoder methods to translate values from the program-visible value to a value of some already-implemented type. For example, you could make a new enumerated type by encoding each element of the enumeration into a corresponding small integer. To define a *physical* type, which is a genuine new type not based on a pre-existing type, a program defines about a dozen methods that control the exact binary representation of the value. For example, the `write-value` method is given a value, an addressor (specifying a record), a word offset, and a bit offset; the method must write the value into the record at the specified location. Other methods read, compare, compute the size, and check the type of values, etc.

8.4.2 Accessing Attributes

`define-entity-type` defines an *accessor function* for each attribute. An accessor function retrieves the value of an attribute of an entity. In the example above, the accessor functions are named `person-name`, `student-dept`, `student-courses`, and so on.

Accessor functions are actually *generic functions* of CLOS. They take one argument, which is an entity handle. For example, suppose the value of the variable `george` is an entity handle for a particular student. The Lisp form (`person-name george`) returns the value of the name attribute of the student, which is a string. `person-name` can be applied to a student, by the usual rules of CLOS inheritance. The Lisp form (`student-dept george`) returns an entity handle that refers to the `department` entity that is the student's department.

`define-entity-type` also defines `setf` methods for updating the values of attributes. The Lisp form (`setf (instructor-salary jones) 20000.0`) sets the value of the `salary` attribute of `jones` to `20000.0`. The `person` attribute is defined with the `:read-only` option, which suppresses the definition of the `setf` method. Because Statice uses Lisp's `setf` mechanism, Lisp's 'place modifier' forms can be used with accessor functions. For example, (`incf (instructor-salary jones) 100.0`) means that Jones gets a raise of $100.00.

Accessor functions for set-valued attributes return lists; for example, `student-courses` returns a list of `course` entity handles. Likewise, the `setf` methods for set-valued attributes accept lists to store the entire set. There are also special forms called `add-to-set` and `delete-from-set` to add or delete one element. For example, (`add-to-set (student-courses george) english-101`) adds `english-101` to `george`'s set of courses. (This example assumes that `english-101` is a variable whose value is an entity handle for an entity of type `course`.)

Statice's accessor functions thus behave and look like accessors for Lisp structures and CLOS instances. The resulting programming style is immediately grasped by Lisp programmers, and fits naturally into programs.

The :inverse-function option to the name attribute defines an *inverse accessor function* named person-named. It takes a name as its argument and returns the person entity, thus doing the inverse of what the accessor function does. students-in-dept is also an inverse accessor function, which takes a department and returns a set of students. In general, the inverse of an *x*-to-*y* function is a *y*-to-*x* function. person-named is one-to-one, and students-in-dept is one-to-many.

8.4.3 Making and Deleting Entities

define-entity-type defines a *constructor function* that makes a new entity of this type. For example, the constructor function for the student type is named make-student. The arguments to the function specify the initial values for the attributes, using keyword arguments, and the returned value of the function is the entity handle for the new entity. Example:

```
(make-student :name 'Fred'
              :dept english-dept
              :courses (list english-101 history-201))
```

Again, this syntax is familiar and natural for Lisp programmers, because it is just like the syntax of constructor functions for Common Lisp structures. The ability to initialize the name attribute is inherited from the person entity type. If no keyword argument is provided for an attribute, the attribute's initial value is taken from the :initform option in define-entity-type, just as in CLOS. If no :initform was provided, the initial value is the null value for single-valued attributes, and the empty set for set-valued attributes.

The function delete-entity takes any entity handle as an argument, and deletes the entity. It also removes from the database any reference to the entity. Suppose we delete entity *e*. If the value of a single-valued attribute is *e*, the value is changed to the null value. If the value of a set-valued attribute contains *e* as one of its members, *e* is removed from the set. Thus, there are never any 'dangling references' to entities in a database. Statice maintains 'referential integrity' [Date82].

Entities are never garbage-collected, because they can never become garbage. If an entity exists, it is always reachable, because you can always use associative access (see below) to find all entities of a given entity type. This is a fundamental difference between the data models of Lisp and Statice.

8.4.4 Associative Access

The for-each special form provides associative access to entities in a database. It iterates over entities of a type or in a set, optionally selecting on the basis of attribute values, optionally sorting by some value. It serves as the 'query language' of Statice.

In its simplest form, for-each iterates over all entities of an entity type. For example, the following form iterates over all students in the database, repeatedly evaluating *body*, with the variable s bound to entity handles for each successive entity:

```
(for-each ((s student))
   ...body... )
```

This syntax is similar to that used by Common Lisp iteration functions such as dolist and dotimes. The body can be an arbitrary sequence of Lisp forms.

for-each can also iterate over the elements of a set-valued attribute. The following example adds up and returns the total number of credits of all the courses being taken by George:

```
(let ((total 0))
   (for-each ((c (student-courses george)))
      (incf total (course-credits c)))
   total)
```

Finding a subset of entities, based on their attribute values, is a more interesting kind of database query. This example adds up the credits of all courses in the English department being taken by George:

```
(let ((total 0))
   (for-each ((c (student-courses george))
              (:where (eql (course-dept c)
                           english-dept)))
      (incf total (course-credits c)))
   total)
```

The next example returns the course named 'Introduction' in the English department:

```
(for-each ((c course)
           (:where (and (string-equal 'Introduction'
                        (course-title c))
                        (eql (department-named
                              'English')
                             (course-dept c)))))
   (return c))
```

The contents of the :where clause is always a valid Lisp form that expresses the condition of the query. for-each allows an extremely restricted subset of Lisp forms in a :where. But by making the syntax a subset of Lisp's syntax, for-each looks natural and is easy to understand.

A query can involve more than one variable. To find every student who is in a department that is headed by Jones:

```
(let ((result nil))
   (for-each ((s student) (d department)
              (:where (and (eql (student-dept s) d)
                           (eql (department-head d)
                                jones)))
```

```
        (pushnew s result))
    result)
```

The `for-each` iterates over each *pairing* of student and department, for all students and all departments in the database, that satisfy the `:where` clause. The body is evaluated for a subset of the Cartesian product of sets, much like a *join* operation in the relational algebra.

`for-each` also does sorting. To call a function for all visiting instructors, in ascending order of salary:

```
(for-each ((i instructor)
           (:where (eql (instructor-visiting i) t))
           (:order-by (instructor-salary i) ascending))
    (some-function i))
```

8.4.5 Transactions

To provide concurrency control and recovery, Statice uses the traditional concept of serializable *transactions*. All operations on Statice databases must be done within the scope of a transaction. Changes made within a transaction are not visible outside the transaction, until the transaction *commits*. When the transaction commits, the changes are made persistent, and made visible to other processes and workstations. If the transaction *aborts*, all effects of the transaction are undone. All changes within a transaction are atomic: either all take place, or none takes place.

The programmer specifies transaction boundaries using a special form called `with-transaction`. Everything inside the dynamic scope of a `with-transaction` happens within the same transaction. If the body returns normally, the transaction commits. If the body returns abnormally (e.g., by doing a Lisp `throw` or `return`, possibly as the result of an error), the transaction aborts.

Transactions are intended to be of short duration, e.g., measured in milliseconds. Many applications in software engineering (and CAD, etc.) need some kind of longer-term concurrency control, spanning durations during which designs are altered, new versions are created, and so on. Several mechanisms for such longer-term concurrency control are discussed in the literature, such as 'checking out', version control, and active user notifications [Chou86,Bancilhon85,Hornick87]. We feel that different applications are likely to require different paradigms for handling these issues, so we have refrained from 'hard-wiring' any one mechanism into the core of Statice. Instead, we plan to supply a library of alternative higher-level concurrency-control mechanisms, built on the basic transactions that Statice provides.

8.5 IMPLEMENTATION

Statice is organized into three layers of modularity. From lowest to highest:

1. *File level* provides a page-oriented file system. It supports transactions and communication between client and server hosts.

2. *Storage level* provides storage allocation for records within files, and index structures.

3. *Function level* implements entities, data types, accessor functions, and query processing.

The overall structure of the implementation is based on ideas from [Cattell83] and [Brown85], with various improvements.

8.5.1 File Level

File level provides a page-oriented file system. The caller can create and destroy files and pages within files, and can read and write the contents of pages. The caller must open a transaction before doing anything, and all side-effects happen atomically when the transaction commits. The file can be located on the local host, or on a remote host connected by a network. File level manages all network communication, allowing any number of local and remote clients to access a file concurrently.

Concurrency control is implemented with two-phase locking on page granularity. Deadlocks are detected when they occur, and cause one of the transactions to abort and restart. Recovery uses a log, storing 'redo' records. A background process performs periodic checkpoint operations to propagate pages from the log to the database, and recover log space used by transactions that have committed, without delaying the operation of transactions.

Contents of pages are kept in page buffers in memory; they are read in from the disk or the network (depending on whether the file is local or remote) as needed. On any client host, there is one buffer for any database page, because all processes on the client reside in the same virtual address space and can use the buffer (under control of the locks, of course).

In most database systems, buffers can only be used for the duration of a transaction, because after the transaction commits and the locks are released, the page might be changed by some other host, rendering the contents of the buffer obsolete. However, it is important to retain these buffers in an object-oriented database, because the same objects are often used in many successive transactions. File level utilizes a novel cache coherence protocol that allows the client to use retained buffers in subsequent transactions, without the need to communicate with the server before using the page. This greatly decreases response time in typical object-oriented database scenarios.

File level also includes a facility to back up databases to magnetic tape or optical disk. The backup mechanism uses the 'fuzzy dump' technique described in [Gray78] so that transactions can continue to run while backup dumping is in progress.

8.5.2 Storage Level

Storage level is built on file level, and is responsible for the physical organization of databases. It provides variable-length *records* to its caller. A record is an arbitrary-length vector of words. There are entry points to create, delete, grow, and shrink a record, and to read words from and write them to a record. Storage level does not concern itself with the contents of records.

The implementation of records is similar to that in System R's RSS [Astrahan76]. Records are addressed by *record identifiers*, or *RIDs*, which contain a page number and an offset into a table of descriptors at the end of that page. The RID for a record never changes, even if the record changes size, and the descriptor can indirect to another page if a record grows too large to fit on its original page. Storage level concerns itself with placement of records onto pages, and its caller never has to deal with the underlying fixed-size pages.

Unlike System R, Statice records can grow to be extremely large. Large records have a tree of blocks, each block within one page; the branch blocks contain RIDs to the next level, and the leaf blocks hold the contents of the record. Large records are important for storing values such as long text strings and image data.

The caller can define several *areas*, and allocate any record in a particular area. Areas are disjoint sets of pages. By allocating records in the same or different areas, the caller can exert some control over locality and clustering.

Storage level provides a sophisticated B*-tree implementation, supporting variable-size keys and multiple associated values. It uses the Prefix B-tree algorithm [Bayer77] and the techniques described in [McCreight77] for efficient handling of variable-size data.

A much simpler B*-tree implementation, called *B-sets*, is also provided. A B-set has one-word keys and no values. Thus, it maintains a sorted set of 32-bit numbers with fast insertion and deletion. Because of its simpler format, it attains a higher branching factor than the general B-trees, and so is more efficient for callers that only need a simple set.

8.5.3 Function Level

Function level provides all the database functionality of Statice, by building on storage level. Each entity is represented by a record (the *entity record*), which contains a pointer to the record representing the type of the entity, and a 96-bit identifier that is unique over all space and time (a *UID*). Values of the single-valued attributes of an entity are stored in the entity record, including values of inherited attributes. Each value of a set-valued attribute is stored in its own *tuple record*, which is like a tuple in a normalized relational database.

Function level uses the B*-trees of storage level to maintain indexes on attribute values. For example, the :inverse-index option of the name attribute of the person entity type tells function level to maintain a B*-tree. Each index entry's key is computed from the name string, and the entry's value is the RID of the entity record. Thus the inverse access function person-named is sped up.

The :multiple-index option of the course entity type makes an index whose keys are formed from the title string and the RID of the dept entity. The :unique option on the index ensures that only one course can have a particular pair of title and department. The key values are computed by function level, a different way for each type, combined using the algorithm described in [Blasgen77], and handed as untyped data to storage level.

There is also a different kind of index, called a *group index*, which function level uses when indexing is based on entity values instead of data values. The :inverse-index option of the instructor attribute of course is an example of a group index. Given an instructor, we want to be able to locate quickly all the courses taught by the instructor. The group index associates with each instructor a set of RIDs, pointing to the entity records of the instructor's courses. When the set is small, function level stores the RIDs in a record; when it becomes larger, it converts the representation to use a B-set. The group index lets the `courses-taught-by` accessor function find the courses by directly following pointers (RIDs). (In relational databases, this kind of indexing is sometimes called *pre-linking*.) Note that finding the instructor of a particular course works by direct pointer-following regardless of indexes, since the course entity record stores the RID of the instructor's entity record.

Entity handles are created by function level when an entity is first referenced. A hash table, keyed on the internal address of the entity, makes sure that only one handle is created for any entity, to preserve the identity property. An entity handle contains the RID of the entity it references, so that accessor functions can go directly to the entity record for attribute values, without any index lookups. This provides the fast 'direct access' mentioned above.

`for-each` uses a query optimizer that checks for the presence of helpful indexes and uses them when appropriate. Indexes can be created or deleted at any time, with no visible semantic effect, allowing the database to be tuned as requirements change over time.

8.5.4 Processes and Processors

Sharing of objects is accomplished by accessing databases on remote workstations, using network communication. This is done by file level. When using a database stored on a remote workstation, the application program calls down through the levels, and file level communicates with the file level on the server host. This means Statice causes little process-switching overhead on the client host: function and storage level, and the client part of file level, all run in the application's process.

There are two reasons for running function and storage levels on the client host instead of on the server. First, in many applications, there is little or no contention for database writes, thus much of the database remains cached on the client host. Because of the cache coherence scheme, the client might only need to wait for a response from the server host once (at commit time), even for a complex transaction. The impressive performance consequences of such an organization were demonstrated in [Rubenstein87]. (Our scheme improves on that of [Rubenstein87] because it does not require the database to be 'single user'.)

Second, in our environment, the client and server hosts use the same kind of processor. Although the server is not more powerful, it is shared by many clients. If the computation of the higher levels took place on the server, there would be a serious danger that the server's processor would be a system-wide bottleneck, with the client processors simply waiting. Instead, Statice takes advantage of the ample processor power available at each client, obtaining better concurrency overall.

8.6 CONCLUSIONS AND STATUS

Statice provides persistent, shared storage for Genera. The object-oriented data model provides data independence, expressive power, and a natural and clear interface to the host language. The implementation provides efficient access, both associative and direct, and transactions.

The implementation is about 36,000 lines, plus 22,000 lines of test suites, all in Symbolics Common Lisp. The present implementation is built on Flavors [Moon86]. When CLOS is fully implemented in Genera, Statice will be upgraded to use it; we expect this to be easy since Flavors and CLOS are very similar, and most of the differences do not affect Statice.

Several small applications have been written using Statice by software developers at Symbolics. Two applications are used by Symbolics to produce software products.

Bug Tracker is a multi-user interactive application for keeping track of bug reports and their subsequent handling. It keeps track of outstanding bug reports and their status. It records the correspondence of reports with actual bugs; this is a many-to-many relationship, since many people might send in reports about the same bug, and one report may refer to several underlying bugs. It is integrated with the Genera electronic mail system, so that incoming mail reporting bugs can be automatically entered into the database, and so messages can automatically be sent to, say, all the people who have sent in reports about a particular bug. Bug Tracker lets cooperating software developers and their managers keep track of tasks and priorities, and helps software support personnel provide up-to-date information.

SRDB stands for Software Releases DataBase. The Software Releases organization is responsible for packaging and shipping software products. SRDB keeps track of the list of customers, products, etc. and generates invoices, packing slips, mailing lists, and so on, for a software release.

Statice is a released commercial product; it has been installed at many customer sites. Future plans for Statice include using it for software development tools closer to the heart of software development, including version control, configuration management, the electronic mail system, source code and object code, the relationships between procedures (*a* calls *b*, *a* uses *b* as a variable, etc.), and so on. These tools will base their data integration on Statice instead of virtual memory. Statice itself will acquire new features and tools, and, like any database system, its performance will always be under improvement.

ACKNOWLEDGMENTS

The authors would like to thank Dave Stryker, Bob Kerns, Sonya Keene, Penny Parkinson, and especially Dave Moon for their contributions to the design of Statice. This work was performed when the authors were at Symbolics, Inc.

9 Programming with Vbase

Tim Andrews

9.1 INTRODUCTION

Vbase is a fully integrated software development platform which supports schema definition and procedural languages built around a central object database. An integrated tool set is also included for program debugging and database browsing. Because Vbase is an object system, it raises the level of abstraction and expressiveness of the tools available to the programmer. The semantics of object code is richer and more directly associated with the actual objects in the application domain. Where conventional systems rely on a relatively weak notion of data value, restricted essentially to numbers and characters, object systems introduce a host of new concepts which provide a powerful foundation for software development.

9.1.1 Fundamental Concepts

In Vbase, an object is very much like a value of one of the built-in data types that are standard in higher-level programming languages, such as the data types `Integer`, `Float`, and `Character`. In the Vbase object system, however, many more built-in types are provided, including aggregate types such as `Set`, `Stack` and `Queue`. Moreover, programmers are provided with the capability to extend the set of built-in types at will. This permits them to include types that represent the kinds of real-world objects they need to manipulate. For example, if the application involves text processing, then `Paragraph`, `Page`, and `Chapter` are likely candidates for user-defined types. Similarly, for a mechanical design system, the type `Part` might be defined by the user.

In an object system, an object of a given type is said to be an instance of the type. For example, integers are instances of the type `Integer`, parts are instances of the type `Part`, and so on. A type in Vbase defines the potential behavior of its instances in the following sense. (1) Each type has an associated collection of operations, the operations that can be performed on its instances. For example, `Stack` is associated with the operations `Push` and `Pop`; `Part` might be associated with operations like `CheckStatus` and `Assemble`. (2) In addition, each type has an associated collection of properties. Properties are roughly analogous to the fields of conventional database technology, but they are more accurately viewed as kinds of associations that may be formed between a given type's instances and other objects. For example, `Stack` defines the property `Cardinality`, which forms an association between a stack and the number of elements it contains. `Part` might define properties such as `PartNumber`, `ParentPart`, and `Subparts`.

A type's operations and properties impose constraints on operation invocations and property associations, specifying the allowable types of the objects involved. The Vbase procedural language is strongly typed, allowing detection of many errors during program compilation rather than at run-time.

Types in Vbase are organized into a subtype/supertype hierarchy. For example, types such as `StructuralPart` and `HydraulicPart` might be defined as subtypes of the type `Part`, and they might define their own associated operations and properties. Each type inherits the operations and properties associated with its supertypes. This means that `Part`'s associated operations can be performed on instances of these two subtypes. And the subtypes' instances can have values for `Part`'s associated properties. In addition, subtypes such as `StructuralPart` and `HydraulicPart` might refine or specially tailor the operations and properties they inherit. These simple mechanisms provide enormous power in modeling applications in a language that is much closer to that of the end user than are conventional languages.

In addition to its use as an environment for software development, the Vbase database serves as a repository for persistent objects. The new types defined for use in an application serve as templates for storing, retrieving, and manipulating data. The basic database operations for creating and deleting objects and for setting and getting property values are system-supplied for all objects, and may be used as is or redefined for application-specific needs.

9.1.2 System Overview

The Vbase system comes with a kernel database containing an initial hierarchy of types. This initial set is quite extensive and is documented in the System Type Library Reference [Ontologic88b]. Besides the database, the system has three major components: TDL (the Vbase Type Definition Language)— used to write definitions of new types. COP (C Object Processor)— an extended version of C that can manipulate Vbase database objects. ITS (The Vbase Integrated Toolset)— provides comprehensive support for debugging and browsing. The Vbase system runs under BSD Unix 4.2 on Sun 3 workstations and under Vax VMS.

9.1.3 Chapter Organization

The next section discusses the process of constructing and supporting applications in terms of the three different kinds of code users write when using Vbase. An example is included which illustrates some of Vbase's basic features. Sections 9.3 and 9.4 provide more detailed discussion of TDL and COP, respectively.

9.2 USING VBASE

There are three kinds of code users write when using Vbase:

1. *Specification* code, or code for the schema or data model. This is code that defines types, properties, and operations. It is written in TDL.
2. *Implementation* code, or method code. This is code that implements an operation. It is written in COP.
3. *Application* code, that is, code that acts strictly as a client of the types, operations, and properties already specified and implemented. This is also written in COP.

This chapter will provide a brief overview of the three different kinds of code, and then discuss an example involving all three.

9.2.1 Overview

To write specification code, the user must think about the types of objects involved in the applications she or he wishes to support. By "objects" here is meant *the real world objects involved in the applications*. The user must divide these objects into categories and subcategories (types and subtypes), and determine what types of associations among objects need to be recorded and accessed (properties), and what types of modification and examination the objects from each category are required to undergo (operations).

These types are then specified in TDL, including specification of the abstract interfaces to the operations and properties. Specification of an abstract interface includes information about what operation invocations or property accesses must be like, formally, and what types must be involved. Abstract interfaces are independent of the storage and implementation characteristics of operations and properties. When the TDL code is compiled, all the specification information is permanently recorded in the database.

Implementation code is written in COP, an object-oriented extension of C, with persistence. In COP, the user can create and delete instances of TDL specified types as well as instances of system-supplied types, and invoke the types' associated operations and access their associated properties. Because COP supports persistence, the creation, deletion, and modification of objects can be automatically recorded in the database, as the user wishes.

Implementation code implements an operation, that is, it determines exactly what an operation does, and what it returns. Implementing an operation can involve invocation of other operations, or even recursive invocation of the operation being implemented. In writing an operation implementation, the user has available all the resources COP provides.

The COP implementation of a given operation consists of a combination of *methods*. The implementation of different operations may overlap; that is, different operations may be implemented by some of the same methods.

Whereas TDL is used to specify the abstract interfaces to operations, methods are used to implement these operations. Vbase enforces a separation of specification from implementation so that an operation's implementation may vary while requiring no modification to the code that invokes the operation. The integrity of code invoking the operation is maintained as long as only the implementation, and not the operation's abstract interface, changes.

Application code is code that is neither specification code nor method code. The types, properties, and operations specified and implemented in the latter two kinds of code are typically of general utility to application programs. Among the application programs are the main programs, which open and close the database.

Application code does not implement a Vbase operation, but, like a method, it draws on the resources provided by COP, as well as on all the information in the database, including the types properties and operations, both user-defined and system-supplied.

Writing software with Vbase generally proceeds roughly from specification to implementation to application, and back to specification, and so forth, for several iterations. In addition, this cycle might apply broadly, i.e., to most of an application's software at once, or it might apply more narrowly, i.e., to each separate type and its associated operations and properties. In practice there will, of course, be countless variations on this general pattern.

Within this writing cycle, the movement back to specification is frequently accompanied by an *enriching* of the data model, that is, by the addition of subtypes of previously defined types, and by the fine tuning or refinement of inherited and previously defined operations.

9.2.2 An Example

We now develop an example that illustrates the three different kinds of coding involved in using Vbase.

Writing specification code. Suppose we need to support a variety of applications which derive information about the various parts of some large collection of devices. Suppose further that we identify the major subcategories of parts as the category of *electrical parts*, the category of *hydraulic parts*, and the category of *structural parts*. We have already formed the beginnings of our data model. The simple type hierarchy we have identified might be diagrammed as in Figure 9.1.

Each of the boxes in the diagram stands for a *type*. Arrows point from a type to its *direct supertype*. Entity here is a system supplied type. Every type, system-supplied or user-defined, is either a direct or indirect subtype of the type Entity.

We have chosen to locate Part as a direct subtype of Entity. But user-defined types are often appropriately located elsewhere in the system-supplied type hierarchy. The considerations that determine the appropriate location of user types in the hierarchy will be elucidated as the discussion proceeds.

Now we must identify the various kinds of association that need to be recorded and accessed. Suppose that parts typically have a part number, a parent part, child

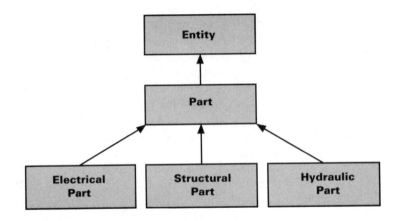

Figure 9.1 A simple type hierarchy.

parts, a reliability factor, and an engineer who is responsible for them. And perhaps for structural parts, in particular, we need to record the material they are made from. And perhaps for hydraulic parts, in particular, we need to record the flowrate and pressure they are designed for, and so on. We might diagram the required associations as shown in Figure 9.2. In this figure, arrows represent properties. The arrows point to the type of object that can serve as a value for the represented property. These types are known as the properties' *valuespecs*.

The valuespecs of these properties include some types not yet considered: the types Integer, Engineer, Material and Real. Integer and Real are system-

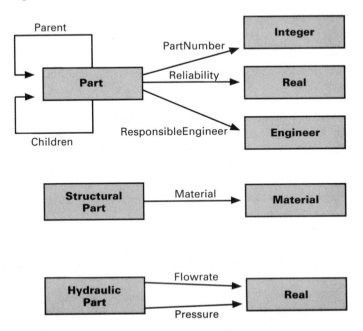

Figure 9.2

supplied types. However, we will have to define the types `Engineer` and `Material` ourselves in TDL.

We might now consider if we will need to record any kinds of associations from instances of these types to other objects. For example, we might need to record the employee ID number and supervisor of each engineer responsible for some part. Since every engineer is an employee, and since employees in general have supervisors and IDs, we can define the type `Engineer` as a subtype of the type `Employee`, and associate `Supervisor` and `EmployeeID` with `Employee` (see Figure 9.3).

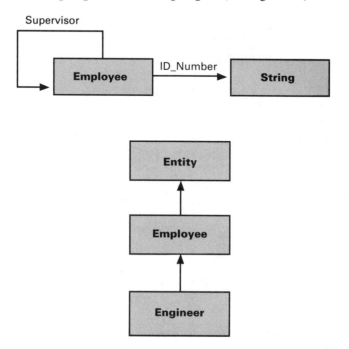

Figure 9.3

Since a type's properties are *inherited* by its subtypes, even *indirect* instances of `Employee` (such as *direct* instances of `Engineer`) can have values for `Supervisor` and `EmployeeID`. Moreover, if we later define new subtypes of `Employee`, they will also automatically inherit these properties. Here is how we might code the schema we've developed so far:

```
define type Part
        supertypes = {Entity};
        properties =
        {       PartNumber: Integer;
                Parent: optional Part inverse
                        Part$Children;
                Children: distributed Set[Part]
                        inverse Part$Parent;
                Reliability: Real;
```

```
                ResponsibleEngineer: Engineer;
        };
end Part;
define type StructuralPart
        supertypes = {Part}
        properties =
        {       Material: Material;
        };
end StructuralPart;
define type HydraulicPart
        supertypes = {Part};
        properties =
        {       FlowRate: Real;
                Pressure: Real;
        };
end HydraulicPart;
define type ElectricalPart
        supertypes = {Part};
end ElectricalPart;
define type Engineer
        supertypes = {Employee};
end Engineer;
define type Employee
        supertypes = {Entity};
        properties =
        {       EmployeeID: String;
                Supervisor: Employee;
        };
end Employee;
define type {Material} is enum (steel, plastic, copper);
```

The significance of much of this code should be apparent. Each code segment enclosed between `define` and `end` contains a TDL type definition statement, which specifies the name of the type being defined, its direct supertype, and its associated properties and their valuespecs. Properties may also be specified as optional or multivalued, and their inverses may be specified.

The last segment above contains a definition of a special sort of type, an enum-Type. An enumType is a type with a fixed number of instances, which are created in TDL. The above definition specifies three instances: *steel, plastic* and *copper*. While COP will be used to create instances of the other types we've defined, it cannot be used to add instances of the type `Material`. Since `Material` is an enumType, it has a fixed set of instances.

Let us now consider the kinds of modification and examination the parts in our applications are required to undergo. Suppose we want to display in a convenient format all the properties of a given part (examination). We might then define an operation, associated with the type `Part`, to accomplish this. The type definition for `Part` needs a simple addition to specify the abstract interface to the `PropertyDisplay` operation:

```
define type Part
        supertypes = {Entity};
        properties =
        {       PartNumber: Integer;
                Parent: optional Part inverse
                        Part$Children;
                Children: distributed Set[Part]
                        inverse Part$Parent;
                Reliability: Real;
                ResponsibleEngineer: Engineer;
        };
        operations =
        {       PropertyDisplay(the_part: Part)
                return(Part)
                method(display_method);
        };
end Part;
```

This new code specifies the type of argument the operation takes, the type of object it returns, and the name of the method that will implement the operation. We now turn to the writing of the COP code for just such an implementation.

Writing implementation code. We want to implement an operation that takes a part as argument, displays its property values, and, for convenience, returns the part. Here is what the code might look like:

```
#define MAXSIZE 500
import Engineer;
enter module Part;
obj Part
method display_method(the_part)
obj Part the_part
{       char c_engineer_ID[MAXSIZE];
        AM_StringToC(c_engineer_ID,
                the_part.ResponsibleEngineer.EmployeeID,
                MAXSIZE);
        printf("Part: %d\n Parent: %d\n Reliability:
                %8.2g\n
                \tResponsibleEngineer: %s\n", (int)
                the_part.PartNumber,
                (int)the_part.Parent.PartNumber,
                (float)the_part.Reliability,
                c_engineer_ID);
        return(the_part);
}
```

This example illustrates some basic points. Since this is an operation implementation, i.e., a method, it contains the reserved word "method", followed by the method-name as specified in the TDL definition of the type that defined the operation. This is preceded by the declaration "obj Part" to indicate the type of object returned by the operation.

The method-name is followed by a formal argument list. In this case, the argument list consists of the formal "the_part" enclosed in parentheses. On the next line, the formal is declared to be of type Part to indicate that actuals must be instances of Part.

In the method body, the second part of the printf statement contains expressions such as "the_part.Parent.PartNumber". These are property get-accesses, using a dot notation similar to that used for C structures. Such expressions designate property values. The expression just mentioned designates the PartNumber of the Parent of the_part. The parent itself cannot be displayed since it is a part. Only strings and numbers can be displayed, so we print the parent's partNumber.

Most of the property values we want to print are objects of type Integer and Real. These are not the same as C values. However, we can cast them to C int and C double, respectively, when we supply them as arguments to printf. A more complicated conversion to perform is from an object string to a C string. To accomplish this, we use the function AM_StringToC.

The two *import* statements near the beginning of the code provide a semantic context for the interpretation of property names, such as "PartNumber". When a given property is accessed, the type that defined it must be imported.

This operation displays the values of the properties associated with parts in general. It does not display values of properties associated with, for example, hydraulic-Parts, although hydraulicParts can be arguments to it. However, it is possible to refine the operation for the various subtypes of Part, so that the values of their associated properties will be displayed as well. Before discussing this further, we will consider a simple application program that utilizes the PropertyDisplay operation.

Writing application code. Suppose we want an application program to read a partNumber as input, and then display the property values of the part with that number. With the PropertyDisplay operation already implemented, this program need only open the database, look up the part with the specified number, and invoke the operation with the part as argument.

If there are many parts to be stored in the database, these parts should probably be stored as members of an *unordered dictionary*. An unorderedDictionary is an aggregate whose members each have an associated index or key. The type Unordered-Dictionary (a system supplied type) defines an operation that, provided with a key, performs an efficient lookup of the dictionary member associated with that key. In this case, each part's key would be its partNumber.

```
extern char *getenv();
import UnorderedDictionary;
import Part;
main()
```

```
{       int c_part_number;
        obj Integer the_part_number;
        obj Part the_part;
        char *db;
        /* Get database name from env variable. */
        db = getenv("DBNAME");
        printf("Begin opening the database\n");
        AM_databaseOpen(db, 2500);
        printf("End opening the database\n");
        scanf("%d",c_part_number);
        the_part_number = c_part_number;
        the_part = UnorderedDictionary$GetElement(
                $PartsDictionary, the_part_number);
        Part$PropertyDisplay(the_part);
        printf("Begin closing the database\n");
        AM_databaseOpen(db, 2500);
        printf("End closing the database\n");
        exit(0);
}
```

The database is opened with a call to AM_databaseOpen. The partNumber
is read with scanf, and the part lookup is performed with the operation Unordered-
Dictionary$GetElement. The call to the PropertyDisplay operation takes
the form "Part$PropertyDisplay(the_part);".

Operation calls use operation *pathnames*. An operation's pathname usually consists
of the name of the type that defined it, followed by "$", followed by the operation name
specified in the TDL.

Finally, the database is closed with AM_databaseClose.

Note also that the types UnorderedDictionary and Part are *imported* near
the beginning of the code to provide a semantic context for operation names.

Refinement and dispatching. As mentioned earlier, each subtype of Part
can refine the PropertyDisplay operation to handle properties specific to it, as well
as the properties associated with parts in general. We can make this change to the
specification and implementation code without changing the application code.

This will involve writing for each subtype a method that implements the specialized
behavior. The full implementation of each refinement will then be a combination of the
subtype's method and the original method for the supertype.

The result will be that an invocation of the operation Part$PropertyDisplay
will involve *dispatching*. Dispatching is the run-time selection of an appropriate operation implementation, based on the direct type of the invocation's first argument. Because
dispatching endows the first argument of an operation invocation with special significance, the first argument is called the *dispatch argument*.

Thus, if the actual argument is a direct instance of Part, only the original method
will be executed. If the actual argument is a direct instance of StructuralPart, the
original method will be executed together with the new method for StructuralPart's

refinement. Similarly, if the actual argument is a direct instance of HydraulicPart, the original method will be executed together with the new method for HydraulicPart's refinement.

A look at the code should clarify this. We begin by specifying the operation refinement for each subtype.

```
define type StructuralPart
        supertypes = {Part};
        properties =
        {        Material: Material;
        };
        operations =
        {        refines PropertyDisplay(the_part:
                        StructuralPart)
                returns(StructuralPart)
                methods(structural_display_method);
        };
end StructuralPart;
define type HydraulicPart
        supertypes = {Part};
        properties =
        {        FlowRate: Real;
                Pressure: Real;
        };
        operations =
        {        refines PropertyDisplay(the_part:
                        HydraulicPart)
                returns(HydraulicPart)
                method(hydraulic_display_method);
        };
end HydraulicPart;
```

The new code here specifies the operation as a refinement with the reserved word "refines". The code for StructuralPart specifies the argument as being of type StructuralPart. The type of the dispatch argument must always be the same as the type defining or refining the operation. StructuralPart is also specified as the return type. Finally, a new method-name is specified. The code for HydraulicPart is similar.

Here is what the new implementation code might look like:

```
#define MAXSIZE 500
import Material;
enter module StructuralPart;
obj StructuralPart
method structural_display_method(the_part)
obj StructuralPart the_part;
```

```
{       char c_material_name[MAXSIZE];
        $$(the_part);
        AM_StringToC(c_material_name,
                        the_part.Material.Name,
                MAXSIZE);
        printf("\tMaterial:%s\n",c_material_name);
        return(the_part);
}
```

The most important new feature of the above code is the $$ call. The result of executing this $$ call is that control is passed to the supertype's method, that is, the original method for the operation defined by Part. When execution of that method is complete, control is passed to the statement following the $$ call in this method. This is how methods are combined in Vbase.

The $$ call could have occurred anywhere in this method. By placing it at the beginning of the method body, we indicate that the general behavior is to take place first, followed by the display of the properties specific to the subtype.

Note the changes in the import and enter module statements, as well as the adjustments in the declarations to accommodate the new dispatch argument type.

Dispatching, in this example, saves us the trouble of conditionally invoking different versions of the operation. But, more importantly, it saves us the trouble of modifying the application code to accommodate the special behavior associated with new subtypes or refinements if they are added later. The application's operation call can be entirely insulated from the evolution of the subtype structure.

While this example illustrates many interesting features of Vbase, we have by no means touched upon them all. The next two sections provide a more in depth discussion of the Vbase schema definition and procedural languages.

9.3 USING TDL

TDL, the Vbase Type Definition Language, is roughly analogous to data definition languages in conventional database systems. It is used to specify a schema or data model for a Vbase application. This is achieved primarily through the creation of new data types which define categories of objects in the database, and through the specification of the abstract interfaces to the operations and properties associated with these types. TDL can also be used to create instances of user-defined or system-supplied types.

Of the various TDL statements, the type definition statement is the most important and most frequently used. It is also the most complicated, and so we devote most of this section to it.

9.3.1 The Basic Form of the Type Definition Statement

A type definition statement is used to establish the existence of a user-defined data type. This statement specifies information about

  1. the location of this new type in the type hierarchy,

2. the properties for which instances of the new type may have values, and

3. the operations which may be performed on the type's instances (or, more precisely, the operations for which the type's instances may be the dispatch argument).

The basic form of a type definition statement is shown below.

```
define type idn
        supertypes = { type-name };
        properties clause
        operation clause
end idn;
```

Every TDL type definition begins with a *header* and ends with a *footer*. The header and footer specify the name of the type being defined. For example, the type definition below establishes the existence of a user-defined type called "Employee".

```
define type Employee
        . . . . . . .
        statement body
        . . . . . . .
end Employee;
```

The name `Employee` here has been supplied by the user. Any idn is legal here. An idn is a string of arbitrary length containing alphanumeric characters plus the underscore, except that the first character cannot be a numeral. By convention, leading underscore names are reserved by Ontologic for system use. Also by convention, type names begin with a capital letter.

The TDL and COP compilers are case insensitive, except for the purposes of reporting. This means, for example, that `Employee` and `emPloyEE` will, in a given context, designate the same object.

The *supertypes* clause is used to establish the location of a new user-defined type in the type hierarchy by specification of a direct supertype for the new type. So, for example, the following type definition statement establishes the existence of a type named Employee as a direct subtype of the type `Person`.

```
define type Employee
        supertypes = {Person};
end Employee;
```

The type name `Person` is a user-supplied idn. A type definition for both Employee and `Person` must be compiled before any COP code involving these types can be compiled, but the TDL for `Employee` may be compiled before, after, or along with the TDL for `Person`.

The type `Entity` may be specified as a new type's direct supertype if no other type has properties or operations that can be usefully inherited or refined by the new type.

The current release of Vbase supports a tree structured network of types, so specification of a type's direct supertype determines its exact location in the hierarchy. Future Vbase releases will allow for more complicated subtyping structures (and more sophisticated inheritance mechanisms), and so specification of more than one direct supertype may be called for. The plural form of the reserved word "supertypes" and the requirement of braces around the supplied supertype lay the syntactic groundwork for this future enhancement.

We now turn to the definition of properties and operations.

9.3.2 Defining Properties

The properties clause of a type definition provides the names of properties for which the defined type's instances are to have values. It does not create any instances of the type, or establish any property values for the type's instances; rather, it simply sets the stage for this to be accomplished by a TDL *entity definition* or by a COP application at run-time.

In addition, the properties clause specifies for each property a *valuespec* which the property's values must satisfy. Often a valuespec will be a type (satisfied by its instances).

The system ensures that the value of a property for any given object satisfies the property's valuespec. The valuespecs of properties are also used by the COP compiler in compile-time type checking.

So, for example, the type `Employee` might define properties such as `Name` and `Supervisor`. To restrict the values of the property `Name` to strings, the property's valuespec can be specified as the type `String`. To restrict the values of the property `Supervisor` to employees, this property's valuespec can be specified as the type `Employee`.

```
define type Employee
        supertypes={Person};
        properties=
        {
                Name: String;
                Supervisor: Employee;
        };
end Employee;
```

Notice that the valuespec for the property `Supervisor` is the type `Employee`, the type we are in the process of defining. This is entirely legal and, in fact, quite common. It simply specifies that any employee's supervisor must be an employee.

In addition to a property name and a valuespec, a property specification can include various combinations of the following:

1. the reserved word "`optional`", to indicate that the property is *optional*,
2. specification of a *default value* for the property,
3. specification of the property's *inverse*,

4. the reserved word "distributed" to indicate that the property is *distributed*,

5. specification of the types of access the property *allows* or *disallows* (initialization, read and/or write access), with the reserved words "allows" and "disallows",

6. the reserved word "refines" to indicate that the property is a *refinement*.

We now consider each of these in turn.

Optional properties. According to the type definition above, each employee, from the moment of its creation and for the duration of its existence, is required to have a value for the properties Name and Supervisor. This does not mean the values cannot change, but rather that there must always be some value or other. However, properties can also be specified as *optional*.

If a property defined by some type is optional, an instance of the type may at any time lack a value for that property. In particular, such an instance may be *created* without any value for the property. The property for this object may be set to some value later, or the object may remain without a value for the property for the duration of its existence. In addition, an object which currently *has* a value for an optional property may at any time be modified so that it *no longer* has a value. A value for an optional property may be set and removed any number of times.

To specify a property as optional, simply include the reserved word optional after the colon in the property specification. Here is an example:

```
define type Employee
        supertypes={Person};
        properties=
        {
                Name: String;
                Supervisor: Employee;
                Telephone_ext: optional String;
        };
end Employee;
```

Here, all the properties are required except Telephone_ext. Some employees may not have a telephone extension, so this property is optional.

Property default values. Instances of a given type can be created either in TDL or in COP. In either case, property values for the new instance may have to be specified at the time of creation.

As stated in the previous section, values for optional properties need not be supplied at creation time. In addition, a value for a property with a *default value* need not be supplied at creation time. The default value will be used to initialize the property if no value is supplied in the entity definition or COP constructor.

A default value can be specified by including after the valuespec- expression in the property specification ":=", followed by a numeral, a string (a sequence of characters enclosed in quotes), or a database name. The default must, of course, satisfy the property's valuespec.

Inverse properties. It is possible to specify a property's inverse in TDL. The inverse of a given property, p, is another property, p′, such that the system ensures that: v is the value of p for object o *if and only if* o is the value of p′ for v.

Suppose, for example, that Dora's office is room 3-226. Then the occupant of room 3-226 is Dora. The properties Office and Occupant can be seen as inverses of one another (see Figure 9.4).

Figure 9.4 Inverse properties.

If two properties are defined to be one another's inverses, then whenever a value for one is established or dis-established, the system updates the other appropriately. Suppose, for example, that Office and Occupant are defined as inverses. Then if a COP application established room 3-226 as the value of Office for Dora, the system would establish Dora as the value of Occupant for room 3-226.

To specify a property's inverse, append the reserved word "inverse" to its property specification, followed by the name of its inverse. The name of the inverse property must be a pathname. The pathname of a property usually consists of (a) the name of the type that defined the property, followed by (b) "$", followed by (c) the short name of the property. The path name of a property usually has the form type-name$short-property-name, where type-name names the type that defined the property.

```
define type Employee
        supertypes={Person};
        properties=
        {
                Name: String;
                Supervisor: Employee;
                Start_date: Date;
                Employee_id_number: Integer;
                Telephone_ext: optional String;
                Office: Room inverse Room$Occupant;
        };
end Employee;
```

Here the property Occupant has been specified as the inverse of Office. Since it is *rooms* which have values for the property Occupant, the type Room must define this property as well, and the property Office must be specified as its inverse. So there are always two different places where properties are specified as inverses of one another.

```
define type Room
        supertypes={Location};
        properties=
```

```
        {
        Room_number: String;
        Occupant: optional Employee inverse
                          Employee$Office;
        };
    end Room;
```

If a property has an inverse, TDL requires both it and its inverse to be optional. To understand why, consider our previous example. Suppose we had not made the property Occupant, defined by Room, optional. And suppose we have so far created neither Dora nor room 3-226, but we want to associate these two objects via this property. If we create the room first, we cannot assign the property its proper value, since the value (Dora) does not yet exist. And we cannot leave it without a value until Dora is created, since the property is not optional. We encounter similar problems if we create Dora first.

In addition, if a property with an inverse is expected to change in value for a given object, its inverse must be optional. To understand why, consider our previous example once again. If we change Dora's office from 3-226 to 3-228, then room 3-226 must be modified to have no value for the property Occupant. This is allowed only if Occupant is optional.

Multi-valued properties. The previous examples involving the type Employee presupposed that each employee has exactly one name, one supervisor, one start date, one employee ID number, one office, and, at most, one telephone extension. But many properties are most naturally viewed as having more than one value. Consider, for example, the property Subparts which might be defined by the type Part. A given part might have, let us say, zero, one, or many subparts. Vbase supports two general approaches to potentially multi-valued properties. One approach involves using a property which is strictly speaking single-valued, but whose value for a given object is a set. This allows the user to think of the set's elements as the property's various values. Here is an example:

```
define type Part
        supertypes={Entity};
        properties=
        {
                Subparts: optional Set[Part];
        };
    end Part;
```

Here, the valuespec expression in the property specification is not just a type-name as in the prior examples. Rather, it is a type-name Set, followed by another type-name enclosed in brackets, [Part]. This is a *parameterized valuespec* expression. It designates a valuespec which is satisfied by any set whose members are parts. In general, a valuespec expression of the form:

```
Set[type-name]
```

designates a valuespec which is satisfied by sets whose members are constrained to be instances of the type designated by the type-name in brackets, i.e., sets that have that type as *memberSpec*.

Now, to establish various parts as subparts of a given part, a set must first be created and established as the value of the subpart property for the given part. Then the various subparts must be inserted into the set. Gaining or losing subparts involves inserting and removing parts from the set.

This approach to multi-valued properties is appropriate for many cases. However, inverses of such properties are not allowed. For, since it is strictly speaking sets which are the values of the property Subparts, the type Set would have to define the inverse. But *kernel types cannot be modified by the user*. In particular, they cannot be modified so as to define an additional property.

The user could define her or his own aggregate type to hold the various subparts, e.g., a subtype of Set:

```
define type SpecialSet[Aggregate$MemberSpec]
        supertypes={Set};
        properties=
        {
                parent: optional Part inverse
                        Part$Subparts;
        };
end SpecialSet;
define type Part
        supertypes={Entity};
        properties=
        {
                Subparts: optional SpecialSet[Part]
                        inverse SpecialSet$Parent;
        };
end Part;
```

But an inverse defined by this new type, in this case, may or may not produce the desired behavior. Let us examine such an inverse closely. It would form an association, not from each of the various subparts to their parent part, but rather from the special-set which contains the subparts to the parent part.

If we want the inverse to form an association from each of the various subparts to the parent, the second approach to multi-valued properties must be used. This approach involves defining the multi-valued property as *distributed*. An example of a non-distributed property is shown in Figure 9.5 and of a distributed property in Figure 9.6.

To define a property as distributed, include the reserved word "distributed" before the valuespec expression in the property specification. The valuespec-expression, as in the first approach, must be of the form "Set [*type-name*]" (or, more accurately, "Set [*valuespec-expression*]").

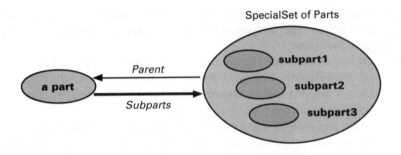

Figure 9.5   A non-distributed property and its inverse.

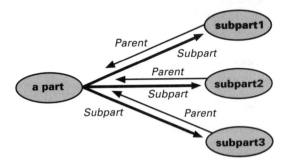

Figure 9.6   A distributed property and its inverse.

```
define type Part
        supertypes={Entity};
        properties=
        {
                Subparts: distributed Set[Part]
                                inverse Part$Parent;
                Parent: optional Part
                                inverse Part$Subparts;

        };
end Part;
```

Notice that since values of the property Subparts are parts, both Subparts and its inverse Parent are mentioned twice within the type definition for Part.

To add and remove objects as values of a distributed property, use the operations Insert and Remove defined by Set as follows. Suppose a_subpart is a part we wish to add as a subpart of a_part (where a_subpart and a_part are COP variables). This can be achieved by the following COP statement:

```
set$Insert(a_part.Subparts, a_subpart);
```

To remove it as a value, the following can be used:

```
set$Remove(a_part.Subparts, a_subpart);
```

The expression a_part.Subparts here denotes a *distributed set* of values of the property Subparts. A distributed set is a special kind of set used to implement distributed properties and their inverses. Unlike the set which held the subparts in our example of a non-distributed property, this set does not need to be created by the user.

Property access. In the examples we've seen so far, access to the specified properties is entirely unrestricted. There are three kinds of access to non-distributed properties: one can read or *get* a property value, one can initialize or *init* a value at creation time, and one can establish or set a property value some time after creation. For distributed properties, the types of access are: read or *get*, add a value or *insert*, and remove a value or *remove*. Any of these types of access can be specified as disallowed. For example, to prevent attempted changes to an employee's start date, we might "disallow set" for that property, as in the following:

```
define type Employee
        supertypes={Person};
        properties=
        {
                Name: String;
                Supervisor: Employee;
                Start_date: Date disallows (set);
        };
end Employee;
```

We could also have said "allows (init, get)" instead of "disallows (set)". Here "Allows..." has the sense of "allows only...". In general, to specify restrictions on property access, use allows or disallows followed by the relevant types of access-expressions (set, get, init, insert, remove) enclosed in parentheses and separated by commas. This should appear after the property's inverse specification (if there is one).

Inheritance and refinement. One of the central purposes of the Vbase type hierarchy is to provide mechanisms for *inheritance* and *refinement*. Inheritance, as it relates to properties, concerns the fact that instances of a type can have values for properties defined by a supertype of that type, i.e., a type inherits its supertypes' properties. Refinement, as related to properties, concerns the fact that a type can modify, in certain ways, the specification of the properties defined by its supertypes, i.e., inherited properties can be refined. Let us consider each of these notions in turn.

Inheritance and Subtyping. Suppose we define a direct subtype of Part called "Pipe". We make Pipe a subtype of Part because pipes are parts of a special kind. Perhaps pipes in particular have a property that doesn't apply to parts generally, say diameter. Then we might define the type Pipe as follows:

```
define type Pipe
        supertypes={Part};
        properties=
```

```
            {
                    Diameter: Real;
            };
    end Pipe;
```

Notice that the supertypes clause specifies `Part` as the direct supertype of `Pipe`. Notice also that the only property mentioned in the properties clause is `Diameter`. But if the type `Part` defines the property `Subpart`, this property is inherited by `Pipe`, and so pipes can be given values for `Subpart` as well as for `Diameter`.

If we define a direct subtype of `Pipe`, say `CopperPipe`, it too inherits the property `Subpart` defined by `Part`. A type inherits properties defined by all of its supertypes, direct and indirect.

If a type is intended to have no direct instances, that is, if any instance of it is to be an instance of some more specialized subtype of it, then the type may be specified as *UnInstantiable* (having no direct instances), by including "`IsInstantiable=$False;`" in the definition of the type.

Refinement. The definition of a given type can specify *refinements* of any of the properties defined by its supertypes. This means that the type's definition can provide a new specification of an inherited property. The new specification will, in most respects, be just like the specification given by the supertype; but it begins with the reserved word "`refines`", and

1. triggers may be added to the access operations (see section 9.3.4),
2. the default value may be changed,
3. the types of property access allowed may be made less restrictive, and
4. the valuespec may be specified as more restrictive, provided the original property was specified as constrainable.

The most common sort of property refinement consists of adding access operation triggers. This is discussed in sections 9.3.4 and 9.4.12. A property is specified as constrainable by including the reserved word "`constrainable`" after the inverse and access specifications. For example, suppose that the subparts of pipes are always themselves pipes. Then we can enhance compile-time type checking by (a) defining `Part` so as to specify `Subparts` as constrainable, and (b) defining `Pipe` so as to refine the property `Subparts`.

```
    define type Part
            supertypes={Entity};
            properties=
            {
                    Subparts: distributed Set[Part]
                                    inverse Part$Parent
                                            constrainable;
                    Parent: optional Part
                                    inverse Part$Subparts;
```

```
                        };
        end Part;
        define type Pipe
                supertypes={Part};
                properties=
                {
                        Diameter: Integer;
                        refines Subparts: distributed Set[Pipe]
                                        inverse Part$Parent;
                };
        end Pipe;
```

Notice the reserved word "refines" preceding the property name. The valuespec
for the refinement is more restrictive, since Pipe is a subtype of Part.

When a type refines a property, its subtypes inherit that refined property, not the
property of which it is a refinement. So, for example, if CopperPipe is a subtype
of Pipe, it inherits the property Subpart with valuespec Pipe (not Part), i.e., it
inherits Pipe's refinement and not the original property defined by Part. In addition,
CopperPipe could further refine the property Subparts, say, to specify its valuespec as CopperPipe, a still more restrictive valuespec, *provided* Pipe had specified
Subparts as constrainable.

A property can be specified so as to *prohibit* refinement of any sort by including
the reserved word "unrefinable" after the access restriction specification.

It can also be specified so as to put a limit on *how much* more restrictive the valuespec can be for its refinements, its refinements' refinements, and so on. This is done by
including, instead of simply constrainable, the reserved words "constrainable
to" followed by a valuespec-expression. Then the valuespec of a refinement (and a refinement's refinement, etc.) will have to be a supertype of the named type or the named
type itself. The named type here must, of course, be a subtype of the original valuespec.

If a refined property includes a constrainable to specification, it must be
compatible with any constrainable to specification for the property of which it is
a refinement.

9.3.3 Defining Operations

Operations are defined in the operations clause of a type definition statement. Each
operation specification in the operations clause must include three things:

1. an idn to serve as the operation's name,
2. an argument list, specifying the operation's formal parameters,
3. specification of a base method, the COP code that implements the operation.

In addition, a property specification can include various combinations of the following:

4. specification of trigger methods, COP code that implements operation pre-
processing and post-processing,

5. the reserved word "iterator" to indicate that the operation is an iterator,

6. specification of the types of exceptions that can be raised by the operation,

7. the reserved word "refinement" to indicate that the operation is a refinement.

Here is an example of a type definition statement with a properties clause and a simple operations clause:

```
define type Employee
        supertypes={Person};
        properties=
        {
                Name: String;
                Supervisor: Employee;
                Start_date: Date;
                Employee_id_number: Integer;
        };
        operations=
        {
                Employment_duration(emp: Employee, date:
                                        Date)
                        returns(Integer)
                        method(employment_duration_method);
        };
    end Employee;
```

In the operations clause above, the operation name "Employment_duration", the argument names "emp" and "date", and the method name "employment_duration_method" are all idns entirely of the user's devising. The types Employee and Date (the argument valuespecs) must be compiled before any COP code involving these types is compiled.

The operation defined here might calculate the length of employment of the specified employee (first argument) as of the specified date (second argument) based on the value of the property Start_date. It might then return this length, say, to the nearest whole number of months.

Since this operation is defined by the type Employee (that is, it is defined within the type definition for Employee), its first argument must always be an Employee, and the valuespec for the first argument must be the type Employee.

Note that although the above statement defines only one operation, any number of operation definitions can be included in an operations clause.

Keyword arguments. Operation arguments in Vbase can be either positional or *keyword* arguments. In our previous example of an operation specification, the arguments are positional. This means that the position of an argument in the argument list determines which formal parameter in the operation's method the argument gets assigned to. For a keyword argument, in contrast, the argument's name determines which formal parameter it gets assigned to (where an argument name is the expression immediately preceding the colon in the argument list).

The keyword arguments are separated from the positional arguments by the reserved word "`keywords`" in the specification of the argument list. The first argument must always be positional, and the argument name and colon are optional for positional arguments.

Optional arguments and default values. Vbase supports optional operation arguments. Only keyword arguments can be declared as optional. An argument is specified as optional by including the reserved word "`optional`" before the argument name.

If an operation is invoked with an optional argument omitted, the argument's associated formal parameter may be left with no value. (The method will typically use the COP "`hasvalue`" construct to see if the formal has a value, and then proceed accordingly.) But it is also possible to ensure that an optional argument's associated formal is assigned a value by declaring a default value for the optional argument. To do this, simply follow the argument's valuespec with "`:=`" followed by a string, numeral or database name. The designated object will then be assigned to the argument's associated formal parameter whenever the argument is omitted from an operation invocation.

Triggers and method combination. The previous example of an operations clause involved an operation implemented by a single method, the *base method*, specified following the reserved word "`method`". But operations can also be implemented with a combination of methods. One way to do this is to specify, in addition to the base method, a *trigger method*. This is a method whose execution begins before execution of the base method. It typically then calls the base method with a special COP statement, consisting of "`$$`" followed by an argument list. When the base method completes execution, control flows back to the trigger method. So the trigger method can be seen as *enclosing* the base method.

To specify a trigger method, include before the reserved word `method` in the operation specification the reserved word "`triggers`", followed by the name of the trigger method enclosed in parentheses. It is also possible to specify several trigger methods by following `triggers` with several method names separated by commas and enclosed in parentheses. Each trigger method encloses the one mentioned after it, except the last, which encloses the base method.

Triggers are frequently added to the implementations of create operations and property access operations. See section 9.4.12 for an example.

Iterators. An iterator is a special kind of operation which operates as a coroutine with a COP iterate loop. At the top of the iterate loop, the iterator is called. The iterator then *yields* an object to be processed by the loop body. While control resides in the loop body, the local state of the iterator is preserved. When the loop body completes execution, the iterator is called again, and its execution begins where it left off, after the yield statement. If the iterator executes a return statement, control is passed to the statement following the iterate loop. All iterators are null-valued (no return value is legal for return statements in an iterator method).

Typically, an iterator operates on an aggregate, and is used to process its elements one at a time. The iterator method uses, e.g., a *for* loop to iterate over the members, yielding an element to its coroutine each time through. When the looping is complete, the iterator returns, and the coroutine is exited. The bounds of the loop are specified in the iterator method (e.g., in the *for* statement). This means an application or operation method which uses a COP iterate loop need not specify these bounds, and so need not be aware of the internal structure of the aggregate being processed.

To specify an operation as an iterator, include the reserved word "iterator" before the operation name. In addition, instead of specifying a *returns* valuespec, specify a valuespec which must be satisfied by any object yielded as follows:

```
yields (vspec-expr)
```

Exceptions. In Vbase, application code or an operation's method can specify that an *exception* be raised at a certain point in the flow of execution. The raising of an exception usually indicates the existence of an error condition, and it triggers execution of an appropriate error handling routine known as an "exception handler".

Each exception is an instance of a special sort of type, an exceptionType. Like other types, it defines properties for which its instances can have values. When an exception is raised, an instance of a specified exceptionType is created by the system, and its property values are established so as to carry certain information about the particular exceptional circumstances which led to its creation. This object is passed to the appropriate exception handler, which can then use its property values to determine how to proceed.

If an operation's method involves raising exceptions of a particular type, (1) this exceptionType must be "known" to the system, and (2) the operation specification must indicate that exceptions of this type can be raised.

(1) There are many predefined exceptionTypes which are known to the system. They are available for general use by user-written methods. But if the properties defined or inherited by these exceptionTypes aren't appropriate to the user's needs, she or he may want to define new exceptionTypes. This is done with TDL exceptionType definition statements.

An exception definition is just like a type definition statement, except that the definition header has the form "define exceptionType idn" rather than "define type idn". Here is an example of an exception definition.

```
define exceptionType BadDate
        supertypes={Exception};
        properties=
        {
        Date: Date;
        };
end BadDate;
```

Notice that the supertypes clause specifies the type Exception as the direct supertype. The hierarchy of types in the Vbase kernel database includes a hierarchy of the predefined exceptions. Exception heads this hierarchy. It is the most general exceptionType; every other exceptionType, predefined or user-defined, must be a direct or indirect subtype of Exception.

(2) When specifying an operation in a type definition statement, the types of exceptions it can raise must be specified. To do this, include , after the "returns" specification, the reserved word "raises", followed by the exceptionType names enclosed in parentheses and separated by commas.

```
define type Employee
        supertypes={Person};
        properties=
        {
                Name: String;
                Supervisor: Employee;
                Start_date: Date;
                Employee_id_number: Integer;
        };
        operations=
        {
                Employment_duration(emp: Employee, date:
                                              Date)
                        returns(Integer)
                        raises(BadDate)
                        method(employment_duration_method);
        };
end Employee;
```

Refinement, dispatching and method combination. A type's operations, like its properties, are inherited from its supertypes. Moreover, inherited operations, like inherited properties, can be *refined*, i.e., a type can provide a new specification of an operation defined by one of its supertypes. The new specification will, in most respects, be just like the specification given by the supertype, but it must differ in the following respects:

- it begins with the reserved word "refines", and
- the first argument's valuespec is the type refining the operation.

In addition, differences of the following sort are permissible:

A. Additional methods:
    1. the refinement can specify a different base method,
    2. triggers can be added,
B. More restrictive valuespecs:
    3. the return valuespec can be more restrictive than in the original,
    4. argument valuespecs can be more restrictive than in the original, provided the original argument was specified as constrainable, by including the reserved word "constrainable" after the valuespec expression,

C. Exceptions:

    5. the exceptions specified may form a subset of the original's exceptions,

    6. an original exception may be replaced with one of its subtypes,

D. Additional arguments:

    7. optional arguments may be added to the argument list.

Refinements provide, roughly speaking, alternative versions of an operation. Their primary usefulness can be understood as follows. The application programmer, writing COP code, can call any version simply by mentioning the operation's *original* version (defined by the supertype), and the system will determine at run-time which version to invoke. The version selected is the one defined by the direct type of the *first* argument. This process of run-time determination of the appropriate version is known as *dispatching*, and so we refer to an operation's first argument as the "*dispatch argument*". Because of dispatching, the application programmer need not even know about the operation's various versions. In fact, new versions can be added without requiring any changes to the application code. An example should help make this clear.

Consider an application involving parts. Suppose some parts are classified as pipes, some are classified as holding tanks, and some parts are not further classified. We might create a type structure consisting of the type `Part` and two subtypes, `Pipe` and `Tank`.

These types might be defined with the following TDL type definitions defining properties for physical dimensions, such as length and diameter and an operation to calculate volume. Figure 9.7 shows the type structure.

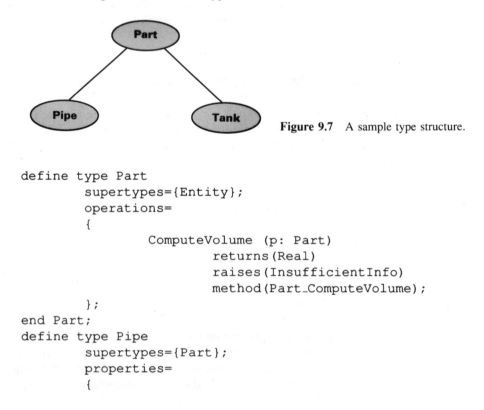

Figure 9.7 A sample type structure.

```
define type Part
        supertypes={Entity};
        operations=
        {
                ComputeVolume (p: Part)
                        returns(Real)
                        raises(InsufficientInfo)
                        method(Part_ComputeVolume);
        };
end Part;
define type Pipe
        supertypes={Part};
        properties=
        {
```

```
                Diameter: Real;
                Length: Real;
        };
        operations=
        {
                refines ComputeVolume (p: Pipe)
                        returns(Real)
                        method(Pipe_ComputeVolume);
        };
end Pipe;
define type Tank
        supertypes={Part};
        properties=
        {
                Width: Real;
                Length: Real;
                Height: Real;
        };
        operations=
        {
                refines ComputeVolume (t: Tank)
                        returns(Real)
                        method(Tank_ComputeVolume);
        };
end Tank;
```

Let us suppose that tanks are box-shaped, so the Tank_ComputeVolume method simply returns the product of the width, length, and height of the specified tank. The Pipe_ComputeVolume method returns the product of the length and pi times half the diameter of the specified pipe. And the Part_ComputeVolume method, let's say, always raises the exception InsufficientInfo, since direct instances of Part don't have property information concerning their physical dimensions.

Now suppose a COP application includes the following statements.

```
obj Part a_part;
    . . .
    . . .
Part$ComputeVolume(p: a_part);
```

The operation explicitly mentioned, here, is the one defined by Part, the "original". (The prefix "Part$" indicates that the operation defined in the type definition for Part is intended.) But if the value of the variable a_part has direct type Tank (i.e., is a direct instance of Tank), the Tank_ComputeVolume method will be used, not the Part_ComputeVolume method. Similarly, if the value of a_part has direct type Pipe, the Pipe_ComputeVolume method will be used. And finally, if the value of a_part is a direct instance of Part, the Part_ComputeVolume method will be used.

In this case, dispatching saves the application programmer the trouble of conditionally invoking the three different versions:

```
switch (a_part.Directype)
{
        case $Tank:
                Tank$ComputeVolume(p: a_part);
                break;
        case $Pipe:
                Pipe$ComputeVolume(p: a_part);
                break;
        case $Part:
                Part$ComputeVolume(p: a_part);
                break;
```

And, more importantly, it saves her or him the trouble of expanding this conditional statement to accommodate additional subtypes of Part which might require still different methods to compute the volume of their instances. The application's operation call can be entirely insulated from information about the various versions.

In the above example, each refinement is implemented by a single method. An operation refinement can also be implemented by method combinations. Trigger methods may be included in the refinement's implementation. In addition, the refinement's implementation may be combined with the implementation of the refinee. This is achieved by including in the refinement's base method a COP $$ call. This passes control to the refinee's first trigger method or, if it has no triggers, to its base method. When all the methods associated with the refinee have completed execution, control flows back to the refinement's base method. So the refinement's implementation encloses the implementation of the refinee.

For each operation which is implemented by a combination of methods, there is an associated *call list*, a list of the methods in the order in which they are to be executed. A $$ call does not specify a method explicitly. Rather, it has the meaning "call the next method on the call list".

9.3.4 Redefining Property Access Operations

To initialize, set and retrieve values of a given property, Vbase uses init, set, and get operations which are associated with the property; and to add or remove values of a distributed property, the property's insert and remove operations are used. These operations are created by the system, and are not typically invoked explicitly by the user. Rather, their invocation is implicit in a variety of statements. For example, in response to a COP statement like

```
x = a_pipe.Diameter;
```

the system invokes the get operation for the property Diameter. These operations may be customized by the user. That is, the user can replace or remove an operation's system-supplied base method, as well as add triggers to the operation's implementation. This is done by including at the end of the property specification the reserved word "define", followed by the name of the operation to be customized (init, get, set, insert or remove), followed by specification of the exceptions, triggers and base method.

This topic is discussed further, with a detailed example, in section 9.4.12.

9.4 PROGRAMMING IN COP

The COP language is a superset of C, extended to permit the manipulation of Vbase database objects. COP includes all the features of standard C (as documented by Kernighan and Ritchie) unchanged. The COP compiler accepts both COP and standard C source code as input. This section presents only COP extensions to C. Since this section is oriented toward the practical use of COP, it does not provide an exhaustive, feature-by-feature description.

9.4.1 Opening and Closing the Database

In order to use any of the resources provided by the database, including the user-defined and system-supplied types, properties and operations, it is necessary to open and close the database. This is typically accomplished in a main application program, by means of the system-supplied functions AM_databaseOpen and AM_databaseClose.

AM_databaseOpen takes two arguments. The first argument is the name of the database to be opened, and the second specifies the cache size in kilobytes. These can be passed on the commandline to main() by means of argv and argc. It is also common to take the database name from the environment variable DBNAME.

AM_databaseClose takes no arguments. It is common to protect the code that closes the database, by putting it in a code block preceded by the reserved word "protect". Protecting the code ensures that it gets executed even if the raising of an exception disrupts the normal flow of control. Exceptions and protected code will be discussed in section 9.4.11.

Here is an example of a main program skeleton:

```
#define CACHESIZE 2500
/* for getting the name of the database */
extern char *getenv();
void my_application();
main()
{
        /* for holding the database name */
        char *db;
        /* get the database name from the env variable */
        db = getenv("DBNAME");
        printf("Begin opening the database \n");
        AM_databaseOpen(db, CACHESIZE);
        printf("End opening the database \n");
        /* my_application contains the example's code */
```

```
my_application();
protect
{
printf("Begin closing the database \n");
AM_databaseClose();
printf("End closing the database \n");
}
exit( 0 );   /*successful termination*/
}
```

9.4.2 Declaring Object Variables

Just as variables that take conventional values must be declared in C programs (as in "int x,y, z;"), variables that take Vbase objects as values must be declared.

Declaring variables with simple type-names. A typical declaration specifies a type and the names of one or more variables, separated by commas. This constrains the values of the variables to be instances of the type.

```
obj  type-name  variable-name, ...., variable-name;
```

Variables are idns, i.e., strings of arbitrary length containing alphanumeric characters plus the underscore, except that the first character cannot be a numeral. By convention, leading underscore names are reserved for system use.

```
obj Real a_real, another_real;
obj Employee the_employee;
obj Part the_part;
```

Declarations such as these specify a type of which values must be instances. That is, values must be either direct or indirect instances of the specified type. For example, suppose part #35224 is a hydraulic part. Since the type HydraulicPart is a subtype of the type Part, part #35224 is an instance of Part as well, an indirect instance. So part #35224 is an allowable value of the variable "the_part", declared above.

Declaring aggregate valued variables. The Vbase library of system-supplied types provides a variety of aggregate types, such as Array, Stack, and OrderedDictionary. If a variable is to have aggregates as values, it usually should be declared, not with a simple type-name, but rather with a parameterized type-name.

These parameterized type-names consist of the name of a type followed by one or two parameters, enclosed in square brackets and separated by commas. For example,

```
obj UnorderedDictionary[Employee, Integer]
                        an_employee_dictionary;
```

The type-name "UnorderedDictionary" indicates that the values of "an_employee_dictionary" must be instances of UnorderedDictionary. But the parameters further constrain the variable's allowable values.

The first parameter, "Employee", indicates the type of members the dictionary must have. Strictly speaking, it indicates that any value of the variable must be an UnorderedDictionary whose value for the memberSpec property is the type Employee. If an aggregate has a given type as memberSpec, this means that its members are constrained to be instances of the type.

Each element of an UnorderedDictionary is associated with an *index* or *key*, an object which serves as a unique identifier for the dictionary element (the index is not itself an element of the dictionary). The second parameter indicates what type of object the dictionary's indices must be. Strictly speaking, it indicates that any value of the variable must be an UnorderedDictionary whose value for the IndexSpec property is the type Integer.

All declarations of aggregate valued variables can use a parameterized type-name, with a parameter indicating the type of members values must have. Only Unordered-Dictionary variables take the second parameter, indicating the type of tag members must have.

Multi-dimensional aggregates are handled by using parameterized type-names as parameters in other parameterized type-names. For example, a variable whose values are matrices of integers would be declared as follows:

```
obj Array[Array[Integer]] the_matrix;
```

Sometimes it may be useful to declare an aggregate-valued variable with a simple type-name, rather than a parameterized type-name, for example, when we need to handle sets whose memberSpecs we have no way of determining before run-time. Then we can use a declaration such as the following:

```
obj Set the_set;
```

Note, however, that this somewhat limits the use of this variable as an operation argument. See the section on operation invocation below.

9.4.3 Valuespecs

The type-name or parameterized type-name in an object variable declaration specifies the variable's *valuespec*. Variables, properties, and operation formal parameters all have associated valuespecs, which are used by the compiler to detect type errors.

A simple type-name designates a simple valuespec, i.e., a type. An object is said to satisfy a simple valuespec if and only if it is an instance of it.

A parameterized type-name designates a *parametricSpec*, which is composed of a *baseType* and one or two *parameters*. The initial type-name specifies the baseType, and the parameters of the parameterized type-name specify the parameters of the designated valuespec. These parameters are themselves valuespecs, simple or parameterized.

An aggregate is said to satisfy a parametricSpec if and only if

- it is an instance of the parametricSpec's base type, and
- its memberSpec is the parametricSpec's first parameter, and its indexSpec is the second parameter (if there is one).

In general the compiler demands a guarantee that no run-time type error will occur (unless an assert is used—see section 9.4.8). For example, consider these two variable declarations:

```
obj Part a_part;
obj HydraulicPart a_hydraulicPart;
```

And consider this assignment statement:

```
a_hydraulicPart = a_part;
```

This will result in a compile-time type error, since the valuespec of the variable "a_part" doesn't guarantee that the value of "a_part" will be an acceptable value for "a_hydraulicPart". In other words, the fact that the value of "a_part" satisfies the valuespec Part doesn't guarantee that it will satisfy HydraulicPart, the valuespec of "a_hydraulicPart".

In contrast, the following assignment results in no error:

```
a_part = a_hydraulicPart;
```

Compile-time type checking generally involves consideration of the following sort of question: *Given that an object satisfies valuespec A, is it guaranteed to satisfy valuespec B?*

If *A* and *B* are simple valuespecs, then a guarantee is provided if and only if *A* is a subtype of *B* or *A* is the same as *B*.

If *A* and *B* are both parametricSpecs, then a guarantee is provided if and only if

- the baseType of *A* is a subtype of the baseType of *B* or *A*'s baseType is the same as *B*'s baseType, and
- *A* and *B* have exactly the same parameters.

If *A* is a parametricSpec and *B* is a simple valuespec, then a guarantee is provided if and only if *A* is a subtype of *B*'s baseType or *A* is the same as *B*'s baseType.

If *A* is a simple valuespec and *B* is a parametricSpec, then no guarantee can be provided.

9.4.4 Writing Methods

A method is similar to the definition of a C function. As discussed earlier (see section 9.2), a method implements an operation. Since there are two types of operations, procedures and iterators (see section 9.3.3.4), there are two kinds of methods, *procedure methods* and *iterator methods*.

Each method begins with a declaration of the type of object returned or yielded by the operation it implements, or, if no object is returned, it begins with the reserved word "void". Then, for procedure methods, the reserved word "method" appears, or, for iterator methods, "iterator" appears. This is followed by the method's name, as introduced in the operations clause of a type definition, and a formal argument list.

Each formal must then be declared. Formals that correspond to keyword arguments (see section 9.3.3.1), must appear in the argument list after all positional formals. In addition, the declaration of keyword formals must begin with the reserved word "keyword".

```
obj {valuespec-expression | void}
{method | iterator} op-name (arg-list)
arg-declarations
{
        method body
}
```

As with C functions, procedure methods can return an object with a *return* statement. An Iterator method yields an element to a COP iterate loop via a *yield* statement.

A method can include a $$ call if it is part of a combination of methods that implement an operation. The argument list in the $$ call must have the same form as the argument list of an invocation of the operation.

Every method must be preceded by an enter module statement:

```
enter module type-name;
```

where "type-name" names the type whose definition introduced the method's name.

9.4.5 Object Creation and Deletion

If an application deals with particular instances of user-defined or system-supplied types (as most applications do), for example, particular parts, then these instances usually need to be *created* using Vbase. Instances of the types String, Integer, and Real don't need to be created. But sets, arrays, employees, and parts, for example, all need to be created. This is done with COP constructors.

A constructor is an operation invocation with a special syntax. The general form of a constructor is

```
type-name$[ argument list ]
```

A constructor followed by ";" constitutes a COP statement. The result of executing it is the creation of an object, along with property initialization, and some other things to be described below. Constructors also "return" the object they create, so they can be used as operation arguments, or be assigned to variables. For example:

```
obj Part the_part
   . . .
   . . .
   . . .
the_part=
        StructuralPart$[PartNumber: 35224,
                        Children: $(PartMod$part_3345,
```

```
                     Part$part_5495),
            Reliability:  0.93,
            ResponsibleEngineer:
                     EngineerMod$peter_smith,
            Material: Material$Steel];
```

Here, the type-name "StructuralPart" indicates the direct type of the object to be created. For example, to create a direct instance of the type HydraulicPart, we would use

```
HydraulicPart$[ argument list ]
```

To create an aggregate, the constructor must begin with a parameterized type-name.

```
parameterized-type-name$[ argument list ]
```

The parameterized type-name indicates the type, the memberSpec and possibly the indexSpec of the object to be created. Constructors for aggregates must specify the memberSpec and, for UnorderedDictionary, the indexSpec in this way.

These parameters have a slightly different form from those used for variable declaration. Each parameter must begin with the reserved word "obj". For example, to create a set whose members are constrained by the system to be parts, we would use

```
Set[obj Part]$[ argument-list ]
```

To create an UnorderedDictionary whose members are constrained to be employees, indexed by integer tags, we would use

```
UnorderedDictionary[obj Part,
                    obj Integer]$[argument-list]
```

The argument list in a constructor is used to specify

- the initial values for properties of the new object,
- for aggregates, the initial members,
- whether or not the object is to be persistent, and
- if persistent, an object with which it is to be clustered in persistent storage.

When creating an instance of a given type, this type must be imported. This allows the system to recognize the names of properties defined and inherited by the type. This is done with the import statement, which should occur outside of a function or code block and before the relevant code. For example,

```
import StructuralPart;
```

In addition, if initial values are specified with database names, the modules whose names form the first part of the database names must be imported. For example,

```
import PartMod;
import EngineerMod;
import Material;
```

Property initialization.   An argument list contains a sequence of *argument-name: expression* pairs, separated by commas. Some of the argument names are the names of properties defined or inherited by the type being instantiated. The expression with which it is paired specifies the property's initial value. An expression can be a numeral, string, variable, property getaccess, or operation invocation.

Properties that are optional or that have default values need not be included in the argument list. If left out, optional properties will have no value for the new object, and properties with default values will have that default as the initial property value.

Some property values are derived by the system, such as the property `Cardinality` defined by `Collection` and the property `DirectType` defined by `Entity`. These properties must be left out of the argument list.

Here is a constructor to create an instance of the type `StructuralPart`, defined in our example in section 9.2.

```
StructuralPart$[ PartNumber: 35224,
                 Children: the_subparts,
                 Reliability: 0.93,
                 ResponsibleEngineer:
                         EngineerMod$peter_smith
                 Material: Material$steel ]
```

Here the partNumber and reliability can be specified with numerals, "35224" and "0.93". The responsibleEngineer is specified with a *database name*. An object's database name is the value of its *Pathname* property, an optional property defined by `Entity`. Instances can acquire database names by setting or initializing this property.

The `Material` is also specified with a database name, "Material$steel". The database name of an instance of an enumType often consists of the enumType's name ("Material"), followed by "$", followed by the idn introduced for the instance in the enumType's TDL definition ("steel").

The initial values of the distributed property `Children` are specified with a variable, "the_subparts", whose value is an aggregate containing those initial values.

To initialize a distributed property, a constructor takes an aggregate argument. The aggregate should contain the desired initial values of the property. This aggregate should be empty if the property is to have no values initially. Any type of aggregate is allowed. However, even if a value is repeated in the aggregate, it will not be repeated as a value. Each object either is or is not a value of a distributed property. The question of how many times it occurs as a value does not apply.

Constructor arguments that correspond to distributed properties are always optional. If such an argument is not supplied, the property will be initialized with no values.

Each formal argument of a constructor has an associated valuespec, which supplied values must satisfy.

If the value is specified with a variable, the compiler will compare the variable's valuespec with the valuespec of the formal argument. The valuespec of the variable must guarantee that the variable's value will satisfy the formal argument's valuespec (unless an assert is used. See section 9.4.8). Otherwise a compile-time type error occurs.

Similarly, if the supplied value is specified with a property getaccess, the property's valuespec must guarantee that the property value will satisfy the valuespec of the formal argument. And if the supplied value is specified with an operation invocation, the operation's return valuespec must make similar guarantees.

Aggregate membership initialization. Constructors for some aggregates have arguments that specify initial elements. For example, the constructor for arrays can indicate that the new array should be filled with a specified value. It can also specify the elements to be associated with each array index. Here is an example:

```
Array[obj Integer]$[UpperBound: 5,
                    init: $(1,2,3,4,5,6) ]
```

This creates an array of integers whose zero-th element is 1, whose 1st element is 2, and so on.

Storage managers. Objects created with Vbase can be either persistent or process local. If an object is persistent, it will be saved in the database, and can be accessed during a later session. A persistent object is typically accessed by its database name (if it has one), which is guaranteed to uniquely identify the object, or by any other property value that will identify it. Persistent objects are also often stored in an UnorderedDictionary and accessed by their dictionary tags.

If an object is process local, it will not be saved in the database, but will exist only for the duration of the process that created it.

To specify an object as process local, include the following argument in the constructor argument list:

```
StorageManager: PloStorage
```

If no StorageManager argument is included, the new object will be persistent. To explicitly specify it as persistent, you can include this argument:

```
StorageManager: OKStorage
```

Object clustering. Persistent objects that are likely to be accessed together can be *clustered* together in disk storage. This means that whenever one of the objects is accessed from disk and brought into the database cache, all objects clustered with it are also brought into the cache. Subsequent access to any of these objects is then a *main memory access* rather than a disk access. Clustering can be used to great advantage to improve application performance.

To cluster a new object with some other object, specify this other object in the "where:" argument of the constructor. Also include the argument "hownear:

$Segment". This indicates that the new object is to be stored in the same *segment* as the specified object. Segments are variably sized atomic units of transfer between secondary storage and database cache.

Create operations. Using a COP constructor for creating an instance of a given type actually involves an implicit invocation of the type's associated *create operation*. Every type has an associated operation used for creating its instances. If the user defines a type in TDL, the system automatically supplies the appropriate create operation when the TDL code is compiled. This operation can be customized by the user through the addition of *triggers* for pre-create and post-create processing.

Object deletion. The type Entity defines the operation Delete, which is inherited by every other type in the hierarchy, system-supplied or user-defined.

The delete operation attempts to negate the existence of its argument. If successful, the entity deleted will become inaccessible, in the sense that no further operations or property accesses may be performed on the entity. The Delete operation may be unsuccessful for a variety of reasons, of which two are common. The first is that the entity is a universal (it is not possible to delete the number 3, for example).

Attempting to delete such an object results in a CannotDeleteUniversal exception. The second typical exception occurs when low-level resources required to effect the delete are temporarily unavailable: for example, if the media on which the entity resides is 'down'. All of these exceptions are subtypes of the CannotDelete exception.

There are several important things to know about deleting an entity. The first is that references to an entity may exist even after the entity is deleted. If, for example, pipe A has a property which connects it to pipe B and pipe B is subsequently deleted, pipe A will continue to refer to pipe B unless explicit action is taken. It is the responsibility of the deletor to ensure that properties referring to the deleted entity are also unset or reset. This is normally done by refining the Entity$Delete operation through the addition of triggers. An attempt to operate on a reference to a deleted entity will raise a NoSuchRef Exception. If uncaught, this will normally cause the process to trap.

9.4.6 Property Access

There are three kinds of access to single-valued properties (non-distributed properties):

- one can initialize or init a property with a value at creation time,
- one can establish or set a value some time after creation, and
- one can read or get a property value.

In addition, multi-valued properties (distributed properties) allow two kinds of access:

- one can initialize or init a property with an aggregate of values, at creation time,
- one can add or insert a value some time after creation, and
- one can take away or remove a property value.

Initializing properties was discussed in section 9.4.5.1, above. We now discuss how the user can use COP to engage in the other four kinds of access.

Property access and imports. In order to access a property, the type that defined the property must be *imported*. This is done with the import statement, which should occur at the beginning of the file in which the relevant code occurs.

```
import type-name;
```

The import provides a semantic context for the interpretation of property names.

For property accesses that involve a variable whose valuespec is a type that inherits or refines the property, this type may be imported instead of the type that originally defined the property.

Setting property values. The general form of a COP statement for setting a property value is

```
variable.property-name = expression;
```

where the expression can be a string, numeral, database name, variable or operation call. Here are some examples:

```
import Employee, Part;
import StructuralPart;
import EngineerMod, PartMod;
{
  obj Part the_part;
  obj Employee the_employee;
  obj Engineer the_engineer;
        the_employee.Pathname =
              "EngineerMod$peter_smith";
        the_engineer.Supervisor =
              EngineerMod$peter_smith;
        the_part.ResponsibleEngineer=the_engineer;
        the_part.ParentPart=
              StructuralPart$[ PartNumber: 35224,
                        Children: the_subparts,
                        Reliability: 0.93,
                        ResponsibleEngineer:
                              EngineerMod$peter_smith
                        Material: Material$steel ];
```

In general, the object designated by the right-hand side of the assignment must satisfy the valuespec of the property referred to in the left-hand side.

If the right-hand side of a property assignment is a quoted expression or a numeral, it will be interpreted as a Vbase string or number (i.e., an instance of the type `String` or an instance of the type `Integer` or `Real`).

So, for example, if the valuespec is `Number` and the supplied value is 3.2, no type error occurs. But if the valuespec is `Integer` and the supplied value is 3.2, a type error does occur.

If the valuespec is the type `Real` and the value is supplied with an expression such as 3, a cast is made. No type error will occur, and the property value will be a Vbase real.

If the right-hand side is a variable, its valuespec must guarantee that its value will satisfy the valuespec of the property being set. If the right-hand side is a property `get-access`, the valuespec of the property mentioned in the right-hand side must guarantee that the value returned by the `get-access` will satisfy the valuespec of the property being set. If the right-hand side is an operation invocation, the operation's return valuespec must make a similar guarantee.

Getting property values. The general form of a simple property `get-access` in COP is:

```
variable.property-name
```

This behaves like an operation invocation that returns the value of the specified property for the object that is the value of the variable. Something of this form can be used, for example, in a variable assignment or as an operation argument. Here are some examples:

```
obj Part the_part, another_part;
obj Employee the_employee;
        the_supervisor = the_employee.Supervisor;
        Part$Assemble(a_part, another_part.Parent);
        if (a_part.Material == Material$Steel)
        { ..... };
```

Chained property `get-access` is also allowed:

```
variable.property-name.   ...   .property-name
```

For example:

```
obj Part the_part;
        if (the_part.ResponsibleEngineer.
                        Supervisor.IDNumber == 377)
        { ... };
```

In a simple property `get-access`, the valuespec of the variable must guarantee that the variable's value will be an instance of the type that defined the property being accessed. Otherwise a compiler type error occurs.

In a chained property `get-access`, the valuespec of the variable must make such a guarantee for the first property accessed. In addition, each other property must be defined by the baseType of the valuespec of the property preceding it. Again, a compile-time type error occurs if these conditions are not met.

Accessing distributed properties. Distributed properties are accessed via the invocation of the operations `Insert` and `Remove`, defined by the type `Set`. Suppose `a_subpart` is a part we wish to add as a child-part of `a_part`. This can be achieved by the following statement:

```
Set$Insert (a_part.Children, a_subpart);
```

To remove it as a value of the property `Children`, the following can be used:

```
Set$Remove (a_part.Children, a_subpart);
```

The expression "`a_part.Children`" here denotes a `distributed set` of values of the property `Children`. A distributed set is a special type of set used to implement distributed properties and their inverses.

Access for optional properties. Optional properties may be left uninitialized or may be unset at any time. To unset an optional property, a statement of the following form can be used:

```
unset ( variable.property-name );
```

The variable's valuespec must guarantee that the value of the variable will be an instance of the type that defined the property being unset.

Since optional properties may be value-less, a `NoValue` exception may be raised at run-time when performing property `get-access`. Therefore, it is always advisable to test an optional property to see if it has a value before performing `get-access` on it. This is done with the `hasvalue` construct:

```
hasvalue ( variable.property-name )
```

This is an expression whose value is the boolean true if the property has a value, and false otherwise.

Property access operations. Property access actually involves implicit invocation of system-supplied operations. With each non-distributed property are associated init, set and get operations. The system supplies each distributed property with an init and get operation, but the operations `Set$Insert` and `Set$Remove` are used for other sorts of access.

Init, set and get operations may be customized by the user. This will be discussed in section 9.4.12.

9.4.7 Operation Invocation

An operation invocation in COP has a form similar to a typical function call. It consists of an operation's pathname followed by an argument list. Each element of the list is an actual argument, possibly paired with an argument name. If the argument is a keyword argument, the actual must be paired with its argument name. If the argument is positional, the actual may or may not be paired with its argument name.

Just as accessing a property requires importing a type that defined, inherited, or refined it, so invoking an operation requires importing an appropriate type. The type explicitly mentioned in the operation invocation must be imported, i.e., the type named in the first part of the operation's pathname. (Because of inheritance and dispatching, the type explicitly mentioned may not be the one that is actually executed at run-time.)

Here are some examples:

```
Import Part;
  {
   obj Part a_part, another_part;
        Part$Assemble(a_part, another_part);
        Part$DisplayProps(a_part.Parent);
  }
```

An actual operation argument can be any object expression, such as a numeral, string, database name, property get-access or operation invocation. Numerals and strings are interpreted as designating Vbase numbers and strings, and integers are cast to reals when appropriate.

As discussed previously, each operation formal argument has a valuespec that is used for compile-time type checking. For numeral, string or database name actual arguments, the designated object must satisfy the valuespec of the operation's formal argument. For property access actuals, the valuespec of the property must guarantee that the property value will satisfy the formal's valuespec. And for operation invocation actuals, the return valuespec must guarantee that the returned value will satisfy the formal's valuespec.

When an operation invocation is the right-hand side of a variable assignment, the operation's return valuespec must guarantee that the returned object will satisfy the variable's valuespec.

9.4.8 The Assert Operator

In some cases, the user will want to suppress detection of a compile-time type error by use of the assert operator. Consider, for example, the following assignment statement:

```
a_structural_part = the_part.Parent;
```

Suppose that the valuespec of the variable "the_structural_part" is StructuralPart, and suppose the valuespec of the property Parent is Part. Then this statement would result in a compile-time type error. But if we have somehow determined that the value of Parent for the_part will indeed be a structural part, we can suppress the type error by use of the assert operator as follows:

```
a_structural_part = assert (the_part.Parent,
                                    obj StructuralPart)
```

In general, to make a COP expression, E1, with one valuespec behave like an expression with another valuespec, replace E1 with the expression

```
assert (E1, obj valuespec-expression)
```

where "valuespec-expression" designates the other valuespec. Such expressions can be used as operation arguments as well as in assignment statements.

9.4.9 Using Iterators

In Vbase, one of the fundamental uses of iterators involves the system supplied *aggregate iterators*. The aggregate iterators allow the user to perform a given routine iteratively, once for each member of an aggregate. The type Aggregate defines an iterator, called "Iterate", which is refined by each of Aggregate's subtypes.

The routine to be performed iteratively is specified as the body of a COP iterate loop.

```
iterate (variable = iterator-name(arg-list))
  { loop body }
```

For aggregate iterators, a short form can also be used.

```
iterate (variable = aggregate-expression)
  { loop body }
```

Here "aggregate-expression" is a COP expression that designates an aggregate (a direct or indirect instance of the type Aggregate).

Each time through the loop, variable is assigned a different member of the designated aggregate. The loop body then uses variable to process the element. The loop ends once all elements have been processed. Control is then passed to the statement following the loop body.

Suppose we want to display the property values of each of the subparts of a given part, using Part$DisplayProps. If Subparts is a distributed property, its value is a distributed set, which we can iterate over to process its elements one at a time.

```
iterate (a_subpart = the_part.Subpart)
  {
        Part$DisplayProps(a_subpart);
  }
```

One advantage of using iterators is that the user need not be concerned with the bounds of the loop. The iterate loop terminates once the iterator returns. So the implementation of the iterator determines the bounds of the iterate loop with which it operates as a coroutine.

9.4.10 Object Keys and Database Lookups

Once a persistent object is created and stored in the database, it must have some key or unique identifier that allows it to be retrieved from the database during subsequent sessions. There are a variety of ways to accomplish this.

Database names. One approach to this problem uses database names as object keys. An object can be given a database name by setting its pathname property. Typically, the user defines a module in TDL to group together database names of related objects. The name of the module should then form the first part of the object's pathname. For example:

```
an_employee.Pathname = ''EmployeeMod$peter_smith'';
```

The system ensures that no two objects get the same pathname. If the user gives an object a pathname already used by some other object, the result is that the pathname property for the other object is unset. Therefore, it is advisable to make sure a pathname is unused before assigning it to an object. How to perform such a check is explained below.

To find the object with a given pathname, the free operation Entity$Name-Lookup can be used. The operation is invoked with a string as argument. Here are some examples.

```
obj Entity the_object;
obj String the_pathname;
      the_object = Entity$NameLookup
                            ("EmployeeMod$peter_smith");
      the_object = Entity$NameLookup(the_pathname);
```

If no object has the specified pathname, a nameNotFound exception is raised.

The Entity$NameLookup operation has a second, optional argument that can be used to specify a module. If a module is specified, only the object's short name need be supplied as the first argument:

```
the_object = Entity$NameLookup
                            ("peter_smith",$EmployeeMod);
```

If an application does frequent lookups, this may not be the most efficient approach. An alternative is described below.

UnorderedDictionary. Objects are commonly inserted into unordered dictionaries to make them easy to retrieve from the database. The type UnorderedDictionary is a system supplied type. It defines an operation that inserts a specified object into a specified dictionary, and associates the object with a specified dictionary key. The object can then be retrieved by using the GetElement operation defined by UnorderedDictionary. This operation returns the element associated with a specified dictionary key in a specified dictionary. The lookup performed by the operation is relatively efficient, since a hash table is maintained for each UnorderedDictionary, with the elements hashed by dictionary key.

Just as modules are defined in TDL to group together names of related objects, unordered dictionaries can be created to group together related objects, and to facilitate access to them. Of course, each UnorderedDictionary itself must have some key by which it can be accessed, such as a database name.

Searches and TypeClasses. Although it is common to use database names or dictionary keys to uniquely identify objects, any property value can serve as an identifier. While Entity$NameLookup and UnorderedDictionary$GetElement are system supplied lookup operations, the user can write her or his own lookup routines.

Such lookup routines will typically involve iteration over a type's typeClass (the class of instances of the type). Suppose, for example, that we want to find the employee with a given IDnumber (where IDnumber is a property defined by the type Employee). Since we know we are looking for an instance of Employee, we can iterate through the typeClass for Employee, checking the IDnumber of each instance until the desired employee is found:

```
the_type = $Employee;
iterate (an_employee = the_type.Class)
   {
           if (an_employee=the_type.Class)
           {
             employee_found = TRUE;
             break;
           }
   }
```

In the above example, once control passes out of the iterate loop, if employee_found is TRUE, the value of an_employee will be the employee we are looking for.

If a type's instances are to be searched through in this way, it is usually desirable for the type's associated typeClass to be explicit. If the user iterates through a typeClass that is not explicit, this may actually require the system to perform a much larger search.

This is because to generate the members of a type's *implicit* class the system finds the nearest supertype that has an explicit typeClass, and iterates through this supertype's associated class checking each member to see if it is an instance of the original type. If no supertype has an explicit typeClass, the system must iterate through *every object in the database*.

9.4.11 Raising and Handling Exceptions

As described previously (see section 9.3.3.5), COP code can indicate that an exception of a specified type be raised at a certain point in the flow of execution. The raising of an exception usually indicates the existence of an error condition (where what counts as an error condition is determined by the programmer).

An exception is raised by use of the COP `raise` statement:

```
raise exceptionType_name(prop_name: expression , ...  ,
                         prop_name: expression);
```

The result of executing such a statement is the creation of an instance of the specified `exceptionType`, and the initialization of the new instance's properties. These properties carry information about the nature of the particular circumstances that led to the raising of the exception.

Once the exception is created, it is passed to an appropriate *exception handler*. This is a portion of code that specifies the action to be taken in response to the error condition. The handler may, for example, print an error message based on the values of the exception's properties.

Each handler is appended to a COP statement or block of statements, and is intended to handle those exceptions of a specified type raised during execution of that statement or block. For example, suppose the operation `Employment_duration` can raise a `BadDate` exception. Then we might append an exception handler for such exceptions to a block in which occurs a call to `Employment_duration`:

```
{
        the_duration = Employment_duration(an_employee);
        printf("%d\n", the_duration);
}
 except (exc: BadDate)
{   /* handler body */ }
```

In this case, if an exception is raised, the assignment and the `printf` statement are not executed, and control is passed to the handler body.

The `except` clause of the handler specifies the type of exception it is intended to handle, and specifies a variable whose value will be the exception passed to the handler. The handler body typically uses this variable to access the exception's properties in order to determine the action to be taken in handling the exception.

When a `raise` statement is executed, the search for an appropriate handler proceeds by first checking the handler (if there is one) for the code block in which the `raise` appears. If there is no handler for the type of exception that was raised, the next enclosing code block is checked for an appropriate handler. If this code block is not nested within another, the function or operation call that led to execution of this last block is checked for an appropriate handler.

The search continues "*outward*" in this manner until an appropriate handler is found. If even the main program has no appropriate handler, a run-time message informs the user of an uncaught exception.

Note that in order for a handler to be "*appropriate*" for a certain exception, its except clause must specify an `exceptionType` of which the exception is a direct or indirect instance.

Several handlers may be appended to the same statement or block, for handling exceptions of different types. During the search for a handler, the first appropriate handler encountered will be used.

When execution of an exception handler completes, control is passed to the statement immediately following the handler, and the exception is deleted. A break statement in the handler body also passes control to the statement following the handler, and results in the deletion of the exception.

It is possible to have more than one exception handler handle a given exception, by re-raising the exception in the body of a handler. This is done with a reraise statement, which has the same form as a raise statement (except the reserved word "reraise" is used instead of "raise"). When such a statement is executed, the search for an appropriate handler continues from where it left off. In addition, the exception's property values may be modified. Note that multiple handlers on the same statement are considered to be in parallel, so that only one of these can ever be used in a single flow.

Notice also that there is no ``;'' after the except clause. Including a semi-colon immediately after the except clause specifies a null handler body. (This is analogous to putting a semi-colon immediately after the for clause of a for statement, thereby specifying a null loop body.)

The properties specified in the raise statement must be defined, inherited or refined by the specified exceptionType. Every exceptionType is a subtype of Exception, which defines the properties ExceptName, ExceptFun, ExceptLine and ExceptFile. These properties are initialized automatically whenever an exception is raised.

Raising an exception interrupts the normal flow of control. This means that some statements that would normally be executed will not be executed if an exception is raised. However, it is possible to ensure the execution of some statements, whether or not an exception is raised. This is done by grouping the protected statements into a block, and preceding the block with the reserved word "protect".

This ensures that if control ever flows to the code block within which the protected block occurs, the protected code will be executed whether or not an exception is raised.

It is common to protect that portion of application code which closes the database. See section 9.4.1 for an example.

9.4.12 Re-Defining Property Access Operations

As discussed in section 9.3.4, it is possible to customize property access operations. It is common to customize get operations to allow property values to be derived rather than stored in persistent storage. It is also common to add triggers to set operations in order to implement property dependencies.

For example, suppose Part defines a property Status whose value is either defective or OK. We might wish to implement the following property dependency: if a part's status is set to defective, its parent's status should also be set to defective. Thus defective status will be transmitted upward through the subpart/parent-part hierarchy. The type Part might be defined this way:

```
define type Part
    supertypes={Entity};
    properties=
    {
```

```
                   Parent: optional Part;
                   Status: Status
                              define set triggers
                                         (transmit_status_method);
              };
       end Part;
```

The set trigger `transmit_status_method` might look like this:

```
void method transmit_status_method(the_part, the_status,
                                                 the_prop)
obj Part the_part;
obj Status the_status;
obj PropType the_prop;
{
            $$(the_part, the_status, the_prop);
            if (the_part.Status==$defective &&
                    the_part.Parent.Status != $defective)
               the_part.Parent.Status = $defective;
}
```

This trigger method first calls the base method of the original set operation. The status of the part is set, and control returns to the trigger method. The trigger checks to see (i) if the part's status was set to defective and (ii) if its parent is not already defective. If both conditions are satisfied, the parent's status is set to defective. This last step involves implicit invocation of the set operation for the property `Status`. So this trigger implicitly calls itself recursively.

10 Abstract State and Representation In Vbase

Craig Damon and Gordon Landis

10.1 INTRODUCTION

One of the potential strengths of the object-oriented programming paradigm is its combination of expressiveness and flexibility provided by such semantic modeling techniques as type inheritance, and strong software engineering principles such as data abstraction.

Type inheritance is a mechanism whereby a type's behaviors can be step-wise extended, via the creation of subtypes. A type provides an abstract specification of its instances' behavior. A subtype of this type can add new pieces of specification, so that instances of the subtype obey not only the subtype's own specifications, but also those defined by the supertype. The behaviors specified by the supertype are said to be inherited by the subtype.

Inheritance provides many benefits. It enhances semantic expressiveness, by providing a natural structure for defining and sharing packets of behaviors. It increases system maintainability, by allowing new behaviors to be added by augmentation, rather than mutation of existing code. And it allows for sharing of code and implementation.

Data abstraction, or the strict encapsulation of implementation details behind an abstract interface specification, enhances both safety and maintainability. Safety is enhanced because there is no way to operate on an object in an inappropriate manner; the only manipulations possible on an object are those defined by its type. Maintainability is enhanced because an object's implementation details are not visible to the user of the object, and therefore the implementation can be changed without impacting other parts of the system.

Object systems to date have fallen short of their potential in the area of data abstraction for a number of reasons. First, their specification mechanisms have focused on abstractly specifying only the operational behavior of objects, providing no way to describe object state as part of an abstract interface specification. This limits the expressive power of the specification language. Second, they have not provided a clean, safe mechanism for mapping an object's specification onto its implementation. These limitations often result in subtle dependencies on implementation details (because the critical pieces of interface information cannot be expressed at the specification level), and sometimes even provoke developers to subvert the data abstraction!

In her keynote address at OOPSLA '87, for example, Dr. Liskov noted the abuse of inheritance at the expense of solid data abstraction by the object community [Liskov88]. In Smalltalk, for example, a new class is frequently defined as a subclass of another, not because its instances fit the semantics that the superclass defines, but because the developer wants to share implementations easily. Dr. Liskov suggested that the existing class should be related to the new class as its representation, rather than its superclass.

One of the major foci of Vbase has been to develop a strong abstract notion of state and its implementation. This chapter will describe the Vbase concepts of abstract state (or properties) and representation. This chapter is divided into four sections. The remainder of section 10.1 provides an overview of Vbase. Section 10.2 describes the model of abstract state that Vbase employs. Section 10.3 discusses the implementation of state in Vbase using a model of representation. Section 10.4 discusses some directions for future work in abstract state and representation.

10.1.1 Vbase Overview

Objects are the central semantic (or specification-level) construct in Vbase. An object has both state and behavior. State is modeled by *properties,* and behavior is modeled by *operations,* both of which are defined by the object's *type*(s). All interactions with an object are based upon the properties and operations that are defined by its type, and made available to the object's clients via the type's abstract interface.

Types also provide implementations for the operations and properties that they define. Operations are implemented by code. Properties are (normally) implemented by allocating and manipulating storage. Operations are implemented via a special type of C function called a *method*. An object's client cannot call one of its methods directly, it can only call the operation defined in the abstract interface, which is translated to the appropriate method call(s) by a process called *dispatching.*

For each operation, there is one *base method* and an arbitrary number of *trigger* methods. The base method is implemented by the supertype that defined the operation. Subtypes may then augment both the specification, for example by adding new arguments, and the implementation, by adding trigger methods. (In fact, the supertype that originally defined the operation may also add trigger methods of its own, for example to separate the implementation into meaningful blocks.)

When an operation is invoked, dispatching is used to determine which implementation (that is, which actual methods) to use, normally by examining the type of the first argument to the operation (called the *dispatch argument*), and using the most specific set of methods applicable to that type.

Properties are implemented by pieces of storage called *representation pieces*. Vbase's strict adherence to data abstraction requires that a client of an object can interact with the object's properties, but not with the underlying storage that actually holds their values. This storage is only accessible to the code that implements the property (which is a part of the type manager that defined the properties).

Typically, an object has one representation piece for each of its types. Thus, if an object O is an instance of type C, which has supertypes B and A, all of which define properties, then O will have three representation pieces, one to store the properties defined by each type. Each representation piece is accessible only to the type that actually defined the properties; the other types must access those properties via their abstract interface, just like any other client would. Figure 10.1 has an example.

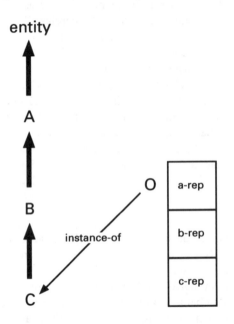

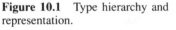

Figure 10.1 Type hierarchy and representation.

In its most general form, an object's representation piece can be *any other object of any type*. Most typically, however, representation pieces are very simple primitive objects, like an array of slots in which property values are stored. This need not normally be of concern to the type implementor at all: the system will automatically define the appropriate representation pieces to implement the type's properties, and will provide code to manipulate that representation. However, the type programmer has the option of defining the exact form and layout of a representation piece.

For example, a STACK type might be implemented by a pair of representation pieces: an array, which holds the values pushed on the stack, and a single value, which indicates the array index of the stack "top". Alternatively, the type implementor could use just the array, and store the integer value indicating the "top" index at array index zero. Only the STACK type accesses these representation pieces directly, so the implementor could even change from one implementation to the other, without impacting any of the type's clients (all of whom interact at the abstract interface, using Push and Pop operations).

In most object-oriented systems the concepts of specification and implementation are merged with classification into a single class concept. In Vbase, these concepts are separated: the tasks of both abstract specification and actual implementation of behavior are accomplished by type Type, while the task of classification is accomplished by the type valuespec. For example, *union(type1, type2)* is a valid ValueSpec, but it does not define or implement any behaviors (it merely mentions other types that do so), so it is not a type. Type is a subtype of ValueSpec, and inherits its classification abilities.

10.2 MODELS OF STATE

Since the earliest days of programming, the computer's ability to store and retrieve data, thus maintaining a form of state, has been one of the programmer's central concerns. Although useful research has been underway in stateless programming, most applications, particularly those employing a database, make extensive use of some notion of state.

10.2.1 Existing Models of State

Various systems, object-oriented and otherwise, have put forth their own notions of state. Among the most influential have been the record field model, the instance variable model, and the entity/relationship model. These models can be evaluated in terms of their expressiveness as specification languages, and in terms of their support for encapsulation and data abstraction.

Record fields. One of the most basic models of state is patterned after the notion of a record with fields. Data entities are modeled by records, and their state is modeled by field values. This model has been used successfully by innumerable standard programming languages, and has been incorporated into certain modern object-oriented languages, which have evolved directly out of existing programming languages.

As a specification language, the record field model has rather primitive semantics, basically supporting just the concept of a named, typed storage location. As an implementation (or representation) language, however, it is also a flexible tool for describing data layouts.

One well-known object-oriented language that uses the record-field model is C++ [Stroustrup86], which is based on the C programming language [Kernighan78]. C++ retains the record field concept from C (called *structs*), and builds around it a concept of object and object state. There are two ways to interact with an object's state: either through its operations (called *member functions*), or by directly accessing the struct fields. In general, direct access to struct fields is prohibited for the sake of encapsulation, but it is possible to make these fields public.

In C++, the operational interface to an object provides a specification of the object's behaviors, but not of its state. The struct fields, on the other hand, provide a specification of the object's state, but this is not an abstract specification, because it is mapped directly onto the implementation. The struct fields are the object's state, and are also the object's representation; there is no way to separately describe these two aspects.

Instance variables. The instance variable concept, as exemplified by the Smalltalk language [Goldberg83], defines a set of private variables which are associated with each instance of an object class. These variables maintain the state of the instance, and are private to the instance. Like the record field model, instance variables support the semantics of a named, typed storage location. Unlike the record field model, though, instance variables do not have any additional power as a representation language, because there is no way to describe the layout of different instance variables with respect to one another.

For the sake of encapsulation, instance variables cannot be accessed except through the operations defined by the object's class. This means, however, that while the operational interface defined by a type provides a specification of the object's behavior, the only state specification that exists is in terms of instance variables, and this specification is only accessible to code internal to a class. Furthermore, the state specification implied by instance variables, like that implied by record fields, is mapped directly onto the implementation layout; there is no way to change the implementation of a piece of state, while keeping its specification unchanged.

Relations. The relation model of state, as exemplified by the Entity-Relationship model of [Chen76], is not an object-oriented model in the sense given by [Wegner87], since it has neither inheritance, nor in fact a strong notion of type or class. This model nonetheless has a good deal of expressive power, combining the record field model with a notion of entity-identity. In the entity-relationship model, an entity is fundamentally represented by a record (as in the record field model), but an entity's state is not limited to that which can be represented directly by field values. Entities may also partake in relationships, which describe their interconnections with other entities. A 1-N or M-N relationship is also modeled by a record with fields, one field of which contains an entity-identifier, which refers to the entity being described.

The incorporation of relations into a basically record-oriented model increases the expressive power of the system, since it makes it possible to represent multi-valued facets of an entity's state. The extended state represented by an entity's associated relations, however, is not directly specified, but must be inferred from the existence of the entity-identifier in these associated relations. And again, the state specified is not an abstract state, in the sense that it is mapped directly onto the representation layout: there is no way to change the representation of state without changing its specification.

10.2.2 Abstract State

An abstract model of state allows specification of object state without implying anything about implementation. In its simplest form, an abstract state definition would have no more expressive power than the record field or instance variable models; but even in its simplest form, it has the advantage over these models that it maintains a separation from implementation details.

One of the hallmarks of object-oriented systems is that they associate operations with data elements. This is normally done by having a type define those operations that will be associated with each of the type's instances. In some object systems (those that provide some level of support for data abstraction), it is possible for a type to change the implementation of an operation without changing its specification. An abstract model of state generalizes on this capability, by allowing types to define state descriptions (as well as operations), and to change the implementation of these state descriptions, without changing their specifications.

Whenever a type defines operations to read and write a piece of information from its instances, this can be thought of as implying the definition of a piece of state. In Vbase, this state is specified explicitly, and is normally modeled as a property. Most properties are characterized by the existence of Get and Set operations to access the property. For example, the type Person might define an Age property, which would have Age$Get and Age$Set operations. Some properties also have an Init operation, which behaves much like a Set operation, but can only be executed once per object instance, at the time when the instance is created.

In its simplest form, a Vbase property definition consists of a property name, and a specification of its value type:

```
propname: typespec;
```

This definition induces two operations, to get and set a property's value. For the sake of this discussion, the specifications of those operations will be taken as follows:

```
Get (basetype)
        returns (typespec);
Set (basetype, typespec)
        returns (basetype);
```

where basetype is the type that made the property definition, and the object returned by the Set operation is the object that was passed as the first argument (this return spec makes it convenient to use Set operations as functions in larger expressions).

10.2.3 The Contract of State

The advantage of defining a property (rather than having the state merely "implied" by the existence of Get and Set operations) is that the property definition provides a guarantee to the user, and makes explicit the relationship between the Get and Set operations. If the Get and Set operations are defined on their own (without a property), then there is no guarantee that they model the same abstraction; in fact, there is no guarantee that they have anything more to do with one another than that they have similar names. The property adds the additional semantics, in effect saying that a state invariant is maintained between Set and Get invocations. If we assume that the type Person defines a property Age, as follows

```
Age: integer;
```

then the Get and Set operations induced by the Age property have these specifications:

```
Age$Get (person)
        returns (integer);
```

```
Age$Set (person, integer )
        returns (person);
```

We can now write the invariant of state as follows:

```
Age$Get (Age$Set (aPerson, anAge) )
          == anAge
```

[This invariant becomes more complex, of course, if we want to describe the effects of intervening operations (between the `Set` and the subsequent `Get` operations), concurrent transactions, etc., but it is sufficient as is for our current purposes.]

This invariant is a contract between the type and its users. It guarantees that the property behaves like a storage location (in so far as what you store in it with a `Set` operation will be there next time you look with a `Get` operation). Note that this contract could be made without an explicit notion of object state, for example by simply stating directly the above invariant. The strength of an explicit notion of state is that it provides a simple way of stating this invariant, and provides a nexus for further contracts between a type and its users.

Unlike the notions of state defined in other object-oriented languages, Vbase properties do not compromise data abstraction. The contract implied by a property definition only guarantees how an object's state behaves, not how it is implemented. While the internal implementation of an object normally includes a representation for the object's abstract state, this internal representation is distinct from the abstract state, and may in fact have a completely different format.

For example, the type `Person` might have a property `Age` as a part of its abstract state-specification. The age of an instance might not be represented directly, however. Instead, it might be computed each time the `Age$Get` operation is invoked, based on the current date and the value of an internally stored `Birthdate` (which could be a part of the object's representation, but not necessarily a part of the abstract state-specification.) And, of course, the implementation of the `Age` property could be changed by the type `Person`, without impacting the application code that uses the type's abstract interface.

The fundamental advantage of promoting an abstraction for state to the level of a type's specification of its instances' behavior is that it provides a simple mechanism to make guarantees about object state. Most existing systems cannot do this: they either have no way of making such guarantees (at least not outside of the type manager itself); or, if such guarantees are made, they are made in such a way that they directly compromise the autonomy of the data abstraction by exporting representation-level information.

An abstraction for object state can be used to express more complex state guarantees than the one described above; the more expressive a specification language, the less often its users will have to go below the level of the specification, and rely on implementation details in potentially dangerous ways.

10.2.4 Inheritance and State

Types inherit the behavior specifications defined by their supertypes. They can augment these specifications by either adding new behaviors of their own, or by refining the behaviors that their supertypes defined.

A great deal of work has been done on defining the legal constraints on subtype and refinement specifications for operations [Cardelli84a]. Because Vbase properties are based directly on an underlying set of operations, many of these results can be applied to subtyping and refinement of properties.

The general rule is that a subtype must obey all of the constraints guaranteed by the supertype, such that users of the supertype will never be unpleasantly surprised if they unknowingly get hold of and operate on an instance of the subtype (and it dispatches to subtype code).

This leads to the (slightly surprising) result that the `typespec` of a property cannot normally be either restricted or expanded by a subtype's refinement. A restricted `typespec` could cause surprises when the user tried to invoke the `Set` operation; and an expanded `ValueSpec` could cause surprises when the user tried to invoke the `Get` operation.

Most commonly, the only change that a property refinement makes is to change or augment the implementation of the `Get` or `Set` operations. For example, a `Set` operation might have a trigger method that updates a cached data structure.

10.2.5 More Complex Constraints

More complex state guarantees can be represented either declaratively, or embedded in code. These behaviors are typically represented only in program code in most systems, but promoting them to the level of an object's state-specification has the advantages of making the constraints explicit, and providing at least the opportunity for the system to automatically implement code to uphold the constraints. The Vbase property specification provides a convenient nexus for such state constraints.

Optional properties. One addition to the contract of state is the notion of optionally valued properties. For example, a useful property of a `Person` might be his/her `Spouse`. Not everyone is married, however, and the case without a spouse is equally as interesting and important as the case with a value. The contract of state can be extended to incorporate this with the aid of exceptions and two additional operations, `UnSet` and `HasValue`.

In these optional properties the `Set` operation remains unchanged. However, the `Get` operations specification must be changed to indicate that this operation may not yield a value at all. This is modeled by allowing the operation to raise an exception rather than returning the value:

```
Spouse$Get (person)
        returns (person)
        raises (NoValue);
```

The programmer is then able to catch the `NoValue` exception and deal with the case of an unmarried person. This is somewhat awkward if the `NoValue` case is in fact the case that the program is currently interested in. For this purpose, the `HasValue` operation is defined as

```
Spouse$HasValue (person)
        returns (Boolean);
```

Now the only remaining problem is being able to remove a value from the person once it has been set. In real life, this is modeled by the Divorce operation, but the general case is modeled in Vbase by the UnSet operation:

```
Age$UnSet (person)
        returns (person);
```

This leads to several additional invariants for optional properties.

```
Spouse$HasValue (
        Spouse$Unset(aPerson))
        == False
Spouse$HasValue (
        Spouse$Set(aPerson,bPerson))
        == True
Spouse$Get (
        Spouse$UnSet(aPerson))
        raises NoValue
```

This is indicated in Vbase by adding the keyword optional to the property definition.

```
Spouse: optional person;
```

Due to a current implementation restriction, the HasValue and UnSet operations are currently only provided as language level features, not true operations. The compiler turns the HasValue construct into a Get and catches the NoValue exception, while UnSet is implemented as a special NoValue value (Null) given as the value to be Set. This restriction should be removed in order to make HasValue and UnSet true model-level, rather than language-level, constructs.

Inverses. One of the most common constraints on object state is that inverse relationships hold between objects. For example, if the type Person has a property called Spouse, which refers to another instance of type Person, then it is often desirable to have a guarantee that this other person's Spouse property refers back. In other words, Spouse is a symmetric property: it is its own inverse.

This sort of information is not easily represented in systems that do not have an explicit notion of abstract state. Behaviors such as inverses are typically represented only in the code that implements an operation (in non-object-oriented systems, it is even worse, because the behavior must be implemented in application code, rather than the object's own operation code). For example, the Spouse$Set operation might have a method associated with it that maintains the inverse, by invoking the Spouse$Set operation in the reverse direction. But since this behavior is only represented in the method code, there is no way to specify to the user of the type that the inverse is maintained.

If we assume arguments and returns analogous to those in the previous section, then the property inverse behavior can be represented by the following invariant:

```
Spouse$Get( Spouse$Get(
        Spouse$Set( husband, wife )))
        == husband
```

This is represented in Vbase by adding an "inverse" clause to the property definition, as follows:

```
Spouse: person inverse Spouse;
```

Cardinality. The other common constraint on object state is cardinality. So far we have only examined single-valued properties. Assume that the type `Person` defines two properties, as follows:

```
GroceryList: list[food];
Child: distributed set[person];
```

Both of these properties are aggregate-valued, but they have very different behaviors (aside from the simple difference that one is list-valued and the other is set-valued). Each instance of `Person` has a single `GroceryList` property, whose value is a list of food items. The keyword "distributed" in the definition of `Child`, however, means that each instance of `Person` has a whole set of `Child` properties, each of whose value is a single person. An example is shown in Figure 10.2.

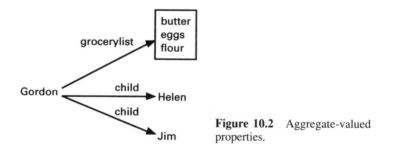

Figure 10.2 Aggregate-valued properties.

The difference between distributed and non-distributed properties becomes most apparent when looking at their interaction with inverses. If both the `Child` and `GroceryList` properties were given an inverse (say, `Parent` and `Owner`, respectively), then there would be `Parent` properties pointing from Jim and Helen back to the parent, Gordon; but there would be only one inverse for the `GroceryList` property, and it would point back from the list itself, rather than from any of the individual food items.

An additional clause (not currently supported in Vbase) on a multi-valued property could be used to specify cardinality range constraints, e.g., that a person must have EXACTLY two parents, or that a building must have AT LEAST 2 fire exits.

10.2.6 AIO, AKO, APO

The three standard relationships that are supported by many semantic data models [Hammer81], "an-instance-of", "a-kind-of", and "a-part-of", represent state that is common to a broad class of objects. In most systems that support these relationships, the relationships are built into the system code, but are not accessible to user inspection or modification.

One of the achievements of object-oriented programming is to make it possible to extend existing systems by adding subtypes with new behaviors. Ideally, then, even the general state characteristics represented by "an-instance-of", "a-kind-of", and "a-part-of" should be user-extensible.

These relationships are simply represented in Vbase as inverted properties. The built-in relationship "a-kind-of", for example, is represented by a pair of inverted properties, just like user-defined relationships:

```
subtypes: distributed set[type]
        inverse supertypes;
supertypes: distributed set[type]
        inverse subtypes;
```

Since these properties are defined by the type `Type`, it is possible for the user to create a subtype of `Type`, which refines these properties, to provide special "a-kind-of" behaviors. In fact, it would even be possible for users of Vbase to develop their own, parallel type hierarchy, with their own notion of subtyping and inheritance.

The relationship "an-instance-of" is modeled through the property `DirectType` on each instance and the property `Class` maintained by each type. In Vbase a `Class` is a "predicate-defined aggregate." That is, the collection of all objects meeting some criterion (as opposed to an explicitly defined aggregate, which is a collection of all objects explicitly inserted into it). The most common kind of `Class` is one where the predicate is just that the members are all instances of a specified type. When a stronger model of multi-valued properties is developed, this `Class` should become a simple (multi-valued) property on `Type`, defined as an inverse to the `DirectType` property of each object.

It is particularly useful to be able to develop specialized "a-part-of" behaviors, because each application domain has its own notion of what a parts-hierarchy consists of and behaves like. Certain general characteristics can be built in at the system level, but most of the details of "a-part-of" state are application specific (like lock propagation behavior). These application-specific behaviors can be represented as refinements of the `Parts` and `PartOf` properties.

10.3 REPRESENTATION

In most cases, the implementation of abstract state requires the actual storage of concrete state values. In Vbase, this state storage is maintained in a series of objects called the *representation* of a base object.

10.3.1 Concept of Representation

Representation is a way of building upon existing work through a form of composing types. Languages such as CLU [Liskov81] and Alphard [Wulf76] have formally brought the concept of representation to the level of a language feature. However, neither of these languages supported inheritance, a notion which has become a cornerstone of object technology.

In our model of representation, the implementation of an object consists of a combination of methods (code) and representation. The representation consists of zero or more ancillary objects, which are used to store the necessary state information to implement the abstract behaviors of object, and are accessed and maintained by the method code. Typically, these objects are automatically created when the object they represent is created, and deleted when the object is deleted.

10.3.2 Simple Representation

Part of the definition of a type consists of descriptions of the representation objects that the type needs to implement an instance. Each of these descriptions, called Representation Descriptors or RepDescs, is used to describe one representation object of the eventual instance. A RepDesc specifies the type and size of the representation object, and identifies an operation that will be used to initialize it. Although a Vbase type programmer may explicitly specify these descriptors, Vbase will typically generate them (and the methods to manipulate them) automatically for the programmer, through the behaviors defined by type Type.

The default representation for a type consists of a single object, either a Record (similar to records in other languages) or an _Array (similar to C arrays). In either case, there is one field or slot in the representation object for each property requiring storage that is defined by the abstract type.

As a simple example, consider the type Person described earlier, which defines two properties, Age and Spouse. The system would generate a single RepDesc describing the one object that would be required to implement this state. This object would be an instance of the generated (unnamed) Record type:

```
define Record
        Age : Integer;
        Spouse : Person;
end;
```

Assuming that Person is a direct subtype of Entity (or, more precisely, that no other type up the supertype chain defines a property requiring storage), an instance of this Record type would be the only representation object required to represent an instance of Person. The more general case, where supertypes also require storage, is described in a later section.

10.3.3 User Specified Representation

Even when only one of the instance's types requires representation, however, the example can be more complex—and more interesting. The type programmer could specify explicitly what representation objects are required. There are at least four different scenarios under which this might make sense.

The programmer might know a more efficient implementation (since the system default may not be the best possible choice in all cases). Or there may be an externally imposed layout on the data structure. There could be some underlying piece of representation required that does not map into any abstract property defined by the type and thus not mapped into the default representation. Finally, the programmer could specify an explicit representation for better control over the clustering of representation pieces.

The first case might come up if the type definer knows of constraints on the semantics of the type that are not specifiable in the type's abstract interface, but that (if known) could be used to generate a more efficient representation. Unfortunately, this will always be possible: no matter how sophisticated the state-specification language becomes, there will be cases that it does not cover. In these cases, type programmers must take matters into their own hands.

For example, if a type defines two properties, but only one of them will have a value for any given instance (determined, let's say, by the value of a third property), then the representation could take advantage of this fact by allocating only one "slot" in the instance's representation. Since Vbase does not currently support specification of this kind of "either/or" constraint in property definitions, it is up to the type definer to implement the space-efficient layout to take advantage of it.

The second case, where the representation is constrained by an externally imposed data layout, typically occurs when there is an existing body of code that is to be shared. For example, if a company has invested time and money in the creation of a large body of finite-element analysis tools, then new object-oriented applications might be designed so that the object representations are in the format expected by the existing tools.

The third case, where an underlying piece of representation is necessary even though it does not map directly onto any abstract property, might be exhibited by a type like pixel image. A pixel image has two properties, `Height` and `Width`, as well as `Display` and `RasterOp` operations (and probably many others). The representation for this type might consist of two objects, one to hold the values for the properties and one to hold the actual set of pixels. The former would probably be an instance of a simple `Record` type similar to the one defined in the `Person` example, but the latter representation piece would be an instance of some low-level type like `Space` (used in Vbase to store an uninterpreted sequence of bytes).

The type `Space` will be discussed more fully in a later section (its actual semantics are not vital here). The obvious question in doing this is why not just promote the representation piece to the abstract interface by defining a third (presumably private) property, which refers to this instance of `Space`. There are a couple of problems with this approach. The first is that it compromises type-safety and semantic integrity of pixel images. It may not be appropriate for any users of `PixelImage` to access this space. All of their manipulations should be through the operations defined by `PixelImage`.

The second problem lies with potential subtypes of `PixelImage`. If, for example, a subtype called `PatternFill` needed only to store the pattern to be filled, not the entire `PixelImage`, it would still need to support this property (and thus the size of the entire pixel image).

The fourth case, where the type definer wants to control the clustering of representation pieces, is another kind of efficient concern. In the example of the `PixelImage`, above, it might turn out that the actual array of pixels is very large, and therefore time consuming to page in and out of memory, while the other representation pieces, records containing `Height` and `Width` information, are small enough that they can be cached in memory at all times. It might be desirable, therefore, to separate these representation pieces into separate "paging units", so that calculations of pixel image size, overlap, and occlusion can be calculated efficiently, and the actual pixel arrays can be brought into memory for only those pixel images that are currently visible.

10.3.4 Representation and Inheritance

In the typical case, the descriptor for this representation object is combined with the descriptors defined on the type's immediate supertype. If all of the `RepDescs` have been generated, the resultant representation will consist of one object for each abstract type of the object which defines one or more properties requiring storage.

If a subtype of `Person` called `Student` was defined with the two stored properties `Major` and `GradePointAverage`, instances of `Student` would have two representation objects, one an instance of the record defined earlier for type `Person`, and the other an instance of a second `Record` type containing the fields for holding the `Major` and `GradePointAverage` property values.

To support inheritance, an operation can be dispatched to ensure that the method(s) actually executed are appropriate for the direct abstract type of the instance being operated on. Only methods which are dispatched should be allowed to access the pieces of representation and then only for the dispatch arguments. The potential problems in accessing representation of other sorts of objects are discussed in the next section.

As stated earlier, each type defines the complete set of objects that is used as the representation for instances of the type. In most simple cases, a type simply adds one or more representation objects to the set already defined by its supertype, using these objects to implement the additional abstract behaviors that it defines. The supertype's methods continue to be used to manipulate its original pieces of representation, with the subtype possibly adding a small piece of behavior to the operation by using a trigger method.

Many models, such as C++, Ada and Vbase, support a notion of public and private state. In C++, private properties have been used as a replacement for representation. The constraint on who can access which representation pieces is one distinction between these models. Any property, even private, is nonetheless a part of the abstract behavior of the object and may be accessed by any of the operations which have the necessary visibility and on any object of that type to which they have access. Touched on briefly earlier, the problems with the private property approach will become more apparent when considering the ability to take over all or part of a supertype's representation.

The concept of using private properties as representation arises from the overuse of inheritance that Dr. Liskov was lamenting. Proper use of inheritance provides a strong framework for specification, allowing new capabilities to be added (as new subtypes) while localizing the changes needed to the code. Inheritance only fortuitously provides a mechanism for sharing implementation and should be used for this purpose only with great care and trepidation. Representation, on the other hand, provides strong support for sharing implementation while not interfering with the abstract specification of a type.

10.3.5 Taking Over Representation

In some cases, however, a type may be able to provide a better implementation for some or all of the behavior that it is inheriting. It then has the freedom to provide the new implementation by replacing some or all of the representation defined by the supertype and all of the methods that access those pieces of representation. This is termed "taking over" the representation.

The `PixelArray` and `PatternFill` example was touched on earlier. `PixelArray` array defines two representation pieces for its instances, referred to here as `BoundsRecord` and `PixelData`. `PatternFill` is a subtype of `PixelArray` whose instances inherit only the representation object `BoundsRecord` from `PixelArray`. In addition, `PatternFill` defines a second representation object for each instance, `PatternData`.

The methods for implementing the `Display` operation for `PixelArray` touches both the `BoundsRecord` and `PixelData` representation objects of its argument. The method which is dispatched to if this argument is a `PatternFill` examines the `BoundsRecord` objects well, but uses the `PatternData` object rather than `PixelData` object. The dispatching mechanism guarantees that only the valid representation objects of the dispatch argument are actually requested by a method.

If access were allowed to the representation of objects other than dispatch arguments, a possible run-time type failure could arise. `PixelArray` might define another operation, XOR, which accepts two arguments, `Data` and `Mask`, only one of which (`Data`) is used in dispatching. The obvious implementation of this operation would access the `PixelData` representation object of the `Mask` argument as well as the `Data` argument. As long as the `Mask` argument was not an instance of `PatternFill`, this operation would succeed. But if the `Data` argument was an instance of `PixelArray` (so no dispatching occurred), but the `Mask` argument was an instance of `PatternFill`, a run-time failure would occur accessing the `PixelData` representation object.

This same mode of failure would occur regardless of whether the object were accessed via a non-dispatched parameter, as in the XOR example above or some other path, such as the value of a property access. Only dispatch arguments can be safely accessed at the representation level. Currently, Vbase does not track which operations access which pieces of representation. Cross checking this information against which operations are re-implemented in a subtype that employs representation takeover would reduce the impact of the selective representation takeover problem discussed earlier.

10.3.6 Accessing Representation

It also provides two mechanisms for selecting a representation object of an instance of a given type: each `RepDesc` is named and this name may be used in some circumstances (see the section on language support) to identify which representation object is intended; each `RepDesc` also contains an integer index which is unique across all of the `RepDescs` for a single type.

Abstract State and Representation In Vbase   Chap. 10

Type representation manager. All control over the representation objects is provided through the mechanisms defined by the type `RepManager`. The operations defined by type `RepManager` give the programmer control over the representation being defined. The principal operations are `GetRep`, `ReleaseRep`, `SetRep`, `MakeRep` and `DeleteRep`.

```
GetRep(object:Entity,
       selector:Integer)
returns (Entity)
```

This, along with `ReleaseRep`, provides the backbone of the representation model. Given an integer selector, the `GetRep` operation returns the representation object with that tag for the object supplied. Some implementations of `GetRep` may leave the object locked (for example, wired down in memory or locked from other writers).

```
ReleaseRep(object:Entity,
           selector:Integer)
```

This is the other half of the `GetRep` / `ReleaseRep` pair. If any part of the object was locked to access the representation, `ReleaseRep` releases it. In some cases, this operation may not have any effect, but for generality's sake, every `GetRep` should be paired with a `ReleaseRep`.

```
SetRep(object:Entity,
       selector:Integer,
       repPiece:Entity)
```

This makes an existing object the representation piece of object with the tag selector. This is normally used only during object creation.

```
MakeRep(object:Entity,
        selector:Integer,
        description:ReqDesc,
        initializers:ArgumentList)
```

This creates a new object using the initializers provided according to description of the representation piece contained in the `ReqDesc`. A `ReqDesc` (short for requirements descriptor) is the object constructed by TDL to describe the requirements the type has for a given representation piece. This operation is semantically equivalent to an abstract create of the new representation piece followed by a `SetRep` operation. The combined operation is useful for both simplification and some efficiency that may be gained in combining the efforts. The `SetRep` operation remains useful in some fringe cases, for example, sharing representation objects between objects.

```
DeleteRep(object:Entity,
          selector:Integer)
```

This operation disassociates the indicated representation piece from the object given, deleting the representation piece if it is not shared. `DeleteRep` is normally used only during object deletion. Other operations defined by `RepManager` are for bookkeeping purposes and for support of the three special properties of each object: its abstract type, representation type and storage type.

Language support.   The `GetRep` and `ReleaseRep` operations are both common and potentially dangerous (as described in the section on Representation Manager), so COP provides a special layer between the programmer and the operations themselves, in the form of the `getrep` statement defined in COP. A `getrep` statement is an executable statement of the form:

```
getrep (variable:name (argument))
       statement
```

`Variable` is a newly introduced variable with a scope of the subordinate statement `statement`. The variable is initialized to the representation piece indicated by the name `name` of the dispatch argument `argument`. COP transforms the name provided into the integer selector of the representation piece indicated. The representation piece is accessed by the `GetRep` operation and the `ReleaseRep` operation is automatically run upon exiting `statement`.

COP validates that the object whose representation is being examined is in fact a dispatch argument of the current method. COP also generates the type of the variable according to the declared type of the requested representation piece.

Under certain rare circumstances, it may not be viable to depend on the `getrep` syntax. Most notably among these are representation level manipulations required during create. The object being created cannot be a dispatch argument to the create operation. COP provides the *protect* statement for cases like this, where a pair of operations (such as `GetRep` and `ReleaseRep`) must both be executed if either is executed. A protect statement is an executable statement of the form:

```
statement1
 protect  statement2
```

If execution begins on the statement `statement1`, COP will guarantee that the statement `statement2` will be executed.

In the current model, Vbase cannot restrict the usage of the `GetRep` (and other potentially dangerous) operations except through the expected use of such special language features. Like many aspects of programming, this has proven to be a double-edged sword. It has prevented any tendency to confine the user unreasonably, but has left a dangerous weapon within reach.

10.3.7 Subtypes of RepManager

In Vbase, every object has three types: its abstract type, which describes its abstract behavior, its storage type, which describes the behavior of the actual storage used in implementing the object [Damon88], and its representation type which describes how its representation objects are manipulated. The representation type (or representation manager) of each object is some subtype of the type RepManager.

RepManager, and its subtypes, are what bring both the flexibility and the simplicity to Vbase's use of representation. They provide a clean encapsulation of an object's implementation, hiding the low-level details needed to manipulate the representation pieces, while leaving the high-level capabilities, such as taking over the representation.

Each subtype of RepManager is tuned to a particular usage and additional ones can be added as needed. A particular object can be created with any representation manager that supports the representation pieces defined by the object's direct abstract type. There is one representation manager that is generalized to support any combination of representation pieces. Other specialized representation managers include one tuned for single, default representation piece objects and others tuned for specific system critical types. A sophisticated programmer may wish to write a specialized RepManager for some other behavior.

One particularly interesting representation manager provided with Vbase is ImmediateRep. This stretches the model of representation and shows the flexibility of it. ImmediateRep is limited to objects who have a single Integer representation piece which is unchangeable. Types such as enumerations and Integer itself use this representation. The representation manager stores all of the information required by each instance directly in the reference, gaining the expected performance benefits while remaining completely within the model.

Besides the tag indicating what representation manager and storage manager this object is, ImmediateRep stores the actual integer value in the object Reference. There is also a second integer value used as an index into an array of types to determine the abstract type of this object. This mechanism gives the high performance expected from basic types like Integers and Booleans without breaking out of the model and allows several interesting additional behaviors.

By writing a new similar representation manager, an enumeration, which uses ImmediateRep by default, could have additional representation object(s) associated with it, allowing arbitrary additional behavior. Assuming the initial Integer representation object remained, this enumeration would continue to display the high performance characteristics common to enumerations, while allowing the additional semantics not normally associated with them.

10.3.8 Primitive Types and Storage Managers

Composing each type out of representation pieces of other types would recurse infinitely if it were not for primitive types. In Vbase, a primitive type is a type whose instances are their own representation. There are three such cases currently, Integer, Real and Space. The types Integer and Real are fairly straightforward, dropping down to the underlying system support for the arithmetic and logical operations defined on them. Space is mildly more interesting. Space is just an abstraction for memory. It does not directly define any properties or operations, instead relying on the storage type to give access to its constituent bytes.

Just as there are many subtypes of RepManager, there are numerous subtypes of the storage type StorageManager. There are three major storage managers provided with the system. `OKStorage` and `OKSharedStorage` provide support for persistent objects, while `PloStorage` supports process local (non-persistent) objects. The distinction between the `OKStorage` and `OKSharedStorage` managers comes in the transaction model each supports. `OKStorage` provides an optimistic concurrency control mechanism, targeted at long, largely autonomous transactions. `OKSharedStorage`, on the other hand, provides a low-level pessimistic concurrency control, targeted at high concurrency and communication (i.e., semaphores) objects. As with `RepManager`, a sophisticated user may wish to tailor a subtype of `StorageManager` for use in a particular application.

10.4 THE FUTURE

There are several additions to the model and its use in Vbase that are worth exploring. Resolving some of the problems discussed above clearly has high priority among these tasks, but there are several other avenues which may prove very fruitful in improving the model.

10.4.1 Improved Multi-Value Properties

The model of properties needs to be expanded to allow more general support for multi-valued properties. There are three primary changes currently being investigated.

One such area would allow other forms of access to the individual property values, similar to the variety of accessors available in a full aggregate hierarchy, such as arrays, lists and dictionaries. Some properties are naturally keyed, so that each value has some tag value associated with it. These values should be directly accessible with the use of this tag. Other properties are naturally ordered, and this order should be maintained by the property, so that at least the correct ordering for iteration is guaranteed.

Another major piece of work is removing the current requirement of an explicit denotable aggregate being available for each multi-valued property. This unduly restricts the type programmers' ability to define the optimal representation. In particular, this largely disallows any real sense of derived multi-valued properties. Finally, and probably most importantly, the operations used by multi-valued properties must be user specifiable. Currently, with the single set-like option, the system default operations must be used. This does not even allow a user written trigger to be combined with the insert or remove operations.

10.4.2 Alternate Representation

Support for alternate representation is the most attractive of these. Alternate representation is the ability for a type to specify a variety of representations, only one of which would be used by any given instance at any given time. Method dispatching would have to be modified to include an understanding of which of the alternative representations the object has. The language CLU already supports a form of alternate representation, but its model does not need to deal with dispatching since there is no inheritance.

The choice among the alternative representations could be made at create time based on an initializer of an immutable property or the representation could be dynamically altered based on a mutable property of the object. Specialized representations for aggregates based on the type of their members (such as sets of integers) is the simplest example of statically allocated representation. Alternate representations based on current size or access patterns to an aggregate would warrant the dynamic representation capability.

Different methods would be written to deal with each of the various alternatives. The dispatcher would then select the appropriate combination of methods based on some indicator of which of the alternative representations the dispatch argument actually utilizes. Typically this indicator would be a property stored in a common representation piece to all of the alternatives, although a new representation manager could be designed to store this information directly in the reference, significantly speeding up the dispatching.

10.4.3 Representation Concurrency Control

Finally, we are investigating the possibility of structuring some forms of concurrency around access to representation objects. In combination with the specification of which operations touch specific representation pieces, this could be the basis of a semantically based concurrency scheme.

10.5 CONCLUSIONS

Vbase combines data abstraction and type inheritance in a single object-oriented framework. The database abstraction mechanism consists of three central features: a strict separation of the specification of behavior from its implementation details, so that users of a type can only interact at the abstract specification level, and cannot touch the representation layout; a specification language that includes an explicit notion of state, so that properties as well as operations can be specified as part of a type's abstract interface; and a model of representation that formalizes the relationship between an object and its implementation.

The type inheritance mechanism makes it possible to define a hierarchy of types, where subtypes can inherit both behaviors and implementation from their supertypes. While the inheritance of specification is strict, however, the inheritance of implementation is not; a subtype can either inherit a supertype's implementation, or it can override the implementation.

Just as an object instance can have many different behaviors, some derived from each of its many types, it can also have many representation pieces, normally one for each of its types.

On the specification side, a type has a flexible mechanism for inheriting and augmenting the behaviors specified by its supertype (by refining operations and properties) as well as for adding new behaviors (by defining new properties and operations).

On the representation side, a type can control which pieces of supertype representation are inherited, and which pieces are overridden. Because of the separation of specification from implementation, and their separate interactions with the inheritance mechanism, a type can inherit a property, potentially augmenting the behavior specification by way of a property refinement, while completely overriding the supertype's representation of the property.

11 Object SQL

Craig Harris and Joshua Duhl

11.1 INTRODUCTION

SQL is a well-known and widely used query language for relational databases. The idea of extending SQL for use in an object processing environment has a certain allure, and a certain notoriety. Like a good marriage, the elements can complement each other and create something of great value. Like a difficult marriage, there can be friction and uneasy compromise.

This chapter explores the areas of synergy in combining SQL with the object paradigm. Because the object paradigm is gaining attention in the programming community, and because SQL already enjoys considerable popularity, we can expect to see various implementations of an object SQL from relational and object system vendors. The discussion here should therefore be of interest to SQL users, to object system users, to SQL and object system developers, and to those simply trying to keep abreast of new developments in database and language technology. To those attempting their own definition and implementation of an Object SQL, we can offer two pieces of advice. First, try to include someone who thinks the whole thing is a silly idea. Second, make sure you have plenty of donuts.

The next section defines what we mean by the "Object SQL", and looks at the benefits provided to the SQL language and to the users and developers of object systems. The remaining sections examine the specific object processing extensions to the SQL query model. Section 11.3 focuses on the general requirements of query processing in an object environment. Section 11.4 describes some reasonable object extensions to SQL. The last section introduces an important class of query optimizations made possible when operating in an object environment.

11.2 OBJECT SQL: WHAT AND WHY

11.2.1 What Is It?

Object SQL is a subset of the ANSI SQL standard with object processing extensions. It is not a traditional SQL which just happens to be implemented using objects. It is a language for posing questions about objects using the SQL paradigm. The term "Object SQL" is used in two contexts throughout this chapter. In this section, we take it to mean any form of SQL which can operate in an object environment. In sections 11.3, 11.4, and 11.5 we also use it to refer to the particular implementation used in Vbase. The latter sense is intended for concreteness, and we hope it doesn't distract the reader from the central theme of the concept of an Object SQL.

11.2.2 What Is a Query?

All databases have protocols for accessing their information content. Many times, these protocols take the form of a programming language or programming language extensions. Vbase, for example, uses an extension of the C language (COP) for manipulating data; and a new language (TDL) for defining the structure of data. A problem with having a programming language as a database interface is that the only people capable of using the database are programmers. The desire to allow individuals with little or no programming expertise to effectively use a database is the primary motivation for the query concept.

In an informal sense, a query is a single interaction between an end-user and a database. The user formulates a request in a non-procedural manner, specifying 'what' to do rather than 'how' to do it. The query processor analyzes the request, and dynamically constructs and executes a program to respond to the request.

11.2.3 Query Languages

A query language is a framework for expressing a query. While query languages are typically non-procedural in nature and implemented as interpreters, they display a wide diversity of interactive protocols. It is probably useful to categorize query languages with respect to two dimensions: the kinds of questions which can naturally be expressed, and the paradigm for posing questions.

Without intending a complete classification, we can identify questions of the forms:

- "What if ...?",
- "Is it true that ... ?"
- "What are all the objects for which a given condition holds?"
- "What is the value of an object's property?"

It's important to realize that questions of one form can generally be couched in another form with a suitable amount of restructuring. The point is one of convenience. Thus, spreadsheet languages such as VisiCalc^{TM}[1] are especially useful for "what if" questions; logic languages such as Prolog handle "is it true" questions smoothly; languages such as QBE^{TM} or SQL are good for filtering groups of things; and object languages like Smalltalk or COP naturally express questions about properties and operations.

Interaction paradigms also fall into rough classes. Both VisiCalc^{TM} and QBE^{TM} present their users with a framework for asking questions which is closely bound to the format of the answers. The former uses a spreadsheet to display the answer to a "what if" question, while the latter uses a tabular skeleton to display the results of a filtered collection. Languages such as Prolog and SQL attempt a happy medium between a mathematically sound formalism (predicate or relational calculus) and a user-accessible syntax.

11.2.4 A Bit of History

The acronym 'SQL' stands for structured query language. SQL was originally proposed by IBM in 1981 as the user interface language to the System R relational database. Their product was not released, however, until 1986. In the interim, RSI Inc. developed ORACLE^{TM}, the first commercial SQL product. Since that time, several other implementations have been marketed, including UNIFY^{TM}, MISTRESS^{TM}, and INGRES^{TM}. Given the rapid introduction of several SQL dialects and the general acceptance of SQL in the early '80s, it is not particularly surprising that ANSI undertook the language's standardization (X3H2).

11.2.5 Why Bother?

To some, the concept of an object-oriented SQL may seem a bit odd. SQL is commonly perceived as being a query language for relational database systems. Why would one want to use it for asking questions about objects? Wouldn't it necessitate a database? Wouldn't it necessitate defining special "relation" objects? This question can be best addressed by approaching it from two perspectives: first by examining what a query language, such as SQL, can provide to an object system, such as Vbase, and then from the other side, what an object system can provide to a query language.

What does SQL bring to an object system?

Existing User Base.   An important practical consideration is that there is a comparatively large base of people who have had some experience using SQL. The number of individuals who have used object systems is probably much smaller. Extending a familiar tool to operate in a new environment is one way to provide a smoother transition.

Ad-Hoc Query Mechanism.   While most object systems provide mechanisms for examining objects, few if any offer mechanisms for formulating and executing ad-hoc queries over this object data. The formulation of ad-hoc queries is a natural feature

---

[1]Editors' note: VisiCalc^{TM} was the first spreadsheet program. It is no longer sold.

of SQL. It provides users the ability to describe criteria for selecting and organizing object data that can result in a perspective of the data that is more naturally oriented towards what the user wants to know from it. Furthermore, users do not have to write code in the data manipulation language (in this case COP) to view their data, but rather can express their query through SQL. Finally, SQL provides the opportunity to have alternative perspectives of the same object data.

Better Aggregate Manipulation. SQL is one of the simplest languages for manipulating groups of things. In Vbase, for instance, objects that contain groups of other objects are termed Aggregates. SQL can perform any operations over any aggregates, and can do so more simply than Vbase's data manipulation language (COP).

Convenient Persistence for Object Language Systems. While Object SQL was developed on a system with an integrated object database, developing an SQL with object extensions seems like a convenient way for object languages to acquire a persistent component. Object languages such as Smalltalk or C++ could employ an extended SQL with an existing relational database product.

What does an object system bring to SQL?

Objects Simplify Queries. Although SQL is one of the simplest languages available for manipulating groups of things, it is still difficult for people to formulate complex queries with multiple join conditions or subqueries. Much of this complexity is attributable to the relational model rather than to SQL. In a schema consisting of people and documents such that one or more people can author one or more documents, a relational system would be likely to have three tables: one for people, one for documents, and one for the author relationships. In an object system, the author relationships might be modeled as properties or instance variables. To find all documents authored by individuals residing in Detroit, the relational SQL user would need to specify a join condition over the people, author, and document tables, viz:

```
Select  doc.title
From    person, author, document doc
Where   residence='Detroit' and
        person.id=author.person and
        doc.id=author.document;
```

The user of an object SQL could phrase the question solely in terms of people:

```
Select  p.authorOf.title
From    person p
Where   p.residence = 'Detroit';
```

The Object Paradigm Solves Some Common SQL Problems. Two problems generally considered difficult for traditional SQLs are "referential integrity" and "the parts explosion problem (tree-structured tables)". Object systems are generally capable of solving the referential integrity without any additional language support. Vbase, for example, provides built-in integrity for a variety of cases including inverse properties. It also provides users with a means of managing more complex cases with its trigger mechanism.

Querying tree-structured tables is another difficult problem for SQL, usually solved by the addition of several new clauses to the basic select command. By generalizing from a 'table' to an 'Aggregate', an Object SQL can obviate the need for additional linguistic support. Specifically, it is possible to define an aggregate whose iterate operation is implemented by computing a transitive closure. Using such an aggregate in a query's *from-clause* will accomplish the effect of walking a tree structure.

Greater Ability to Direct Query Processing. The standard form of SQL does not give the user much opportunity to indicate how a query should be processed. Although this is quite arguably a feature, it should be noted that an Object SQL can offer the user more flexibility in this regard. By generalizing the traditional notion of a *relation* to the object notion of *aggregate,* a user can identify a limited portion of a whole relation. By permitting indices to be types of aggregates, an Object SQL can permit a user to select a particular index in the from-clause of a query.

11.3 INTEGRATION OF A QUERY LANGUAGE WITH AN OBJECT DATABASE

11.3.1 Query Processing Requirements

On the surface query processing is simple: ask a question, get an answer. But what if we find ourselves asking the same question periodically? Entering the same query over and over entails needless work, and is prone to error. Furthermore, if the query takes a while to process and we know we will want to ask it again later, we may want to optimize it. What if we want to save the answer for subsequent processing? What if we want to report the same answer in a different format, or to define a common format for the answers to several different questions?

Query processing in an object environment occasions an additional desire for extensibility. While we certainly need to handle an extended set of data types (discussed in section 11.4), we may also wish to allow extensions in the way queries are evaluated. In order to satisfy the desires for persistence and for extensibility, Object SQL defines types for queries, for query results, and for the format of a report. Users of Object SQL may freely define subtypes and supertypes so as to replace, refine or redefine the query processing operations.

Stored queries. Object SQL defines a type called Query, whose operations include Create and Evaluate. The Create operation takes arguments corresponding to the major SQL selection clauses, validates that the query is well-formed, and returns a "query" object. The Evaluate operation takes a "query" object and an optional naming environment (for processing nested queries), and returns a "QueryResult" object. While there is no Optimize or Compile operation in the initial implementation, it would be reasonable to add one. The query object is a means for saving a query which is to be used repetitively. Once created, it can be named and evaluated or reevaluated programmatically.

Query results.   A QueryResult is an object which holds onto the results of evaluating a query. Logically, it is a collection of records, whose fields correspond to the expressions in the select-clause of an SQL query. It defines an iterator called NextResult, which yields successive records—grouped and ordered as specified in the query. QueryResult objects are created during the evaluation of a query, and cannot be updated without taking special measures (importing a private interface).

In the initial implementation of Object SQL, record types were not available, and arrays were used to represent the resulting tuples instead. While records are definitely preferable, their use gives rise to some interesting issues. The fields of a record must be named. The obvious choice for a field name is the title of a select expression component. The problem is that this may limit the class of strings which can be used for titles to those which can be used for field names (i.e., no embedded spaces, etc.).

Reports.   A report object is a format definition. Type Report defines a Create operation and a Print operation. The latter takes a report format and a QueryResult, and prints the results. The Create operation allows the specification of overall title and font, along with column specific information (title, data type, width, position, font, justification, etc.). The assumption is that reports will look roughly like a table of data. This assumption and the overall behavior of type Report can be extended or modified by the use of subtypes and supertypes.

11.3.2 Issues with a Programmatic Interface

There are numerous ways in which to specify and execute a query within an object language. In an "embedded" approach, the host object language syntax is extended to recognize SQL keywords and constructs. A variation on this theme is to utilize the pre-processor or macro facility of the host language (if it has one) or to build a special-purpose pre-processor. An alternative is to use the "module language" approach endorsed by the ANSI SQL standard. The idea here is that the query looks to the host language like a procedure invocation (message event, lambda expression, etc.). The variations on this idea play with the nature of the query-procedure arguments, and the point at which query validation occurs. While the initial version of Ontologic's Object SQL does not support programmatic queries, our intent is to follow the spirit of the ANSI standard with a module language approach.

11.4 LANGUAGE ADAPTATION ISSUES (SYNTAX AND SEMANTICS)

In extending SQL to Object SQL, our overall aim was to provide a useful tool for an object environment while maintaining compatibility with the SQL standard. To this end, we have left the keywords and clause-level syntax of the language intact, while generalizing the semantics of the language's commands, and the syntax and semantics of its expressions, and names.

Where the language definition relies on relational concepts, we have tried to generalize the concepts into their object equivalents. Thus we treat *relations* as Vbase Aggregates, and *attributes* as Vbase PropertyTypes. We have also generalized the permissible expressions for particular clauses. Where the from-clause used to expect the names of *relations*, it now accepts aggregate-valued expressions; and where the select-clause in traditional SQL required expressions of *attributes*, Object SQL accepts any expression whether or not the expression's terms include a PropertyType. In order to provide the degree of extensibility expected in an object system we have expanded the syntax of expressions to allow for arbitrary procedure invocations. Finally, because object systems permit the denotation of individual entities (relational systems do *not* support tuple references), we extended the rules for name construction and interpretation. The following three sections examine the extensions to the language's commands, expressions, and naming system.

11.4.1 SQL Commands: Select, Insert, Update and Delete

The primary data management actions of SQL include the select, insert, update and delete commands. The initial version of Object SQL provides support only for the first of these; but as indicated in section 11.2, the extensions to the legal select expressions allow for the semantics of insert, update and delete within the context of a selection. While the Object SQL select command may be sufficient to accomplish any data management action, support for the insert, update and delete commands is important both for user convenience and for compatibility with the standard. The following sections explore the semantics of these commands.

Selection. In a general sense, selection in SQL transforms one or more groups of things into another group of things. The groups which form the source of this transformation may be called the *discourse domain* (sometimes abbreviated to "DD"), because they constitute the set of things about which a question is asked (and also because the name has a "techie" ring to it). We'll call the result of the transformation the *target domain*. The transformation itself consists of several optional phases:

1. **Combination**—If there is more than one group in the DD, the elements of each group are combined into a single group in what is known as a *join*.
2. **Filtering**—The DD is filtered according to some criteria on an instance by instance basis.
3. **Grouping**—The resulting collection is grouped such that each group member has the same value for some attribute.
4. **Filtering**—The resulting groups are again filtered, this time by a criterion which applies on a group by group basis (for example, groups with more than two members).
5. **Ordering**—The result is ordered on the basis of one or more attribute values.
6. **Projecting**—Each attribute in the target domain is computed by applying a function to each member of the result.
7. **Duplicate Elimination**—Duplicates in the result are filtered out.
8. **Naming**—A name/title is given to each attribute in the target domain.

While the transformations listed above are optional, they must occur in the given order (at least logically), if they occur at all. This is *not* to say that opting for a given transform, say grouping, requires that all preceding transformations be specified. The actual order of processing may sometimes be altered slightly for efficiency, but the result of the query should correspond exactly as if the order of these phases were maintained.

Specifying the Target and Discourse Domains with Select and From. As described above, all queries must minimally identify a discourse domain and a target domain. In SQL, these are introduced with two separate clauses. The from-clause lists all the groups in the discourse domain, and the select-clause describes the attributes of the target domain.

Let's start with the from-clause. Its basic syntax is as follows:

```
From   <comma separated list of aggregate-valued
          expressions >
```

as exemplified by:

```
From Person.Class                    % All People
From BostonWhitePages                % An OrderedDictionary
From Type.defprops, Type.defops      % Two DistributedSets
From $ComputeListOfMyFavoriteThings() % An operation
                                     % returning a List
```

The purpose of the from-clause is to identify a portion of the database as being pertinent to the current query. It's important to understand that this is an identification of both data (the members of the aggregates) *and* schema (the MemberSpecs of the aggregates). The transformation phases discussed in the previous section can be partitioned into two classes, according to whether they operate on the data or the schema of the discourse domain. The various filters, groupers, and sorters operate on the data. The projections and renames map the discourse domain schema onto the target domain schema. One final point about the from-clause. It's very common to wish to select from the class of a type. Rather than requiring users to enter $< type - name >$. Class (as above), Object SQL will accept a type name in the from-clause, and interpret it as a reference to its class.

The select-clause is used to specify a target domain. Its basic syntax looks like:

```
Select <comma separated list of expressions, usually of
          PropertyTypes>
```

as exemplified by:

```
Select Name, Age, Salary         % some properties of
                                 %             type Person
Select *                         % all properties
Select Salary + Commission       % an expression of two
                                 %             properties
Select List$Remove($FavoriteThings, $Rain) % an
                                 %   arbitrary expression
```

There's an important difference between components of a select-clause, and those of a from-clause. The latter are expressions which evaluate to real, existing aggregate objects. The former are expressions of PropertyTypes, which need not denote real, existing PropertyType objects. Essentially, a select-clause defines a record type, and individual select expressions define the fields of the record type. The point is that these definitions occur during query evaluation, and thus the results of a selection query are not objects which existed prior to the query. This is similar to the situation in relationally based SQLs, where the result of a query is not a table, even though it looks like one.

We just asserted that a select-clause is composed of expressions of PropertyTypes. This is not quite correct. It's composed of expressions of only those PropertyTypes which have been introduced by an associated from-clause. If the types in the union of the MemberSpecs of the aggregates of the from-clause (whew!) do not define or inherit a PropertyType, it is illegal to refer to that PropertyType in the select-clause.

Joins: Combining Elements in the Discourse Domain. When more than one aggregate is specified in a from-clause, SQL combines the aggregates' data and schema into a single group in an operation called a join. Joins are logically constructed by forming the cartesian product of the constituent aggregates. Suppose a from-clause referenced two aggregates $A1$ and $A2$ with MemberSpecs $MS1$ and $MS2$, whose basetypes were $T1$ and $T2$; and that $T1$ has $NP1$ number of PropertyTypes and $NI1$ number of instances; and that $T2$ has $NP2$ number of PropertyTypes and $NI2$ number of instances. The result of joining $A1$ with $A2$ would be a group with $(NP1 + NP2)$ number of properties, and $(NI1 * NI2)$ number of instances. The total number of values would be $((NP1 + NP2) * (NI1 * NI2))$. It's not hard to see that joins get big fast! The elements of a join consist of all possible combinations of $T1$ instances composed with $T2$ instances. If this sounds semantically meaningless, well, you don't need a hearing aid. The virtue of a join as a logical construction is that 1) it loses no information, and 2) that it maps two separate groups into a single group. The transforms of discourse domain to target domain all rely on mapping one group into another, so this initial combination is essential. While the definition for forming joins has been partly responsible for the poor reputation of relational database performance, it should be noted that no real vendor of relational databases actually performs joins this way. It's almost always possible to avoid forming cartesian products through the suitable use of references and hash table or btree access methods.

In object databases, it's rarely necessary to even express joins—much less have to optimize around them. The reason for this is that objects can directly refer to one another through their properties. In relational systems, tuples 'refer' to other tuples by storing an identical attribute value. The practical necessity of the join concept is to deduce an interrelationship from a common value.

Instance Filters: The Where-clause. The first permissible transformation on the discourse domain is an instance by instance filtering. The where-clause consists of a boolean expression, generally parameterized by at least one property of the discourse domain. The expression is evaluated in the context of each instance. If it evaluates to true, the instance is kept in the DD; otherwise, it is rejected. Though the precise description of boolean expressions is deferred until later, we'll just note here that SQL provides special syntax for comparing numbers, strings, and aggregates. This syntax is further extended to allow for database operations which return boolean objects. The where-clause is probably the most frequently used transform. One could go a long way with a subset of SQL which included only select, from and where.

Classifying: The GroupBy-clause. After applying an optional instance level filter, the user can choose to partition the DD into groups according to a common property value. The GroupBy-clause takes a list of PropertyTypes defined over the DD. All instances with the same value for the first such PropertyType are grouped together in the result. If a secondary grouping is specified, then all instances *within* a group which have a common value for the second PropertyType mentioned will be organized into subgroups, and so on. Such groupings can be useful in and of themselves to facilitate the visual assimilation of a query's results. If we wished to know whether defensive talent at the game of foosball among Ontologic employees was evenly distributed among tasks, we could ask:

```
Select Task.name
From Foosball_Players
Where Employer = Ontologic and DefensiveSkill = $High
Group By AssignedTask;
```

What we'd probably do with the result is count and record the number of results with the same task. This would be a bit easier because results with the same task would be printed together; but there's even a better way:

```
Select Task.name, count(*)
From Foosball_Players
Where Employer = Ontologic and DefensiveSkill = $High
Group By AssignedTask;
```

This would return one result for each task, consisting of the task name and the number of talented defensive specialists in that task. The count function in the select-clause is one of five aggregate functions with explicit syntactic support. The others are sum, avg, min, and max.

Filters on Groups: The Having-clause. If the DD has been grouped, it can be desirable to apply another level of filtering, to weed out uninteresting groups. The Having-clause is used for this purpose. It can only appear in conjunction with a GroupBy-clause. Its form is similar to the where-clause in that it consists of a parameterized boolean expression. It differs from the where, however, in that the parameter may only be referenced as an argument to an aggregate expression, as in

```
Select Task.name
From Foosball_Players
Where Employer = Ontologic and DefensiveSkill = $High
Group By AssignedTask
Having count(*) > 1;
```

which reports only those tasks whose members include more than one defensive specialist.

Ordering the Results: The OrderBy-clause.   The last transform applied strictly to the DD is ordering. Note that the target domain cannot be explicitly ordered. In most cases, the projection of the discourse domain onto the target domain preserves ordering; but this is not guaranteed. The mechanism for specifying an ordering is the OrderBy-clause. It consists of a list of pairs, where the first member of a pair is a PropertyType in the DD, and the second member is an optional specification of direction. The default direction is ascending (indicated by the `asc` keyword), but it is possible to request a descending ordering (`desc`) as well. When more than one $< PropertyType, direction >$ pair is given, the first acts as a major sort, and the remaining as minor sorts.

In typical relational implementations, all SQL data types support an ordering operation. This is not the case in Object SQL, where PropertyTypes may have valuespecs with an unordered domain. In Object SQL, the OrderBy-clause is only legal when the base type of the valuespec of the PropertyType defines (or inherits) an operation named "GreaterThan".

Projecting the Results: Field Specifications.   Projection is a phase which always occurs in an SQL query. It is the process of mapping the discourse domain (possibly filtered, grouped, filtered again, and sorted) onto the target domain. It is also the point in selection processing where object identity is lost. All of the previous transformations have mapped groups of instances onto smaller groups of instances based on some function of instance property values. Here the focus changes from the instances themselves to expressions of the instances.

In the initial discussion of the select-clause, it was asserted that the purpose of the select was to identify a target domain. An alternative way of looking at the function of the select-clause is to specify a projection matrix. In the general case, for each field or attribute in the target domain (it is no longer applicable to speak of PropertyTypes in the target domain), there is a function over potentially all of the PropertyTypes in the discourse domain.

Insertion.   In extending the semantics of the SQL *from* and *Insert into* clauses to permit any aggregate expression, we've introduced an ambiguity. In a relational framework, an insert-clause logically encapsulates two actions: the creation of a tuple, and the insertion of the tuple in a particular table. Anything else wouldn't make sense, as a tuple is always a part of one and only one table in a relational system. In an object system however, an object may be a member of several aggregations, and in some systems, need not be a part of any aggregation. Thus we have the problem of deciding whether or not to create an object before inserting it into the specified aggregate. This problem can be somewhat ameliorated by variations on the standard syntax of an insert command. A syntactic form such as:

```
Insert into <aggregate-of-person>
        values (name:'Harry', eyeColor:$Blue);
```

could be interpreted as first creating a person named Harry and then inserting Harry into the specified aggregate. A syntactic form such as:

```
Insert into <aggregate-of-person>
        select * from Person where name = 'Harry';
```

could be taken to mean "find the person named Harry, and insert him into the aggregate." But here we get back to the problem that the result of a selection is a record-type, not a pre-existing object. What's the solution? We don't know, but we hope there's a way to avoid coupling creation with aggregate insertion.

Deletion. As was the case with insertion, we encounter an ambiguity with the semantics of the Object SQL delete clause: should we simply remove the object from its aggregate, or should we destroy it as well? In this case, however, the resolution is simpler. We specify the meaning of removing an object from its type's class as destroying the object. Removing an object from a collection does not imply the destruction of the object. Thus, assuming "$Part" is the name of a type,

```
Delete From $Part
Where partNumber=345;
```

will destroy the part whose number is 345 (concomitantly removing it from its class), while will

```
Delete From $MyAssembly.part
Where partNumber=345;
```

remove the part whose number is 345 from the aggregate of parts in the object called "$MyAssembly", without destroying it.

There's a second issue involved with extending the semantics of delete: not all aggregates support a delete/remove operation. Indeed, the concept is inappropriate for fixed-size arrays and immutable sequences. Some aggregates, defined by insertion order (such as stacks and queues) support removals in only a limited sense (such as the top or first element). Furthermore, indexed and explicitly-ordered aggregates (such as dictionaries and lists), require additional information (a key or position) in order to perform a removal. In fact, the only aggregates which always permit removal are those defined by the identity of their elements (such as bags and sets).

One way of approaching this problem is to limit the types of aggregate permissible in the from-clause to bags, sets and classes. While this is plausible, it is perhaps more friendly to permit any aggregate specification, and to expand the meaning of the where-clause to be appropriate for the given type of aggregate, so long as it exports a remove operation. Thus

```
Delete From $MyList
Where position>2 and position <=7;
Delete From $MyDictionary
Where tag > ''osprey'' and tag < ''pelican'';
```

would remove the 3rd through 7th elements of a list in the first case, and all items associated with tags "osprey" through "pelican" in the latter case.

11.4.2 Expressions

Most of the major SQL clauses require associated expressions. The where-clause, for example, introduces a boolean-valued expression used as an instance filter. In Object SQL, the semantic basis for all expressions is the Vbase Procedure. Anywhere an expression is permitted, a procedure invocation using COP syntax may be employed. The following are all legal where-clause expressions:

```
Where  Entity$Equal (aPerson, $GeorgeWashington)
Where  List$IsMember ($GeorgeWashington, $USPresidents)
Where  Boolean$Not (Person$isMarried$Get (aPerson,
                          Person$isMarried))
```

Choosing Procedures as the semantic basis for expressions is an important extension for an object-based SQL. In relational systems, the number of data types is fixed. In object systems, the number of data types and their behavior is user-definable. Procedure based expressions allow SQL to keep up with user extensions. The fact that arbitrary procedures can have arbitrary side-effects is both a strength and a weakness. We could require that all expressions run in their own sub-transactions, and abort after returning their results (in order to undo any side-effect); but this seems unnecessary (in fact, since Transaction$Abort is itself a procedure, a user could achieve this effect if so desired). It is interesting to note that the procedural basis of expressions allows the effects of the insert, update, and delete commands to be achieved within the context of a select expression as in the following examples:

```
select Person$Create($Person, name:'Harry') from
                          type.supertypes;
select Person$Name$Set ($Harry, 'Fred', Person$Name)
                          from type.supertypes;
select Person$Delete ($Fred) from type.supertypes;
```

This sequence of queries causes a person named Harry to be created (logically, an insert command), then changes his name to Fred (logically, an update command), and then deletes him from the database (logically, a delete command). Note that the from-clause in these examples is used simply as a counter. In Version 1.0 of Vbase, types can have only one supertype, and this ensures that each of the select-clauses are evaluated only once. While the syntax for procedure invocations is all that is strictly necessary in formulating an expression, the examples above should illustrate its unwieldiness. Object SQL supports the forms of expressions in the ANSI SQL standard (translating them into the appropriate procedure invocations):

```
+, -, *, /        Number${Add,Subtract,Multiply,Divide}
=, <>             Entity$Equal, Boolean
                          $Not(Entity$Equal(...,...))
>, >=, <, <=      <type>$GreaterThan
```

In addition, Object SQL extends the dot notation used in the ANSI standard to indicate (possibly chained) property access. Thus:

```
aPerson.Mother Person$Mother$Get(aPerson,Person$Mother)
A.B.C          BType$C$Get(AType$B$Get(A,Atype$B),BType$C)
```

Allowing "chained" property access as in the example above may introduce a problem when any non-terminal property ("B" in the example) is multi-valued. In the collective interpretation of a multi-valued property (substitute Person$Children for "B"), the result is a Collection, and the succeeding property ("C") must be appropriate for the particular kind of collection (e.g., "Cardinality"). In the distributive interpretation of a multi-valued property (substitute Person$Child for "B"), the sub-expression "A.B" is itself multi-valued (it would have to evaluate to a different entity for each of A's children). Object SQL does not permit this case, and reports an ill-formed expression whenever a distributed property is non- terminal.

11.4.3 Naming

Name classes and construction. In environments with individually deno-table entities (i.e., object systems), there must be additional classes of names over and above those used in the SQL standard. Object SQL classifies names by the duration of their bindings: persistent, SQL-session specific, and query-local.

Persistent-named entities are those whose names span SQL queries and sessions. In Vbase, such names are recognized by an embedded '$', as in "Stack$Push" and "$MyFavoriteThings$WhiskersOnKittens". Depending on the context, names without an embedded '$' may still be interpreted as database names. This can occur in from- and select-clause expressions as discussed in the next section.

Many objects don't have a user-specified name. In Vbase this situation gener-ally arises when an object is created programmatically (i.e., in a COP program or via ITS or SQL) without assigning the Entity$Pathname property. When the result of an Object SQL query contains such objects, they are reported to the user via a session-specific generated name. In an ECAD domain, for example, a query which reports the connections between two pins might give a result such as "#4Connection". This name denotes a particular connection, and may be referenced in subsequent queries within a given SQL session. The query "select * from Connection c where c = #4Connection", for example, would list all the property values of #4Connection. Session-local names such as these are recognized by the presence of a leading '#' char-acter. They are generated by the SQL processor and may be referenced by a user. If a user specifies a session-local name which has not been previously reported by the SQL processor, the system will report a NameNotFound error.

 The final class of names are those local to a given query. The from-clause intro-duces named iteration variables over the discourse domain. In a clause such as "From President p", the name "p" may be used in any other clause (e.g., select- or where-) to denote the next President. In a clause such as "From President", the name "President" may be used as "p" in the previous example—to denote the next President in another clause of the same query. Query-local "variable" names are recognized as character strings without embedded '$' signs and without leading '#' characters, providing they are introduced in the from-clause.

Use and interpretation. The use and interpretation of query-local names in Object SQL is intended to follow the ANSI standard, which is oriented towards ease of use rather than conceptual simplicity. The precedence rules for introducing and interpreting such names are as follows:

1. When encountered in a from-clause, simple names (those without '$' or '#' signs) are always treated as variable declarations.

2. When encountered in expressions in other clauses, simple names are interpreted either as variable references or as property references.

3. When the expression is a chained property access ("A.B.C"), the second through the last components are always interpreted as property references.

4. When the simple name is the first component of a chained property access, or an argument to a function/procedure, or simply appears by itself, the system first tries the variable reference interpretation, and if that fails, then tries the property reference interpretation.

5. When interpreted as variable references, the binding of the simple name is to the next element of the discourse domain (the next tuple in the cartesian product). In the queries "select p.name from Pin p;" and "select Pin.name from Pin;", the 'p' in the select-clause takes on a different binding for each instance of type Pin in the first query, and "Pin" has the same interpretation in the select-clause of the second query.

6. When the variable reference interpretation fails, the system tries to interpret the name as a Property defined by the Type of the members of one of the discourse domain components (in Vbase terminology, the baseType of the memberSpec of one of the aggregate expressions in the from-clause). If no such property can be found, the query is ill-formed. If more than one such property can be found, the system selects the property based on the order of from-clause expressions. In the query "select coordinate ... from Pin, Transistor ...", the name "coordinate" is interpreted as a property of the ith Pin (if type Pin has such a property) or of the ith Transistor (if type Pin does not have such a property but type Transistor does).

7. The from-clause consists of a comma separated list of "FromExpressions", where a FromExpression consists of an AggregateExpression and an optional variable name. If the AggregateExpression is a simple name, the processor tries to interpret it as the persistent name of an aggregate. If this fails, it tries to interpret it as the persistent name of a type (whose class is to be taken as the aggregate). If the variable name is present and the AggregateExpression is a simple name, then both names may be used subsequently to denote the same element of the iteration.

Scoping. Object SQL permits arbitrary nesting of queries. A nested query is one which appears in the where-clause of another query. The naming environment of a nested query is inherited from its containing query, and may be extended with its own local variable definitions. When the nested query introduces a name (in its from-clause) which is identical to an inherited name (from the from-clause of its containing queries), the local definition takes precedence within the scope of the nested query.

11.5 SOME OPTIMIZATION EXTENSIONS

Like other 4GLs, SQL provides users with a means of specifying what should be done but not with a means of specifying how to process a request. In many cases there are different possible answers to the how question, each with different performance characteristics. When we speak of query optimizations, we're really talking about the methods chosen by the query processor for fielding the users' requests. Perhaps the most important optimizations are those which reduce the effective cardinality of the discourse domain, either by eliminating unnecessary discourse domain components or by avoiding the necessity of computing a full cartesian product. When SQL is brought into an object environment, new possibilities for such optimizations naturally arise.

11.5.1 A Bit of Theory Regarding the Optimization of Equi-Joins

Consider the case of an equi-join condition such as "$Where f(x) = g(y)$". The obvious means of dealing with this filter is to enumerate all $< x, y >$ tuples, while passing on those for which the expression "$Entity\$Equal(f(x), g(y))$" returns $\$True$. But unless the number of $< x, y >$ tuples is very small, there is always an important and easily applicable optimization here. The key point is to note that the functions "f" and "g" must have the same range-domain in order to be comparable by entity equality. Let's call that range domain "RD". Now suppose there existed a function "h" such that "h" was the inverse function of "g." The "h" function would take an element from "RD" and map it back to an element in the domain of "y". If the SQL processor knew of such a function, then it could eliminate "y" from the where-clause and compute "$Where f(x) = g(h(f(x)))$" instead. More to the point, it could simply yield a tuple of the form $< x, h(f(x)) >$.

11.5.2 Finding Inverse Functions in an Object System

This may be of theoretical interest, but how can the SQL processor know how to find such an inverse function? There are two answers to this question. The first is that in Vbase (and perhaps other object systems as well), there is a concept of an inverse property. Consider a query such as

```
select p.Name
from Company c, Person p
where c.CEO= p.wife;
```

which finds the names of all men whose wives are the CEO of a company. Noting that the `Person$Wife` property has an inverse called `Person$Husband`, Object SQL can transform the query into the simpler

```
select c.CEO.husband.name
from Company c
where hasvalue (c.CEO.husband);
```

In the new formulation, the cardinality of the discourse domain has been reduced from ($|Company| * |Person|$) to ($|Company|$). The number of property accesses per iteration, which was previously three (one for `p.name`, one for `c.CEO`, and one for `p.wife`) can be kept the same through the use of common subexpression optimizations (the expression "`c.CEO.husband`" need only be evaluated once per iteration).

11.5.3 Constructing Inverse Functions Using Unordered Dictionaries

What if the inverse function "h" does not already exist, or cannot be located by the Object SQL processor? Well, then it can be constructed on the fly via the use of hash tables. The idea here is that we compute $f(x)$, and store the pair $< f(x), x >$ in an Unordered-Dictionary where $f(x)$ is the key and x the value. Then we iterate over the "y" domain, computing the function $g(y)$, and yield the tuple $< theDictionary[g(y)], y >$. The hash table acts as the inverse function "h", constructed during the iteration over the x domain and used during the iteration over the y domain. The computational cost of this approach is ($(C1 * |x|) + (C2 * |y|)$), where $C1$ is the cost of computing $f(x)$ plus the cost of insertion into the hash table, and $C2$ is the cost of computing $g(y)$ plus the cost of hash table retrieval. The important point here is that the cost of hash table insertion and retrieval is relatively constant (actually, the linear hashing algorithm used in Vbase varies in cost between narrow constant bounds), partly because it uses fixed-size object references for both key and data. By way of contrast, the unoptimized approach has a cost proportional to $|x| * |y|$ rather than $|x| + |y|$.

11.6 CLOSING REMARKS

Providing an SQL with object extensions is an idea with plausible merit. From the standpoint of an SQL user, an object paradigm can serve to radically reduce the complexity of formulating a query. For those who follow the evolution of the SQL language, object extensions may obviate the need for special syntactic support for the "parts explosion" problem, provide built-in support for the maintenance of referential integrity, and allow for a new class of optimizations. The users and developers of object systems should find that an Object SQL provides a convenient mechanism for manipulating groups of things and for posing ad hoc queries without needing to write a program to find and display results.

ACKNOWLEDGMENTS

The authors would like to acknowledge the help of Laurie Bruce, Paul Martel and Bob Strong for their assistance both with the design of Object SQL and with the review of this chapter.

12 Integrating an Object Server with Other Worlds

Alan Purdy, Bruce Schuchardt and David Maier

12.1 INTRODUCTION

During the last three years a team at Servio designed and implemented an object-oriented database server (or object server) called GemStone[1] [Maier85, Maier86a, Maier86b]. GemStone delivers to application developers a database subsystem with a Smalltalk-like object model instead of one of the more traditional record-oriented models (e.g., relational, hierarchical). This object model allows applications to manage information (e.g., documents, pictures, sound) not easily handled by more traditional database systems.

The GemStone server provides neither graphics nor terminal handling support for building end-user interfaces to database applications. Instead of trying to support fast-response user I/O from a central machine, we assume that application development and application use is centered at a personal workstation such as an IBM-PC[2] or a Smalltalk machine (Figure 12.1). The workstation, in turn, communicates with a GemStone object server (and other servers) over a network. The workstation's dedicated processing power provides the capabilities required for high-quality interfaces to application users (e.g., bitmap graphics, mouse, windows), while the object server provides modeling power and efficient sharing of persistent objects. The computing environments on these workstations represent the "other worlds" with which the GemStone object server must be integrated.

We begin this chapter with a review of the GemStone system, covering the motivation for GemStone, the object model, the OPAL[3] language, and GemStone's database

---

[1]GemStone is a registered trademark of Servio Logic Development Corporation.

[2]IBM-PC is a registered trademark of IBM Corporation

[3]OPAL is a registered trademark of Servio Logic Development Corporation.

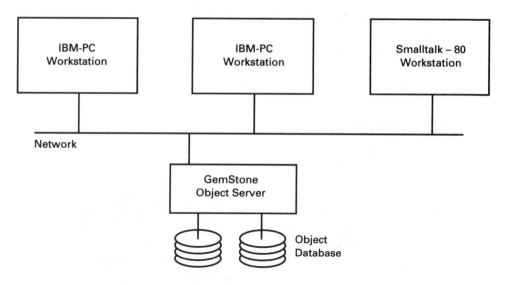

Figure 12.1 System topology.

features. We then describe an interface to GemStone from the "procedural world" of a language such as C or Pascal. This interface supports both the application development tools delivered with GemStone and application programs running on the workstation.

The GemStone system architects ultimately wish to provide a single "seamless" environment to application developers working in an "object-oriented world," such as Smalltalk, and wishing to use GemStone's features. Although integrating GemStone with another "object world" would seem easier than integrating it with a "procedural world", this task is more complex than it first appears. We discuss the requirements for a seamless integration and then present a design framework based on passive and active "agents" [Decouchant86, Woo85] for GemStone objects. We conclude with a discussion of our progress toward the "seamless" goal, and the open research issues concerning a seamless integration.

12.1.1 Motivation for GemStone

The limitations imposed by the record-oriented data model of most database systems severely restrict the kinds of information that can be easily managed by these systems. GemStone was designed to greatly increase the data-modeling power of a database component with the hope of vastly reducing the development time of applications with complex information needs. Such applications include office information systems, computer-aided design, documentation of complex mechanical systems (automobiles, air-frames), and artificial intelligence knowledge bases. Such a system's data model should support the definition of new data types, rather than constrain designers to a fixed set of predefined types. Also, the bounds on the number and size of data objects should be determined only by the amount of secondary memory, not primary memory. Such a system should also provide shared access to persistent data in a multiuser environment with the usual database amenities such as concurrency control, recovery, authorization, and system management functions. Finally, the system should have an interactive interface for defining new database objects, writing database routines, and executing ad hoc queries.

By combining the capabilities of an object-oriented language with the storage management functions of a traditional data management system we assumed that we would meet these goals and provide an environment that would reduce application development effort and promote data sharing among applications.

12.1.2 GemStone Object Model

GemStone's object model is identical to that of Smalltalk-80[4] [Goldberg83]. The three principal concepts of the GemStone object model are *object, message,* and *class*. These correspond roughly to *record, procedure call,* and *record type* in conventional systems. An object is a private memory with a public interface. The private memory of (most) objects is structured as a list of *instance variables* containing their values. Instance variables are like field names in a record or indices in an array; their values are references to other objects. Objects communicate with other objects only by passing messages among themselves. These messages are requests for an object to change its state, to return a value (i.e., another object), or to perform some sequence of actions. The set of messages to which an object responds (the public interface) is called its *protocol*. An object may only inspect or change another object by sending a message to it. Each object responds to a received message by executing a *method* written in the OPAL language. Objects sharing the same format and methods are grouped into a *class* and called *instances* of the class. The methods and format of a class's instances are factored and stored once, giving a single object describing the class, the *class-defining object*. Each instance of a given class contains a reference to its class definition. The classes in GemStone are arranged in a *class hierarchy*, with each subclass inheriting behavior and structure from its superclasses. When a message is received by an object, the object consults with this class (and potentially its superclasses) to locate the proper method for execution.

12.1.3 OPAL Language

The OPAL language syntax and semantics are nearly identical to the Smalltalk language presented by Goldberg and Robson [Goldberg83]. OPAL and Smalltalk share two major language constructs: message expressions and method definitions. Each is discussed below.

Message expressions. All message expressions look like <receiver> <message>. Each receiver is either a variable identifier, a literal, or another expression denoting an object that receives and interprets the message. Each message contains a *selector* (a procedure name) and possibly message *arguments*. When a message expression is executed, another object is returned as the value of the message expression. Thus a message receiver may be an expression that, when evaluated, returns an object that is then sent another message.

OPAL supports three kinds of messages: unary, binary, and keyword. Unary messages have no arguments and have a single identifier as a selector, for example,

```
5 negated
```

[4]Smalltalk-80 is a registered trademark of Xerox Corporation.

This expression sends the unary message composed of the unary selector `negated` to the object 5 and returns the object whose value is −5. Binary message expressions have a receiver, one argument, and a message selector that comprises one or two nonalphanumeric characters. For example, to multiply 8 by 3, we send the message "*3" or "multiply by 3" to the receiver "8":

```
8 * 3
```

This binary expression returns the object 24. In this example, the binary selector * is used for multiplication. Comparisons are binary messages too:

```
emp1 salary<=emp2 salary
```

This binary expression demonstrates precedence. The two unary messages with the selector `salary` have precedence over the binary message whose selector is <=. Thus, the salaries of `emp1` and `emp2` are compared with the binary message. Keyword messages have one or more arguments and multipart selectors composed of alphanumeric characters and colons. For example, to set the third component of an array held in anArray to the string 'Ross', we use

```
anArray at 3 put: 'Ross'
```

In this example, the selector is read as "at:put:" with the two arguments of 3 and 'Ross'.

Methods. Methods define all execution in GemStone. Each method corresponds to one message selector and is defined within the scope of the class instance that is the receiver of the message. Thus, a method can directly access the named instance variables of the receiving object. A method (like a Pascal function) has a formal declaration, an optional declaration of temporary variables, and a body composed of a sequence of OPAL message expressions. The method body always returns a value to the sender of the original message. The following example defines a method whose unary selector is `wholeName`. This method first defines a temporary variable named `temp`. The method body assigns an instance variable named `first` to the temporary, then concatenates the temporary, a blank, and the value of the instance variable `last`. Finally, it returns the result of that concatenation to the sender of the message.

```
wholeName
    |temp|
    temp := first.
    ↑temp + ' ' + last
```

12.1.4 GemStone Database Features

GemStone combines the database management features common to most commercial database systems (e.g., Ingres [Stonebraker86b], IMS [IBM74]) with the object-oriented data model provided by the Smalltalk-80 system. GemStone's main features are:

Sharing of Objects. GemStone provides each user with a distinct list of dictionaries called a `symbolList`. Although this list is private to each user, the dictionaries it contains can be shared. Thus a dictionary shared by two users allows the sharing of the objects contained in that dictionary. A dictionary is a collection of key-value pairs and supports the naming of objects. In this context a dictionary acts much like a file directory.

Resilience to Common Failure Modes. The data in a database often represent a significant capital expense. Most database users, including users of GemStone, expect their databases to survive all power failures that do not permanently damage the secondary storage media. In addition, if the reliability of the disk drives is insufficient, users can selectively replicate the stored objects on line, ensuring that the database survives single-point disk failures.

Multiple Concurrent Users. The standard mechanism for sharing a database requires the concept of a transaction. Intended changes to a database become visible to others when a user successfully commits changes. GemStone uses an optimistic concurrency control policy [Kung81].

Security. Database systems must secure information from unauthorized change or access. GemStone secures the object database by first authenticating each user through a user name and password. Along with user authentication, groups of objects may be explicitly marked as either read only, read/write, or no privileges for selected users.

Centralized Server. GemStone is a centralized server for a database of objects. It currently does not allow a database to be distributed among several GemStone servers.

Primary and Secondary Storage Management. GemStone hides from application designers the paging of objects between secondary and primary memory, and supports objects larger than what can fit in the server's primary memory.

Method Execution. GemStone supports a Smalltalk-like execution model on the server. This capability gives the application designer using GemStone a choice: copy an object's state to the workstation for manipulation or execute messages remotely on the GemStone server.

Uniform Language. GemStone presents one language, OPAL [Maier85, Maier86a], to its users. Through OPAL the user manipulates the information in the database (Data Management Language), defines new classes (Data Definition Language), writes portions of application programs (General Computation Language), and controls the GemStone server (System Command Language).

Fast Associative Access. Database systems are traditionally efficient at finding all members of a set meeting a selection criteria. GemStone allows users to dynamically add (or remove) associative access structures to accelerate such membership tests [Maier86b].

12.1.5 An Example Application

To illuminate the ideas in this chapter, we present a simple document archiving system. For this example a set of documents is stored on GemStone in a user-specific dictionary. The application accesses this set to find a given document, update a document, and call a new document. A document set is hierarchical: it can contain both documents and other sets of documents. A user can move documents between sets and can have the same document appear in multiple sets. The main classes in this example are Dictionary, SetOfEntries, and Document. A Dictionary is a subclass of Set and stores an unordered collection of Associations between a name and any arbitrary object. SetOfEntries is a subclass of Array that stores list of Associations. SetOfEntries differs from Dictionary in that it maintains a user-specified order on its entries. Each entry in a `SetOfEntries` associates the name of an entry with the value of an entry. In our example, the value will be either an instance of `Document` or another instance of `SetOfEntries`. A document has two instance variables, `header` and `body`; both are instances of `String`. A more complete system would impose further structure, such as headings, sections, and paragraphs, on the body of a document. Figure 12.2 illustrates a database containing pieces of manuals. Note that one of the documents is shared by two entries in `Manuals`.

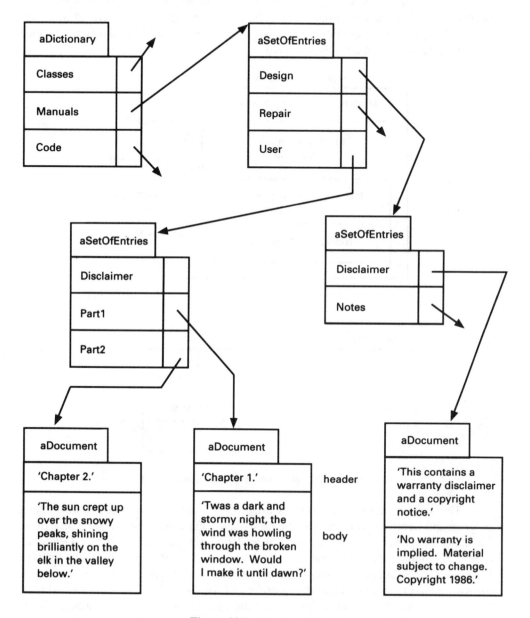

Figure 12.2 Structured documents example.

12.2 INTEGRATING GemStone WITH A PROCEDURAL ENVIRONMENT

To support applications in the "procedural world", GemStone provides a C and Pascal callable object module (Figure 12.3), which the designer links with applications running on an IBM-PC. The Procedural Interface Module (PIM) implements remote procedure calls [White86] to functions supplied by the GemStone object server. The PIM hides the network communications protocols and provides calls to GemStone for controlling sessions, transporting object states between the two environments, and sending messages to objects residing on GemStone. The calls in each category are described in Tables I-III. Although these descriptions somewhat simplify the actual PIM functions supplied by GemStone, the essentials are preserved.

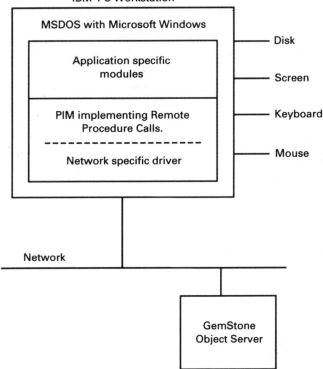

Figure 12.3 Workstation details showing PIM.

The session-controlling functions establish a connection between a workstation program and GemStone, control GemStone sessions, and control GemStone transactions. The other categories of functions allow workstation procedures to reference GemStone objects by unique identifiers that are represented in C or Pascal by variables of type Oop (for Object-Oriented Pointer). Before sending a message to a GemStone object, the workstation must first obtain the identifiers of the receiving object, the desired message selector (which will be an instance of the class Symbol), and the message's arguments. To use the object transportation, the designer must know how to interpret

GemStone's objects when their state is "fetched" into the application process on the PC. Knowledge of the following object formats is sufficient for building applications: Number, Character, Boolean, UndefinedObject, byte objects, pointer objects, and class-defining objects. All the functions take a session identifier as an argument, which we have omitted for simplicity.

TABLE I. SESSION CONTROLLING FUNCTIONS

`Logon(UserID, Password)`	Create a virtual circuit to the object server, and authenticate the user. The PIM hides from the application the details of the actual communications protocol
`Logoff`	Abort the current transaction, log the user off the server, and disconnection the session's virtual circuit
`AttemptCommit`	Attempt to commit the changes since this user's last transaction. If the transaction succeeds, true is returned; otherwise, false is returned
`Abort`	Tell GemStone to discard all the intended changes to the database since this transaction began. Begin a new transaction
`SignalInterrupt`	This function is an asynchronous action that signals the server to stop whatever it is doing for this user and await further instructions
`Resume`	Tells the suspended GemStone session to continue from where it was suspended

TABLE II. REMOTE MESSAGE SENDING FUNCTIONS

`SendMessage (ResultId, ReceiverId, MessageId)`
Send the given message to the indicated receiver object. The server executes the indicated method and returns the result. Each argument to SendMessage is in the form of a GemStone object identifier. Internal to the IBM-PC, these are represented as 32-bit values

`ExecuteStatements (ResultId, StatementsId)`
Send a sequence of OPAL statements in text form to the object server, which compiles it, executes it, and returns the result

TABLE III. OBJECT TRANSPORTING FUNCTIONS

`Fetch (ObjectId, From, To, Buffer)`
Copy the given object's state from the server to the application process buffer. The caller may selectively move a fragment of the object

`FetchInfo (ObjectId, Size, ClassId, Form)`
Return an object's metainformation to the application process, including its size in bytes or pointers, its class, and its format (bytes, pointers, atoms)

`Store (ObjectId, From, To, Buffer)`
Copy the given object's state from the application process' buffer to the server. The caller may selectively move a fragment of the object

`Instantiate (ClassId, NewObjectId)`
Create a new object of a given class and return its object identifier to the application

For the primitive GemStone classes of SmallInteger, Character, Boolean, and Undefined Object, the state (or value) of an instance is directly encoded in its Oop. The PIM includes utility functions to convert between C or Pascal values and their equivalents for instances of these classes. The PIM also includes functions to convert between GemStone floating-point and large integer values and their Pascal or C equivalents. Applications access information about other GemStone objects by sending messages to objects (for execution on GemStone) or by fetching object states from the object server into the Pascal or C address space. An object's state will be formatted either as an array of bytes (e.g., instances of String or Symbol) or as an array of Oops, each of which identifies another GemStone object. Although giving an application direct access to the internal state of a GemStone object violates the integrity of an object, such access is necessary for efficient copying of objects between GemStone and the workstation. For example, without these transporting functions, access to each character in a String instance would require a separate PIM call. Because class definitions and methods are themselves objects and respond to the same functions as other objects, the PIM supports class and method definition. In practice, a designer rarely defines these directly through the PIM. Classes and methods are more often defined through the browser in the OPAL Programming Environment or through some other application written on top of the PIM.

12.2.1 Example of PIM's Use

This section provides Pascal code fragments for the application described above in section 12.1.5. This application accepts from the user a path to a document such as User/Part1, copies the given document's body to a local file called MyManual-Body for editing, then moves the edited string back to GemStone as the document's new body before committing the transaction. The OPAL compiler accesses a user's symbolList (See section 12.1.4) when compiling OPAL source code submitted by the user. We assume that all users of this application have an object named Manuals in one of their symboList dictionaries. Thus any OPAL code sent to ExecuteStatements that mentions Manuals will obtain an object corresponding to that name.

```
{Include the PIM external declarations}
PROCEDURE TransferString(AnOop: OOP; Size: INTEGER;
FileName: STRING);
{Move a string from a GemStone database to a local file}
   CONST MaxChunk = 512;
   TYPE
      ChunkRange = 1 . . MaxChunk;
      Chunks = ARRAY[ChunkRange] OF BYTE;
   VAR
      Next: INTEGER; Chunk: Chunks;
      ChunkSize: ChunkRange; Outfile: FILE OF Chunks;
   BEGIN
   Next   :=  1;
   ChunkSize    :=    MaxChunk;
   OPEN(OutFile, FileName);
   WHILE Next <= Size DO BEGIN
      IF(Size - Next + 1) < MaxChunk THEN
```

```
                ChunkSize   := Size - Next + 1;
            Fetch(AnOop, Next, Next + ChunkSize - 1, Chunk);
            Write(OutFile, Chunk: ChunkSize);
            Next  := Next + ChunkSize;
            END;
        CLOSE(OutFile);
    END;
    PROCEDURE ExampleProgram;
        VAR Body, Class: OOP; Size, Form: INTEGER;
            Path: STRING;
            Success: BOOLEAN;
        BEGIN
            IF Logon('Alan', 'SwordFish') THEN BEGIN
                {Logon with Id, Password}
            ReadLn(Path);
            ExecuteStatements(Body, 'Manuals find.
                            '''+Path+''') body');
            {The preceding assumes the existence on GemStone
             of a method named find: for a SetOfEntries that
             takes a path argument (such as 'User/Part1') and
             returns the appropriate object.  It also assumes
             that a Document responds to body by returning
             the body's string.}
            FetchInfo(Body, Size, Class, Form);
            IF Class = StringClassOop THEN BEGIN
                TransferString(Body, Size, 'MyManualBody');
                {...  Edit the Body}
                {...  Transfer it back to GemStone}
                END;
                Success := AttemptCommit;   {Try to commit the
                                               changes}
            Logoff;
            END
    END;
```

12.2.2 A Critique of the PIM in Practice

Servio found the Procedural Interface Module adequate for building the applications that constitute the OPAL Programming Environment (OPE) that runs on the IBM-PC under Microsoft Windows[5]. The OPE includes

- *Class browser*, which allows a user to examine, add, and modify GemStone class and method definitions (this browser is similar to the class browser in the Smalltalk-80 programming environment [Goldberg84]);

---

[5]Windows is a registered trademark of Microsoft Corporation.

- *Bulk loader/dumper*, which allows a user to transfer formatted data with fixed record types between PC-based files and GemStone;
- *Workspace editor*, which allows a user to enter, edit, and execute OPAL expressions.

Each of these OPE applications accesses information stored on the GemStone object server. In each case the designer wrote the user interface code for the application in Microsoft C, accessed GemStone through the PIM, and accessed the user through Microsoft Windows. Once our designers became familiar with these tools, the delivery of a new application often became primarily an exercise in specification. For example, a document archive application similar to the preceding example took one developer three days to design, code, and test.

This ease of development is not without a high training and education cost. The GemStone object server requires the application designer to be familiar with GemStone's PIM, its OPAL language, transactions, and other concepts of database management. Although Microsoft Windows vastly improves the quality of an application's human interface, windows imposes its own long learning curve.

The option of two execution environments (PC or GemStone) complicates the application design process: The designer must decide whether to copy an object to the PC for processing or to forward messages for execution on the server. This decision is rarely simple. It often requires an intimate understanding of the relative speed of the two execution environments, the bandwidth connecting the two machines, and the degree of competition for that bandwidth. GemStone offers relatively fast access to the structure of objects, but it is slower than most implementations of Smalltalk for general computation. Thus, extensive arithmetic and string operations are best performed on the PC. The path parsing code we referenced above (find:) would probably execute more quickly on the PC if we ignored the time required to transfer instances of SetOfEntries. Because of this transfer time, however, the find: function would probably take less clock time if it executed on GemStone. Also, when an object's state is copied to the PC, the application designer must ensure that any changes to that copy are transferred to GemStone at the appropriate point (i.e., prior to committing a transaction).

The PIM does not provide certain functions needed by most applications. For example, the PIM lacks the following:

Control of Cached GemStone Objects. If the object states cached in the PC were managed directly by the PIM, then two modules of an application accessing the same object would access the same state. As the PIM currently stands, if two modules each cache object states, the designer must guard against the same object being cached twice. This is especially important if both modules are modifying objects in their cache.

Functions to Transfer Large Objects. Applications often move large objects between local files on the workstation and the GemStone object server. The example above demonstrates the kind of function needed.

Transitive Transfers. Because a GemStone object can be composed of references to other GemStone objects, we also need standard procedures for transporting all the objects transitively reachable from a given object.

Before we provide these functions in the "procedural world," we first wanted to prototype them in a Smalltalk-80 integration with GemStone. Smalltalk's "object world" is more supportive of such experimentation. In the next section we discuss the design and prototype implementation of this integration.

12.3 INTEGRATING THE GemStone AND Smalltalk-80 ENVIRONMENTS

The task of integrating GemStone with the Smalltalk-80 environment appears easy because both share similar data models and similar languages. However, this task offers several difficult challenges. In this section we first define the goals of such an integration, then describe a design framework based on *agents*, which are Smalltalk representatives of GemStone objects. These agents are of two kinds: *proxies*, which are little more than a transparent packaging of the PIM remote message sending functions for the Smalltalk environment, and *deputies*, which take a more active role in implementing various policies for caching the state of GemStone objects in Smalltalk's object memory. Pasco's encapsulators [Pasco86] have characteristics similar to this agent model.

12.3.1 Integration Goals

We want to provide developers with the illusion of one uniform application development environment quite unlike what the PIM provides to Pascal and C developers. Such a "seamless" integration would combine Smalltalk's development environment with GemStone's ability to easily access and modify persistent, shared, and secure objects. This integration has the following specific goals:

Object Transparency. Object transparency allows developers to design and implement applications without caring where an object is located or where a method is executed. Object transparency frees most developers from dealing with difficult caching and communication issues that arise when transporting objects or messages between Smalltalk's object memory and GemStone's stable storage. For example, the method that adds a new entry to a SetOfEntries in the document archive example should not need to test whether the SetOfEntries is cached in the Smalltalk workstation.

Automatic Database Object Creation. Objects created in the Smalltalk environment should continue as Smalltalk objects until they are referenced by a GemStone object. All Smalltalk objects referenced by a GemStone object should be converted automatically to GemStone database objects. In our example application a seamless system should automatically convert a new Smalltalk document to a GemStone document when it is added to a GemStone SetOfEntries.

Tuning Options. Sophisticated designers should be given techniques for increasing the performance of working applications. For tuning reasons a designer may wish to change the policies for caching the states of selected GemStone objects in Smalltalk's object memory. Also, because GemStone and Smalltalk-80 both provide an environment for method execution, a designer should be given control of where a method is executed. However, designers need reasonable defaults for such choices to allow them to ignore these concerns in the initial implementation stages. Note that this tuning goal conflicts with the object transparency goal.

Transparent Garbage Collection. The Smalltalk-80 environment frees application developers from explicitly deallocating the space occupied by unreferenced objects. An integrated system should continue to perform this function in an invisible fashion.

Session and Transaction Control. GemStone is a transaction-based database system. Thus developers need control of transactions (atomic actions) and control over the GemStone session from within the Smalltalk-80 environment. In addition, the integrated system should automatically synchronize GemStone object states cached in the Smalltalk-80 object memory with their states within GemStone when a transaction commits or aborts.

Transparent Exception Handling. The Smalltalk-80 environment provides several ways to handle exceptional conditions. The application developer should see a uniform exception handling mechanism independent of the machine where the exception occurs.

Uniform Name Binding. The Smalltalk-80 system binds names to Smalltalk objects at several distinct times: during compilation, during method initiation, and during method execution. Persistent GemStone objects should also participate in each of these binding times. For instance, we noted before that GemStone maintains a `symbolList` of symbolic names on behalf of each GemStone user. Those names should be available whenever name binding occurs in the Smalltalk-80 environment.

12.3.2 A Design Overview

Our design for integrating the Smalltalk-80 environment with a GemStone object server is based on a new Smalltalk class called `Agent`. An agent is often defined as someone authorized to act in another's interest. The other party is sometimes called the principal. In our design, instances of `Agent` (always Smalltalk objects) act in the interest of principals, which are GemStone objects. An agent knows the GemStone Oop of the principal it represents. Messages sent to a GemStone object from within the Smalltalk environment are directed through the object's Smalltalk agent. `Agent` is an abstract class (only its subclasses have instances) having the subclasses `Proxy` and `Deputy` (Figure 12.4). Although both *proxy* and *deputy* seem to be synonyms for *agent*, their connotations differ. Proxies usually act on behalf of their principal in a very constrained and limited capacity, such as voting shares of stock or standing in for a bride or groom at a marriage ceremony where the principal cannot be present. In contrast, deputies often have much more authority to make decisions on behalf of their principal. For example, a deputy foreign minister may be authorized to negotiate a trade agreement with perhaps only the final terms subject to ratification by the principal.

Instances of our `Proxy` class act only as forwarding agents, keeping no local information about their principal, other than its GemStone Oops and GemStone class. Each `Proxy` instance forwards messages that it receives to its principal for execution on GemStone and routes the result back to the sender of the Smalltalk message. These proxies offer Smalltalk programmers a substantial improvement over the PIM style of interface because they package messages and arguments in proper form for network communication, unpackage the results, and perform simple translations between Smalltalk and GemStone messages. Such a generic proxy performs correctly with a principal of any GemStone class. Using a minor variant of the proxy scheme, Servio has reimplemented

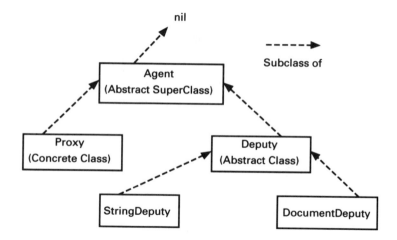

Figure 12.4 Relationship among kinds of agent classes.

many of the OPE tools for the Smalltalk environment, but with much less programming than the original effort, which used C, Windows, and the PIM.

Deputies implement more sophisticated policies for message handling. Deputies may cache all or part of their principal's state in the Smalltalk object memory. Thus different subclasses of `Deputy` can implement distinct policies for message processing and cache management. Some may decide always to cache a GemStone object's state in Smalltalk's object memory and execute messages locally in the Smalltalk environment. Others may selectively execute some messages in the Smalltalk environment and forward others for execution in GemStone. We consider the implementation options for `Deputy` subclasses in more detail later in this chapter.

The last new Smalltalk class in our design is `GemSession` (Figure 12.5), whose instances represent active database sessions with GemStone. An instance of `GemSession` provides all the functions of the PIM. However, only proxies and deputies will use those functions listed in Tables II and III. Most applications will send messages directly to a GemSession only for session and transaction control (i.e., PIM functions in Table I) and for error control. An application may register an error block with a `GemSession` to be executed in the Smalltalk environment with the appropriate error code whenever GemStone raises an exception. A `GemSession` ensures that each GemStone principal represented by a Smalltalk object has at most one agent, via a list called `registered-Agents` that associates each Smalltalk agent with its principal. Before a new agent is created for a GemStone object, `GemSession` consults `registered-Agents` to see whether an agent for that object already exists. This list also supports cache consistency for deputies. When a `GemSession` receives a commit message, it notifies all deputies of its intent to commit. Each deputy then flushes any modified cached state to GemStone. A `GemSession` also notifies deputies whenever a transaction aborts, telling each deputy to invalidate its cached GemStone object state.

Two new Smalltalk objects complete this design. The first is called the **import-Equivalents**. This set maps GemStone classes to their equivalents in the Smalltalk environment, typically a deputy or proxy class. GemSession uses `importEquivalents`

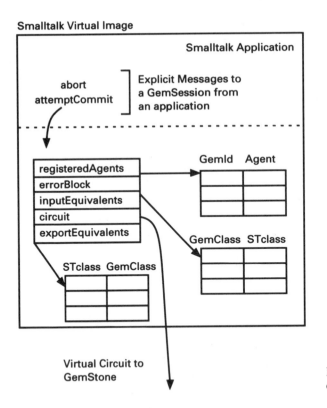

Smalltalk Virtual Image

Smalltalk Application

abort
attemptCommit

Explicit Messages to
a GemSession from
an application

registeredAgents
errorBlock
inputEquivalents
circuit
exportEquivalents

GemId   Agent

GemClass   STclass

STclass   GemClass

Virtual Circuit to
GemStone

Figure 12.5 A GemSession object
detail.

to decide what kind of a Smalltalk object to create when a GemStone object is first referenced from the Smalltalk environment. For immutable GemStone objects that have well-known behavior, the equivalent import class need not be a subclass of Agent. For example, in the cases of numbers and characters, GemSession returns a reference to an equivalent Smalltalk object.

The second new Smalltalk object is called **exportEquivalents**. This set maps Smalltalk classes to their equivalents in the GemStone environment. GemStone uses this set to decide what kind of GemStone object to create when a new Smalltalk object is first exported to GemStone. Ideally, if a Smalltalk object does not already have an equivalent GemStone class in the exportEquivalents set, GemSession will create a new GemStone class of the same name, recompile its methods in the GemStone environment, update exportEquivalents, and add a proxy class for the new GemStone class to importEquivalents. This new proxy class simply forwards all messages. Most Smalltalk methods require only slight syntactic modification before recompilation in the GemStone environment.

The preceding design meets the goals of object transparency, automatic database object creation, tuning options, and session and transaction control. Existing Smalltalk applications can use agents without noticing that they are such; agents present a protocol much as any other Smalltalk object, yet, they are actually manipulating persistent, shared GemStone objects. Designers can experiment with new caching policies without modifying the application by creating new deputies and modifying importEquivalents.

12.3.3 Implementation of Agents

In an agent's masquerade, it forwards to its principal on GemStone most of the messages that it receives. For efficiency reasons, however, agents (and especially deputies) execute some messages in the Smalltalk environment, particularly those that depend on the principal's identify or class. Selectors like = = (test of identity) and isNil (test for nil) are among the many that all agents can process locally.

An Agent must first examine a message intended for its principal before deciding whether to invoke a local Smalltalk method or forward the message for execution on GemStone. Because a class usually inherits messages from all its superclasses (in the agent's case, Object), this examination is not always easy. Methods inherited from Object do not provide an opportunity for the agent object to decide where work is to be performed. Unfortunately, all sorts of behavior are implemented in Object that, in the proxy's case, should be forwarded to GemStone. To handle these inherited messages properly, agents could reimplement all messages inherited from Object and forward selected messages on to GemStone.

The scheme above will not work for a generic proxy that forwards any arbitrary message to its principal. This case can be managed if we alter the standard message lookup behavior by putting nil in the agent's superClass variable and rewrite the instance method doesNotUnderstand:. Thus, when a message is sent to an agent, no instance method corresponding to the message is found. Smalltalk in this case sends the doesNotUnderstand: message to the original receiver and passes the original message as its argument. The new doesNotUnderstand: can establish a default behavior for all messages an agent receives (e.g., always forwarded in the case of a proxy). This same technique can be used to forward messages not reimplemented for each deputy.

Whenever GemStone returns one of its object's Oops to the Smalltalk environment, GemSession ensures that an agent exists for that object by performing the following steps:

1. See whether this GemStone principal already has an agent by looking in registeredAgents. If so, return that agent. Some immutable objects such as Number and Character instances do not need agents. For such instances, return their Smalltalk equivalents.

2. Otherwise, create a new agent for the GemStone object. Look in the importEquivalents to find which kind of agent to create. If no agent equivalent is found, use a generic proxy that forwards all messages for execution in the the GemStone environment.

3. Add the new agent to the registeredAgents list.

Each new subclass of Agent must respond to the class message import: aGemOop, which should create and initialize a new agent instance for the principal with the given Oop.

12.3.4 Deputy Implementation Criteria

Designers tuning an application by creating deputies with custom behavior for selected class instances should first examine how those database objects are being used in the application. Designers should consider the following aspects of object usage:

Object Size. Smalltalk does not do well with big objects. Thus, creating a deputy that completely caches a big object's state in the Smalltalk object memory may not make sense. Deputies for such cases may cache fragments of the principal. However, this fragmentation increases the complexity of local methods.

Relative Immutability. Rarely modified objects are easier to manage than volatile ones. In order to manage caches properly, all deputy methods executed locally must mark the cached object appropriately if they modify the cache. This marking can be computationally expensive. Objects known to be immutable can be managed in special ways. For example, `Symbols` in GemStone can be imported directly as `Symbols` in Smalltalk without the need for an agent because they are never changed; their behavior is constant across environments.

Complexity of Behavior. Simple objects with complex methods (e.g., strings) are often worth caching because of the faster execution of methods in the Smalltalk environment.

Interobject Connectivity. Sets of objects that are highly connected may be inefficient to cache in the Smalltalk environment because of the time required to create a proxy or deputy for each member of the set.

Desired Transaction Rate. One difficulty of having many objects with state cached in Smalltalk is that all the dirty ones must be flushed prior to committing a transaction.

Mixing Forwarding with Local Execution. Applications must do so carefully. If a deputy decides to forward a message to GemStone, it cannot know whether the GemStone method depends on another GemStone object that might also have a Smalltalk deputy with a dirty cache. Also, when a forwarded message returns from executing on GemStone, the deputy has no way of determining whether any GemStone objects have been modified as a side effect. One of these modified GemStone objects might have a deputy with an outdated cache.

Bandwidth between Machines. If the channel connecting GemStone with Smalltalk has low bandwidth, then it may be practical to transfer only a few objects between the two environments.

12.3.5 Deputy Strategies

When designers create new deputy classes, they need to be aware of the interdependence of cache management, transaction management, and message management. This section discusses the options available for each of these, and how the various options interact.

Cache management. Each deputy has the option of caching a GemStone object's state in the Smalltalk object memory. The designer has several choices on how to manage these caches:

Transitive agent creation. When a deputy caches the state of a GemStone pointer object, it can also create an agent for each object transitively referenced by the cached state. In our example application, when a document deputy is created, both the header and the body can also be converted to deputies, each with its own cached state.

Leaves. A large object-oriented memory (LOOM) leaf [Stamos82] can be seen as a generic agent that knows nothing about its principal other than its identifier. Such an agent can delay creating the correct agent until it intercepts its first message meant for its principal. In our example application each entry in a `SetOfEntries` could be treated this way.

Partially cached state. For large objects, a deputy can cache a fragment of the GemStone object. In the example application a document body could be cached in relatively small fragments.

Delayed agent creation. A deputy can always delay creating an agent for part of its internal state if a method that modifies the receiver is not forwarded and operates on the cache. Thus a cache of a GemStone object will reference a Smalltalk object. These references must be changed to agent references, and the referenced objects must be converted to GemStone objects when the cache is flushed to GemStone.

Transaction management. Deputy caches must be synchronized with their principal's state prior to committing a transaction. This implies that each Smalltalk object referenced from a deputy cache must be exported to GemStone before a commit begins. In our archive example, the application creates a Smalltalk document with a body and header and then adds that document to a `setOfEntries`. The document, its body, and its header must all be converted to GemStone objects because they are transitively reachable from the `SetOfEntries`.

When an application attempts to commit a transaction, GemSession transitively traverses the deputy's cached state, converting all referenced objects to GemStone objects. Then, GemSession flushes dirty deputy caches to GemStone.

Message management. A proxy that always forwards messages to GemStone never has a problem with cache management. A deputy that caches its principal's GemStone state in the Smalltalk object memory has several options with regard to how it handles messages. For messages it chooses to support with local methods, we see these basic strategies:

1. *Write-through.* Perform the method in Smalltalk on the cache, then transmit any changes in the cache to GemStone prior to returning to the sender. Alternatively, the deputy could delay the write-through until just prior to a commit.

2. *Read-back.* For all methods that change a cache, a deputy could perform the work on GemStone, then refresh the cached state after the forwarded messages return to the deputy. Thus all reading messages operating in Smalltalk would see the correct state of the cache.

3. *Send-through.* Perform the work in both places; that is, both forward the message for execution on GemStone and perform an equivalent method locally. Send-through is an attractive alternative when a single message can cause large changes in a single object's state, such as a global replacement of a substring in a string.

12.4 CONCLUSION

In this section we evaluate the success of the agent framework, discuss some open research issues with respect to the presented design, and briefly discuss the status of the integration project.

12.4.1 Summary

The design presented in this chapter succeeds at meeting many of the goals for a seamless integration of GemStone with Smalltalk, especially if an application can live with the default behavior of proxies. For those designers not content with the efficiency of the resulting application, this design provides a reasonable factoring to allow incremental tuning by creation of custom deputies. The deputy model allows easy experimentation of alternative cache management strategies. We suspect that once the major classes supplied with GemStone have pretuned Smalltalk deputies, this custom tuning process should not be a difficult chore.

12.4.2 Open Research Issues

We see the following areas in need of further research before the Smalltalk and GemStone environments behave well as one seamless system:

Unification of Object Models. The Smalltalk and GemStone data models differ in three significant areas: object formats, method execution environments, and language features. GemStone supports objects significantly larger than what most Smalltalk implementations can accommodate and stores large unordered collections (such as `Set` and `Bag`) in a format quite different from Smalltalk. Unlike Smalltalk, GemStone users can declare the type of instance variables in a class definition and declare the type of a collection's elements. Classes provided in the Smalltalk virtual image and in the GemStone "initial" database that share the same name do not necessarily share the same behavior or format. For example, although both environments have an `Array` class, GemStone arrays grow dynamically, whereas Smalltalk arrays grow by using `become:`. Also, GemStone does not implement the `become:` message but does allow an instance to change its class. Further, each system supplies classes not supplied by the other. The process of automatically converting a Smalltalk class to its equivalent GemStone class is complex because of these differences.

Smalltalk Snapshots. The Smalltalk snapshot mechanism is at odds with GemStone's session and transaction control. If a user creates a snapshot of a Smalltalk virtual image while a GemStone session is active or while a transaction remains uncommitted, that snapshot can be inconsistent with the state of the GemStone database when the snapshot restarts. An integrated system should discard the snapshot notion entirely and replace it with a stable object in GemStone that describes the state of the workstation environment. This state information can then be read when the Smalltalk workstation loads the virtual machine. If this state is stored centrally, then the user can resume work previously suspended on a different workstation.

Transaction Transparency. If one transaction strategy has been shared by a group of applications, then certain deputies or groups of deputies can implement transaction control directly, removing some burden from the application designer.

Symmetric Interface. The interface between the GemStone and Smalltalk environments is asymmetric. Requests for activity always arise from outside the GemStone environment. The two execution environments are in a master-slave relationship, with

GemStone being the slave. GemStone objects do not "know" about external environments, nor can they initiate communication with external objects. This asymmetry limits the strategies available for synchronizing state between Smalltalk and GemStone objects, particularly after a message is forwarded to GemStone.

Dirty Cache Identification. Unlike most primary memory subsystems, the Smalltalk-80 object memory does not provide a "changed bit" for identifying modified memory segments. Management of modified caches is very inefficient without such an indicator.

Better Cache Management Policies. If one can modify the Smalltalk-80 virtual machine, more intelligent cache management strategies might be attempted. For example, some multilevel memory schemes (e.g., virtual memory caches [Denning70]) keep the lower layers updated by "writing through" the faster higher layers. These "write through" operations can be asynchronous with the main line process. If we apply this technique to the situation at hand, we reduce the time taken to flush dirty proxies prior to forwarding messages for GemStone execution, by exploiting the workstation's unused CPU cycles during the transaction.

Better Exception Handling. The existing GemStone does not support processes and semaphores in the general manner of Smalltalk. Thus the metaphors for exception handling in the Smalltalk-80 virtual image cannot be used on the GemStone side of an integrated system.

Integrated Development Environment. In order to create a seamless development environment, all the development tools provided in the standard Smalltalk-80 environment must be modified. These tools must be changed because none of them currently have the appropriate menus for handling transaction committing and aborting. Also, each of these tools (browser, inspector, debugger, and workspace) is written to take advantage of only one name dictionary—Smalltalk.

Integrated Name Binding. The opportunities for name binding are different between the GemStone and Smalltalk-80 environments. Most applications will want to present the richer GemStone naming environment to their users. To implement this change, the Smalltalk-80 compiler and the mechanism for creating and resuming snapshots must be modified. Also, the objects named in the Smalltalk virtual image must be merged with the objects named in GemStone.

12.4.3 Project Status

Servio currently has a working version of the Smalltalk-GemStone integration. The current version reflects the design as presented in [Schuchardt86]. Another implementation along the lines suggested by this chapter is in progress.

ACKNOWLEDGMENTS

The authors wish to thank Paul McCullough, Allen Otis, Mun Tuck Yap, Tom Ryan of Hewlett-Packard Laboratories, and the reviewers for helping improve the style and presentation of this chapter.

Eds: This article, "Integrating an Object Server with Other Worlds," by Alan Purdy, Bruce Schuchardt, and David Maier appeared in the ACM Trans. on Office Information

Systems, vol. 5, no. 1, January 1987, pp. 27-47. Alan Purdy and Bruce Schuchardt were affiliated with Servio Logic Development Corp., 15025 S.W. Koll Parkway, Beaverton, OR 97006 and Dave Maier was affiliated with Servio Logic Development Corp. and Oregon Graduate Center at the time of writing this article. Copyright 1987 Association for Computing Machinery, Inc., reprinted here by permission.

13 The Development of a Framework for VLSI CAD

Rajiv Gupta, Rajesh Gupta, Wesley H. Cheng, Ido Hardonag, Sheng Y. Lin, Ellis Horowitz, and Melvin A. Breuer

13.1 INTRODUCTION

Over the last few years, research in semantic data models and object-oriented databases has reached a considerable degree of maturity and sophistication [Hammer81,Stefik86]. Early research prototypes as well as commercial object-oriented databases are already becoming available [Banerjee87a & b,Fishman87,Maier86a,Ontologic88a]. Concomitantly, developments in portable network-transparent windowing software such as X-windows have made feasible the integration of applications operating in a heterogeneous environment. These developments will undoubtedly have a large impact on how design data is stored and processed in the computer-aided design (CAD) world.

Cbase, the subject of this chapter, is a VLSI CAD framework for storing design and test information[1]. The primary goal of this chapter is to explore the suitability of object-oriented databases for CAD applications as well as to document our experience in using such a database for this application domain in particular. Cbase has a sophisticated user interface that allows interactive access to design data and CAD tools. Several design-for-test applications which interact with this framework have been built or are under development. These applications include a test methodology selection system, a serial scan design system, a built-in self-test system, and a functional test system. Our experience confirms some of the key advantages of the object paradigm, viz., modeling power, ease of integration, generic programming features, and access to meta-data.

The remainder of this chapter is organized as follows. In this and the following sections we discuss the merits and demerits of various ways of storing CAD information. The third section details the layered architecture of Cbase. In the fourth section we

---

[1] Unless mentioned otherwise, throughout this chapter Cbase refers to the version 2.1 of the framework.

describe the value of object-oriented programming with specific examples taken from Cbase code.

13.2 WHY A CAD DATABASE?

VLSI design data has some unique characteristics which makes its management difficult. Typically, circuit design data tends to be hierarchically organized. A circuit consists of components or cells, which in turn may be composed of lower level cells. Also, the same design object may have multiple views, i.e., different aspects of the same information may be required by different applications. Views may be thought of as windows or perspectives on the design data. Multiple views can be used to provide easy retrieval and manipulation of related subsets of data, possibly via reorganization or temporary data structures. For example, a structural or schematic view of a full adder may indicate the manner in which half adders are interconnected to form the full adder; a behavioral view may express the truth table (i.e., the function) associated with the full adder; a physical view may consist of rectangles in the mask layout of the adder; and so on. Clearly, powerful modeling capabilities are needed to describe and manage the variety of information associated with a circuit. In addition, design data is processed by several CAD tools (synthesis tools, design-for-test (DFT) tools, layout editors, simulators at various levels, etc.). Since these tools may be written in a diverse set of languages, interfaces to many programming environments are essential. Last but not least, a very large volume of design information is associated with each VLSI system. It is essential that the design environment can quickly access and retrieve such a large amount of information.

Historically, a number of separate files with distinct formats have been used to store circuit design data at various levels of description. This approach suffers from several drawbacks, not the least of which is the lack of integration among CAD tools operating at different design levels. Recently there have been moves towards integrating all the information about a design into a common store. This has resulted in the development of languages, formats, and design databases such as VHDL [Aylor86], EDIF [EDIFmanual87], and OCT/Vem/RPC [Harrison86,Cavin87]. The use of a unified design database provides several potential advantages including the integration of all application tools, a single representation for design information, code reusability among applications, generic programming, elision (data hiding), and access to meta-information.

The choice of a database to implement the above-mentioned common store is significant. If (disk) files with a common format (such as EDIF) were used to store the design information, then each application would be forced to have parsing and lexical analysis capabilities in its front end. Relational (or record-based) databases, though excellent for business data processing, suffer from several drawbacks when used for modeling CAD objects and the CAD development process; these have already been summarized by Horowitz and Wan in Chapter 7.

To varying degrees of conviction, most researchers in this area believe that object-oriented databases (OODBs), which closely resemble semantic data models [Hammer81], are suitable for storing and manipulating design information [Banerjee87b,Fishman87,Ontologic88a,Stefik86]. The object-oriented paradigm supports several key concepts useful in CAD applications. The diversity of information types requires the database object types and their properties to be defined and modified rather frequently. The object type hierarchy, with the inheritance of an object type's properties by its sub-types, facilitates many levels of data abstraction. *Operations* and *methods* defined under an object type capture its behavior and allow CAD programmers to manipulate design data in an abstract way without referring to the implementation details. A *triggering* mechanism helps enforce integrity checking and makes event monitoring feasible. These concepts will be dealt with in detail later in this chapter.

13.3 CBASE ARCHITECTURE

Cbase is a VLSI CAD database built on top of an object-oriented database (Vbase from Ontologic [Ontologic88a], as presented in Chapter 9). It consists of a multilayered system which provides a common repository of both VLSI CAD objects and their associated operations, a tool interface for writing new applications, and a user interface for invoking applications or viewing objects in the database. Cbase provides a platform for creating, displaying, manipulating and maintaining large digital designs via a friendly, window-based, graphic tool and user interface.

Figure 13.1 shows the organization of the various layers of Cbase. The communication between various system layers follows a strict but extendible protocol. The Cbase layers are described below.

1. CAD Object Repository (CORe)—contains type schemas for various VLSI circuit objects. CORe is described in detail in section 13.3.1.

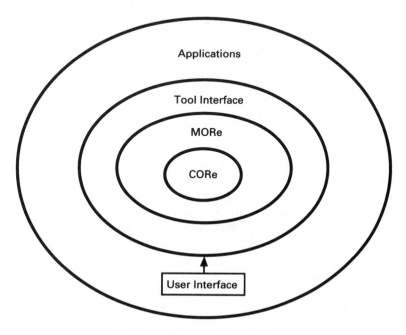

Figure 13.1 Architecture of Cbase.

2. Method Object Repository (MORe)—contains methods for maintaining objects in CORe (section 13.3.2).

3. Tool Interface—a layer that implements a standardized *protocol* for accessing objects in CORe (section 13.3.3). All tools use the generic functions provided by this protocol.

4. Application Programs—written by application developers using the tool and user interfaces (section 13.3.4). The user Interface is a special application that allows users to create/update circuits using the keyboard and mouse, and invoke CAD tools to operate on them. This program interacts with the database just like any another application and uses the protocol provided by the tool interface.

13.3.1 CORe

CORe is the innermost layer of Cbase. Objects in CORe consist of schemas or type definitions for circuit elements. The object schemas have been defined in the Type Definition Language (TDL) provided by Vbase. A part of the *Is-A* hierarchy provided by the Cbase CORe is shown in Figure 13.2. In this figure, the types shown in italic font are provided by the Vbase kernel; bold-faced types are Cbase extensions.

Cell is the basic component abstraction in Cbase at the register-transfer level. Each cell has a Name and an associated graphic Image. IModeType and MiscProp-Type are object schemas for holding I-modes [Abadir85] and miscellaneous properties (type, style, functional attributes, etc.) of a Cell, respectively. Each Cell can have Ports attached to it, which in turn can be attached to Buses. In this way, Cells can be organized in a circuit graph using Ports and Buses. Cells can be further organized into a component hierarchy using subCells and isCellOf properties defined for each Cell. The mechanisms for building the circuit graph hierarchy are inherited by all the subtypes of Cell. In the defined schema, Ports and Buses are collections of Terminals and Nets, respectively. Both Terminal and Net are refinements of Port and Bus.

Types Cell, Port and Bus allow the user to create a hierarchical hyper-graph that can be annotated with any user-defined attributes. Since these types can be further refined, it is feasible to make more complex structures by specializing the nodes of this hierarchical graph. In fact, any data structure in Cbase can be thought of as an edifice built on top of a denotable, hierarchical hyper-graph.

Several *exceptions* (not shown in Figure 13.2) are also defined. Exception is a special type of object created whenever an abnormal condition is detected. The corresponding exception handler catches and processes the exception raised.

Note that in Cbase 2.1 Gate is not a subtype of Cell. Ideally, one would like to extend the notion of Cell to include the smallest circuit element, such as a switch, and the largest circuit element, such as a complete system. But this might defeat the purpose of factoring out common properties so that many methods can be shared. In addition, the corresponding data structure might not be space-efficient.

Making Gate a subtype of CKtBaseType illustrates a pragmatic compromise. We use a fairly rich definition of Cell by including all the properties that can be used to represent a hierarchical circuit description for each cell. However, in our circuit model a Gate object will never have subcells; on the other hand it may have properties such

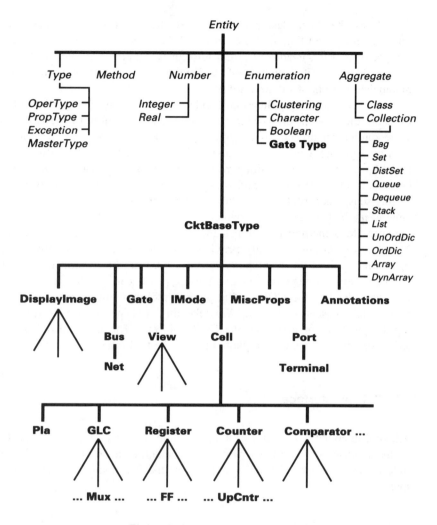

Figure 13.2 Cbase Is-A hierarchy.

as gate type that pertain only to `Gate` objects. Thus the information required to be associated with a `Gate` object does not have much in common with the information to be associated with a general `Cell` object.

13.3.2 MORe

MORe (Method Object Repository) is a collection of methods associated with circuit object types. The basic purpose of MORe is to insulate the application developer from internal changes in CORe. The methods are written in COP, an object-oriented extension of C discussed in Chapter 9. Methods for creating, deleting, and maintaining the object types shown in Figure 13.2 have been implemented. We have also implemented methods for loading and unloading PLAs, as well as gate-level and register-transfer level descriptions of circuits to and from disk files.

Cbase has been designed to be as resilient as possible to changes in the object schema during the lifetime of the system. Whenever a new object schema, say for a new subtype of register, is added to the CORe, new methods will have to be written for it in MORe. However, it is undesirable to have to change existing applications that need to manipulate objects of the new subtype.

We insulate the application developer from future changes in CORe and MORe by using the concept of *type polymorphism*, which refers to the ability to invoke the same routine on objects of different types. For example, the *generic method* `Display(Object)` can be invoked on all the object types shown in Figure 13.2. If a new object type is added, along with a routine for displaying it, this routine must also be bound to the generic method `Display` in the TDL specification of the new object. In this sense each routine is tightly bound both to the object type it acts on and to a generic method name through which it can be called. In Vbase, the type of the first argument to a method determines the type to which this method will be dispatched. This mechanism automatically provides a degree of insulation between schema developers and application developers. This is because the generic method name remains the same, even though the set of object types it can act on increases when new objects are added to the CORe. The generic programming concept will be discussed in more detail in section 13.4.4. We take this concept one step further by standardizing the protocol for accessing the CORe objects. The standardized protocol, which is still under development, is implemented by the tool interface described in the following section.

13.3.3 Tool Interface

The tool interface is a library of access/maintenance routines for the database. It allows all the applications and the user interface to manipulate circuit objects in a generic, type-independent manner. The following is a partial list of methods that constitute the tool interface:

- `Create (ObjectType: Type)`—creates an empty, default instance of ObjectType and returns a reference to it.
- `Edit (Object: Entity)`—helps in editing Object graphically.
- `Delete (Object: Entity)`—deletes Object and all references to it.
- `Display (Object: Entity)`—non-graphic display of properties of Object.
- `DisplayRecursive (Object: Entity)`—same as Display but recursive.
- `Draw (Object: Entity)`—graphic display routine for Object.
- `DrawRecursive (Object: Entity)`—same as Draw but recursive.
- `Attach (Object1: Entity, Object2: Entity)`—has different semantics depending on the types of Object1 and Object2.
- `Detach (Object1: Entity, Object2: Entity)`—opposite of Attach with analogous semantics.

- Flatten (Object: Entity)—returns the leaf level objects of the same type as Object in the circuit hierarchy rooted at Object. For example, for a cell it returns the subcells at the leaf level.

- Copy (Object: Entity)—creates and returns a duplicate copy of the circuit hierarchy rooted at Object.

- ExportToFile(Object: Entity, Format: FormatType)—produces a file with the description of Object in the format specified by Format.

- ImportFromFile (ObjectType: Type, Format: FormatType, FileName: FILE)—returns an object of type ObjectType by loading its description from the file FileName organized in the format specified by Format.

- Simulate (Object: Entity)—propagates the values at the input ports to the output ports using the behavior of Object and the value on the control ports.

Methods in MORe that act uniformly on all objects are automatically available at the tool interface level. However, several tool interface methods such as Attach (O1, O2) can be bound to MORe routines based on the type of all the arguments (and not just based on the type of the first argument, the feature provided by Vbase). This extra complication in dispatching is handled by the tool interface layer. To that extent this layer provides for standardization and *two-level dispatching* to overcome restrictions imposed by Vbase's model of polymorphism.

13.3.4 Application Subsystems

The main purpose behind Cbase is to provide a framework for integrating diverse VLSI CAD applications. Currently, Cbase supports several. Figure 13.3 shows all the application programs that are currently linked to Cbase. Most of the present applications are for testability analysis and design-for-test. The database, however, is not biased towards any particular application domain within VLSI CAD and can be used to build tools for other CAD activities.

In order to provide an interface with existing applications, any circuit in the Cbase database can be *exported* into text files using a hierarchical register transfer-level description format. Specialized formats are used for storing PLA descriptions and gate-level cell descriptions. Circuit descriptions created by the applications in files can also be *imported* as new cells into the database.

Applications linked to Cbase via files (indicated in Figure 13.3 by IF in the tool interface) include PLA-TSS, TDES, TGS, and LAGER. Since these programs were written to interact via files, the present interface to these systems is file-based. PLA-TSS takes the description of a PLA as input and suggests possible testable design methodologies (TDMs) for making it testable based on user-specified goals and constraints [Zhu86]. TDES (Testable Design Expert System) takes a register transfer level design and makes it into a testable design based on certain predefined TDMs [Abadir85]. TGS, which is written in Pascal, is an integrated test generation system for combinational circuits [Lee89].

In order to generate a mask layout for a design, a file interface to a silicon assembly system is required. The present interface allows one to export a Cbase circuit into Structure Description Language (SDL) [Jain88], which can be processed by the LagerIV

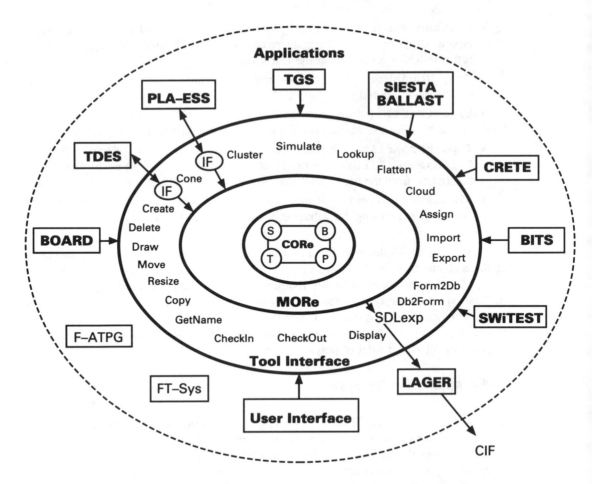

Figure 13.3 Applications interfaced to Cbase.

silicon assembly system to perform layout-level macro-cell generation, placement, and routing.

    Several applications which work directly off the database are currently under development. These include a full scan system (CRETE), a partial scan system (SIESTA/ Ballast) and built-in self-test system (BIST). A complete description of the test related applications is beyond the scope of this chapter. In order to illustrate how an application can benefit from the facilities provided by the framework, we discuss one application, viz. the user interface, in detail in the following section.

13.3.5 The Cbase User Interface

Any user interface should observe the following criteria as closely as possible. First, it should accommodate growth in types, tool interface and applications with minimal changes in the interface code. For example, if we define a new object type called `BILBOlatch`, a user should be able to `Create`, `Attach` and `Delete BILBOlatch` objects from the same interface after simply recompiling the system. In other words, the user interface should not be hard-coded with the state of the object type hierarchy and the knowledge of the associated methods at the time of its creation. In the Cbase user interface, a user who wishes to create a new object can ask the system to display the hierarchy of all object types currently defined; at this point the system retrieves the current object type hierarchy directly from the database.

A second desirable feature in the user interface is that the same set of routines should be called by the user interface and the application programs. For example, it should not be the case that the user interface calls the MORe routine `PlaAttach` while application programs must call a generic tool `Attach` to attach a PLA to something. In effect, both the user interface and the application programs have the same view of the database objects; this ensures that they are fully compatible with respect to circuits created and/or manipulated by each other.

Cbase provides a multi-window user interface built using the X-11 windowing package to access predefined subsystems and circuits in the database (see Figure 13.4). A structural view editor allows a user to interactively create and manipulate circuits in the database by working with a schematic display. All circuit objects have graphic image properties. To display and edit non-graphic properties of objects, data entry forms are used. A user can work with a hierarchical circuit by moving up and down the hierarchy.

Cbase is an open framework. One can replace the default operations inherited by a type with ones that perform the desired operations. The same is true of the user interface. The user interface for Cbase is easily customizable. Much of the code is declaration of widgets and their callback procedures. As the user has access to all the callback routines and declarations, he or she is free to declare new items in the panel or graphic command icons to make new functions available. This method of "mix and match" using the toolkit has many advantages, not the least of which is that it provides high-level constructs such as Text Widgets with full Emacs editing capability, scroll bars, and forms with a minimum amount of programming.

As mentioned earlier, one of the distinguishing features of the Cbase user interface is the fact that new object types and their associated operations can be added to the system with little change to the existing code. In this section we describe the capabilities of the user interface and the programming concepts that lead to its extensibility.

Figure 13.4 shows the user's view of the user interface. In addition to the status line, the current directory and the scroll buttons, it has three major parts. These are: the central graphics window, the command icons to the left, and the system operation panel on top. In the following, we discuss their function, what is novel about their implementation, and how the object paradigm facilitated their implementation.

Main Graphics Window. The graphics window in the middle of the screen is used for displaying and interactively manipulating various views of the circuit. Routines for doing this are written using the Xlib calls. The circuits created in Cbase are hierarchical, with no limit imposed on the depth of the hierarchy. One level of the hierarchy or the full hierarchy associated with a circuit may be displayed by appropriately setting the `Detail` toggle.

At present, only the schematic view of the circuit may be displayed in the main graphics window. However, the code is completely generic and can easily be extended

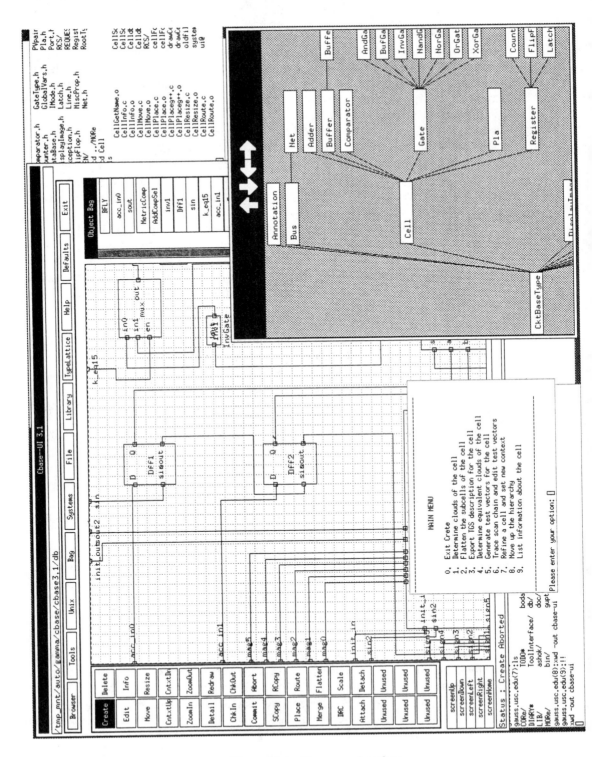

Figure 13.4 Cbase user interface.

The Development of a Framework for VLSI CAD   Chap. 13

to other views. In order to draw, display, or edit objects in the main graphics window, generic calls provided by the tool interface are used. Run-time dispatching, based on the types of arguments passed to these type-independent routines, determines the actual procedure that will be invoked. If the classes describing the other views are derived from the existing classes, and their interface related methods are bound to the generic calls used by the user interface, the same code can be used for editing and browsing other views. From this point of view the user interface is completely extensible.

In order to manipulate objects in the main graphics window the tool interface provides methods such as `giInit()` for mapping and initializing most of the window objects, `giRedraw()` for refreshing the screen, `giDraw()` for interactively drawing any object, `giDisplay()` for displaying a particular view of any object, and so on. In that sense, most of the code for maintaining the main graphics window is simply a "driver" for the facilities provided by the underlying framework. Note that the above operations act on any object in any context.

Command Icons. The graphics command buttons (or icons) activate routines that manipulate the objects in the graphics window. Routines to graphically `Create`, `Delete`, `Edit` (the non-graphic properties), `Copy` (full hierarchical copy), `Move`, `Resize`, `Refine`, `Move-up`, `Zoom in/out`, `Detail` (recursive display), `Redraw`, and `Check in/out` (archive) objects are provided. The `Refine` command allows the user to go down to a lower level in the component hierarchy while `Moveup` will move the current context up by one level. The `Check in/out` commands are used to move circuits back and forth from an archival space.

There is a "callback" routine associated with each widget implementing a command icon. A callback procedure is a routine which is activated upon detecting a certain event in a widget. For instance, clicking the left mouse button inside the Create icon will activate its callback routine. All the callback routines in the user interface have been written using the type-independent protocol provided by the tool interface.

Consider, for example, the callback routine for any generic operation OP associated with the OP icon. The following is the pseudocode associated with this routine:

```
OP_CallBack
{  Prompt user to click on object;
   theObject = giSelect();
   OP(theObject)
   except (Xption: CannotOP)
   { Exception handler for improper OP.}
}
```

The actual binding of the OP operation to a type-specific OP is done at run-time. This type of late binding minimizes future changes to the user interface code. Polymorphism, as the above phenomenon is sometimes called, forms the basis of extensibility for most of the callback routines. Type-sensitive dispatching, however, may not always guarantee complete extensibility. Consider, for example, the create operation associated with a type. Clearly, the generic create cannot be a dispatched operation as there is no object to dispatch on. This logical anomaly is handled differently in different systems. Solutions include sending create messages to the meta-class or having free create procedures. In the next section we will show how the meta-information associated with an object-oriented database can be used to make object creation a generic operation.

System Operation Panel. In addition to the graphic command icons, the user interface provides several panel operations. The following is a description of various panel items and their associated operations.

Object Querying and Browsing The Vbase panel item provides access to a fourth generation query language called Object SQL (see Chapter 11) and a textual database browser. The availability of these two packages is a direct consequence of using a persistent data structure stored in a database.

Using Object SQL a user can request information from the database. A typical query consists of three items: a specification of what kind of information is desired, the domain that must be searched for obtaining that information, and the condition that the information must satisfy. For example, a query may request names and types (kind of information) of all the cells (domain of information) which have more than a given number of subcells (condition). SELECT, FROM, and WHERE clauses are used to form a query. The following are some example queries:

```
SELECT Name, Width, isOnCell.Name
FROM    $Port
WHERE   Width > 10;

SELECT Name, MiscProps.Type, MiscProps.Style
FROM    $Set$Intersect($systemCell.subCells,$Library);

SELECT isOnCell.Name
FROM $Port
WHERE extBus.Name = "PHI1";
```

The first query above requests the name, width, and the cell name for all ports which have more than 10 terminals. The second query asks for the name, type and style of all the library cells which are used as the subcells of the $systemCell. The $systemCell is a global, predefined cell whose use is similar to that of '/' directory in UNIX. All circuits in the system are subcells of the $systemCell which forms the root of the cell hierarchy in the database. The third example generates the list of all the cells which are connected to the clock PHI1.

From the above examples, the ease with which the database can be queried should be obvious. Note that there is no concept of tables or records in object-oriented databases. In Object SQL, the basic clauses of SQL had to be extended to regard object instances (over some domain) as the rows of the table and their properties or members as the columns of the table. Also, note the use of dot notation to access members of composite objects.

Using the textual **Browser** one can move around in the database from object to object and display the attributes of any object, without doing any programming. For example, the following browser commands list the contents of the $systemCell, the list of its subcells, and the contents of its only subcell. The commands typed in by the user are preceded by the 'its>' prompt.

```
its> show value $systemCell
  define $Variable $systemCell
    vspec = $Cell;
    binding = #0Cell;
    directType = $Variable;
    repmanager = $HeaderRep;
    storagemanager = $OkStorage;
    name = "systemCell";
    symbol = #0Symbol;
    pathName = "$systemCell";
  end $systemCell;
its> show value #0Cell.subCells
#0Cell.subCells = #1DistributedSet %{#1Cell}
its> show value #1Cell
  define $Cell #1Cell
    name = "TestCell";
    hasPorts = #3DistributedSet; %{}
    subCells = #4DistributedSet;
                    %{#2Cell,#3Cell,#4Cell}
    isCellOf = #0Cell;
    interconnect = #5DistributedSet;
                    %{#0Bus,#1Bus,#2Bus}
    image = #1DisplayImage;
    miscProps = ; % No Value
    copyOfCell = ; % No Value
    permission = ; % No Value
    directType = $Cell;
    repmanager = $HeaderRep;
    storagemanager = $OkStorage;
    name = ; % No Value
    symbol = ; % No Value
    pathName = ; % No Value
  end #1Cell;
```

The above examples illustrate the ease with which data can be accessed. Using the browser one can display several other entities such as the stack, exceptions and status information along with the contents of user-defined objects. The browser generates symbolic pointers such as #2Cell and #0Bus (for example, see the #4DistributedSet associated with the subcells of #1Cell above) to refer to composite objects pointed to by members of the object being displayed. In addition, the browser also gives a fair amount of meta-information about the objects. In fact one can display the definition of any type (which are instances of type Type) using the show value command. For example, 'show value $Cell' will display all the properties and methods defined for objects of type Cell.

Tool Invocation Several often used tools are provided by the `Tools` panel item. This widget is associated with such functions as circuit partitioning, hierarchical clustering and highlighting objects in the current context. All the operations which pop-up from this panel item take the current context (typically a Cell) as the argument and operate on it.

Application Invocation The `Systems` panel option is provided for accessing various CAD application subsystems listed earlier (Figure 13.3). A typical application takes one or more object pointers from the current context as input and produces results which will be visible (if it alters the schematic associated with the current context) after the next `Redraw` operation.

There is a key difference between a tool invoked through the `Tools` panel item and an application invoked using the `Systems` panel item. While the tools operate in the context of the user interface, the systems typically reopen the database as another user. Needless to say, for the latter case, multi-user operation of the framework is extremely important. In addition, since two applications are operating on the database simultaneously (the user interface and the other application) using the same persistent data structure, care must be taken to preserve database integrity. Vbase provides objects of type `Lock` with associated operations `Acquire` and `Release` to implement a user-devised concurrency control mechanism. The present user interface, however, simply disallows user operations while another application is working on the database, in order to ensure data integrity. Future versions will implement a more elaborate concurrency control mechanism.

Object Referencing In systems with a global name space and a user-defined unique key to identify each object, one can unambiguously refer to any object using its key. Object-oriented systems, however, have no such key to serve as object identity. An object-id, which is typically invisible to the user, provides programmatic access to the objects. However, a system assigned object-id is not a convenient way to refer to objects from the user interface. The Cbase user interface provides the capability to point directly to a desired object in the current context.

The object bag provides a context-independent reference to objects selected by the user. It is used as a scratch pad for objects that are either nongraphical in nature, or are from other levels of the hierarchy and therefore not directly accessible from the current context. One can use the bag to hold object pointers from one circuit, switch over to another circuit, and still have reference to objects that were placed in the bag. The bag may also be used for parameter passing when invoking CAD applications.

Interface to Alien Applications and Files The `File` panel item provides menu options for exporting/importing circuits to and from files. An extensible format with LISP-like syntax that resembles EDIF (Electronic Data Interchange Format) [EDIFmanual87] is used for storing design information in files. As mentioned earlier, several applications such as TDES and PLA-ESS take their inputs in this format and produce their output in the same format.

A file-export routine, in general, is easy to write as its job is to convert structured information stored in a data structure to an unstructured stream of ASCII characters. On the other hand, a file-import routine can be quite complex as it has to process an input stream of characters to recognize the tokens, organize the tokens into language constructs and recognize them, and then extract the information out of the recognized constructs and store it in the internal data structure. A typical import routine is patterned after a compiler. It is driven by a grammar with semantic actions associated with each production rule of the grammar. These semantic actions incrementally construct a parse-tree as the input file is processed.

The Cbase import routine does all the above operations with the difference that the parse tree constructed is a persistent one and corresponds to the Cbase data structure. The following code segment taken from the import routine illustrates the essence of the process. The code for parsing is written in COP and is processed by YACC (Yet Another Compiler Compiler) to generate the parser.

```
typeValue:
  _comb
     {
       $$ = "comb";
       $GlobalCell.miscProps.cellType =
             $CircuitType$Combinational;
     }
```

The above code illustrates how the production typeValue $\rightarrow$ _comb is processed. The associated semantic action (enclosed between curly braces) simply assigns combinational to the cellType property in the miscProps of the cell currently being processed ($GlobalCell). This code will remain the same in a typical import routine except the references would be to volatile objects. Thus there is no extra programming overhead in importing or exporting a file because of the persistence of the data structure.

Library A typical design contains several standard circuit components such as flip-flops and multiplexers which are repetitively used. The Cbase user interface provides facilities to enter any part of a design into a *library* for future use. The Library menu item allows for entering, displaying, removing and instantiating subcircuits from the library.

There are two ways of instantiating a library component. One can instantiate a *shallow copy* of the component. In this case only the top-level cell of the component, along with all its interface information and a pointer to the actual copy in the library, is copied into the design in progress. Any change to a component in the library is reflected in all its shallow copies in use. Clearly, if this type of instantiation is used, no application program should attempt to modify two copies of the same component differently. Alternatively, one can instantiate a library component using *deep copy*, in which case the complete cell hierarchy associated with the component will be copied.

Other Utilities Several frequently used operating system calls are provided by the Unix panel item. Using Tdl one can display the *IS-A* hierarchy in the Cbase CORe rooted at any type, and display properties and methods defined in any type declaration. Finally, Help, Defaults and Exit perform the conventional operations.

13.4 OODB FEATURES THAT AID CAD FRAMEWORK DEVELOPMENT

Several OODB features aided in building the Cbase prototype. In this section we discuss these features. We illustrate each OODB concept with the help of examples from our code and show how its absence would have resulted in more design effort, more code, or both.

13.4.1 Modeling Power

One of the major advantages of using the object-oriented paradigm is increased modeling power. The objects and their interrelationships in OODBs align very closely to the real world objects and their interrelationships. On the other hand, conventional data modeling paradigms such as file formats or relational data models entail considerable effort in forcing real world objects into fixed programming constructs. Thus, there is a semantic gap between how information is stored and the way in which it will be put to use. Relational databases, in particular, have been shown to be inadequate for storing complex information structures such as the ones encountered in CAD [Kent79].

Consider, for example, the task of modeling many-to-many relationships. In order to make the example concrete, consider Cell and Port types. In general, a cell can have many ports, and a port can be on many cells. (In Cbase 1.0, a port can be shared between a cell and its subcell.) The TDL segments shown below indicates the relevant parts of the definitions of Port and Cell.

```
define Type Cell
       . . . . . . . .
       hasPorts: distributed Set[Port]
              inverse $Port$isOnCell;
       . . . . . . . .
end Cell;
define Type Port
       . . . . . . . .
       isOnCell: distributed Set[Cell]
              inverse $Cell$hasPorts;
       . . . . . . . .
end Cell;
```

Here the inverse clause helps maintain the two-way pointers between ports and cells. Thus the insertion

```
$Set$Insert(aPort, aCell.hasPorts)
```

where aPort and aCell are Port and Cell objects respectively, would (i) include aPort in the set aCell.hasPorts, as well as (ii) include aCell in the set aPort.isOnCell. In the relational model, the Port and Cell definitions would roughly correspond to a relation for each. However, to model this relationship, one would have to introduce an extra relation (or an intersection record). Furthermore, in order to retrieve combined information, a join over these relations may be required. The gain in both modeling power and object access time in the case of OODBs is substantial.

OODBs typically provide a set of predefined system types such as Set, Queue, Stack, List, and OrderedDictionary. Many of the routinely used data structures and their associated operations such as Insert, Push and Pop are provided in Vbase. This simplifies the modeling effort as the designer can concentrate on the problem at hand and not let the solution be cluttered with data structure specific routines.

Another advantage of having a powerful data structure directly stored on the disk is that most applications now do not need a local, memory-resident data structure. When accessed, the relevant information about an object is automatically cached into memory. Clearly, no code for loading and mapping disk information to memory data structures is needed. If the same information were stored using a file format such as EDIF [EDIFmanual87], the front end of every application would have to be a parser/loader utility. Note that this advantage does not apply to object-oriented *languages* such as C++, Smalltalk, and Objective-C that lack object persistence.

In order to clarify the above point, consider the task of drawing a circuit consisting of cells, ports and buses. All one has to do is iterate over those circuit objects in the database and draw each one of them. This is exactly how one would like to think of drawing a circuit, without having to build a set of queries to extract the data from the database, load them into local data structures, and then display them.

Relationships among Objects. If too many concepts are modeled using a limited set of constructs, loss of exact meaning is inevitable. OODBs provide several mechanisms to model different relationships among objects.

Classification is the ability to relate an object to a group of objects via the *Is-Instance-Of* relationship. In order to check the class (or Type) to which an object O belongs, one simply has to check O.DirectType. Also, the function TypeOf(O) (which is defined on Entity and hence, inherited by every object) returns the type of the object O.

Object Specialization/Generalization refers to the ability to organize object types in an *Is-A* hierarchy. For example, in Cbase, Register is a Cell, which in turn is a CktBaseType, which is an Entity (see Figure 13.2).

Aggregation allows the programmer to model an object as an aggregate of its constituent objects. This type of relationship is known as the *Is-Part-Of* relationship and is specified in TDL by defining appropriate properties of an object. For example, the constituent objects in a Cell are given in the properties clause of the Cell TDL, as shown below.

```
define Type Cell
    supertypes = {CktBaseType};
        properties = {
                name:          String;
                subCells:      distributed Set[Cell]
                               inverse $Cell$isCellOf;
                interconnect: optional Set[Bus];
```

```
        image:           optional DisplayImage;
        . . . . . . . . . . . . . . . . . .
        };
  end Cell;
```

Research in artificial intelligence and semantic data modeling has shown that these three classes of relationships are sufficient to model many real world situations. Also, the ability to represent different relationships directly without overloading any single construct (as must be done in conventional models due to the small set of fixed types of a particular language) leads to a clearer model and cleaner code. This in turn helps cut down development effort.

Data Abstraction and Data Hiding. With the advent of "3rd-generation" programming languages (such as CLU), it was realized that a clear distinction should be made between the storage structures associated with the data and the logical structure of the information. Data hiding refers to the idea of insulating the programmer from the actual structure in which the data is stored. Typically this is achieved by providing constructs to control accessibility of various data members and methods associated with a type. Data abstraction refers to the extreme case of this separation where the only access to the storage structure is through a set of predefined operations.

In TDL, a set of operations is defined for each VLSI object in Cbase. For example, the partial Cell definition shown below lists some of the allowable operations on a cell—Delete, CreDrawEdit, DisplayForm, etc.

```
define Type Cell
        supertypes = {CktBaseType};
        operations = {
                refines Delete (c: Cell)
                        raises (CannotDelete)
                        triggers (CellDeleteTrigger);
                refines CreDrawEdit (c:Cell)
                        method (CellCreDrawEdit);
                refines DisplayForm (c:Cell)
                        method (CellDisplayForm);
                . . . . . . . . . .
                };
  end Cell;
```

Data abstraction and data hiding are advocated as good programming practices even in conventional languages by defining record types, giving meaningful names to variables, and writing routines to manipulate fields in a record. There is no way to enforce this in conventional languages. In OODBs, completely encapsulating an object with its data and operations forces the programmer to use the correct operations on all objects. In addition, a programmer does not need to know the details about objects created by other programmers.

Interface Modeling. The object paradigm was also found to be useful in modeling the user interface of Cbase. Using the X-11 toolkit, building the user interface was a simple task of using the predefined widgets in the toolkit. Programming with widgets consisted mainly of their declarations and attaching call-back routines. The toolkit allows one to declare several types of widgets (such as label widget, command widget, etc.), attach them to an appropriate parent widget, set the size and position of the windows, and link the routine that should be invoked (the call-back routine) when a particular widget is selected. Dynamic creation or destruction of a widget is performed with a single call to the Create/Destroy procedures. The toolkit provides mouse pointing facilities, text widgets with Emacs editing functions, and several other features that take the chore out of user interface implementation.

13.4.2 Code Reusability

Object-oriented languages allow a programmer to write less code and implement the same functionality by reusing modules of code. This is not just a matter of changing parameters to a procedure: Vbase offers the capability to paste together modules as required to form larger modules. In addition, OODBs also support the porting of objects from one version to another while the system is under development. Types can be automatically migrated to a new database, thereby eliminating the task of updating and copying the object definitions.

Predefined Routines. The simplest form of code reusability is to use any predefined routines that already exist in the system. OODBs typically provide a wide set of predefined types and their associated operations. For instance, in Vbase the predefined Stack object has a set of routines such as $Stack$Push, $Stack$Pop, and $Stack$Delete, which can be used directly.

Property and Operation Inheritance. Property/operation inheritance implies that an object type automatically has all the properties/operations of its parent type. This is one of the fundamental differences between OODBs and relational databases. As one can notice, all the operations for Cell listed earlier are refinements of the operations on its parent type. Thus the behavior that a type shares with its supertype does not need to be re-implemented. More importantly, this allows one to assign default behavior to objects. For example, most of the operations for Register have not yet been implemented in our system. However, one can create or delete a register, or invoke several of the operations defined for Cell that have been inherited by Register since Cell is the supertype of Register. In fact, once the subtype–supertype link is established in the *Is-A* hierarchy, a large amount of code is automatically available to the object, even before a single line of code specific to the new object type has been written.

13.4.3 Method and Trigger Combination

Method and trigger combination refers to the idea of writing several small modules of code and using these modules in different combinations to form methods for different types and situations. Such a building block approach has been used successfully in other disciplines such as hardware design. In software engineering, however, the use of replaceable software modules is still not commonplace. A part of the problem has been the inability to make code generic enough. In conventional programming, this would involve many checks which would make the code inefficient.

However, with OODBs, the automatic dispatching mechanism (see next section) allows programmers to combine modules by triggering them at the appropriate places. Each object-specific operation module is designed so as to simply handle its additional set of properties, then invoke the corresponding module for its supertype. Note that all modules are invoked using the same generic call irrespective of the type of the argument. This is illustrated in Figure 13.5 for the operation of displaying data entry forms on the user interface, for `Register`, `Cell` and `CktBaseType` objects.

13.4.4 Generic Programming

Generic programming refers to the style of writing code modules to be as general as possible in order to be usable by different types of objects. The object paradigm has two essential features—polymorphism and access to meta-information—that help in generic programming.

Polymorphism. Polymorphism is the facility to automatically dispatch a call to an appropriate routine according to the type of the parameters passed. This feature is illustrated in Figure 13.6 for the `delete` procedure provided by the tool interface. Depending on the type of the arguments, the appropriate `delete` procedure in the MORe is invoked. This feature makes the code upward compatible and resilient to modifications.

Polymorphism is also evident in the trigger and method combination example (Figure 13.5). A call to `DisplayForm` is automatically dispatched to either `CBTdisplayForm`, `CellDisplayForm`, or `RegDisplayForm` according to the type of the object passed. Almost all the callback routines associated with command icons in the user interface are made generic using polymorphism. A notable exception is the create icon discussed below.

Accessibility of Meta-Information. As mentioned earlier, the create operation cannot be a dispatched operation as there is no object to dispatch on. This problem can be solved by providing access to the meta-information, i.e., the information about the database schema itself. In OODBs the user-defined types are actually objects that are compiled into the database. They are therefore available to a program just like any other object.

In order to see the usefulness of meta-information in implementing the create icon in the user interface, consider the call-back routine `createsub()`. When a user clicks on the `Create` icon, the complete *IS-A* hierarchy associated with the system is regenerated and displayed in a separate window (see Figure 13.4). The user then selects the type of the object to be created. The selected type is returned to the callback routine `createsub()`. This routine can now access the operations associated with this type. It selects the create operation for the selected type and invokes it to create a default object. Normal dispatching can then be used to do the remaining operations associated with object creation, such as providing the initial image and values for non-graphic properties. The following code implements `createsub()`.

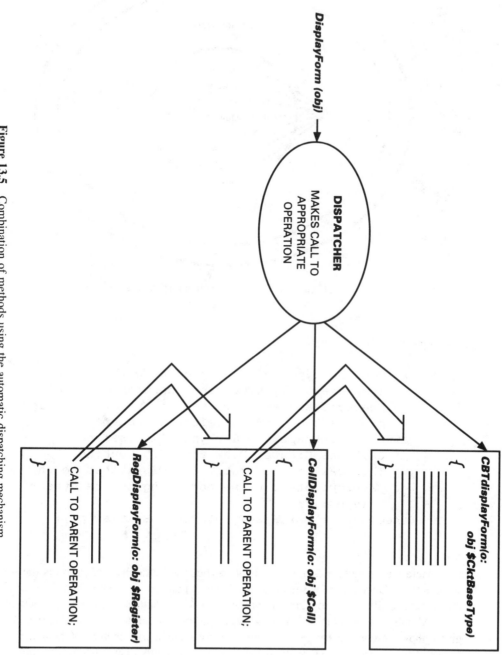

Figure 13.5 Combination of methods using the automatic dispatching mechanism.

257

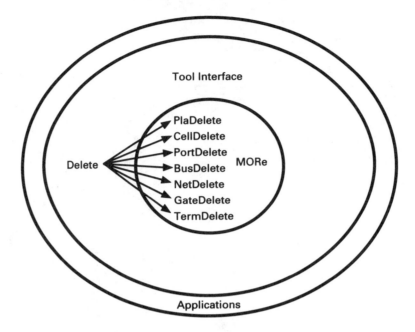

Figure 13.6 Type-sensitive dispatching.

```
createsub()
{
    /* Get the type to be created by clicking in the
       type hierarchy tree. The function GetType displays
       the type hierarchy rooted at its argument and
       prompts the user to select a subtype. */
    aType = $CktBaseType$GetType($CktBaseType);
    /* Call the Create, Draw and Edit routine.
       This call is automatically dispatched to the
        appropriate routine according to the type of
       "aType". */
    $theObject = $CktBaseType$CreDrawEdit(aType);
}
```

Here the procedure GetType displays the *Is-A* hierarchy and prompts the user to select a type. Once a type is selected, an object of that type is created and the user draws the object and fills in its non-graphic properties using a data entry form for objects of this type. All this is done by the CreDrawEdit routine. Note that the createsub() code given above is completely generic and will not change irrespective of how the CORe grows. The generic call to CreDrawEdit is automatically dispatched to the appropriate method, such as CellCreDrawEdit, based on the type of the object passed to it. The binding between the generic call and the object-specific routine is done in the TDL. It is our experience that the whole user interface can be developed in such a generic manner.

Notice that the above "trick" is possible only because of the availability of the meta-information. The type hierarchy display routines read the types from the database at the start of each session and create an internal data structure for graphical display. This ensures that the information displayed by the program is always consistent with the current *Is-A* hierarchy used in the database.

13.4.5 Language and Environment Features

Several language features are known to accelerate programming by catching errors early in the code-compile-test cycle. Both TDL and COP comply with some of these features and we discuss them briefly.

Although C itself is a weakly typed language, the COP compiler ensures that database objects can be manipulated only by procedures attached to them. Strict type checking of this nature results in early elimination of several hard-to-catch bugs.

The advanced exception handling capability of OODBs comes in handy in rapid prototyping. Typically, the final version of an application would have a large amount of code dealing with erroneous input data or other anomalous situations. In an early prototype, one would like to avoid such detailed error handling. If exceptions are also treated as objects, one can initially write a very simple exception handler for the most general type of exception. This default exception handler can then be gradually refined as the prototype grows. This was indeed done in Cbase 1.0 (the first prototype), where most exception handling was restricted to a print statement when an exception of type Failure (the most general type of exception in Vbase) was caught. Several of these exception handlers have since been refined to perform context-sensitive error handling.

13.5 DRAWBACKS AND LIMITATIONS

13.5.1 OODB Limitations

The above discussion might lead one to believe that the object paradigm is a panacea for all the woes of software engineering. The paradigm, however, does suffer from drawbacks and should be viewed in the context of its limitations.

One of the disadvantages of using object technology seems to be the long learning curve. Most programmers trained in the conventional school of programming can pick up a new language fairly quickly. However, object programming seems to require a longer gestation period. Our experience is that it normally takes several months before programmers are skilled enough to start on a project.

Another problem, which is to be expected in the initial stages of any budding technology, is the unavailability of robust and reliable tools such as source-level debuggers and fast compilers. With packages such as X-11, which are based on the client-server model and process client requests asynchronously, there is another associated problem in dealing with bugs. Error latency may camouflage the real bug since the source line at which a program fails may not be the line in error. Even with synchronous packages such as Vbase, errors in user code are often reported as some abstruse error in system code.

Yet another potential problem lurks in the nature of abstraction. While it shields applications from low-level details, it also makes them dependent on the reliability of the abstraction layer. A well-hidden bug in this layer will show up as a rare malfunction in the application layer. Since the application programmer does not have implementation-level knowledge of the lower layer, the bug may be almost impossible to isolate and eradicate, especially if it is disguised by asynchrony.

Performance is another issue one has to consider carefully. As can be expected, OODBs occupy more space and are in general slower than the file-based systems currently in widespread use in the CAD industry. Files offer a raw form of access to data. In an OODB, a considerable amount of semantic information is stored, leading to a larger storage requirement for the same data. Compile time performance is also poorer in OODBs because of strict type checking (with respect to a persistent data structure).

Our experience with Vbase reveals that default object creation/manipulation operations provided by the environment may not deliver the desired level of performance. Fortunately, since OODBs are in general open systems, most default operations can be substituted by user-defined, object-specific operations. In addition, there exist provisions for clustering objects on the disk so as to improve access performance.

13.6 CONCLUSION

By far the most important contribution of object-oriented technology to the development of Cbase was its modeling power. Complex CAD structures and concepts were implemented exactly as perceived in the real world, without the need to force them into any predefined constructs. In addition, the gradual refinement and evolutionary approach offered by OODBs was particularly suitable for rapid prototyping of an application such as Cbase. Features such as generic programming and code reusability also helped the rapidity with which the prototypes could be completed. However, the environment is not perfect; some special problems do exist due largely to the newness of the technology, and lack of user education and experience with this new paradigm.

With the increasing complexity of VLSI systems, one of the major requirements of CAD frameworks is that they have the power to model complex circuit designs. Our experience in this project shows that the object paradigm eminently meets this need, and it can be a great asset in developing a framework that caters to a range of application programs across various levels of the VLSI design problem.

ACKNOWLEDGEMENTS

This work was supported in part by AT&T, and in part by the Defense Advanced Research Projects Agency under contract no. N00014-87-K-0861 and monitored by the Office of Naval Research. The views and conclusions contained in this document are those of the authors and should not be interpreted as necessarily representing the official policies, either expressed or implied, of AT&T, DARPA or the U. S. Government. A preliminary version of this work appeared in IEEE Computer, May 1989; the details of Cbase 1.0 were presented at ICCAD-88, November 1988, and the user interface was detailed in the Proceedings of 1st Intl. Conf. on System Integration, April 1990.

14 Object Database Support for CASE

Lung-Chun Liu and Ellis Horowitz

14.1 INTRODUCTION

The software development process involves numerous types of information and enormous amounts of data. These data items can be maintained in various formats and media. Source programs follow strictly their languages' syntax, object code and binary executables are machine dependent but can be stored in systems other than the target machines, documents are in textual or typesetting format, and communication between project personnel are in written memos or electronic mail. It is believed that integrated database support will greatly reduce the efforts spent in maintaining this data and improve the overall productivity for software product development [Eastman81, Katz84, Bernstein87]. Such an environment database has been identified as the core of any automated Software Engineering Environment (SEE) and is vital to the success of a Computer-Aided Software Engineering tool (CASE) [Penedo86, Stenning87].

In contrast to the large volumes of data produced by the development process, the relationships among these data items are far more complicated to maintain. Usually these relationships are loosely coupled. For instance, when a function needs to be changed in the specification or new features are added in, a caucus must be held to determine what documents have to be reviewed, what activities must be reinitiated, what program modules and manual pages will be affected, who are the project staff to be involved in these tasks, and what will be their responsibilities. This management level information is more likely to be held in chapter form or in people's minds and be exchanged orally without records. For a project of long duration, staff turnover is the norm and effective project management becomes threatened due to the lack of sufficient information.

Several mechanisms and tools have been proposed for dealing with different aspects of the software life cycle data. Consider just some examples: SCCS [Rochkind75] and RCS [Tichy86] for source code and document version control, the *Make* utility [Feldman79] for program dependency and installation, SODOS [Horowitz86a] for document definition and manipulation. These tools provide systematic approaches to managing specific types of information or performing targeted activities. However, most of them are mainly concerned with a single phase or a single function of the software life cycle, such as requirement analysis, programming, documentation, version control, or configuration management. Management information, though at a coarser level of granularity, is not fully captured in these tools.

Traditional project management tools (e.g., Gantt chart, CPM and PERT algorithms) only focus on activity scheduling plus, to a certain degree, resource cost computation. The iterative nature of software development requires that activities be re-scheduled and re-initiated. Such a capability has still not been furnished in these traditional tools. Furthermore, most existing management tools use their own file formats and are unable to share or interchange data with other life cycle tools. A recent research direction is the exploration of an underlying project database which models all information(or knowledge) produced through the entire life cycle [Penedo86].

To overcome the deficiencies of traditional management tools and construct an extensible database core for an integrated SEE, a model, called DesignNet, has been derived to support this need [Liu87]. The DesignNet model is a hybrid model for describing and monitoring the software development process. The aim of this model is to provide the conceptual basis for a higher level integrated software project management environment. It utilizes AND/OR structural operators to describe the *work breakdown structure (wbs)* and Petri net notation to represent the dependencies and parallelism among activities, resources, and products. It is an event-driven model since the project state is changed only when some events happen (e.g., spec changes, reported bugs, departure of personnel). When such events are submitted to the modeled project, the desired reactions will be automatically triggered according to a predefined project plan. Meanwhile, the relationship between the event and the triggered activities will be tracked in the underlying database. Thus, a complete project history log is maintained without manual intervention.

This chapter describes the object-oriented database support for the DesignNet model. Other implementations of engineering design databases [Wong79, Stonebraker83, Penedo86] are based on the relational model, although their conceptual models are either defined with abstract data types, entity-relationship, or object-oriented methodology. The examples here and our prototype use Ontologic's Vbase product [Ontologic88a], one of the first of few object-oriented databases available. It describes the actual definition and construction of the database layer of the DesignNet model based on an object-oriented development environment.

The chapter begins with justification for choosing an object-oriented approach versus a record-oriented approach. Next, the elements of the DesignNet model are described in terms of object types. The object type hierarchy is also presented. The following sections discuss the techniques used in accomplishing various management functions, such as work breakdown structure representation, time stamping mechanism, project history recording, event triggering, and concurrent activity monitoring. The final section presents our conclusions regarding the strengths and weaknesses of an object system for maintaining software project management information.

14.2 SOFTWARE PROJECT MANAGEMENT DATA REQUIREMENTS

To choose the mose suitable database approach for supporting software project management, the data management requirements must be identified first. This section investigates these issues and then, based of the desired capabilities, concludes that an object-oriented database is most appropriate.

The project work breakdown structure is the central target for management. A large, complex system cannot be tackled without being decomposed into several major tasks. Depending on its complexity, each major task can be further decomposed into the next level subtasks. This decomposition may extend several levels below. Any task in the hierarchy is an aggregate entity of its next level of constituents. Aggregate information of a task can be collected recursively from the subhierarchy rooted at this task (e.g., the man hours spent, the cost, and the duration of a task). This hierarchical structure does not exist only for the activities executed, but also for the staff involved, documents generated, and reports issued. Thus, representation of hierarchical data and aggregate entities is essential.

The hierarchical nature of the wbs also introduces the concept of *level of data abstraction*. For example, suppose that we uniformly treat all the data elements generated in the development process as *product*. Then, we can categorize them into several specific types such as requirements document, functional specification, module design description, test plan, program module, and instruction manual. Each type may need more classification (e.g., the module design description contains both the module interface description and the control flow description). The resultant structure is the *object type hierarchy* where lower level subtypes can share and inherit common properties of their supertypes. This generalization/specification, aggregation, and classification abstraction [Smith77, Mylopoulos80] has been used for a long time to represent knowledge in artificial intelligence. Employing such a knowledge representation scheme not only helps us in organizing the data, but also lets us enforce integrity constraints on different object type levels.

In a design environment, data entities can incur a long period of evolution. While one version of the project is in operation, bug fixes, newly added features, plus new configurations may spawn several divergent products. Different versions of programs and documents must be sustained so that later examination and comparison are possible. On the management level, in order to reason about the progress of activities, maintaining the entire project's chronological records is inevitable. The project manager should be able to look back at any point in time and see what state the project was in. Keeping a single state of a data object is not sufficient. Versioning, historical recording, and alternatives must be handled properly by the supporting database.

Current project management tools are *centralized* management tools in the sense that all project changes are collected together into the system by a single authority. For a large project with hundreds of activities, such management methodology demands substantial manual efforts. The DesignNet model defines a triggering mechanism to automate the activity initiation, replanning, and rescheduling when activities have to be redefined and/or reinitiated. Project personnel report the events directly to the system. The system will trigger actions depending upon these events. For example, a specification change requires the design activity to be reinitiated or the completion of implementing a program module initiates the testing activity of this module. Thus, the database needs to model the behaviors as well as the possible interaction among objects.

Having looked at the related issues, the decision is apparent. An ideal database model for this purpose should have the following capabilities: the power to model hierarchical data and aggregate objects, the distinction between data type and instance, the inheritance of properties and operations down the wbs hierarchy, the ability to handle design evolution including version and alternative control, and a procedure triggering mechanism. Current record-oriented models such as the hierarchical, network, and relational database models have deficiencies in supporting all the above notions and mechanisms. The recent development of object-oriented database models, which combine the power of object programming and the efficient management of data, provides a feasible solution for the issues described above.

14.3 MODELING THE SOFTWARE LIFE CYCLE USING THE DesignNet MODEL

Software projects usually do not progress in a simple, linear manner from application concept to operational system [Dowson87]. Repetition of the same activities, due to change of the previous decisions, seems to be central to the software process. Besides errors and mistakes, the evolution of a software system (e.g., new release with enhanced features) also leads to iterations of the process. Several approaches were proposed to describe the software development process. The traditional Waterfall model [Royce87] views software development as a manufacturing process. Each step is a phase, and the completion of one phase leads to another. Back pointing arrows show the possible backtracking to previous phases. In [Osterweil87], all software activities are viewed as being aimed at the creation and/or alteration of software products. Software processes are viewed as software objects, and products of other processes.

This section briefly describes how the DesignNet model is used to represent the project wbs, activity dependencies, and historical records. The detailed definition of the DesignNet model is described in [Liu87]. We will show how the software life cycle phases are modeled in DesignNet after this description.

DesignNet is composed of three basic components, a set of places, a set of structural operators, and a set of execution transitions. Places are further categorized into five subtypes: project, activity, resource, product, and status report. Each subtype represents a specific information type that is involved in the project development cycle. Structural operators connect places of the same type into a hierarchical decomposition via directed structural links. They allow aggregate information to be collected automatically at different levels of detail. Transitions together with the dependency links define the precedent relationships among different information entities.

Figure 14.1 shows an example of a design net. The activity places *activity, driver design & imple.*, and *driver testing* together with the AND operator form an activity wbs. The product places *product, graphic command spec., test plan & procedure, driver code, operation manual, baseline code*, and *version description*, also form a product wbs. The *driver design & imple.* activity is initiated either when a new version of the graphic specification is generated or when the testing shows a failure. Both situations require the resource *system programmer* to be involved in the design task. This example also shows

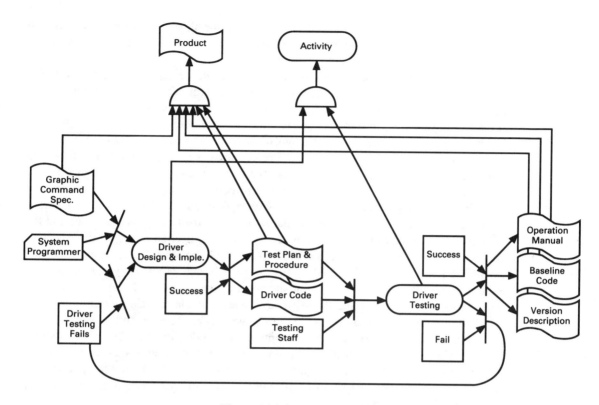

Figure 14.1   A DesignNet example.

that a possible iterative backtracking exists from testing to design. If the driver code fails to pass its functional testing, the plotter driver design activity will be reinitiated.

The places plus the structural operators, the transitions, and the connections only define the static description of a project. It depicts the project plan and only serves as a template. Due to the iterative nature of a software project, a planned activity or planned product can be executed/generated more than once. To distinguish the planned entity and the actual execution occurrence, tokens are used to store the execution dependent information. Tokens are objects with specific properties. DesignNet permits any number of tokens to reside at a place, and each token would represent an instance of the place where the token was created. A project executes by firing transitions. The transition firing is a nonvolatile process and creates new token instances with time dependent information. An instance of the fired transition is also created to keep track of the tokens that enable this transition and the tokens that are created after the firing. The tokens and fired transition instances delineate the project execution history.

Depending upon the management methodology and life cycle phases chosen by a project manager, one can specify many predefined activity, resource, and product types to enforce the software development discipline. These definitions include the rules that activities of individual phases must follow, the cost measurement criteria for different resource categories, and the formats that various documents should obey. These predefined types are used as organization-wide standard templates and are elaborated to lower level details while a specific project plan is built up. The aim is to build standardized internal development discipline while the flexibility for extension is still preserved. This goal cannot be achieved in conventional databases where type inheritance and procedural properties are not supported.

Under current DesignNet prototype development, we have chosen the waterfall model [Royce87] as the methodology to experiment with. Other life cycle models are equally well represented. It contains six major life cycle phases. Different personnel skills and development disciplines are required for different phases. Also, each phase has its own product types. A full DesignNet representation of this model is defined in [Liu87]. Figure 14.2 shows the graphical representation of these six phases. Based on this representation, several predefined objects are constructed as life cycle templates.

The resource and document types required before an activity can be initiated and the product types generated after an activity is finished are defined with transitions before and after that activity. In the initial *requirement analysis* phase, the user and the system analyst are involved in defining the system specification based on the customer contract. Tools for automating the requirement and specification development, such as SREM [Davis77], can be used at this stage. During *preliminary design*, system engineers take the specification as input and generate the functional design document, the interface control document and the test plan of each module. Special design tools (e.g., PSA/PSL [Teichroew77]) can be used at this stage. In *detail design* and *implementation*, programmers translate these design descriptions into code modules. The code modules together with test plans and testing procedures generated in earlier stages are then tested (*testing* phase) by testing engineers and quality assurance staff. When the final product goes into *operation*, product control staff and the software manager are in charge of the update and document change.

This template provides the typical behaviors that activities of each phase should follow. Various predefined triggers are attached to certain transition types. They are invoked when certain events are detected. For example, a delta operation into the SCCS [Rochkind75] is attached to the transition type after the testing phase activity, so that the version of a code module is updated after being modified and debugged. Other triggers implement design rule checking across development phases. These triggers assist in handling constraints and enforcing consistency checking.

What management questions can be answered in DesignNet that are either impossible or difficult to answer using conventional tools? To address this issue, we have divided the management questions into six areas: activities, documents, people, cost, project history and project analysis. Under *activities* we can ask: given the wbs, what nodes (at any level) are complete, incomplete, or not yet started. Under *documents* we can ask: what is the status of all documents, in particular what version is complete, started but not complete, or not yet begun. Document creation is modeled in the wbs and specific versions are tracked. Under *people* we can ask: who is responsible for a specific activity, or what time was spent by some person on a specific activity. These are simple resource questions. A more difficult one would be: what people were involved in the same generic activity, but at different occurrences. Under *project cost* we can ask: how much has been spent, how much needs to be spent to complete the next phase, what are various categories of expenditures. Under *project history* we can ask: how long did it take to achieve a certain milestone, how much money was required and how many people were involved. Under *project analysis* we can ask for all critical activities,

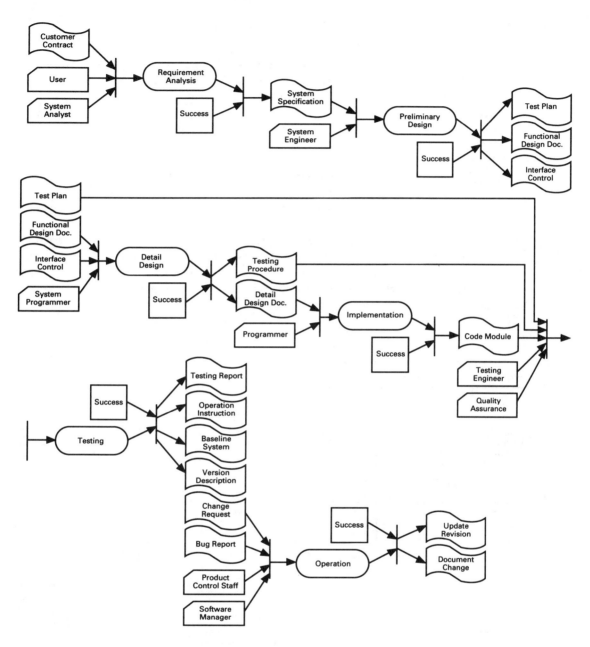

Figure 14.2 DesignNet of Life Cycle Phases.

all late activities, all re-scheduled activities, or all activities that have been re-executed more than once. Also, we can ask: what activities will be affected given that a change in specification has occurred. Most of these questions are difficult to answer using existing software project management tools. They all depend upon accurate and timely capturing of the data.

14.4 THE DesignNet MODEL IN TERMS OF OBJECTS

Utilizing an object-oriented database to design an application system is a two-stage task. The object type hierarchy design comes first and the application program design comes next.[1] However, these two stages are coupled together closely since the operations and procedures that manipulate objects must also be included in the type definitions. The type hierarchy is analogous to the conceptual schema of conventional database systems except that type definition contains more behavior description for each object type such as methods, operations, exceptions that can be raised, and triggers for integrity enforcement. To the application system, only the name of the object and the functions that can manipulate the object are known. This *data abstraction* concept is a means of implementing information hiding and is a powerful feature in object programming.

Under the current prototype implementation, all components in DesignNet are represented as object types in the database. Several subtypes are defined under each component. Figure 14.3 shows the object type hierarchy. The hierarchy describes the type structure of all objects included in DesignNet. On the leftmost part of the hierarchy are three object types for time object representation and manipulation. The execution transi-

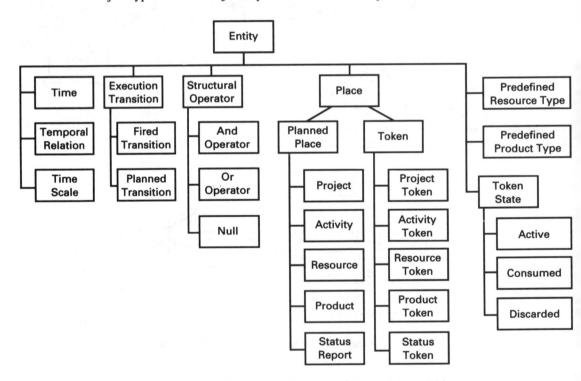

Figure 14.3 Object type hierarchy of DesignNet.

[1]The current release of Vbase does not support run-time type definition update. Any type definition change must be done in the first stage.

tion type has two subtypes, the planned transition and the fired transition. The structural operator is an enumerative object and has three alternatives. The planned place and the token are the major object types that encapsulate project information. The information associated with project planning is stored within the planned place objects, while the execution dependent information is stored within tokens. For instance, in Figure 14.1, the driver design activity requires a system programmer resource. This resource is specified in the planned place prior to the activity place. When the project gets executed, different staff with the necessary skills may be assigned to the same activity at different executions. A token is generated for each occurrence. Place is a supertype of the planned place and the token. Both types are further decomposed into five subtypes for more specific information types. The token state is also an enumerative object that corresponds to the possible token states: the active, the consumed, and the discarded state. Several predefined resource and product types are also included. Since their definition depends on the life cycle phases chosen by the project manager, their subtypes are not shown here.

14.5 RELATIONSHIPS AMONG OBJECT TYPES

In conventional databases, the information is usually modeled as records. Relationships among data entities are constructed through primitive references to related records. To set up a one-to-many or many-to-many relationship among several record types in the relational model, a new record type is introduced and the key fields of associated record types are used to designate records that make up the relationship. In the network and hierarchical model, links are used in connecting occurrences of the associated records.

Object-oriented databases use different approaches in capturing relationships between objects. They allow more complicated relationships. For example, an association between entities may itself be considered as an entity and further relationships can be built upon this entity. In Vbase, there is no need to define an explicit object type for establishing relationships between objects. Instead, properties of an object can have highly complicated constructs and can be used for this purpose. A property can be a primitive type object(e.g., a number or a string), a reference to another object, or an aggregate object in which individual elements are references to other objects. The latter two cases are usually the way relationships are modeled.

The hierarchy in Figure 14.3 only shows the supertype and subtype relations of objects in a generalization and specialization manner. In this section, we will define the relationships among objects that are necessary for the DesignNet model. Identifying all desired relations is a crucial task in designing any application system that utilizes an object-oriented database approach.

Figure 14.4 shows the relationships defined among object types in DesignNet. The *place, transition, time,* and *structural operator* types are the top-level object types. Their relationships are shown in Figure 14.4(a). Since the time a place is created in the project plan and the time a transition is defined to connect places is important for tracking the project planning, they both have a *createtime* property to denote when they are created. The wbs of a project is maintained by three associations. The *decomposetype* of a

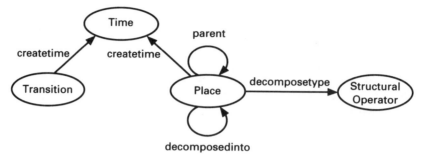

(a)

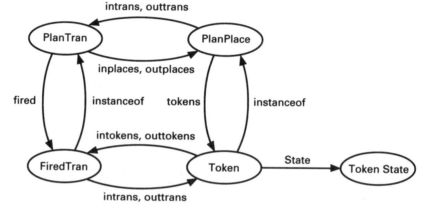

(b)

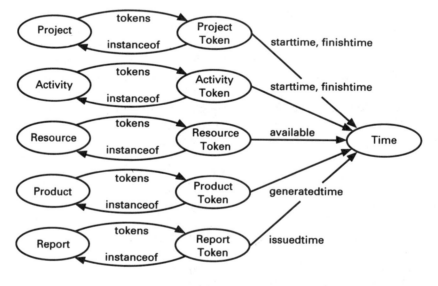

(c)

Figure 14.4 Relationships among object types in DesignNet.

place is initialized to be the NONE operator which means no decomposition. When a place is decomposed, the decomposetype specifies either an AND or an OR structural operator. The *decomposedinto* together with the *parent* associations sustain the one-to-many decomposition relationship. The decomposedinto is a set object containing all the places that a place is decomposed into. The parent is an object reference to a place where the current place is decomposed from.

As a result of iteration in design projects, the same element in a project plan may have several occurrences (e.g., an activity being executed more than once, a code module having multiple versions). There exists a one-to-many relationship between the plan elements and their actual execution elements. Figure 14.4(b) shows the one-to-many relationship between planned places and tokens (the *fired* and *instanceof* property) as well as the one-to-many relationship between planned transitions and fired transitions (the *tokens* and *instanceof* property).

The connection among transitions and places encapsulates the dependencies between different project information. The *intrans* property of a place links to the transitions where it can be triggered from. The *outtrans* property of a place connects to the transitions where it will enable after an active token is generated. The *inplaces* and *outplaces* properties of a transition connect to its input and output places. All the above relations are represented through set objects since they are many-to-many mappings.

The planned place object type is further refined into five lower level types, namely the project, activity, resource, product, and report types. Accordingly, the token object type is also refined to five lower level token types. The original relationships between planned places and tokens must also be refined to reflect this subtype specialization. Figure 14.4(c) shows the redefined mappings among these subtypes. The refined token types also have newly defined relations with time objects. The project token and activity token have two associated time stamps, the *starttime* and *finishtime*. The resource token keeps track of the time that a resource is *available* (i.e., the time assigned to an activity). The product token keeps the generation time and the report token keeps the issued time.

14.6 TIME NOTATION AND STAMPING MECHANISM

One crucial element in the project development cycle is the recording of all events. This recording relies heavily on a time basis and is necessary for both the planning and executing phases of a project. During the project planning stage, we must put down the time when every piece of the plan is constructed by the project manager and supervisors of tasks. This helps us to review, evaluate, and modify the project plan. When a project is being executed, an activity can be initiated more than once and a document can have several revisions. The time an activity is initiated and the time a document is created must be stored with their corresponding instances. Therefore, most objects in DesignNet have to be associated with time.

Since the current Vbase release does not support a time object and time stamp mechanism, the first task is to define a generic time notation and the manipulating operations. Figure 14.5 shows the TDL (Type Definition Language) definition of the desired properties and operations for time.

```
 1   % Time object and manipulating operations definition
 2   define Type TemporalRelation is enum (BEFORE, AFTER,
                                                      EQUAL);
 3   define Type TimeScale is enum (MINUTE, HOUR, DATE,
                                              MONTH, YEAR);
 4   define Type Time
 5       supertype = {Entity};
 6       properties =
 7       {
 8             tstamp: Integer;
 9             minute: Integer;
10             hour:   Integer;
11             date:   Integer;
12             month:  Integer;
13             year:   Integer;
14       };
15       operations =
16       {
17             Stamp (type : Type,
18                  keywords
19                      minute: Integer,
20                      hour:   Integer,
21                      date:   Integer,
22                      month:  Integer,
23                      year:   Integer)
24                  raises (StampOverflow)
25                  returns (Time)
26                  method (TimeStamp);
27
28             Comparison (t1: Time, t2: Time, granularity:
                                      TimeScale)
29                  returns (TemporalRelation)
30                  method (CompareTime);
31       };
32       define procedure Current()
33             returns (Time)
34             raises (SystemTimeFailure)
35             method (CurrentTime)
36       end Current;
37   end Time;
```

Figure 14.5   Time object type and operation definition.

Three object types (*TemporalRelation, TimeScale, Time*) and three basic operations (*Stamp, Comparison, Current*) have been defined for this purpose. The *tstamp* property (line 8) of the *time* object contains a time value measured in seconds starting from the clock initiated time chosen by the system (which is 00:00:00 GMT, January 1, 1970 on our UNIX system). It keeps a global time-of-day reference in the second level of granularity which is quite enough for most applications. The calendar values of year, month, date, hour, and minute (lines 9-13) are also stored within the time object. Presumably these values can always be computed from the global clock tstamp reference. However, current Vbase does not support virtual property fields and there is also a tradeoff between space and time. If all calendar fields are computed whenever they are accessed, computation overhead can degrade the system performance.

Figure 14.6 shows a COP (C Object Processor) language implementation of the *Current* operation which is implemented by the method *CurrentTime*.

```
1    #include <time.h>
2    enter module $Time;
3
4    method obj $Time CurrentTime()
5    {
6        struct tm *time;
7        long tstamp;
8        obj $Time currentTime;
9
10       tstamp = time ((long *) 0);
11       time = localtime (&tstamp);
12       currentTime = $Time$[stamp:  tstamp,
13                            minute: time->tm_min,
14                            hour:   time->tm_hour,
15                            date:   time->tm_mday,
16                            month:  time->tm_mon,
17                            year:   time->tm_year];
18       return (currentTime);
19   }
```

Figure 14.6 COP program segment for current time operation.

It retrieves the current global time in seconds (line 10), translates it into calendar format (line 11), creates a time object with the associated time values (lines 12-17), and returns it. This operation can be attached to an object's time property as an *init* (initialization) operation such that whenever an instance of that object is created, it will be automatically time stamped. For instance, suppose a document object has a *timecreated* property to denote the time when its instances have been created. The following definition will cause a time stamp to be transparently attached to the document:

```
define Type Document
    properties =
```

```
{
    timecreated: $Time
                 define init method(CurrentTime);
    ...
}
```

On the other hand, the *Stamp* operation (lines 17-26 in Figure 14.5) permits an arbitrary time setting given the calendar time. It is used for the time setting on a value other than the current time (e.g., an activity is expected to finish on Jan. 10, 1988). The *Comparison* operation (lines 28-30) takes two time objects and compares them on the given time granularity. The granularity parameter allows one to compare the time on the desired time scale. For example, we can ask if two activities start on the same month (a large granularity) or if one code module is generated earlier than the other (a small granularity). This operation returns three possible temporal relations (line 2)—before, after, or equal.

The above definitions merely provide primitive manipulation functions. Higher level functions can be built upon these operations without difficulty. One major extension is the comparison of two time durations and their temporal relations. We can determine if an activity starts before or after another activity. Or we can ascertain if two activities overlap, meet, or contain each other. We can also decide if two activities have the same start date, end date, or duration.

Keeping a complete historical record is the basis for the satisfaction of project auditing. This record should maintain a wide range of information. With the time stamp mechanism, DesignNet provides the version development traceability at a coarse level of granularity. Since tokens in the same place denote different occurrences of that place, time dependent properties stored with each token provide flexibility for building finer level version control. For example, a version index is stored with the token of a code product place. We can incorporate any source code version control system (e.g., SCCS) and use the version index to locate the version generated at a specific time.

14.7 WORK BREAKDOWN STRUCTURE REPRESENTATION

For a complex project, the wbs may extend many levels deep in the hierarchy. Most existing project management tools [SuperProject86, Microsoft86] use an artificial coding method for distinguishing different level entities (e.g., an eight digit code for a maximum of eight-level hierarchy). This mechanism can be implemented easily under relational databases. Nevertheless, users can only select certain code combinations that group the required entities together for report generation purposes. Neither the automatic aggregate data collection nor the unlimited level representation is considered. Under the object-oriented scheme, the capabilities of defining aggregate objects and procedure attachment afford a better solution.

In DesignNet, the wbs is represented through structural operators and links. A structural operator connects places of the same type where its output arc points to a single place for the node to be decomposed and its input arcs come from nodes denoting the constituents. It is always a one-to-many mapping from a place to its decomposed places. On the object type definition, since a structural operator merely carries the logical one-to-many decomposition and no property is associated with it, defining it as an enumerative literal object is sufficient. The link then can be defined as a property of the place object. With no extra level of structural operator object being created, we can save half the object accessing time during the wbs traversal.

Figure 14.7 shows the TDL definition of the structural operator object and the links used to construct the wbs. The structural operator is defined as an enumerative object with three literal values (line 2). The place object contains three properties for wbs links. When a place is originally created, it is not decomposed and its default structural `decomposetype` is null (line 8). If a place has been decomposed into lower level places, the operator type is defined and saved in the `decomposetype` property. All constituents of this place are stored as a set in the `decomposedinto` property (lines 10, 11). The `parent` property (line 9) is a reference to its parent place where this place is decomposed from. If this property has a null value, then this place is the root of a wbs hierarchy. The `decomposedinto` property provides a top-down traversal link while the `parent` property provides a bottom-up traversal link. Maintaining a two-way link allows efficient access in either direction. The `inverse` clause in the `decomposedinto` property guarantees that whenever a child place is added into this set, the `parent` property will also be updated. It enforces the integrity between the double links.

```
1   % Structural Operator definition
2   define Type SOperator is enum (None, And, Or);
3   define Type Place
4       supertype = {Entity};
5       properties =
6       {
7           . . .
8           decomposetype:  SOperator := None;
9           parent:         optional Place;
10          decomposedinto: optional distributed
                                        Set[Place]
11                          inverse $Place$parent;
12          . . .
13      };
```

Figure 14.7 Structural operator and *wbs* link definition.

For those properties that must be aggregated from lower level places, a method is defined for the property's *get* operation. This method checks if the place has been decomposed into lower level places. If yes, it will recursively retrieve an individual constituent's value and perform the desired aggregate function to yield the final property value. Figure 14.8 shows one such example, the computation of an activity's cost. Part (a) shows that the method ActCost is attached to the cost property's get operation (line 7). Part (b) is the COP code for this operation. If an activity is not on the bottom level (i.e., a task), its cost is a summation of the cost from its AND'ed children activities (lines 12-16) or the maximum cost among all its OR'ed children activities (lines 17-22). Attaching a retrieving method to an aggregate property ensures that the data is always collected from the current state of the database. An alternative way to achieve the data integrity is to attach a modification method (i.e., the *set* operation) such that when the property value is updated, the method invokes higher level entities' computation method recursively and propagates the change upward to the topmost level entity.

```
1   define Type Activity
2        supertype = {Place};
3        properties =
4        {
5            ...
6            cost: $Real
7                    define get method(ActCost);
8            ...
9        };
```
             (a) Activity object type definition

```
1   enter module $Place;
2   enter module $Activity;
3   method obj Real ActCost(act)
4   obj $Activity act;
5   {
6       obj $Real total;
7       obj $Activity curAct;
8
9       total = 0;
10      if (act.decomposetype == $SOperator$None)
11          total = act.cost;
12      else if (act.decomposetype == $SOperator$And)
13      {
14          iterate (curAct = act.decomposedinto)
15              total += curAct.cost;
16      }
17      else if (act.decomposetype == $SOperator$Or)
18      {
19          iterate (curAct = act.decomposedinto)
20              if (curAct.cost > total)
21                  total = curAct.cost;
22      }
23      return (total);
24  }
```
             (b) Activity cost computation method

Figure 14.8   Activity cost computation method.

Due to the nature of a design project, the same activity may be executed multiple times depending on various conditions. To avoid destroying the project history, different instances of the same activity must be created whenever it is reinitiated. This process can be automated since the project state is changed only when new tokens have been created or existing tokens' values have been updated (both cases indicate the occurrence of an *event*). This section describes what object types and their properties have been defined to accomplish this event-driven management methodology.

Initially, the project manager only defines the dependencies among activities, resources, and products through the transition connections in the project plan. An instantiation mechanism has been defined in DesignNet such that a newly occurred event will always trigger its associated transition during the project execution period. This transition checks whether all its input places have active tokens. If so, it fires itself by creating a fired transition instance of itself, one token for each of its output places, and connections among the input and output tokens. All these operations are handled automatically by the system.

To distinguish between the project plan and actual initiated instances, both the transition and the place object have two subtypes defined under them. Figure 14.9 shows the two subtype definitions of the execution transition — the planned transition subtype PlanTran (lines 1-23) and the fired transition subtype FiredTran (lines 25-42).

```
1    % Planned Transition definition
2    define Type PlanTran
3        supertypes = {Transition};
4        properties =
5        {
6            fired:      optional distributed
                         Set[FiredTran]
7                        inverse $FiredTran$instanceof;
8            inplaces:   optional distributed Set[Place]
9                        inverse $PlanPlace$outtrans;
10           outplaces:  optional Set[Place]
11                       inverse $PlanPlace$intrans;
12       };
13       operations =
14       {
15           Fire (type: Type, keywords transition:
                         PlanTran)
16               raises (NotEnabled)
17               method (TranFiring);
18
19           EnabledCheck (type: Type, keywords intoken:
                         Token)
20               raises (Enable)
21               method (CheckTranEnable);
```

```
22       };
23   end PlanTran;
24
25   % Fired Transition definition
26   define Type FiredTran
27       supertypes = {Transition};
28       properties =
29       {
30           instanceof: PlanTran;
31           intokens:   optional Set[Token];
32                       inverse $Token$outtran;
33           outtokens:  optional Set[Token];
34                       inverse $Token$intran;
35       };
36       operations =
37       {
38           refines Create (ft: FiredTran)
39               triggers (ConsumeInTokens)
40               triggers (DiscardOutTokens);
41       };
42   end FiredTran;
```

Figure 14.9   Transition subtypes definition.

A one-to-many mapping exists between the planned transition and the fired transition since a planned transition can be fired more than once. This mapping is implemented with a set property `fired` (lines 6, 7) in the planned transition and a single value property `instanceof` (line 30) in the fired transition. The `fired` property contains all fired instances associated with this planned transition. The `instanceof` property is a backward link to its planned transition. Again, the `inverse` clause guarantees the integrity of this double linked mapping. The separation of one representative object entity (e.g., the planned transition) and its actual members (e.g., the fired transition) into two subtypes provides us a work around approach in the systems that do not support run-time object type creation. On the other hand, this distinction requires that all subtypes under these two subtypes be separated as well. In DesignNet, a place can denote five different information entities. Under this separation, two parallel subtypes are defined for each information type and a total of ten subtypes result.

Since a transition can be enabled by conjunctive conditions and can trigger more than one event after its firing, the transition and place have a many-to-many relationship. Both the planned transition and the fired transition have multiple links to their inputs and outputs. For a planned transition, the inputs and outputs are planned places (lines 8-11). For a fired transition, the inputs are tokens that enable this transition and the outputs are tokens created after its firing (lines 31-34).

Two operations are defined with planned transition. The `EnabledCheck` operation (lines 19-21) checks to see if all the input places of the transition have active tokens. If yes, an `Enable` exception is raised. This operation is invoked when any of its input places has a newly created token. The `Fire` operation (lines 15-17) will fire the planned transition by creating a new fired transition instance and perform the token bindings. The fired transition has two trigger functions attached to its create operation (lines 39, 40). One function (`ConsumeInTokens`) changes all the active input tokens to consumed state to prevent the same transition being fired once more. The other function (`DiscardOutTokens`) checks to see if output places already have active tokens, and if so, puts them into a discarded state. This trigger guarantees that only one token can be in an active state at a time. Such a situation happens when one activity is ongoing and new changes from earlier phases require reinitiation of this activity. Having more than one active token in the same activity means that redundant efforts are spent on the same task and may result in inconsistent products. If any token is already in an active state, the `DiscardOutTokens` trigger sends mail to the responsible staff notifying them of the existence of the situation.

Places are the entities containing the primary information involved in the project development cycle. Figure 14.10 shows the subtypes definition of the place object. The place type also has two subtypes, the `PlanPlace` (lines 1-12) for planned place and the `Token` (lines 14-31) for actual instances generated during execution. A one-to-many relationship mapping exists between the planned place and the token since a planned place can have multiple copies of information due to reinitiation (e.g., a specification changed or a bug being found). This mapping is maintained by the `tokens` property (lines 6, 7) of the planned place and the `instanceof` property (line 20) of the token. The `tokens` property is a set object that collects all object references of tokens associated with this planned place. The `instanceof` property is a backward link from the token to its template.

```
1    % Planned Place definition
2    define Type PlanPlace
3        supertypes = {Place};
4        properties =
5        {
6            tokens:     optional distributed
                         Set[Token]
7                        inverse $Token$instanceof;
8            intrans:    optional Set[Transition];
9            outtrans:   optional Set[Transition];
10           refines decomposedinto: optional
                                     Set[PlanPlace];
11       };
12   end PlanPlace;
13
14   % Token definition
15   define Type TokenState is enum (Active, Consumed,
                                     Discarded);
16   define Type Token
17       supertypes = {Place};
18       properties =
```

```
19      {
20          instanceof: PlanPlace;
21          state: TokenState := Active
22                  define set triggers (TokenStateSet);
23          intran:     optional FiredTran;
24          outtran:    optional FiredTran;
25      };
26      operations =
27      {
28          refines Create (t: Token)
29              triggers (ForwardEnable)
30      };
31  end Token;
```

Figure 14.10   Planned place and token definitions.

Similar to the transition firing, the planned place has multiple links to inputs and outputs since a place denotes an event that can be triggered from disjunctive events and may enable other transitions depending upon the project state. For a planned place, the inputs and outputs are planned transitions (lines 8, 9). On the contrary, only a single input and output fired transition is necessary for a token since a token is created due to the firing of a transition even though its associated planned place may have more than one input transition. Thus, the intran and outtran properties (lines 23, 24) of a token are single-valued properties while the intrans and outtrans properties of a planned place are set variables.

A trigger operation ForwardEnable is attached to the default create operation, (lines 28, 29). This trigger checks if any other transition will be enabled due to the creation of this token. Firing a transition creates tokens on all its output places and these tokens may further enable transitions of later life cycle phases. A chain reaction can result. For example, when a programmer reports the completion of a code module, a transition is fired to upgrade the new version code into the system, and this new code will also fire another transition to initiate the testing of this code module.

14.9 SUMMARY AND CONCLUSIONS

DesignNet is a model that provides a framework for describing the software development process. Project managers can have a hierarchical view of projects though the wbs decomposition. Relationships and interaction among different project information types (activity, product, resource, and status report information) are defined in Petri notation. Its most novel feature is that it allows for the reinitiation of activities and for the restructuring of the plan, two phenomena that are common for software development, but are not addressed in any existing models. Since this paper is focused on the database support of the model, DesignNet is not described in full detail here. For a complete description, please see [Liu87] and [Liu88b].

This paper has identified several key software management issues that must be modeled by any integrated SEE database. They are: work breakdown structure, project history, event monitoring, and reinitiation of tasks. Whether a CASE tool can model these concepts is a crucial factor in reducing the manual efforts spent on manipulating management level information. Though object-oriented databases appear to offer superior modeling power for describing the concepts, these concepts still require realization in such a system. We have proposed the DesignNet model which considers all these issues, and discussed several representation techniques for supporting the database layer of this model, including a time stamp mechanism, the use of set variables, and the use of multiple instances and triggers.

Utilizing an object-oriented development environment which combines both language and database features provides a number of important advantages for the SEE application. The object type hierarchy and property inheritance offers many levels of data abstraction. Operations and methods defined under an object type capture its behavior and fulfill the information hiding goal. A triggering mechanism allows the enforcement of integrity checking. It also makes automatic event monitoring feasible. The provision of composite objects assists in representing a project's work breakdown structure.

A prototype system of DesignNet has been implemented on a Sun workstation. The user interface is based on X-windows and the object database is Vbase. The program will visually display a DesignNet similar to that shown in the first two figures of this chapter. It is possible to incrementally augment the wbs or to view any segment of the project. We have not yet applied DesignNet to an actual project since not all the higher level modules are completed.

Several shortcomings of the current version of the object database that we use can be cited. First, the diversity of management information types requires dynamically defining and modifying the database object types and their properties. In Vbase, the TDL definition and COP program must be recompiled after any property modification and existing object instances will be incompatible to new object types. It requires shutting down the system to migrate existing object instances to their new type definitions. This is intolerable for an operational system. A work around approach is available to resolve this. We can create an object subtype that includes all the property changes and perform the recompilation. The data migration then can be performed by copying existing object instances to this new subtype while the system is still operating. Once all objects are moved, the old object type is removed and the subtype replaces the actual object definition. Several dynamic object type evolution management methodologies have been proposed [Banerjee87b] and [Penny87]. A future release of Vbase will also provide such a feature. Their effectiveness needs to be studied before we can conclude which approach is superior.

A second weakness is the lack of support for object version control. The engineering design task is usually a process of long duration. An object instance's evolution needs to be recorded for later examination. The object history recording mechanism described in this paper, namely creating multiple object instances and time stamping, introduces redundancy and space overhead. The approach of an incremental differential representation of object versions can eliminate this problem [Banerjee87b]. However, it introduces extra computation overhead. Several existing object-oriented databases plan to support this feature in various ways in the future. Another shortcoming is the lack of multiple inheritance along the type lattice where an object type has several supertypes. This representation does exist in software design information. Conflicts arise with the property inheritance in a lattice structure: for example, if two supertypes have defined the same property names with different value specification. Similar conflicts also arise in the inheritance of operation.

Commercially available OODB systems are just now appearing. In this chapter we have shown how one can begin to base a SEE targeted to software project management on such a system. We have identified several techniques for accomplishing the required object modeling. Some of these techniques are required because of the limitations of the current systems. We expect to see in the future more comprehensive solutions to these problems as more insight is gained by doing applications like the one we presented here.

15 An Object-Oriented Model for Network Management

Soumitra Sengupta, Alexander Dupuy, Jed Schwartz,
Yechiam Yemini

15.1 INTRODUCTION

Networks have become a principal means for information sharing and transfer in large corporations and institutions. The recent direction towards large enterprise-wide computing is a direct consequence of the interconnection and the ease of availability of computing resources in large numbers. The complexity of interconnections has risen sharply in the past few years. Consequently, management of the connectivity subsystems has become a matter of paramount importance in order to support resilient and efficient information flow in today's networks.

A network, in simplistic terms, consists of physical connections between many computing entities, and sets of protocols for information exchange over these connections. The number of computing entities, the richness of interconnections, and the heterogeneity of protocols, all contribute to the complexity of a network and its management. While geographic distribution and functional isolation of different domains within a network make it impractical to employ a centralized network management strategy, a distributed solution, by its very nature, adds to the complexity of monitoring and coordination of network entities.

Current solutions for network management are mostly restricted to a single set of protocols executing on a single platform of hardware and connections supported by a single vendor. Most networks, however, consist of a heterogeneous mixture of components that communicate using a variety of protocols. Even when it is possible to reconcile the heterogeneity, the volume of management information from the network itself can be overwhelming, which makes the task of extracting correct and meaningful conclusions extremely hard.

The **NetMATE** (Network Management, Analysis, and Testing Environment) project at Columbia University addresses these and other issues related to effective network management. The fundamental purpose of NetMATE is to provide a model of a network, whether real or simulated, that can be manipulated and studied. NetMATE is being developed as a set of software tools that monitor the functional and performance behavior of large scale distributed network systems, analyze these behaviors, identify and isolate erroneous operational conditions, report them in a meaningful manner to operators, and support operator-directed, semi-automated network management. NetMATE is a natural extension of **NeST**, Columbia's Network Simulation and Prototype Tool system [Bacon87, Dupuy88], which is a portable simulation environment consisting of two parts: a monitor and a simulator. The monitor permits graphical iconic interaction and management of simulated network scenarios; and the simulator executes detailed simulated processes in accordance with the parameters set by the monitor and process definitions. NeST has been ported to many sites including universities, industrial and governmental research and development laboratories, corporation development and operations teams.

In this chapter, we discuss the design of a specific module in NetMATE which deals with the issues of modeling a network to create and store a permanent repository of generic and specific properties of network entities. **Vbase**, an object-oriented database [Ontologic88a], is chosen for the purpose of defining and storing the models of real network entities, their interrelationships, and dependencies. Vbase is an excellent and complete object-oriented software system with a clean architecture and supports a rich set of data value and aggregate types (and associated operations) and relationships. One of the most useful features of Vbase is that the types themselves are objects, and hence can be manipulated to a very high degree. Given the intricate structure and behavior of a network, Vbase has been a very useful tool and database in implementing the NetMATE network model.

The remainder of the chapter is organized as follows. In section 15.2, we specify the functional requirements of NetMATE and discuss the sophistication required to fulfill the requirements. NetMATE architecture is presented in section 15.3, where we discuss the different modules that support the required functionality. Section 15.4 elaborates on the data model. Specifically, the generic relationships between the network entities and their representation in the data model are detailed. We also briefly touch upon the representation of information required by various modules of NetMATE. A discussion of the Vbase database with respect to the NetMATE project follows in section 15.5. The current status of NetMATE is presented in section 15.6, and we conclude in section 15.7.

15.2 FUNCTIONAL REQUIREMENTS

The functional requirements of the NetMATE system are derived from the needs of various users of the system such as operators, administrators and researchers. There are few fundamental necessities, however, that are desired by all users. In order for the NetMATE to be a generic tool for network management, it must support these functions, and more importantly, be extensible in accommodating future needs.

Configuration Management — A network management system should be able to define, confirm, and exercise control over the configuration of network entities. Automatic validation of a configuration should be possible which includes validation of connectivity and other network relationships. For instance, the system must recognize that a standard *modem* cannot be attached to a generic *ethernet* but it can be connected to an *asynchronous line*; and if a modem is defined to be connected to an asynchronous line, then the system must confirm the actual connection in the network.

Configuration Management requires definition of static information regarding generic network entities such as modems, hosts, terminal servers, link protocols, transport protocols, and so on. Furthermore, it requires definition of properties of specific entities within a generic class to check the validity of a configuration accurately.

Fault and Performance Management — NetMATE functions should include fault management facilities such as fault tracing and reporting, event logging and execution of diagnostic tests. Similarly, it should be able to monitor and evaluate the performance of the network by collecting and disseminating performance data and maintaining performance logs. The provision of these functions requires real-time management of large amounts of network information by NetMATE, and an expert system capable of diagnosing faults and performance degradations.

Flexibility and Extensibility — NetMATE must be flexible enough to accommodate the wide variety of vendor products, connection schemes and protocols abundant in today's heterogeneous networks. The generic nature of NetMATE tools must provide mechanisms to adapt to such diversity with ease, and provide both generic and specific reasoning about configurability and fault analysis. One of the important strategies of NetMATE implementation is to take advantage of existing network management systems that control only a single, homogeneous network (e.g., **NetView** – an SNA network management system [Willett88]).

Distributed Network Management — In a large network, it is impractical to enforce a centralized network management system for mainly two reasons: vulnerability of the central system to failure, and an overwhelming flow of network management information that would slow the real-time management and fault analysis processing. The distribution of management functions, however, gives rise to typical distributed systems' problems such as concurrent network commands (updates) issued to the same entity by two different management systems. NetMATE systems should have clear and possibly non-overlapping management domains, and a coordination policy to avoid such problems.

Research and Planning — Besides managing a real network, NetMATE should support design and evaluation of new networks and protocols through simulation of the same under various test conditions such as traffic patterns, loads, and failures. For real networks, this facility would allow a configuration to be tested before actually installing the network, and thus aid in the planning process. For researchers, the simulation techniques would be beneficial in modeling and verification of correctness and interoperability of protocols.

The OSI model of network management [ISO87] includes the first two functions as requirements. Two other functions are mentioned—accounting and security management. The NetMATE system, however, concentrates on the more fundamental requirements mentioned above, and we believe that the additional functions can be accommodated in NetMATE later.

15.3 NETMATE ARCHITECTURE

Let us examine the architecture of the NetMATE system in terms of its system modules and their functions. The functional capabilities of NetMATE mentioned above are not implemented individually by the modules; instead, a subset of NetMATE modules cooperate to support a specific function. This is desirable in order to make use of existing capabilities and to avoid duplication of effort.

Conceptually, there are five major components of a NetMATE installation: the *Physical Network*, the *Simulated Network* (or *Simulator*), the *User Interface* (*UI*), the *Expert Analyser* (*EA*), and the *Modeler*. The Modeler is the heart of the installation in the sense that it holds the network model and other information in a database; all other components function as clients to the Modeler. Thus the Modeler serves as the hub of the system, and provides the essential glue by being a central repository of information. The Modeler may interact with the Physical Network through *Network Control Points* (NCP) which control a specific subset of the network. In a distributed implementation, the Modeler also provides services to other installations in the system and takes part in joint coordination of information flow with other Modelers. Figure 15.1 depicts the NetMATE architecture.

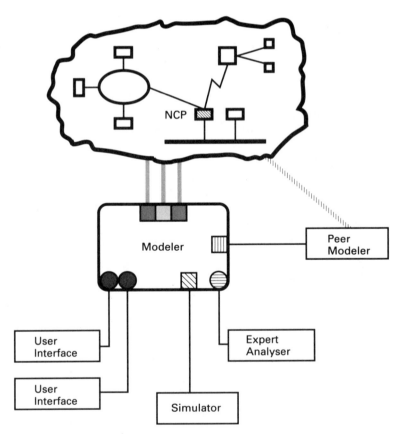

Figure 15.1 NetMATE architecture.

NetMATE architecture policy dictates that each module individually be as independent as possible. This allows for distributed execution of the modules. (The Expert Analysis module, possibly, is the only exception due to efficiency reasons.) The Modeler, in addition to the network information, also holds information for each client, and thus acts as a database server for its clients. It also serves as a conduit for information flow between its clients.

The definition of interfaces between the Modeler and other client modules is of considerable importance. They are defined by a set of information transfer units, and the invocation procedures to initiate the transfer. Ideally, a Simulator-Modeler interface should be similar to a NCP-Modeler interface so that there are minimal differences between a physical network and a simulated network. Different UI-Modeler interfaces may implement different views of the network to different users (for security as well as user-sophistication level reasons). A Modeler-Modeler interface could include only a specific view (and thus have a superset of a UI-Modeler interface). The architecture of NetMATE is such that an interface may be reused for different clients, thus providing ease of use and flexibility in the system.

NetMATE implements a network management control and information flow which is shown in Figure 15.2. A real network element is governed by NCPs which have detailed knowledge about the entity. (A simulated network entity is governed by the Simulator.) The NCPs (and the Simulator) relay information to the Network Manager(s)

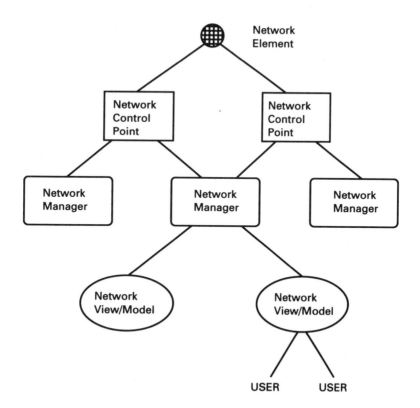

Figure 15.2   Network management control/information flow.

(implemented by the model in the Modeler and the logic in the Expert Analyser module). In absence of an explicit NCP, the Network Manager functions as an NCP to the entity. The Manager ultimately provides the information to the users through different views implemented by the UI-Modeler interfaces.

It is important to note that the hierarchy depicted in Figure 15.2 does not necessarily have a tree structure. Indeed, for information flow, it may be desirable to send critical information to more than one Network Manager. However, for the control flow, which demands strong consistency, it may be necessary to superimpose a strict and unique hierarchy structure by which one network element is controlled by a single Network Manager.

15.4 THE MODELER: AN OBJECT-ORIENTED DATABASE

In this section, we elaborate on the model chosen for the network and other information as implemented by the Modeler. A network (real and/or simulated) is subdivided into *Network Management Domains* consisting of physical devices and connections. Selection of a domain is based upon any reasonable criterion, such as geographic proximity, or similar family of communication protocols (TCP/IP compatible, SNA-compatible, etc.) For control purposes, the management functions associated with a network entity may not overlap different domains. The network model in the Modeler represents a network management domain. Multiple Modeler systems interchange network information and carry out management functions cooperatively to meet the goals of the NetMATE project. The management domain approach is motivated by [ISO87], and has appeared in other network management designs [Feridun88, Klerer88].

A Modeler consists of a *Network Model*, which describes the network entities in the domain being managed; a *Network Management Model*, which defines the network control points and managers of sub-domains or peer domains; and an *Organization Model*, which contains information about the clients of the Modeler. Associated with each model, there is a group of cooperative processes that maintain the integrity of, and provide services for, the model. The models are realized by an object-oriented database, and collectively form the basis for an integrated network management tool for a specific domain.

15.4.1 Network Model

A Network model is partitioned into two modules: *Network Configuration*, and *Network Definition*. Network Configuration consists of model instances that correspond to the actual network entities in the domain. Network Definition consists of pre-defined classes for these entities from which the instances in the Network Configuration partition are realized. Consider an example where there exists a class called **Modem** in the Definition, and there are three modems in the domain. Then there exist three instances of the Modem class in the Configuration representing the three modems.

Network configuration. Network Configuration stores two kinds of information: generic network topology, and specific information about network entities. While the specific information is realized from the class hierarchy defined in Network Definition, the topology information requires a generic class hierarchy of its own in the Network Configuration. This hierarchy is partially depicted in Figure 15.3.

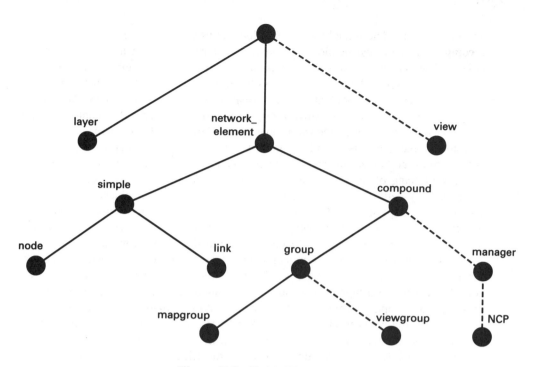

Figure 15.3 NetMATE generic type hierarchy.

The generic network entities in a domain are nodes, links, and protocol layers. A node object in the model represents a node entity which may be a machine, protocol engine, process or application in the network. Similarly, a link object represents a link entity which is a channel through which node entities can communicate. Therefore, node and link objects model abstract notions of endpoints and connectivity among the endpoints in the domain. The classes **node** and **link** are subclasses of a **simple** class, and a relationship called *connection* exists between pairs of nodes and links.

Since the behavior of node and link entities are governed by a pre-defined, layered communication protocol, the Network model defines a **layer** class of objects. A layer object represents the properties of an installed protocol and specifies a set of node and link objects in the Configuration partition that follow the protocol. A node or a link is contained exclusively in a layer, that is, they cannot be shared among multiple layers. This is an important concept in NetMATE as we conceive the endpoints of communication to be more than just physical devices and the connectivity between endpoints to be more than just a physical connection. Indeed, the nodes and links in the *physical* layer do represent physical devices and connections; but in a higher level layer, they represent endpoints and connections specific to that layer. For example, in a *X.25* layer, there may be *X.25* nodes and *X.25 Virtual Circuit* links. The model will usually include a number of layers with a clear semantics of ascendancy of layers.

A second level of abstraction within a layer is achieved by a group object (an instance of the **group** class) which represents a collection of nodes, links, and other groups in the same layer. This aggregation gives rise to a simple hierarchy with parent-child relationship. A group, as such, has no pre-defined network semantics. Its properties and functions are determined by its definition and use. The class **group** is a subclass of a **compound** class, and defines a *grouping* relationship between itself and its children objects. The classes **simple** and **compound** are subclasses of a **network_element** class.

A relationship called *membership* is established between layer and network_element objects representing the fact that a layer consists of nodes, links and groups. Additionally, a *mapping* relation is defined between objects in different layers. The mapping relationship represents the correspondence of objects at different levels of abstraction (layers) in a protocol suite. Objects (simple or group) at a "higher" layer map to objects (simple and/or group) at "lower" layers. The mappings, thus, model the functional dependency of the well-being of the objects at one layer to the well-being of the objects at lower layers, and by definition, determine the ascendancy of the layer objects. A subclass of group, called mapgroup, is defined to realize the mapping relationship. An object at a higher layer maps to a set of mapgroups, which individually represent the lower layer they belong to and the group of objects involved in the mapping in that layer.

The relationships *connection* and *grouping* are many-to-many, whereas the *membership* relationship is one-to-many. The mapping relationship is one-to-many when considered between a higher layer object and mapgroups. However, an object (simple or group) in a mapgroup may also be a member in other mapgroups in the same layer, and if considered between objects in different layers, the mapping relationship is many-to-many. The network class hierarchy is shown in Figure 15.4 and these relations are shown in Figure 15.5, and are implemented as properties of the classes in the hierarchy. The instances of all objects representing the generic network entities in a domain and explicit representation of the relationships among the objects conceptually construct the topology of the network.

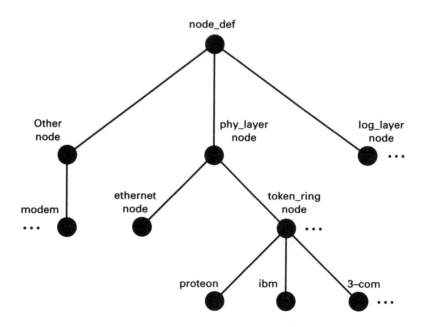

Figure 15.4 NetMATE definition type hierarchy (sample).

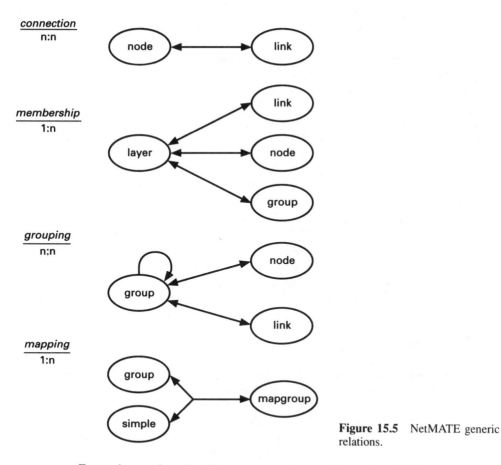

connection
n:n

membership
1:n

grouping
n:n

mapping
1:n

node → ← link

link
layer → ← node
group

node
group → ← link

group
simple → mapgroup

Figure 15.5 NetMATE generic relations.

For each generic node, link, group and layer object, NetMATE makes use of additional specific details about their properties other than the generic relationships mentioned above. A node object may represent, for example, a host computer, a gateway, or a modem. Similarly, a link might represent an Ethernet bus, a virtual circuit, or a TCP connection. A gateway node may send management information which differs significantly from the information sent by a bridge node, and usually, they will support different sets of management commands. It is therefore necessary to associate specific information about the capabilities of the generic network entities, and this is accomplished by the *kind_of* relationship for layer, simple, and group objects. The objects at the other end of the kind_of relation are instantiated from the class hierarchy defined in the Network Definition Model, and are the place holders for the specific properties.

Network definition. Network Definition consists of (relatively) static information about the properties of layers and other network entities. It aids in construction of a Network model in two majcr ways: creation of objects for specific properties in Network Configuration; and integrity maintenance of the defined model. In a specific Network model, only a subset of the Definition model that represents the actual network entities in the domain may be chosen to instantiate the specific properties in the Configuration model.

Sec. 15.4   The Modeler: An Object-Oriented Database   **291**

The Definition partition provides property templates (by defining classes and associated attributes), and defines restrictions on relationships (by specifying allowable values for attributes). Additionally, the operations defined for the classes provide network management commands such as querying for status. Thus the partition functions as a dictionary of entity-specific definitions of network management and control information supported by each entity. This is a very flexible approach which allows the different classification schemes to be introduced in the Definition model in a semi-dynamic fashion. One example of classification could be a vendor-specific management scheme. Figure 15.4 shows a sample Network Definition class hierarchy for the nodes in the domain. Once a generic node object is defined in the Network Configuration, it may be assigned a specific node class in the Network Definition, upon which one (or many) property templates are instantiated from the chosen class which are then linked to the generic node through its kind_of relationship.

The partitioning of the Network model into two modules allows NetMATE to provide generic services at the user level, which are subsequently translated into different sets of specific procedures for different entities with minimal knowledge requirement from the user. This flexibility is extremely important in an heterogeneous network domain because it allows common network analysis functions to be specified at a high-level of abstraction, and then continually refined at the lower levels.

15.4.2 Network Management Model

The Network Management model represents the management structure, and is also partitioned, similar to the Network model, into two modules: Definition and Configuration. The Management model defines, and has instances of, Network Control Points which represent other network management systems. The protocols by which the Modeler communicates with an NCP are captured by the operations defined for that **NCP** class.

In a distributed network management implementation, a Modeler may request information from another Modeler. In this scenario, the latter Modeler behaves as a Network Control Point of the former. Therefore, many properties of the NCP class are applicable for peer Modelers acting as servers. This architecture is easily extendable to form a management hierarchy of Modelers consisting of local, peer and parent managers. In the Management model, one is interested in a **manager** class, a subclass of **compound**, instances of which represent a set of manager objects with a *managing* relationship. Note that NCP thus becomes a subclass of manager class (Figure 15.3). For NetMATE managers, the class will have the NetMATE Network Management Protocol routines defined in its operations and will include appropriate interface definition. An interesting aspect of the management model is that by specifying the Network Management Protocols as a set of layer objects, and nodes and links that implement the management activities in the Network model, it should be possible to monitor the performance of the Network Management Protocol itself.

It is useful to differentiate between Network Management model information and the Network model information for various reasons. Management information is required for the distributed implementation of NetMATE, and also to model NCPs. The hierarchical structure reduces the data flow between every network entity and a single Modeler (and thus supports filtering), and allows the integration of vendor-specific network management subsystems in a uniform fashion.

15.4.3 Organization Model

The Organization model keeps information about the various client modules of NetMATE that are using the services of the Modeler. This model is also used by the clients, if desired, to store information related to their operations. Not all information in this model related to a client need be persistent; it may be sufficient to keep the information as long as the client requires services from the Modeler. While a detailed design of the Organization model has not been finalized, some of the important issues follow.

Important information related to a client includes communication protocol and associated interface, outstanding requests, outstanding replies, and event triggers. Among these, the outstanding requests and replies imply asynchronous, message-based communication protocol between clients and the Modeler. Event triggers require a mechanism for definition of event objects (which may be persistent), evaluation of associated procedures and appropriate interruption of the client. Additionally, the Organization model routines are responsible for maintaining the consistency of the Network and Network Management models as they are accessed by the clients. A partial class hierarchy for the User Interface appears in Figure 15.3.

A user interface client may choose to store display information in the Organization model that corresponds to the objects in the Network model. The class hierarchy defined for display information includes **view** (instantiates a window object), **viewgroup** (instantiates a group containing objects that are displayed in a view), and **appearance** (instantiates an object representing the graphical image of an element on the screen). A set of processes in the Modeler may be dedicated for the user interface client for manipulation of such display objects.

The major function of modules in an Expert Analyser is to provide automatic decision making in fault and performance bottleneck analyses. For this, an Expert analyzer must understand the Network model in great detail. It is the principal client of the event reporting services, and the principal requester of information from the network.

An Expert Analyser consists of a generic knowledge base which consists of rules for problem determination in a generic model of a network such as the Network model described earlier. However, in order to be applicable on a live (real or simulated) network, many rules would require network entity-specific attribute values to be substituted in real time. In some cases, where generic rules are not possible, the rules must be entity-specific to effectively handle an entity-specific problem. Thus an Expert Analyser client may consist of rules that are best defined in the Network Definition, along with other entity-specific attributes and operations. Although these rules would be a part of the Network model information, their invocation and evaluation will be controlled by the Expert Analyser client.

15.5 THE MODELER AND VBASE

The preceding description of the Modeler architecture clearly demonstrates the need for an object-oriented system supporting an object-oriented data model for network management systems. A relational model for elements in a network is impractical and unwieldy mainly due to heterogeneity, and the large number of, and different, ways network elements have to be managed. For example, the properties of, and applicable operations on, a node differ widely depending upon the layer it belongs to (and hence the protocol it executes), its own type hierarchy within a layer (for instance, whether it is a **gateway**, or a **bridge**, or a **host** object in the *physical layer*), and possibly the vendor network management facilities it provides. Since NetMATE is designed as a generic set of tools, it is therefore necessary to isolate these dependencies in different collections of properties and associated sets of specific operations for ease and portability in network management. Vbase supports the required modularization capability of the NetMATE models to a very high degree and has been an invaluable tool for developing the NetMATE prototype.

Vbase, as a general-purpose object-oriented database, supports properties, operations, and inheritance for abstract data types defined in a type hierarchy. Besides using the basic features to define the network element types in NetMATE, we have made good use of the convenient *many-to-many* relationship construct in Vbase (implemented as "distributed set"). The exception and trigger concepts, rarely found in other systems, have proven quite valuable in the Modeler development. Although at the current prototyping stage we have had no need for concurrency control, the synchronization mechanisms available in Vbase also seem quite adequate for that task.

The clean structure of Vbase is most evident in its design that the same constructs that Vbase supports, are also used in its implementation. One useful consequence of this is that the user-defined types and methods themselves are *objects* of system types **Type** and **Method**. We have exploited this feature by being able to use the object id of a type at run-time to efficiently refer to, and exchange information about, that type across computers and disparate object-oriented systems.

Some desirable Modeler functions that are not currently possible through Vbase follow. Dynamic modification of the type hierarchy and definition in the Network Definition model, even in a restricted form, is required. We expect this function to be supported by the object-oriented database through dynamic schema updates. Secondly, it is desirable to have Structured Query Language (SQL)-like features in the interface between different modules and the Modeler. This can be made possible by having the Object SQL queries invoked and evaluated from the procedures in Vbase. Finally, a distributed implementation of Vbase (which probably is more of a research issue) will be extremely helpful in the distributed NetMATE system.

15.6 CURRENT IMPLEMENTATION

The NetMATE system currently has prototypes for a User Interface module and a Modeler. The User Interface module is implemented in the X Window system and is written in C++. It makes use of the Interviews window system interface library. At present, dynamic creation and deletion of generic nodes, links and groups are supported. It is possible to define connections and groupings. The user of the system is able to move the graphical representation of objects on the screen at will.

The interface between the Modeler and the User Interface is developed using the SUN RPC/XDR interface protocol [RPC-manual]. This interface allows the UI to invoke remote procedure calls to the Modeler to get services performed on its behalf. This interface was chosen for the prototype since it is easy to use, and appropriate at the present time. It is our intention to follow ISO ASN.1 standards for information exchange when appropriate tools to do so become more available. Until then, we will use two

RPC interfaces for bi-directional communication between the Modeler and each of its clients.

The Modeler, implemented in Vbase, currently has the generic Network Configuration. In this prototype version, it includes creation and deletion of nodes, links and groups, connections between nodes and links, and addition and deletion of simple and group objects to and from a given group. It also returns objects that a given node or link is connected to, children objects of a given group, parent objects of a given group or a simple object, and so on. As mentioned earlier, while VBase is not a distributed database, it has been fairly easy to exchange objects between the Modeler and the User Interface as 64-bit object IDs defined in VBase. A preliminary design for the User Interface information to be stored in the Organization model of the Modeler is complete.

For the second version of NetMATE, we have decided upon the structure of the Network Definition partition for an X.25 network and the interface between the User Interface and the Modeler that allows the User Interface to inquire about the specific properties of nodes and links, and their values. Our next goal is to define the same for a TCP/IP local area network and attach the NetMATE system to a physical network.

15.7 CONCLUSION

In today's heterogeneous network environment, network management is a challenging and complicated task. Our preliminary design and implementation results for NetMATE have demonstrated the utility and flexibility of an object-oriented approach to model not only a network but also the network management and organization structures. The modular development of NetMATE will allow a distributed, efficient and portable solution to manage diverse networks, both real and simulated.

16 An Object-Oriented Geographical Information System

Ronald Williamson and Jack Stucky

16.1 OVERVIEW OF OBJECT-ORIENTED GRAPHICAL INTERFACE

16.1.1 Overview of the Application

This chapter describes a generic Geographic Information System (GIS) effort supporting Earth resource imaging analysis. A generic GIS consists of i) a graphic, raster and text interface, ii) a database containing maps, images and graphical and textual descriptors, and iii) a collection of processes which transform the representation and content of each of the data objects in the GIS. The focus of this particular effort was to analyze the effectiveness of object-oriented design and implementation technologies (in particular Vbase, from Ontologic, Inc.) in representing, accessing and updating the data elements in a GIS. Toward this end we have designed an object-oriented representation and a prototype implementation of such an object-oriented GIS.

The scenarios relating to the Earth resource analysis prototype system involve tracking changes in the environment based on man-made and natural events. The information required to represent these changes and the impact of these changes includes Landsat raster imagery, vector map information at a variety of resolutions, temporal relationships, spatial relationships, descriptions of targets impacting the environment (such as major cities, civilian / military airports, military bases, chemical factories, oil refineries, pipelines and drilling wells, etc.). Each of these factors must be represented such that an Earth Resource Analyst can query for relevant information on a particular geographic area, feature or time-period and perform an analysis based on the resulting information. The analyst then updates the information in the database based on the conclusions of his analysis. Our objective in this task is to determine the benefits to the Earth Resource Analyst of object-oriented interfaces and representations. Specific measures of the effectiveness of the object-oriented approach include:

- Improved quality of reports, database updates, and analysis.
- More timely access to widely dispersed information.
- A more intuitive interface with the information in the database.
- Necessary minimum training level of the analysts.
- Reduced costs for maintenance and update of the overall system.

16.1.2 Overview of Methodology

In the design of an object-oriented database system and analyst interface, one important consideration must be addressed: the specialization of sub-types from their parent types. Choosing a generic type for an object allows flexibility, but diminishes the impact of the strong typing that is a virtue in many object-oriented systems. Picking the correct point in this spectrum is an important element in object-oriented design. A major effort was devoted to the use of abstract types. Abstract types are intermediate types which will never be instantiated as objects, but exist as semantic placeholders to group common properties and operations of children types. Abstract types have no additional cost in Vbase, and they add much to constructing a rich representation within the database. When sibling object types share common properties, the properties are grouped in a parent type. The most common methodology for designing an object-oriented database schema is to lay out the type specialization hierarchy first, add the relevant properties second, and finally define the methods or operation to act on the type instances. The methods are usually apparent once the implementation is begun. The design description in this chapter was partitioned into three general areas: graphic objects, geographic objects and data objects. Each concept is described in the following sections. The top-level type hierarchy is shown in Figure 16.1.

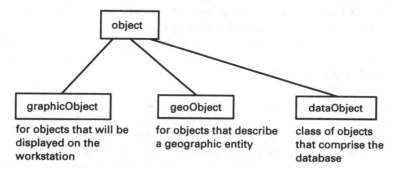

Figure 16.1 Top-level type hierarchy.

16.1.3 Graphic Objects

Graphic objects are those entities that represent things displayed on the workstation display. Examples for this database include images and maps, as well as icons, cursors, and drawings. The original SRIP prototype was highly dependent on its representation of images and maps, and this design reflects that dependency. Figure 16.2 depicts the type hierarchy for graphic objects.

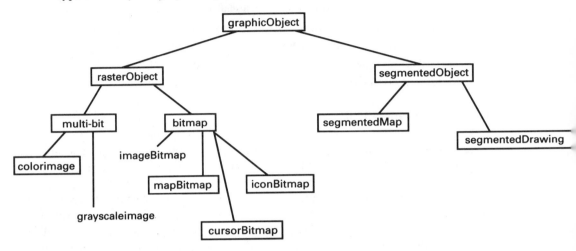

Figure 16.2 Graphic object type hierarchy.

The end nodes of the hierarchy are instantiated with objects. Bitmaps can be represented by images, maps, cursors and icons. Images can also be represented by colors and gray scale. Segmented graphics can be represented for maps and drawings. Properties for each of the types are shown in Figure 16.3.

16.1.4 Geographic Objects

Geographic objects, as depicted in Figures 16.4 and 16.5, represent the geographic description of objects. The most important children of this type are the concepts of point, line and area. Latitude and longitude are also represented so that future implementations of these types can be changed with little intervention.

This hierarchy allows the programmer to describe point, line and aerial features.

16.1.5 Data Objects

Data objects contain the conceptual information embedded in the database. Examples of data objects are readouts (target descriptions which change over time), observations within the imagery and the conceptual description of geographic and graphic entities (such as country boundaries, coastlines, rivers, etc.). Data objects are defined using the types set up by the graphic and geographic type hierarchies (see Figure 16.6).

Several types of data are represented in this hierarchy. The 'feature' type is analogous to the SRIP subregion data entity. Specializations of this type are permanent objects associated with other data objects such as cities or airports. Additional specialization can be performed for each type, for example, by delineating the types of buildings into terminals, barracks, etc. Each feature can have properties such as composition, role, status, etc. The activity type is distinguished from the feature type in that it represents those

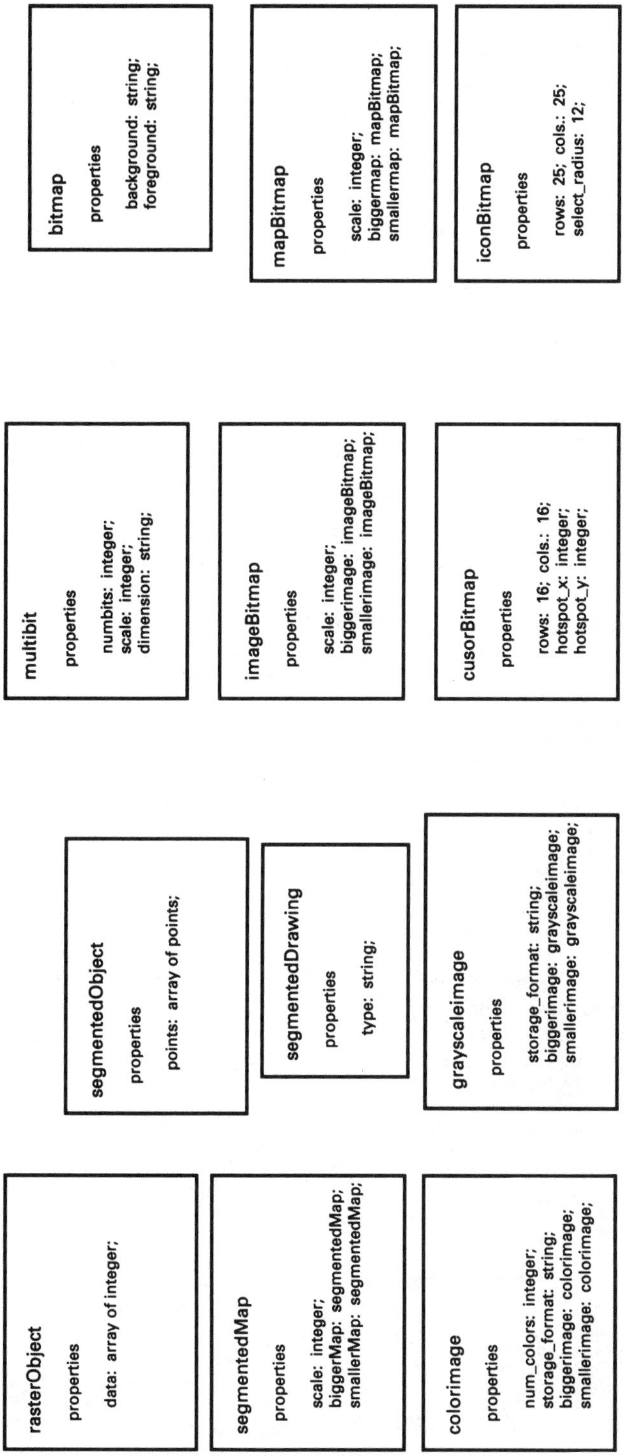

bitmap

properties

    background: string;
    foreground: string;

mapBitmap

properties

    scale: integer;
    biggermap: mapBitmap;
    smallermap: mapBitmap;

iconBitmap

properties

    rows: 25; cols.: 25;
    select_radius: 12;

multibit

properties

    numbits: integer;
    scale: integer;
    dimension: string;

imageBitmap

properties

    scale: integer;
    biggerimage: imageBitmap;
    smallerimage: imageBitmap;

cusorBitmap

properties

    rows: 16; cols.: 16;
    hotspot_x: integer;
    hotspot_y: integer;

segmentedObject

properties

    points: array of points;

segmentedDrawing

properties

    type: string;

grayscaleimage

properties

    storage_format: string;
    biggerimage: grayscaleimage;
    smallerimage: grayscaleimage;

rasterObject

properties

    data: array of integer;

segmentedMap

properties

    scale: integer;
    biggerMap: segmentedMap;
    smallerMap: segmentedMap;

colorimage

properties

    num_colors: integer;
    storage_format: string;
    biggerimage: colorimage;
    smallerimage: colorimage;

Figure 16.3   Type attributes.

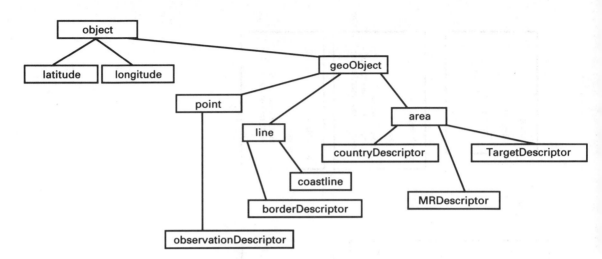

Figure 16.4 geoObject type hierarchy.

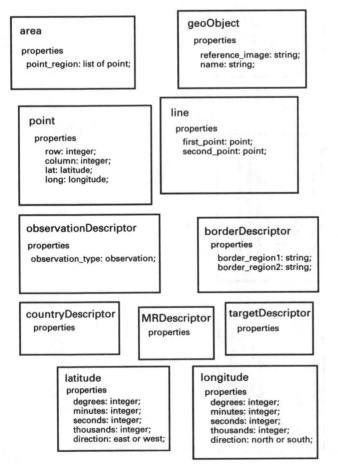

Figure 16.5 geoObject type properties.

300

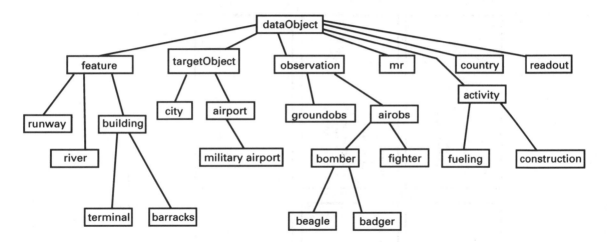

Figure 16.6 dataObject type hierarchy.

dynamic events associated with the status of the data object. Activities take up an area (unlike observations) and are part of the readout object. Example activities are construction, smokestack venting, and fueling. The 'country', 'state' and 'targetObject' types contain the conceptual information. These objects contain attributes that point back to the associated geographic and graphic descriptions. They are also linked together hierarchically so that it is possible to find the military objects within a country, and the targets within a military region. The observation type contains the hierarchy of man-made objects. Each observation has an associated icon, as well as associated properties such as confidence and multiplicity. The readout type contains the textual information comprising the readout. That object also is linked to other readouts for a target. Figure 16.7 lists the properties associated with some of the types in this hierarchy. Several of the types associated with properties are denoted simply as 'string'. This is a generic type that can be embellished with the actual implementation. For example, instead of representing observation confidence with a string, a type can be defined confidence_type, that can have values of 'confirmed', 'probable' and 'possible'. This additional type checking allows for a more robust system. Figure 16.7 describes the data type attributes.

16.2 MAP REPRESENTATION

A `SegmentedMap` Object is a subtype of a `GraphicObject`. A `SegmentedMap` can represent such things as coastlines, international boundaries, states, etc. A `SegmentedMap` inherits properties from its parent, `SegmentedObject`. These include a list of `Areas`, a list of `Lines`, and a list of `Points`. `Areas`, `Lines`, and `Points` are all subtypes of `GeoObject`(Figure 16.8). `Areas` are composed of `Lines` and `Points`, while `Lines` are composed of `Points`. The TDL follows for a `SegmentedObject`, `SegmentedMap`, and a `GeoArea`. In addition, a hierarchy diagram similar to the overview is presented in Figure 16.8 showing how object types were implemented.

airobs

properties

wingspan: integer;
payload: integer;

features

properties

location: area;
target: target;
date_of_entry: date;

hanger

properties

capacity: string;
hardening: string;
roof_type: string;

observation

properties

location: point;
multiplicity: integer;
confidence: string;
icon: iconBitmap;

fighter

properties

armaments: string;

building

properties

composition: string;
length: integer; width: integer;
purpose: string;

construction

properties

construction_type: string;
equipment_used: string;
modified_feature: feature;

country

properties

imagery: garphicObject;
descriptor: countryDescriptor;
population: integer;
borders: list of country;
name: string;
targets: list of target;

targetObject

properties

name: string;
type: string;
location: latitude, longitude;
readpits: list of readout;
description: text file;
parentMR: mr;
parentCountry: country;

activity

properties

location: area;
date_of_start: date;
date_of_completion: date;

readout

properties

month: int. day: int. year: int;
analyst string: BEnum: string;
missionID: string; frameNum: string;
imagery: graphicObject;
target: target;
activities: list of activity;
observations: list of observations
nextReadout readout,
lastReadout readout,

mr

properties

name: string;
population: integer;
imagery: mapBitmap;
targets: list of target;
borders: list of country;
parentCountry: country;

Figure 16.7 dataObject type attributes.

```
define Type SegmentedObject
        supertypes = {GraphicObject};
        properties = {
                Name:String;
                VectorList: optional Dynarray[Line];
                PointList: optional Dynarray[Point];
                AreaList: optional Dynarray[GeoArea];
                };
        operations = {
                refines display (aseg : SegmentedObject)
                        method (SegmentedObjectDisplay);
                };
end SegmentedObject;
define Type SegmentedMap
        supertypes = {SegmentedObject};
        properties = {
                MapResolution: optional Integer;
                LargerMap: optional SegmentedMap;
                SmallerMaps: optional array[SegmentedMap];
                };
        operations = {
                refines display (aseg : Segmentedmap)
                        method (SegmentedMapDisplay)
                };
        define procedure mapimport()
                method(SegmentedMapImport)
        end mapimport;
end SegmentedMap;
define Type GeoArea
        supertypes = {GeoObject};
        properties = {
                PointList: optional array[Point];
                LineList: optional array[Line];
                AreaName: optional String;
                };
        operations = { };
end GeoArea;
```

Segmented maps also have properties that are particular to themselves, such as LargerMap and SmallerMap. If a particular segmented map was of Sweden, then a LargerMap would represent say Europe and a SmallerMap might represent a particular group of rivers. In this way, it is possible to form a tree hierarchy of a large area without having to replicate the same data. An example is shown in Figure 16.9 which is a rough outline of how Europe might be stored. Notice that Area 3 might be

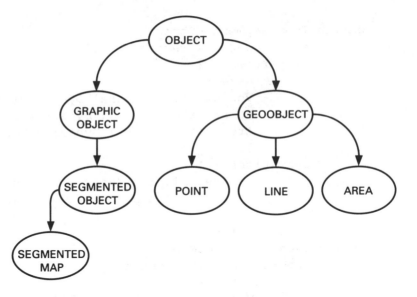

Figure 16.8 SegmentedMap type hierarchy.

the border between Norway and Sweden. Rather than have two sets of identical data, it is easy enough for Norway and Sweden to both point to Area 3.

Figure 16.10 shows an example of exactly how a country's boundaries would be represented through the use of SegmentedMaps and its subcomponents. The type hierarchy is shown in Figure 16.8. Our example is a country named 'X'. The boundaries of 'X' are represented by two SegmentedMaps. This was done because the east border of 'X' just happens to be the western boundary of country 'Y'. By the definition of a Country, we would assume among other things that a list of SegmentedMaps would be one of its properties. Other properties of Country could be items such as name, political system, terrain, etc. The segmented maps in our example have 3—9 areas

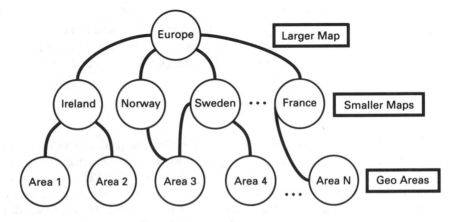

Figure 16.9 Country map hierarchy.

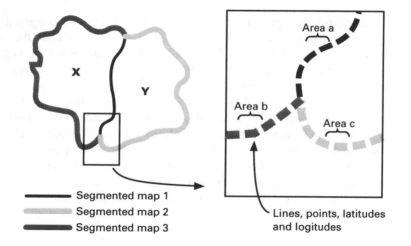

Figure 16.10 Segmented map description.

each. These areas might contain some geographical significance which separates them logically. Each of these areas is comprised of lines (vectors). Further still, the lines are comprised of points, which in turn are comprised of a Latitude and Longitude for the given point. One issue of concern while storing segmented maps is whether access time will be too large for a given map. Currently, there are several ideas on how to retrieve maps more intelligently than simply reading in the data. These methods are clustering, bitmap representation, and low-level storage representation. Clustering a segmented map involves storing related maps, areas, lines, points in the same location on the disk, allowing a single disk access of say 50K to retrieve an entire area or map. The problem with clustering is that maps, areas, lines, points can be shared among different logical entities such as countries X and Y above. In this case normal clustering won't be as efficient for one or the other countries due to the common border being clustered with only one country. A solution to this problem might be replication of the common boundary, although this would involve multiple updates when anything in the common segment changes.

Bitmap representation involves keeping a bitmap picture of a particular segmented map in memory along with the actual data. As long as the original data stays unchanged, the map may be displayed by simply dumping the bitmap image. When a change is made to the data, the bitmap is updated as well. The beauty of this idea is that from an application point of view, the programmer need not be aware of the bitmap representation. To the programmer, maps are composed only of real data points. Underlying triggers and display routines do the work of keeping the bitmap and real data in sync. This concept can be added at any time without having to change one line of the application programmer's code. Low-level storage representation involves digging into the underlying storage structures of Vbase. One may rewrite the access routines for objects in any way desired. If map data was more efficient to retrieve and display in some particular binary form, then we could store it in this form in Vbase and write our own retrieval routines. This would allow object-oriented programming while also decreasing our retrieval and display time. The only drawback with this method is that the way the data is stored would be very application specific. For instance, if a different application wanted to use the same map system, but was interested only in computations on the data, then the new storage representation we developed might not be the optimal method for this task. Currently predefined segmented maps can be read into Vbase. This is a separate program that accesses the database and is only used to populate it with instances of SegmentedMaps, Areas, Lines, and Points. The data read in is from a World Data Bank II tape. The data has been converted from ASCII format degrees, minutes, seconds to a binary radian format. These maps can then be retrieved through the window interface (whose design is given in Section 16.4). The maps are drawn in a graphics window under X11. In addition to retrieving this graphical data from Vbase itself, a segmented map may be read in from the raw binary file. This is done to show a comparison of speed. Once a map is in a Graphic window, the map window may be resized, iconified, and scrolled. Selection of different actions such as Display, Create, Quit, etc. are done through pop-up menus and text lists.

16.3 RASTER IMPLEMENTATION

RasterObject, a subtype of GraphicObject, is a raster (bit image) description of an image to be displayed on the screen (see Figure 16.11). There are two subtypes in RasterObject: GreyScaleImage and ColorImage. Currently, only the GreyScaleImage type is implemented. The RasterObject type is defined using the Vbase type definition language (TDL). It contains properties of a bit image that is common to the two subtypes. The end node descriptions (i.e. GreyScaleImage and ColorImage) are those that will actually be instantiated. The objects and type definition of these end nodes contain more specific properties that will allow a full unique display of the image. The hierarchy of RasterObject is presented in Figure 16.11.

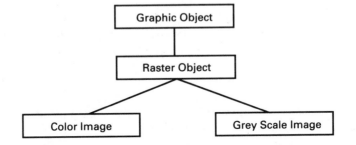

Figure 16.11 Top-level raster object type hierarchy.

The basic TDL for RasterObject, GreyScaleImage for the above tree description is as follows:

```
define type RasterObject
    supertypes={GraphicObject};
                    /* This object inherits all the
                        properties of GraphicObj*/
        properties={
            name:String;        /* The name of the image */
```

```
            filename:String;    /* File that  the data was
                                   imported from  */
            num_rows: Integer; /* The number of rows in the
                                   image */
            num_cols:Integer;   /* The number of columns in
                                   the image */
            image:Dynarray[Space];   /* The actual image
                                        data */
       };
    end RasterObject;
    define type GreyScaleImage
       supertypes={RasterObject}; /* Inherits the properties
                                     of RasterObject */
       properties={
            bitsperpixel:Integer;
            scale:Integer;        /* eqvlt to the resolution
                                     of the image */
       };
    operations = { /* The operations allowed on a
                      GreyScaleImage */
            Display (image:GreyScaleImage);  /* display the
                                       image to the screen */
            method(GreyScaleImage_Display);
            GSImport(); /* Store an image into the
                           database */
            method(GreyScaleImage_Import);
       };
    end GreyScaleImage;
```

Since the image object will actually be instantiated with the GreyScaleImage type, the properties defined in that type will inherit all the properties of its supertypes, thus containing all the properties and information that fully describe that particular image instance. The field bitsperpixel is used for defining the grey level in the image, i.e., the number of bits that each pixel contains. If bitsperpixel=1, then you have a bit image, with only two levels, black or white. If bitsperpixel=8, then you have a full grey level image with 256 levels of grey shading. The field, scale, refers to detail or scale of the image. It is possible to have more images of the same image at different levels. If scale=1, then you have the fullest best possible resolution of the image. If scale=2, then the image is smaller with fewer pixels, usually with a loss of resolution, because the resolution is usually based on the image with the scale of 1. A graphic description of the use of the scale property is shown in Figure 16.12.

The operations define the actions that are allowed on the GreyScaleImage. In our prototype, we have the Display operation, which displays an instance of the image on the screen and the Import operation, which brings new instances of an image into the database. Currently the image format file imported is a Sun Microsystems raster format file, which is a binary file with a Sun-defined header. All the operations are

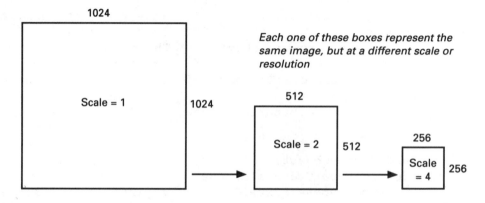

Figure 16.12 Description of the scale property.

implemented in COP code. The ColorImage portion has not been implemented, but can easily be added to our database in a similar fashion; the following is an outline:

```
define type ColorImage
    supertypes={RasterObject};
    properties={
        more detailed description to define a color
        image such as color  map, bits per pixel, etc.
    };
    operations={
        ColorImport ( image : ColorImage )
                    /* For importing color  image
                       files.*/
                method( ColorImage_Import);
        Display ( image : ColorImage )
                    /* Displaying the color image
                       instance */
                method( ColorImage_Display );
    end ColorImage;
```

Because of the nature of objected-oriented databases, the color image type and its operations can be added without needing to change the other types and operations. Another subtype of RasterObject that has been suggested but not implemented is BitMap. Its subtypes are specific instances of user-defined graphics, e.g., a particular cursor symbol, icons, images, etc. Again, these can easily be added when the need arises. Using an object-oriented database, the common information of a particular instance is placed as high as possible in the type hierarchy, and the closer you get to the nodes, the more detailed the description (properties) gets. This makes it easy to add new types and functionality without having to change everything in the database. In the GreyScaleImage type both bitmaps and 8-bit images can be stored and displayed, The Import method (operation) imports a Sun raster file, which translates into a $512 \times 512 \times n$

bit image. Current user input for the `Import` operation consists of the file name to be read, and the name of the image (which the user can use as a comment). Maximum size is 132 characters. The `Display` method (operation) will display the image with a fixed window and image size.

16.4 WINDOW INTERFACE

The function of the window interface is to provide a view hierarchy for each object instance in the database. Each object has unique display properties which are defined by the object's type. Each window is a separate display control process which accesses the Vbase database. The windowing model hierarchy for the GIS prototype is illustrated in Figure 16.13. The analyst interface hierarchy is shown in Figure 16.14.

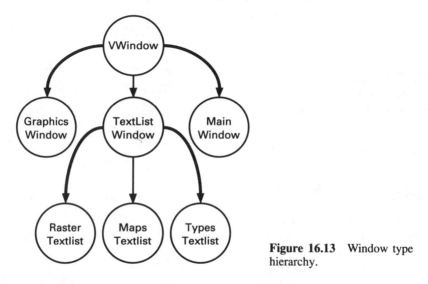

Figure 16.13 Window type hierarchy.

The object `VWindow` contains general information about windows, i.e., initial location, size, font, border, background and foreground color, as specified in the following TDL code:

```
define VWindowType VWindow
       supertypes = {Entity};
       properties = {
               position_x: Integer;
                       /* screen location of startup */
               position_y: Integer;
               name: String;
                       /* window name */
               number: Integer;
                       /* unique window number */
               font: String;
               foreground: Integer;
```

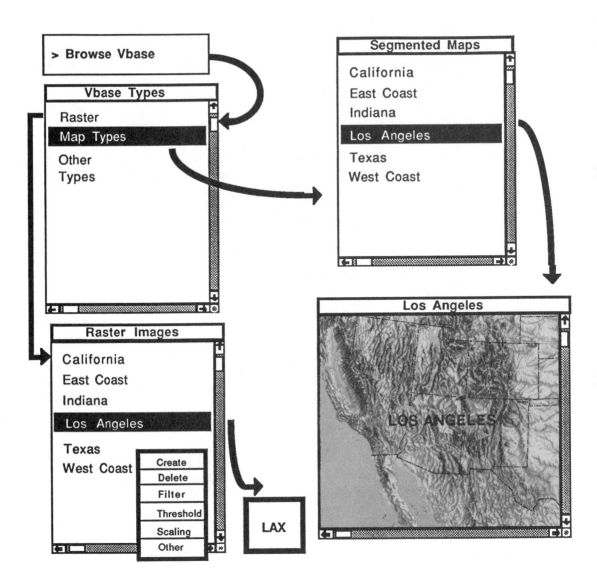

Figure 16.14 Analyst Interface to the Type Hierarchy.

```
background: Integer;
textcolor: Integer;
width: Integer;
        /* default window size */
height: Integer;
};
```

Information about a window object becomes further refined as we traverse down the hierarchy, for example a `TextListWindow` definition expands on the `VWindow` definition as follows:

```
define VWindowType TextListWindow
        supertypes = {VWindow};
        properties = {
                namelist: optional array[String];
                        /* list of items */
                popupmenu: optional array[String];
                        /* list of pop up items */
        };
```

Associated with each window object is a control method which is redefined for each subtype. An initial process, Main, is responsible for instantiating an instance of the first window to appear in the GIS environment. This instance is then stored in an unordered dictionary ($WindowDict), using the Vbase variable ($WindowNumber) as the unique key index. Main then creates a child process (window) and passes the unique key associated with the newly generated instance. Every window created will first invoke a window method to retrieve or remove the particular window instance associated with the process. After retrieving this instance, the method then dispatches to a control routine based on the type of window object found. The window control routines are entered through dispatching on the particular instance. Once inside the control method, new X-Windows can be created, pop-up menus invoked, scrollable lists of text (TextListWindows) displayed. In addition to doing its own windowing, the control procedure can instantiate other subtypes of VWindow based on user input. The top-level control loop is illustrated as follows:

```
Main process
->  Open(Vbase);
->  Acquire Lock to Vbase
    Instantiation of object
->  Trans-Commit(Vbase);
->  Release Lock to Vbase
    Fork Child(window)
->  Close(Vbase);
    Exit
Window process
->  Open(Vbase);
->  Acquire Lock to Vbase
    Retrieve Object (window instance)
->  Release Lock to Vbase
    Dispatch Control to appropriate control routine
                                based on type
->  Close(Vbase);
    exit
Control Code (in general)
Window Initialization, etc.
User Input
```

```
->    Acquire Lock to Vbase
      Instantiate instance based on input of some kind
->    Trans-Commit(Vbase);
->    Release Lock to Vbase
      Fork Child(window)
continue until getting user input until some ending
condition (popup menu, quit selection, etc.)
return to window
```

16.5 FUTURE RESEARCH

Segmented maps are a small part of the analyst interface, although a significant underlying structure. The logical combination of segmented maps and Data Objects is the next step. The association of an air field, city or forest with a particular map is an example of object combination. Performance tuning and benchmark definition is still in progress. We expect that the methods discussed above will contribute to better performance for our GIS application. A combination of secondary access mechanisms and Vbase optimizing will be necessary.

17 Using an Object Database to Build Integrated Design Environments

Timothy Andrews

17.1 THE DESIRE FOR INTEGRATED ENVIRONMENTS

The desire to build integrated product development environments is a natural outgrowth of the development of sophisticated but disparate analytical tools. Previously, efforts were concentrated on building tools to ease various activities in the development cycle, for example finite element analysis packages and process planning packages. In fact, each of these tools is quite complex and efforts continue to improve them individually. However, the availability of a set of basic development tools has enhanced the desire to build an integrated environment containing all of the tools.

There are two primary reasons for wanting an integrated environment. The first is the simple but fundamental point that each of the development activities is contributing to a single goal: the end product. There may be radical differences in perspective during each phase; when building an airplane, there is a MCAD 3-D design phase, stress analysis phase, tooling and manufacturing phase, testing phase, and maintenance phase, just to name a few.

The realization that there is a direct payback from integrated environments also motivates their development. Simple systems which begin to integrate design and process planning have been shown to be effective in reducing overall costs significantly. In a similar manner, this concept can be applied to the life-cycle cost model for the product, feeding back information from the field maintenance and repair analysis all the way back to the initial design, resulting in products whose life-cycle costs are lower. In the case of a product, such as an airplane, where life-cycle costs are dominated by post manufacturing phases, this can result in substantial savings.

The reason for these savings is that adjustments made earlier in the design process are far less costly. As a product moves through the various stages of development and deployment, the cost of changing a feature from an earlier stage increases exponentially (see Figures 17.1 and 17.2).

Thus, allowing the changes to be instituted early via a feedback mechanism can be extremely effective. This in turn requires a simulation environment in which all the phases of the development and deployment of the product are integrated.

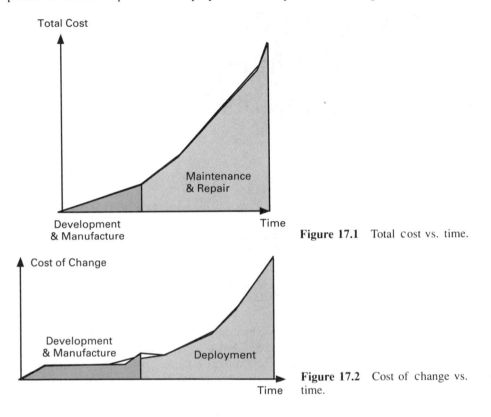

Figure 17.1 Total cost vs. time.

Figure 17.2 Cost of change vs. time.

17.2 DIFFICULTIES IN BUILDING INTEGRATED ENVIRONMENTS

Human nature is such that as we grow older we become more set in our ways. Nowhere is this more apparent than in our homes. The longer we live in a home, the more it becomes a permanent domicile. As we acquire more "stuff", our home becomes more comfortable, and even though it may not be ideal, it is home. With each passing year, each new piece of furniture, each room that was repainted, it becomes more difficult to consider moving. Moving would mean packing up all the "stuff"; an adventure fraught with peril. Many can recount the treasures lost or broken during a move. And, of course, the more "stuff", the greater the trauma.

Product development, manufacturing, and even maintenance environments (product environments, for short) share much in common with the above scenario. We start with a small apartment (few tools, no customization). Slowly we acquire more and better tools. As we become more sophisticated we tailor the tools to match our needs more closely, and our environment becomes more of a "home": we have more "stuff" in the form of tools and applications, and we have put more into "remodeling" in the form of customized features. Thus our incentive to stay put is great. The advantages of "moving" must be significant, or must solve some problem that cannot be solved in our current "home".

This is perhaps the most fundamental problem with building integrated product environments: it requires "moving". In order to understand why, we need to examine existing situations more closely. A set of applications that might be involved in making a satellite is shown in Figure 17.3.

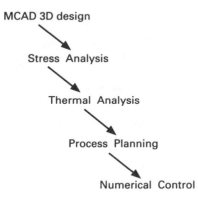

MCAD 3D design

Stress Analysis

Thermal Analysis

Process Planning

Numerical Control

Figure 17.3 Design phases in building a satellite.

In each area tools are applied to ease the process for the engineer. In the MCAD stage there are 3D modeling tools which work on technical workstations. These packages have greatly increased the productivity of design engineers by allowing them to interactively change product designs and see the results rendered accurately before them on the screen, all in real time. Very sophisticated and accurate stress analysis and thermal analysis packages are also used. These packages have also greatly increased the effectiveness of analytical engineers by allowing precise simulation of the system in its anticipated real world use. At each stage this situation exists: there is a package or set of packages, highly tailored to the specific task, and greatly increasing the productivity of that stage.

The success of these individual applications has led to wide use, and therefore those wishing to build integrated environments must incorporate these existing tools. However, each tool was typically developed without thought for communication with other tools or a common storage model. As stated, the major reason for this is simply that the tool solves a particular problem, and is not concerned with the world beyond the problem.

Since the primary desire for integration is because there is, in fact, one model of the overall process, the first problem with individual tools is that they lack the generality of a global perspective. There is typically no abstract model even of the problem domain which the tool is designed to address, much less enough generality to support the overall paradigm. Largely, this is due to the lack of abstract modeling capability in the software systems used to develop the applications. Standard development languages such as C provide little support for conceptual modeling, and, thus, the model on which the tool is based is soon lost in the implementation.

Database Management Systems (DBMSs) provide some support for conceptual modeling of data, and consequently could provide a mechanism for integration. However, here a second problem arises. Most of the vendors of these specialized tools tried to use commercial DBMSs, but found them unsatisfactory for reasons of performance or lack of modeling capability [Ketabchi86, Sidel80]. As a result, most of the data formats of the individual packages are tailored to the specific application, and thus incompatible, making integration a difficult task.

Traditional DBMSs have other drawbacks in this regard. Perhaps the most serious is that DBMSs provide only data management, and only within their data storage and retrieval system. This means that using a DBMS for integration requires migrating all of the relevant data to the DBMS: or "moving". Traditional DBMSs provide some separation between the abstract model (schema) and the implementation (storage), but rarely support an open architecture which allows the replacement of the storage managers with those of existing applications. It is this latter capability which is crucial to providing an incremental capability. We wish to express the model in abstract notation, giving us a clean conceptual framework both to accurately reflect the current model and to provide a uniform description for new applications. However, we wish access to be translated to the existing tools so that these tools and their clients can continue to work unimpeded (see Figure 17.4).

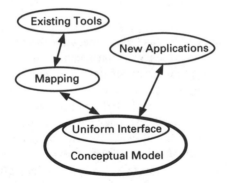

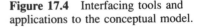

Figure 17.4 Interfacing tools and applications to the conceptual model.

Another drawback of current DBMSs as an integration platform is that they model only certain types of data, forcing new types to be developed outside of the DBMS. This is one of the reasons why these systems were rejected by the tool developers in the first place: their limitation to dealing only with very regular, well-behaved data, and their corresponding lack of ability to deal with funny shapes and sizes of data. As an integration environment needs to be extremely flexible in order to accommodate existing systems as they are, an extensible type mechanism is very important.

Finally, traditional DBMSs do not provide support for general behavioral semantics. They model only data, thus making the incorporation of operational semantics to enforce constraints impossible. Again, when trying to meld disparate tools, this can be significant, as several tools may have different internal representations for the same entities. The natural way to integrate this is to build a uniform model with underlying operations embedded in the database to keep all internal representations synchronized.

17.3 AN OBJECT DATABASE AS AN INTEGRATION PLATFORM

The best candidate system upon which to base an integrated system is thus one which supports good modeling, an open architecture, and database features. A new wave of products is coming to fruition that satisfies many of these demands: object database systems. There are several currently under development, and a few are already commercially available. All of these products are potential bases for a product integration system. One such product will be examined in some detail to study examples of how the theory described above can be put into practice.

Vbase [Andrews87, Ontologic88a] features many of the capabilities needed to provide a practical framework for integrating design applications. The object model [Wegner87] is an excellent abstract modeling technique. It provides a clean conceptual schema containing both data structure and behavioral information, and is extensible to accommodate change and addition to the system.

Object databases differ from object languages in offering database support for objects. Further, they provide a very clean separation between the model and the physical implementation, making it possible to gracefully accommodate existing tools and data formats [Damon88a]. This means the construction of a unified product development system can proceed incrementally: remodeling rather than moving.

The concepts discussed in this chapter are general and apply to most object database systems. In order to provide a concrete demonstration of the theory expounded in an existing system, the text and examples in the rest of this chapter will refer specifically to the Vbase object database system.

17.4 MODELS OF INTEGRATION

17.4.1 Common Aspects of All Models

It cannot be overemphasized that the primary goal of building an integrated environment is to establish a uniform model of the overall system. The primary advantage of an object system is realized in this area. Objects provide a mechanism for expressing a computer model in much the same fashion as an analytical model. Object systems provide a rigorous formal interface which hides implementation details and protects clients from changes in those implementations. Object systems also provide a natural modularization capability which makes large systems more manageable.

17.4.2 Translation Models

The simplest integration model is one based on translation between the objects in the object database system and the various formats desired by the existing tools. The model is developed in the object database system, and the objects are stored there. Translation behaviors for the objects are implemented so that existing applications can request and store information in their standard format.

Two universities are currently using a translation model. At USC, researchers in the computer science and electrical engineering departments are cooperating to build an integrating environment for integrated circuit development [Gupta89] (see Chapter 13). They have developed an object model with a uniform interface for all tools. A layer using the interface is wrapped around existing tools to provide for translation to and from the object database; new tools make direct use of the interface and deal only with objects (see Figure 17.5).

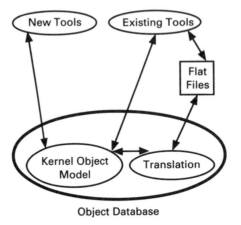

Object Database   **Figure 17.5** Translational model.

This method of integration requires the least "remodeling"; only the layers around the existing tools to do the translation are necessary. This effort is relatively straight-forward as Vbase provides an extension of the C programming language for object manipulation. In most standard systems such as Unix and VAX/VMS, communication protocols are provided in C which make it simple to invoke other applications. Thus existing tools remain completely intact.

Now all CAD information is stored in the object database and is available to new tools or can be accessed directly by the object database browser and query tools.

Another example of this technique is underway at the University of Connecticut [Demurjian88] (see Figure 17.6). The researchers there are building a CASE system for software design and development. The first step is to decompose Pascal programs into objects. Then existing editing and compiling tools are integrated.

Again the basic goals are the same: a global model of the development process shared by all tools, and incorporating existing tools smoothly. Here the translation is from the objects describing the semantic structure of a Pascal program to the textual representation demanded by standard editors and compilers.

17.4.3 Storage Replacement Models

The other extreme is to integrate by replacing the object storage with existing storage management systems (Figure 17.7). Obviously, this approach lends itself to an environment where there are multiple DBMSs already in use. However, this technique can also be used when the tools use only standard flat files as well. As always, a conceptual model is established as the cornerstone of the system. However, instead of translating to and from the objects in the object database system, the information is stored directly in the existing storage formats and is never stored as objects. Importantly, applications use

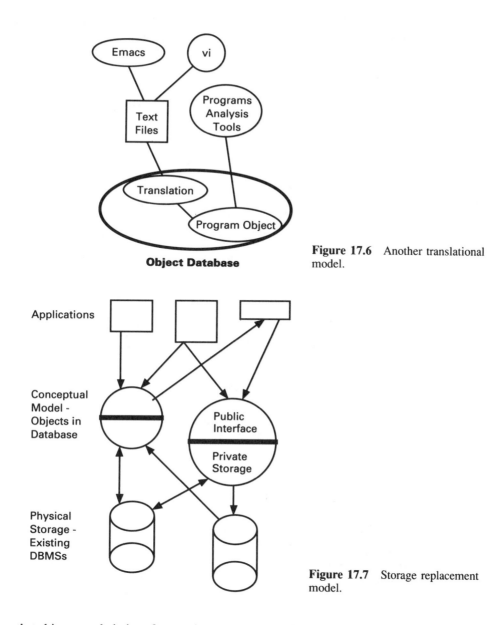

Figure 17.6 Another translational model.

Object Database

Figure 17.7 Storage replacement model.

the objects as their interface and are unaware that the object storage is being provided by external systems.

Large corporations, such as those in the aerospace industry, find this approach very attractive as they typically have several DBMSs in use with large investments in applications written against them. This investment prevents them from adopting new technology on a large scale, yet at the same time it is difficult to extend existing software or develop new applications, resulting in large backlogs of requests for software development.

Object databases allow the design of a conceptual model through the definition of object types, and the subsequent manipulation of instances of those types. For example, consider a simple model as shown below:

```
Assembly
        parent: Assembly
        tailNoLow: Integer
        tailNoHigh: Integer
        relKeyNo: Integer
```

Applications can write code such as this:

```
if(anAssembly.parent.tailNoLow > 10
   && anAssembly.parent.tailNoHigh < 50)
then
    printf("This Part Must be Recalled\n");
```

The application writes standard property access notation, oblivious to where the data is stored. The object type Assembly can actually get its values from anywhere. Thus, the implementor of the object type assembly can write:

```
{
 y = anAssembly.relKeyNo;
 exec-SQL(``Select TailNoLow into $x
                From Assembly
                Where Assembly_id=
                Select Parent_id
                From Assembly
                Where Assembly_id=$y'');
 return(x);
}
```

Note the highlevel of code that applications can write without being concerned with the details of the implementation. Further, since Vbase supports the full object model there is great flexibility in mapping the high-level code of the application to the actual storage mechanism. This is an important point as there are many existing data models with very different semantics, the hierarchical and relational data models, for instance. Attempting to provide a mapping between these two models with a limited language may prove problematic. The SQL language, which is currently being proposed as an integration language, is an example of a language which may lack the flexibility necessary [Date86]. In contrast, the object model can easily support the semantics of both the relational and CODASYL models [Osborn88].

17.4.4 Mixed Storage Models

Between the two models described one can architect a system where some information is stored in the object database while some remains external. For example, most technical workstations support a windowing environment which contains interfaces to display bitmapped images onto the screen. Typically, these images are stored in raster files for which the system provides access procedures.

Now consider building an application to model information on people, including a bitmap image of the person. The desire is that the bitmap image appear to the application as an object which is part of a person object. However, since the system reads and writes raster files, it would be much easier to store the bit image directly in a raster file rather than as an object in the database. This can easily be done as follows:

```
/* Object definition of Image object */
define Type SunBitImage
        supertypes = {Entity}
        properties = {
        prFileName: optional String;
        pixRect: optional Pointer;
        width: Integer := 0;
        height: Integer := 0;
        };
        operations = {
        display(b: SunBitImage,
                w: Pointer, at: Point)
                method(SunBitImageDisplay); }
end SunBitImage;
/* Object definition of Person object */
define Type Person
        supertypes = {Entity};
        properties = {
        LastName: String;
        FirstName: String;
        Age: Integer;
        BirthPlace: String;
        Sex: String;
        BitImage: optional SunBitImage;
        };
        operations = {
        DisplayImage(p: Person)
                method(Person_DisplayImage); }
end Person;
/* Internal code in Image object */
method
void
SunBitImageDisplay (aSunBitImage)
obj $SunBitImage aSunBitImage;
{
FILE *imageFile;
char buffer[256];
Pixwin *pw;
struct pixrect *thePixRect;
Canvas theCanvas;
```

```
            AM_stringToC(aSunBitImage.prFileName,
                 buffer, sizeof(buffer);
        if(imageFile-fopen(buffer, ''r'')) == NULL {
                 printf("Couldn't open %s\n",buffer);
                 return; }
        thePixRect=pr_load(imageFile,NULL);
        fclose(imageFile);
        aSunBitImage.pixRect = (obj $Pointer)thePixRect;
        aSunBitImage.width=thePixRect->pr_size.x;
        aSunBitImage.height=thePixRect->pr_size.y;
        theCanvas=(Canvas)aCanvasObj;
        pw=canvas_pixwin(theCanvas);
        thePixRect=(struct pixrect*)aSunBitImage.pixRect;
        pw_write(pw, (int)aPoint.x, (int)aPoint.y,
                 (int)aSunBitImage.width,
                    (int)aSunBitImage.height,
               PIX_SRC, thePixRect, 0, 0);
    }
    /* Application code to display image. */
    void
    displayimage()
    {
            obj $Pointer canvasObj;
            $SunBitImage$Display(currentPerson.BitImage,
                    canvasObj, $Point$[]);

    }
```

This is an example of how the clean break between the specification, or interface, and the implementation makes the application developer's job much easier. The person's image does indeed appear to be just another object, a property of the person object bound to the variable `currentPerson` in the above piece of code. Access is just as it would be for any other property, and displaying the image is a simple matter.

Internally, the `SunBitImage` object type defines some information which is often needed locally, such as the `width` and `height` of the bit image in pixels. However, rather than storing the bit image directly, the name of the raster file containing the image is stored instead. This makes the job of writing the display routine much easier as the Sun facility `pr_load` loads the raster file into the appropriate memory structure, and the `pr_write` procedure actually displays the image.

17.5 ISSUES

In all the modeling discussed above performance may be an important issue. Using an object database system, such as Vbase, for the conceptual model while using existing tools for data storage and retrieval limits the performance of the system to that of these underlying tools.

How much of a problem this represents is subject to considerable debate. One can argue that the only current method of integration involves human processing: someone is asked for information and manually extracts the data from the separate environments, collates the results and returns the answer. Compared to this, any computerized solution is orders of magnitude faster.

In Vbase, more creative solutions are possible. Dual representations with complex caching can be used to improve performance while hiding the low-level details from the applications. Again, the open architecture combined with the separation of implementation from specification is critical to this approach. The open architecture allows different caching schemes to be used for different underlying tools. The separation feature allows these caching schemes to be altered without affecting client code so that incremental approaches to improving performance can be taken.

17.6 CONCLUSION

Object databases offer a good base upon which integrated environments can be built. This is because the object model is rich enough to encompass virtually all models existent in today's separate tools. Further, as the Vbase example shows, if the object database also supports a good separation of the storage model from the conceptual model, then an attractive environment can be built with a uniform abstract model for all tools. Performance may be an issue, but again, the separation noted can provide opportunities for caching and using alternate representations that can improve performance without changing the abstract model. A number of these environments are currently under development, and their progress will begin to answer some of the remaining questions.

ACKNOWLEDGEMENTS

The editors wish to thank Prof. Fulton of Georgia Institute of Technology for permission to reprint this article.

18 A Quickstart Introduction to C++

Rajiv Gupta

18.1 INTRODUCTION

C++ is an object-oriented programming language. Neither is this the definition of C++, nor does C++ circumscribe what object orientation ought to mean. However, most practitioners of the art would agree that C++ brings to C many features that have customarily been associated with the object paradigm. The merger of this paradigm, with its theoretical elegance from the software engineering viewpoint, and an efficient and popular language such as C is one of the most significant developments of the past decade.

Most of the enhancements that C++ makes to C in order to facilitate writing "good" programs can be "simulated" in other languages. However, as observed by Bjarne Stroustrup, one "can write structured programs in Fortran, write type-secure programs in C, and use data abstraction in Modula-2, but it is unnecessarily hard to do so because these languages do not *support* these techniques" [Stroustrup87a]. In that sense, C++ supports object-oriented programming while most other languages merely enable it.

C++ is, for the most part, a superset of C. C operators, control structures, pointers and records are supported fully to maintain upward compatibility. It retains the flexibility, portability and efficiency of C while providing several additional features, foremost among which is the support for object-oriented programming.

Besides several minor syntactic alterations that were long due, C++ brings four major concepts to C. These are: abstract data types, encapsulation, class (or type) hierarchies with inheritance, and polymorphism. These conceptual extensions to C eminently support good programming practices such as code reusability, information hiding, generic programming and natural extensions to the host language. We have already discussed these concepts in the context of object-oriented databases. In this chapter I shall describe how C++ implements them.

Abstract data types were invented by programming language theorists to separate storage structures (a bunch of memory locations) from the abstract behavior of data objects such as stacks and queues. The idea is simple but powerful. An abstract data type encompasses not only the implementation of an object type but also a full set of operations that are allowed on an instance of that data type. The operations are intended to insulate the users of the abstract data type from its implementation details. For example, a stack S of objects of type T may be implemented as an array of objects with a pointer to the top of S. However, from the users' point of view, the only operations that may be meaningful on S are `createStack()`, `delete(S)`, `push(Obj,S)`, `pop(S)`, and `isEmpty(S)`, where `Obj` is an object of type T. By defining all the storage management associated with S as private, and allowing access to it only through the above operations (also known as methods), one can localize future changes to the implementation of the stack.

In C++, abstract data types are defined as classes. Classes provide the facilities to define well-encapsulated object types with their operations. To reflect the fact that operations are a part of the object, they are accessed just like the data associated with it. For example, if `aCircle` is an instance of the class `Circle` which has a method `draw` defined on it, `draw` can be invoked as `aCircle.draw()`.

Encapsulation refers to the ability to make parts of the implementation details inaccessible to the user. As we will see, in C++ parts of an object defined by a class may be made private, while others can be accessed publicly. Also, there exist mechanisms for controlling the visibility of the contents of an object by declaring *friends* of its class or by making some of its members *protected*. Since a class is a well-encapsulated unit (i.e., all the data and function constituents of its instances may not be available to the user), C++ provides mechanisms to initialize and clean up objects of any class when they are created or deleted.

Many high-level languages provide a facility for defining simple types and using them to build more complex types. From that point of view, C++'s class concept is not much different from that offered by other languages such as Modula-2. Though this is a great improvement over languages that do not allow self-contained "modules" as fundamental language constructs, modeling a module purely as an abstract data type suffers from a serious limitation. By definition, a module is a black box which may be available to the user only as object code. This implies that the users have no way of adapting a module to future changes. Even incremental additions can be incorporated only by defining a completely new module which replicates most of the code of the old module.

What distinguishes C++ from most other languages is its facility for "deriving" one class from another and arranging classes in a lattice. A class Y is said to be a derived class of X if every instance of Y is also an instance of X. C++ provides constructs and semantics for deriving a class from another class by explicitly specifying a subclass/superclass relationship. A derived class (also known as subclass or subtype) *inherits* all the properties and operations of its parent class (in C++ parlance, all the members of its parent class). One can additionally define extra members or alter existing inherited members while defining a derived class.

Polymorphism—the facility to automatically dispatch a call (or a message) to an appropriate routine according to the type of the arguments passed—is another major concept implemented in C++. This feature makes the code upward compatible and resilient to modifications. It also makes application programs more generic by making them independent of low-level, type-specific implementation details. C++ provides for polymorphism via the ability to define special types of functions called *virtual functions* for any base class. When other classes are derived from this base class, and the virtual function appropriately redefined for each one of them, a call to the virtual function will be automatically routed to the appropriate routine. We will study virtual functions and operator overloading (another form of polymorphism) in greater detail later in this chapter.

One of the greatest accomplishments of C++ is its implementation of the above object-oriented concepts without compromising the efficiency of C. Other object-oriented languages such as Smalltalk cannot make this claim. In fact, the run-time efficiency of C++ code, and the space required by user-defined objects, are comparable to those of C. A call to a non-virtual function is as fast as a C call. Calls to virtual functions (which are bound at run-time) typically involve a few extra memory references.

The purpose of this chapter is to introduce the reader to C++'s implementation of the above concepts. It is meant to be a summary of C++ features rather than a definitive guide to the language syntax and usage. The exposition is brief and assumes a knowledge of C. The features of C++ that do not differ significantly from C receive only minimal coverage. Though it is not meant to be a complete treatise on C++, readers familiar with C should be able to write simple C++ programs after reading this chapter. Readers are referred to [Wiener88, Stroustrup86, 87a, 89b] for more detailed descriptions.

C++ is an evolving language. Some of the more recent features such as multiple inheritance, recursive definition of assignment and initialization, and protected members are detailed in [Stroustrup87b, 87d, 89a], while several possible future additions such as container and parameterized classes, templates, exception handling, persistence, and storage management are discussed in [Stroustrup87c, 88b]. Problems involved in type-safe linkage of separately compiled modules, in generating names for overloaded functions, and in library building are discussed in [Stroustrup88c].

The remainder of this chapter is organized as follows. In section 18.2 I shall describe several features of C++ that enhance C without making any fundamental modifications to its semantics and capabilities. Issues such as program structure, built-in types, declarations, control statements, functions, input/output facilities and storage management are covered. Section 18.3 discusses the object-oriented extensions to C. The concepts such as classes, class lattices, inheritance, data hiding and virtual functions are elaborated. Finally, some limitations of C++ are briefly discussed in the last section.

18.2 THE BASICS

18.2.1 Program Structure and Organization

A typical C++ program consists of one or more header files and a set of program files. The header files contain the definition of classes and other declarations to be used in the program, and the program files contain the bulk of executable code (i.e., the main program and the method definitions). Each program must contain one (and only one) function called `main`. This function, which cannot be overloaded, designates the start of the program. Typical `main` definitions are:

```
int main() { ...main body... }
int main(int argc, char* argv[]) { ...main body... }
```

The main program "includes" the header files, declares variables, and manipulates them via expressions, statements, and method invocations. I shall briefly describe what is new about the basic constructs such as declarations, expressions and statements before discussing the constructs that support object-oriented programming.

18.2.2 Types and Declarations

C++ supports all the fundamental types such as `int`, `short`, `long`, `float`, `double` and `char` supported by C. The type of a variable, constant, or expression determines the functions and operations that may be applied to it.

Another fundamental type, which cannot be instantiated, is `void`. It is used to indicate that a function does not return a value, or, in case of a pointer declaration, the pointer is to an object of unknown type. A pointer of any type can be assigned to a pointer to `void` (i.e., a variable of type `void*`).

There exist constructs that enable derivation of new types from the fundamental types. The keyword `const` appearing in front of any basic type converts it to a type whose behavior is identical to the original type except that its instances can be initialized only once. The operators `*`, `*const`, `&`, `[]` and `()` can be applied to basic types in order to form pointer to, constant pointer to, reference to, vector of, or function returning the basic type, respectively, as illustrated below. The following are some legal C++ declarations. Note that "`//`" tells the compiler to ignore the remainder of a line. Thus comments can be introduced in a program either using `//` or the traditional `/* .... */`.

```
const double e = 2.71828;        // a constant
const double* ptr2const_e = &e;  // pointer to a
                                 //            constant
char *const Err_Msg_Ptr =
          "Error: You cannot change this pointer\n";
                                 // constant pointer
char* c_wizards[3] = {"B. Stroustrup",
                 "B. Kernighan", "D.M. Ritchie"};
double (*centi2faran)(double);   // pointer to
                                 // function returning double
```

All constants must be initialized. In general, it is good programming practice to initialize all variables. The operator `&` allows derivation of an alternative name for an object. If `T` is a type, `T&` is a *reference to* `T`. For example,

```
long  US_population = 203184772;
long& US_pop_ref = US_population; // a reference to
                                  // US_population
```

defines US_pop_ref as an alternate name for the location containing the long integer. The ability to have references is extended to parameter passing in functions and call by reference is allowed.

As in C, a function, a type, a class, a label, or any other object in C++ has a name. Names are introduced into the program through declarations such as the ones described above. The position where a name is declared, and other qualifiers such as extern, determine the regions of the program where the name can be used. This region, called the scope of the name, may be the block in which it was declared (local), the file in which it was declared, or the class in which it was declared.

In C, if a local variable has the same name as a global variable, the global variable is completely overshadowed in the scope of the local variable. For example, if a program contains a variable X, and a subroutine in it also has a local variable named X, the value of the global variable X cannot be accessed from within the subroutine. In C++, one can refer to the global variable as ::X, using the scope qualifier operator ::.

Storage associated with objects may be allocated upon an entry into the scope in which they are valid (automatic) or it may be allocated for the entire duration of the program execution (static). The former is typically allocated on the run-time stack while the latter is allocated from the heap.

C++ also provides enumeration, records and unnamed unions. For example, one can define a named enumeration as follows.

```
enum CoordinateSystems {Cartesian, Polar};
```

Even though the struct construct of C has largely been overridden by the class construct (to be discussed shortly), it is supported by C++ (as a class with no member functions and all other members public) for upward compatibility.

If certain fields in a record are mutually exclusive (i.e., only one of them may be present at any time) *unions* can be used to save space. C++ allows both named and anonymous unions. This is similar to the concept of varient records in Pascal. A union is like a structure of members whose size is large enough to contain the largest member. At any time, at most one of the members can be stored in a union. For example, one may define a record to store the coordinates of a point on a plane as follows. Here, it is assumed that for any point either Cartesian or Polar (but not both) coordinates will be stored.

```
struct xy_coord {double x, y;};
struct rt_coord {double r, theta;};
struct coordinates {
  CoordinateSystems coord_type;
  union {
        xy_coord xy_coordinates;   // used when
                              // coord_type==Cartesian
        rt_coord rt_coordinates;   // used when
                              // coord_type==polar
  };
};
```

18.2.3 Expressions and Statements

C++ supports all standard C mathematical and boolean operators such as +, -, *, /, ++, --, !, & and %. Several new operators such as new, delete, delete[], and :: are also introduced. The reader is referred to [Stroustrup86a] for a complete list. Explicit type conversion to produce a value in one type given the value in another is feasible using either the traditional cast notation or a new functional notation. Thus, both

```
double d = (double) anInt;
```

and

```
double d = double(anInt);
```

achieve the same result.

All C control statements such as if, if-else, while, do-while, switch, return, for and goto are also supported by C++. Other than the object-oriented constructs, C++ programs look very similar to C programs and have the same structure.

18.2.4 Input/Output: The Stream Library

C++, like C, does not provide any built-in facilities for input/output. A standard library called the stream library is provided for this purpose. The overloaded operators << and >> in this library are responsible for conversion of values or arbitrary types into character streams. The << symbol indicates "put to", while the >> symbol indicates "get from". Three standard streams cin, cout, cerr, which are somewhat akin to the Cstdin, stdout and stderr, are provided.

The following example illustrates the use of the stream library and some other features described above:

```
#include <stream.h>
const int AbsoluteZero = -273;
main() {
  float    fahr;               //convert from
                               //Fahrenheit to Celsius
  char*    ErrMsg=
     "Temps less than absolute zero are not allowed.\n";
  cin >> fahr;                 //input temp in Fahrenheit
  int cent=5*(fahr-32)/9;      //convert to Celsius
  if (cent < AbsoluteZero)
     cerr << ErrMsg;
  else
     cout << cent << "\n"; //output Celsius  value
}
```

This program reads in a floating point number (the temperature) from the standard input stream, converts it from Fahrenheit to Celsius and, if it is in proper range, outputs it. Note that the operator << works on both cent (an int) and ErrMsg (a character string).

The above example also illustrates the use of constants and inline declaration of variables. Both of these are not allowed in C. By using constant declarations, the #define of C can be completely avoided. Also, the declaration of variables such as cent, within a { } block and possibly after some statements, helps put the declaration of a variable closer to its use. This is allowed as declarations are treated like statements.

18.2.5 Functions

Type checking. C++ performs considerably more static type checking than C. The function definition syntax has been extended so that the conformity of a function call can be checked against its declaration. Thus, one can declare a function, dot_product() along with the types of formal arguments, as:

```
float dot_product(float vec1[], float vec2[], int
        dimension=100)
        { .... function-body .... }
```

This function can be invoked by the call dot_product(v1, v2, dim). The compiler will automatically verify that v1, v2, and dim are of proper types. In fact one can also invoke this function as dot_product(v1, v2), in which case a default value of 100 will be passed for dim. In this manner C++ allows one to specify a set of default values for the trailing parameters in a function declaration. In addition, C++ provides for type-safe linkage between separately compiled modules.

Inline function substitution. Functions allow one to write code that can be reused in many places. Each function call, however, entails the overhead of a context switch which may be unacceptable for very small functions. To remedy this C++ allows inline substitution of functions. This can increase speed and totally removes the need for the use of C preprocessor macros. In order to tell the compiler that a function should be expanded inline, the function definition is preceded by the keyword inline. For operations associated with a class, if the body of the operation is included in the class declaration, it is automatically expanded when called.

Function and operator overloading. Most languages disallow operators such as + and − to be used on user-defined types. C++ goes a long way in elevating user-defined types so that they "look and feel" like system-defined types. Operator overloading is one mechanism that facilitates this. For example, one can define a class for complex numbers and overload operators +, −, =, / and * with functions to perform the corresponding operations on complex numbers. With these and few other overloaded operators, complex numbers can be treated just like int and double.

C++ also allows the use of the same name to perform different functions on different types. As an example, consider

```
int add(int,int);
double add(double,double);
```

When the function `add()` is called the compiler determines which of the two add functions is to be called based on the number and types of the parameters. For example, if one calls `add(1,1)`, the function `add(int, int)` will be invoked.

The set of resolution rules that allow binding a call with an actual function are rather elaborate and will not be repeated here. These rules try to find the "best" match for a given call from the list of overloaded functions with the same name. The quality of a match is independent of the order in which the functions were declared; it depends on features such as the number of type conversions required to match the formal argument types to actual argument types, and whether the conversions are unavoidable, standard, or user-defined. Certain functions that are too close (for example, those that differ only in the type of the return argument) cannot have the same name. If the resolution rules come up with two functions that match a call, the call is ambiguous and the compiler reports an error.

Call by reference. As mentioned earlier, C++ allows an alternative name or a reference to an object of type `T` via `T&`. For example, the declaration

```
circle& sameCircle = aCircle;
```

introduces a synonym `sameCircle` for `aCircle`. Here it is assumed that `aCircle` has already been declared. Since an alternative name cannot be used without the object for which it is an alternate name, every reference must be initialized. Also, every operation on a reference is an operation on the base object.

This type of name aliasing is extended to function parameters. If the formal argument to a function is a reference, at the time of call it temporarily becomes an alternative name for the actual parameter. For example, if a function defined as

```
void updateBalance(double&  balance) {  .....  };
```

is invoked as `updateBalance(myBalance)`, `balance` becomes an alternative name for `myBalance`, allowing the latter's value to be changed from within the function. If a function returns a reference (instead of a value), it can be used both as an lvalue and an rvalue (i.e., it can be used on both sides of an assignment operation). This facility is invaluable in defining complex user-defined types such as streams.

Variable number of parameters. Function overloading along with default arguments to functions typically takes care of most of the parameter passing needs. However, there are instances when neither the number of arguments nor their types can be specified at the time of writing the function. The function `printf()` is one such example. C++ permits an arbitrary number of arguments to a function if the argument list terminates with ellipsis (...). As is to be expected, type checking is suppressed for the arguments that are not specified. A set of macros is provided for accessing the unspecified arguments.

18.2.6 Storage Allocation and Deallocation

Storage associated with an object can be either automatic or static. In C, the standard library functions such as `malloc()` and `free()` are used to allocate storage for the latter type of objects. In C++ storage allocation and deallocation are done by calls to `new` and `delete`. An object created by `new` on the free store persists until it is explicitly destroyed by the `delete` operator. `new` and `delete` are typically used to build the nodes of dynamic data structures such as trees and linked lists.

The operators `new()` and `delete()` can be overloaded, just like any other operator or function, if a user wants to take over free-store management.

18.3 SUPPORT OF OBJECT-ORIENTED PROGRAMMING

18.3.1 Classes

The C++ class provides the programmer with the ability to create new types and define operations on those types. The user-defined classes behave in exactly the same way as the system-defined classes such as `int` and `float`, and to that extent the class construct can be viewed as a language extension construct rather than a programming construct.

A class is a user-defined type that is typically used to introduce a new concept not supported by the host language. A class prescribes the attributes that its instances can have and methods that can act on them. The names declared within a class (both the attributes and the methods) are called the *members* of the class. A member can be referenced only within the scope of other member functions of the class, unless special actions are taken to increase its visibility (for example, by declaring it `public`, `protected`, or `friend`).

Classes provide data abstraction and hiding, user-controlled memory operations, dynamic typing, and several other useful features. One can view a class as a template that specifies data and operations associated with an object type. A non-member function can access only the public portions of the objects instantiated using a given class template and manipulate it only through the defined set of public operations. In the terminology of object-oriented programming, these operations represent the messages that can be sent to the object.

A C++ class can contain objects of other classes, pointers to objects of other classes, or even pointers to objects of its own class. Any method may be defined inline for reasons of efficiency. The language also provides syntax for pointing to the individual members of a class.

As an example, consider a class which stores a person's name, social security number, and date of birth.

```
class person
    {                           // This part is private.
                char*   name;
                char*   social_sec_no;
        protected:              // This part is accessible to
```

```
                        // the member functions
                        // of subclasses of person.
            date*       date_of_birth;
    public:             // This is visible externally.
                        person();  //constructor
                        person(char*, char* date*);
                            //constructor
                        ~person();  //destructor
            void        setname(char*);
            char*       getname();
            void        setSSN(char*);
            char*       getSSN();
            void        setDOB(date*);
            int         getAge();
    };
```

As mentioned earlier, a method is accessed and invoked via the object it acts on. Within the body of any method, all the members of the object through which this method was invoked are accessible directly. For example, if getAge was invoked using aPerson.getAge(), any references to name, social_sec_no or date_of_birth inside this procedure refer to those attributes of aPerson.

In order to provide an explicit access to the object via which a method is invoked, the reserved word this is used. this, whose type is T* in the context of every function associated with the class T, can be thought of as a hidden argument to every method defined on T.

In a class definition, one can define static data members for those attributes of which only one copy should exist for the whole class rather than an individual copy for each instance. Class variables, as they are sometimes referred to, not only associate the static objects with the classes they logically belong to, they also help reduce the clutter in the global name space. The latter is true because in the absence of static members, objects which are global to a class will have to be declared in the global name space. In newer versions of C++ not only data members but even function members can be static, thus reducing the number of globally declared function names. This facility is very useful in building libraries, as one does not have to be concerned about user-defined function names colliding with the internal functions used in the library. Heretofore, ingenious techniques such as embedding underscores or dollar signs in the function names have been used by library builders.

Consider the following declaration:

```
const person aPerson;
```

If the function setSSN() were allowed on aPerson, it would render the declaration of aPerson as a constant meaningless. On the other hand, if all operations on constants such as aPerson were disallowed, it would also suppress access to functions such as getSSN() which do not change the object they act on. In the function declaration, the keyword const as a suffix to the argument list tells the compiler that this function is allowed to act on constant instances of this class. Thus the definition of `person` should really be changed to include the following modified members, if constant instances of `person` are to be used:

```
char*    getname()  const {return name};
char*    getSSN()   const {return social_sec_no};
int      getAge()   const {/* compute age */};
```

18.3.2 Data Hiding and Friends

As illustrated in the definition of the class `person`, a class may contain three types of members. Members of a class may be *public*, *private* or *protected*.

Any function, irrespective of whether it is a member function of a class X or not, can manipulate instances of X through the members declared in its public section. Non-member functions cannot use the private members of a class. (There are ways to cheat by trying to locate them via their locations in memory; however, that is not the intended access method for class members.) In the above example, the six `get` and `set` operations can be invoked by any member or non-member function while the private members `name` and `social_sec_no` can only be accessed in the body of the member functions. The `protected` members, which are pertinent for derived types, will be discussed in the next section.

For reasons of efficiency, it may sometimes be desirable to allow a non-member function to directly access non-public data of an object rather than expend the overhead of a function call. The `friend` construct provides a way of granting a non-member function access to private and protected portions of a class. Friends of a class have the same access to its members as the member functions. For example, if one were to modify the definition of `person` to include

```
public: friend void SupervisoryFunction(char*,
                    char*, date*);
```

then `name`, `social_sec_no` and `date_of_birth` can be initialized in this function even though it is not a member function.

18.3.3 Constructors and Destructors

Since non-member functions cannot access all parts of a class definition, some way of initializing instances of a class is essential. Clearly, one can provide suggestively named member functions such as `Init_Person` to provide for object initialization; however, this is inelegant and errorprone. A user might simply forget to call this function after object creation.

C++ provides a useful construct called a constructor for this purpose. Constructors are functions with the same name as the class in which they are defined. They provide for automatic initialization of class objects as they are automatically called when the scope in which the object is declared is entered. Multiple constructors for a class object are permitted (this is just another form of overloading).

Destructors, which take the name of their class preceded by the ~ character (e.g.,~ClassName), perform the reverse operation; they provide for automatic deallocation of the storage occupied by an object. Destructors are invoked when the block containing the object is exited.

Constructors and destructors permit the class programmer to take control at storage allocation/deallocation time. A sophisticated programmer can thus allocate and deallocate objects of known types very efficiently. An object whose size is unknown at compile time can also be allocated using this mechanism. C++ does not provide any other mechanism for garbage collection.

18.3.4 Inheritance

As indicated earlier, C++ allows an abstract data type, provided as a class, to be further customized by the user. In C++ parlance, the original class is called the base class and the new one a derived class. A derived class inherits all the members of the base class. One can define new members for the derived class in addition to the ones inherited from the base class. Thus the derived classes provide the basis for inheritance and customization of abstract data types represented as classes. The terms derived class, subclass and subtype are used synonymously in the object-oriented programming literature; similarly the terms base class, superclass, supertype, parent class/type are used interchangeably; and so are they here.

Earlier C++ compilers supported only one direct superclass per derived class, though many classes could be derived from a superclass. This restriction gives rise to a hierarchical organization (also known as *Is-A* hierarchy) among classes and the resulting inheritance scheme is termed *single inheritance*.

In many real world situations, however, the objects naturally tend to belong to more than one class. A powerful feature, which has been added to the language since its first release in the mid-'80s, allows a class to have more than one direct base class. This feature, which is commonly referred to as *multiple inheritance*, results in a lattice (or a directed acyclic graph) of classes. I shall introduce the single and multiple inheritance features of C++ and several other associated details with the help of an example taken from philology. In the following example, some of the assumptions about the evolution and characteristics of natural languages are made purely for pedagogical reasons and may not withstand close philological scrutiny.

Single inheritance. Consider the class definitions a linguist or a philologist may use to store characteristics of different families of languages. The characteristics that need be stored about a given language in a family may involve attributes such as complexity of the grammar, phonology, size of the vocabulary, number of people speaking that language, set of symbols in the alphabet, size of the alphabet, geographical regions where it is spoken, etc. Clearly, not all the attributes apply to all the language families. For example, if a set of languages contains only spoken languages with no script, a set-valued attribute to store symbols in the alphabet is superfluous. Thus, for different families of languages, different attributes are relevant.

It was postulated by the German philologist August Schleicher that most languages originated from a common root called the Proto-Indo-European language. The characteristics of this proto-language were inherited, sometimes with modifications, by all the languages that originated from it. The fundamental assumption, which was made by many classical philologists, is that when one family of languages evolves from another, it only acquires new characteristics. Thus, the basic evolution paradigm is divergence with addition. This is also the basic mechanism embodied in single inheritance.

Given this scenario, if the philologist interested in designing a schema for languages is also knowledgeable about object-oriented languages, he or she will define a *base class* called `Proto_Indo_European` to represent the family of these ancient languages, and derive all the other language classes from it. This class may look something like this:

```
class Proto_Indo_European {
  public:
    Boolean           isPhonetic;
    ScriptType        scriptType;
    SymbolSet         *alphabetSet;
    int               no_of_speakers;
    MapWords2String   *dictionary;
          . . . . . . . . . .
    virtual    void      printAlphabet();
    virtual    int       alphabetSize();
    virtual    Boolean   containsWord(Word&);
          . . . . . . . . . .
}
```

The above class declares common attributes and functions that will be inherited by all its subclasses. The meaning of the keyword `virtual` will be explained in the next section.

Two families of languages evolved from the Proto-Indo-European languages: the Slavo-Germanic languages and the Aryan-Greco-Italo-Celtic languages. For the sake of exposition, assume that the languages in the former family share a trait called `Type-OfVerbConjugation` which can take a value from a finite domain (an enumeration) called `verbConjEnum`; and for the latter family an integer-valued attribute called `lex-icalComplexity` needs to be stored in addition to the attributes of the Proto-Indo-European languages. To provide for these new attributes we derive two classes for these families as follows:

```
class Slavo_Germanic: public Proto_Indo_European {
  public:
    verbConjEnum TypeOfVerbConjugation;
}
class Aryan_Greco_Italo_Celtic: public
          Proto_Indo_European {
  public:
    int lexicalComplexity;
}
```

Several features of the above derivations are important and worth discussing. First, note the keyword `public` following the derived class name. If the derivation is public, the private, public and protected members are inherited with the same access control features as those in the base class. However, if the keyword public is omitted, even the public members of the base class cannot be accessed by the non-member functions of the derived class. For example, if Slavo_Germanic was derived without the keyword public, then the assignment

```
aLanguage.no_of_speakers = 0;
```

is improper for a variable aLanguage of type Slavo_Germanic. However, even when the derivation is private, it is possible to explicitly specify access control for the members of the base class. In the above example, one can make the assignment to aLanguage.no_of_speakers legal by including

```
public: Proto_Indo_European::no_of_speakers;
```

in the definition of class Slavo_Germanic. As is to be expected, one cannot grant more access to a member in the derived class than that provided by the base class.

One can develop, with enough research on the evolution of language characteristics, a class hierarchy similar to the one indicated in Figure 18.1. There are three types of users for the classes in this hierarchy. First we have the class programmers who are charged with writing the member functions. They clearly have access to all the members of a class. Then there are those users who wish to instantiate and manipulate objects of a class via its public interface. The ability to derive one class from another introduces yet another type of users, viz., those who are interested in providing a new class of objects by customizing an existing class. Protected members discussed next are relevant to this third class of users.

Protected members. The private members of a class are inaccessible to the member functions of any class derived from it, even if the derivation is public. Thus, for certain members, the classification merely into private and public may be too restrictive. Two constructs, friend and protected, are used to overcome the difficulties imposed by this strict discipline.

We have already seen the use of friends of a class. The protected members allow selective access to the base class. Any member function of a class derived publicly from a base class can access members declared as protected in the base class; protected members are inaccessible to the non-member functions just like the private members. For example, if we publicly derive a new class called Aquarian from the class person declared earlier, the member functions of Aquarian can access the date_of_birth while the non-member functions cannot access this member, either in an instance of person or that of Aquarian.

It should be emphasized that a protected member in a base class is also a protected member in the derived class only if the derivation is public. It becomes a private member otherwise. Also, note that "protected" derivation (though it is quite reasonable and consistent) is not allowed. In addition, the access to a protected member is through a statically determined access pointer; the object should be explicitly known to be an instance of the derived class in order for a protected member to be accessible in a member function of the derived class.

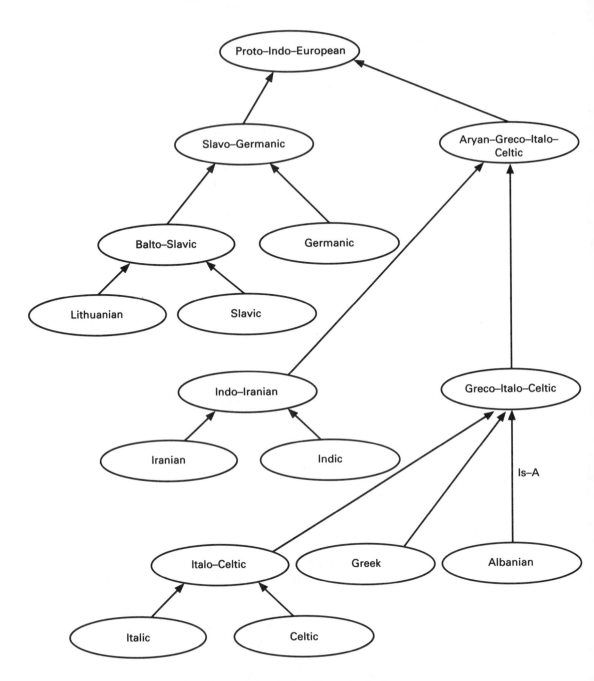

Figure 18.1 A class hierarchy for languages.

Multiple inheritance.   The basic assumption in our language example has been that a family of languages can evolve from only one parent family. This assumption is not strictly valid for natural languages. Multiple inheritance, which allows a class to inherit behavior from more than one base class, can be used to model this situation more realistically. Since more than one base class is allowed, the classes in a program written in a language that supports multiple inheritance can be organized in a *class lattice*. It is widely believed that multiple inheritance is a powerful structuring mechanism that leads to cleaner software organization.

The contribution of C++ with respect to multiple inheritance is in coming up with a clean and efficient implementation of this powerful concept. I shall now discuss the basic multiple inheritance scheme, the rules for resolving ambiguities that arise because of naming conflicts in the parent classes, and the handling of multiply included classes.

Assume that we have specialized the language classes of Figure 18.1 down to the Italic, Rumanic, Franco, Espano and Portuguese families. All these classes evolved from Vulgar Latin as shown in Figure 18.2. Instances of these classes can be used to denote individual languages such as Castilian and Catalan (instances of Espano family), Modern French (an instance of Franco), and so on.

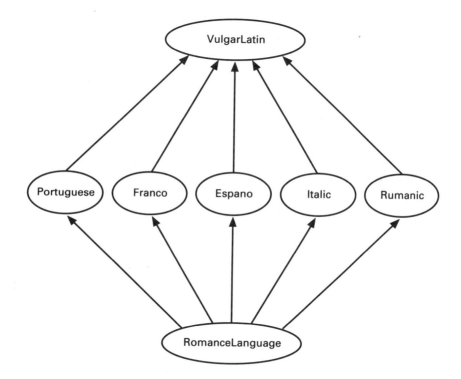

Figure 18.2 Class derivation using multiple inheritance.

Now consider the derivation of the class of Romance languages. These languages, which also developed from Vulgar Latin, have instances such as Italian, French, Spanish and Rumanian. Clearly, it is desirable that this class be derived from the five classes shown in Figure 18.2. In addition, there are other lesser known Romance languages. These include Rhaeto-Romanic (a language spoken in parts of southern Switzerland and northern Italy), Provençal (the literary language of troubadours in Provence of France) and

Sardinian (spoken on the island of Sardinia in the Mediterranean Sea). Thus, additional members may be required to store attributes and functions relevant to these languages.

One can derive a new class called RomanceLanguage as follows:

```
class RomanceLanguage:
   public Franco, public Italic, public Rumanic,
   public Portuguese, public Espano{
     // Additional members
   };
```

In this manner, one can combine several disparate concepts in a composite new class. All the ambiguities arising because of the combination are detected and reported at compile time. For example, if all the five base classes above have a function `printAlphabet()`, then the usage `aRLang.printAlphabet()` is ambiguous for a variable aRLang of type RomanceLanguage. In such a situation, one has to qualify, using `::`, which `printAlphabet()` is actually intended. For example, `Franco::printAlphabet()` refers specifically to that function associated with the class Franco. When multiple base classes can cause ambiguity, it is good programming practice to add a function with the same name to the derived class. This function may in turn invoke one or more of the corresponding functions from the base classes.

It should be noted that combining classes in a manner that can lead to a name conflict is *not* an error. Only when a member name is invoked ambiguously (i.e., when a name can be traced to two distinct members in the parent classes) does the compiler report an error. Also, the members of the base class are explicitly referred to using the `::` notation rather than referring to them as "my-parent-class" as is done in Smalltalk, or using the $$ syntax of COP (see Chapter 9).

A less obvious side effect of the above derivation is that each object of type RomanceLanguage contains five subobjects of type VulgarLatin. This may be acceptable, even useful, in some instances where one is interested in representing a composition of independent concepts. (Because of this, the above type of inheritance has been referred to as *independent multiple inheritance* [Stroustrup87d].) However, in most cases a more explicit control over subobject shareability is required. *Virtual base classes* provide mechanism for achieving this; they provide a way of indicating to the compiler that a base class must be included in the final derived class only once, even if it occurs several times in the list of base classes, either directly or indirectly. For the above example, if we define the descendents of VulgarLatin as

```
class X: public virtual VulgarLatin { ... };
```

where X is substituted with Franco, Italic, Espano, Portuguese and Rumanic, respectively, then the derivation

```
class RomanceLanguage:
   public Franco, public Italic, public Rumanic,
   public Portuguese, public Espano {
     // Additional members
   };
```

will give rise to a class whose instances will have only one subobject of type VulgarLatin. It should be emphasized that the keyword virtual is a qualifier for the derivation and not for the base class itself. This base class behaves exactly as a non-virtual base class for all other purposes.

While initializing an object in a given class, special syntax exists for initializing the members of the base classes and the members of its own class. The members of the base classes are initialized first. They are initialized in the order in which they appear in the declaration of the derived class; the members of the derived class are initialized later. For the most part, the order of initialization should not matter as far as the final object is concerned.

18.3.5 Polymorphism and Virtual Functions

Sometimes it is not possible to write a function for a base class even though it is known that such a function will be needed by all the derived classes. For example, a function called printAlphabet() should be provided by the class Proto_Indo_European, even though this function can only be written when class-specific knowledge pertaining to each derived class is available. Virtual functions allow the programmer to declare functions in a base class that can be redefined in each derived class. The compiler will find the appropriate class for each call of the virtual function.

When a virtual function is called, the interpretation of the call depends on the type of object for which it is called. For a virtual function that is redefined more than once as one moves down the class lattice, the version from the most derived class is used. This rule also applies in the case of multiple inheritance.

Consider, for example, a virtual function printAlphabet() that is defined by VulgarLatin and redefined by Italic. For any object aRLanguage of type RomanceLanguage, aRLanguage.printAlphabet() dispatches to the redefinition in the class Italic. Curiously, even (Franco)aRLanguage.printAlphabet() dispatches to the same function. This latter case illustrates the fact that a call through one path may result in the invocation of a function redefined in another path.

The rule to remember here is that when virtual base classes are used, there is only one shared subobject corresponding to the virtual base class. The functions in this subobject may have been overridden due to derivation and any amount of casting would not change that fact.

All redefinitions of a virtual function must occur on a single path when one moves down from a virtual base class in the class lattice. If this condition is not satisfied, an ambiguity will result, since the rule "use the function redefinition in the most derived class" will not result in a unique function definition.

18.3.6 Abstract Classes

There are instances in which one is interested in defining a class solely for the purpose of derivation; no instances of this class will ever be used by the application. Typically, such classes are needed to represent the core properties and methods inherited by all classes in a type lattice. Abstract classes provide this functionality. One declares a class as abstract by explicitly assigning to one or more virtual functions in its definition a value zero. For example,

```
class abstClass {
    // data members
  public:
      virtual void f() = 0 // a pure virtual function
}
```

defines an abstract class.

18.4 SOME LIMITATIONS AND OTHER CAVEATS

I end this chapter by pointing out some of the limitations of C++. Some of these features mentioned below are still under consideration and may be included in future versions of the language. On the other hand, quite a few of these features were deliberately left out because they were deemed too expensive, in terms of the overhead, when compared with the utility they would provide.

C++ does not support persistent objects. Objects created by C++ programs are destroyed when the program terminates. Much research is being done to extend the language to support persistent objects, thus upgrading it to an OODB. In Chapters 20 and 21 we will study two attempts at making a database out of C++ by providing object persistence.

In addition, C++ provides no specialized constructs for exception handling, parameterized classes, or iterators for aggregates. We have already seen such constructs in the context of COP and Vbase. Unfortunately, it is not possible to cleanly "simulate" all these features while remaining within the confines of the language. The next chapter will discuss these limitations in greater detail and contrast C++ features with those of COP.

Early in this chapter we mentioned that C++ is a superset of C. This is not strictly true as there are some minor incompatibilities in the two languages. For one, C++ has many more keywords than C does. This invalidates some variable names which are allowed in C.

Another incompatibility exists because C++ makes function calls more secure by checking types and number of arguments. In C, the declaration

```
char*  GetName();
```

declares a function that accepts an arbitrary number of arguments. In C++, the above statement declares GetName to be a function with no arguments. Also, there are differences in the name space associated with structures in the two languages.

Other than these minor incompatibilities, the two languages can be easily intermixed. Most C++ compilers allow command line flags (for example, -fno-strict-prototype in GNU g++) so that C programs can be compiled and linked with little or no change. This is very important as it makes many extensive libraries, which have been developed for C programs, directly accessible to C++ programs.

ACKNOWLEDGEMENTS

I wish to thank Abhijit Khale for helping with a preliminary draft of this paper. Rajesh Gupta proofread the final manuscript and his efforts are gratefully acknowledged.

19 C++ and COP: A Brief Comparison

Craig Damon

19.1 INTRODUCTION

Recently, designing an object-oriented language that you can call your own has been all the rage. Some of these (e.g., Eiffel [Meyer85] and Trellis/Owl [Schaffert86]) are completely new languages, while the majority (e.g., Objective-C [Stepstone86], Object-Pascal [Tesler84] and Flavors [Moon86]) are extensions to existing languages. And in at least one case, an existing language became an object-oriented language by proclamation. The rationale in that case seems to run "The committee thought to put in every other feature ever considered in the history of computer languages, surely they must have included this as well".

This chapter will briefly discuss some criteria for determining whether a language is object-oriented and how some of the above languages do (and don't) meet those criteria. Then two apparently similar languages, C++ and COP, will be probed in more depth. Their real similarities and differences will be examined over a spectrum of language issues: basic structure, type checking, model of inheritance, model of state and model of storage.

19.1.1 What is an Object-Oriented Language?

With all the hoopla surrounding objects, a solid definition of the term object-oriented has been difficult to discern. However, a number of papers and presentations recently have been solidifying around a few central themes. Wegner [Wegner87] argues that an object-oriented language must meet three key criteria: a concept of objects; a concept of class or type to describe these objects; and the notion of inheritance. Stroustrup [Stroustrup87a] describes object-oriented programming as combining data abstraction with inheritance. He goes on to describe a set of features considered important for supporting data abstraction: constructors and destructors for all object creation and deletion; parameterized types; an exception mechanism; object coercions and iterators.

These definitions, while not in exact agreement, do point in a very similar direction. To reasonably be considered object-oriented, a language must support some notion of independent entities, commonly referred to as objects. The behavior of these objects must be defined by a type which can be defined by a programmer using that language. These types must be able to be related through an inheritance mechanism.

19.1.2 Categories of Existing Object-Oriented Languages

Many, but not all, of the languages claimed to be object-oriented do in fact meet these criteria to some reasonable degree. The existing set of object-oriented languages (and it's probably growing day by day) can be classified in a number of ways. These languages differ in their inheritance models, type checking models, compiler technologies and support for application specific needs. Each of these qualities could be used for differentiating the languages. Wegner developed a quite admirable classification scheme in [Wegner87].

At the OOPSLA (Object-Oriented Programming Systems, Languages and Applications) conference in 1987, a natural classification of object-oriented languages emerged in several of the workshops. The first group, composed of the Smalltalk aficionados, was constantly at odds with the second group, composed of the proponents of strong type checking. Meanwhile, the third group, consisting of those with Lisp orientation, watched on with some bemusement. This seems to make a good rough classification, since it appears that, in reality, many (if not most) people choose among these categories first and then investigate the alternatives within one of these groups more seriously.

The first group is dominated by Smalltalk [Goldberg83]. Other, more recent languages, such as Self [Ungar87] also seem to belong here. Of course, the various Smalltalk derivatives, such as OPAL [Maier86a] would fit here as well. Objective-C is a little schizoid along these lines and might be classified here or it might be classified with the other C-based languages in the second group.

The second group is just beginning to settle. The one common thread, the notion of strong static type-checking, is nearly dominated by many differences between the languages falling in this group. Some languages have been based on an existing procedural language, usually C, while others have developed from scratch. Although no single language clearly dominates the group, C++ is moving into a position to become the one dominant language.

Within the Lisp world, the object wars are over, having settled on the CLOS [DeMichel87] standard.

19.1.3 Biases

No article is written without biases and this one is no exception. In particular, the author of this chapter was the principal designer of the language COP and many of the abstraction mechanisms that it is built upon. This chapter will attempt to evaluate the differences between COP and C++ and will many times (but by no means always) favor the COP approach. This side will be chosen because the arguments are still largely the same as when the design decisions in COP were made, not because of any pride of authorship. Because of familiarity with the issues in COP, many of the comparisons will be cast into the framework of the decisions made there. This may introduce its own form of bias into the evaluation.

Bjarne Stroustrup graciously agreed to review this chapter, making it possible to remove a number of the lingering biases. He also clarified a number of points concerning C++ and provided a number of corrections relating to the latest releases of C++. The author wishes to extend his thanks for Mr. Stroustrup's contribution to this chapter.

19.2 BASICS

Within the C corner of the strong type checking group lie the languages C++ and COP. They make a good basis for comparison because of their basic similarities. They are roughly the same age; they both have solid commercial implementations and are in reasonably wide use (although C++'s use is more than an order of magnitude greater); and in many cases, they are being used for similar tasks (computer-aided engineering applications, for example). Both languages were designed to be general purpose programming languages. Within that criteria, C++ chose to focus on extremely high performance in its low-level constructs, while COP chose to focus on modeling support. Its initial inclusion as a part of an object-oriented database product required COP to also focus on tight integration with the database. The similarity of the features in each language have attracted similar types of programming projects, most notably computer-aided engineering applications and language processors.

Because of these similarities, the differences between these languages provide fertile ground for experimentation and growth in both languages. In the longer term, they may well (and probably should) grow towards each other, creating a single object C language.

19.2.1 History of C++

C++ [Stroustrup86] was developed at Bell Laboratories by Bjarne Stroustrup, with the help of others, in an effort to develop a better C. As such it is heavily based on the language C [Kernighan78]. Simula [Dahl70] was the principal source from which the extensions were drawn, although Algol68 is credited as the source of the operator overloading concepts found in the language.

The earliest version was known as C with Classes and was first used in 1980. It lacked many of the current features and was only used within Stroustrup's group at Bell Labs.

In 1983, the language acquired the name C++ and was released for use in other groups at Bell Labs. In 1985, it was made commercially available and is now supported by several independent vendors as well as AT&T.

19.2.2 History of COP

The language COP [Ontologic88] (for C Object Processor) has a very different origin. The language was designed from the start to be a portion of a commercial product, in particular, an object-oriented database. This influenced many of the most basic decisions, not the least of which was the choice of extending C, rather than defining a new language or extending some other language.

The initial version of the language was primarily designed by Robert Handsaker, Gordon Landis and Thomas Atwood, with Stanley Zdonik serving as a consultant. The first processor based on this design was used in 1984.

A near business failure in 1985 gave the surprisingly positive opportunity to re-evaluate all of the work done on COP and the underlying abstraction mechanisms during a six month period with little or no other demands. During that period, Craig Damon and Robert Handsaker led the language design effort with consulting help from Toby Bloom. Out of that work came the current COP language, with the first external user in 1986 and the commercial release of the Vbase product (including COP) in early 1988.

The language CLU [Liskov79] was the spiritual driving force behind the language design. Many of the concepts of data abstraction, as well as the iterator and exception models, were brought over in some form from CLU. To this, the notions of inheritance, type hierarchy and dynamic binding were added. These were primarily influenced by the work done in Smalltalk.

19.2.3 Basic Similarities

Two particularly obvious similarities dominate at first glance. Both languages are a tightly integrated extension to C, attempting to stay within the mind set of the underlying language. And both languages support a basically similar model of inheritance, although as will be noted later, the differences are actually quite significant.

As an implementation and porting simplification, both languages have been implemented as preprocessors to the host system's C compiler rather than as native compilers. Recently, however, some true compilers for C++ have appeared. The initial decision to generate C code has had some effects on the feature set of both languages.

Both languages support a notion of object state, not a universal capability across all object-oriented languages. In both languages, the state can be declared as either publicly visible or private. Publicly visible behavior can be accessed by any code, while private behavior is more protected; only the code implementing the type (and possibly selected other places) can access it.

A type in either system may define behavior in the form of operations or functions to manipulate the member objects of that type. These operations may either be directly implemented, or may dynamically choose an implementation at run-time based on the actual type of the object.

There are many similarities in syntax because of the common choice of base language and the effort to stay consistent with it. Both use the dot notation to access state and the parentheses notation to indicate an operation invocation. Although the underlying mechanism is somewhat different in most cases, both languages make heavy use of the other common syntactic forms such as = and + to express concepts in their respective extensions. This tends to give the programmer a similar feel when reading code in either language.

Finally, both languages require and give reasonable support for both constructors and destructors of objects. Neither language implements automatic garbage collection, requiring an action to remove an object (either explicitly deleting the object or in some cases in C++, an action which exits the scope which defines an object).

19.2.4 Minor Differences

There are a range of minor differences between the languages that could distract from a comparison. None of these differences have much bearing on the languages themselves, and for the most part, the languages could change sides in these issues with little real effect on either language.

The first one encountered is the difference in terminology. These differences are widespread. Where C++, consistent with most of the object community, calls its types Classes, they are called Types in Vbase. C++ classes declare Member Functions, while Vbase types define Operations. COP distinguishes non-dynamically bound operations by calling them Non-Dispatched Operations, while C++ takes the opposite tact and names the dynamically bound member functions Virtual Functions. The individual pieces of state are referred to as Fields in C++, while they are called Properties in COP. The function which creates an object in C++ is called a Constructor and the function which deletes an object a Destructor, while the corresponding operations are considered Create and Delete operations in COP.

The terms class and constructor, which have one meaning in C++ (as given above), are each used for a different concept in COP. In COP, a class is an aggregate referring to all the objects which meet some criteria. Usually this criteria is "being an instance of type X", so that the class is an aggregate referring to all of the instances of a given type. In COP, a constructor is the syntactic form generally used to invoke a create operation.

There are also a handful of minor syntactic differences. While COP chose to use a dollar sign ($) to separate levels of naming, C++ chose two colons (::). Because of the potential conflict with system defined names, the C++ choice is far preferable. C++ adds the keyword `class` to indicate the new extended type system, while COP chose the keyword `obj`. C++ chose to pull a single distinguished argument out of the call to member functions. It was decided not to make that distinction in COP, as this prohibits the possibility of multiple argument dispatching. C++ also treats this argument specially in the function definition. The argument is not directly named in the parameter list, but instead can be referred to by the new keyword `this`. Fields on the object pointed to by `this` can be referred to directly, without the normal dot or points at (->) syntax. Similarly, member functions can be directly invoked without indicating the base object for the member function. In agreement with the lack of special syntax for operation invocation, COP gives no special treatment to the dispatch argument within a method either.

Although both systems support the idea of optional arguments, they do it in a very different manner. COP adds keyword arguments to C, which are bound to the formal parameter by an identifying tag rather than by their position in the argument list. Any keyword argument may be defined to be optional or provided with a default value. C++

allows the type to define the last n arguments to be optional by declaring default values for them. Although this by itself lacks a great deal of the expressive power of the keyword argument paradigm, this is largely overcome by C++'s function overloading capabilities.

Somewhat because of the difference in their age, the two languages have differed in their interactions with the emerging ANSI C standard. C++ has an admirable heritage of interchange with the ANSI standard, both providing new features for the standard and borrowing ideas from it. Unfortunately, Stroustrup has asserted that the remaining differences will not be changed in C++, leaving a language that will not accept the vast body of existing C (ANSI and otherwise) code. COP has committed to tracking the ANSI standard and currently supports the standard except for minor preprocessor differences.

Traditionally, a C++ source level debugger has not been available, while a COP level debugger was considered essential to the product. This was somewhat necessitated by the greater level of transformation performed by the COP compiler. This situation is beginning to be remedied with the recent arrival of C++ debuggers with some new compilers.

19.2.5 Reference Semantics

Common to almost all, if not all, object systems is the notion of reference. In some systems the reference is explicitly visible, while in others it is never apparent without looking under the covers. A reference provides a means of denoting a specific object with all access to the object using this reference. This reference, rather than the object, is assigned and moved about as the object is passed to and from various functions and variables. In this sense, object references are equivalent to pointers in a language like C.

Whereas COP allows access to objects only through these references, C++ allows local variables to hold the objects themselves. This can seriously break the polymorphism that is a cornerstone of an object-oriented system. For a simple example of this, consider a class named `Shape` that defines the virtual function `Area`. If a class `Circle`, providing the new field `Radius` and a new implementation for `Area`, were to be derived from `Shape`, problems can arise. If an instance of `Circle` is assigned to a `Shape` variable, the `Radius` field will be lost. In current implementations at least, `Circle`'s version of `Area` will be used on this `Shape` variable, causing a reference to random memory locations. The latest release of the compiler patches the virtual function pointer on this assignment, forcing the `Shape` variable to use the version of `Area` defined by `Shape`. However, calculating the area of a `Shape`, rather than one of its derived classes, is not necessarily a well-defined concept.

On the positive side, it does give C++ a straightforward notion of stack based objects, a feature sorely missing from the current version of COP. The concept of value based objects also simplifies the work required by the compiler to generate efficient code for local objects.

To maintain some reasonable sense of polymorphism, a C++ programmer must use a C pointer as an object reference. Although this has positive performance benefits, it also severely limits the future growth of the language. It limits the maximum object space to the memory limitations of the host machine and prohibits objects from ever being moved within memory. It also prevents any form of reference validation, disallowing the detection of dangling references as well as simple garbage references, both common programming errors.

The strong data abstraction that C++ should provide is endangered by the tight association of reference and pointer, particularly because of the freedom that C gives a programmer to manipulate pointers. This is especially true since C++ allows the programmer to obtain the address of a field within a C++ object and use that as a general pointer.

Because of the defined relationship between structs and classes, the actual layout of an object in memory is absolutely fixed. This is a clear violation of the concept of data abstraction, and unreasonably ties the implementation to the specification. It also creates problems with variable sized objects. (They cannot have any virtual functions; see [Sakkinen88]). Still more problems with this approach will be discussed in the sections on state and storage.

19.3 HIGH LEVEL DIFFERENCES

Despite their similarities (both are C based preprocessors generating C code), the two languages have several basic structural differences. These differences range from the way that types are declared to some basic features in the languages.

19.3.1 Type Definition

The basic way types are defined varies rather markedly between the languages. C++ chose to add a handful of new syntax plus some new semantics to C itself so that the definition of a class is written in the same language as the code that manipulates its instances. C++ has defined classes to be a minor extension of structs, allowing private as well as public portions of the declaration. C++ has also added the capability to define member functions for structs, and thus for classes. This form of extension has allowed C++ to maintain a single type system, reducing programmer learning time. Typically, the class definitions are written in separate files which are included in each application that requires them.

In Vbase, a separate language was invented to define types. This language, TDL or Type Definition Language, is a purely declarative language having a very different feel from COP. There were three reasons for this choice.

First, we could do it. Because COP is integrated with a database, there was an external store that could hold type definitions (and in fact, had to hold the type definitions). As the definitions had to be placed into the database, requiring them to be separately compiled simplified the issue of deciding when they were being redefined (simplified for the compiler, not the programmer).

Secondly, it seemed difficult, if possible at all, to cleanly integrate all of the semantics desired in Vbase's type modeling into C. Whereas a declarative language like TDL utilizes a number of adjective and modifying phrases, their use in C would seem quite strange. The only solution seemed to be a language targeted at specification, rather than one so clearly targeted at implementation, as C is.

Finally, we wanted to allow Vbase to have other language interfaces. A common independent type definition language simplified the demands on the subsequent language processors.

This separation required (and enabled) a sharper distinction of what interfaces from the type system were being used by the COP code. Two new declarations were added to COP to support this distinction. One of these, `import`, gives visibility to the behavior of instances of the indicated type. By default, it gives visibility only to the public behavior, although it is possible to `import` the private interface as well. The `enter module` declaration is used when defining some portion of the implementation of the indicated type. It is used to define the methods for the operations defined by the type. The `enter module` declaration grants full visibility to the names defined in the type to all of the subsequent COP code.

This system of type defined interfaces imported by interested code takes an opposite approach to controlling visibility from the one used by C++. C++'s paradigm is that a class explicitly declares which other classes (and thus their member functions) are granted private visibility (through the `friend` specification). This gives the type much tighter control over external poking and prodding about. The interface concept allows the type to grant more specific access (any number of interfaces can be defined), but gives no control over what code actually imports which interfaces. It also does not require foreknowledge of all of the code which is to be exposed to the private portion of a type. The representation model, discussed later, also significantly changes the usage pattern of private properties between the two systems. The decision to split the languages has been a mixed blessing. Several users have appreciated the forced separation of specification from implementation (truly an unintended benefit). Others have complained of the confusion and headaches expected of requiring two languages to be learned and used. Some of the problems should be helped by the recently improved handling of imports.

This type mechanism in COP has one clear advantage not directly related to the separate language issue. A type is a first-class object in Vbase, meaning that the schema information is directly available from any code written in COP. This, combined with a general run-time operation invocation mechanism, allows general meta-data manipulation and run-time generation of actions. A number of interesting projects have been implemented using these capabilities. Since C++ has no run-time incarnation of classes, such work is difficult, when possible at all, in C++.

19.3.2 Exception Mechanism

An exception mechanism has proven a powerful programming tool in a number of languages that have supported it. But beyond this, having the exception mechanism integrated with the specification mechanism yields significant wins. Rigorous use of inheritance requires that all of the behavior defined by the supertype be supported by all instances of any subtypes. This occasionally conflicts with the need to model systems where such behavior is not guaranteed. By incorporating exceptions into the specification, it is possible to describe such situations.

As an example, consider the case of the type `Stack` and its operation `Pop`. The `Pop` operation is specified to accept a `Stack` as its sole argument and to return an element from the `Stack`. Fairly simple, but what happens when the `Stack` is empty?

The two standard methods for dealing with this problem are to return a second "did it work" value, or to define a magical invalid return value. Neither solution is very satisfying and in the second case, the specification does not describe what the error case is (at least with the specification capabilities provided in most languages). The more natural solution is to state that the Pop operation will return an element, if it returns successfully, but that it may also raise the exception StackEmpty under the error condition.

Such situations are even more complicated when the defining type will never, in fact, fail to complete the operation successfully, but when a subtype might fail. For example, suppose the type Person is defined to have a MakeFriend operation, which will say that the Person given as the first argument considers the Person supplied as the second argument as a friend. Surely this operation would never fail. But later, a subtype of Person, Snob, is defined, which will only accept rich or famous persons as their friends. If the MakeFriend operation was specified to possibly raise an exception, this new subtype would not break any existing code (any code that was well-formed at least).

C++ provides no exception mechanism. Stroustrup [Stroustrup87c] has discussed adding an exception mechanism to the language, but to date it appears that one will not be added. This is one of the significant omissions in the language.

A rich exception mechanism is integrated into the COP model. Exceptions can be raised, caught and reraised. An exception is an object (not quite first-class in the current implementation) and a subtype of Type called ExceptionType exists to create types of exceptions. Exceptions thus gain two major pieces of functionality from the general model of objects, properties and inheritance.

Raising an exception entails creating the exception object, possibly giving a list of initializers for the properties of the exception, followed by the actual raise operation on the exception object, transferring control to the closest (dynamically defined) enclosing handler for this type of exception. COP provides the raise statement, which combines these two behaviors.

A handler is declared using the except statement. Its handler will catch exceptions which are raised by the execution of the statement being guarded. A particular handler is defined to catch all exceptions within a particular subtree of the exception type hierarchy. At the top of the exception hierarchy is the ExceptionType exception. Any handler declared to catch Exception will catch any exception. Multiple parallel handlers may be declared for a single statement, in which case only the handler declaring the most direct type of the exception, if any, will be chosen. A local variable is also declared as part of the handler. The exception object being raised is assigned to this variable when the handler is selected by the raise operation.

Within a handler, any arbitrary actions can be taken, including any manipulations of the exception object itself. From within a handler, the exception may be reraised (using the reraise statement), propagating the exception to the next closest enclosing handler, not including any parallel handlers. If the exception is not reraised by the handler, the exception object is automatically deleted upon termination of the handler and execution continues sequentially with the code following this handler (and any handlers parallel to this handler). Unfortunately, this mechanism does not currently allow for resumption of the code following the raise of the exception.

One more statement is provided to help in dealing with exceptions. The `protect` statement associates a handler with a protected statement. If execution begins on the protected statement, the handler is guaranteed to be run upon termination of the protected statement. Termination can be of any form, ranging from the normal completion of the statement to a goto or return to an exception being raised or even a termination signal to the process. The `protect` statement has proven a great boon in simplifying management of numerous problems regardless of the presence of exceptions, and has been almost essential in the face of potential exceptions.

To keep the proliferation of exceptions in check and allow for better specification of behavior, each operation specifies what exceptions it might raise. A given implementation may only raise an exception of one of the specified types (or one of its subtypes). Although this constraint is not currently enforced by the compiler or the run-time system, it is considered a bug in the program to break this specification and in very bad taste in any circumstances.

19.3.3 Iterators

In most traditional procedural languages, a programmer wishing to examine the contents of some type of aggregate, such as a linked list or hash table, must be aware of the underlying data structure used to implement the aggregate. This causes dependencies on the actual implementation chosen to be scattered throughout the application. To allow for strong data abstraction, a system must provide a mechanism for abstract looping. In Smalltalk, this capability is provided by the ability to pass code blocks into a loop method. In COP, this is accomplished through the use of an iterator.

An iterator is a special form of operation. It is a true co-routine, communicating with the invoking process at well-defined points only. In COP, an iterator is invoked through a special `iterate` statement. This statement is similar to many of the looping constructs in C, with a controlling expression and a statement which serves as the body of the loop. The controlling expression has three portions: a variable to receive each value yielded by the iterator; the name of the iterator itself (this may be defaulted in some cases); and the initial arguments to the iterator.

When an `iterate` statement is executed, the iterator operation is invoked with the arguments given. The yielded value, if any, is then assigned to the controlling variable and the body of the loop is executed. Upon completion of the body, the iterator is requested to yield another value, this value is assigned to the control variable, and the loop body is executed again. This pattern repeats until the iterator halts (by returning without yielding a value). The body of the loop may also break this cycle through one of the C branching statements or by raising an exception. Through all of this, the iterator method maintains its own state, both local variables and order of execution, yielding values as they become available through the use of the `yield` statement. When the iterator method executes a `return` statement, the iteration is terminated and no more values are yielded.

As was noted earlier, the loop may also be terminated by any of the standard C branching constructs or by raising an exception. In any of these cases, the iterator is terminated, running any handlers of `protect` statements that are currently active in the iterator.

This construct has also proven to be quite efficient, requiring only a single heap allocation upon initial invocation and a handful of extra instructions for each iteration.

C++ provides no abstract looping construct. Several possible work-arounds have been discussed, but each has serious drawbacks associated with it. The most common suggestion has been the use of begin, next, and end member functions that use only the state held in the object being iterated over. This has several problems. It is a non-reentrant solution, leading to potentially disastrous bugs if used in a recursive calculation. It requires exactly one base object being iterated over. Iterators have proven more generally useful, with ones defined taking no arguments to ones taking several "base" objects.

19.4 TYPE CHECKING ISSUES

One of the major differences between languages is their type system, how it is evaluated, and what it allows (and disallows) programmers to do and what problems it detects. The concept of type checking in COP and C++ is quite different at points. A few of these differences have already been noted, but several more differences remain to be discussed. Although these differences could be resolved in either language without apparently changing a great deal of the language, they make up a large part of the "feel" of each language, particularly C++.

19.4.1 Parameterization

COP, however, supports a simple model of parameterized operations and types that supports most of the cases that are encountered. It is exceedingly difficult, when possible at all, to write generic structures such as sets and lists without system support for parameterization. C++ provides no support for any form of parameterization. The lack of first-class types and run-time type checking further complicates the issue, since this would at least allow the possibility of a slow, but complete implementation. A model of parameterization for C++ [Stroustrup88c] is currently being explored.

In the COP model, types can describe a list of parameters that can be used for classifying their instances. Each parameter maps to an unsettable property of the object. Typically, this parameter would be something like the memberspec property defined on the type Array. Each element of an array is guaranteed to be an instance of the value of the memberspec property of the array. For example, a specific array might be said to be an array of fish. This means that the value of the memberspec property is the valuespec Fish and that all of the elements of the array are instances of Fish.

Operation specifications may be written to either require a specific parameterization or accept a generic parameterization, referred to as an UnboundParameter. In the latter case, this UnboundParameter may then be used as the valuespec of any of the other parameters to this operation or the valuespec of the return value. When such an operation is type checked, the value of the property underlying the type parameter is used in place of this UnboundParameter. Returning to the earlier example, the SetElement operation on array is defined to take a generic Array of T as its first argument, while its second argument, the actual value to store in the array, must be an instance of T. Thus, if an array of Fish was supplied as the first argument, the second argument must be an instance of Fish, since the UnboundParameter T has been bound to Fish.

When this type checking is performed at compile time, only the compile time declared type of the expression used as the value of an argument is used, rather than the actual run-time binding of the parameter. If an UnboundParameter describing the valuespec of a parameter to the operation cannot be bound at compile time, a type checking error is reported by the compiler. If the UnboundParameter which cannot be bound describes the return value of the operation, the most general valuespec Entity is assumed. When run-time type checking is used, through Procedure$Invoke for example, the actual binding is always used.

This model does leave a number of holes that remain to be plugged. The most common of these is the desire to parameterize the valuespec of properties and to bind an UnboundParameter to valuespecs other than those derived directly from parameterized arguments to the operation.

19.4.2 Type Conversions

Automatic type conversions can be a great boon. Most languages (although by no means all) have accepted the conversions between real and integer values as basic and mandatory. Generalized support for such conversions breaks down one of the remaining barriers to a truly programmer definable type system. Unfortunately, these benefits are not the only side of the issue. "Coercions are essentially a form of abbreviation that may reduce program size and improve readability, but may also cause subtle and sometimes dangerous system errors [Cardelli84a]."

C++ supports a rich system of type coercion capabilities. Automatic conversions may be generated between different user defined types or between user and language defined types. Such automatic conversions are quite important to C++, given the copy-on-assignment semantics of many objects. Conversions may also be explicitly requested using the standard C cast syntax or an alternative syntax. Although this new syntax does tie together nicely with the constructor concepts in C++ and allows for more general conversions (multiple arguments are possible), the need for yet another piece of special syntax here is questionable.

In this generality, the C++ model of coercion leaves itself open to potential ambiguity. Ambiguities arise from two sources. If multiple levels of coercion are used, there may be several different intervening classes for which the appropriate coercions are defined. For this reason, C++ disallows multiple levels of automatic coercions, avoiding the problems.

The other source of ambiguity comes from the combination of automatic coercion, multiple arguments for coercions and general operator overloading issues. If the actual combination of types given to the coercion operator has not been defined in any of the actual coercion functions, several paths may exist, each depending on converting a different one of the arguments. C++ reports any ambiguity here as a type checking error, taking the safe route and losing little of the functionality.

COP provides only limited support for type coercions beyond the predefined C conversions. The object types which have direct equivalents to standard C types (Integer, Real, etc.), are implicitly converted to and from their C equivalent type as needed in a manner very similar to the coercions defined in C for the arithmetic types. The one exception to this automatic coercion is the conversion from a String object to a C string. No assumptions are made about the lifetime of the created C string, so the memory management of this string is left to the programmer. Because of this, a predefined function is required to perform this conversion rather than an automatic coercion. These conversions are required by the double type system (C and Vbase) available in COP, but largely alleviate the problems such a system introduces.

No user defined types will be automatically converted to or from other object types or C types. The former case is easily handled by an operation (although the resulting code is not as readable as if an implicit coercion were supported), but the latter case (converting to and from C types) is much more problematic in COP. This lies in the fact that TDL (and thus all user written object types) can only describe other object types, not any of the C types. Since COP has bridged the world for the predefined C types, this only becomes an issue for user defined C types, such as enums and structs, but can be a nuisance in these cases.

19.4.3 Operator Overloading

Much like type coercions, operator overloading gives tremendous power to the programmer, while opening the potential for terrible abuse.

Again, C++ supports a full and rich model for user extensibility here. Essentially any of the predefined C unary and binary operators can be overloaded, although the precedence and number of operands cannot be changed. The overloaded operator maps to either a member function or a friend function, but not both. No new in-line operators may be defined. The standard relationship between operators is not maintained and C++ will not assume the meaning for any of the operators from these relationships. Most notably, the appropriate assignment operators (such as +=) could be overloaded appropriately if the underlying operator (in this case +) is overloaded.

The C++ model also includes general function overloading, so that the programmer may define multiple specifications for a given function name, with the compiler choosing the appropriate binding based on the compile time type of the arguments. Note that this is very different from the dynamic binding used for virtual functions, where the actual type (not the declared type) of a single argument is used to find the appropriate binding.

COP provides only minimal support for operator overloading. A specified subset of C operators ([], >, >=, <, <=, ==, ! =) may be overloaded by an object type. This association is done implicitly by a predefined, operator specific name, for example an operation named GreaterThan is used for the operator >. The operands of the operator are bound, in order, to the parameters of the operation.

One notable distinction between the C++ model and the COP model is the handling of left-hand side operators (specifically [] on the left-hand side of an assignment). The C++ solution uses its reference notion to generalize the two cases (left- and right-hand side), while COP recognizes these as two separate operations (SetElement and GetElement).

The C++ solution has the advantage of requiring only one function to be written, although it is a slightly more complicated function. But this generality also introduces difficulties that the COP approach avoids. The first is an apparent small hole in the type checking. The second problem becomes more apparent when looking at storage managers, persistence and concurrency. Since the function cannot know whether it is modifying the current state of the object or not, it cannot communicate this information to the other portions of the system.

19.4.4 Static Type Checking

Prior to now, C++ has done type checking only within a compilation unit (top-level source file). The latest compiler, however, will do cross module type checking at link time.

COP uses the database to hold information about the object type system, so that only a single definition is in use. While this definition may be altered over time, leaving open the types of mismatches that C++ is susceptible to, an automatic tool can detect these inconsistencies in an already compiled module.

COP leaves loopholes in the compile time type checking, allowing the programmer to explicitly request run-time checking. This is made possible by the first-class nature of the type objects. Built-in support for run-time type checking comes in two basic forms: the `assert` operator and dynamic operation invocation using `Procedure$Invoke` or a related operation.

The `assert` operator takes two operands, an object to be type checked and a `valuespec` that it is expected to be an instance of. If the assertion succeeds, the expression yields its first operand with the new compile time declared type of the `valuespec` indicated. If the assertion fails, the exception `IllegalAssert` is raised.

`Procedure$Invoke` is an operation which takes two arguments: a `ProcedureType` (`ProcedureType` is a subtype of `OperationType` that excludes iterators) and an argument list. It then invokes the operation after having validated that the proper number and type of arguments were supplied. A corresponding iterator, `Iterator$Invoke`, is provided to allow run-time iteration using an arbitrary iterator.

19.5 MODEL OF INHERITANCE

Inheritance is one of the key features of an object-oriented system. But there have been a multitude of different models of inheritance. Although COP and C++ fall into the same basic corner of the inheritance world (both use inheritance, not delegation and both allow for inheritance of state), there are subtle differences between them that account for fairly large differences in their actual behaviors and capabilities.

19.5.1 Refinement

Refinement is an addition to inheritance that allows the inherited behavior itself to be extended, rather than just adding completely new behavior. In certain cases, such as object deletion, this ability is an absolute necessity. In other cases, such as refining state, it allows the program to stay much closer to the world to be modeled.

C++ gives only a small amount of support for refinement, targeting the absolute minimum requirements. The principal support is for constructor and destructor functions.

In a constructor, the base class's constructor functionality is automatically combined with any functionality of the derived class, allowing the derived class to refine the behavior of the base class. Equivalent support is offered for destructors. In both of these cases, the refinement cannot provide an alternative implementation for base class's behavior; instead it can only extend that behavior. This is directly tied to the lack of a model of representation in C++ and will be discussed at greater length in that section.

C++ also offers some support for refining functions. Refinements could take place on either virtual or statically bound functions, but the static binding may mask the behavior inappropriately in non-virtual functions. Function refinement is more general (either additional or replacement implementations may be used) than the refinement paradigm given for constructors and destructors, but is more complicated and error prone to use. The limitations here will be discussed further when considering the method combination capabilities of the two languages.

COP offers general support for refinement. Any dispatched operation may be refined by a subtype. Free operations may also be refined by using the subtyping mechanism, although this has the same potentially undesirable problem of not guaranteeing that the refinement code will be executed for instances of the subtype providing the refinement. In either case, these refinements may provide additional behavior or they may entirely replace the implementation used by the supertype.

In addition, properties may be refined. This refinement may involve changing the valuespec of the property in some cases or it may just be a change in the implementation. The most common property refinement is to add some simple piece of behavior, typically either an additional validation of the value or maintaining some index into the class of instances based on the value being set.

19.5.2 Method Combination

Method combination is the ability to combine multiple pieces of code into a single logical function. In the ultimate method combination system (and Flavors [Moon86] came pretty close), the combination would take two pieces, a new method and an existing logical function, and a description of how the combination should take place. The simplest options are to execute the new method before, after or instead of the logical function. To protect a piece of code from external changes, the method should not be dependent on the exact hierarchy above (or below) its defining type. Rather, the combination should mask this knowledge, simply requiring recombination rather than recoding on a change to the hierarchy. Any type should be able to provide any number of methods to be used in the combination and these methods should be sharable by any number of combinations.

C++ provides only a minimal support for this type of combination, largely because no clear distinction is drawn between the specification of a function in the class definition and the code implementing it. When a member function is refined, the definition for that function becomes, by default, a replacement for the implementation provided in the base class. The programmer may explicitly call the base class's implementation, giving the ability to combine the new function before the base function, after it or both. However, this requires hard coding knowledge of the hierarchy in the code. Only one function may be added per type and no capability for sharing this code between different classes or different member functions within a class is provided.

COP, on the other hand, provides a reasonable approximation to the full capabilities described above. COP operations are specifications of function-like behavior. It is this specification that is referred to by a programmer desiring to call the operation. The code itself lives in methods, any number of which can be combined to make up the implementation for an operation. These methods are classified according to usage into two categories: trigger methods and base methods. When a method is used as the logical function by itself, it is considered a base method. Any method which is combined with a logical function to define a new logical function is considered a trigger. So, all operations are implemented by one base method and zero or more trigger methods. The defining type and each refining type may define a base method and add any number of triggers. The defining type must provide a base method if the operation is to be executable by instances of the defining type or if any trigger methods are provided. If a refining type defines a new base method, the implementation defined by the supertypes is discarded and a new logical function is defined.

Trigger methods, like refinements in C++, can be defined to be executed before the remaining logical function or after the remaining logical function. This is controlled by a special identifier, $$, which refers to the remaining logical function. When the trigger method wishes to pass control onto the remaining logical function, a call to $$ is made using the standard call syntax. Iterator operations cannot currently have trigger methods provided for them.

Methods may be shared between any number of operations. This has been used extensively within the implementation of standard COP operations such as object creation and inverse property maintenance. The requirement for sharing, however is an agreement between the method signature and the signature operations being implemented, which greatly reduces the opportunity for method sharing. If COP provided a better model for parametric method signatures, the opportunities for method sharing would be greatly enhanced, with a corresponding increase in programmer productivity and decrease in image size.

The run-time performance of this method combination has been quite acceptable. In the current COP implementation, the overhead is roughly four times the cost of the normal function call overhead itself, with this cost generally only being paid on the calls made within the logical function itself, but not on the external call into the logical function, so no cost is usually paid when no combination is used. Even this overhead is dominated by the cost of several other features within the COP world, notably run-time extensibility, reference validation and support for persistent objects. In a model such as C++, this method combination capability would require only a single memory dereference in addition to the normal function call overhead.

19.5.3 Multiple Inheritance

Multiple inheritance is the ability to inherit from several nominally unrelated types. In a number of cases, this is the only clean way to model the desired behavior. It leads to more polymorphic code and to better code sharing. There are a number of problematic areas with multiple inheritance, such as operations refined on multiple branches and ambiguous naming from coincidentally named functions or fields, problems to which various systems have provided an assortment of answers.

Although as of this writing, neither system supports multiple inheritance, Stroustrup has published a description [Stroustrup87b] of the support C++ will be giving for multiple inheritance. This system takes a reasonable minimalist approach with a few otherwise unexpected behaviors.

Multiple inheritance is fairly straightforward when two classes are unrelated, a situation found in C++, since it, unlike most object-oriented systems, does not have a single, common top of the hierarchy. If a name conflict appears, and is actually used, the ambiguity is considered an error. Virtual functions behave as expected.

The situation is more complicated when inheriting from two classes which share, at some point in the hierarchy, a common base class. Ambiguities arising from virtual functions being refined on multiple paths are disallowed, simplifying the problem, but removing much of the inherent power of multiple inheritance. The C++ model defines two basic forms of multiple inheritance. The programmer can use the same mechanism as was used for the simpler case, which leaves double copies of the common base class's state. Alternatively, the inheritance can be declared as virtual inheritance. With virtual inheritance, there is only one copy of the state from the common base class. With non-virtual inheritance, all of the expected problems of multiple copies of data are experienced, both in synchronization and object size. Unfortunately, the default behavior is non-virtual and it must be declared on the super classes of the multiply-inherited class, not on the multiply-inherited class itself. Because of this, a programmer defining a class should know in advance whether there will be subclasses common to this and any other sibling subclasses.

19.6 MODEL OF STATE

One of the major uses of computers, and thus primary jobs of most programming languages (but not all), is recording information by maintaining some form of state. Different languages have surprisingly large variations in the way they model state, if they model state at all. Within the object-oriented world, little attention has been paid to this area and few of the systems have an extensive model.

19.6.1 Abstract State

Abstract state is the ability to separate the specification of the state from the implementation of that state. Different systems that support some notion of abstract state vary significantly in the level of specification they support.

C++ provides no concept of abstract state, leaving no distinction between the specification of the state and the implementation chosen. Beyond the lack of separation, C++ provides no support for any of the additional behaviors that can be specified in other systems, such as inverses and additional constraints. Some workarounds are possible to emulate some of these features. Most of these require defining a new unique class to be the type of the field, overloading all of the appropriate C operators and making extensive use of the automatic coercion capabilities. These efforts tend to be difficult to implement initially and grow increasingly difficult to maintain as a larger number of these unique classes are defined.

A model of abstract state is one of the primary foci of Vbase [Damon89]. Properties are defined only as a nexus of information for the operations (Get and Set) actually implementing the property. When a property is accessed, the Get operation is run and when a property is modified, the Set operation is run. These operations are general operations in the Vbase sense, giving all of the refinement and method combination behavior found in the model. A property may disallow direct setting of the property, allowing for immutable and derived properties.

The method combination feature has proven particularly useful, allowing arbitrary triggers to be written on property access. These are typically added to Set operations, being used as either an additional validation procedure for the new value of the property or as a method of updating external objects which refer to the subject of the property because of or through the value of the property. The other commonly used operation behavior that is frequently used is that of providing an alternative implementation, in particular for the Get operation. By default, the system provides an implementation for the Set operation that actually stores the value on the object and a Get operation that retrieves it from that slot on the object, similar to what happens with a traditional model of state. But the programmer could specify an alternative implementation, either in the initial definition or in a refinement of the property. When not directly stored, these properties are called derived properties.

Several particularly useful behaviors have been moved into the declarative capabilities within TDL, crossing the boundary from implementation detail into specification. Vbase supports a concept of optional properties, parallel to the notion of optional arguments discussed earlier. A property can be declared as the inverse of another property, with a system provided trigger guaranteeing this relationship is maintained. And the system provides support for multiple valued properties, which greatly simplifies a number of modeling concerns and enhances the value of the inverse behavior.

This model of abstract state is one place where a significant performance price is paid for the functionality. As the optimization work in COP progresses, these costs are being minimized for properties which do not take advantage of any of the additional behaviors, but this remains a serious performance drawback to using Vbase.

19.6.2 Model of Representation

Representation is the underlying implementation of abstract state. Since the actual storage required for properties is not clearly discernible from the specification of the properties, some other mechanism for declaring these requirements must be provided. Representation is a means of describing these requirements by utilizing the specifications provided by other types.

In C++, the concept of representation is less useful since there is no notion of separating the specification of state from its implementation. The system, of course, makes a decision about the representation to be used, but the programmer has no control over this decision. This becomes a particular problem in C++ when a class is derived from a base class which itself defines a large amount of storage. In many cases, the need for this storage is superseded by some other implementation in the derived class, but it must be carried along regardless. Some effort can be made to make private fields refer to this representation, allowing derived properties to not initialize these fields, but this has problems when dealing with objects which are not the object to a virtual function.

In COP, a full model of representation has been implemented. An object can be composed of an arbitrary set of other objects, with dependencies only on their abstract specifications. Two capabilities in particular enhance the performance tunability of COP applications. The first of these is representation takeover, allowing a subtype to provide a completely different (and presumably more efficient) implementation from the one provided in the supertype. The ability to cluster different portions of the object, through segregation into different rep pieces, is extremely valuable when dealing with applications with a large amount of data.

19.7 STORAGE MECHANISMS

In the end, all state maps down to some concept of raw storage. Different systems handle storage very differently. Allocation mechanisms vary widely. Some languages depend on an active garbage collection scheme, while others require explicit deletion of objects. Again, both COP and C++ are similar in this regard. Both support an explicit allocate/deallocate paradigm instead of a garbage collection one.

19.7.1 Storage Managers

Many languages support multiple concepts of storage. C, for instance, supports multiple concepts of storage (static versus automatic in C, for example) which are independent of type. These generally are not user extensible, being limited to the group of storage types defined by the language. Other languages allow for user defined storage mechanisms, but only for use by all of the instances of a single type.

C++ falls into the latter camp. In the currently released version, the allocator and deallocator operators `new` and `delete` can be replaced on a type by type basis, allowing some flexibility in memory allocation. This is particularly useful for giving a more efficient memory allocator for specific object classes. In an upcoming release of C++, the dereference field operator $(->)$ can be taken over, allowing a different mapping to memory. However, the model presented still ties the basic storage manager too close to the host machine's model of virtual memory.

Vbase allows for general user written storage managers independent of an object's abstract type. A set of manipulation routines, such as `allocate`, `dispose`, and `resize` define the basic capabilities of all storage managers, while the standard operations `wire` and `unwire` provide the mapping between the model of storage and the local machine's model of virtual memory. The `wire` operation locks an object's storage into virtual memory and returns a virtual memory pointer to this storage. `unwire` performs the inverse action, unlocking the object storage. Each of these operations is defined (but not implemented) by the type `StorageManager`. A subtype of `StorageManager` defines a new storage type, providing an implementation for each of these operations. These operations are dispatched based on the storage type of the dispatch argument, rather than the abstract type of the argument. In this manner code written using the `StorageManager` operations will in fact execute the code for the correct storage type.

The ability to nearly arbitrarily mix different storage managers and abstract types allows a great deal of simplification and code reduction, particularly in the face of persistent objects. In general, this orthogonality of storage manager from abstract type (the only compiler known type information) has a small but not insignificant performance hit. An abstract type, however, may restrict the set of valid storage managers for its instances. If this set is restricted to one, no performance penalty is paid and if the indicated storage manager is built directly on top of the system virtual memory, traditional storage performance characteristics are obtained.

19.7.2 Persistence

Persistence is the ability to maintain the state of objects between process invocations. There are two basic means of accomplishing this behavior: giving the programmer explicit read and write semantics for objects; or by providing a way of directly referring to persistent objects. The former case is by far the easier to implement, but leaves the burden on the application programmer and results in problems with object identity across invocations.

C++ does not directly support any form of persistence. A number of object read/write mechanisms have been and are being written for C++, but they all exhibit the difficulties mentioned above. There are several difficulties in the basic model of C++ in trying to define any form of persistence that is more tightly integrated. The biggest of these is the tight tie between pointers and references that was discussed earlier. If it is possible to arbitrarily obtain the virtual memory address of an object, that object must be locked down in memory until the process exits. This association also limits the maximum object space to some portion of all of virtual memory, a significant drawback when objects can live forever. The lack of distinction between left-hand side and right-hand side uses of operators makes tracking when and how an object has been modified exceedingly difficult.

Since COP is part of a database system, cleanly integrated support for persistence was essential. There are several storage managers provided with the system, including a process local, heap based manager, and two persistent storage managers. Since all memory references go through the storage manager `wire` and `unwire` operations, this can be done cleanly. To allow for a large enough object space, all object references in COP are 64 bits, with 56 of these bits available for object address. The system provided storage managers utilize an intervening cache, but a user written storage manager need not do this.

19.7.3 Concurrency

If a system supports persistent data, a means of controlling concurrent access and updates to that data must also be provided. Numerous models of concurrency and transactions have been developed over the years in the database world, but little of that work has made it into the language side of computer software. In C++, since there is no support for persistence, there is no need for concurrency control mechanisms.

The persistent storage managers for COP provide the actual concurrency control mechanisms. One of these supports transactions and detects conflicts between different processes, while the other manipulates objects which are extra-transaction and whose changes are immediately visible in all related processes. This latter storage manager tends to be used for semaphores and other communication objects, while the vast majority of persistent objects use the transaction based storage type.

19.8 CONCLUSIONS

Despite their basic similarities, the two languages have a large number of differences. Partly this is because the original goals of the two languages differed markedly. In building C++, Stroustrup attempted to build a better C (and succeeded admirably). Ontologic instead attempted to define a language that allowed for tight integration of persistent data into the application and provided a rich set of modeling capabilities. Perhaps surprisingly, the size of the extensions made (as measured by the number of new keywords and constructs) are approximately the same in the two languages.

In the design of both languages, the ultimate efficiency of the generated code was considered extensively in deciding what new features could be added and what they would look like. In the C++ case, this criterion argued for fewer features. In the case of COP, several extenuating circumstances alleviated some of these performance concerns. The expectation of a significant portion of the data living initially on disk rather than in virtual memory reduces the performance expectations (and potential) noticeably. A heavy dependency on user performance tunability led to many features such as the representation model and helped pay back some of the performance price of the other features. And a great deal of emphasis was placed on features which could be compiler optimized, creating a slower compiler, but one which is capable of gaining back some more of the performance cost required by some of the features included.

Overall, an application with no persistent data can be expected to run two times slower in COP than C++ when a comparable effort toward performance has been applied. However, if a significant amount of the data is persistent, this advantage will quickly disappear or even reverse. As the compiler for COP matures and new features are added to C++, this differential should also diminish. At some point, it is imaginable that the additional declarative power of TDL and the underlying persistence in the compiler will allow the performance of COP to surpass that of C++, but that is not expected in the near future.

C++ is more tightly integrated with C and has made more extensions within the non-class portions of the language. Perhaps because of this tighter integration, many of the changes in C++ seem to be more ad hoc and less motivated by a single strong object model.

COP, on the other hand, makes extensions which are much more internally consistent and more closely based on an object model. Furthermore, COP allows a much sharper separation between specification and implementation than was apparently the goal of C++. In so doing, COP cleanly integrates storage management, data abstraction, and inheritance into a single object model.

Both languages have a great deal to offer and they continue to improve over time as experience with them grows and time is available to mutate the languages. Hopefully over these changes, the languages can learn from each other and grow together. Already over their brief histories, the two languages have seen significant movement towards each other. Perhaps at some point, there will be no significant distinction between the languages and they can be truly merged, helping to reduce the risk of another Tower of Babel explosion of languages.

20 ODE (Object Database and Environment): The Language and the Data Model

R. Agrawal and N. H. Gehani

20.1 INTRODUCTION

The object paradigm is a natural way of organizing data as it allows users to structure, retrieve and update data in terms of the application domain. ODE is a database system and environment based on the object paradigm. The database is defined, queried and manipulated using the database programming language O++ (it was called O in earlier versions of this chapter). O++ is based on C++ [Stroustrup86]; it borrows and extends the object definition model of C++. This chapter is an introduction to the linguistic facilities provided in O++ and the data model it supports.

Although conventional programming language objects and database objects are similar in that they encapsulate object properties, there are several differences. For example, database objects persist beyond the lifetime of the program creating them. Many database applications, such as computer-aided design and software management, require the capability to create and access multiple versions of an object [Atwood85, Dittrich87a, Katz86, Tichy86]. Object versions are also important for historical databases, such as those used in accounting, legal, and financial applications, that must access the past states of the database [Copeland84, Rowe87]. Support for active databases, such as those used in computer integrated manufacturing, power distribution network management, and air-traffic control, requires the capability to attach to objects conditions and actions that are triggered when the conditions are satisfied [Dayal88a, Stonebraker88]. Finally, the ability to associate constraints with objects is necessary to ensure database integrity [Nikhil88]. Programming languages typically do not support persistent objects (with the exception of files) or multiple object versions, nor do they provide facilities for associating constraints and triggers with objects. Consequently, if a conventional programming language is to be used as a database programming language, it must be augmented with facilities that support the needs of database systems.

O++ provides one integrated model for both database and general purpose manipulation. We use the C++ object model, called the *class*, as the basis for the object model of O++. The class facility supports data encapsulation and multiple inheritance. O++ extends C++ classes by providing facilities for creating and manipulating persistent objects and their versions, and associating constraints and triggers with objects. A major criticism of the current object-oriented databases and languages is that they lack the capability to pose arbitrary "join" queries, and that query processing "smells" of pointer chasing as in CODASYL database systems [Neuhold88]. O++ alleviates these problems by providing iterators that allow sets of objects to be manipulated almost as declaratively as the database query languages based on relational calculus. The set iteration facility of O++ also allows the expression of recursive queries [Agrawal88, Bancilhon86], a major concern in deductive databases. The iterators can be qualified with clauses that specify iteration subsets and order, which can be used to advantage in query optimization. Many of the O++ facilities can be found in other languages and systems. Our major contribution lies in providing a clean fusion of the advances in both database and programming language research within an object-oriented framework.

Virtues of object-oriented database systems have been extolled elsewhere (see, for example, [Banerjee87a, Diederich87, Dittrich87a, Ege87, Fishman87, Hornick87, Hudson87, Lecluse88, Maier86a, Manola86]. O++ shares with these systems the goals of providing a rich type system to model complex and composite objects. It provides encapsulation to hide implementation details, supports multiple inheritance for organizing objects in taxonomies in which the more specialized objects inherit the data and functions of more generalized objects, separates type definition from type instantiation, allows explicit specification of relationships between objects, and supports object identities that allow persistent database objects to have an existence independent of their values. Some extensible database projects, such as [Batory88, Carey88b, Paul87, Rowe87, Schek86, Schwarz86] also have similar goals. O++ is in the same spirit as the work done in designing database programming languages, such as [Andrews87, Bancilhon87, Copeland84, Nixon87, Rowe79, Schlageter88, Schmidt77, Smith83, Wasserman79]; it strives to be the single language for data definition, data manipulation and general computation to avoid the problems arising out of "impedance mismatch" [Copeland84]. O++ also shares the concerns of the persistent programming languages, such as [Albano85, Cardelli84b, O'Brien86, PPRG85, Richardson88, Richardson89]; persistence is a property of object instances and not types, and persistent objects are accessed and manipulated in much the same way as volatile objects. O++ is related to the language E [Richardson88, Richardson89] in that O++, like E, also uses the C++ object model and adds persistence to it. Vbase [Andrews87] and O2 [Lecluse88] also seek to blend an object-oriented data model with C.

In this chapter, we concentrate on the data modeling and the query processing aspects of O++. We do not cover concurrency issues and some systems-oriented features such as schema evolution, authorization, security, etc. We also do not discuss the environment and the implementation strategies. These issues will be discussed in future papers. We have tried to be precise with the language constructs, but omitted details when they were obvious. Although we will occasionally refer to transactions, we do not discuss them in this chapter. For the purpose of this chapter, any O++ program that interacts with the database will be considered to be a single transaction. The rationale behind the design of O++ is discussed in [Agrawal89a].

The organization of the rest of the chapter is as follows. Section 20.2 describes the data structuring facilities provided in O++. Section 20.2.1 gives an overview of the object definition facility, section 20.2.2 discusses the inheritance model, section 20.2.3 presents the persistence model, section 20.2.4 discusses how persistent objects of the same type are grouped together in a cluster, and section 20.2.5 describes the set data type.[1] Section 20.2.6 discusses persistence in some related C-based languages/systems: E, Vbase, and O2. Section 20.3 presents the query processing facilities. Section 20.4 presents our versioning model, and sections 20.5 and 20.6 discuss the facilities for associating constraints and triggers respectively with objects. Our conclusions are presented in section 20.7.

20.2 DATA STRUCTURING CONSTRUCTS

A database is a collection of persistent objects, each identified by a *unique* identifier, called the object identifier (id) that is its *identity* [Khoshafian86]. We shall also refer to this object id as a *pointer to a persistent object*. We visualize memory as consisting of two parts: volatile and persistent. *Volatile* objects are allocated in volatile memory and are the same as those created in ordinary programs. They are allocated on the program stack or on the heap and their lifetime is bounded by the life of the program. *Persistent* objects are allocated in persistent store and they continue to exist after the program that created them has terminated. Interaction with these objects is routed through an object manager, but this is hidden from the programmer. The medium used for persistent memory is implementation dependent.

20.2.1 Object Definitions: C++ Classes

Class declarations consist of two parts: a specification (type) and a body. The *specification* represents the class "user interface". It contains all the information necessary for the user of a class, and also for the compiler to allocate class objects. The *body* consists of the bodies of functions declared in the class specification but whose bodies were not given there.

Class specifications have the form

```
class  name {
    private components
public:
    public components
};
```

[1]Readers familiar with C++ may skip sections 20.2.1 and 20.2.2.

The *private* components of a class are data items and functions that implement class objects. These represent internal details of the class and cannot be accessed by the user of a class.

The *public* class components can be data items, constructors, destructors, member functions (operators), and friend functions (operators). The public components, which represent the class user interface, are the components that the user of a class can reference. Constructors are functions that are called automatically to construct a class value. Member and friend functions are used to manipulate class objects.[2] Destructors are functions that are called automatically when a class object is explicitly deleted or when its scope is left. Constructors and destructors can be used to respectively guarantee initialization of objects and cleanup upon deallocation.

We illustrate the use of the class facility by defining a class item. Here is its specification:

```
#include "db.h"
#ifndef ITEM
#define ITEM 1
class item {
    Name nm;
    double wt; /* in kg */
public:
    item(Name xname, double xwt);
    Name name();
    double weight_lbs();
    double weight_kg();
};
#endif
```

The private part of the specification of class item consists of the declarations of two variables: nm and wt. The public part consists of a constructor function item (has the same name as the class name) and three member functions name, weight_lbs and weight_kg.

Here are the bodies of the member functions:

```
#include "item.h"
item::item(Name xname, double xwt)
{
    nm = xname;
    wt = xwt;
}
Name item::name()
{
    return nm;
}
```

---

[2]In this chapter, we shall not distinguish between member and friend functions except to say that their syntax is slightly different; see [Stroustrup86] for details.

```
double item::weight_kg()
{
    return wt;
}
double item::weight_lbs()
{
    return (wt * 2.205);
}
```

Here is an example definition of an `item` variable:

```
item cpu(Name("intel 80386"), 0.005);
```

This definition automatically invokes the constructor function `item` to properly initialize the newly created object. Note that the first argument for the constructor `item` is the expression

```
Name("intel 80386")
```

which calls the constructor function `Name` of class `Name` (not shown here) to convert a string into a `Name` object.

The public components of a class are accessed using the selected component notation, e.g.,

```
cpu.weight_lbs()
```

20.2.2 Inheritance

Inheritance allows objects to be organized in taxonomies in which the more specialized objects inherit properties, i.e., the data and functions, of more generalized objects. Similar objects with a few different properties can be modeled by specifying a common part, called the base (super) class, for the common properties and then deriving specialized classes from this base class. Derived classes can be used to construct heterogeneous data structures such as lists with different types of elements because a pointer to a class can point to any object whose type is derived from this class.

A derived class is specified by following its name with the name of the base class. A derived class inherits the data items as well as the member functions of the base class. As an example, consider the following class `stockitem` that is derived from class `item`:

```
#include "db.h"
#include "item.h"
class stockitem: public item {
    int consumption;   /*qty consumed per year*/
    int leadtime;      /*lead time in days*/
public:
    int qty;
```

```
    double price;
    stockitem(Name iname, double iwt, int xqty,
              int xconsumption,
              double xprice, int xleadtime);
    int eoq();          /*economic order quantity*/
};
```

stockitem is the same as item except that it contains other information such
as the quantity in stock, its consumption per year, its price and the lead time necessary
to restock the item. Also, stockitem has its own constructor function and additional
member functions.[3]

Class item was made a *public* base class of stockitem so that every public
member of class item becomes a public member of class stockitem. A *private* base
class is declared by using the keyword private in which case member functions of
the derived class can reference the public members of the base class, but these members
are not directly accessible to the users of the derived class.

Multiple inheritance. Multiple inheritance allows a new class to be derived
from multiple classes. For example, class stockitem can be derived from the two
classes item and supplier, as a result of which stockitem will have the properties
of both item and supplier. First, here is the specification of class supplier:

```
#include "db.h"
#ifndef SUPPLIER
#define SUPPLIER 1
class supplier {
    Name nm;
    Addr addr;
public:
    supplier(Name xname, Addr xaddr);
    Name name();
    Addr address();
};
#endif
```

Here is the new specification of class stockitem:

```
#include "db.h"
#include "item.h"
#include "supplier.h"
class stockitem: public item, public supplier {
    int consumption;
    int leadtime;
public:
```

---

[3]We have not shown the bodies of the member functions; unless necessary, we will not give the function
bodies in the rest of the chapter.

```
        int qty;
        double price;
        stockitem(Name iname, double iwt, int xqty,
                int xconsumption, double xprice,
                int xleadtime, Name sname, Addr saddr);
        int eoq();  /*economic order quantity*/
        int reorder_level();
        Name itemname();
        Name suppliername();
        Name name();
};
```

Note that each of the base classes item and supplier has a member function named name. Ambiguities are resolved by using explicit qualification as shown below, for example, in the bodies of the member functions itemname and suppliername:

```
Name stockitem::itemname() { return item::name(); }
Name stockitem::suppliername() { return
                                supplier::name(); }
```

If an application requires that the name member function for stockitem yield the supplier's name, then name can be redefined as follows:

```
Name stockitem::name() {return supplier::name();}
```

20.2.3 Persistent Objects

When incorporating persistence in O++, we kept the following principles in perspective:

1. Persistence should be a property of object instances and not types.
2. It should be possible to allocate objects of any type (including user-defined types) in either volatile or persistent store.[4]
3. There should be no difference between accessing and manipulating persistent and volatile objects.
4. It should be possible to move objects from persistent store to volatile store in much the same way as it is possible to move objects from the stack to the heap and vice versa.

Persistent objects are referenced using pointers to persistent objects (that is, their identities); these pointers can be allocated in either the heap or the stack but persistent objects must themselves be allocated in persistent store. Persistent objects are allocated and deallocated in a manner similar to heap objects. Persistent storage operators pnew

---

[4]Components of an object that are pointers to volatile objects may not always (e.g., across program invocations) be meaningful if the object is allocated in persistent store.

and pdelete are used instead of the heap operators new and delete. If successful, pnew returns a pointer to the persistent object created by it; otherwise, it returns the null pointer. Here is an example:[5]

```
persistent stockitem *psip;
....
psip = pnew stockitem("1m dram", 0.05, 5000, 10000, 7.50,
                      15, "at&t", "berkeley hts, nj");
```

Note that psip is pointer to a persistent stockitem object, and *not* a persistent pointer to a stockitem object. Thus, syntactically the keyword persistent is a type qualifier (like const and volatile in ANSI C [ANSI-C88]) and not a storage specifier, even though it refers to a type of storage. Also, psip is allocated on stack (not in the persistent store), but pnew allocates the stockitem object in persistent store and its id (returned by pnew) is saved in psip.

Persistent objects can be copied to volatile objects and vice versa using simple assignments:

```
*sip = *psip; /*copy the object pointed to by psip*/
              /*to the object pointed to sip       */
*psip = *sip; /*and vice versa */
```

One can also write:

```
stockitem si = ("250k dram", 0.05, 500, 1000, 2.50, 15,
                "at&t", "berkeley hts, nj");
*psip = si;
```

A persistent object can be deleted with the pdelete operator, e.g.,

```
pdelete psip;
```

deletes the object pointed to by psip.

Persistent object accesses can be as fast as volatile object accesses but typically they are likely to be slower (for example, persistent objects may be stored on disk). An implementation may speed up access of persistent objects by caching them but this is not guaranteed. To speed up accesses to persistent objects, a user can copy a persistent object to volatile memory, operate upon it and store it back in persistent memory.

---

[5]Creation of a persistent object is syntactically similar to the creation of a volatile object:

```
stockitem *sip;
....
sip = new stockitem("512 dram", 0.05, 7500, 15000, 5.00,
                    15, "at&t", "berkeley hts, nj");
```

20.2.4 Dual Pointers

Pointers to persistent objects always refer to persistent objects and ordinary pointers to volatile objects. Consequently, it is not possible to write a function that accepts as an argument a pointer to either a volatile or persistent object. To allow writing of such functions, we introduce the notion of a dual pointer: one that can refer to a volatile or persistent object. Whether the object referenced is volatile or persistent is determined at run-time. Pointers to volatile and persistent objects can be assigned to dual pointers. But dual pointers that refer to volatile objects can only be assigned to pointers to volatile objects and dual pointers that refer to persistent objects only to pointers to persistent objects. Here is an example illustrating the use of dual pointers:

```
class node {
    ....
    dual node *next;
public:
    ....
    dual node *add(dual node *n);
};
persistent node *p, *proot; /*proot refers to a list in
                               persistent store*/
node *v, *vroot;            /*vroot refers to a list in
                               volatile store*/
....
proot = proot->add(p);
vroot = vroot->add(v);
```

20.2.5 Clusters of Persistent Objects

All persistent objects of the same type are grouped together into a *cluster*; the name of a cluster is the same as that of the corresponding type, that is, clusters are type extents [Buneman86]. Before creating a persistent object, the corresponding cluster must exist; it is *created* by invoking the `create` macro[6]—in this program or in another program:

```
int create( type-name);
```

type-name is the name of the cluster being created.[7] Create returns 1 if successful; otherwise, it returns 0.

A cluster can be destroyed by invoking the destroy macro:

```
int destroy( type-name);
```

---

[6]Eventually we intend to extend the `create` macro to allow the programmer to give additional information to assist the object manager in implementing efficient accesses to objects.

[7]The ODE environment can be queried about the clusters that exist in persistent store. In the case of classes, it can also be asked to display the specification of the objects in the cluster, i.e., the public part of the class specification.

type-name is the name of the cluster being removed. Note that all the objects in the cluster are destroyed. `destroy` returns 1 if successful; otherwise, it returns 0.

Subclusters. Sometimes it may be desirable, for logical organization or efficiency reasons, to group objects in a cluster into subclusters so that they can be collectively referenced. For example, subclusters can be used to partition a `student` cluster into groups corresponding to the dorms in which the students live.[8] Subclusters are also created and destroyed with the `create` and `destroy` macros. A subcluster name is a string qualified by the corresponding cluster (object type) name, e.g.:

```
create(student::"Cascadilla Hall");
destroy(student::dorm);   /*dorm is a string variable*/
```

Objects are specified to belong to a specific subcluster when they are allocated in persistent store, e.g.,

```
sp = pnew student("Jack")::"Cascadilla Hall";
```

20.2.6 Sets

O++ supports multisets (sets whose elements do not have to be unique). Sets are a convenient mechanism for manipulating a collection of objects. Sets can be simulated by arrays, but such a simulation makes it harder to write clear code and reduces the potential for optimizing a set implementation and accessing a subset of the set elements. Set declarations are similar to array declarations but, unlike arrays, set subscripting is not allowed. Here are some examples:

```
persistent part *partset<MAX>;   /*MAX is the set size*/
real s<100>;
```

When declaring set parameters, the maximum number of elements in a set need not be specified:

```
userid users<>;
```

The set operations supported are assignment, union, difference, insertion, and deletion. Set elements are accessed by using the set iteration facility (discussed later).

20.2.7 Related C-based Approaches

The database implementation language E [Richardson88, Richardson89] also started with C++ and added persistence to it. In E, persistent objects must be of special types called "db" types. Objects of such types can be volatile or persistent. Persistent objects can be

---

[8]The type inheritance mechanism can also be used to simulate the effect of subclusters but this may require the creation of a large number of types, e.g., one type for each dorm.

allocated statically by using the storage class `persistent` in object definitions or they can be allocated dynamically by using the predefined db class `file`. Other features of E include generic classes and iterators.

Vbase [Andrews87] combines an object model with C. It presents to the user two languages: the type definition language TDL for specifying classes and operations, and the C superset COP for writing methods to implement the operations. The O2 system [Lecluse88] also integrates an object model with C. Type definitions are written in one language and methods are written in the C superset CO2. A class in O2 implicitly owns a persistent collection of objects of the class.

20.3 QUERY PROCESSING CONSTRUCTS

One misgiving researchers have with the current object-oriented databases is that they may take us back to the days of CODASYL databases in which data is accessed by "using pointers to navigate through the database" [Neuhold88]. In object-oriented databases, the pointers are the object ids. By introducing clusters, sets, and high-level iteration facilities for accessing objects in clusters and sets, O++ provides an alternative to using object ids to navigate through the database. Another criticism of object-oriented databases is that they lack the capability to express arbitrary "join" queries [Neuhold88]. In O++, arbitrary joins can be expressed by iterating over the clusters to be joined and the join conditions can be specified as the iteration conditions.

20.3.1 Iterating Over Sets and Clusters

Values of the elements of a set, a cluster or a subcluster can be accessed with a `for` loop of the form.[9]

```
for i in set-or-cluster-or-subcluster
    [ suchthat-clause ] [ by-clause ] statement
```

The loop body, i.e., *statement*, is executed once for each element of the specified set, the cluster or the subcluster; the loop variable i is assigned the element values in turn. The type of i must be the same as the element type.

The *suchthat-clause* has the form

```
suchthat( e_st )
```

and the *by-clause* has the form

```
by( e_by [, cmp ])
```

---

[9] The square brackets [and] indicate an optional item. The `suchthat` and `by` clauses are based on similar clauses in SQL [Chamberlin76] and Concurrent C [Gehani86]. Similar `for` loops have been provided, among others, in Pascal/R [Schmidt77], Rigel [Rowe79], Plain [Wasserman79], Trellis/Owl [O'Brien86], and Vbase [Andrews87].

The suchthat and by expressions *e_st* and *e_by* must contain the loop variable *i*. If the suchthat and by expressions are omitted, then the for loop iterates over all the elements of the specified grouping in some implementation-dependent order. The suchthat clause ensures that iteration is performed only for objects satisfying expression *e_st*. If the by clause is given, then the iteration is performed in the order of non-decreasing values of the expression *e_by*. If the by clause has only one parameter, then *e_by* must be an arithmetic expression. If the by clause has two parameters, then the second parameter *cmp* must be a pointer to a function that compares two elements of type *t*, where *t* is the type of the by expression *e_by*. *cmp* compares its arguments and returns an integer greater than, equal to, or less than 0, depending upon whether its first argument is greater than, equal to, or less than its second argument.

As an example, here is a program segment that illustrates iteration over clusters and sets. It prints the name of people along with the names of their children whose profession is computer science (CS):

```
class person {
public:
    Name name;
    char sex;
    Name Profession;
    persistent person *children<>;
};
....
for p in person
    for c in p->children suchthat(c->Profession ==
                                  Name("CS"))
        printf("%s %s\n", p->name, c->name);
```

Although the suchthat and by clauses can be simulated by using an *if* statement within the loop body and by sorting the set of values in volatile memory, these clauses facilitate optimization, similar to those performed in relational database systems, as follows: we expect to pass these clauses to the object manager to select only the desired object ids and deliver them in the right order for the for loop.

Iterating over cluster hierarchies. Clusters mirror the hierarchy relationship of the corresponding types. If type *x* is derived from type *y*, then the corresponding clusters also have the same relationship. It is sometimes necessary to collectively access objects in a cluster and those in related "derived" clusters.[10] This can be done with the forall loop which has the form

> forall *oid* in *cluster* [*suchthat-clause*] [*by-clause*]
> *statement*

---

[10]POSTQUEL [Rowe87] allows a * to be specified after the relation name to retrieve tuples from the named relation and all relations that inherit attributes from it. Orion [Banerjee87a] also provides similar functionality.

Except for the inclusion of objects in derived clusters, the semantics of the `forall` loop are the same as those of the `for` loop for iterating over a cluster. Thus, given the class `item` and the derived class `stockitem` as defined in section 20.2, the statement

```
for ip in item
    tot_wt += ip->weight_kg;
```

computes the weight of only objects of type `item`, but the statement

```
forall ip in item
    tot_wt += ip->weight_kg;
```

computes the weight of all items including stock items.

Arbitrary joins. The `for` and `forall` loops can have multiple loop variables:[11]

```
for i_1 in set-or-cluster-or-subcluster-1, ...,
    i_n in set-or-cluster-or-subcluster-n
    [suchthat ( e_st)] [by ( e_by)] statement
forall oid1 in cluster-1, ..., cluster-n
    [suchthat ( e_st)] [by ( e_by)] statement
```

The loop body, i.e., *statement* will be executed for every combination of values for the loop variables that satisfy the `suchthat` expression and in the order specified by the `by` clause.

These loops allow the expression of operations with functionality of the arbitrary relational join operation. For example, we can write

```
for e in employee, d in dept
            suchthat(e->dno == d->dno)
    printf("%s %s\n", e->name, d->name);
```

to print the name of the employee from the `employee` object and the name of the department from the `dept` object.

Type test. The object type can be determined with the `is` operator which has the form

```
e is type
```

This expression evaluates to true if expression *e* is of the specified type, and to false otherwise. Note that if *e* is of a dual pointer type, then the `is` operator will return true if *type* is the dual pointer type, or either the corresponding ordinary pointer type or

---

[11]RIGEL [Rowe79] also allows multiple loop variables in its `for` loop.

the corresponding persistent pointer type depending upon whether *e* refers to a volatile object or a persistent object.

This test is particularly useful when iterating over objects in a cluster and in hierarchically related clusters using the `forall` loop. For example, suppose that we want to compute and print the average income of university employees and, separately, that for faculty and students in a university database (employees can be other than faculty and students, e.g., staff). Class `person` has the member function `income`, and classes `student` and `faculty` have been derived from it. Here is the code to perform the above computation:[12]

```
np = ns = nf = incomep = incomes = incomef = 0;
forall p in person {
    incomep += p->income(); np++;
    if (p is persistent student *)
        { incomes += p->income(); ns++;}
    else if (p is persistent faculty *)
        { incomef += p->income(); nf++;}
}
printf("%g %g %g\n",
        incomep/np, incomed/nd, incomef/nf);
```

20.3.2 Fixpoint Queries

Aho and Ullman [Aho79] have shown that the least fixpoint operator is an essential addition to the relational query languages, and considerable research has been devoted to developing notations for expressing least fixpoint queries and designing algorithms for evaluating them (see, for example, [Agrawal88, Bancilhon86]. When iterating over a set or a cluster, we allow iteration to also be performed over the elements that are added during the iteration, which allows the expression of recursive queries [Aho79]. Thus, given the class `person` as above, the following statements find all the descendents of abraham:

```
for p in person suchthat(p->name == Name("abraham"))
    descendants = p->children;    /*basis for recursion*/
for d in descendants
    descendants += d->children;   /*recursion*/
```

Modifying a set or a cluster while iterating over it makes the by clause inoperative because such modification is likely to destroy the ordering. Deleting an element from the set or cluster means that the loop will not iterate over this element provided such an iteration has not already taken place or is not currently taking place.

---

[12]One can simulate this task using C++ virtual functions, but this may require modification of existing class definitions to add appropriate functions. Hence this approach is not appropriate for posing arbitrary queries.

20.4 VERSIONING

Many database applications, such as computer-aided design and software management, require the capability to create and access *multiple versions* of an object [Atwood85, Dittrich85, Katz86, Tichy86]. Object versions are also important for historical databases, such as those used in accounting, legal, and financial applications that require accesses to the past states of the database [Copeland84, Rowe87].

In ODE, all persistent objects can have versions and there is no pre-defined limit on the number of versions that an object can have.[13] The current version of an object is updatable, but old versions may be read-only depending upon the implementation. As in the case of persistence, versioning is an object property and not a class property. Objects belonging to the same class can have different numbers of versions.

Depending upon the application, one may want to access the current version or a specific version. For example, an address-book object that keeps track of current addresses would like to reference the latest versions of person objects (to access their latest addresses). On the other hand, a software configuration object may want to reference specific versions of objects representing component modules.[14]

Our version model supports both of these modeling requirements. An object and all its versions are treated as one logical object with one id. A pointer to a persistent object can refer to a logical object in which case it is called a *logical* id or to a specific version of an object in which case it is called a *version* pointer. Accessing an object using a logical object id results in access to the current version of the object.

Thus, the address-book object can refer to the current versions of `person` objects using logical ids. When the address of a person is changed and a new version of the `person` object created, no change is required to the address-book object. On the other hand, version pointers are used to refer to specific versions, e.g., in the software configuration object. O++ provides macros for coercing version pointers to logical object ids and vice versa.

Updating a persistent object does not automatically create a new version. A new version is created explicitly by calling the macro `newversion`. The effect of the call

```
newversion(p)
```

where p is a logical object id is to create a new version of the specified object.[15] Henceforth, p refers to the new version. Logically, the contents of the new version, i.e., *p, will be identical to those of the previous version.

Macro `previous` can be used for accessing different versions of an object. It takes a pointer to a persistent object and a non-negative integer n and returns a pointer

---

[13]We are assuming that we have a large, if not infinite, persistent store. Persistent store may be hierarchically organized and old versions may be flushed out to a slower medium. An implementation may impose a limit on the number of versions that can be created.

[14] Orion [Banerjee87a] and Iris [Beech88] also provide facilities for specific reference to a particular version and generic reference to a versioned object.

[15]In this chapter, we will only describe the linear versioning mechanism. O++ allows the version graph of an object to be a tree; see [Agrawal89b] for details.

to the nth previous version; if there is no such version, then `previous` returns the null pointer. Thus, the total salary over the last five years of an employee can be computed as:

```
persistent Employee *e, *ve;
....
for(i=0; i < 5; i++)
    if ((ve = previous(e, i)) == NULL)
        error("%s has not been with company for 5
                years\n", e->name);
    total += ve->salary;
}
```

Given a logical object id, operator `pdelete` deletes the object and all its versions. Given a version pointer, `pdelete` deletes the specified version.[16]

20.5 CONSTRAINTS

Constraints are used to maintain a notion of consistency beyond what is typically expressible using the type system [Nikhil88]. Updates that violate the specified constraints should not be permitted. Interpretations of consistency are usually application specific and may be arbitrarily complex. Constraints, which are Boolean conditions, can be associated with classes. Objects must satisfy all the constraints associated with the corresponding class.

Constraints are specified in the constraint section of a class definition as follows:

```
constraint:
    constraint_1;
    constraint_2;
      ....
    constraint_n;
```

constraint_i is a Boolean expression that refers to components of the specified class. Constraints are checked at the end of constructor and member (friend) function calls. Therefore, although we do not prohibit accessing components of an object directly (if the components are specified to be public), it is the programmer's responsibility to ensure that such accesses do not violate any constraints (because no checking will be done automatically).

Here is an example of a constraint:

```
constraint:
    supplier_state == Name("NY") ||
                      supplier_state == Name("");
```

---

[16]Implementations may choose not to allow the deletion of specific versions.

If a constraint is not satisfied, then the access is aborted[17] and the object restored to its original state.

20.5.1 Constraint Inheritance

A derived class inherits the constraints of its parent class and new constraints can be added. Consequently, constraints can be used to specialize classes, as in

```
class female: public person {
public:
    ....
constraint:
    sex == 'f' || sex == 'F';
};
```

Such constraint-based specializations are useful in many applications, e.g., in frame-based knowledge representation systems [Brachman85b].

20.6 TRIGGERS

Triggers (also called alerters or monitors), like integrity constraints, monitor the database for some conditions, except that these conditions do not represent consistency violations [Nikhil88]. When trigger conditions become true, the associated trigger action is executed. Triggers are necessary for supporting active databases, such as those used in computer integrated manufacturing, power distribution network management, air-traffic control, etc., and are found in many database systems such as POSTGRES [Stonebraker88], HiPAC [Dayal88a], Sybase [Darnovsky87], Vbase [Andrews87], and OOPS [Schlageter88].

Triggers are associated with objects. There are two types of triggers: *once-only* (default) and *perpetual* (specified using the keyword perpetual).[18] A once-only trigger is automatically deactivated after the trigger has "fired", and it must then be reactivated explicitly if desired. On the other hand, a perpetual trigger is automatically reactivated after being fired.

Triggers are specified within class definitions:

```
trigger:
    [perpetual]  T1 ( parameter-decl-1: trigger-body-1
    [perpetual]  T2 ( parameter-decl-2: trigger-body-2
        ....
    [perpetual]  Tn ( parameter-decl-n: trigger-body-n
```

---

[17]Violation of a constraint will cause the transaction of which this access is a part to be aborted and rolled back as in Cactis [Hudson87]; at a later time, we may provide additional exception handling mechanisms which will allow the class designer or the user to respond to the violation of a constraint.

[18]POSTGRES [Stonebraker88] has similar triggers.

Ti are the trigger names. Trigger parameters can be used in the trigger bodies which have the form

```
trigger-condition ==> trigger-action
within expression ? trigger-condition ==> trigger-action
              [: timeout-action]
```

The second form is used to specify a timed trigger. Once activated, the timed trigger must fire within the specified period (floating-point value specifying the time in seconds); otherwise, the timeout action, if any, is fired.

Triggers are set by explicitly activating them after the object has been created. A trigger *Ti* associated with an object whose id is *object-id* is activated by the call

```
object-id -> Ti( arguments)
```

The trigger activation returns a trigger id (value of the predefined class `Trig-gerId`) if successful; otherwise it returns a 0. The object id can be omitted when activating a trigger in the body of a member function. Note that there can be more than one activation of a trigger in effect.

An active trigger fires when its condition becomes true. Firing means that the action associated with the trigger is "scheduled" for action. Unlike [Stonebraker88], a trigger action is not considered part of the transaction that causes the trigger to be fired (triggering transaction). Each trigger firing results in the creation of an independent transaction with the trigger action being the transaction body. Conceptually, trigger conditions are evaluated at the end of each transaction. Transactions representing trigger actions are executed after (but not necessarily immediately after) the triggering transaction, i.e., there is "weak coupling" [Dayal88a] between the triggering transaction and the trigger action. If the triggering transaction is aborted, the trigger actions generated by it are aborted.

Triggers may be deactivated explicitly before they have fired as follows:

```
~ trigger-id
~ object-id -> Ti( arguments)
```

The first form deactivates a trigger whose trigger id is specified as the argument (this trigger id must have been returned by a successful trigger activation). The second form deactivates a trigger that was activated with the specified arguments. If a trigger is not active, then deactivating it has no effect. The object id can be omitted when a triggee is referenced within the body of a member function.

We provide one special macro, named `changed`, for use in trigger conditions. This macro returns true if the value of its argument (which must be a data component of the object containing the trigger) has been changed in the current transaction and false otherwise.

Note that the perpetual triggers cannot be simulated with once-only triggers by re-activating the trigger in the trigger action. The problem with doing this is that the trigger action is executed as a transaction at some later time. As a result, the trigger will be inactive for the period between the firing of the trigger and the activation instruction in the trigger action is executed.

As an example of a once-only trigger, consider the following class `inventory`:

```
include "db.h"
#include "item.h"
#include "supplier.h"
#include "stockitem.h"
class inventitem: public stockitem {
public:
    inventitem (Name iname, double iwt, int xqty,
                int xconsumption, double xprice,
                int xleadtime, Name sname, Addr saddr);
    void deposit(int n);
    int withdraw(int n);
    ....
trigger:
    order(): qty < reorderlevel() ==> place_order(this,
                            eoq());
                        /*"this" refers to the object
itself*/
    };
```

Trigger `order` is activated in the constructor function `inventitem` and in the member function `deposit`:

```
#include "invent.h"
inventitem::inventitem(): (Name iname, double iwt,
        int xqty, int xconsumption,
        double xprice, int xleadtime, Name sname,
        Addr saddr)
{
    ....
    order();  /*trigger activation*/
}
void inventitem::deposit(int n)
{
    qty += n;
    order(); /*trigger activation*/
}
```

The action associated with the trigger `order` will be executed after its condition becomes true (as result of executing the `withdraw` operation whose body is not shown).

As an example illustrating a perpetual trigger, consider a securities broker's database. For each customer, a portfolio is maintained. When the customer wants to buy or sell shares, a buy or sell order is issued by sending an appropriate message to the "market maker". Amongst other objects, the market maker's database has an object for each stock which stores such information as the stock price, and buy and sell orders for that stock from various brokers. The stock price is continuously updated based on the buy and sell orders. Here is the specification of class `stock`:

```
class stock {
    list-of-outstanding-orders;
    void fillorders();
public:
    Name stockname;
    double price;
    stock(Name xname, double xprice);
    void update(double xprice);
    void sell(Name broker, int orderid, int amount,
                double lowlimit);
    void buy(Name broker, int orderid, int amount,
                double highlimit);
    ....
trigger:
    perpetual fill(): changed(price) ==> fillorders();
};
```

Member function `sell` checks the current stock price, and if it is above the lower limit specified for selling the stock, the stock is sold immediately; otherwise, the sell order is added to the list of outstanding orders. Similarly, member function `buy` causes stock to be bought immediately if the current stock price is below the upper limit specified for buying the stock; otherwise, the buy order is added to the list of outstanding orders.

The stock price is updated by member function `update`. The trigger condition `changed(price)` becomes true whenever `price` changes, and the trigger action `fillorder` is executed:

```
void stock::fillorders()
{
    for each order a  in the list-of-outstanding-orders
        if (price >= a.lowlimit) {
            sellstock(this, a.amount, price);
            message(a.broker, a.orderid, a.amount,
                        price, "sold");
            delete a  from the list-of-outstanding-orders
        }
        if (price <= a.highlimit) {
            buystock(this, a.amount, price);
            message(a.broker, a.orderid, a.amount,
                        price, "bought");
            delete a  from the list-of-outstanding-orders;
        }
}
```

Timed triggers can be used to specify time limits within which the order is to be executed:

```
class stock {
public:
    Name stockname;
    double price;
    stock(Name xname, double xprice);
    void update(double xprice);
    ....
trigger:
    sellorder(Name broker,int orderid,int
                amount,double lowlimit,double time):
        within time ?  price > lowlimit ==>
            {
                sellstock(this, amount, price);
                message(broker, orderid, amount,
                        price, "sold");
            }
    buyorder(Name broker,int orderid,int amount,double
                        highlimit,double time):
        within time ?  price < highlimit ==>
            {
                buystock(this, amount, price);
                message(broker, orderid, amount,
                        price, "bought");
            }
};
```

When the triggers `sellorder` and `buyorder` are activated, the time limit (parameter `time`) within which the trigger must fire is specified.

20.7 CONCLUSIONS

An important goal of research in programming languages design is to provide a better fit between problems and programming notation. We have tried to do this for databases by using one unified data model for data definition and data manipulation. We started with the object-oriented facilities of C++ and extended them with features to support the needs of databases, putting to good use all the lessons learned in implementing today's database systems. The resulting database programming language O++ makes available to database objects the full range of type-structures and multiple inheritance found in C++ and, at the same time, provides features such as persistence, iterators, fixpoint querying capabilities, versions, constraints, and triggers.

This chapter presented the linguistic facilities for specifying and accessing data provided in O++. As mentioned, the rationale for our design decisions is discussed in

[Agrawal89a]. We have begun a prototype implementation of O++, and we hope to report on the implementation strategies and experiences in the near future.

ACKNOWLEDGMENTS

The persistence model was influenced by discussions we had with Steve Buroff and Mike Carey. David DeWitt's suggestions lead us to modify the chapter that made our presentation more complete. We are also grateful to J. Annevelink, S. Buroff, H. T. Chou, A. R. Feuer, D. H. Fishman, R. Greer, L. M. Haas, H. V. Jagadish, J. D. Jordan, K. Kelleman, B. W. Kernighan, D. E. Perry, A. Singhal, D. Shasha, W. P. Weber, and A. L. Wolf for their comments and suggestions.

The first author was a member of the technical staff at AT&T Bell Laboratories, Murray Hill, at the time of writing this paper. "ODE (Object Database and Environment): The Language and the Data Model," by R. Agrawal and N.H. Gehani appeared in the Proceedings of ACM–SIGMOD 1989 International Conference on Management of Data. Copyright 1989 Association for Computing Machinery, Inc., reprinted by permission.

Tim Andrews, Craig Harris and Kiril Sinkel

21.1 INTRODUCTION

This chapter reviews the ONTOS object database. ONTOS is designed to be an efficient and practical data manager. It integrates many of the object mechanisms and techniques that were just recently seen exclusively in research systems [Atkinson87b, Halbert86, Stonebraker86, Carey86b].

ONTOS also breaks new ground in several key areas. It incorporates a version and alternative mechanism that is inexpensive in database overhead and transparent to the application most of the time. It introduces a shared transaction mechanism which allows cooperating processes to share information within the confines of a single transaction. It also updates standard out-of-line exception handling by adding a concept of hierarchy to exceptions. Finally, it pioneers in its query processing by adding "navigational" extensions to SQL predicate calculus semantics and enlarging the SQL notion of table to include arbitrary collections of objects such as classes and aggregates.

Some of these features have been pioneered in Vbase [Andrews87], the predecessor system to the ONTOS object database. Perhaps one of the biggest shifts from Vbase to ONTOS can be seen in the philosophy guiding system design. The guiding principle behind the ONTOS design is that the system should allow the user to make the appropriate trade-off between performance, safety and formalism. Compared to Vbase, it is in some senses a lower level product, with fewer layers of indirection. It gives the programmer the same access to the underlying hardware that is available through C++. While it provides a rich set of abstractions it does not prevent the programmer from "breaking the rules" and using more primitive mechanisms when performance or other considerations require it. Thus it gives the programmer direct control over cache memory management, data clustering and the scope of database to memory transfers when it is critical to performance or application design.

Briefly, here are salient features of ONTOS:

Object Model. ONTOS is object-oriented in its internal architecture. However the object model that it exports is that of the language selected by the user. Initially, ONTOS will support two language interfaces. A C++ interface is the major application program interface [Stroustrup86]. The interface consists of a relative handful of member functions linked into the users's application and a small class library. An SQL interface will also be supported for programmatic queries. Support for other languages will be added in subsequent releases.

The C++ interface is enhanced with additional modeling power via a class library. The class library provides classes of Aggregates and Iterators as well as classes for schema definition and support of versions and alternatives.

Performance. The ONTOS design goal is to achieve a 500 fold performance improvement over that of relational databases for certain classes of applications. We believe such an improvement is attainable through the combination of better reference semantics of the object model, caching directly in process heap memory, the availability of virtual memory pointers, and user control over low-level details when these are critical to performance.

Distribution and Concurrency. ONTOS is designed around the requirements of the local area network and the window-based workstation. Its client-server architecture allows transparent distribution of the database across nodes. A database registry makes it unnecessary to know the physical location of the data in advance, insulating the application from the details of network configuration. Its concurrency control and transaction mechanisms insure data consistency and arbitrate among potentially conflicting users. However, they also have special features to promote data sharing among cooperating processes characteristic of multi-window, multi-process applications. Typically, these are poorly supported by standard databases.

Development Environment. ONTOS development environment uses standard languages and development environments. Development cycle times for compiling and debugging depend on the user's selection of commercial compilers and tools. The schema loader operates on C++ class definitions directly, eliminating the need for a separate schema definition language.

Platforms. ONTOS has been targeted for a variety of hardware platforms and operating systems early in its product life. To reduce the chances of platform dependencies inadvertently creeping into the design, initial development was carried out on two somewhat disparate hardware/operating system environments—UNIX on Sun workstations and OS/2 on 386 PCs.

21.1.1 Object Model

ONTOS uses an object model internally [Wegner87, Booch86a, Lam88]. Thus it directly expresses the complex relationships between data. It provides aggregate classes for modeling one to many relationships. It resolves references directly and presents objects that are fully C++ compatible at the C++ interface.

To achieve this, the ONTOS class library introduces an Object class. It is the parent of all persistent classes. Object defines a constructor for creating objects in the database and a destructor for deleting them. It also defines properties for an object name (ONTOS objects can be referenced by name as well as by reference) and for the physical clustering of objects in the database.

Aggregates. ONTOS provides the developer with a number of generally useful aggregate classes. These include `Dictionaries`, `Sets`, `Arrays` and `Lists`. For instance, dictionaries are implemented as hash tables or B*trees. These data structures are available as general abstractions eliminating all the programming normally required to create, access and maintain them.

Schema Representation. In C++, as in most programming languages, there is no standard mechanism for representing class data definitions for run-time use. The ONTOS class library provides classes for expressing properties, member functions and their arguments and the overall class definitions themselves. These classes are used to represent schema definitions to the database in a machine independent way and also are useful in program development.

Versions and Alternatives. In many applications it is natural to think of a single object as having a number of valid versions and to form collections of such objects into particular configurations. ONTOS allows exactly this kind of behavior. Object state is not copied when a new version is created, and thus, the overhead is very low.

Access to Functions. Among the schema representation classes are classes needed to express member function declarations. These classes allow key algorithms to be packaged in the database rather than with the application code. The behavior of the application can then be changed without changing the application programs themselves. For instance a text processing application might conveniently support multiple (natural) languages by placing all language-dependent functions into the database.

21.1.2 Performance

A database's effect on overall system performance goes far beyond the speed with which it can fulfill information requests. In fact there are really three aspects to the performance of a database. The first is concerned with data organization. The question might be phrased as: "How closely does the organization of the data, as it is stored, match the typical access patterns of applications that use it?" In addition to the logical organization of the data in secondary storage, we must also be concerned with its physical organization. Thus the second issue affecting performance has to do with the efficiency with which data is brought from secondary storage into main memory. Since efficient units of disk transfer are usually larger than the units of data requested, reasonable data clustering and buffering can improve performance substantially. Finally, once data has been presented to the application, how available is it? How much work does it require before it is put into structures that the application can use?

Logical organization. ONTOS provides random access within a one-dimensional address space based on object id (UID). The granularity of reference is a single object. Further, aggregates (container objects) are themselves denotable as objects.

These properties lead directly to a number of simplifications and optimizations. For instance a single address space simplifies references a great deal and makes it practical and inexpensive to store properties in the form of references to other objects.

Secondly, objects, as atomic units of reference, are naturally clustered and thus always read in a single disk operation unless they are very large. This compares to perhaps four or five reads required to assemble the tuples comprising the complete representation of the object in a relational system.

Finally, aggregates have a great potential for improving performance, since they express the one to n relationship directly, without the expense of join operations for instance.

Physical clustering. Efficient clustering at the level above the object level usually takes some knowledge of the dominant access patterns of the data. For example, in a CAD application it may be common to access a part object and the object representing its image property together. There is no general way of predicting this access pattern. Therefore the strategy adopted in ONTOS is to allow the programmer to specify clustering and to provide tools for reclustering when more experience with the application permits better choices to be made.

Availability of data. In many applications, data is highly interrelated and structured. In general, data structures are expressed as graphs whose edges are frequently implemented by memory references. ONTOS is very convenient for such implementations since it supports direct translation between virtual memory references and object UIDs.

21.2 ONTOS ARCHITECTURE

ONTOS is a distributed database and uses the client-server style of data interaction [Hornick87, Carey86a] (see Figure 21.1). The server side manages the data store; the client side provides the interface to user processes and manages the mapping of data to the application process's virtual memory space. The client and server communicate over the network. (When both reside on the same node, the network is bypassed and direct inter-process communication is used.)

A third component of the architecture is the registry. The registry keeps track of all databases in the network. It also maintains user profiles and access rights for database security.

21.2.1 Server Architecture

The ONTOS database is probably best thought of as a logical object store. Each object is identified by an identifier (UID) guaranteed to be unique within the database. The entire database, whether it is all contained on a single node or distributed over several nodes, has a single UID space and thus operates as a single, very large, random-access memory.

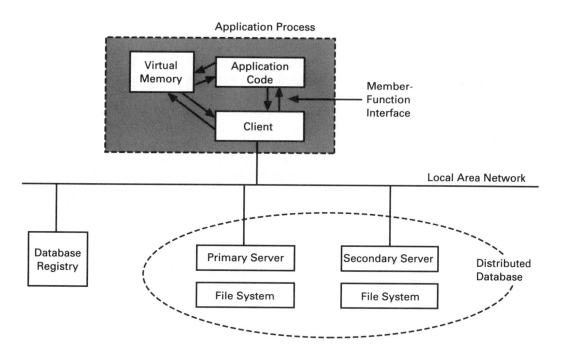

Figure 21.1 ONTOS client-server architecture.

In addition, each object also may have a name. Names are mapped to UIDs by a hierarchy of name directories. Thus an object's full name is a pathname, tracing a path from the root directory to a leaf directory containing the object name. The pathname is similar to pathnames in systems such as UNIX. However, there is an important difference. The directory structure, and in fact the entire database, are logical entities that are independent of such physical devices as processor nodes and disk volumes. None of the path elements express any physical location information. Therefore network reconfiguration and the movement of data from one node to another do not require any changes in object names.

An ONTOS database may be contained on a single node or distributed over a number of nodes in a network. The database is controlled by a primary server. It may be distributed over other nodes as well; if so, each of the other nodes has a secondary server managing local storage.

The task of the server process is to manage the underlying storage of its portion of the database and respond to client requests over the network. In addition, the primary server of each database maps objects to their respective servers. It is also responsible for all operations global to the database. These include database open and close requests and the control of multi-server commits.

The storage that each server controls is divided into one or more areas. Present plans for both UNIX and OS/2 are to implement areas as files. However, in the future they may be implemented as disk partitions or in other ways. This change will not affect any higher level functionality.

21.2.2 Client Architecture

The client is implemented as a function and class library that is linked into the application process. It manages communication between the application and one or more servers over the network. It also provides the application with various virtual memory management services and translates object references between their UID form and virtual memory addresses used during processing. Most of these services are optional so that the application can manage as few or as many of the housekeeping functions as it chooses. For example, when objects are activated (i.e., brought into virtual memory) the client can allocate memory or let the application manage that function. Similarly, when a transaction is closed, the client can manage flushing stale data or allow the application to take care of that task. The goal is to allow the application to manage tasks when it can make special optimizations while providing intelligent defaults that make programming simpler when no particular optimizations are involved.

The interface between the application and the client itself is composed of a relatively small set of functions and classes. The major functions are Database Open and Close, Transaction Start, Commit and Abort and the object read and write functions. These are Get and Put Object, Get and Put Logical Cluster and Get and Put Closure.

21.2.3 The Registry

In a distributed database, it is convenient to reference resources by their logical names rather than by physical location since logical names are much more durable and are not affected by network reconfigurations. The registry provides this facility. For instance, it maintains a directory of primary servers and their node addresses. The registry also maintains Access Control Lists used to implement database security features.

21.3 C++ OBJECT INTERFACE

21.3.1 General

One may think of ONTOS objects as consisting of collections of properties and functions. Each object is identified by its own identifier or UID, guaranteed to be unique and consistent within an ONTOS database. Each object's properties are either embedded in the object or represented by UID references to other objects.

21.3.2 Activation and Deactivation

Objects are transferred from the database to the application's memory and vice versa by operations known as activation and deactivation.

Activation involves transferring object state from the database to memory. All references contained by the activated object to other read objects are translated from their UID form to high performance virtual memory-based references. Also, all the references to the newly-activated object from other read objects are similarly translated. (The Transparent Reference scheme, discussed below, makes this process very inexpensive.) The function signatures for activating a single object, logical cluster and closure are given below.

```
Entity* VB_getObject    (
                         char* objectName,
                         LockType lock=ReadLock,
                         void* storage=0,
                         unsigned long amount=0
                        )
Entity* VB_getCluster   (
                         char* clusterName,
                         LockType lock=ReadLock,
                         void* storage=0,
                         unsigned long amount=0
                        )
Entity* VB_getClosure   (
                         char* closureName,
                         LockType lock=ReadLock,
                         void* storage=0,
                         unsigned long amount=0
                        )
```

Deactivation is the reverse process—the translation of memory references back to UIDs and the writing of objects back to the database. (ONTOS has a transaction mechanism. Thus actual changes to database state are pended until the transaction is committed, as described later in this paper.)

Because activation can critically affect performance, the number of objects activated is placed under the control of the programmer. The programmer may choose to activate a single object, a logical cluster of objects or a closure—that is the graph of all objects reachable directly or transitively from a given object. The same options apply to deactivation as well.

The first two techniques—activation of single objects and of logical clusters are more efficient in most cases in that they allow restricting the reading of objects to only those that are likely to be needed by the application. However these techniques do have the disadvantage of leaving at least some references unresolved.

Conversely, closure is the safest technique since all references are guaranteed to be translated. It is useful when a sufficient number of objects in the closure will be needed and the closure is known to be of a manageable size. In general, objects are connected to other objects through references (See Figure 21.2). The graph of objects reachable from any particular object directly and transitively may be quite large and can, in the limit, include the entire database. It is therefore not always practical to transfer all reachable objects whenever an object is read. Wholesale reading and automatic reference translation of all affected objects will frequently be impractical; this leaves dangling references at the periphery of the read objects.

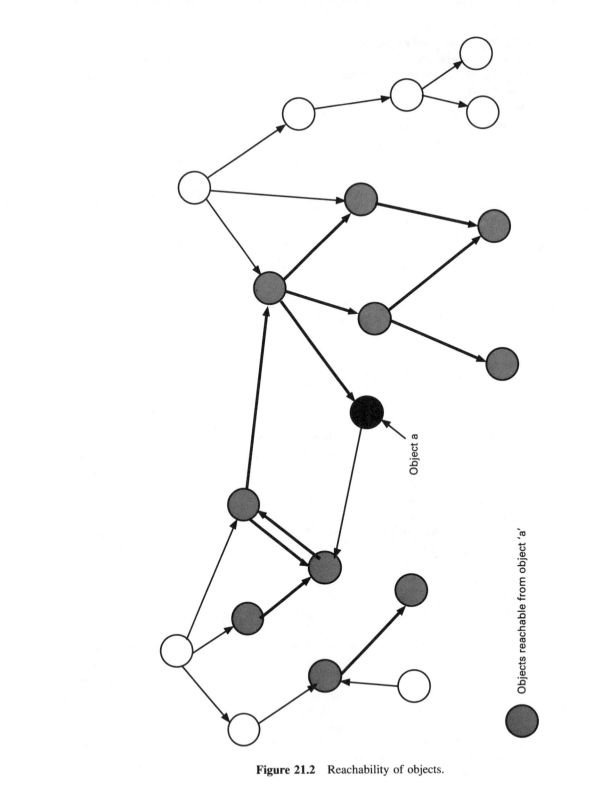

Figure 21.2 Reachability of objects.

Object a

Objects reachable from object 'a'

Because of these different situations, ONTOS provides two mechanisms for handling reference translation and the concomitant task of keeping track of valid and invalid references—Transparent References (or TRefs) and Direct References.

21.3.3 Transparent References

TRefs go through one level of indirection and thus are always safe. If an object referenced by a TRef is inactive, it is activated automatically by the system. While the indirection and reference validity checking does incur a small overhead, it is probably no higher than what the application would frequently incur in performing the task separately. Thus the cleanness of code and the convenience of using TRefs are expected to make them the reference of choice in almost all cases.

21.3.4 Direct References

However, one of the tenets of the ONTOS design philosophy is to provide a direct mechanism in all cases where an abstract mechanism forces a performance trade-off. Thus ONTOS also supports direct references. If direct references are specified in an object's class definition, when the object is activated references to previously read objects are translated to standard C++ virtual memory pointers while references which cannot be translated are set to the special system constant Inactive.

If a closure is read or if the application has other techniques for determining valid references, these references may be used directly, without testing, and will have the same performance as C++ references. The references may still be checked for validity, of course, though if that must be done in most cases the performance advantage compared to TRefs will be lost.

In order to see the difference in using TRefs and direct references, consider the code segment given below. It gives two alternate definitions for a circuit class. The first definition uses the TRef mechanism for references while the second uses direct references. To eliminate function call overhead, inline member functions are defined. Note, that in both cases the member function 'Symbol' returns a memory pointer. Thus from the standpoint of client code, the two methods are equivalent.

```
class Circuit: Entity{
   TRef* theSymbol; // actually of type GraphicalObject
   TRef* subComponent;     // tree of subcomponents
                                      stored as array
public:
   GraphicalObject* symbol()
      {return((GraphicalObject*) theSymbol->binding());}
   void draw()            // retrieval
      {return(symbol()->draw());}
   void symbol(GraphicalObject*newSymbol) // assignment
      {theSymbol = newSymbol->FindTRef();}
};
```

```
class Circuit: Entity{
   GraphicalObject* theSymbol; // iconic representation
                                              of Ckt
   ComponentArray* subComponent;
              // tree of subcomponents stored as array
public:
      GraphicalObject* symbol()
          {return(theSymbol);}
      void draw()
          {return(symbol()->draw());}
};
```

21.3.5 Memory Management

Often the user will want to control memory allocation. For instance, when many small objects are involved, it is usually more efficient to allocate a large common block of memory and store the objects contiguously rather than to allocate space individually for each object. Thus all activation functions have arguments for a memory pointer and memory size. Objects are transferred into this memory area contiguously until the transfer is complete or memory is exhausted. An error is returned in the latter case.

21.4 TRANSACTION MODEL

The activation and deactivation of objects discussed so far implicitly assumed a single user. In a database system with many concurrent users, conflicts between users must be detected and resolved. ONTOS handles such conflicts through a transaction mechanism discussed below.

The ONTOS transaction mechanism provides a number of features. In common with most transaction mechanisms, it insures atomicity of change. Either all changes comprising a transaction are made or none are made. This prevents the database from becoming inconsistent.

ONTOS allows transactions to be nested [Moss86]. Each level of nesting is atomic on its own. This makes it much easier to provide a general undo facility. The undo scopes, in fact, can be nested to an arbitrary number of levels.

ONTOS also supports cooperating processes. Multiple processes may join in a single transaction. As described below, a shared transaction combines the changes made by several processes into a single atomic change while providing the processes themselves a common datapool for sharing and exchanging information.

21.4.1 The Lock Mechanism

Object activation calls (getObject, getLogicalCluster and getClosure) all specify a lock argument. This argument may specify a read lock, a write lock or no lock at all. The granting of locks follows the usual lock management protocol. A read lock is granted as long as the object is not locked for writing. Write locks are exclusive—an object may not be locked for writing or reading. Finally, when an object is deactivated, a write lock is obtained (if not already held) before the modifications are installed in the database.

Obtaining a read lock insures that no modification to an object will occur until the lock is released. If that is not important, an object may be read with a non-restrictive read lock. This type of lock reduces the likelihood of conflict in the database.

Conflict resolution.   The action that should be taken in the event of a lock conflict varies in different situations. A conflict might lead the application to abort the current transaction, wait and try to obtain the lock later or simply continue processing without having obtained the object. Thus the application can specify the action taken upon conflict as part of the `TransactionStart` call. It is function valued and can be one of the system supplied functions or a function provided by the user.

21.4.2 The Basic Transaction

The interface to the transaction mechanism consists of three functions—`Transaction Start`, `TransactionCommit` and `TransactionAbort`. The function signatures starting, committing, and aborting transactions are given below.

```
void TransactionStart(
                VFP conflict=WaitOnConflict,
                char* name=0,
                VFP buffering=DefaultBuffering);
        void TransactionCommit
                (VFP cleanup=DeferCleanup);
        void TransactionAbort
                (VFP cleanup=CleanCache);
```

TransactionStart.   The `TransactionStart` call defines the beginning of a transaction scope. Multiple `TransactionStart` calls without intervening commits or aborts create nested transaction scopes.

`TransactionStart` also defines several parameters for the transaction. It specifies a transaction name used to join shared transactions. It defines a buffering protocol. The default is to activate objects into the process heap and to buffer deactivated objects until the transaction is committed. However, other options might be used for shared transactions. Finally, it defines a function for dealing with any conflicts that may arise in reading or writing objects during the transaction.

TransactionCommit.   The `TransactionCommit` call ends the transaction. In the case of nested transactions, all changes made within the transaction are now visible to the outward transaction. If this is the outermost transaction, an attempt is made to write all deactivated objects to the database.

TransactionAbort.   `TransactionAbort` also ends the transaction. No changes are made to the database (or to the state of any encompassing transaction scopes).

Post-transaction Cleanup. In general, an application will have made copies of object state in the heap, in static memory, on the stack or even exported it in the form of displays and printouts. If the transaction is aborted, this state is potentially invalid and leads to what is commonly called the dirty cache problem. Careful design is required to ensure that this state is not erroneously used in subsequent processing. To assist in dealing with this problem, the `TransactionCommit` and `TransactionAbort` calls provide for an optional function-valued cleanup argument. One of four system-supplied functions can be used or a user-written function may be specified.

The `CleanCache` function invalidates all implicit object references and frees the heap space that was used. It can be used to cleanup the cache after transaction aborts. It might also be used after a successful commit as a way of automatically cleaning out all objects to limit unbounded cache growth.

In the case of a successful commit, cached objects reflect the new state of the database and need not be reread in the subsequent transaction provided no intervening commits have been made elsewhere in the network. Two functions, `DeferCleanup` and `AbortNextIfDirty`, make this optimization safely.

`DeferCleanup` dispenses with refreshing cached objects if there have been no intervening transactions and thus no possibility for another process to corrupt the cached data. If there have been intervening transactions, however, it safely reactivates each object the first time it is referenced.

The `AbortNextIfDirty` function assumes that the cached objects will remain valid. It postpones checking for conflicts until cached objects are again deactivated. (This is commonly known as an optimistic protocol.) If it detects conflicts at that time, it aborts the present transaction. `AbortNextIfDirty` imposes the least overhead and is appropriate when the chance of conflicts is small.

The user may also supply customized functions if the system-supplied functions are inappropriate.

21.4.3 Nesting Transactions

Transactions can be combined in several ways as shown in Figure 21.3. Nested transactions, which will be discussed in this section, are a clean way to implement such functions as undos. Shared transactions, to be discussed in the next section, provide atomicity for cooperating processes.

Transactions may be nested to create units of atomicity within a larger transaction. The initial state of a child transaction is exactly the state of its parent transaction at the time it is initiated. At the end of the child transaction the parent's state includes either all the changes made by the child, in the case of a commit, or none of those changes in the case of an abort. Furthermore, a child's changes are not visible outside the parent until the parent commits successfully.

As we have seen, nested transactions are a convenient mechanism for implementing an undo facility. They also make long transactions more practical. Since ONTOS checks for conflicts globally, nesting can be used as a technique to get early warning of conflict. By nesting a series of short transactions within an overall long transaction, it is possible to progressively check for conflicts during the course of the long transaction and thus reduce the impact of aborts caused by data conflicts.

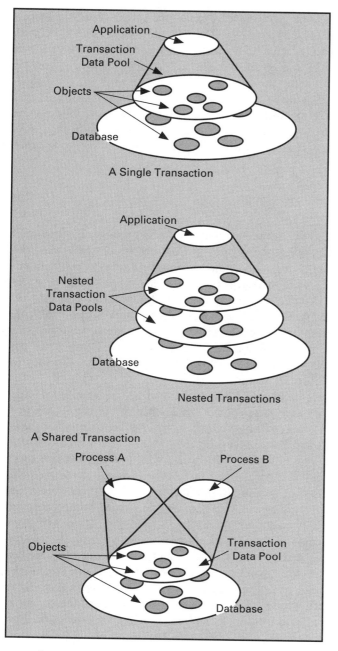

Figure 21.3 Combining transactions.

21.4.4 Shared Transactions

Cooperating processes can share a single transaction. This facility allows dealing with tasks which are atomic from the standpoint of changes to the database but are implemented more easily by a number of cooperating processes. It is particularly convenient for multiple window applications in which a separate process operates each window.

Recall that transactions may be given names. Names make it possible for a process to join a transaction that is already in progress. The first process to issue a `Trans-actionStart` call with a particular name argument simply initiates the transaction. Subsequent processes issuing a `TransactionStart` call with the same name join the existing transaction.

The shared transaction makes the work of all participating processes atomic. For the shared transaction to commit and its changes to be made visible outside it, all processes sharing it must commit successfully. Transaction commits are pended until the last of the cooperating processes commits. A transaction abort by any process aborts the entire transaction.

21.5 EXCEPTION HANDLING

Object programming allows code to be more robust, more interchangeable and more portable than it can be using non-object techniques. It is reasonable to expect, therefore, that object programs will need a better defined, more regular and robust exception handling mechanism as well. The common system of passing error codes back as special values within the domain of a function's return value has well-known drawbacks.

However the largest drawback of the traditional system arises because the code detecting the error cannot, in the general case, recover from it. Frequently, the point in the program at which there is enough context for error recovery is in a high-level function while actual error detection occurs in a low-level function. The two may be separated by arbitrarily many levels of function calls.

An elegant solution to this problem [Miller88] that can be implemented without any language extensions uses a two part protocol. The essence of the protocol is this: The high-level function specifies an exception scope. It specifies an exception handler and execution paths for normal and abort processing.

If any function that runs within this scope detects an error, it dispatches directly to the error handler. The error handler either corrects the problem and returns to the point at which the exception was raised or determines that the error cannot be corrected and aborts processing. An abort involves cleaning up data objects created in the exception handler scope and taking the abort branch.

This protocol is implemented in ONTOS in an object-oriented form. In its non-object form, the exception space is flat—that is, an exception handler must be specified for every type of error condition to be handled. In the ONTOS object-oriented implementation, however, error conditions are specified by classes. The root class, called `Failure`, defines the necessary error raising functions. (Exception handling occurs as a side effect of the creation of a `Failure` object.) More specific errors are represented by classes derived from `Failure`.

Thus the exception handling facility allows the definition of a systematic hierarchy of exception conditions that the system will handle and the linking of these exception conditions with appropriate exception handling functions. When an error is detected, system mechanisms dispatch to the exception handler and, if an abort is required, handle the cleanup gracefully.

The exception handling facility involves three library classes. `Failure` objects are created to raise an exception condition. `ExceptionHandlers` relate `Failure` classes to error handling functions. `CleanupObj`, the root of the Client Library and thus of all persistent objects, keeps track of objects created in each `ExceptionHandler` scope so they can be cleanly deleted if an exception ends in an abort. Here is how these classes function in the overall exception mechanism. An exception processing example is given in Figure 21.4.

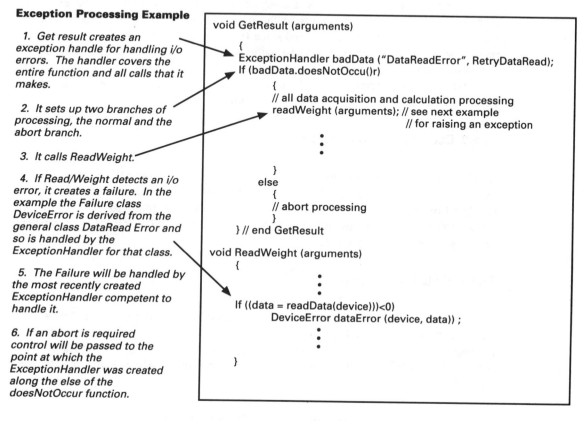

Exception Processing Example

1. *Get result creates an exception handle for handling i/o errors. The handler covers the entire function and all calls that it makes.*

2. *It sets up two branches of processing, the normal and the abort branch.*

3. *It calls ReadWeight.*

4. *If Read/Weight detects an i/o error, it creates a failure. In the example the Failure class DeviceError is derived from the general class DataRead Error and so is handled by the ExceptionHandler for that class.*

5. *The Failure will be handled by the most recently created ExceptionHandler competent to handle it.*

6. *If an abort is required control will be passed to the point at which the ExceptionHandler was created along the else of the doesNotOccur function.*

```
void GetResult (arguments)
{
    ExceptionHandler badData ("DataReadError", RetryDataRead);
    If (badData.doesNotOccu()r)
    {
        // all data acquisition and calculation processing
        readWeight (arguments); // see next example
                                // for raising an exception
            •
            •
            •
    }
    else
    {
        // abort processing
    }
} // end GetResult

void ReadWeight (arguments)
{
            •
            •
            •
    If ((data = readData(device)))<0)
            DeviceError dataError (device, data)) ;
            •
            •
            •
}
```

Figure 21.4   indexException processing.

21.5.1 Failure Objects

`Failures` carry information used in recovering from errors. `Failure` classes might be provided, for instance, for handling problems with file storage (e.g., file not found), memory allocation problems, i/o problems and many others. Each `Failure` class defines data structures to be used by an Exception Handler in recovering from the `Failure`. For instance, a `File Failure Class` might contain the file pathname, the nature of the attempted operation and the operating system error return codes.

21.5.2 ExceptionHandler Objects

`ExceptionHandler` objects provide the second half of the error handling mechanism. `ExceptionHandlers` are defined for specific classes of `Failures`. They relate a `Failure` class to an exception handler function. The exception handler function is considered competent to handle all failures of the failure class specified by the exception handler and of all failure classes derived from that failure class. This allows the natural inheritance mechanism to be used to manage error handling as well as normal programming.

The function that creates the `ExceptionHandler` also defines the execution path for an abort. An abort returns to the point at which the `ExceptionHandler` was created and deletes objects created since that point. It then takes the alternate abort path rather than the direct path. (These paths are created in the code by branching on the return from either of two functions: `Occurs ( )` or `doesNotOccur ( )`. See the code example in this section.) The `ExceptionHandler` object catches a failure and passes it to its exception handling function as an argument.

21.5.3 ExceptionHandler Stack

In addition to being related to a failure class, `ExceptionHandlers` also have an execution, or temporal, scope. Creation of an `ExceptionHandler` object causes it to be placed on the exception stack; its deletion causes it to be removed. When a failure occurs, this stack is searched top down for the first `ExceptionHandler` competent to deal with the class of the `Failure`.

21.5.4 Handling Failures

The handling of failures is controlled by system code invoked by the `Failure` constructor. It is this code that searches the exception handling stack and, when it finds a competent `ExceptionHandler`, calls the exception handling function associated with it. In general, executing an exception handling function may have one of three outcomes:

1. The function may correct the problem. In that case control is returned to the code which originally raised the exception.

2. It may request that the exception be reraised. By returning `FALSE` it requests that the `Failure` be passed to the next competent `ExceptionHandler` earlier in the exception stack. This new function may also terminate in the same three ways. If it aborts, however, it aborts at an earlier point in the application's processing stream.

3. It may decide that no recovery is possible and call the `abort ( )` member function defined on `Failure`. Abort causes the system to clean up all stale data and resume processing from the point at which the `ExceptionHandler` was created. After an abort, control passes to the abort side of the `Occurs ( )` or `doesNotOccur ( )` branch.

Abort handling brings us to the last element of the exception handling facility—cleanup objects and the cleanup object stack.

21.6 VERSIONING MECHANISM

The ONTOS versioning and alternatives mechanism allows a single object to exist in any number of versions [Landis87, Skarra86]. All objects of the same version are collected into a Configuration object. Configurations are related to each other through derivation links. Each configuration (except the first) has a parent and may have any number of children. Thus both alternatives and serial versions are supported. Objects in leaf configurations may be changed freely; objects in inner configurations are immutable (see Figure 21.5).

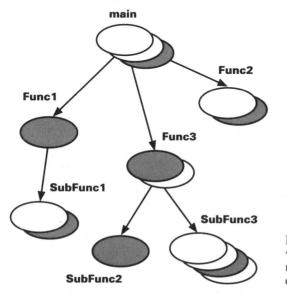

Figure 21.5 A software system with versions. The shaded versions represent one correct system configuration.

Inner configurations can be deleted however. When an inner configuration is deleted, its parent inherits all the children of the deleted configuration. The parent and child states are preserved as before and only the record of intermediate states is lost.

Applications create new configurations by specifying a derivation link between the desired new configuration and some existing previous configuration. When created, a new configuration consists of the state of all objects as they exist in its parent configuration. Thus creating a new configuration is inexpensive; object state is not copied.

Objects are written into a configuration implicitly. All object deactivations are made into the application's currently active configuration. Thus versions of individual objects are not denotable; rather configurations are denotable.

This approach is well-suited to applications where most object references are made within a particular configuration. It allows objects to be referenced directly, without regard to their version history. It does make accessing different versions of the same object less direct, however. Most interest in versioning systems we have encountered falls into the first category—working within a configuration, making this approach preferable.

21.7 CLASS LIBRARY

ONTOS provides a library of classes for its own internal use and for the user's convenience. The library contains:

Persistence. All the properties and member functions that an object needs to support database storage and retrieval are defined by the class Object. All objects that are direct or indirect instances of Object can be stored in ONTOS.

Aggregates. Aggregate objects generalize common data structures such as arrays, lists, sets, hash tables and B*trees.

Schema. Schema classes give a machine independent ways to represent the structure of an object. They are used by ONTOS and are useful in any situation where run-time knowledge of the structure of an object is needed.

21.7.1 Describing Schema

In C++, as in many other languages, class definitions are only accessible to the compiler. They are not accessible at run-time. Thus any code that needs access to information on field offset and field types must use a separate hand-coded representation of the class. ONTOS provides five schema classes to represent class definitions in a machine independent and run-time accessible way. Furthermore, Classify, an ONTOS utility, is provided to generate schema objects from standard C++ class definitions. These objects are loaded into the database to represent the schema and are accessible both to ONTOS and to the application. The classes are:

Type. Represents the overall class definition. Its properties are the type of the classes superclass and aggregates containing the class's properties and procedures.

Property. Represents a property's type and denotes if the property is a reference to another object. The latter allows reference conversion to be made when necessary.

Procedure. Represents a member function. Contains a reference to the function's code and argument list. Essentially procedure allows run-time binding of function calls.

ArgumentList. Represents a member function's argument list so that run-time argument passing and type checking may be done.

Argument. Represents the type and default value of an individual argument in a member function argument list.

21.8 PROGRAMMATIC SQL INTERFACE

The SQL interface adds a predicate-based iteration style of interaction to the database, to the navigational style characteristic of object systems generally, and C++ specifically. The programmatic interface described is intended both for access from applications programs when the SQL style of query is more convenient and as a back-end for an interactive end-user query facility.

The query facility is designed around a persistent `QueryIterator` class, allowing queries to be stored as objects in the database. The following code segment gives `QueryIterator` class definition and an example:

```
class QueryIterator: public Object
   {
   public
       QueryIterator(char* queryText);
       void reset (char* queryText=0);
       int SQLCODE(); //std error code
       Boolean moreData();
       int yieldRow( ... );
       Boolean yieldRowAsString
         (char* header, int length);
       int numberOf Columns();
   };
Entity *state, *zipcode;
Employee* mgr;
QueryIterator aQuery = (
   "Select address.state,
       address.zip,
       manager
   From employee");
while (aQuery.moreData())
   {
   aQuery.yieldRow (state, zipcode, mgr);
    // process data
   }
```

Each instance of the iterator represents a particular query. (The `QueryIterator` constructor argument is an SQL query string.) The results of the query are obtained by calling the `yieldRow` member function. `yieldRow` accepts a variable number of arguments; it specifies a C++ argument for each field in the row. Each time it is called, it returns another row of the query until all rows have been returned.

There is also a string form of the iterator function, `yieldRowAsString`, which returns the row in string form for direct display to the user.

21.8.1 SQL Extensions

Object systems frequently model one-to-many relationships with `Aggregate` objects rather than procedurally through join operations. To be able to handle such relationships easily, Object SQL will extend the SELECT, FROM and WHERE clauses of standard SQL.

In standard relational SQL, the SELECT clause specifies the columns that are to be chosen; the FROM clause specifies the tables that are to be searched and the WHERE clause uses a constraining expression to further filter the resulting search. In the extended SQL, the arguments permitted in the three clauses are expanded.

In addition to accepting class names (the object analog of tables in relational systems) the FROM clause will accept any argument that evaluates to a collection of objects. For instance it will search `Aggregates` of the class, iterators defined for such `Aggregates`, or an explicit list of objects.

Similarly, the SELECT clause will accept property names (analogous to relational columns) as well as member function invocations and "navigational style" property chain expressions. An example of the latter is person.mother.mother.name for grandmother's name.

Finally, the WHERE clause is extended to allow arbitrary Boolean expressions including member function calls that return Boolean values.

These extensions allow the additional expressiveness of object systems to be used inside traditional SQL queries.

21.9 CONCLUSION

ONTOS is designed with practical usefulness as the paramount consideration. It supports C++ because that appears to be the language of choice among those who are using or planning to use an object language for production applications. It provides support for a distributed environment and for cooperating processes because this is the current environment in which workstation systems operate. Performance is extremely important because, though available processing power has grown at a phenomenal rate, the growth in our appetite for functionality seems to have exceeded it. There seems to be little room left for trading more powerful data abstraction for performance.

Within these constraints ONTOS delivers very clean and high performance reference semantics, raising the level of information that may be captured in the data. ONTOS also makes improvements in the level of abstraction at which programmers work, contributing to improving programmer productivity.

References

[**ABADIR85**] M. S. Abadir and M. A. Breuer. A knowledge-based system for designing testable VLSI chips. *IEEE Design and Test of Computers*, 2(4):56–68, August 1985.

[**ABITEBOUL87**] S. Abiteboul and R. Hull. IFO: A formal semantic database model. *ACM Transactions on Database Systems*, 12(4):525–565, 1987.

[**ABRIAL74**] J. R. Abrial. Data semantics. In J. W. Klimbie and K. L. Koffeman, editors, *Database Management*, pages 1–59. North-Holland, 1974.

[**AFSARMANESH85A**] H. Afsarmanesh, D. Knapp, D. McLeod, and A. Parker. An extensible, object-oriented approach to databases for VLSI/CAD. In *Proceedings of the International Conference on Very Large Databases*. VLDB Endowment, August 1985.

[**AFSARMANESH85B**] H. Afsarmanesh, D. Knapp, D. McLeod, and A. Parker. An approach to engineering design databases with applications to VLSI/CAD. In *Proceedings of the International Symposium on New Directions in Computing*. IEEE, August 1985.

[**AFSARMANESH85C**] H. Afsarmanesh. The 3-dimensional information space (3DIS): An extensible object-oriented framework for information management. Technical Report CRI-85-21, Computer Research Institute, University of Southern California, Los Angeles CA, October 1985.

[**AFSARMANESH86A**] H. Afsarmanesh, D. Knapp, D. McLeod, and A. Parker. Information management for VLSI/CAD. In *Proceedings of the IEEE International Conference on Computer Design: VLSI in Computers and Processors*. IEEE, October 1986.

[**AFSARMANESH86B**] H. Afsarmanesh and D. McLeod. A framework for semantic database models. In G. Ariav and J. Clifford, editors, *New Directions for Database Systems*, pages 149–167. Ablex Publishing Company, 1986.

[**AGRAWAL87**] R. Agrawal. Alpha: An extension of relational algebra to express a class of recursive queries. In *Proc. IEEE 3rd Int'l Conf. Data Engineering*, pages 580–590, Los Angeles, CA, Feb. 1987. Also in *IEEE Trans. Software Eng.* 14, 7 (July 1988), 879-885.

[**AGRAWAL89A**] R. Agrawal and N.H. Gehani. Rationale for the design of persistence and query processing facilities in the database programming language O++. In *2nd Int'l Workshop on Database Programming Languages*, Oregon Coast, June 1989.

[**AGRAWAL89B**] R. Agrawal and N.H. Gehani. Version managment in ODE. Technical memorandum, AT&T Bell Laboratories, Murray Hill, NJ, 1989.

[**AHAD85**] R. Ahad and D. McLeod. An approach to semi-automatic physical database design and evolution for personal information systems. Technical Report CRI-85-11, Computer Research Institute, University of Southern California, Los Angeles CA, September 1985.

[AHAD86] R. Ahad and D. McLeod. Performance optimization techniques for an object-oriented semantic data model. Technical Report CRI-86-21, Computer Research Institute, University of Southern California, Los Angeles CA, July 1986.

[AHAD88] R. Ahad. The object shell: An extensible system to define an object-oriented view of an existing database. In K. R. Dittrich, editor, *Advances in Object-Oriented Database Systems*, pages 174–192. Springer-Verlag, 1988.

[AHLSEN84] M. Ahlsen et al. An architecture for object management in OIS. *ACM Transactions on Office Information Systems*, 2(3), 1984.

[AHO76] A. Aho, J. Hoftcraft, and J. Ullman. *The Design and Analysis of Computer Algorithms*. Addison-Wesley Publishing Company, 1976.

[AHO79] A.V. Aho and J.D. Ullman. Universality of data retrieval languages. In *Proc. 6th ACM Symp. Principles of Programming Languages*, pages 110–120, San-Antonio, TX, Jan. 1979.

[ALBANO85] A. Albano, L. Cardelli, and R. Orsini. Galileo: A strongly-typed interactive conceptual language. *ACM Transactions on Database Systems*, 10(2):230–260, June 1985.

[ANDREWS87] T. Andrews and C. Harris. Combining language and database advances in an object-oriented development environment. In *Proceedings of the Conference on Object-Oriented Programming Systems, Languages, and Applications*, pages 430–440, Orlando, FL, October 1987. ACM.

[ANSI-C88] ANSI C. *Draft Proposed American National Standard for Information Systems—Programming Language C*, 1988.

[ARISAWA86] H. Arisawa and T. Miura. On the properties of extended inclusion dependencies. *IEEE Transactions on Software Engineering*, SE-12(11), 1986.

[ASTRAHAN76] M. M. Astrahan et al. System R: Relational approach to database management. *ACM Transactions on Database Systems*, 1(2):97–137, June 1976.

[ATKINSON87A] M. P. Atkinson and P. Buneman. Database programming languages. *ACM Computing Surveys*, 19(2):105–190, June 1987.

[ATKINSON87B] R. Atkinson, B. Liskov, and R. Scheifler. Aspects of implementing CLU. In *ACM National Conference Proceedings*, 1978.

[ATWOOD85] T.M. Atwood. An object-oriented DBMS for design support applications. In *Proc. IEEE 1st Int'l Conf. Computer-Aided Technologies*, pages 299–307, Montreal, Canada, Sept. 1985.

[ATZENI86] P. Atzeni and D.S. Parker. Formal properties of net-based knowledge representation schemes. In *Proceedings on Data Engineering Conference*, 1986.

[AYLOR86] J. Aylor, R. Waxman, and C. Scarratt. VHDL: Feature description and analysis. *IEEE Design and Test of Computers*, 3(2), April 1986.

[BACON87] D. Bacon, A. Dupuy, J. Schwartz, and Y. Yemini. NEST: A network simulation and prototype tool. In *Proceedings Usenix Conference Winter 87*, Dallas, Texas, 1987.

[BALLOU88] N. Ballou et al. Coupling an expert system shell with an object-oriented database system. *Journal of Object-Oriented Programming*, 1(2), 1988.

[BALZER85] R. Balzer. Automated enhancement of knowledge representations. In *Proceedings of the International Joint Conference on Artificial Intelligence*, pages 203–207, August 1985.

[BANCILHON85] F. Bancilhon, W. Kim, and H. Korth. A model of CAD transactions. In *11th Int'l Conference on Very Large Data Bases*, pages 25–33. Morgan Kaufmann, 1985.

[BANCILHON86] F. Bancilhon and R. Ramakrishnan. An amateur's introduction to recursive query processing strategies. In *Proc. ACM-SIGMOD 1986 Int'l Conf. on Management of Data*, pages 16–52, Washington D.C., May 1986.

[BANCILHON87] F. Bancilhon, T. Briggs, S. Khoshafian, and P. Valduriez. FAD, a powerful and simple database language. In *Proc. 13th Int'l Conf. Very Large Data Bases*, pages 97–105, Brighton, England, Sept. 1987.

[BANCILHON88] F. Bancilhon, G. Barbedette, V. Benzaken, C. Delobel, S. Gamerman, C. Lecluse, P. Pfeffer, P. Richard, and F. Velez. The design and implementation of O2, an object-oriented database system. In K. R. Dittrich, editor, *Advances in Object-Oriented Database Systems*, pages 1–22. Springer-Verlag, 1988.

[BANERJEE86] J. Banerjee, H.J. Kim, W. Kim, and H.F. Korth. Schema evolution in object-oriented persistent databases. In *Proceedings of the 6th Advanced Database Symposium*, 1986.

[BANERJEE87A] J. Banerjee, W. Kim, H.J. Kim, and H.F. Korth. Semantics and implementation of schema envolution in object-oriented databases. In *Proceedings of the ACM SIGMOD International Conference on Management of Data*, pages 311–322. ACM SIGMOD, May 1987.

[BANERJEE87B] J. Banerjee, H. Chou, J. Garza, W. Kim, D. Woelk, N. Ballou, and H. Kim. Data model issues for object-oriented applications. *ACM Transactions on Office Information Systems*, 5(1):3–26, January 1987.

[BARDIN87] B. Bardin. Layered virtual machines and object-oriented design: A balanced refinement methodology. In *Proceedings AIAA Computers in Aerospace VI Conference*, pages 389–92, 1987.

[BARTH88A] R. Barth and B. Serlet. A structural representation of VLSI design. In *Proceedings of ACM/IEEE 25th Design Automation Conference*, pages 237–242, Anaheim Convention Center, Anaheim, CA, June 1988.

[BARTH88B] R. Barth, B. Serlet, and P. Sindhu. Parameterized schematics. In *Proceedings of ACM/IEEE 25th Design Automation Conference*, pages 243–249, Anaheim Convention Center, Anaheim, CA, June 1988.

[BARTH88C] R. Barth, L. Monier, and B. Serlet. PatchWork: Layout from schematic annotations. In *Proceedings of ACM/IEEE 25th Design Automation Conference*, pages 250–255, Anaheim Convention Center, Anaheim, CA, June 1988.

[BATINI86] C. Batini, M. Lenzerini, and S. Navathe. A comparative analysis of methodologies of database schema integration. *ACM Computing Surveys*, 18(4):323–364, December 1986.

[BATORY84] D. Batory and A. Buchmann. Molecular objects, abstract data types, and data models: A framework. In *Proceedings of the International Conference on Very Large Databases*. VLDB Endowment, August 1984.

[BATORY85] D. Batory and W. Kim. Modeling concepts for VLSI CAD objects. *ACM Transactions on Database Systems*, 10(3):322–346, September 1985.

[BATORY88] D. Batory, J. Barnett, J. Garza, K. Smith, K. Tsukuda, B. Twitchell, and T. Wise. GENESIS: An extensible database management system. *IEEE Trans. Software Eng.*, Nov. 1988.

[BAYER77] R. Bayer and K. Unterauer. Prefix B-Trees. *ACM Transactions on Database Systems*, 2(1):11–26, March 1977.

[BEECH88] D. Beech and B. Mahbod. Generalized version control in an object-oriented database. In *Proc. IEEE 4th Int'l Conf. Data Engineering*, pages 14–22, Los Angeles, CA, Feb. 1988.

[BERNSTEIN87A] P. Bernstein. Database system support for software engineering—an extended abstract. In *9th International Conference on Software Engineering*, Monterey, CA, April 1987.

[BERNSTEIN87B] P.A. Bernstein, V. Hadzilacos, and N. Goodman. *Concurrency Control and Recovery in Database Systems*. Addison-Wesley, 1987.

[BERRE88] A. Berre, T. L. Anderson, and D. Maier. The HyperModel benchmark. Technincal Report 31/88, Dept. of CSE, Oregon Graduate Center, Beaverton, OR, 1988.

[BITTON83] D. Bitton, D. DeWitt, and C. Turbyfill. Benchmarking database systems—a systematic approach. Technical Report #526, University of Wisconsin Madison, WI December 1983.

[BLAHA87] M. Blaha, W. Premerlani, and J. Rumbaugh. Relational database design using an object-oriented methodology. *CACM*, 31(4), April 1988.

[BLASGEN77] M. W. Blasgen, R. G. Casey, and K. P. Eswaren. An encoding method for multifield sorting and indexing. *CACM*, 20(11):874–878, November 1977.

[BOBROW83] D.G. Bobrow and M. Stefik. *The LOOPS Manual*. Xerox PARC, 1983.

[BOBROW86] D.G. Bobrow, K. Kahn, G. Kiczales, L. Masinter, M. Stefik, and F. Zdybel. CommonLoops: Merging LISP and object-oriented programming. In *Proceedings of the Conference on Object-Oriented Programming Systems, Languages, and Applications*, pages 17–29. ACM, March 1986.

[BOEHM81] B.W. Boehm. *Software Engineering Economics*. Prentice Hall, Englewood Cliffs, NJ, 1981.

[BOOCH86A] G. Booch. Object-oriented development. *IEEE Transactions on Software Engineering*, SE-12(2), February 1986.

[BOOCH86B] G. Booch. *Software Engineering with Ada*. Benjamin/Cummings, Menlo Park, CA, 1986.

[BORGIDA85] A. Borgida and K. Williamson. Accommodating exceptions in databases and refining the schema by learning from them. In *Proceedings of the International Conference on Very Large Databases*. VLDB Endowment, August 1985.

[BORGIDA86] A. Borgida, T. M. Mitchell, and K. Williamson. Learning improved integrity constraints and schemas from exceptions in databases and knowledge bases. In M. L. Brodie and J. Mylopoulos, editors, *On Knowledge Base Management Systems*, pages 259–286. Springer Verlag, 1986.

[BORGIDA88] A. Borgida. Modeling class hierarchies with contradictions. In *Proceedings of the ACM SIGMOD International Conference on Management of Data*, pages 434–443. ACM SIGMOD, June 1988.

[BOTTCHER86] S. Böttcher, M. Jarke, and W. Schmidt. Adaptive predicate management in database systems. In *Proceedings of the International Conference on Very Large Data Bases*, 1986.

[BRACHMAN84] R. Brachman and H. Levesque. The tractability of subsumption in frame-based description languages. In *Proceedings on AAAI84*, 1984.

[BRACHMAN85A] R. J. Brachman and J. Schmolze. An overview of the KL-One knowledge representation system. *Cognitive Science*, 9:171–216, 1985.

[BRACHMAN85B] R.J. Brachman and H.J. Levesque, editors. *Readings in Knowledge Representation*. Morgan Kaufmann, 1985.

[BREUER88] M. A. Breuer, W. H. Cheng, R. Gupta, I. Hardonag, E. Horowitz, and S. Y. Lin. Cbase 1.0: A CAD database for VLSI circuits using object-oriented technology. In *Proceedings of IEEE International Conference on Computer-Aided Design, ICCAD-88*, pages 392–395, November 1988.

[BRODIE81] M. Brodie. On modeling behavioral semantics of data. In *Proceedings of the International Conference on Very Large Databases*. IEEE, September 1981.

[BRODIE84A] M. Brodie, J. Mylopoulos, and J. Schmidt, editors. *On Conceptual Modeling*. Springer-Verlag, 1984.

[BRODIE84B] M. Brodie. On the development of data models. In M. Brodie, J. Mylopoulos, and J. Schmidt, editors, *On Conceptual Modeling*, pages 19–47. Springer-Verlag, 1984.

[BRODIE86] M. Brodie and J. Mylopoulos, editors. *On Knowledge Base Management Systems*. Springer-Verlag, 1986.

[BROWN85] M. R. Brown, K. N. Kolling, and E. A. Taft. The Alpine file system. *ACM Transactions on Computer Systems*, 3(4):261–293, September 1985.

[BUNEMAN79] P. Buneman and R. Frankel. A functional query language. In *Proceedings of the ACM SIGMOD International Conference on Management of Data*, pages 52–57. ACM SIGMOD, May 1979.

[BUNEMAN86] P. Buneman and M. Atkinson. Inheritance and persistence in database programming languages. In *Proc. ACM-SIGMOD 1986 Int'l Conf. on Management of Data*, pages 4–15, Washington D.C., May 1986.

[CAMMARATA86] S. Cammarata and M. Melkanoff. An information dictionary for managing CAD/CAM databases. In *Database Programming & Design*, pages 26–35. Miller Freeman Publications, San Francisco, CA, March 1986.

[CARBONELL83A] J. Carbonell. Learning by analogy: Formulating and generalizing plans from past experience. In R. Michalski, J. Carbonell, and T. Mitchell, editors, *Machine Learning: An Artificial Intelligence Approach (Volume 1)*, pages 137–162. Tioga Publishing Company, 1983.

[CARBONELL83B] J. Carbonell, R. Michalski, and T. Mitchell. An overview of machine learning. In R. Michalski, J. Carbonell, and T. Mitchell, editors, *Machine Learning: An Artificial Intelligence Approach (Volume 1)*, pages 3–24. Tioga Publishing Company, 1983.

[CARDELLI84A] L. Cardelli. A semantics of multiple inheritance. In G. Kahn, D. B. MacQueen, and G. Plotkin, editors, *Semantics of Data Types*. Springer-Verlag, 1984.

[CARDELLI84B] L. Cardelli. Amber. Technical memorandum, AT&T Bell Laboratories, Murray Hill, NJ, 1984.

[CARDELLI85] L. Cardelli and P. Wegner. On understanding types, data abstraction and polymorphism. *ACM Computing Surveys*, 17(4), 1985.

[CARDENAS79] A. Cardenas. *Database Management Systems*. Allyn and Bacon, 1979.

[CAREY86A] M Carey, D. Dewitt, J. Richardson, and E. Shekita. Object and file management in the EXODUS extensible database system. In *Proceedings of the 12th VLDB Conference*, Kyoto, Japan, August 1986.

[CAREY86B] M. Carey, D. Dewitt, D. Frank, G. Graefe, J. Richardson, E. Shekita, and M. Muralikrishna. The architecture of the EXODUS extensible DBMS. In *Proceedings of the International Workshop on Object-Oriented Database Systems*, Pacific Grove, CA, September 1986.

[CAREY86C] M. J. Carey and D. J. DeWitt. Extensible database systems. In M. L. Brodie and J. Mylopoulos, editors, *On Knowledge Base Management Systems*, pages 297–314. Springer-Verlag, 1986.

[CAREY88A] M. J. Carey, D. J. DeWitt, and S. L. Vandenberg. A data model and query language for EXODUS. In *Proceedings of the ACM SIGMOD International Conference on Management of Data*, pages 413–423. ACM SIGMOD, June 1988.

[CAREY88B] M.J. Carey, D.J. DeWitt, G. Graefe, D.M. Haight, J.E. Richardson, D.H. Schuh, E.J. Shekita, and S.L. Vandenberg. The EXODUS extensible DBMS project: An overview. Technical Report Computer Sciences Technical Report #808, Univ. Wisconsin, Madison, WI Nov. 1988.

[CATTELL80] R. G. G. Cattell. An entity-based database user interface. In *Proceedings of the ACM SIGMOD International Conference on Management of Data*, pages 144–150. ACM SIGMOD, 1980.

[CATTELL83] R. G. G. Cattell. Design and implementation of a Relationship-Entity-Datum data model. Technical Report CSL-83-4, Xerox PARC, May 1983.

[CATTELL88] R. G. G. Cattell. Object-oriented DBMS performance measurement. In K. R. Dittrich, editor, *Advances in Object-Oriented Database Systems*, pages 364–367. Springer-Verlag, 1988.

[CAVIN87] Ralph K. Cavin III and A. Richard Newton. Data management for IC design. In *SRC Workshop*. Semiconductor Research Corporation, November 1987.

[CCADAPLEX84] Computer Corporation of America, Cambridge, MA. *Daplex User's Manual*, 1984. CCA-84-01.

[CERI84] S. Ceri and G. Pelagatti. *Distributed Databases: Principles and Systems*. McGraw Hill, 1984.

[CHAMBERLIN75] D. Chamberlin, J. Gray, and I. Traiger. Views, authorization, and locking in a relational database system. In *Proceedings of the National Computer Conference*, pages 425–430. AFIPS, June 1975.

[CHAMBERLIN76] D.D. Chamberlin, M.M. Astrahan, K.P. Eswaran, P.P. Griffiths, R.A. Lorie, J.W. Mehl, P. Reisner, and B.W. Wade. SEQUEL 2: A unified approach to data definition, manipulation, and control. Technical Report RJ 1798, IBM, June 1976.

[CHEN76] P. P. Chen. The Entity-Relationship model: Toward a unified view of data. *ACM Transactions on Database Systems*, March 1976.

[CHEN88] G.-D. Chen and T.-M. Parng. A database management system for a VLSI design system. In *Proceedings of ACM/IEEE 25th Design Automation Conference*, pages 257–262, Anaheim Convention Center, Anaheim, CA, June 1988.

[CHOU86] H.-T. Chou and W. Kim. A unifying framework for version control in a CAD environment. In *12th Int'l Conference on Very Large Data Bases*, pages 336–344. Morgan Kaufmann, 1986.

[CLEMM85] G. Clemm, D. Heimbigner, L. Osterweil, and L. Williams. Keystone: A federated software environment. In *ACM SIGPLAN Symposium on Programming Languages and Programming Environments*. ACM SIGPLAN, May 1985.

[CLOCKSIN81] W. Clocksin and C. Mellish. *Programming in Prolog*. Springer-Verlag, 1981.

[CODD70] E. F. Codd. A relational model for large shared data banks. *Communications of the ACM*, 13(6):377–387, 1970.

[CODD79] E. F. Codd. Extending the database relational model to capture more meaning. *ACM Transactions on Database Systems*, 4(4):397–434, 1979.

[CONKLIN87] J. Conklin. Hypertext: An introduction and survey. *IEEE Computer*, September 1987.

[CONNORS88] T. Connors and P. Lyngbaek. Providing uniform access to heterogeneous information bases. In K. R. Dittrich, editor, *Advances in Object-Oriented Database Systems*, pages 174–192. Springer-Verlag, 1988.

[COPELAND84] G. Copeland and D. Maier. Making Smalltalk a database system. In *Proceedings of the 1984 ACM SIGMOD Intl. Conf. on Management of Data*, pages 316–325, Boston, MA, June 1984.

[COX86] B. Cox. *Object-Oriented Programming: An Evolutionary Approach*. Addison-Wesley, 1986.

[CURRY84] G.A. Curry and R.M. Ayers. Experience with Traits in the Xerox Star workstation. *IEEE Transactions on Software Engineering*, SE-10(5), 1984.

[DAHL70] O.-J. Dahl, B. Myhrhaug, and K. Nygaard. *SIMULA-67 Common Base Language*. Norwegian Computing Center, Oslo, 1970.

[DAMON88A] C. Damon. Data abstraction and objects: A model of representation. Internal memo, Ontologic, Inc., 47 Manning Road, Billerica, MA 01821, 1988.

[DAMON88B] C. Damon and G. Landis. Abstract types and storage types in an OO-DBMS. In *Digest of papers, spring CompCon '88*. Computer Society Press, 1988.

[DANIELL89] J. Daniell and S.W. Director. An object-oriented approach to CAD tool control within a design framework. Research Report CMUCAD-89-15, Electrical and Computer Engineering Department, Carnegie Mellon University, Pittsburgh, PA, March 1989.

[DARNOVSKY87] M. Darnovsky and G. Bowman. *TRANSCT-SQL User's Guide, Document 3231-2.1*. Sybase, Inc., 1987.

[DATE82] C. J. Date. *An Introduction to Database Systems: Volumes 1 & 2*. Addison-Wesley, 1982.

[DATE86] C. J. Date. A critique of the SQL database language. In *Relational Database: Selected Writings*, pages 269–311. Addison-Wesley, 1986.

[DAVIS77] C.G. Davis and C.R. Vick. The software development system. *IEEE Transactions on Software Engineering*, 3(1):69–84, January 1977.

[DAYAL78] U. Dayal and P. Bernstein. On the updatability of relational views. In *Proceedings of the International Conference on Very Large Databases*. IEEE, September 1978.

[DAYAL84] U. Dayal and H. Hwang. View definition and generalization for database integration in a multi-database system. *IEEE Transactions on Software Engineering*, SE-10(6):628–645, November 1984.

[DAYAL86] U. Dayal and J. M. Smith. PROBE: A knowledge-oriented database management system. In M. L. Brodie and J. Mylopoulos, editors, *On Knowledge Base Management Systems*, pages 227–257. Springer-Verlag, 1986.

[DAYAL88A] U. Dayal, B. Blaustein, A. Buchmann, U. Chakravarthy, M. Hsu, R. Ledin, D. McCarthy, A. Rosenthal, S. Sarin, M.J. Carey, M. Livny, and R. Jauhari. The HiPAC project: Combining active databases and timing constraints. In *ACM-SIGMOD Record*, volume 17, 1, pages 51–70, March 1988.

[DAYAL88B] U. Dayal, A. P. Buchmann, and D. R. McCarthy. Rules are objects too: A knowledge model for an active object-oriented database system. In K. R. Dittrich, editor, *Advances in Object-Oriented Database Systems*, pages 129–142. Springer-Verlag, 1988.

[DECOUCHANT86] D. Decouchant. Design of a distributed object manager for the Smalltalk-80 system. *ACM SIGPLAN Not.*, 21(11):444–450, November 1986.

[DELISLE86] N. Delisle and M. Schwartz. Neptune: A Hypertext system for CAD applications. In *Proceedings of the ACM SIGMOD International Conference on Management of Data*, pages 132–141, 1986.

[DEMICHIEL87] L. G. DeMichiel and R. P. Gabriel. The Common Lisp Object System: An overview. In *ECOOP Conference Proceedings*, pages 201–220, June 1987. Also published as a special issue of Bigre, No. 54, June 1987.

[DEMURJIAN88] S. A. Demurjian. A database systems environment for supporting computer-aided software engineering. Internal memo, Computer Science and Engineering Department, University of Connecticut, Storrs, CT, 1988.

[DENNING70] P.J. Denning. Virtual memory. *ACM Computing Surveys*, 2(3):153–189, September 1970.

[DIEDERICH87] J. Diederich and J. Milton. ODDESSY: An object-oriented database design system. In *Proc. IEEE 3rd Int'l Conf. Data Engineering*, pages 235–244, Los Angeles, CA, Feb. 1987.

[DITTRICH85] K. Dittrich and R. Lorie. Version support for engineering database systems. Technical Report Rep. RJ4769, IBM Research Lab., San Jose, CA, July 1985.

[DITTRICH86] K. Dittrich, W. Gotthard, and P. Lockemann. DAMOKLES—A database system for software engineering environments. In *Proceedings of IFIP Workshop on Advanced Programming Environments*, Trondheim, Norway, June 1986.

[DITTRICH87A] K.R. Dittrich, W. Gotthard, and P.C. Lockemann. DAMOKLES—A database system for software engineering environments. In *LNCS 244*, pages 353–371, 1987.

[DITTRICH87B] K. R. Dittrich, W. Gotthard, and P. C. Lockemann. Complex entities for engineering applications. In S. Spaccapietra, editor, *Proceedings of the International Conference on the Entity-Relationship Approach*, pages 421–440. North-Holland, 1987.

[DOWSON87] M. Dowson. Iteration in the software process. In *Proceedings of the 9th International Conference on Software Engineering*, pages 36–39, Monterey, CA, March–April 1987.

[DUHL88] J. Duhl and C. Damon. A performance comparison of object and relational databases using the Sun benchmark. In *Proceedings of the Conference on Object-Oriented Programming Systems, Languages, and Applications*. ACM, 1988.

[DUPUY88] A. Dupuy and J. Schwartz. NeST system overview. Technical Report CUCS-375-88, Department of Computer Science, Columbia University, New York, NY, 1988.

[EASTMAN80] C. Eastman. System facilities for CAD databases. In *Proceedings of the 17th Design Automation Conference*, 1980.

[EASTMAN81] C.M. Eastman. Database facilities for engineering design. *Proceedings IEEE*, 69(10), October 1981.

[ECKLUND87] D. Ecklund and E. Ecklund. CAD performance requirements for persistent object systems in a distributed environment. In *Proceedings of the Workshop on Persistent Object Systems: Their design, implementation and use*, Appin, August 1987.

[EDIFMANUAL87] EIA. *EDIF Specification*. EDIF Steering Committee, May 1987.

[EGE87] A. Ege and C.A. Ellis. Design and implementation of GORDION, an object base management system. In *Proc. IEEE 3rd Int'l Conf. Data Engineering*, pages 226–234, Los Angeles, CA, Feb. 1987.

[ESWARAN86] K.P. Eswaran, J.N. Gray, R.A. Lorie, and I.L. Traiger. The notions of consistency and predicate locks in a database system. *Communications of ACM*, 19(11), 1976.

[FARMER85] D. B. Farmer, R. King, and A. Myers. The semantic database constructor. *IEEE Transactions on Software Engineering*, SE-11(7):583–591, 1985.

[FELDMAN69] J. A. Feldman and P. D. Rovner. An Algol-based associative language. *Communications of the ACM*, 12(8), 1969.

[FELDMAN79] S.I. Feldman. Make—A program for maintaining computer programs. *Software Practice and Experience*, March 1979.

[FERIDUN88] M. Feridun, M. Leib, M. Nodine, and J. Ong. ANM: Automated network management system. *IEEE Network*, 2(2):13–19, March 1988.

[FININ84] T. Finin and D. Silverman. Interactive classification. In *Proceedings of IEEE Workshop on Principles of Knowledge-based Systems*, 1984.

[FISHMAN87] D. Fishman, D. Beech, H. Cate, E. Chow, T. Connors, T. Davis, N. Derrett, C. Hoch, W. Kent, P. Lyngbaek, B. Mahbod, M. Neimat, T. Ryan, and M. Shan. Iris: An object-oriented database management system. *ACM Transactions on Office Information Systems*, 5(1):48–69, January 1987.

[GALLO86] F. Gallo, R. Minot, and I. Thomas. The object management system of PCTE as a software engineering database management system. In *Second ACM Software Engineering Symposium on Practical Software Development Environments*, pages 12–15, Palo Alto, CA, December 1986.

[GARG87] P. Garg and W. Scacchi. On designing intelligent hypertext systems for information management in software engineering. In *Hypertext '87*, page 409, 1987.

[GARG88] P. K. Garg. Abstraction mechanisms in hypertext. *Communications of the ACM*, 31(7):862–870, 1988.

[GEHANI86] N.H. Gehani and W.D. Roome. Concurrent C. *Software—Practice & Experience*, 16(9):821–844., 1986.

[GENERA88] Symbolics Inc., Cambridge, MA. *Programming the User Interface*, 1988. Genera 7.2 documentation.

[GIBBS83] S. Gibbs and D. Tsichritzis. A data modeling approach for office information systems. *ACM Transactions on Office Information Systems*, 1(4):299–319, October 1983.

[GOLDBERG83] A. Goldberg and D. Robson. *Smalltalk-80: The Language and its Implementation*. Addison-Wesley, 1983.

[GOLDBERG84] A. Goldberg. *Smalltalk-80: The Interactive Programming Environment*. Addison-Wesley, 1984.

[GOLDMAN85] K. J. Goldman, S. A. Goldman, P. Kanellakis, and S. B. Zdonik. ISIS: Interface for a semantic information system. In *Proceedings of the ACM SIGMOD International Conference on Management of Data*, pages 328–342. ACM SIGMOD, May 1985.

[GRAEFE88] G. Graefe and D. Maier. Query optimization in object-oriented databases: A prospectus. In K. R. Dittrich, editor, *Advances in Object-Oriented Database Systems*, pages 358–363. Springer-Verlag, 1988.

[GRANACKI85] J. Granacki, D. Knapp, and A. Parker. The ADAM advanced design automation system: Overview, planner, and natural language interface. In *Proceedings of the 22nd Design Automation Conference*, 1985.

[GRAY78] J. Gray. Notes on database operating systems. In R. Bayer, R. Graham, and G. Seegmuller, editors, *Operating Systems: An Advanced Course*, volume 60 of *Lecture Notes in Computer Science*, pages 393–481. Springer-Verlag, 1978.

[GRIFFITHS76] P. Griffiths and B. Wade. On an authorization mechanism. *ACM Transactions on Database Systems*, 1(3), 1976.

[GUPTA88] M. A. Breuer, W. Cheng, R. Gupta, E. Horowitz, I. Hardonag, and S. Y. Lin. Cbase 1.0: An object-oriented CAD database. In Rajiv Gupta, editor, *Proceedings of the Vbase User's Group Meeting*. Ontologic, Inc., May 1988.

[GUPTA89] Rajiv Gupta, Wesley Cheng, Rajesh Gupta, Ido Hardonag, and Melvin Breuer. An object-oriented VLSI CAD framework: A case study in rapid prototyping. *IEEE Computer, Special Issue on Rapid Prototyping*, pages 28–37, May 1989.

[HALBERT-86] D. Halbert and P. D. O'Brien. Using types and inheritance in object-oriented languages. Draft from Object-Based Systems Group, 1986.

[HAMMER75] M. Hammer and D. McLeod. Semantic integrity in a relational database system. In *Proceedings of the International Conference on Very Large Databases*. IEEE, September 1975.

[HAMMER76] M. Hammer and D. McLeod. A framework for database semantic integrity. In *Proceedings of the International Conference on Software Engineering*. IEEE, October 1976.

[HAMMER78] M. Hammer and D. McLeod. The semantic data model: A modeling mechanism for database applications. In *Proceedings of the ACM SIGMOD International Conference on Management of Data*. ACM SIGMOD, June 1978.

[HAMMER80] M. Hammer and D. McLeod. On database management system architecture. In *Infotech State of the Art Report: Data Design*, volume 8 of *Infotech State of the Art Reports*, pages 177–202. Pergamon Infotech Limited, Maidenhead, United Kingdom, 1980.

[HAMMER81] M. Hammer and D. McLeod. Database description with SDM: A semantic database model. *ACM Transactions on Database Systems*, 6(3):351–386, September 1981.

[HARRISON86] D.S. Harrison, P. Moore, R.L. Spickelmier, and A.R. Newton. Data management and graphics editing in the Berkeley design environment. In *Proceedings of IEEE International Conference on Computer-Aided Design, ICCAD-86*, pages 24–27, 1986.

[HASKIN82] R. Haskin and R. Lorie. On extending the functions of a relational database system. In *Proceedings of the ACM SIGMOD International Conference on Management of Data*. ACM SIGMOD, 1982.

[HASS83] N. Hass and G. Hendrix. Learning by analogy: Formulating and generalizing plans from past experience. In R. Michalski, J. Carbonell, and T. Mitchell, editors, *Machine Learning: An Artificial Intelligence Approach (Volume 1)*, pages 405–428. Tioga Publishing Company, 1983.

[HAWRYSZKIEWYCZ84] I. Hawryszkiewycz. *Database Analysis and Design*. Science Research Associates, 1984.

[HEILER88] S. Heiler and S. Zdonik. Views, data abstraction, and inheritance in the FUGUE data model. In K. R. Dittrich, editor, *Advances in Object-Oriented Database Systems*, pages 225–241. Springer-Verlag, 1988.

[HEIMBIGNER81] D. Heimbigner and D. McLeod. Federated information bases—a preliminary report. In *Infotech State of the Art Report: Database*, volume 9 of *Infotech State of the Art Reports*, pages 383–410. Pergamon Infotech Limited, Maidenhead, United Kingdom, 1981.

[HEIMBIGNER85] D. Heimbigner and D. McLeod. A federated architecture for information systems. *ACM Transactions on Office Information Systems*, 3(3):253–278, July 1985.

[HORNICK87] M. F. Hornick and S. B. Zdonik. A shared, segmented memory system for an object-oriented database. *ACM Transactions on Office Information Systems*, 5(1):70–95, January 1987.

[HOROWITZ86A] E. Horowitz and R.C. Williamson. SODOS: A software documentation support environment—Its definition. *IEEE Trans. on Software Engineering*, SE-12(8):849–859, August 1986.

[HOROWITZ86B] E. Horowitz and R.C. Williamson. SODOS: A software documentation support environment—Its use. *IEEE Trans. on Software Engineering*, SE-12(11):1076–1087, November 1986.

[HUDSON87] S. Hudson and R. King. Object-oriented database support for software environments. In *Proceedings of the ACM SIGMOD International Conference on Management of Data*, pages 491–503, San Fransisco, CA, May 1987. ACM SIGMOD.

[HUDSON88] S. Hudson and R. King. An adaptive derived data manager for distributed databases. In K. R. Dittrich, editor, *Advances in Object-Oriented Database Systems*, pages 193–203. Springer-Verlag, 1988.

[HULL87] R. Hull and R. King. Semantic database modeling: Survey, applications, and research issues. *ACM Computing Surveys*, 19(3):201–260, September 1987.

[IBM74] IBM Corporation, IBM Corp., White Plains, NY *IMS-VS general information manual, GH20-1260*, April 1974.

[IBM81] IBM Corporation, GH24-5013-0, File No. S370-50. *SQL/Data System: Concepts and Facilities*, 1981.

[ISO87] ISO TC97/SC21/WG4/N399 Management Framework Editing Meeting. Position paper concerning OSI management domains, June 1987.

[ISRAEL84] D. Israel and R. Brachman. Some remarks on the semantics of representation languages. In M. Brodie, J. Mylopoulos, and J.W. Schmidt, editors, *On Conceptual Modeling*. Springer-Verlag, 1984.

[JAGANNATHAN88] D. Jagannathan, R. L. Fritchman, B. L. Guck, J. P. Thompson, and D. M. Tolbert. SIM: A database system based on the semantic data model. In *Proceedings of the ACM SIGMOD International Conference on Management of Data*, pages 46–55. ACM SIGMOD, June 1988.

[JAIN88] Rajeev Jain. *LagerIV Distribution 1.0*. Electronic Research Laboratory, University of California, Berkeley, CA, June 1988.

[KATZ81] R. ·H. Katz and N. Goodman. View processing in multibase—a heterogeneous database system. In P. Chen, editor, *An Entity-Relationship Approach to Information Modelling and Analysis*, pages 259–280. ER Institute, 1981.

References

[KATZ82] R. H. Katz. A database approach for managing VLSI design data. In *Proceedings of the 19th Design Automation Conference*, 1982.

[KATZ84] R.H. Katz, W. Scacchi, and P. Subrahmanyam. Development environments for VLSI and software. *Journal of Systems and Software*, 4:13–26, 1984.

[KATZ86] R. H. Katz, E. Chang, and R. Bhateja. Version modeling concepts for computer-aided design databases. In *Proceedings of the ACM SIGMOD International Conference on Management of Data*, Washington, D.C., May 1986. ACM SIGMOD.

[KEMPER87] A. Kemper and M. Wallrath. An analysis of geometric modeling in database systems. *ACM Computing Survey*, 19(1), 1987.

[KEMPF86] J. Kempf and A. Snyder. Persistent objects on a database. Technical Report STL-86-12, Hewlett-Packard Laboratories, September 1986.

[KENT79] W. Kent. Limitations of record-oriented information models. *ACM Transactions on Database Systems*, 4(1):107–131, March 1979.

[KERNIGHAN78] B. Kernighan and D. Ritchie. *The C Programming Language*. Prentice Hall, 1980.

[KERSCHBERG84] L. Kerschberg, editor. *Proceedings of the International Workshop on Expert Database Systems*. ACM, October 1984.

[KETABCHI86] M. Ketabchi. A matrix of CAD applications requirements/DBMS capabilities. Internal memo, Department Of Electrical Engineering and Computer Science, Santa Clara University, Santa Clara, CA, 1986.

[KHOSHAFIAN86] S.N. Khoshafian and G.P. Copeland. Object identity. In *Proc. OOPSLA '86*, Portland, OR, Sept. 1986 and 406-416.

[KIM87] W. Kim, J. Banerjee, H. T. Chou, J. F. Garza, and D. Woelk. Composite object support in an object-oriented database system. In *Proceedings of the Conference on Object-Oriented Programming Systems, Languages, and Applications*, pages 118–125, 1987.

[KIM88A] W. Kim and H. Chou. Versions of schema for object-oriented databases. In *Proceedings of the International Conference on Very Large Databases*. VLDB Endowment, IEEE, ACM SIGMOD, September 1988.

[KIM88B] W. Kim, N. Ballou, H. Chou, J.F. Garza, and D. Woelk. Integrating an object-oriented programming system with a database system. In *Proceedings of the Conference on Object-Oriented Programming Systems, Languages, and Applications*, pages 142–152, 1988.

[KIMBLETON78] S. Kimbleton, H. Wood, and M. Fitzgerald. Network operating systems—an implementation approach. In *Proceedings of the National Computer Conference*, pages 773–782. AFIPS, June 1978.

[KIMBLETON79] S. Kimbleton, P. Wang, and E. Fong. XNDM: An experimental network data manager. In *Proceedings of the Berkeley Workshop on Distributed Data Management and Computer Networks*, pages 3–17. University of California, Berkeley, CA, August 1979.

[KING82] R. King and D. McLeod. The event database specification model. In *Proceedings of International Conference on Improving Database Usability and Responsiveness*, June 1982.

[KING84] R. King and D. McLeod. A unified model and methodology for information system design and evolution. In M. L. Brodie, J. Mylopoulos, and J. W. Schmidt, editors, *Perspectives on Conceptual Modeling*. Springer-Verlag, 1984.

[KING85A] R. King and D. McLeod. A database design methodology and tool for information systems. *ACM Transactions on Office Information Systems*, 3(1), January 1985.

[KING85B] R. King and D. McLeod. Semantic database models. In S. B. Yao, editor, *Principles of Database Design*, pages 115–150. Prentice Hall, 1985.

[KLERER88] S.M. Klerer. The OSI management architecture: An overview. *IEEE Network*, 2(2):20–29, March 1988.

[KNAPP83] D. Knapp, J. Granacki, and A. Parker. An expert synthesis system. In *Proceedings of the International Conference on Computer-Aided Design*, pages 419–424. ACM/IEEE, September 1983.

[KNAPP85] D. Knapp and A. Parker. A unified representation for design information. In *Proceedings of the Conference on Hardware Description Languages*. IFIP, 1985.

[KOENIG88] A. Koenig. Associative arrays in C++. In *Proc. of 1988 Summer USENIX Conference*, 1988.

[KOLLARITSCH89] P. Kollaritsch, S. Lusky, D. Matzke, D. Smith, and P. Stanford. A unified design representation can work. In *Proceedings of ACM/IEEE 26th Design Automation Conference*, pages 811–813, Las Vegas Convention Center, Las Vegas, NV June 1989.

[KROENKE83] D. Kroenke. *Database Processing*. Science Research Associates, 1983.

References

[KUNG81] H.T. Kung and J. Robinson. On optimistic methods for concurrency control. *ACM Trans. Database Syst.*, 6(2), June 1981.

[LAM88] H. Lam, S. Y. W. Su, A. M. Alshqur, and M. S. Guo. OSAM*: A departure from tuple/record oriented databases. Technical report, Database Systems Research and Development Center, University of Florida, Gainesville, FL, 1988.

[LANDIS87] G. Landis. Maintaining design evolution and history information in an object-oriented CAD/CAM database. In *Proceedings of IEEE COMPCON*, 1987.

[LANDIS88] G. Landis. Abstract state and object behavior. Internal memo, Ontologic, Inc., Billerica, MA, 1988.

[LECLUSE88] C. Lecluse, P. Richard, and F. Velez. O2, an object-oriented data model. In *Proceedings of the ACM SIGMOD International Conference on Management of Data*, pages 424–433, Chicago, IL, June 1988. ACM SIGMOD.

[LEDGARD81] H. Ledgard and M. Marcotty. *The Programming Language Landscape.* Science Research Associates, 1981.

[LEE89] K.-J. Lee. Test generation system (tgs) user's manual. Technical Report CENG 89-03, University of Southern California, Department of Electric al Engineering–Systems, June 1988.

[LENZERINI87] M. Lenzerini. Covering and disjointness constraints in type networks. In *Proceedings on Data Engineering Conference*, 1987.

[LEVESQUE86] H. Levesque and R. Brachman. A fundamental tradeoff in knowledge representation and reasoning. In *Readings in Knowledge Representation.* Morgan Kaufman, 1986.

[LI88A] Q. Li and D. McLeod. Object flavor evolution in an object-oriented database system. In *Proceedings of the Conference on Office Information System.* ACM, March 1988.

[LI88B] Q. Li and D. McLeod. Supporting object flavor evolution through learning in an object-oriented database system. In *Proceedings of the International Conference on Expert Database Systems*, April 1988.

[LIEN78] Y. E. Lien and J. H. Ying. Design of a distributed entity-relationship database system. In *Proceedings of the International Computer Software and Applications Conference*, pages 277–282. IEEE, November 1978.

[LIN85] Herbert Lin. The development of software for ballistic-missile defense. *Scientific American*, 253(6):46–53, December 1985.

[LINDSAY80] B. Lindsay and P. Selinger. Site autonomy issues in R*: A distributed database management system. IBM Research Report RJ2927, IBM Research Laboratory, San Jose, CA, September 1980.

[LISKOV77] B. Liskov, A. Snyder, R. Atkinson, and C. Schaffert. Abstraction mechanisms in CLU. *Communications of the ACM*, 20(8):564–576, August 1977.

[LISKOV81] B. Liskov, R. Atkinson, T. Bloom, E. Moss, C. Schaffert, R. Scheifler, and A. Snyder. *CLU Reference Manual.* Springer-Verlag, 1981.

[LISKOV88] B. Liskov. Data abstraction and hierarchy. *ACM SIGPLAN Notices, Addendum to the Proceedings of OOPSLA '87*, 23(5), 1988.

[LITWIN80] W. Litwin. A model for distributed databases. In *Proceedings of the ACM Second Annual Louisiana Computer Exposition*, pages 1–36. ACM, February 1980.

[LITWIN81] W. Litwin. Logical design of distributed databases. Technical Report MOD-I-043, INRIA, Paris, France, July 1981.

[LIU87] L.C. Liu and E. Horowitz. A formal model for software project management. Technical Report CRI 87-41, University of Southern California, Los Angeles, CA, 1987. Also *IEEEE Trans. on S/W Engr.* 10/89

[LIU88A] L.C. Liu and E. Horowitz. Object database support for a software project management environment. Technical Report CRI 88-71, University of Southern California, 1988. Also appeared in *ACM SIGSOFT '88: Third Symposium on Software Development Environments.*

[LIU88B] L.C. Liu. *An Integrated Systems Approach for Software Project Management.* PhD thesis, Computer Science Dept., University of Southern California, Los Angeles, CA, 1988.

[LIU88C] L.C. Liu. A graphic oriented Vbase object type hierarchy browser. In Rajiv Gupta, editor, *Proceedings of the Vbase User's Group Meeting*, May 1988.

[LOCHOVSKY85] F. Lochovsky, editor. *Database Engineering (Special issue on object-oriented systems)*, volume 8. IEEE Computer Society, December 1985.

[LOOMIS87] M. Loomis and J. Rumbaugh. An object-modeling technique for conceptual design. In *ECOOP-87*, 1987.

[LORIE81] R. Lorie. Issues in databases for design applications. IBM Computer Science Research Report RJ3176, IBM, July 1981.

[LORIE83] R. Lorie and W. Plouffe. Complex objects and their use in design transactions. In *Proceedings of the ACM SIGMOD International Conference on Management of Data*, May 1983.

[LYNGBAEK83] P. Lyngbaek and D. McLeod. An approach to object sharing in distributed database systems. In *Proceedings of the International Conference on Very Large Databases*. VLDB Endowment, October 1983.

[LYNGBAEK84A] P. Lyngbaek and D. McLeod. Object sharing in distributed information systems. *ACM Transactions on Office Information Systems*, 2(2):96–122, April 1984.

[LYNGBAEK84B] P. Lyngbaek and D. McLeod. A personal data manager. In *Proceedings of the International Conference on Very Large Databases*. VLDB Endowment, August 1984.

[LYNGBAEK86] P. Lyngbaek and W. Kent. A data modeling methodology for the design and implementation of information systems. In *Proceedings of the International Workshop on Object-Oriented Database Systems*, pages 6–17. ACM/IEEE, September 1986.

[MAIER85] D. Maier, A. Otis, and A. Purdy. Object-oriented database development at Servio Logic. *Database Eng.*, 8(4), December 1985.

[MAIER86A] D. Maier, J. Stein, A. Otis, and A. Purdy. Development of an object-oriented DBMS. *ACM SIGPLAN Not., Proceedings OOPSLA '86*, 21(11), November 1986.

[MAIER86B] D. Maier and J. Stein. Indexing in an object-oriented DBMS. In *Proceedings of the 1986 International Workshop on Object-Oriented Database Management Systems*, Asilomar, Calif., September 1986. IEEE Computer Society Press, Washington, DC.

[MAIER87] D. Maier. Data model requirements for engineering applications. In *1st Workshop on Expert Database Systems*, 1984.

[MANOLA86] F. Manola and U. Dayal. PDM: An object-oriented data model. In *Proc. of the Int'l Workshop Object-Oriented Database System*, Asilomar, CA, Sept. 1986.

[MCCREIGHT77] E. M. McCreight. Pagination of B*-Trees with variable-length records. *CACM*, 20(9):670–674, September 1977.

[MCLEOD76] D. McLeod. A framework for database protection and its application to the INGRES and System R database management systems. In *Proceedings of the International Computer Software and Applications Conference*. IEEE, October 1976.

[MCLEOD77] D. McLeod. High-level definition of abstract domains in a relational database system. *Journal of Computer Languages*, 2(3):61–73, 1977.

[MCLEOD82] D. McLeod. A database transaction specification methodology for end-users. *Information Systems*, 7(3):253–264, 1982.

[MCLEOD83] D. McLeod, K. V. Bapa Rao, and K. Narayanaswamy. An approach to information management for CAD/VLSI applications. In *Proceedings of the ACM SIGMOD International Conference on Management of Data*, May 1983.

[MCLEOD85] D. McLeod and S. Widjojo. Object management and sharing in distributed, autonomous databases. *IEEE Database Engineering*, 8(4):83–89, December 1985.

[MCLEOD86] D. McLeod. An object-oriented approach to databases for VLSI/CAD. In *Proceedings of the Workshop on Information System Support for Integrated Design and Manufacturing Processes*, April 1986.

[MCLEOD88] D. McLeod. A learning-based approach to meta-data evolution in an object-oriented database. In K. R. Dittrich, editor, *Advances in Object-Oriented Database Systems*, pages 219–224. Springer-Verlag, 1988.

[METCALFE76] R. Metcalfe and D. Boggs. Ethernet: Distributed packet switching for local computer networks. *Communications of the ACM*, 19(7):395–404, June 1976.

[MEYER85] B. Meyer. Eifel: a language for software engineering. Technical Report TRCS85-19, University of California, Santa Barbara, CA, 1985.

[MEYER88] B. Meyer. *Object-oriented Software Construction*. Prentice Hall, New York, 1988.

[MEYROWITZ86] N. Meyrowitz. Intermedia: The architecture and construction of an object-oriented hypermedia system and applications framework. In *Proceedings of Object-Oriented Programming Systems, Languages, and Applications*, 1986.

[MICHALSKI83A] R. Michalski, J. Carbonell, and T. Mitchell, editors. *Machine Learning: An Artificial Intelligence Approach (Volume 1)*. Tioga Publishing Company, 1983.

[MICHALSKI83B] R. Michalski and R. Stepp. Learning from observation: Conceptual clustering. In R. Michalski, J. Carbonell, and T. Mitchell, editors, *Machine Learning: An Artificial Intelligence Approach (Volume 1)*, pages 331–364. Tioga Publishing Company, 1983.

[MICHALSKI86A] R. Michalski. Understanding the nature of learning. In R. Michalski, J. Carbonell, and T. Mitchell, editors, *Machine Learning: An Artificial Intelligence Approach (Volume 2)*, pages 3–25. Morgan Kaufmann, 1986.

[MICHALSKI86B] R. Michalski, J. Carbonell, and T. Mitchell, editors. *Machine Learning: An Artificial Intelligence Approach (Volume 2)*. Morgan Kaufmann, 1986.

[MICROSOFT86] Microsoft Corporation, Bellevue, Washington. *Microsoft Project*, 1986.

[MILLER88] W.M. Miller. Exception handling without language extensions. In *USENIX C++ Conference Proceedings*, 1988.

[MILLER89] J. Miller, K. Gröning, G. Schulz, and C. White. The object-oriented integration methodology of the Cadlab workstation design environment. In *Proceedings of ACM/IEEE 26th Design Automation Conference*, pages 807–810, Las Vegas Convention Center, Las Vegas, NV, June 1989.

[MOON86] David A. Moon. Object-oriented programming with Flavors. In *OOPSLA Conference Proceedings*, pages 1–8. ACM, November 1986. Also published as SIGPLAN Notices, (21):11, November, 1986.

[MOON88] D. A. Moon. The Common Lisp object-oriented programming language standard. In W. Kim and F. Lochovsky, editors, *Object-Oriented Concepts, Applications, and Databases*. Addison-Wesley, 1988.

[MOSS81] E. Moss. *Nested Transactions: An Approach to Reliable Distributed Computing*. PhD thesis, Massachusetts Institute of Technology, Cambridge MA, April 1981.

[MOSS86] E. Moss. The theory of nested transactions. Technical report, University of Massachusetts, Amherst, MA, 1986.

[MOTRO81] A. Motro and P. Buneman. Constructing superviews. In *Proceedings of the ACM SIGMOD International Conference on Management of Data*. ACM SIGMOD, April 1981.

[MOTRO84A] A. Motro. Browsing in a loosely structured database. In *Proceedings of the ACM SIGMOD International Conference on Management of Data*, pages 197–207. ACM SIGMOD, April 1984.

[MOTRO84B] A. Motro. Query generalization: A technique for handling query failure. In *Proceedings of the International Conference on Expert Database Systems*, 1984.

[MOTRO86A] A. Motro. SEAVE: A mechanism for verifying user presuppositions in query systems. *ACM Transactions on Office Information Systems*, 4(4):312–330, October 1986.

[MOTRO86B] A. Motro. BAROQUE: A browser for relational databases. *ACM Transactions on Office Information Systems*, 4(2):164–181, April 1986.

[MOTRO88] A. Motro, A. D'Atri, and L. Tarantino. KIVIEW: An object-oriented browser. In *Proceedings of the International Conference on Expert Database Systems*, March 1988.

[MYLOPOULOS80A] J. Mylopoulos, P. Bernstein, and H. K. T. Wong. A language facility for designing database-intensive applications. *ACM Transactions on Database Systems*, 5(2):185–207, June 1980.

[MYLOPOULOS80B] J. Mylopoulos. An overview of knowledge representation. In *Proceedings of Workshop on Data Abstraction, Database, and Conceptual Modeling*, Pingree Park, CO, June 1980.

[NARAYANASWAMY88] K. Narayanaswamy and K. V. Bapa Rao. An incremental mechanism for schema evolution in engineering domains. In *Proceedings of the International Conference on Data Engineering*, pages 294–301. IEEE, January 1988.

[NAVATHE76] S. Navathe and J. Fry. Restructuring for large databases. *ACM Transactions on Database Systems*, 1(2):138–158, June 1976.

[NAVATHE80] S. Navathe. Schema analysis for database restructuring. *ACM Transactions on Database Systems*, 5(2):157–184, June 1980.

[NAVATHE82] S. Navathe and S. G. Gadgil. A methodology for view integration in logical data base design. In *Proceedings of the International Conference on Very Large Databases*. VLDB Endowment, 1982.

[NEUHOLD77] E. Neuhold and H. Biller. POREL: A distributed database on an inhomogeneous computer network. In *Proceedings of the International Conference on Very Large Databases*, pages 380–395. IEEE, October 1977.

[NEUHOLD88] E. Neuhold and M. Stonebraker. Future directions in DBMS research. Technical Report Tech. Rep.-88-001, Int'l Computer Science Inst., Berkeley, CA, May 1988.

[NIKHIL88] R.S. Nikhil. Functional databases, functional languages. In M.P. Atkinson, E P. Buneman, and E R. Morrison, editors, *Data Types and Persistence*, pages 51–67. Springer-Verlag, 1988.

[NIXON87] B. Nixon, L. Chung, D. Lauzon, A. Borgida, J. Mylopoulis, and M. Stanley. Implementation of a compiler for a semantic data model. In *Proc. ACM-SIGMOD 1987 Int'l Conf. on Management of Data*, pages 118–131, San Francisco, CA, May 1987.

[O'BRIEN86] P. O'Brien, P. Bullis, and C. Schaffert. Persistent and shared objects in Trellis/Owl. In *Proc. Int'l Workshop Object-Oriented Database System*, pages 113–123, Asilomar, CA, Sept. 1986.

[ONTOLOGIC88A] Ontologic, Inc., 47 Manning Road, Billerica, MA 01821. *Vbase Reference Manual—Vbase Release 1.0*, 1988.

[ONTOLOGIC88B] Ontologic, Inc., 47 Manning Road, Billerica, MA 01821. *COP Reference Manual*, 1988.

[OPPEN83] D. Oppen and Y. Yogen. The Clearinghouse: A decentralized agent for locating named objects in a distributed environment. *ACM Transactions on Office Information Systems*, 1(3):230–253, July 1983.

[OSBORN88A] S.L. Osborn. Identity, equality and query optimization. In K. R. Dittrich, editor, *Advances in Object-Oriented Database Systems*, pages 346–351. Springer-Verlag, 1988.

[OSBORN88B] S. L. Osborn. An object-oriented critique of traditional database models. Internal report, University of Western Ontario, 1988.

[OSTERWEIL87] L. Osterweil. Software processes are software too. In *Proceedings of the 9th International Conference on Software Engineering*, pages 2–13, Monterey, CA, March 30-April 2, 1987.

[PASCO86] G.A. Pasco. Encapsulators: A new software paradigm in Smalltalk-80. *ACM SIGPLAN Not.*, 21(11), November 1986.

[PATON88] N. W. Paton and P. M. D. Gray. Identification of database objects by key. In K. R. Dittrich, editor, *Advances in Object-Oriented Database Systems*, pages 280–285. Springer-Verlag, 1988.

[PAUL87] H.B. Paul, H.J. Schek, M.H. Scholl, G. Weikum, and U. Deppisch. Architecture and implementation of the Darmstadt database kernel system. In *Proc. ACM-SIGMOD 1987 Int'l Conf. on Management of Data*, pages 196–207, San Fransisco, CA, May 1987.

[PENEDO86] M. H. Penedo. Prototyping a project master database for software engineering environments. In *Proceedings of the ACM SIGSOFT/SIGPLAN Software Engineering Symposium on Practical Software Development Environments*, pages 1–11, December 1986.

[PENNEY87] D. J. Penney and J. Stein. Class modification in the GemStone object-oriented DBMS. In *Proceedings of the Conference on Object-Oriented Programming Systems, Languages, and Applications*, pages 111–117, 1987.

[PORTER88] H. H. Porter, E. F. Ecklund, D. J. Ecklund, T. L. Anderson, and B. Schneider. A distributed object server. In K. R. Dittrich, editor, *Advances in Object-Oriented Database Systems*, pages 43–59. Springer-Verlag, 1988.

[PPRG85] Persistent Programming Research Group, Computing Science Dept., Univ. Glasgow, Glasgow, Scotland. *The PS-Algol Reference Manual*, 2nd ed, tech. rep. ppr-12-85 edition, 1985.

[PURDY87] A. Purdy, B. Schuchardt, and D. Maier. Integrating an object server with other worlds. *ACM Transactions on Office Information Systems*, 5(1):27–47, January 1987.

[REITER78] R. Reiter. On closed world databases. In H. Gallaire and J. Minker, editors, *Logic and Databases*, pages 55–76. Plenum Press, 1978.

[RICHARDSON88] J.E. Richardson and M.J. Carey. Persistence in the E language: Issues and implementation. Technical Report Computer Sciences Tech. Rep. #791, Univ. Wisconsin, Madison, WI Sept. 1988.

[RICHARDSON89] J.E. Richardson, M.J. Carey, and D.H. Schuh. The design of the E programming language. Technical Report Computer Sciences Tech. Rep. #824, Univ. Wisconsin, Madison, WI Feb. 1989.

[ROCHKIND75] M.J. Rochkind. The source code control system. In *Proceedings of the First National Conference on Software Engineering, IEEE, New York*, pages 37–43, 1975.

[ROSENKRANTZ80] D. Rosenkrantz and Harry B. Hunt III. Processing conjunctive predicates and queries. In *Proceedings of International Conference on Very Large Databases*, 1980.

[ROTHNIE77] J. Rothnie and N. Goodman. A survey of research and development in distributed database management. In *Proceedings of the International Conference on Very Large Databases*, pages 48–62. IEEE, October 1977.

[ROTHNIE80] J. Rothnie, P. Bernstein, S. Fox, N. Goodman, M. Hammer, T. Landers, C. Reeve, D. Shipman, and E. Wong. Introduction to a system for distributed databases (SDD-1). *ACM Transactions on Database Systems*, 5(1):1–17, March 1980.

[ROWE79] L. Rowe and K. Shoens. Data abstraction, views, and updates in Rigel. In *Proceedings of the ACM SIGMOD International Conference on Management of Data*, pages 71–81, Boston, MA, May 1979. ACM SIGMOD.

[ROWE87] L.A. Rowe and M.R. Stonebraker. The POSTGRES data model. In *Proc. 13th Int'l Conf. Very Large Data Bases*, pages 83–96, Brighton, England, Sept. 1987.

[ROYCE87] W.W. Royce. Managing the development of large software systems. In *Proceedings of the 9th International Conference on Software Engineering*, pages 328–338, Monterey, CA, March 30–April 2 1987.

[RPC-MANUAL] Sun Manual, Sun Microsystems. *Remote Procedure Call/External Data Representation, Network Programming.*

[RUBENSTEIN87] W. Rubenstein, M. Kubicar, and R. Cattell. Benchmarking simple database operations. In *Proceedings of the ACM SIGMOD International Conference on Management of Data*, pages 387–394, 1987.

[SAKKINEN88] M. Sakkinen. On the darker side of C++. In *Proceedings of ECOOP '88, European Conference on Object-Oriented Programming.* Springer-Verlag, 1988.

[SCHAFFERT86] C. Schaffert, T. Cooper, B. Bullis, M. Kilian, and C. Wilpolt. An introduction to Trellis/Owl. *ACM SIGPLAN Notices, Proceedings OOPSLA '86*, 21(11), 1986.

[SCHEK86] H.J. Schek and M. Scholl. The relation model with relation-valued attributes. *Information Sys.*, 11(2), 1986.

[SCHLAGETER88] G. Schlageter, R. Unland, W. Wilkes, R. Zieschang, G. Maul, A M. Nagl, and R. Meyer. OOPS—An object-oriented programming system with integrated data management facility. In *Proc. IEEE 4th Int'l Conf. Data Engineering*, pages 118–125, Los Angeles, CA, Feb. 1988.

[SCHMIDT77] J.W. Schmidt. Some high-level language constructs for data of type relation. *ACM Trans. Database Syst.*, 2(3):247–261, Sept. 1977.

[SCHMIDT87] J.W. Schmidt, J. Paredaens, and P. DeBra. Database models, where they are going? (Summary of panel discussion). In J. Biskup, J. Demetrovics, J. Paredaens, and B. Thalheim, editors, *Proceedings of 1st Symposium on Mathematical Fundamentals of Database Systems (MFDBS87), Lecture Notes in Computer Science*, pages 239–240. Springer-Verlag, 1987.

[SCHUCHARDT86] B. Schuchardt. GemStone to Smalltalk interface. From Poster Session of ACM OOPSLA-86 Conference, 1986.

[SCHWARZ86] P.M. Schwarz, W. Chang, J.C. Freytag, G.M. Lohman, J. McPherson, C. Mohan, and H. Pirahesh. Extensibility in the Starburst database system. In *Proc. Int'l Workshop Object-Oriented Database System*, Asilomar, CA, Sept. 1986.

[SHIPMAN81] D. Shipman. The functional data model and the data language DAPLEX. *ACM Transactions on Database Systems*, 6(1):140–173, March 1981.

[SHOPIRO89] J.E. Shopiro. An example of multiple inheritance in C++: A model of the Iostream library. *ACM SIGPLAN Notices*, 24(12):32–36, December 1989.

[SIDEL80] T. Sidel. Weaknesses of commercial data-base management systems in engineering applications. In *Proceedings of the 17th Design Automation Conference*, New York, NY 1980. ACM.

[SIEPMANN89] E. Siepmann and G. Zimmermann. An object-oriented datamodel for the VLSI design system PLAYOUT. In *Proceedings of ACM/IEEE 26th Design Automation Conference*, pages 814–817, Las Vegas Convention Center, Las Vegas, NV June 1989.

[SKARRA86] A. H. Skarra and S. B. Zdonik. The management of changing types in an object-oriented database. In *Proceedings of the Conference on Object-Oriented Programming Systems, Languages, and Applications*, pages 483–495, 1986.

[SMITH77] J. M. Smith and D. C. P. Smith. Database abstractions: Aggregation and generalization. *ACM Transactions on Database Systems*, 2(2):105–133, June 1977.

[SMITH80] J.M. Smith, S.A. Fox, and T. Landers. ADAPLEX: Rationale and reference manual. Technical Report CCA-83-08, Computer Corporation of America, 1983.

[SMITH81] J. M. Smith, P. Berstein, U. Dayal, N. Goodman, T. Landers, K. Lin, and E. Wong. Multibase: Integrating heterogeneous distributed database systems. In *Proceedings of the National Computer Conference*, pages 487–499. AFIPS, June 1981.

[SMITH83] J.M. Smith, S. Fox, and T. Landers. *ADAPLEX: Rationale and Reference Manual, 2nd ed.* Computer Corp. America, Cambridge, MA, 1983.

[SMITH87] K. Smith and S. Zdonik. Intermedia: A case study of the differences between relational and object-oriented database systems. In *Proceedings of the Conference on Object-Oriented Programming Systems, Languages, and Applications*, pages 452–465. ACM, 1987.

[SMITH88] W.D. Smith, J.R. Jasica, M.J. Hartman, and M.A. d'Abreu. Flexible module generation in the FACE design environment. In *Proceedings of IEEE International Conference on Compter-Aided Design, ICCAD-88*, pages 396–399, Convention Center,Santa Clara, CA, November 1988.

[SNYDER86] A. Snyder. Inheritance and the development of encapsulated software components. In *Proceedings of the Nineteenth Annual International Conference on System Sciences*, 1986.

[STAMOS82] J.W. Stamos. A large object-oriented virtual memory: Grouping strategies, measurements, and performance. Research Report SCG-82-2, Xerox Palo Alto Research Center, Palo Alto, CA, May 1982.

[STEELE84] G.L. Steele Jr. *Common Lisp: The Language.* Digital Press, 1984.

[STEFIK86] M. Stefik and D. Bobrow. Object-oriented programming: Themes and variations. *AI Magazine*, 6(4):40–62, 1986.

[STEMPLE88] D. Stemple, A. Socorro, and T. Sheard. Formalizing objects for databases using ADABTPL. In K. R. Dittrich, editor, *Advances in Object-Oriented Database Systems*, pages 110–128. Springer-Verlag, 1988.

[STENNING87] V. Stenning. On the role of an environment. In *Proceedings of the 9th International Conference on Software Engineering*, pages 30–34, Monterey, CA, March 30-April 2 1987.

[STEPP86] R. Stepp and R. Michalski. Conceptual clustering: Inventing goal-oriented classifications of structured objects. In R. Michalski, J. Carbonell, and T. Mitchell, editors, *Machine Learning: An Artificial Intelligence Approach (Volume 2)*, pages 471–498. Morgan Kaufmann, 1986.

[STEPSTONE86] Stepstone, Inc., Sandy Hook, CT. *Objective-C Reference Manual*, 1986.

[STONEBRAKER76] M. Stonebraker, E. Wong, P. Kreps, and G. Held. The design and implementation of INGRES. *ACM Transactions on Database Systems*, 1(3), 1976.

[STONEBRAKER77] M. Stonebraker and E. Neuhold. A distributed database version of INGRES. In *Proceedings of the Berkeley Workshop on Distributed Data Management and Computer Networks*, pages 19–36. University of California, Berkeley, May 1977.

[STONEBRAKER82] M. Stonebraker and J. Kalash. TIMBER: A sophisticated relation browser. In *Proceedings of the International Conference on Very Large Databases*. VLDB Endowment, September 1982.

[STONEBRAKER83] M. Stonebraker, B. Rubenstein, and A. Guttman. Application of abstract data types and abstract indices to CAD databases. In *Proceedings of the ACM SIGMOD International Conference on Management of Data*, May 1983.

[STONEBRAKER86A] M. Stonebraker and L.A. Rowe. The design of Postgres. In *ACM SIGMOND Record*, volume 15, 2, pages 340–355, June 1986.

[STONEBRAKER86B] M. Stonebraker, editor. *The Ingres Papers: Anatomy of a Relational Database System*. Addison-Wesley, 1986.

[STONEBRAKER88] M. Stonebraker, E.N. Hanson, and S. Potamianos. The POSTGRES rule manager. *IEEE Trans. Software Eng.*, 14(7):897–907, July 1988.

[STROUSTRUP86] B. Stroustrup. *The C++ Programming Language*. Addison Wesley, 1986.

[STROUSTRUP87A] B. Stroustrup. What is object-oriented programming? In *Proceedings of ECOOP '87, European Conference on Object-Oriented Programming*, 1987.

[STROUSTRUP87B] B. Stroustrup. The evolution of C++, 1985 to 1987. In *USENIX Proceedings and Additional Papers, C++ Workshop*, USENIX Association, PO Box 2299, Berkeley, CA 94710, 1987.

[STROUSTRUP87C] B. Stroustrup. Possible directions for C++. In *USENIX Proceedings and Additional Papers, C++ Workshop*, USENIX Association, PO Box 2299, Berkeley, CA 94710, 1987.

[STROUSTRUP87D] B. Stroustrup. Multiple inheritance for C++. In *Proc. of EUUG Conference*, Helsinki, May 1987.

[STROUSTRUP88A] B. Stroustrup. What is object-oriented programming? *IEEE Software*, pages 10–20, May 1988.

[STROUSTRUP88B] B. Stroustrup. Parameterized types for C++. In *USENIX Proceedings and Additional Papers, C++ Workshop*, USENIX Association, PO Box 2299, Berkeley, CA 94710, 1987.

[STROUSTRUP88C] B. Stroustrup. Type-safe linkage for C++. In *USENIX Proceedings and Additional Papers, C++ Workshop*, USENIX Association, PO Box 2299, Berkeley, CA 94710, 1987.

[STROUSTRUP89A] B. Stroustrup. The evolution of C++: 1985 to 1989. Technical Report CSTR #144, AT&T Bell Labs, 1989.

[STROUSTRUP89B] B. Stroustrup. *C++ Reference Manual*. AT&T Bell Labs, 1989.

[SU80] S. Y. W. Su and D. H. Lo. A semantic association model for conceptual database design. In *Entity-Relationship Approach to Systems Analysis and Design*, pages 147–171. North-Holland, 1980.

[SUN86] Sun Microsystems, Inc., 2550 Garcia Avenue, Mountain View CA. *SunView Programmer's Guide*, 1986.

[SUPERPROJECT86] Computer Associates. *SuperProject: Project and Resource Management System*, 1986.

[SWARTOUT78] D. Swartout and J. Fry. Towards the support of integrated views of multiple databases: An aggregate schema facility. In *Proceedings of the ACM SIGMOD International Conference on Management of Data*, pages 132–143. ACM SIGMOD, May 1978.

[SYMBOLICS84] Symbolics Inc., Cambridge, MA. *FLAV Objects, Message Passing, and Flavors*, 1984.

[TANENBAUM81] A. Tanenbaum. *Computer Networks*. Prentice Hall, 1981.

References   **421**

[TEICHROEW77] D. Teichroew and E.A. Hershey. PSL/PSA: A computer-aided technique for structured documentation and analysis of information processing systems. *IEEE Trans. on Software Engineering*, SE-3(1):41–48, 1977.

[TESLER84] L. Tesler. *Object-Pascal Report*. Apple Computer, 1984.

[TICHY86] W. Tichy. RCS: A system for version control. *Software Practice and Experience*, 15(7):637–654, July 1986.

[TSICHRITZIS77] D. Tsichritzis and F. Lochovsky. *Database Management Systems*. Academic Press, 1977.

[TSICHRITZIS81] D. Tsichritzis. Integrating database and message systems. In *Proceedings of the International Conference on Very Large Databases*, pages 356–362. IEEE, September 1981.

[TSICHRITZIS82] D. Tsichritzis and F. Lochovsky. *Data Models*. Prentice Hall, 1982.

[ULLMAN82] J. Ullman. *Principles of Database Systems*. Computer Science Press, 1983.

[ULLMAN85] J. Ullman. Implementation of logical query languages for databases. *ACM Transactions on Database Systems*, 10(3):289–321, September 1985.

[UNGAR87] D. Ungar and R. Smith. Self: The power of simplicity. *ACM SIGPLAN Notices, Proceedings OOPSLA '87*, 22(12), 1987.

[VEGDAHL86] S.R. Vegdahl. Moving structures between Smalltalk images. In *OOPSLA Conference Proceedings*, pages 466–471. ACM, November 1986. Also published as SIGPLAN Notices, (21):11, November, 1986.

[WALKER87] J. H. Walker, D. A. Moon, D. L. Weinreb, and M. McMahon. The Symbolics Genera programming environment. *IEEE Software*, 4(6), November 1987.

[WASSERMAN79] A. Wasserman. The data management facilities of PLAIN. In *Proc. ACM-SIGMOD 1979 Int'l Conf. on Management of Data*, Boston, MA, May-June 1979.

[WEGNER87] P. Wegner. Dimensions of object-based language design. *ACM SIGPLAN Notices, Proceedings OOPSLA '87*, 22(12), 1987.

[WEINREB88] D. Weinreb, N. Feinberg, D. Gerson, and C. Lamb. An object-oriented database system to support an integrated programming environment. Internal report, Symbolics, February 1988.

[WHITE86] J.E. White. A high-level framework for network-based resource sharing. In *Proceedings of the National Computer Conference, (New York, NY)*. AFIPS Press, Reston, VA, June 1986.

[WIEDERHOLD80] G. Wiederhold and R. El-Masri. Structural model for database design. In *Entity-Relationship Approach to Systems Analysis and Design*. North-Holland, 1980.

[WIEDERHOLD82] G. Wiederhold, A. Beetem, and G. Short. A database approach to communication in VLSI design. *IEEE Transactions on Computer-Aided Design of Integrated Circuits and Systems*, 1(2):57–63, April 1982.

[WIENER88] R. S. Wiener and L. J. Pinson. *An Introduction to Object-Oriented Programming and C++*. Addison-Wesley, 1988.

[WILLETT88] M. Willett and R.D. Martin. LAN management in an IBM framework. *IEEE Network*, 2(2):6–12, March 1988.

[WIRFS-BROCK88] A. Wirfs-Brock. An overview of modular Smalltalk. In *Proceedings of the Conference on Object-Oriented Programming Systems, Languages, and Applications*, pages 123–134. ACM, 1988.

[WOELK86] D. Woelk, W. Kim, and W. Luther. An object-oriented approach to multimedia databases. In *Proceedings ACM SIGMOD Conference on the Management of Data*, 1986.

[WOELK87] D. Woelk and W. Kim. Multimedia information management in an object-oriented database system. In *Proceedings of the International Conference on Very Large Databases*. VLDB Endowment, September 1987.

[WOLF89] W.H. Wolf. How to build a hardware description and measurement system on an object-oriented programming language. *IEEE Transactions on Computer-Aided Design*, 8(3):288–301, March 1989.

[WONG79] S. Wong and W. Bristol. A computer aided design database. In *Proceedings of the 16th ACM/IEEE Design Automation Conference*, June 1979.

[WOO85] C.C. Woo and F.H. Lochovsky. An object-based approach to modeling office work. *Database Eng.*, 8(4), December 1985.

[WOODS75] W. A. Woods. What's in a link: Foundations for semantic networks. In D. Bobrow and A. Collins, editors, *Representation and Understanding: Studies in Cognitive Science*, pages 35–82. Academic Press, 1975.

[WULF76] R. A. Wulf, R. L. London, and M. Shaw. Abstraction and verification in Alphard: Introduction to language and methodology. Technical Report ISI/RR-76-46, University of Southern California, 1976.

[YAO85] S. B. Yao, editor. *Principles of Database Design: Volume 1—Logical Organizations*. Prentice Hall, 1985.

[YU81] K. I. Yu. *Communicative Databases*. PhD thesis, California Institute of Technology, Pasadena, CA, June 1981.

[ZDONIK84] S. Zdonik. Object management system concepts. In *Proceedings of the ACM-SIGOA Conference on Office Information Systems*, pages 13–19, 1984.

[ZDONIK88] S. Zdonik. Data abstraction and query optimization. In K. R. Dittrich, editor, *Advances in Object-Oriented Database Systems*, pages 368–373. Springer-Verlag, 1988.

[ZHU86] Xi an Zhu. *A Knowledge-Based System for Testable Design Methodology Selection*. PhD thesis, Department of Electrical Engineering–Systems, University of Southern California, 1986.

Author Biographies

Rakesh Agrawal
K55/801, IBM Almaden Research Center
650 Harry Road
San Jose, CA 95120

Rakesh Agrawal received the M.S. and Ph.D. degrees in Computer Science from the University of Wisconsin, Madison (U.S.A.) in 1983. He also holds a B.E. degree in Electronics and Communication Engineering from the University of Roorkee, Roorkee (India) and a two-year Post Graduate Diploma in Industrial Engineering from NITIE, Bombay (India). From 1983 to 1989 he was with the AT&T Bell Laboratories, Murray Hill, where he was a member of the technical staff in the Computing Systems Research Laboratory. He is presently with IBM Almaden Research Center, San Jose. Dr. Agrawal has published extensively in technical journals and conferences. His current research interests include object-oriented database systems, deductive database systems, distributed and parallel processing, distributed operating systems, and computer architecture.

Dr. Agrawal is a member of the Association for Computing Machinery and the IEEE Computer Society.

T. Lougenia Anderson
Servio Logic Development Corporation
15025 S.W. Koll Parkway
Beaverton, OR 97223

Lougenia Anderson received her Ph.D. in computer science from the University of Washington in 1981. Since that time she has worked for Burroughs Corporation (now Unisys), Tektronix, and Servio Logic, holding both management and technical positions. Her research interests include data semantics, object-oriented databases, the time dimension of information, CAD/CAM databases, user interfaces to databases, and database design methodology.

Tim Andrews
Ontologic, Inc.
Three Burlington Woods
Burlington, MA 01803

Timothy Andrews is currently Product Manager for Ontologic Inc. Mr. Andrews was born in 1957. He received an A.B. in engineering science from Dartmouth College in 1978. He did graduate study at the Sloan School of Management, MIT, in advanced finance theory. Mr. Andrews was previously with Think Technologies, where he was project leader of an object-oriented database effort being designed under contract to Apple Computer. Prior to that he was a project leader at Prime Computer with responsibility for the specification, design and implementation of a relational database product, INFORMATION.

Arne-Jorgen Berre
Center for Industrial Research
P.O. Box 124
0314 Oslo 3, Norway

Arne-Jorgen Berre is a research scientist in the Department of Distributed Information Systems at the Center for Industrial Research in Oslo, Norway. His research interests include distributed system architectures, object-oriented systems, engineering information systems and engineering databases. Berre received the M.Sc degree from the Norwegian Institute of Technology in 1984, where he currently is a part-time PhD-student. He was a visitor at Oregon Graduate Center during the "Database-Year" 1987 to 1988.

Melvin Breuer
Department of Electrical Engineering—Systems
University of Southern California
Los Angeles, CA 90089-0781

Melvin A. Breuer is a Professor of Electrical Engineering and Computer Science at the University of Southern California, Los Angeles. His main interests are in the area of computer aided design of digital computers, fault tolerant computing, and VLSI circuits.

Dr. Breuer is the editor and co-author of *Design Automation of Digital Systems: Theory and Techniques*, Prentice-Hall; editor of *Digital Systems Design Automation: Languages, Simulation and Data Bases*, Computer Science Press; co-author of *Diagnosis and Reliable Design of Digital Systems*, Computer Science Press; and co-editor of *Computer Hardware Description Languages and their Applications*, North-Holland. He has published over 100 technical papers and was formerly the editor-in-chief of the Journal of Design Automation and Fault Tolerant Computing, the co-editor of the Journal of Digital Systems, and was the Program Chairman of the Fifth International IFIP Conference on Computer Hardware Description Languages and Their Applications.

Dr. Breuer is a member of Sigma Xi, Tau Beta Pi, Eta Kappa Nu, a Fellow of the IEEE, and was a Fulbright-Hays Scholar in 1973. He received both his B.S. in Engineering with Honors and his M.S. in Engineering from the University of California, Los Angeles, in 1959 and 1961, respectively. He received his Ph.D. in electrical engineering from the University of California, Berkeley, in 1965.

Craig Damon
Juniper Software Corporation
23 Longmeadow Road
Chelmsford, MA 01824

Craig A. Damon, born in 1958, was the Project Leader, C-interfaces for Ontologic Inc. Mr. Damon graduated from Bowdoin College in 1981 with a B.A. in physics and philosophy. Earlier, he worked for Mosaic's workstation program, where he built the Pascal compiler, rewrote National Semiconductor's loader and assembler, and built an optimizing code generator for the common intermediate language being used by Mosaic's C, Fortran, and Pascal compilers. Prior to joining Mosaic, Mr. Damon was a project leader with Urban Data Processing. He was responsible for product definition, development, documentation and maintenance.

Joshua Duhl
Ontologic, Inc.
Three Burlington Woods
Burlington, MA 01803

Joshua Duhl is a Member of the Technical Staff at Ontologic. He is a co-designer of Ontologic's interactive Object SQL for Vbase. His areas of interests include user interface management systems, graphical database development tools, and database performance. He co-authored "A performance comparison of object and relational databases using the Sun benchmark," delivered at the 1988 Conference on Object-Oriented Programming Systems, Languages and Applications. Mr. Duhl received his B.S. in Computer Science from Haverford College.

Alexander Dupuy
Department of Computer Science
Columbia University
New York, NY 10027

Alexander Dupuy is a researcher for the Distributed Computing and Communications project in the Computer Science department at Columbia University. He designed and developed Nest, a network simulator distributed by Columbia and now being used at dozens of research organizations around the world.

Wesley Cheng
36-LR, Application Support Division
Hewlett Packard
100 Mayfield Ave
Mountain View, CA 94043

Wesley Cheng is a software development engineer at Hewlett-Packard. His current interests include windowing systems, object-oriented technology, and architectures for parallel processing. He completed his B.S. in Computer Engineering at the University of the Pacific and his M.S. in Computer Engineering at the University of Southern California.

Neil Feinberg
Xerox PARC
3333 Coyote Hill Road
Palo Alto, CA 94304

Neil Feinberg is a Senior Member of the Technical Staff at Symbolics, where he continues to work on Statice and other software products. Previously he was one of the principal developers of Spice Lisp, at Carnegie-Mellon University. His research interests include productivity tools, object-oriented databases, and user interface technology.

Narain Gehani
AT&T Bell Labs
Murray Hill, NJ 07974

Narain Gehani got his Ph.D. in Computer Science from Cornell University in 1975. Since 1978, Dr. Gehani has been with AT&T Bell Laboratories, Murray Hill, NJ. Previously, he was on the computer science faculty at SUNY/Buffalo.

Dr. Gehani's research interests include concurrent programming, programming methodology, programming language design, office automation formal specifications, compilers and databases. He has been involved in the design and development of Concurrent C, a tool for distributed programming. His current work involves the design and development of Exceptional C, a tool for writing reliable programs, and ODE, an object-oriented database.

Dr. Gehani has published many research papers in computer science journals. He has written and edited several books. He is currently an ACM National Lecturer (1982).

Dan Gerson
Xerox PARC
3333 Coyote Hill Road
Palo Alto, CA 94304

Dan Gerson is a research staff member in Xerox's Palo Alto Research Center. At Symbolics, he built the file level of Statice, the virtual memory software for the 36xx workstations, and other software products. Previously, he worked at SRI International and at MIT's Laboratory for Computer Science. His research interests include developing persistent object-oriented languages and databases to support collaborative authoring environments, language and programmer support for both short and long-term coordination between processes and users, virtual and persistent memory management, and operating systems architecture.

Rajesh Gupta
Department of Electrical Engineering—Systems
University of Southern California
Los Angeles, CA 90089-0781

Author Biographies

Rajesh Gupta is a Research Assistant in the Department of Electrical Engineering at the University of Southern California, Los Angeles. His interests are in the area of VLSI design automation, design for testability, and applications of AI in design. He received the B.Tech. degree in Electrical Engineering from the Indian Institute of Technology, Madras, in 1985, and the M.S. degree in Computer Engineering in 1987 from the University of Southern California. In 1979 he was awarded the National Talent Scholarship by the Government of India.

Rajiv Gupta
GE Corporate R&D
KW-C313, P. O. Box 8
Schenectady, NY 12301

Rajiv Gupta received his B.E. (Hons.) and M.Sc. (Hons.) from Birla Institute of Technology and Science, Pilani, India, in January 1982. He was a Junior Software Engineer in Tata Burroughs Ltd, Bombay, from March 1982 to July 1982. Gupta received his M.S. and Ph.D. in Computer Science from the Department of Computer Science at the State University of New York at Stony Brook where he was a Research Assistant from August 1982 to July 1987. He joined the Department of Electrical Engineering Systems at the University of Southern California as a Post Doctoral Research Fellow in the VLSI Test Group. He was a Research Assistant Professor in the same department from June 1988 to May 1990. He is presently a Computer Scientist at the GE Corporate R&D Center. Gupta has published numerous research articles on subjects ranging from system reconfiguration, fault diagnosis, VLSI testing, and logic programming to object-oriented databases for VLSI CAD. His research interests include object-oriented frameworks for VLSI CAD, VLSI testing, system-level fault diagnosis and reconfiguration, and fault-tolerant computing. Gupta is a recipient of the National Science Talent Search Scholarship awarded by the Government of India.

Ido Hardonag
Elan Computer Group, Inc.
888 Villa Street, 3rd Floor
Mt. View, CA 94041

Ido Hardonag is currently a software development engineer at Elan Computer Group. He was a graduate student and a Research Assistant in the Computer Science Department at the University of Southern California at Los Angeles. His research interests are in the areas of CAD and user interfaces using object-oriented databases. Hardonag received his B.S. in Mathematics and Computer Science from Tel Aviv University in 1985.

Craig Harris
Ontologic, Inc.
Three Burlington Woods
Burlington, MA 01803

Born in Japan to a poor family of psychotherapists, Craig Harris received an A.B. degree from Dartmouth College in 1978. His undergraduate thesis focused on an object-oriented approach to natural language understanding, which more or less explains his obscure style of exposition. For the last ten years he's worked on relational and object-oriented database products, most recently as a founder of Ontologic Inc., the makers of Vbase. An avid skier, flamenco guitarist and chess player, Mr. Harris will jump at any opportunity to avoid real work.

Ellis Horowitz
Department of Computer Science
University of Southern California
Los Angeles, CA 90089

Ellis Horowitz received his B.S. degree from Brooklyn College and his Ph.D. in computer science from the University of Wisconsin. He was on the faculty there and at Cornell University before assuming his present post as Professor of Computer Science and Electrical Engineering at the University of Southern California. He is a past chairman of the Computer Science Department at USC. Dr. Horowitz is the author of six books and the past editor of the Computer Software Engineering Series for Computer Science Press. In addition, he has published over sixty research articles on computer science subjects ranging from data structures, algorithms, and software design to computer science education. He is a past associate editor for the journals *Communications of the ACM* and *Transactions on Mathematical Software*.

Hyoung-Joo Kim
School of Information and Computer Sciences
Georgia Institute of Technology
Atlanta, GA 30093

Hyoung-Joo Kim received the B.S. degree in Computer Engineering from Seoul National University, Seoul, Korea, in 1982 and the M.S. and Ph.D. degrees in Computer Sciences from the University of Texas at Austin, in 1985 and 1988, respectively. He was a post-doctoral research fellow at the University of Texas at Austin from April, 1988 to September, 1988. Since September, 1988, he has been with Georgia Institute of Technology, where he is an assistant professor of Information and Computer Science. His current research interests include object-oriented systems and databases, deductive databases, user-friendly graphical environments and computer security. He is a member of ACM, IEEE and AAAI.

George Konstantinow
Delco Systems Operations
6767 Hollister Ave.
Goleta, CA 93117

George Konstantinow is a software engineering and information management specialist from Santa Barbara, California.

Dr. Konstantinow received his B.A. in Mathematics from New College, Sarasota, and his Ph.D. in Computer Science and Biomedical Computing from the University of North Carolina, Chapel Hill. He served on the faculty of Duke University with technical and clinical research interests in medical imaging and software engineering, and managed the RNA Computing Laboratory in the Department of Surgery at the Duke University Medical Center.

After leaving Duke, Dr. Konstantinow became a software configuration management specialist for a Southern California software engineering firm and independent software consultant. He advanced to Member of Technical Staff in Information Systems for Hughes Aircraft Company, Santa Barbara Research Center. His responsibilities at Hughes included designing engineering and manufacturing database applications, establishing data administration procedures, building software engineering environments, and investigating new software technologies for engineering support. Dr. Konstantinow is presently Senior Engineer in CAE Development at Delco Systems Operations, where he is responsible for developing corporate engineering information systems.

Dr. Konstantinow is a member of the IEEE, ACM, and MAA. He is currently co-chair of the IEEE Design Automation Standards Subcommittee, Working Group on Design Management. He has published extensively in the fields of design management, software engineering, and biomedical computing; has participated actively on national committees; and has given presentations at international conferences and seminars in various engineering fields.

Charles Lamb
Object Design, Inc.
One New England Executive Park
Burlington, MA 01803

Charles Lamb is a software developer and co-founder of Object Design, where he is building a high-performance object-oriented database system based on C++. At Symbolics he built and improved many parts of Statice. Previously, he worked at Computer Corporation of America as a technical lead on a distributed CAD/CAM data management facility. Mr. Lamb holds S.B. and S.M. degrees in Computer Science from MIT and is a member of ACM.

Gordon Landis
Object Design, Inc.
One New England Executive Park
Burlington, MA 01803

Gordon Landis was born in 1960. He received an A.B. from Dartmouth College in 1981 with a double major in mathematics and computer science. Mr. Landis worked for Prime Computer as a software engineer and led a development team to enhance the performance of the database interface for Prime's electrical CAD applications. At the Boston Database Group, Mr. Landis held the position of systems programmer; he was responsible for the design of a query language for a relational database management system. Mr. Landis was the principal architect of the object manager component of Vbase.

Qing Li
Department of Computer Science
Australian National University
Canberra, ACT 2601, Australia

Qing Li received B.S. from Hunan University, China in July, 1982, and his M.S. from the University of Southern California (USC) in May 1985. He received his Ph.D. from the Department of Computer Science at USC while working with Prof. Dennis McLeod as his advisor. His dissertation was on object-oriented database evolution through applied machine learning techniques. Li's research interests include database design, modeling, and user interfaces.

Sheng Yaw Lin
Advanced Hi-Tech Corp.
2221 W. Rosecrans Ave.
El Segundo, CA 90245

Sheng Yaw Lin received the B.S. and M.S. degrees from National Chiao Tung University, Taiwan, in 1980 and 1982, respectively. He was a graduate student in the Department of Computer Science at the University of Southern California where he received his M.S. in August, 1986. He is currently a Senior Supervisor in Advanced Hi-Tech Corp., El Segundo, CA. His research interests include functional testing of VLSI/LSI circuits, database technologies and design automation.

Lung-Chun Liu
Senior Member of Technical Staff
Silicon Graphics
2011 North Shoreline Blvd.
Mountain View, CA 94039

Lung-Chun Liu received the B.S. degree in Computer Science from National Chiao-Tung University, Taiwan, Republic of China, in 1980, and the M.S. degree in Electrical Engineering from National Taiwan University, Taiwan, Republic of China, in 1982. He received the Ph.D. degree in 1988 from Computer Science Department at the University of Southern California. His dissertation was in the area of software project management. Liu's principal research interests include design and application of object-oriented databases, project management tools for software development, and integrated software engineering environment.

David Maier
Oregon Graduate Center
19600 N.W. Von Neumann Drive
Beaverton, OR 97006-1999

Dr. David Maier is a Professor of Computer Science & Engineering at Oregon Graduate Center, Beaverton, Oregon. He joined the faculty there in 1982 after spending four years as Assistant Professor of Computer Science at the State University of New York at Stony Brook. Dr. Maier has served as program chair of the ACM International Conference on the Management of Data, and on the program committees of the ACM Symposium on Principles of Database Systems and the first conference on Object-Oriented Programming Systems, Languages and Applications. He did the initial data model design for the U.S. Department of Energy's Energy Emergency Management Information System, and has been a consultant or contractor with Tektronix, Inc., Servio Logic Corporation, the Microelectronics and Computer Technology Corporation (MCC), Digital Equipment Corporation, Altair, MAD Intelligent Systems, Object Design and Brookhaven National Laboratories. He is the author of books on relational databases and logic programming, as well as papers in database theory, object-oriented databases and user interfaces. He received a Presidential Young Investigator Award from the National Science Foundation. His Ph.D. was awarded in Electrical Engineering and Computer Science by Princeton University.

Dennis McLeod
Department of Computer Science
University of Southern California
Los Angeles, CA 90089

Dennis McLeod received his B.S., M.S., and Ph.D. degrees in Computer Science from the Massachusetts Institute of Technology in 1974, 1976, and 1978, respectively. He joined the faculty of the University of Southern California in 1978, where he is currently an Associate Professor of Computer Science. His principal research interests include: database system modeling, design, and evolution; distributed databases and database networks; information protection and security; knowledge management; applied machine learning; and information management environments for computer-supported cooperative work and engineering design. Dr. McLeod has published widely in the areas of database systems, knowledge management, and office information systems; he is particularly noted for his work on semantic data modeling and federated databases. He has also served as an advisor and consultant to a variety of private and public sector organizations.

Alan Purdy
Instantiations, Inc.
921 S.W. Washington
Suite 312
Portland, OR 97205

Alan Purdy is currently president and co-founder of Instantiations, a corporation that develops and supplies services and technologies to clients who develop object-oriented systems and applications. Prior to this, Alan was a member of the research staff at Xerox PARC, where he lead a team in integrating database technology with object-oriented languages.

Alan was a co-founder of Servio Logic, and was chief architect of Servio's Gem-Stone object server. Prior to that, he was a computer scientist at Comshare, where he designed language compilers, operating systems, and database systems. After graduating from college, he was chief programmer at the University of Michigan's Human Performance Center, where he programmed a PDP-1 (yes, 1). In 1986 Mr. Purdy served as co-chairman of ACM's first conference on Object-Oriented Programming Systems, Languages, and Applications (OOPSLA-86). He holds a B.S. in Science Engineering from the University of Michigan.

Bruce Schuchardt
Servio Logic Development Corporation

15025 S.W. Koll Parkway
Beaverton, OR 97006

Mr. Bruce Schuchardt has been active in the design of programmer tools and language interfaces to Servio Logic's object-oriented database, GemStone, for the past five years. He received his M.S. and B.S. degrees, both in Computer and Information Science, from the University of Massachusetts and the Oregon State University. He has also served time in data processing shops. He is currently working on end-user productivity tools for GemStone.

Jed Schwartz
Department of Computer Science
Columbia University
New York, NY 10027

Jed Schwartz directs the Large Scale Systems Lab in the Computer Science Department at Columbia University. His research interests include computer networking, network management, and human interfaces. He received an MS in Computer Science from Columbia University, and a BA in Religion and Philosophy from Princeton University. He lives and thrives in New York City.

Soumitra Sengupta
Department of Computer Science
Columbia University
New York, NY 10027

Soumitra Sengupta is an Associate Research Scientist at Columbia University and holds a joint appointment in the Computer Science Department and the Center for Medical Information Sciences. His research interests include distributed processing and networks, and building integrated information management systems. He received his MS and Ph.D. in Computer Science from SUNY at Stony Brook in 1984 and 1987, respectively.

Kiril Sinkel
Ontologic, Inc.
Three Burlington Woods
Burlington, MA 01803

Biographical sketch not available at the time of printing.

Jack Stucky
Hughes Aircraft Corp.
Building E-52,C227
El Segundo, CA 90245

Jack Stucky received a BS in Computer Science and a BS in Mathematics from Purdue University in 1987. He is currently working as a Member of the Technical Staff for Hughes Aircraft Company. His interests lie in object-oriented programming, portable UNIX systems, X-Windows, C programming, algorithms, and high speed graphics.

Qiang Wan
Department of Computer Science
University of Southern California
Los Angeles, CA 90089

Qiang Wan graduated from Tsinghua University, China in 1984 with a B.S. degree in computer science. He received his M.S. for the University of Southern California in 1987. He is currently a doctoral student in the computer science department of USC where he is pursuing research in object-oriented databases. In particular he is working on a standardized user interface and programmer's toolkit for an OODB. Qiang's other research interests include human-computer interactions, database technologies and software engineering.

Daniel Weinreb
Object Design, Inc.
One New England Executive Park
Burlington, MA 01803

Dan Weinreb is a software developer and co-founder of Object Design, where he is building a high-performance object-oriented database system based on C++. At Symbolics, he was the leader and principal designer of Statice. He was a co-founder of Symbolics, where he worked on a wide range of software development and management roles. Mr. Weinreb holds a B.S. degree in Computer Science from MIT and is a member of ACM and IEEE.

Ronald Williamson
Hughes Aircraft Corp.
Building E-52,C227
El Segundo, CA 90245

Ronald C. Williamson received the M.A. degree in applied mathematics from the University of California, Los Angeles, in 1976, and the Ph.D. degree in computer science from the University of Southern California, Los Angeles, in 1984. He joined Hughes Aircraft Company in 1978, where he is a Program Manager for Information Processing projects within AI Technology Department. The areas of technology he has pursued are artificial intelligence applied to database environments, user interfaces, object-oriented design and programming, image understanding, and expert system development within a situation assessment domain.

Dr. Williamson is a member of the Association for Computing Machinery, the American Association for Artificial Intelligence, and the IEEE Computer Society.

Yechiam Yemini
Department of Computer Science
Columbia University
New York, NY 10027

Yechiam Yemini is an Associate Professor with the Computer Science department at Columbia University. His main research interests include distributed computing and communications systems. At present, he is primarily interested in software tools for the design and management of communication systems. He published extensively in these areas and won international awards for some of this work. He is the editor of two books in the field. Professor Yemini received his Ph.D. in Computer Science from UCLA in 1979.

Index

L

LAGER, 243
Landsat, 296
Language uniformity, 220
Large object–oriented memory, 232
Large records, 127
Lattice, 325
Learning curve, 226
Learning from exception, 64
    instruction, 64
    observation, 64
Leaves, 232
Lifecycle, 313
Limitations of record–oriented data model,
    217
Liskov, 179, 191
List, 253, 389
Locality, 127
Lock mechanism, 396
Logical organization, 390
Logical schema design, 26
LOOM, 232
Looping constructs, 352
Low–level storage, 305

M

Machine learning, 63
Maintainability, 178
Major components of a NetMATE installa-
    tion, 286
Making and deleting entities, 123
Management, 100
Many–to–many, 18, 269, 290, 294
    relationships, 252
Many–to–one, 18
Map representation, 301, 303, 305
Mapping compatibility, 74
Maps, 296
MCAD, 315
Member functions, 181
Memory management, 396
Merge, 67
Mesa, 3
Message, 107, 218
    expressions, 218
    management, 232–33
Message–based communication, 293
Meta–data/schema integration, 73
Meta–information, 102, 256

Method, 138, 162–63, 179, 218–19
    code, 132
    combination, 106, 153, 158, 357
    definitions, 218
    execution, 220
    Object Repository MORe, 240
    and trigger combination, 255
Methodology, 99
Mixed storage models, 320
Mixing forwarding with local execution,
    232
Modalities, 17
Model of representation, 360
Modeler, 288–89, 291
Modeling power, 252, 260
Model of integration, 317, 319, 321
Model of state, 181, 183, 185, 187, 359
Modula–2, 3
Modularization, 317
MORe, 240–41
Multi–dimensional aggregates, 161
Multipart selectors, 219
Multiple concurrent users, 220
Multiple database context, 72
Multiple inheritance, 28, 282, 335, 338,
    358, 370
    constraint, 34
Multisets, 374
Multi–value properties, 146, 196, 212

N

Name classes, 212
Name lookup, 77, 83
Naming, 205, 212
    conflicts, 73
NeST, 284
Nested query, 213
Nested transactions, 396, 398
NetMATE, 283, 287
    organization model, 293
Network, 14, 269, 283
    communication, 128
    configuration, 288
    management, 283, 287
    management model, 292
    model, 288
new, 332
Null value, 120

O

O++, 365
  comparison with other systems, 366, 374
  data structuring constructs, 367
Object, 218, 317
  activation, 392
  classification, 16–17
  clustering, 166
  creation and deletion, 163
  database, 130, 317
  deactivation, 392
  definitions, 367
  deletion, 167
  flavor evolution, 62
  generalization, 253
  identification, 105
  identifier, 367
  identity, 16
  keys, 173
  manager, 367
  model, 320, 388
  modeling technique, OMT, 78
  querying, 248
  referencing, 250
  representation, 188
  size, 232
  specialization, 253
  SQL, 199, 200, 202–3, 248
  state, 346
  transparency, 227
  type conversions, 106
  type hierarchy, 239, 262
  type hierarchy design, 268
  uniformity, 17
  version control, 281
Objectify, 68
Objective–C, 253
Object–oriented, 12–13, 17
  database design steps, 32
  database models, 16
  database schema, 297
  design, 95
  development requirements, 93
  methodologies, 93, 262
  pointer, 222
  programming language, 96, 343
  software, 92
OCT/Vem/RPC, 238
ODE, 365
Once–only triggers, 381

One–to–many, 18, 269, 271, 278–79, 290
  relationships, 390
One–to–one, 18
ONTOS, 387–88
  architecture, 390–91
  client architecture, 392
  development environment, 388
  object model, 388
  performance, 389
  platforms, 388
  server architecture, 390
OODB: (*See also* object-oriented)
  features, 251–53, 255, 257
  limitations, 259
OPAL, 107, 109, 216
  language, 218
  programming environment, OPE, 225
Open architecture, 316
Opening and closing the database, 159
Operation:
  arguments, 152
  invocation, 105, 170
  specification, 22
Operational component, 14
Operations, 151, 294
  clause, 153
Operator ::, 328
Operator overloading, 330, 355
Optimistic concurrency control, 220
Optimization, 214
  of Equi-Joins, 214
Optional, 143
  argument, 106, 153, 347
  properties, 144, 170, 185
OrderBy–clause, 209
OrderedDictionary, 253
Ordering, 205
  the results, 209
ORION, 29, 115
Overloading, 254

P

Page buffers, 126
Parameterization, 106, 353
Parameterized operations, 353
  type, 160
  valuespec, 146
Parent–child relationship, 289
Partially cached state, 233
Partition–control instance variable, 47

SQL, 106, 199–201, 294, 320
  commands, 205
  extensions, 405
  transforms, 205
SREM, 266
Stack, 131, 253
State invariant, 183
State representation, 188
Statements, 329
Static type checking, 330, 356
Statice, 117
  implementation, 125
stderr, 329
stdin, 329
stdout, 329
Storage:
  allocation and deallocation, 332
  managers, 166, 361
  mechanism, 320, 361
  replacement models, 318
  type, 194
Stored functions, 113
Stored queries, 203
Stream library, 329
Stress analysis, 315
Strong typing, 104
Stroustrup, Bjarne, 96
struct, 328
Structural operators, 264–65, 269, 271
Structured analysis, 93
Structuring, 16
Subclassing, 27, 46–47, 49, 51, 53
  algorithms, 47
  condition management, 55, 57
  conditions, 27, 47
  for an instance with no existing class, 55
  for new instances with more than one
      class, 53
  for partitioning instances, 51
Subclusters, 374
Subsumption algorithm, 38
Subsumption between methods, 39
Subtype, 139, 149, 179
  relations, 269
Subtypes of RepManager, 194
Subtype/supertype hierarchy, 131
SunView, 71
Superclasses, 28
Supertype, 141–42, 150, 179
Symbolics, 117

Symmetric interface, 234
System command language, 220
System management functions, 217
System/R, 26, 127
System–supplied functions, 159

T

Target domain, 205, 209
TAXIS, 28
Taxonomy of restriction, 47
TCP/IP, 288, 295
TDES, 243
TDL, 103, 132, 136, 141, 254, 275, 281,
    301, 306
Temporal relationships, 296
Testing the membership;
  of CCs, 41
  of DCs, 41
  of SICs, 41
  of SICs and MICs, 41
TextNode-Editing, 87
TGS, 243
Third normal form, 15
Time stamps, 262, 271
Timed triggers, 385
Tokens, 265
Tool interface, 240, 242
Tool invocation, 250
Tools, 100
Traceability, 274
Trailing parameters, 330
Training cost, 226
Transaction, 125
  management, 232–33
  mechanisms, 388
  model, 396–97, 399
  time, 102
  transparency, 234
TransactionAbort, 397
TransactionCommit, 397
TransactionStart, 397
Transition, 264, 265, 278, 280
  firing, 280
Transitive:
  agent creation, 232
  closure, 203
  transfers, 226
Translation models, 317
Transparent exception handling, 228
Transparent garbage collection, 228